£37.50

ML

tur

OXFORD GEOLOGICAL SCIENCES SERIES

Series editors

P. Allen
E. R. Oxburgh
B. J. Skinner

Mineral resources appraisal

Mineral endowment, resources, and potential supply: concepts, methods, and cases

DEVERLE P. HARRIS

CLARENDON PRESS · OXFORD · 1984

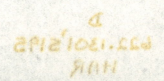

Oxford University Press, Walton Street, Oxford OX2 6DP

London Glasgow New York Toronto
Delhi Bombay Calcutta Madras Karachi
Kuala Lumpur Singapore Hong Kong Tokyo
Nairobi Dar es Salaam Cape Town
Melbourne Auckland
and associates in
Beirut Berlin Ibadan Mexico City Nicosia

Oxford is a trade mark of Oxford University Press

Published in the United States
by Oxford University Press, New York

British Library Cataloguing in Publication Data
Harris, DeVerle P.
  Mineral resources appraisal. —
  (Oxford geological science series)
  1. Mines and mineral resources —
  statistical methods
  I. Title
  622′.13′015195   TN260
  ISBN 0-19-854456-1

Library of Congress Cataloging in Publication Data
Harris, DeVerle P.
  Mineral resources appraisal.
  (Oxford geological science series)
  Bibliography: p.
  Includes index.
  1. Mines and mineral resources. 2. Mine valuation.
I. Title. II. Series.
TN263.H28 1983   622.1   83-11445
ISBN 0-19-854456-1

Printed in Northern Ireland at The Universities Press (Belfast) Ltd.

PREFACE

This book results primarily from the need for an account of quantitative methods for the estimation of mineral and energy resources. In a larger sense, it reflects an interest which initially was fostered by my reading of the seminal work of Maurice Allais and subsequently intensified by exposure to the ideas of John C. Griffiths on geostatistics and operations research. This interest led directly to my own doctoral research and to a continuing interest in the development of this relatively new field of inquiry and analysis.

My first attempt at a book, which was completed in 1977, was basically an extension of a survey and critique of appraisal methods for the US Energy Research and Development Administration. The political and economic events at that time had created a keen interest in energy and resource issues; as a result of that interest, I received requests from all quarters of the world for the 1977 document. Satisfying these requests soon exhausted the limited stock. In recognition of the very rapid evolution of ideas and appraisal methodologies during the period from 1975 to 1981, the 1977 document was updated and extensively rewritten to form the manuscript for this book.

Paramount among considerations of content and style of this book is the identification and description of a conceptual framework that defines the field and enriches understanding of the highly varied contributions, most of which are applications of one or more quantitative methods. By virtue of the compound nature of mineral and energy resources, this framework must bring together elements from economics, geology, and technology. Furthermore, because of uncertainty about the existence and characteristics of undiscovered mineral deposits, appraisal of mineral resources involves issues of statistical estimation. Consequently, the sweep of topics covered in this book is very broad. Accordingly, some sections of the book will be of interest primarily to geologists, others to economists, and still others to statisticians and systems analysts. The reader, regardless of his major discipline, will I hope be rewarded for his effort.

DV.P.H.

Arizona
December 1983

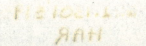

ACKNOWLEDGEMENTS

The contents of this book reflect intellectual contributions of many early and contemporary scientists to this relatively new field of endeavour, loosely referred to as mineral resource appraisal. Acknowledgement is due the US Department of Energy for financial support of research on methods of mineral resource appraisal; especially, I am appreciative of the encouragement and assistance provided by Jack Ellis as project monitor for this research.

Special acknowledgement is made of the contribution of Alice Yelverton, who not only typed the manuscript in all its stages of evolution but also supervised the proofing and coordinating of the manuscript. The magnitude of her effort is exceeded only by its quality.

I am indebted to Professor Brian Skinner of Yale University for the suggestion that an earlier manuscript be reworked and published as a book, and I am grateful to the Oxford University Press for undertaking the publication of a book dealing with a subject as specialized as mineral resource appraisal.

Finally, I am indebted to my wife, Sandra, for sustenance and encouragement during the preparation of this book.

CONTENTS

Dedicated to the memory of my mother,
and to the influence of her
uncommon intellectual curiosity

1 INTRODUCTION: MINERAL RESOURCES AND MINERAL RESOURCE ANALYSIS

1.1. Perspective on mineral resources

The term 'mineral resources', which is in the title of this book, conveys little information without additional qualification; at best, it identifies the general subject to be materials that are sources of one or more minerals. In this book, 'mineral' is used in a loose sense to include metals, nonmetallics, and hydrocarbons. Accordingly, a mineral resource is a material from which a metal, a nonmetallic element, or a hydrocarbon can be extracted. Where greater specificity is required, one of these classes of minerals will be employed as a qualifier of resources, e.g. metal resources or oil resources. When no distinction is desired and the statement could apply to metals, nonmetallics, or hydrocarbons, the term mineral is used as a qualifier, e.g. mineral resources, mineral supply, or mineral endowment.

Mineral resources exist only with respect to an economic and technological framework. A useful statement on mineral resources must also be a statement on specific *economic conditions*, *technological capabilities*, and the *state of nature*.

The term 'mineral' resources includes reserves, those accumulations of a mineral that are known and have been explored to the extent that there is reasonable assurance that the mineral could be produced from them economically, and minerals in known deposits that cannot be exploited economically. Together, these two kinds of mineral resources comprise the category of known resources. Most of our study and analysis traditionally has been devoted to this category of resources, for these are the resources that we know most about and for which we have an immediate interest because of their support of current and near-future economic activities.

Appraisal of *unknown resources*, the category of resources that we know *least* about, is the subject of this book. These resources consist of both economic and subeconomic unknown resources. Obviously, the motivation for the appraisal of unknown resources must stem from issues that relate to a moderate- or long-term time frame. Such issues may include resource adequacy and mineral policy, issues that recently have received considerable attention and, in the case of oil, have become topics of household conversation. While these issues may be of primary concern to governments, because of the time lag from exploration to production, the large mineral firm also may be motivated to examine the long-term outlook for mineral consumption and potential mineral supply, hence mineral resources.

There is no elegant nor ultimately definitive means for estimating unknown mineral resources short of direct sampling of the earth's crust, e.g. drilling at a spacing sufficient to locate and delineate the mineral deposits. While such a programme would most assuredly provide the best possible data for the appraisal of resources, it has not been demonstrated to be the most efficient means for appraisal, although some scholars urge its implementation (Ridge 1974). Arguments justifying such a programme on the basis of economics have so far been superficial. At present, and probably in the future, unknown resources are inferred by models, hopefully founded on fact, of aspects of the economic–physical system within which resources are defined.

The conceptual framework and the resource terms of the following section are developed and stated with respect to only one of the major classes of minerals, metals. While in general, mineral can be substituted for metal without violation of concepts that are developed in this chapter, some of the terms employed are appropriate only for metal resources. This conceptual framework and the definitions of resource terms could have been generalized to apply to metal, nonmetallics, and hydrocarbons simply by considering any member of these three classes of mineral substances to be a chemical compound. Then, grade would be the concentration of the particular chemical compound within the rock, irrespective of whether the compound is a hydrocarbon or a metal sulphide. Following such a general scheme would lead to the statement of the quantity of resources either in terms of an element of the chemical compound, such as copper contained in chalcopyrite ($CuFeS_2$), or in terms of the chemical compound. Adoption of one of these alternatives violates practice in either the metals industry or the hydrocarbons industries. For example, metal resources are generally stated in terms of the quantity of metal, but oil resources are stated in terms of the quantity of the basic hydrocarbon compound.

An alternative to the general development is a separate development of the conceptual framework and definitions of terms for metals, nonmetallics, and hydrocarbons. But, since much of the conceptual framework is identical for each of these classes of minerals and many of the terms are similar, such a presentation would be repetitive and monotonous. Consequently, the decision was made to develop the conceptual framework and definitions of terms on only one of the classes of minerals, metals.

1.2. A conceptual framework for resources and resource analysis

1.2.1. *Definitions of resource terms and identification of useful concepts*

The earth's crust can be considered as one large deposit of metal, a deposit having an average grade (concentration of metal) equivalent to the measure of crustal abundance but possessing considerable variation in grade. Of course, the tonnage of a given metal in this deposit is extremely large. The term *resource base* (Schurr, Netschert, with Eliasberg, Lerner, and Landsberg 1960) has been used to refer to the totality of a metal in the earth's crust. While resource base is useful as a concept, the term has little use in actual resource analysis, for concentrations many times that of crustal abundance are available in smaller quantities and constitute the deposits that are exploited and provide our supply of metal. Fortunately, we have not yet had to turn to extremely low-grade deposits.

Our experience has shown that the ultimate deposit of a metal consists of many smaller deposits occurring in varied geological environments and possessing various characteristics of grade, size, shape, chemical combinations, depth, host rock, etc. The entire collection of such deposits (known plus unknown) is referred to as RB. Suppose that for specified factor price and product price and for currently feasible or near-feasible technology of production (exploration, mining, and processing) those deposits of a metal in RB that could be produced profitably could be identified. The sum of the amount of the metal that could be recovered from these deposits is referred to as resources rs. Critical in the definition of resources is that resources exist for *specified economic* conditions and *currently feasible* or *near-feasible* technology of production. The

economic conditions need not be those that currently prevail.

Specification of economic conditions and technology of production equal to those that currently exist identifies a subset of deposits that could be mined at a profit. The sum of the metal that could be recovered from these deposits is referred to as economic resources rs'.

At any given time, man has only partial knowledge of resources and economic resources. Qualifiers of these two terms are needed to convey the degree of knowledge. Correct and liberal use of these qualifiers is imperative for proper communication.

$$\left.\begin{array}{l}\text{Known economic resources}\\\text{Known subeconomic resources}\end{array}\right\}\text{Known resources}$$

$$\left.\begin{array}{l}\text{Unknown economic resources}\\\text{Unknown subeconomic resources}\end{array}\right\}\begin{array}{l}\text{Unknown}\\\text{resources}\end{array}$$

When the term resources is used without a qualifier, it is to be interpreted as referring in total to all of the above categories of resources.

Known economic resources are commonly referred to as ore reserves. This general category of resources is subdivided into classes, e.g. proved, probable, and possible, to indicate degree of certainty about the estimated quantity and grade of ores. Such refinement is not needed for the subject matter of this book; therefore ore reserve terminology will not be discussed here. A comprehensive treatment of ore reserve and resources terminology has been provided by Schanz (1975).

The relations of economics, technology, and degree of knowledge to categories of resources were summarized in a tableau (see Table 1.1) by Schurr *et al.* [1] (1960). This tableau captures the important dynamics of resources: a change in product or factor prices or an improvement in technology of production causes a change in resources. Although resource base conceptually is an absolute, resources are not absolute; they are a function of economics and technology.

The most widely cited resource classification scheme is attributed to Vincent E. McKelvey (1973), past director of the US Geological Survey (see Fig. 1.1). The diagram of this classification has become known as the 'McKelvey box'. While the 'McKelvey box' is a refinement of the Schurr–Netschert tableau in that it defines a greater number of categories of resources, it is a less complete representation of resource relations than is the tableau. For example, technology, factor prices, and product price are all

TABLE 1.1. *A tabulation of reserve–resource terminology.* (*Source: Schurr* et al. *1960, p. 298.*)

Terms	Aspects		
	Occurrence	Economic	Technological
Reserves	Known	Present cost level	Currently feasible
Resources	Known and unknown	Any cost level specified	Currently feasible and probable future feasibility
Resource base	Known and unknown	Irrelevant	Feasible and infeasible

lumped into one effect, economics. Furthermore, closing the box at the base of submarginal resources leaves out of this classification some of the material referred to by Schurr and Netschert. For example, material which has a sufficient concentration of the element or compound sought but for which there is no existing or near-feasible technology for production is not a resource according to the definition of resources provided by Schurr and Netschert, but it is a part of the resource base. Since the McKelvey box does not specify a nonresource category, it does not include this material. Finally, there is some question as to what is included in submarginal resources.

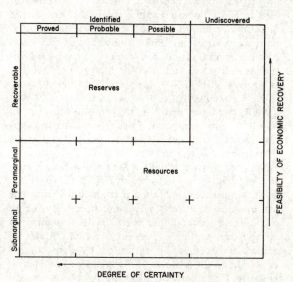

Fig. 1.1. Classification of mineral reserves and resources. Degree of certainty increases from right to left, and feasibility of economic recovery increases from bottom to top. (Source: McKelvey 1973.)

The foregoing discussion stressed the importance of economics and technology in the concept of resources. These factors impart a special character to resources, for the economic structure and the employable or near-feasible technology of a nation are dynamic—they change with time. Consequently, that which today is a non-economic resource may be an economic resource five years from now. Such a result can be due to increased demand and higher prices, a cheapening of the real cost of labour and capital for a given technology, the adoption of newly conceived technology, or all of the foregoing. In a sense, resources can be created by man's economic activities and his scientific and engineering genius. Similarly, they can be destroyed by unfavourable economics, which includes the availability of low-cost, foreign supplies and policies on taxation, trade, environmental protection, mineral leasing, etc. As the identity of economic resources changes with economic conditions and technological improvement, the conditions of interest for the identification and appraisal of resources change.

An additional term, metal endowment, is used in this book. A definition of this term is provided here. Consider each occurrence of the metal in *RB*, the collection of occurrences that constitute the resource base, to have *NC* characteristics, such as concentration, size, chemical combination, mineral assemblage, host material, depth, geometric form, geological association, etc. In theory, *NC* is large, for it is the number of all characteristics of the occurrences of the metal. Suppose that only a few *NCM* of these *NC* characteristics are selected as classification criteria, such as concentration, size, and depth, and that a minimum acceptable level for each of the *NCM* characteristics is identified. The collection of all occurrences having levels of the *NCM* characteristics at least as good as those identified is referred to as D. The sum of the metal contained in all occurrences which constitute D is termed metal endowment and is designated m. Thus, metal endowment is a purely physical measure and is not dependent upon economics and technology as is resources. Provided that the criteria selected to define D are less favourable than those implied by the stated economic conditions and the currently feasible and near-feasible technology, D includes the occurrences upon which rs, resources, is computed. Consequently, m is a more comprehensive and inclusive concept than is rs, for rs could be formed from the occurrences which constitute D simply by selecting those occurrences of D that could be produced economically, given the stated conditions.

While there is nothing in this definition of metal endowment that stipulates that the collections of metal occurrences upon which resources are defined is a subset of D (the collection of occurrences upon which metal endowment is defined), such a relationship is assumed in the use of the term in this book: metal endowment includes resources. The primary need and usefulness of the term arises when an inventory of occurrences having specified physical characteristics is estimated as an initial step to appraising resources and potential supply. Given this motivation, it makes little sense to select the levels of the physical characteristics used to define D and hence metal endowment, such that resources for the economic and technological conditions of interest exceed the physical inventory, metal endowment.

An appraised quantity of metal resources is an estimate of the metal that could be recovered if all deposits were known. Generally, neither the cost of exploration nor the fact that only some fraction of the deposits would be found by exploration, as currently practised, are considered in the estimation of the quantity of unknown resources. The term, potential supply, is used to refer to the quantity of metal in known deposits and in deposits expected to be discovered. In establishing proper perspective for potential supply, it is helpful to imagine that exploration is conducted by one large firm, so that exploration of the same ground is not repeated, but that unit costs and efficiency of exploration by this firm otherwise are typical of the average firm. Then, given the specified status of technology and factor prices and given that markets are unlimited at the specified product price, the optimum amount of exploration EX^* would be the sum of the nonnegative net present values of deposits that constitutes rs and would be discovered. Thus given these conditions, there is an optimum exploration expenditure EX^*.

To contribute to potential supply, deposits must be of a quality such that their exploitation covers production costs and the costs of discovering them. Allocating to each deposit discovered its share of the exploration effort EX gives a net present value (net of exploration and production costs). Naturally, increasing EX to a higher level than EX^* discovers more deposits, but since EX is allocated to those deposits discovered, increasing EX beyond EX^* loses more economic and discoverable resources than are gained. For a given exploration technology and at any progression of exploration, the deposits which remain to be discovered require a greater expenditure per unit of resources than those already discovered.

This interacting of exploration and exploitation with endowment is a 'one-shot' kind of optimization in which the sequential timing of incremental exploration expenditures is suppressed; there are no 'sunk' exploration costs. Therefore, diminishing returns to exploration, due to the greater difficulty of discovery of progressively larger fractions of the endowment, means that exploration costs allocated to the deposits discovered increase while at the same time additional deposits are discovered by a greater expenditure. Thus, conceptually, there is an optimum expenditure, an expenditure that trades off the poorer-quality discovered deposits against more difficult to locate but higher-quality deposits. This optimum expenditure is EX^*. Potential supply ps is the sum of the quantity of metal in those deposits of rs which would be discovered by an exploration effort of EX^* and could be produced economically, including exploration as well as production costs. Like rs, ps is a stock, not a flow; it is an inventory under specified conditions. Conceptually, ps and rs can be equal, but equality requires that the region is totally (in an absolute sense) explored. Since conducting exploration incurs a cost and is less than perfectly effective, ps in general is less than rs.

Suppose that we designate the cumulative exploration expenditure up to time t as EX_t. If we now relax the assumption of unlimited markets but invoke the assumptions that the single large firm will seek to maintain prices and that there is no technological change across time, then exploration would be spread across time as warranted by demand and depletion. Thus, at time t, EX_t would be less than or equal to EX^*; consequently, the set of known and exploited deposits would be some subset of those that constituted ps. The sum of metal in those deposits discovered by the exploration effort represented by EX_t is referred to as supply s_t. Supply, as here defined, is a stock, not a flow per unit of time. s_τ represents the cumulative production plus reserves of all identified deposits at the current time $t = \tau$.

This completes the definition of resource terms. A more formal definition of these terms is provided in § 1.6.

1.2.2. *The appraisal of resource adequacy, a means for examining resource relations and issues*

An appraisal of mineral resources may serve several objectives, four of which are

1. An assessment of resource adequacy—the ability of a region to meet expected consumption requirements to some designated time in the future;
2. The stimulation of exploration for and production of mineral resources in a region;
3. The evaluation of the economic impact of pending mineral policy;
4. The assessment of the regional economic impact of a government-sponsored development programme, such as the construction of infrastructure.

The first of these four objectives, the assessment of resource adequacy, has been the primary motivation of the greatly increased demand of recent years for resources appraisals. The experience of the OPEC oil embargo projected the science of energy and mineral resources appraisal before the public eye. The urgent need and demand for information on the size of our domestic resources of oil and gas focused the attention of policy-makers, economists, engineers, and physical scientists on not only the estimates made by various persons or agencies but also upon the different methods by which these estimates were made. The fact that past estimates of undiscovered petroleum resources have varied by as much as a multiple of ten encouraged the investigation of methods.

The assessment of resource adequacy is worthy of some intellectual probing because of the use of the assessed state of adequacy by society and government in the establishing of policies for domestic resource development, international trade, environmental protection, and for the general preservation or enhancement of the 'quality of life'. Furthermore, the assessment of resource adequacy serves as a useful 'window' through which to view economics and technology and their relations to resources.

What does the term 'resource adequacy' mean? To most of us, it conveys a general impression that all is well, that consumption requirements can be met. Only a moment's thought is necessary to find that additional information is required: *the cost of resource adequacy*. If the OPEC oil embargo taught the American public anything, it was that it makes a difference whether adequacy is achieved at a fourfold increase in consumer price or at no-price change. It was common to hear, prior to the embargo, remarks like the following: 'We are not "running out" of anything; it is only a matter of cost (price); let the price rise and sufficient supplies will be generated'— thus dismissing concern for resource adequacy. These statements are technically correct. Even for a mineral for which (1) the native endowment is very limited relative to current consumption requirements and (2) the resource is homogeneous with respect to quality, this endowment technically is sufficient if cost is no issue and the time frame of the evaluation is sufficiently long. For, given these conditions, competition by industrial consumers would eventually bid up the price to that level at which resources are sufficient. High prices would lead to substitution of the mineral material by some other material, if substitution is feasible, or to the creation and adoption of new manufacturing or process technology not requiring the mineral. Additionally, an increased price for the mineral and an increase in the price of the final product can lead to a reduction in its consumption, hence a reduction in the derived demand for the mineral. For those minerals having a wide range in quality of resources, high prices could lead to a very large expansion of the quantity of resources, contributing to a condition of adequacy of resources. Thus, eventually by communication through the market and through technological change, supply and demand would reach an equilibrium for which resources are adequate. As long as man's personal welfare is not involved in the decision of adequacy of resources, in the long run, adequacy of resources of a given commodity does not seem to be a pressing issue. Of course, man's welfare is involved. Cost is a consideration because it affects man's standard of living. Furthermore, in the short run, technology is fixed and an interruption or reduction of supply could have serious consequences, consequences that may be unacceptable to society.

The point to be made here is that adequacy of resources is undefined unless the terms at which that adequacy is achieved are explicitly stated. These terms include the time frame of the evaluation, the acceptable level of imports, the states of the economic factors, and the levels of the various technologies.

If this designated time is far in the future, an assessment of resource adequacy is a challenging and difficult task, for it requires an assessment of the future course of man's economic activities and policy decisions as well as an estimation of the endowment of the region in that mineral of interest. Furthermore, the assessed states of some of the economic conditions affect consumption as well as resources. For example, unless the mineral industry is highly concentrated, an equilibrium product price reflects the combined effects of resource depletion, advances in technology, factor prices, and the demand for the product. A change in any one of these, *ceteris paribus*, can cause a new price. A comprehensive assessment of resource adequacy must deal in some fashion with this system of interrelated components and its dynamic behaviour over time as well as with the size of the mineral endowment and the progression of exploration. Unfortunately, appraisals of resource adequacy have not always met these requirements. Furthermore, some of these appraisals have not acknowledged the dynamics of resources, focusing instead solely upon estimates of known economic resources (reserves).

A common mistake in some analyses of resource adequacy is the comparison of *quoted reserves* to projected consumption requirements. Such a comparison can foster a misconception of resource adequacy, particularly if the assessment of adequacy is for a long time frame, for it considers only reported economic resources under current economics and technology. From the foregoing conceptualization of the dynamics of resources, it is apparent that an assessment of resource adequacy for some future time should not be based solely upon the current perception of known economic resources. At best, such an assessment is biased because it ignores resource dynamics and the contribution of future exploration to identifying presently unknown deposits. Matters are much worse than this. First, known economic resources, as interpreted from available data, often are not what they seem to be. Reserve data on existing properties seldom represent the total economic resource indicated to exist within the deposit. Data provided by mineral producers usually represent only that part of the economic material *proved* [2] to exist by development work. Since proving a reserve requires drilling or underground excavation and sampling, a producer commonly proves only that quantity sufficient to support his operation for a selected number of years. Generally, this number of years ranges from five to ten. Thus, it is common to find that the proved reserves reported by a producer for a given deposit are about the same as they were five years earlier, even though considerable ore was produced during the five-year period. Therefore, even if economics and technology were to remain static, the passage of time creates reserves as the depletion of proved reserves fosters additional development work and the proving of additional reserves within the known deposits to maintain a proved reserve equal to some multiple of annual production.

Second, more favourable economics and improved technology may create additional reserves in the deposit as time passes, particularly if the deposit is characterized by a wide range of grades. Eventually reserve expansion ceases, either because the deposit becomes physically exhausted or because the cost of mining progressively more inaccessible material exceeds product price. The point to be emphasized here is that either of these ultimate terminal conditions may imply a much greater resource than indicated by currently reported reserves.

Finally, even the relatively well-explored traditional areas of production have considerable potential for the discovery of additional deposits. Assessment of resource adequacy by the simplistic comparison of reserves to consumption requirements ignores the potential of these areas and the potential of as yet nonproducing areas for providing additional resources.

1.3. An overview of resource models and estimation procedures

1.3.1. *Classification of resource models*

Venturing from concepts to measures brings about a confrontation with the harsh reality that the very foundation upon which mineral endowment, resources, potential supply, and supply rest, RB (the collection of mineral occurrences that constitute the resource base) is largely unknown. If RB is not known, rs, ps, and s_t for $t > \tau$ are unknown. Faced with this dilemma, man has had to employ models of those aspects of resources about which his experience provides insights.

Five broad categories of resource models can be recognized: economic, quantity–quality, geological, geostatistical, and compound. The following comments provide a brief and very general idea of the nature of the models in these five classes. Details of models in each of these categories are provided in subsequent sections.

1.3.2. *Economic resource models*

Economic resource models focus upon some aspect of s_t, $t < \tau$, such as a time series of historical data on the primary production of a metal. A time series of production relates to the stock measure s_t as

$$Q_t^s = s_t - s_{t-1} - b_t, \quad 0 \le t \le \tau,$$

where b_t is the quantity of reserves added during the time period $t-1$ to t, Q_t^s is the production during the time period $t-1$ to t, and τ is current time.

One kind of an economic resource model is the 'life-cycle' model. This model depicts the pattern of Q_t^s, $t = 0, \ldots, \infty$ as a 'bell'-shaped curve or as a 'skewed bell' curve. The appropriate model is selected by examining the historical record of Q_t^s, $t = 0, 1, 2, \ldots, \tau$. The total quantity of undiscovered recoverable resource, $F(\infty)$, is estimated by computing the area under the fitted curve $f(t)$ from $t=0$ to $t=\infty$. Subtraction of s_τ from $F(\infty)$ gives an estimate of the quantity of unknown resources which will be discovered in the future and will be economic to produce. By the basic premise of this model, the time series of that production ultimately will define a 'bell'- or 'skewed bell'-shaped curve; economically recoverable resources ultimately will be exhausted. Judgement about the adequacy of resources for a more relevant time frame, say 30 years from now ($\tau + 30$), is made by comparing the difference $F(\tau+30) -$

$\sum_{t=0}^{\tau} Q_t^s$ to forecast consumption requirements minus an acceptable or target size of imports. While these models provide for 'sharp conclusions' in the short run, because they forecast actual production, for very long-term studies, they require that the effects of man's economics and technology interacting with a basic endowment will behave in the future according to trends observable in historical data.

Another kind of economic resource model, an econometric model, explicitly relates Q_t^s to economic variables. Some of these models consist of many equations which represent the system of interrelated activities of the economy or of a sector of the economy. One of the equations within the system would define Q_t^s. Through statistical analysis of historical data, Q_t^s, $t = 0, 1, 2, \ldots, \tau$, or some transformation of Q_t^s, generally is described as a linear function of selected economic variables. In the short run, these economic variables commonly include product and factor prices and relate primary production, imports, and secondary production to demand. Long-term models include variables which represent in some form the determinants of supply and de-

mand; for given a long-term time frame, the determinants change, accounting for the dynamics of the economy. In addition to endogenous variables, such as price, these models may include exogenous variables, such as industrial production, gross national product, population size, per capita income, etc., variables which hopefully can be forecast to the selected time horizon. The general idea of this approach is to forecast the exogenous variables outside of the model by some appropriate means (rate of growth, trend extrapolation, etc.) and let the model determine the levels of the endogenous variables, such as product price. Scarcity of resources is indicated by increased real prices for the forecast horizon.

Commonly, econometric models do not include one aspect of supply which in very long-term analysis is important to resource adequacy, the size and quality of the remaining endowment and the effects of technological change in creating resources from this endowment. The perspective of econometric models is that the effects of resource depletion and of technology in creating resources is present in the variables which represent the dynamics of the economy. While in the short or moderate term, such an assumption is acceptable, for very long-term analysis, a time frame which typifies studies of resource adequacy, this assumption may be somewhat suspect.

1.3.3. *Quantity–quality models*

The relationship of the quantity of a resource measure to its quality has been employed variously to describe aspects of resource availability. Lasky (1950) originated the idea that a model of this relationship could be useful in estimating the ore reserves of porphyry copper deposits as cut-off and average grades are lowered. As a result of his pioneering study, he proposed that the logarithm of cumulative tonnage of reserves R is a linear function of average grade $\bar{q}$

$$\ln R = \alpha_0 + \alpha_1 \bar{q},$$

where α_0 and α_1 are parameters, such that $\alpha_1 < 0$.

While Lasky's objective was primarily to model the quantity–quality relationship for ore reserves, Musgrove (1971) sought to generalize Lasky's idea as a resource estimation model. He examined the relationship of cumulative production plus reserves to average grade for entire regions, such as the United States, and employed this relationship to estimate the quantity of mineralized rock and metal that would be available at considerably reduced average grades.

Recently, Cargill, Root, and Bailey (1980) have modelled cumulative production of ore as a power function of average grade. Their original work developed a model to estimate the quantity of mercury available at reduced grades. This work has been extended to other metals and to oil and gas (Cargill, Root, and Bailey 1981).

Singer and DeYoung (1980) explored estimates by Lasky-type models, based upon cumulative production plus reserves, as average grade is lowered to crustal abundance.

With respect to the resource terms defined in § 1.2, it is difficult to provide a simple classification of the estimate by a quantity–quality model. For the polar case in which the deposit is in production, the model estimates reserves, provided the average grade employed is associated with a cut-off grade for which variable costs equal price. For lower average grades, the estimate includes subeconomic known resources. Consider another polar case. All deposits in a region are known. Then, a model of the quantity–quality relationship for this aggregate of material would describe endowment at some specified cut-off grade and associated average grade. But, when the inventory of mineralized material does not include all deposits, the quantity estimated by this type of a model for a specified quality cannot be classified clearly as resources, endowment, or potential supply unless strong assumptions are made about the undiscovered endowment.

Quantity–quality models also are known as tonnage–grade models. However, the models that are loosely known by this term include distributions of size, distributions of grade, and the correlation across deposits of average grade and tonnage per deposit. These are statistical relationships, and they are very different from the quantity–quality relationship. The tonnage–grade relations of the statistical variety are special topics in geostatistical and compound models and are examined in sections dealing with these topics.

1.3.4. Geological resource models

Some of the geological resource models used as a basis for the appraisal of resource adequacy are at the opposite extreme from economic resource models. Considerable attention is given to the geology of the earth as a basis for appraising the remaining resources or endowment, but the economic evaluation of the estimated stock is often naïve, confused,

or nonexistent. Geological resource models employ various methods for estimation, ranging from statistical correlations of geological variables with some form of mineral occurrence (number of mines, number of deposits, tonnage of metal, value of metals, etc.) to simple measures of density, such as the tons of metal or number of deposits per cubic mile of the earth's crust.

Typically, estimates of undiscovered resources reflect the progression of exploration and the economic conditions at the time of the appraisal, for the densities or correlations employed are based upon known economic resources at that time. Since the economics of resources is implicit to the estimation procedure, it is difficult to comment in economic terms upon adequacy of resources to meet projected consumption requirements to a time horizon, say 30 years from the date of the analysis, for the economics and technology at that time will differ from that at the time of the appraisal. Since the economics and technology are not treated explicitly, evaluation of resource adequacy for conditions different from those at the time of the appraisal cannot be made directly. For example, consider the appraisal by the US Geological Survey (Miller, Thomsen, Dolton, Coury, Hendricks, Lennartz, Powers, Sable, and Varnes 1975) of the undiscovered oil and gas resources of the United States. This appraisal was made by subjective analysis of the geology and known resources of the various regions of the United States. The estimates of quantity of undiscovered resources were made for economic and technologic conditions at that time, which included a recovery factor of 32 per cent. An appraisal of the resource adequacy for a time horizon in the future is relevant only if economic relations and the state of technology at the forecast time were to be the same as they are at the time that appraisal was made. Discernment of the effect of a price increase or an improvement in the recovery rate cannot be made directly.

One kind of geological resource model is based upon the notion of crustal abundance, the average concentration of an element in the crust of the earth. Appraisal of endowment consists of examination of the relationship of reserves of elements at current time to their crustal abundance. Thus, the relationship of a time-variant measure, known economic resources, to a time-invariant measure, crustal abundance, is used as a basis for estimating unknown economic resources of a particular element in a region. Even if the physical underpinnings of this approach were correct, an assessment of resource adequacy using this relationship and a forecast of consumption requirements would be relevant only for economic conditions prevailing at the time of the analysis, $t = \tau$. There is no way that an economic assessment of adequacy of resources could be made directly for conditions different from those at τ.

1.3.5. Geostatistical models

The term geostatistical model is used here in a broad sense to refer to those models which describe some aspect of mineral occurrence probabilistically. These models include subjectively estimated probabilities as well as formal probability models, such as the normal, lognormal, Poisson, and binomial. For example, Brinck (1967) models the endowment of a region in copper by a lognormal distribution having as one of its parameters the median abundance of that metal in the continental crust of the region. Allais (1957) models the number of mining districts in a region by the Poisson distribution, and Slichter, Dixon, and Myer (1962) model number of mines by the negative binomial and exponential distributions.

Geostatistical models include multivariate models, such as those that employ multiple regression analysis (Agterberg, Chung, Fabbri, Kelly, and Springer 1972) or multiple discriminant analysis (Harris [3]) to describe the relationship between geological variables and some measure of mineral occurrence, e.g. number of mines, mineral wealth, tonnage of metal, or number of deposits.

Models that define the structure and uncertainties of the geologist's decision-making process or his inference from geological information to mineral occurrence (Harris and Carrigan [4]) are included as geostatistical models.

The need of executives and policy-makers to have a statement of the uncertainty about estimates has generated a great demand for geostatistical estimation and description of resources, endowment, and potential supply. Consequently, much of this book is devoted to geostatistical models.

1.3.6. Compound models

An approach to resource analysis which represents a sort of compromise between the purely geological evaluation of endowment and the purely economic models is here referred to as a compound model. This model employs geostatistical methods to estimate the unknown endowment, not resources. The unknown endowment is represented by probability distributions of aspects of endowment, e.g. number of deposits, total metal in the regions, deposit size, and deposit grade. These distributions represent the earth in the region being evaluated. Resources and potential supply from the unknown endowment are estimated by interacting economics and technology with this endowment through computer simulation.

Exploration models simulate the effectiveness and cost of exploration practice to determine the deposits that would be discovered given specified economic and technological conditions. The exploitation model ascribes capital and operating costs to each simulated deposit and performs a cash flow analysis to determine if the deposit discovered would be economic, given the specified conditions. By varying the economic and technologic conditions, the models provide synthetic data on the variation of potential supply with the conditions. Statistical analysis of these synthetic data provides response functions which describe potential supply as a function of the economic and technologic factors (variables). Substitution of forecast values of the economic variables provides an estimate of potential supply ps.

Recall from § 1.2.1 that ps is the stock of metal that would be discovered and would be economic to produce given an optimum exploration effort for the stated economic conditions and given an unlimited size of market. Thus, estimated ps for stated economic conditions is not a forecast of cumulative production to the forecast horizon. Therefore, it does not provide for the sharp conclusions about resource adequacy in terms of anticipated economic conditions that an econometric model would provide if the econometric model adequately represented endowment constraints and resources dynamics. On the other hand, estimating potential supply with a compound model, as here described, does service the notion of a basic endowment of a region which consists of deposits having various physical characteristics; furthermore, it describes the effect of specified economics in the transformation of endowment to supply if a host of economic factors which influence actual production are ignored, such as competition between firms, industrial organization, and market structure. In this approach, the dynamics of resources caused by man's economic activities and technological genius are represented through the forecast levels of the economic variables and the parameters of the cost functions of the simulators of exploration and exploitation. An appraisal of resource adequacy consists of comparing the potential supply indicated by the response function (evaluated on the forecast levels of the economic variables) with forecast consumption requirements. Of course, these consumption requirements should be consistent with the product price used for the estimation of potential supply. As applied so far, compound models of potential supply have not represented, except simplistically, the interdependency of the economic system. Major emphasis has been given to wedding the physical aspects of endowment with *some* of the economic factors that affect costs of production and exploration, and to describing by a response function how potential supply computed by the compound model varies as economic parameters are changed.

Generating a response function for potential supply by statistical analysis of the output of a compound model for various levels of the economic variables makes it possible to describe potential supply probabilistically. By employing, as is commonly done, the assumption that deviations from the response function (regression equation) are normally distributed, probabilities for potential supply, conditional upon the specified economic conditions, can be computed by employing the estimate of potential supply $\widehat{ps}$ and the standard error $\hat{\sigma}$ of the response function conditional on E_t (the economic conditions of time t)

$$P(ps'' \leq PS \leq ps' \mid E_t) = F\left(\frac{ps' - \widehat{ps}}{\hat{\sigma}}\right) - F\left(\frac{ps'' - \widehat{ps}}{\hat{\sigma}}\right),$$

where ps'', ps', and PS are, respectively, the lower class limit, the upper class limit, and the random variable for potential supply conditional upon E_t. $\widehat{ps}$ is the expected value for potential supply, given E_t. This is the value of the response function evaluated at E_t. $\hat{\sigma}$ is the standard error of PS conditional upon E_t.

1.4. A brief description of two compound resource models

1.4.1. *Perspective*

In § 1.3 five classes of resource models were recognized: economic, quantity–quality, geological, geostatistical, and compound. One important class of compound models describes metal endowment probabilistically and is referred to as geostatistical endowment models. The compound model interacts an endowment model with an economic model. Through the economic model, product price, the cost of and effectiveness of exploration, and the costs of exploitation are interacted with the estimated endowment to generate an estimate of potential supply. The value of this modelling approach is that it allows the analyst to model the geology-endowment relationship in whatever form and complexity seems

indicated and then to translate this inferred endowment to potential supply by interacting the endowment and economic models. §§ 1.4.2 and 1.4.3 provide two examples of the *use* of geostatistical models of endowment as part of a compound model for potential supply. Presentation of examples of the *use* of compound models before providing an understanding of the structure of the models may seem a distortion of orderly exposition. The motivation for such a presentation is, in a manner of speaking, to see what is at the end of the road. This is particularly useful when providing a perspective for compound models. Suppose, for example, that there is a desire to have an estimate of potential supply of a metal as price varies, or an estimate of the impact of infrastructure development on the contribution of a region's mineral resources to economic development. The idea which motivates the design of a compound model is that even though the objective is an economic description or analysis, this objective may be achieved, at least in certain cases, by modelling the mineral endowment and then simulating the economic activities of exploration, mine development, and exploitation. The behaviour of this compound model or system as economic parameters are changed can be summarized by equations which describe the measure of interest as a function of the economic parameters. Thus, a compound model combined with statistical estimation of response functions presents an alternative to econometric analysis if the objective is to describe some aspect of resource economics. Although the primary motivation in this chapter has been the appraisal of resource adequacy, the two examples presented here address the more specific issue of infrastructure development and its economic effects on resources. Nevertheless, they demonstrate the main feature of compound models of resources: the wedding of a geostatistical endowment model with an economic model.

1.4.2. *The mineral endowment of the Canadian North-west*

In 1969, the Canadian government was assessing the merits of constructing a railway line extending north from Vancouver through British Columbia and across the Yukon Territory. Several different routes had been proposed for the railway. The Canadian government desired the identification of the optimum route of the proposed set, optimum in the sense that its construction over a 25-year period would generate the greatest net benefits to the region. Benefits were to be measured comprehensively in accordance with procedures of regional accounting and economic analysis.

The chief benefits were considered to derive ultimately from three basic industries: agriculture, forestry, and mining. As the proposed railway routes more or less traversed mineral-producing regions, it was apparent at the beginning that mineral resources must receive careful attention. Since the building of the railroad was to take place over an extended time period, these potential benefits must include those from known economic and subeconomic resources and those from unknown resources. The need to factor into the economic analysis the anticipated benefits from unknown deposits forced attention on the estimation of endowment.

The time allowed for the execution of the study was extremely short, only a few months. Consequently, some modelling options were ruled out. With respect to metal endowment, time constraints would permit only spatial, metal density, and subjective probability models. Multivariate geostatistical models and analyses could not be done, given the time and data constraints. The decision was made to employ subjective probabilities, estimated by geological experts, for various levels of mineral endowment. Besides severely constrained time, factors influencing this decision included the following: (1) the importance of the location of the endowment, and (2) the need for tonnage and grade estimates for the economic analysis. Neither spatial nor metal density models provide this information.

The overall plan for analysis was that a master simulator would be developed that would simulate the building of the railway and the flow of agricultural, forestry, and mineral products over the hypothetical railway and existing railways; in addition, it would perform the accounting of benefits and costs for the regions. In order to expedite the study, the system simulation was designed so that the endowment appraisal and its economic evaluation would be done prior to the main simulation and regional accounting. The interfacing of the mineral resource analysis with the main simulator was made via probability distributions for each cell for mineral concentrates and for present value for each metal and nonmetal for each of several transportation rates.

The format for the mineral endowment appraisal included 14 mineral commodities in 11 groups— copper–moly, lead–zinc, molybdenum, nickel, tungsten, asbestos, coal, iron, uranium, mercury, and silver–gold. Probability distributions were obtained from the respondent for each of the cells for each mineral group. Only one round of polling was made of 20 respondents.

There was no analysis of the mineral endowment in subeconomic grades beyond including a marginally economic grade interval in the survey form. The multiple responses (a set of probability distributions from each of the 20 respondents) were processed to yield a composite set of distributions for each cell. These distributions were subjected to analysis by the economic model, which included exploration and exploitation submodels, discounted cash flow analysis, and an algorithm for optimization of exploration expenditures.

The regional exploration model described the probability for the discovery of a deposit, given its presence, as a function of the tonnage of the deposit, the size of the exploration effort, the type of terrain, and the cover (alluvium, ice, etc.). The cost of testing multiple discoveries resulting from regional exploration was specified separately. The relationships of the exploration model were defined from data acquired by questionnaires from 18 explorationists. The exploration model was linked to the exploitation model.

The exploitation model described production costs and relationships for each mineral group: capital and operating costs for open pit and underground mining, milling charges and recovery, and production rate or mine life. Capital costs and operating costs for mining were defined as the sum of two components, one determined by the size of ore body, the other a stochastic component. This stochastic component represents variation in costs due to effects of all other variables that were not specified in the model, such as depth to deposit.

Transportation costs were specified and varied systematically in a sensitivity fashion, for effects of these costs provided the interfacing with the master transportation simulator. All of these cost components were analysed in a detailed discounted cash-flow model. These models were all interrelated in such a manner that exploration could be optimized in a loose sense at the cell level: the regional exploration expenditure was varied until it equalled the present value surplus of all deposits discovered, given that all deposits could be produced at once. Although the primary motivation of the independent endowment and resource analysis was to provide input to the master simulator and regional accounting model, the simulator developed for the resource analysis provided a means for exploring the sensitivity of various aspects of potential supply to economic factors. For example, for two rows of cells along the Yukon– British Columbia border, the resource simulator was manipulated to provide data upon which response functions were developed that showed the effects of price and transportation costs on potential supply (tons of concentrate) of copper and asbestos, given a regional exploration expenditure of US $4 000 000 per cell and the existing infrastructure (Harris, Freyman, and Barry 1971)

Copper

$$\log(T) = 7.9256 + 0.8255 \log(P) - 0.7606 \log(K)$$

Asbestos

$$\log(T) = 7.1407 + 0.2246 \log(P) - 1.0274 \log(K)$$

where T represents short tons of ore or concentrate (ore for asbestos, concentrate for copper), P is the price, and K is a multiple of the basic transportation cost as indicated by the current infrastructure.

As would be expected *a priori*, because of variation in bulk of the commodities, the elasticity [5] of tonnage of concentrate with respect to transportation costs is a much greater negative value for asbestos (−1.0274) than it is for copper (−0.7606).

1.4.3. *Infrastructure and base and precious metal resources of Sonora, Mexico*

The objectives of this study were

1. To appraise the metal resources, giving explicit consideration to infrastructure capital costs and carrying costs;
2. To assess the overall adequacy of the infrastructure of northern Sonora, Mexico, with respect to its base and precious metals resources;
3. To perform a cost–benefit analysis of constructing a road giving direct access to Hermosillo;
4. To explore modelling of infrastructure development within the construct of simulation of metal endowment and resource development;
5. To express metal resources in terms of infrastructure variables.

The metal endowment was appraised by subjective probability methods, methods differing in some respects from those described for the Canadian Northwest, but having a similar end result (for details of the survey design, method of analysis, and estimates of endowment, see Harris 1973).

The economic model was very much like that for the Canadian North-west with respect to the design of its component models: exploration, exploitation, and cash-flow analysis. However, the endowment and economic models interacted through an explicit transportation model. The transportation model determined the path over the terrain from the centre of the cell to the nearest transportation net. In addition, the cost of constructing this linkage to the net and the carrying charge per unit of product to a common destination was determined. These were communicated to the economic model and included in the economic analysis.

In order for the transportation model to determine the transportation linkage internal to the model, the topography was expressed within the model as a two-dimensional array of topographical elevations. The path of the linkage was determined by dynamic programming. Given a gradient constraint, the dynamic programming algorithm determined a discrete approximation to the shortest route across the terrain to a transportation net (for further explanation, see Harris and Euresty (1973) and Euresty [6]).

This system provided a means for exploring various relationships, such as the relationship of base and precious metals resources to prices, mining costs, capital costs for infrastructure, and carrying costs for each cell. Of particular interest in this study was the relationship of potential metal supply (economic resources that would be discovered) to infrastructure and transportation variables.

Suppose that a basic scenario for the economic variables is established and that this scenario is not altered. Then, given an appraised metal endowment, the estimated potential metal supply of the area will vary with the capital cost for the construction of the transportation linkage from the cell to the transportation net and with the charge per ton mile for transportation of the concentrate to its postulated destination; in this study that destination was Hermosillo. A possible model for this relationship is [7]

$$ps_j = B_0 \cdot (TR)^{-B_1} (CC)^{B_2} (h_j/r_j)$$

where B_0 is a constant, B_1, B_2 are the elasticities of ps_j with respect to TR and CC, respectively, h_j is the value proportion for the jth metal of the 5-metal aggregated value, i.e. that fraction of the total value of a ton of ore that is due to the value of the jth metal, r_j is the price of the jth metal, ps_j is the potential supply of the jth metal (economic resources that would also be discovered by exploration), TR is the transportation rate, and CC is the transportation capital cost.

A priori reasoning suggests that these elasticities B_1 and B_2 vary with construction distance, CD, and transportation distance, TD

$$B_1 = \alpha_0 TD^{\alpha_1}$$

$$B_2 = \omega_0 CD^{\omega_1}.$$

In other words, a more general formulation of the potential supply of a cell would describe it as a function of TD and CD as well as TR and CC

$$ps_j = B_0(TR)^{\alpha_0 TD^{\alpha_1}} \cdot (CC)^{\omega_0 CD^{\omega_1}}(h_j/r_j). \quad (1.1)$$

Of course, without numerical values for the parameters B_0, α_0, α_1, ω_0, and ω_1, eqn (1.1) constitutes no more than a conceptual model. For this model to be useful in estimating the potential supply of the jth metal for a region, we must first estimate these parameters. The compound model makes this possible. For the region of interest, a set of values for the variables TR, TD, CC, CD, and for metal prices, is specified. Then, given these values, exploration and exploitation are simulated on the mineral endowment, which is described probabilistically, and the resulting quantity of the metal that could be discovered and produced economically is determined by the model and recorded. By repeating this procedure for many different specified values of the parameters, a data file of the quantity of potential supply and the levels of associated economic and transportation variables is generated. Statistical analysis of these data provides estimates of the unknown parameters, B_0, α_0, α_1, ω_0, and ω_1.

Once these parameters have been estimated, eqn (1.1) can be used to provide estimates of potential supply for specified levels of the economic and transportation variables. For example, given the estimated endowment for cell 39, the basic price, the capital and operating costs relationship of the economic model, the basic infrastructure capital costs, and the carrying cost per mile, the potential supply of base and precious metals for this cell can be described as

$$\widehat{ps_j} = (7 \times 10^8) \cdot \{(TR)^{-TD^{2.59}/7.12}\}$$
$$\cdot \{(CC)^{-CD^{0.41}/2.14}\} \cdot (h_j/r_j) \quad (1.2)$$

where $\widehat{ps_j}$ is the estimated potential supply of the jth metal and TD and CD are in units of 100 miles.

Suppose that CD is zero and TD is 400 miles, then from eqn (1.2), we have

$$\widehat{ps_j} = (7 \times 10^8)TR^{-36.2/7.12}(h_j/r_j).$$

The elasticity of $\widehat{ps_j}$ with respect to TR, the multiple of the basic carrying rate, is approximately $-5 \approx -36.2/7.12$.

For $CD = 0$ and $TD = 200$, we have

$$\widehat{ps_j} = (7 \times 10^8)TR^{-6.03/7.12}(h_j/r_j),$$

indicating an elasticity of approximately 0.85, a much reduced elasticity of $\widehat{ps_j}$ with respect to TR.

Suppose the following $TR = 1.5$, $CC = 1.5$, $TD = 2.0$, $CD = 2.0$, $h_1 = 1.0$, $h_2 = h_3 = h_4 = h_5 = 0$, and $r_1 = US \$0.56/lb$ (the basic price). The implication of setting $h_2 = h_3 = h_4 = h_5 = 0$ and $h_1 = 1.0$ is that the resource appraisal will be in terms of copper equivalent, i.e. all metal implied by geological favourability is considered to be copper. Then

$$ps_j = \frac{(7 \times 10^8)(1.5)^{-0.85}(1.5)^{-0.62}}{0.56}$$

$$= 690\,600\,000 \text{ lbs copper equivalent.}$$

This quantity is approximately 14 per cent of the metal expected to occur in the cell (metal endowment) and about 58 per cent of potential supply when transportation and carrying distances are near zero.

The expected metal endowment of the 64-cell (400 square miles each) area was 66×10^6 tons of copper. Of this quantity, under economic conditions and the infrastructure at that time, 17×10^6 tons of copper were estimated to constitute potential supply, economic resources that would be discovered.

1.5. A summary of resource definitions and concepts

Resource base. The totality of a mineral in the earth's crust of a region is referred to as the resource base of that region.

Endowment (m). Conceptually endowment is intermediate to resource base and resources. The endowment of a region refers to that quantity of mineral in accumulations (deposits) meeting specified *physical* characteristics such as quality, size, and depth. Thus, endowment conceptually is purely physical and is not dependent directly upon economics and technology. The original endowment of a region for specified conditions is immutable with time or man's economic pursuits, although it may be more or less unknown to man.

Resources (rs). Resources refer to that quantity of mineral contained in deposits, which, if they were discovered, could be produced under stated economic conditions and currently feasible technology or technology which will be feasible in the near future. Hence resources are a function of some original endowment, economics, and technology. Mineral resources can be viewed as a part of the more inclusive term, endowment: $rs \leq m \leq$ resource base.

Economic resources (rs'). Economic resources refer to that quantity of metal that could be produced economically given *current economic* conditions and *current technology*. Thus, economic resources are a part of resources rs: $rs' \leq rs \leq m \leq$ resource base.

Potential supply (ps). Potential supply is considered to represent that part of resources that would be discovered by an optimum amount of exploration, given the specified economics and unconstrained markets. Thus, $ps \leq rs \leq m \leq$ resource base.

Supply (s_t). Supply as defined here is a stock measure, not a flow. Specifically, it is the total quantity of mineral to be discovered (cumulative production plus reserves) by time, t. It can be envisioned as a part of potential supply: $s_t \leq ps \leq rs \leq m \leq$ resource base.

Summary of relations. The important relations of these terms can be symbolically summarized as

1. $rs' \leq rs \leq m \leq$ resource base;
2. $rs = rs' + rs''$, where rs' is economic resources, and rs'' is subeconomic resources;
3. $s_t \leq ps \leq rs \leq m \leq$ resource base.

Using k to designate known resource and u to designate unknown resource, the following resource categories and relationships can be identified

1. Combinations of resources by economics and knowledge:
   $rs'_k =$ known economic resource (equivalent to total reserves),
   $rs''_k =$ known subeconomic resources,
   $rs'_u =$ unknown economic resources,
   $rs''_u =$ unknown subeconomic resources;
2. Resources classified by economics only:
   $rs' = rs'_k + rs'_u =$ economic resources,
   $rs'' = rs''_k + rs''_u =$ subeconomic resources;
3. Resources classified by knowledge only:
   $rs_k = rs'_k + rs''_k =$ known resources,
   $rs_u = rs'_u + rs''_u =$ unknown resources.

The subject matter of this book deals primarily with the estimating of rs'_u and rs''_u.

The description in Chapter 1 of resources, endowment, potential supply, and supply has three values

1. It stresses the dynamic nature of what is termed mineral resources and emphasizes the role of economics and technology in defining the magnitude of our resources;
2. It clarifies terms of resources, potential supply, and mineral endowment, terms that will be employed in this book; one of these terms, endowment, is a relatively new term and is used extensively hereafter;
3. It provides a conceptual tie from the physical system, the Earth, to economic measures and hence a framework of reference when discussing various resource appraisal methods.

1.6. Appendix: A formal statement of definitions and some concepts

This section is a restatement in more formal terms of the definitions and some of the concepts in § 1.2.

The earth's crust can be considered as one large deposit of metal, a deposit having an average grade (concentration of metal) equivalent to the measure of crustal abundance but possessing considerable variability in *grade*.

Consider, for convenience, at a given point in time, a single metallic element in a single region of the earth, so that notationally we may ignore both time, metal varieties, and places. Our experience has shown that the ultimate deposit of this metal in that region of the earth consists of many smaller deposits occurring in varied geological environments and possessing various characteristics of grade, size, shape, mineralogy, depth, host rock, etc.

Suppose that there are NM of these deposits and that they constitute a set RB

$$RB = \{r_1, \ldots, r_{NM}\}.$$

Let us represent our knowledge about the ith member of set RB by a set Z_i of NC characteristics

$$Z_i = \{k_{i1}, \ldots, k_{i,NC}\}.$$

The set of NC characteristics includes all physical properties of the NM metal deposits.

Suppose that RB were partitioned solely on the basis of only NCM of the NC characteristics, $NCM \leq NC$, with no thought given to economics or technology. The set of metallizations so formed is D, and the quantity of metal in D is referred to as m, metal endowment

$$m = \sum_D \gamma(r_i)$$

where [8] D is a subset of RB, $RD = D \cup \bar{D}$, such that $r_i \in D$ requires that $k_{i,j} \geq k'_j$, $j = 1, 2, \ldots, NCM$. $NCM \leq NC$. Otherwise, $r_i \in \bar{D}$.

For future reference, let us refer to the level of the NCM conditions used to define D as Z'. Thus, for every $r_i \in D$, $Z_i \geq Z'$.

Suppose that a function, f, is known, which for specified economic and technological conditions describes the present value, v_i, for each $r_i \in RB$.

$$v_i = f(k_{i1}, k_{i2}, \ldots, k_{i,NC}; e_1, e_2, \ldots, e_{NE}),$$

or in vector notation

$$v_i = f(z_i, E)$$

where Z_i is the set of NC characteristics of the ith deposit, as previously described and E is the set of NE economic factors,

$$E = \{e_1, e_2, \ldots, e_{NC}\}.$$

The set E includes operating costs, capital costs, prices, rate of return, etc. Naturally some of these factors reflect the state of technology.

Suppose that levels of the NE economic conditions for currently feasible and near-feasible technology are specified. While these levels must reflect currently feasible and near-feasible technology, some of them, such as product price, need not be those that currently prevail. Then, given RB and the function, f, the present value for each $r_i \in RB$ can be computed, giving rise to the set, V^R

$$V^R = \{v_1, v_2, \ldots, v_{NM}\}.$$

V can be employed to partition RB into two subsets, R and $\bar{R}$

$$RB = R \cup \bar{R}$$

$$R = \{r_i, \ldots, r_{NR}\},$$

where $r_i \in R \rightarrow v_i \geq 0$, $r_i \in \bar{R}$, otherwise, and $NR \leq NM$. That is, R contains all deposits in RB that could be produced economically given the specified economic conditions and given currently feasible or near-feasible technology. Let us designate rs as the quantity of metal in R

$$rs = \sum_R \gamma(r_i).$$

The quantity, rs, measures the magnitude, usually by weight, of the metal resource.

The set R can be considered to be a subset of D if Z', the required levels of the NCM characteristics, is specified so that none of the metallizations excluded from D would be economic to produce given the conditions for R. For example, if grade, one of the elements of Z', were set at an order of magnitude lower than that which would allow profitable mining for conditions specified for R, then $R \subset D$; $D = R \cup \bar{R}$. For such a circumstance, $rs \leq m$. For one class of resource models, that which is based upon estimating metal endowment, this is a useful perspective and is the view of metal endowment as it is employed in this book. While there is nothing in the definition of metal endowment, as previously given, that stipulates this relationship between R and D, the primary need for the term arises when an inventory of deposits having specified physical characteristics is estimated as an initial step to appraising resources and potential supply. Given this motivation, it makes little sense to set Z' such that resources for the economic and technological conditions of interest exceed the physical inventory, the metal in deposits belonging to D. It will be assumed that the term metal endowment is a more inclusive term than resources in the sense of the metal occurrences that are implied by the term. Thus, given an estimate of D and m, resources (rs) can be determined by using the value function f and the economic and technical conditions E to compute a present value, v_i, for all $r_i \in D$, creating a set V^D which contains only NMM elements

$$V^D = \{v_1, v_2, \ldots, v_{NMM}\},$$

where NMM are the number of metallizations in D and $NMM \leq NM$.

By selecting all v_i in V^D which are greater than or equal to zero, the set of NR metallizations that constitute R (the same set as was formed from RB) is formed from D

$$R = \{r_1, r_2, \ldots, r_{NR}\},$$

where $r_i \in R \rightarrow v_i \geq 0$, $r_i \in \bar{R}$ otherwise, and $NR \leq NMM \leq NM$. Thus, given the perspective described, which is that employed in this book, $R \subset D \subset RB$, and $rs \leq m \leq$ resource base.

Suppose that a set $V^{R'}$ is formed by specifying fully the currently prevailing economic conditions and technology. Then a new set R', can be formed from R by selecting all $r_i \in R$ for which $v_i \geq 0$ for the current status of economics and technology

$$R' = \{r_1, r_2, \ldots, r_{NER}\},$$

where $R = R' \cup \bar{R}'$, $r_i \in R \rightarrow v_i \geq 0$, $r_i \in \bar{R}'$ otherwise, and $NER \leq NR \leq NMM \leq NM$.

Let us designate rs' as the quantity of metal in R' and rs'' as the quantity of metal in $\bar{R}'$. Then

$$rs' = \sum_{R'} \gamma(r_i).$$

Similarly,

$$rs'' = \sum_{\bar{R}'} \gamma(r_i).$$

The quantity rs' is economic resources, while rs'' is subeconomic resources. Thus, $R' \subset R \subset D \subset RB$; $rs' \leq rs \leq m \leq$ resource base; and $rs = rs' + rs''$.

Potential supply ps can be formed directly from R or indirectly from D. Consider set R, which contains those metal ocurrences which would be economic to produce for specified economic conditions and currently feasible or near-feasible technology, if the occurrences were known. Suppose that R were partitioned to R^d and $\bar{R}^d$ such that R^d contains those metal occurrences of R that would be discovered by an optimum exploration effort EX^*

$$R = R^d \cup \bar{R}^d,$$

where $r_i \in R^d \rightarrow v_i - c_i \geq 0$ and discovery $r_i \in \bar{R}^d$, otherwise. Then, c_i is the share of EX^* for the ith metal occurrence that was discovered by EX^* and $ps = \sum_{R^d} \gamma(r_i)$. Thus, $R^d \subset R \subset RB$ and $ps \leq rs \leq$ resource base.

Suppose that D were formed from RB by specifying Z' such that $R \subset D$. It has already been shown that by consideration of exploration, R^d, the subset of metal occurrences of R that would be discovered, can be formed from R. Then, $R^d \subset R \subset D$. Since ps is the sum of metal in R^d, the relationship between ps and metal endowment m is obvious: $R^d \subset R \subset D \subset RB$ and $ps \leq rs \leq m \leq$ resource base.

Let us examine further the concept of an optimum level of EX. To contribute to potential supply, deposits must be of a quality such that their exploitation covers production costs and the costs of discovering them. Allocating to each deposit discovered its share of the exploration effort, EX, gives a net present value (net of exploration and production costs). Naturally, increasing EX to a higher level than EX^* discovers more deposits, but since EX is charged against only those deposits discovered, increasing EX beyond EX^* loses more economic and discoverable resources than are gained. This is because at any progression in the optimizing path of exploration, the deposits which remain to be discovered require a greater expenditure per unit of resources than those already discovered, and because when interacting exploration and exploitation with endowment in a 'one-shot' or 'single contract' kind of optimization in which the sequential timing of incremental exploration expenditures are suppressed, there are no 'sunk' exploration costs. Therefore, diminishing returns to exploration, due to the greater difficulty of discovery of progressively larger fractions of the endowment, means that exploration costs allocated to the deposits discovered increase while at the same time additional deposits are discovered by a greater expenditure. Since the set R^d consists of only those occurrences that would be discovered by EX *and* would be economic to produce when all exploration and exploitation costs are considered, then there is an optimum level of EX, EX^*.

If we now relax the assumption of unlimited markets but invoke the assumptions that the single large

firm will seek to maintain prices and that there is no technological change across time, then exploration would be spread across time as warranted by demand and depletion. Thus, at any point in time, EX_t would be less than or equal to EX^*; consequently, the set of known and exploited deposits $\tilde{R}_t^d$ would be some subset of R^d

$$R^d = \tilde{R}_t^d \cup \bar{\tilde{R}}_t^d.$$

Of course, the sum of metal in deposits of $\tilde{R}_t^d$ must be less than or equal to the sum of metal in deposits belonging to R^d

$$\sum_{\tilde{R}_t^d} \gamma(r_i) \leq \sum_{R^d} \gamma(r_i).$$

Let us designate this concept of supply as a stock as s_t

$$s_t = \sum_{\tilde{R}_t^d} \gamma(r_i).$$

Then, at any point in time in our simplified and hypothetical world, supply is less than or equal to potential supply

$$s_t \leq ps.$$

Obviously,

$$\lim_{t \rightarrow \infty} (s_t) = ps.$$

In terms of an individual area and a single metallic ore type hypothesized here, the more intensely the area has been explored the more closely s_t will approach ps. The relationships of the stock terms from resource base to supply can be summarized as follows

$s_t \leq ps \leq rs \leq m \leq$ resource base
$$\Rightarrow R_t^d \subset R^d \subset R \subset D \subset RB.$$

References

Agterberg, F. P., Chung, C. F., Fabbri, A. G., Kelly, A. M., and Springer, J. S. (1972). *Geomathematical evaluation of copper and zinc potential of the Abitibi area, Ontario and Quebec.* Paper 71–41, Geological Survey of Canada.

Allais, M. (1957). Method of appraising economic prospects of mining exploration over large territories: Algerian Sahara case study. *Management Sci.* **3**(4), 285–347.

Brinck, J. W. (1967). *Note on the distribution and predictability of mineral resources.* Euratom 3461, Brussels.

Cargill, S. M., Root, D. H., and Bailey, E. H. (1980). Resource estimation from historical data: mercury, a test case. *J. int. Ass. Math. Geol.* **12**(5), 489–522.

——, ——, and —— (1981). Estimating usable resources from historical industry data. *Econ. Geol.* **76**, 1081–95.

Harris, D. P. (1973). A subjective probability appraisal of metal endowment of Northern Sonora, Mexico. *Econ. Geol.* **68**(2), 222–42.

—— and Euresty, D. E. (1973). The impact of transportation network upon the potential supply of base and precious metals from Sonora, Mexico. *Proc. 10th Int. Symp. Application of Computer Methods in the Mineral Industry*, pp. 99–108. The South African Institute of Mining and Metallurgy, Johannesburg.

—— Freyman, A. J., and Barry, G. S. (1971). A mineral resource appraisal of the Canadian Northwest using subjective probabilities and geological opinion. *Proc. 9th Int. Symp. Techniques for Decision-Making in the Mineral Industry*, Special Vol. 12, pp. 100–16. Canadian Institute of Mining and Metallurgy, Montreal.

Lasky, S. G. (1950). How tonnage and grade relations help predict ore reserves. *Engng Mining J.* **151**(4), 81–5.

McKelvey, V. E. (1973). Mineral resource estimates and public policy. In *United States mineral resources* (ed. D. A. Brobst and W. P. Pratt), pp. 9–19. Geological Survey prof. paper 820, US Geological Survey, Washington, DC.

Miller, B. M., Thomsen, H. L., Dolton, G. L., Coury, A. B., Hendricks, T. A., Lennartz, F. E., Powers, R. B., Sable, E. G., and Varnes, K. L. (1975). *Geological estimates of undiscovered recoverable oil and gas resources in the United States.* Circular 725, US Geological Survey, Washington, DC.

Musgrove, P. A. (1971). The distribution of metal resources (tests and implications of the exponential grade-size relation). *Proceedings of the Council of Economics of AIME*, pp. 349–417. New York.

Netschert, B. C. (1958). *The future supply of oil and gas.* The Johns Hopkins University Press, Baltimore. (For Resources for the Future, Inc.)

Ridge, J. D. (1974). *Mineral resource appraisal and analysis.* Geological Survey prof. paper 921, US Geological Survey, Washington, DC.

Schanz, J. J. (1975). *Resource terminology: an examination of concepts and terms and recommendations for improvement.* Electric Power Research Institute, Palo Alto, California.

Schurr, S. H. and Netschert, B. C., with Eliasberg, V. F., Lerner, J., and Landsberg, H. H. (1960). *Energy in the American economy, 1850–1975*, The Johns Hopkins University Press, Baltimore. (For Resources for the Future, Inc.)

Singer, D. A. and DeYoung, J. H., Jr. (1980). What can grade-tonnage relations really tell us? In *Ressources minérales—mineral resources* (ed. Claude Guillemin and Philippe Lagny), pp. 91–101, 26th CGI, Bur. Recherches Géol. et Minières Mém. 106, Orleans, France.

Slichter, L. B., Dixon, W. J., and Myer, G. H. (1962). Statistics as a guide to prospecting. *Proc. Symp. Mathematical and Computer Applications in Mining and Exploration*, pp. F1-1–F1-27. College of Mines, University of Arizona, Tucson.

Notes

1. Netschert (1958) originated the term resource base and defined its relations to reserves and resources.
2. As commonly used in exploration and mining, for material to qualify as a proved reserve requires that it has been sufficiently well sampled in three dimensions so that there is little doubt about the amount of ore that can be produced under current economics and technology.
3. Harris, D. P. (1965). An application of multivariate statistical analysis to mineral exploration. Ph.D. dissertation, The Pennsylvania State University.
4. Harris, D. P. and Carrigan, F. J. (1980). A probabilistic endowment appraisal system based upon the formalization of geologic decisions—final report: demonstration and comparative analysis of estimates and methods. US Dept. of Energy, Grand Junction Office, Colorado.
5. In general, the elasticity of y, $y = f(P)$, with respect to P is given by $(\partial y/\partial P) \cdot (P/y)$. When the relationship of y to P is log–log, elasticity is simply the coefficient of P.
6. Euresty, D. E. (1971). A systems approach to the regional evaluation of potential mineral resources using computer simulation, with a case study of the impact of infrastructure on potential supply of base and precious metals of Sonora, Mexico. Ph.D. dissertation. The Pennsylvania State University.
7. The presence of r_j, the price of the jth metal, in the denominator seems to contradict economic theory. However, a change in r_j is accompanied by a change in h_j; consequently, the overall effect of a price change must be described by h_j/r_j.
8. The function γ maps the characteristics of the ith deposit, r_i, into m_i, which is the quantity of metal in deposit r_i. $\bar{D}$ means 'not D'. $D \cup \bar{D}$ means union of sets of D and $\bar{D}$. $r_i \in \bar{D}$ means r_i belongs to set $\bar{D}$.

2 RESOURCE APPRAISAL BY MODELS OF ECONOMIC ACTIVITIES

2.1. Overview

This chapter describes those methods and models that have been used to estimate some stock measure of a mineral resource *indirectly* by employing a model of an economic relation or activity. These models are not stochastic, and they do not employ geological factors or physical descriptions of the resource. Estimates of resource abundance are implied only, as indicated by the economic model. Here, the term economic model is used in a loose sense to refer to any relation that includes (1) economic factors, e.g. price, supply, and demand, or (2) the result of economic activity, such as quantities of a mineral commodity that are discovered or produced.

Contrasted to the implicit approach of economic models to describing resource abundance is the explicit approach in which the resources are viewed basically as a physical phenomenon having secondary economic characteristics. The explicit approach to estimation is quite different: metal endowment is estimated, and then the impact of economics on the translating of the endowment to an inventory of resources or potential supply is evaluated. Methods for explicit estimation are described in subsequent sections.

For completeness, this chapter begins with a discussion of supply–demand analysis as a means of inferring resource adequacy. While this discussion is a useful commentary on resource economics, it also serves to demonstrate the limitations of supply–demand analysis as a means of describing *quantitatively* the magnitude of potential supply, resources, and endowment. Because of these limitations, this chapter deals primarily with the applications of life-cycle models of discovery and production and with the applications of discovery-rate models. These models describe potential supply as a limiting value of cumulative production (life-cycle models) and cumulative discovery (discovery-rate models).

2.2. Supply and demand—econometric models

The structure of an econometric model varies with the objective of the model and its time reference. The richest models in terms of economic theory and measures are referred to as structural models, models designed to examine such things as elasticities of demand and supply to economic factors, such as product price, income, factor prices, etc. For example, a single short-run econometric model of a metal market might be of the form

$$Q^s = \phi_s(P; C_1, C_2, C_3),$$
$$Q^D = \phi_D(P; P_1, P_2, Y),$$
$$Q^s = Q^D,$$

where P is the price of the metal, P_1, P_2 are the prices of substitute metals, C_1, C_2, C_3 are the costs of factors of production, Y is the income measure, and Q^s, Q^D are quantities supplied and demanded, respectively.

A model of this nature is of interest because, from the coefficients of the explanatory variables, measures can be obtained that reflect the responsiveness of demand and supply to change in economic variables. Econometric models express metal supply as a flow quantity per unit of time, Q_t^s, not as a stock. Usually, data are available only on the flow per year or, at best, quarter year. Relative to the conceptual framework for mineral resources and supply, the quantity Q_t^s is a function of s_t

$$Q_t^s = s_t - s_{t-1} - b_t,$$

where Q_t^s is the quantity supplied in time period t (usually a year), s_t, s_{t-1} is the cumulative production to time t and $t-1$, respectively, as defined in the conceptual framework for resources, and b_t are reserves added during the period $t-(t-1)$.

A model devised by Burrows (1975) of Charles River Associates for the world tungsten market serves as an example of a model that contains some economic structure and dynamics for a moderate time frame. In this model, the tungsten supply functions for the countries involved took on various forms, as demonstrated by the supply functions for Australia and Brazil

Australia.
$$\log{(Q_t^s)} = 0.0949223 + 0.265807 \log{(\bar{P}_t)}$$
$$+ 0.0302115t + 0.253721X_t,$$

where $\bar{P}_t = (P_t + P_{t-1})/2.0$, an average price of the current and previous time periods, t is time, and X_t is a dummy variable [1].

Brazil.

$$\log(Q_t^s) = -0.344874 + 0.430798 \log(\bar{P}_t)$$
$$+ 0.779576 \log(Q_{t-1}^s) + 0.00944708t,$$

where $\bar{P}_t = (P_t - P_{t-1})/2.0$ and Q_{t-1}^s is the supply in the previous time period.

The point to be made by these examples is that supply equations for a time frame other than the short term commonly contain price and variables describing dynamics of the structure of supply. Dynamics may be expressed in the supply models by direct and indirect means. The presence of price in equations explaining quantities demanded or supplied needs no explanation because of its critical role in economic theory. Accordingly, price appears in both models. In the case of the supply of tungsten for Australia, the time variable t accounts for change in structure, technology, depletion, etc. The supply equation for Brazilian tungsten contains two proxies for dynamics: the variable t, as was the case for Australian tungsten, and the variable Q_{t-1}^s. The use of Q_{t-1}^s is in essence relating supply of the current period t to the supply of the last period, but allowing for some modification by economic factors in the current time period. In resource adequacy studies, the time frame is sufficiently long that the determinants of supply and demand can change. Therefore, resource models often are designed to include some form of dynamics.

Models of demand commonly express the fact that the demand for a metal is a derived demand—derived from the demand for producer and consumer goods that in part consist of metal. For example, a conceptually simple model might consider supply to be a function of price of the metal and grade of the resources, and demand a function of price of the metal and the level of industrial activity

$$Q^D = \phi_D(P, I),$$
$$Q^s = \phi_s(P, q),$$

where I is some measure of industrial activity or some measure of the end use of a metal, P is the price, and q is the grade.

Of course, to use such a model for forecasting would require auxiliary relationships for the forecasting of P, I, and q. Consequently, econometric models for long-term forecasting often are simplistic, tying demand to quantities that have stable time trends, such as GNP, industrial production, population, etc.

The modelling of supply for long-term forecasting often requires even greater sacrifice of economic structure, and may at times be devoid of structure, being modelled strictly as a trend, a function of time

$$Q_t^s = \phi_s(t),$$

where t is time.

As an example of an evaluation of resource adequacy from an economics perspective, consider the following description of the demand projections made by Netschert and Landsberg (1961, p. 9)

> The projection of automobile production, an item affecting a multitude of metals, may help explain the procedure. The starting point is the projected adult population as the essential clue to automobile ownership in the future. A declining rate of growth in ownership, based upon the experience of the past three decades and logically supported by the limitations of time and space, is applied to the population data to obtain number of vehicles. To this is added the replacement demand, based upon assumed vehicle life and attrition rates. Aggregate vehicle production is thus obtained and, by use of a bill of materials, dissected into the component metals. Future substitution in this bill of materials and assumptions regarding future scrap supply are the final factors taken into account that affect the estimated primary metal demand projected to arise out of automobile production.

This description emphasizes the derived demand for metal; in this case, some part of total metal demand is derived from the demand for automobiles, which are constructed in some part from the metal of interest. Notice that although the future supply of metals was the central issue of their work, Netschert and Landsberg performed demand analysis as part of the analysis of supply, for supply and demand are related through price, and the state of one implies some state of the other. Netschert and Landsberg did not describe mathematical models; the following symbolic representation of the relations they described is the author's interpretation and is presented solely as a summary of the concepts of their analysis. Let $Q_{l,t}^D$ be the new metal demand for the lth metal, a demand derived from the demand for product A in the tth time period

$$Q_{l,t}^D = f_D(A_t, O_t, R_t, Z_t, t),$$

where A_t represents automobile production, O_t automobile ownership by the population, R_t replacement automobiles, Z_t scrap availability, and t the time period.

Prediction of $Q_{l,t}^D$ requires prediction of the explanatory variables. For prediction purposes, the following relations were employed

$$A_t = f_A(POP_t)$$
$$POP_t = f_{POP}(t)$$
$$O_t = f_O(t)$$
$$Z_t = f_Z(t)$$
$$R_t = f_R(A_{t-y}),$$

where POP is the population and y the assumed life of automobiles. A derived demand for the lth metal exists for each of the k_l consumer products that use the lth metal. This can be represented by an additional subscript j, one ranging over the k_l products, $Q^D_{l,j,t}$.

The total demand for the lth metal to time t consists of the summation of the demands for the metal in all consumer products over the years of the forecast period

$$\bar{Q}^D_{l,t} = \sum_{r=t_0}^{t} \sum_{j=1}^{k_l} Q^D_{l,j,r},$$

where t_0 is the year from which projection was made, k_l the number of end uses (consumer goods) for the lth metal, $Q^D_{l,j,t}$ the demand for the lth metal derived from the jth consumer product in the tth time period, and $\bar{Q}^D_{l,t}$ the total derived demand for the lth metal in period t. Notice that basically the demand for a metal is tied in some fashion to time trends in the explanatory variables; therefore, the model could be restated as

$$Q^D_{l,j,t} = f_D(f_A(t), f_O(t), f_R(A_{t-y}), f_Z(t)).$$

Obviously, prediction of $Q^D_{l,j,t}$ is only as reliable as are the trends in these explanatory variables.

Now, consider the appraisal of supply and resource adequacy as set out by Netschert and Landsberg (1961, p. 10)

The projected United States demand for primary metal from 1960 through 2000 is then cumulated and compared with United States reserves and resources as currently estimated by the government or by other authoritative sources. Domestic primary production of the metal cannot be projected, however, because of the indeterminable effects of government policy on imports and of private decisions between domestic and foreign investment in the production of the metal. It is, in other words, indeterminate with respect to the basic economic assumptions used to project demand. Domestic primary production is therefore cumulated on the arbitrary assumption that it continues through 2000 at current levels.

Cumulative production is then compared with reserves to obtain an indication of the needed discoveries if the assumed output level were to be maintained, and also compared with identified resources. Where possible, the potential cost effects of turning to presently potential ore are indicated.

Basically, this analysis supposes that demand and supply will equilibrate, but, as pointed out by Netschert and Landsberg, it is impossible to predict the contribution of domestic supply to total supply because of the impact of governmental policies on the size of imports. An appraisal of resource adequacy is relevant only to *some* level of imports, the polar case being for zero imports. The assumption made by Netschert and Landsberg was that domestic production would continue at present levels, meaning that the increase in new metal requirements would all be supplied from foreign sources. Conceptually, this model can be represented as

$$Q^s_{l,t} = \Delta s_{l,t} - b_{l,t} = c_l,$$

where $\Delta s_{l,t} = s_{l,t} - s_{l,t-1}$, $s_{l,t}$ is the cumulative production and reserves of the lth metal at time t, $b_{l,t}$ the reserve additions during the time period $t-(t-1)$, and c_l is a constant value for the lth metal.

Resource adequacy was appraised by comparing the sum of $Q^s_{l,t}$ over the forecast period with reserves

$$\sum_{r=t_0}^{t} Q^s_{l,r} = (t-t_0) \cdot c_l \le b_{l,t_0} \Rightarrow \text{Adequacy}.$$

If this condition is met, then it is reasonable to expect adequate metal supply without price increases. But, if $\sum_{r=t_0}^{t} Q^s_{l,r} > b_{l,t_0}$, then it was assumed, *ceteris paribus*, that the *required additional supply would be forthcoming from 'potential ore.'* Judgement was made as to the price increase required to generate the supply from yet unknown resources (new discoveries).

The main issues addressed by supply models are quantity and quality of the metal resources. In the case of resource adequacy studies, because of their long-time horizon, these issues become enigmatic, for they are the quantity and quality of metal resources that are *known and unknown*. In econometric modelling these issues are treated by projection of trends directly or indirectly within an economic structure. The weakness of this approach to a resource adequacy study having a long-time horizon is the assumption that trends of the past that are reflected in available data will continue into the future. The more distant the future, the greater the possibility that structural and technological change unforeseen at the present will change metal consumption and metal resources. Consumer preferences in end-product can modify the demand for a metal; manufacturing technology can shift the demand for a metal for a given product; new extraction technologies can create new resources either by a process that can extract metal from previously untreatable ores or a less costly, more efficient process of refining or smelting; mining may allow the mining of lower-grade conventional ores; new technologies of exploration can provide greater detection capabilities for currently known modes of occurrence; and advances in scientific knowledge may identify modes of occurrence of a metal that were not previously known. Obviously, it is asking the impossible for *any* modelling effort to foresee all of these possibilities for a long-time horizon. We must accept the fact that every model becomes less reliable rapidly as the time horizon is extended.

Nevertheless, it is a reasonable judgement that econometric models are relatively rigid and not easily manipulated for contingency issues when such issues are more than a mild departure from the experience of the past. For this reason, there is incentive to examine alternative means of minerals modelling, such as explicit models. However, before turning to the explicit models, it should be carefully noted that the very nature of econometric models that makes them inflexible for 'creative' contingency analysis makes them very useful for short and even moderate time frames. This is particularly important if the desired objective is some aggregate economic characteristic, such as price elasticity of supply for an industry, whether of a national or local scope. Explicit models cannot substitute for econometric models in providing such measures.

In the conceptual section, metal resources were defined directly, emphasizing their physical, economic, and technological aspects. Economics and technology were represented as partitioning or sorting operations upon the physical system. Of course, the magnitude of metal endowment is never known, but can only be estimated; hence the true impact of economics and technology in the partitioning operation can never be known in an *a priori* sense. The implicit approach to resource estimation *does not seek to estimate resources* at all. Econometric models at the most describe *resources indirectly* only to the extent that an extrapolation of supply relations to meet projected demand requirements implies the existence of the sources of the metal supplies beyond known reserves. If the sum of projected supply flows exceeds the quantity of known reserves, then the forecast of supplies is a kind of indirect estimate of resources, resources that are defined in terms of the prices and technology either stated explicitly or implicitly in the econometric models.

2.3. Simple life-cycle (time series trend) models

2.3.1. *Concepts and modelling issues*

A trend equation can be considered a very simple, aggregate economic model in which it is assumed that the dynamics of the economy are reflected in a time series of metal production or discoveries.

Trend analysis and extrapolation require a history of production sufficient to estimate the parameters of a curve that represents the time series and then the extrapolation of the equation to some future time horizon.

The assessment of the total, ultimate production of a mineral by the life-cycle model makes no attempt to define that which exists in the region, its endowment. Instead, the model estimates the total that will be produced, given the assumption that trends of the past will continue into the future. Of course, this general assumption is all-encompassing. To facilitate the demonstration of the magnitude of this general assumption, let us turn to a symbolic representation. Let us designate dp/dt as the production during dt, and let us propose that this quantity is a function of m economic variables: $e_1, e_2, \ldots, e_m$. Then, in symbolic notation dp/dt is related to the economic variables through function γ

$$dp/dt = \gamma(e_1, e_2, \ldots, e_m).$$

In the real world, the function γ changes over time as technology changes and as the economic processes adjust to the changes in the structure of the economy and to depletion of the original endowment. Nevertheless, let us assume γ is known and does not change, and let us restrict the future behaviour of each of these m economic variables to a pattern defined by some secular trend

$$e_1 = \phi_1(t),$$
$$e_2 = \phi_2(t),$$
$$e_m = \phi_m(t).$$

Then, $dp/dt = \gamma[\phi_1(t), \ldots, \phi_m(t)]$ or $dp/dt = f(t)$, where the new function f reflects the sum effect of the m individual trends as they relate to dp/dt.

If $dp/dt = f(t)$, it must follow that $dp = f(t)\,dt$. And,

$$p_t = F(t) = \int_0^t f(\tau)\,d\tau.$$

Ultimate production, p_∞, is the value of the integral at $t = \infty$

$$p_\infty = \int_0^\infty f(\tau)\,d\tau = F(\infty).$$

The definitions set forth in Chapter 1 are related to the life-cycle quantities as

$$s_t - s_{t-1} - b_t \to f(t),$$

where s_t is the cumulative production plus reserves at time t and b_t the reserve additions during period, $t-(t-1)$.

$$\text{Limit}_{t \to \infty} [s_t] = ps = F(\infty),$$

where ps is the potential supply and $F(\infty)$ the ultimate production. Undiscovered, recoverable resources at time t are defined as $F(\infty) - F(t)$, which is analogous to $ps - s_t$.

Potential supply evaluated by the life cycle, however, is vaguely defined, for extrapolation of F implies *not current* economic conditions but *those future economic conditions* (prices, costs, grade, etc.) *that would prevail if current trends* in the economic factors continue. In other words, the strong assumption is made that trends of the past will continue in the future. Obviously, the farther away the future is, the less credible is this assumption and the less useful is the estimate of potential supply for the extrapolated period. This general assumption covers a wide spectrum of specific conditions, which include the following.

1. Technological change will continue in a pattern similar to that of the past.
2. The effectiveness of technological innovations in translating resources to reserves will be similar to that of the past.
3. Tonnage and grade characteristics of new resources will change over time in accordance to patterns reflected in the production time series.
4. Changes in the structure of the economy will continue along past trends.

The point to be made here is that extrapolation of F to time t in reality implies the continuation of many past trends—trends in economics and technology of exploitation, exploration, and utilization, trends in the activity of exploration, and trends in the characteristics of mineral deposits. When interpretation of F is not conditional upon mode of occurrence in a region and is considered to represent cumulative supply in general, its use carries additional assumptions, the assumptions that there are no other modes of occurrence nor new supply areas. Obviously this unconditional use and interpretation of F, evaluated at $t = \infty$, as an estimate of total potential supply implies very binding conditions.

The secular trend of an industry may be described by any of a number of curves, including linear, parabolic, modified exponential, logistic, Gompertz, or exponential, depending upon the maturity of the industry and the length of the time series examined. The use of trend analysis for the estimation of resources requires extrapolation of some observed trend of the past into the future. This imposes constraints upon circumstances for which trend extrapolation can be effectively used for resource appraisal.

1. The selected mathematical relationship of production to time must not only fit the time series reasonably well but also must behave in a reasonable manner when extrapolated.
2. There must be a history of production sufficient to define the pattern of trend or, stated equivalently, to estimate the parameters of the mathematical function.

In essence, responding to these constraints forces the analyst to specify a *model* of metal production across time. Although economic theory does not dictate the form of the model, history documents that the time series of many phenomena exhibit a 'life cycle'. With reference to metal production of a region, mine, mining district, or nation, this cycle is characterized by the following phases:

(1) small absolute size of production as deposits in the region are discovered and an exponential increase in production as the mines come on stream and increase production to capacity;
(2) continued increase in production, but at a declining rate, as the discovery of the premium deposits is completed;
(3) maximum production and zero rate of increase as depletion offsets new discoveries;
(4) decline in magnitude of production as all major deposits are in production and depletion increases. Additional discoveries are of small, associated deposits;
(5) rapid decline, at an exponential rate, as mines approach exhaustion.

This concept of life cycle is used as a benchmark for the specification of the trend model.

The concept of a life cycle seems to have an intuitive appeal to persons engaged in mining, for if there is one thing that seems a certainty, it is that an orebody being mined will one day be exhausted. The life cycle is simply an expression of the wasting feature of a mineral deposit as it is produced. The logic that supports the life-cycle representation of a mine, under certain conditions, supports argument for the existence of a cycle for metal production from a mining district, region, or a nation. In fact, Hewett (1929) proposed that such cycles can ultimately be found in all phases of metal production (see Fig. 2.1). For example, Fig. 2.2 is a graph of annual production, smoothed by a moving average, of an actual

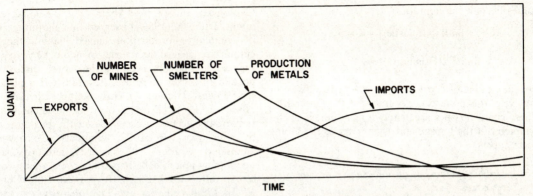

Fig. 2.1. Cycles in metal production. (Source: Hewett 1929, p. 89.)

mining district in Arizona (Harris [2]); the bell-shape of the time series is very marked.

It is common to select a mathematical model that describes a bell or skewed-bell shape to represent this life cycle of metal production. Curves that have this form and often are employed are the first derivative logistic (symmetric bell) or the first derivative Gompertz (skewed bell).

In practice, it is often the integral curve, the logistic or Gompertz, that is fitted to the time series data (cumulative)

$$\text{Logistic: } p_t = \frac{K}{1+e^{a+bt}},$$

$$\text{Gompertz: } p_t = yb^{c^t}.$$

The first derivatives of these curves describe the symmetric (logistic) and skewed (Gompertz) bell shapes. As indicated, they usually are fit to the cumulative production time series. Given the appropriate signs of their parameters, each of these

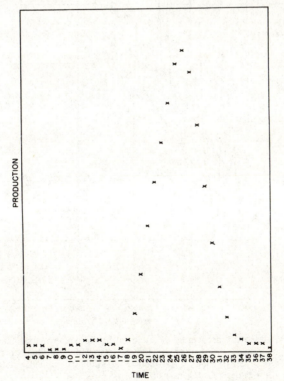

Fig. 2.2. Moving average graph of production of an exhausted mining district. (After Harris [2].)

curves becomes asymptotic

$$\lim_{t \to \infty} [p_t(\text{logistic})] = K = p_\infty,$$

$$\lim_{t \to \infty} [p_t(\text{Gompertz})] = y = p_\infty.$$

The flex point of the logistic is reached halfway in the cycle; this point occurs earlier for the Gompertz. These characteristics are simply a restatement of the symmetry of the logistic and asymmetry of the Gompertz curves.

2.3.2. *Hubbert's analysis of domestic crude oil resources*

One of the leading exponents of trend analysis for the assessment of various mineral resource issues is M. King Hubbert (1967, 1969, 1974). Trend methods recently have received considerable attention as a result of Hubbert's analysis of the ultimate production of US crude oil and the subsequent conflict between him and other scientists of the US

Geological Survey over their very dissimilar estimates. Hubbert (1969) observed that the time series of cumulative production lagged behind that of cumulative-proved discoveries by about 12 years (see Fig. 2.3). He observed further that discoveries peaked in 1957; therefore, he predicted a peak in US domestic crude oil production, exclusive of Alaska, in 1969. History proved this prediction to be remarkably accurate, as it missed the peaking date by one year. In 1957, cumulative discoveries amounted to 85.3×10^9 barrels; therefore, based upon an assumed, bell-shaped life cycle, there would remain after 1969, 85.3×10^9 barrels. Equivalently, $F(\infty) \approx 170.6 \times 10^9$ barrels. This quantity was much smaller than recoverable resource estimates made at that time by others for the lower 48 states: 590×10^9 barrels by Zapp [3] of the US Geological Survey and 380×10^9 barrels by L. G. Weeks (1959). Hubbert's analysis of trends in discovery, production, and reserves and the basically accurate prediction of the peaking of oil production was most artfully done. For

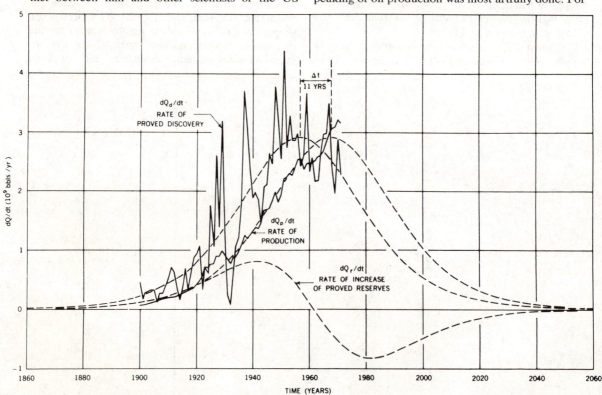

Fig. 2.3. Annual production and proved discoveries of crude oil in the conterminous United States from 1900 to 1971 superposed on the theoretical curves (dashed) derived from Hubbert's logistic curves—see Fig. 36 in Hubbert (1974). (Source: Hubbert 1974.) *Note:* Equivalences of Hubbert's and the author's notations are as follows: $dQ_p/dt = dp/dt$; $dQ_d/dt = ds/dt$; and $dQ_r/dt = dr/dt$.

this analysis, he deserves much credit. However, successful analysis of the turning point in a time series of production does not necessarily imply that extrapolation of the perceived trend will provide an accurate or useful estimate of undiscovered, recoverable oil resources. There is a wide chasm separating these two very different objectives, and bridging this chasm with a life-cycle model of production requires some rather strong assumptions and conditions.

Although Hubbert's approach has received some favourable response, particularly since the energy crisis, it also has been sharply criticized as a method for the appraisal of ultimate production or undiscovered, recoverable resources. Ryan (1965, p. 5) concluded his criticism of trend extrapolation with this general comment

> There is widespread agreement that reliable estimates of ultimate production would be of great value in formulating corporate and government policies. Since adequate subsurface data are not available, however, efforts have been made to develop estimates by various purely statistical devices. Two of the more prominent efforts involve fitting analytical functions and then extrapolating the fitted curves. Such purely mechanical approaches have no logic foundation, however, and should not be used as a basis for policy.

In counterargument to Ryan's criticisms, Moore [4], who performed an analysis similar to that of Hubbert, claimed that too much had been made of the forecast of ultimate production and that his primary interest in the fitting of the Gompertz curve was the projection of the rate of activity. Hubbert argued similarly that the beginning and end of the cycle are not critical, but the turning point from increasing supply to decreasing supply is important and that this turning point was his primary objective. With respect to this argument, Ryan (1965) comments that the ultimate discoveries need not necessarily be twice cumulative discoveries at the time of the peak of discovery, for the multiple of two implies that there is only one peak in production, which may not be so, and that if there is one peak it is at the midpoint of a symmetric curve, a property of the logistic.

Brooks (1976, pp. 166, 167) summarizes Netschert's (1958, pp. 35–8) criticisms

> Netschert's first criticism is that ... the technique depends on data developed from past discoveries; therefore, he says it carries with it the implication that these trends will continue and that further technologic progress will exert no influence.
> A second and related criticism .... is that it is difficult at best to determine where one is on the curve . . . . a point recognized by Hubbert (1965, p. 1721) when he

states that, 'Prior to the peak in the rate of discovery these criteria are relatively uninformative.'
> Netschert's third and most fundamental criticism . . . . is that institutional and market forces, not just resource endowment, determine the course of the time rates of discovery and production.

While the latter two of Netschert's criticisms, as summarized by Brooks, appear to be well taken, the first one may not be totally accurate. The extrapolation of a production or discovery trend does not imply that further technologic progress will exert no influence; rather, it implies that progress in technology will occur at the same rate and be of the same kind as in the past. However, trend extrapolation does not allow for the innovation of a totally new technology; in this regard Netschert's criticism is valid.

The foregoing comments deal generally with the very foundations of resource estimation by life cycle; namely,

(1) the proposition that the complex of economics, technology, and depletion can be captured and prescribed by a mathematical function of time—a life cycle;
(2) the shape of the cycle, assuming there is one;
(3) selection and fitting of the appropriate mathematical curve.

This last issue, model selection and estimation, was the focus of a thorough investigation by Mayer, Silverman, Zeger, and Bruce (1979) of Hubbert's analysis. They point out that while Hubbert uses the derivative logistic as a life-cycle model of production, he never really fitted the logistic to production data. Instead, he derived his production life-cycle model by applying a time shift to a logistic curve which had been estimated from cumulative discovery data—this is to compensate for the lag of the production cycle (see Fig. 2.3). Consequently, Mayer *et al.* (1979) carried out two levels of analysis.

In the first level, they took as given that the logistic is the correct life-cycle model and investigated the effect of using rigorous statistical methods to estimate its parameters from Hubbert's discovery data. They concluded that because of autocorrelation in cumulative discovery data, the most appropriate statistical approach would be to estimate the parameters of the derivative logistic from the time series on annual, instead of cumulative, discoveries. Interestingly, estimation of the life-cycle model from annual discovery data also provided a better fit than Hubbert's logistic or a logistic fitted to *cumulative* discoveries by statistical means. The ulti-

TABLE 2.1. *Parameter estimates from analysis of discovery data.* (*Source: Mayer* et al. *1979, p. 23.*)

Model	Ultimate production (×10⁹ bbl)		Peak year	Residual sum of squares
	Estimate	Confidence interval		
Logistic	154	148–61	1954	2.07×10^9
Generalized logistic	153	138–68	1954	2.00×10^9
Hyperbolic	178	143–213	1950	1.931×10^9

mate recoverable crude oil estimated by the best fitting model (discovery data) was found to be 154×10^9 bbl, a quantity even less than Hubbert's 170×10^9 bbl.

Still employing discovery data, Mayer *et al.* (1979) relaxed the assumption that the logistic is the correct life-cycle model and examined the fit of the generalized logistic and hyperbolic curves. The results of this investigation are reported in Table 2.1.

In their second level of analysis, Mayer *et al.* (1979) investigated the logistic, complex logistic, and hyperbolic curves as life-cycle models for the time series of annual production. The results of this investigation are reported in Table 2.2. As a consequence of the analysis of production data, the authors concluded that life-cycle modelling of production data of crude oil does not yield reliable results: models which fit the data equally well lead to widely different results.

Mayer *et al.* (1979, p. iii) offer the following general conclusions

> Hubbert's results are not greatly affected by consideration of alternative models of cumulative discovery or issues of statistical methodology.
> Hubbert's approach is weakened by the fact that direct analysis of the cumulative production cannot support his estimate of ultimate production.

TABLE 2.2. *Parameter estimates from analysis of annual production data.* (*Source: Mayer* et al. *1979, p. 26.*)

Model	Ultimate production (×10⁹ bbl)	Peak year	Residual sum of squares
Logistic	157	1966	2.43×10^8
Generalized logistic	125	1969	1.55×10^8
Hyperbolic	220	1969	1.55×10^8

2.3.3. *Other life-cycle studies and comments on application*

In spite of difficulties and problems mentioned in the previous section, life-cycle models have their place among the tools employed for the analysis of mineral resource issues. When prudently applied and when interpreted properly, this method can be useful.

Prudent application includes fitting of an appropriate curve to a time series of a mature industry; in other words, a time series of a duration such that the parameters of the mathematical equation to be fitted can be estimated reliably from the data. Proper interpretation must stress extrapolation for only a moderate time period—time periods short enough that change in technology and economic structure cannot be severely disruptive to the trend. If the industry is mature, even significant price changes may not necessarily be severely disruptive to trend. Just how great an effect such price change would in fact have varies with the maturity and physical underpinnings of the industry and the period of the forecast. For a mature industry which is founded on a mineral resource that has been actively explored and is not characterized by a strong relationship between quantity and quality of the resource, price increases may have a small effect. The weight of previous production may be too great to be markedly affected by additional material to be produced by deposits whose reserves at previous prices were depleted, and, if exploration has been rather thorough, future discoveries resulting from the incentives of higher prices may not significantly modify the overall pattern that has already been established.

Prudent application and interpretation would encourage as elementary a specification of the trend as possible. The smaller the region, the more mature is the industry, and the more specific the definition of the population being modelled, the less likely that the trend will not be realized. Specificity is important. For example, a total fossil fuels production time series for the US would reflect heavily the influence of the depletion of the oil and gas deposits of conventional supply areas. A forecast of the potential supply of coal and crude oil and natural gas based upon the extrapolation of a time series of aggregate production would be highly questionable, given recent developments; but 15 years ago, such a procedure might have been accepted, because coal was not considered too important in future energy supply. Recent developments mark a potentially significant change in economic structure and the importance of various energy sources other than oil and gas.

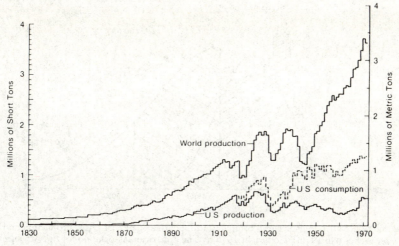

Fig. 2.4. Production of primary lead in the world and in the United States, 1830–1971, and consumption of lead, including scrap, in the United States, 1918–71. Data from US Geological Survey, US Bureau of Mines, and American Bureau of Metal Statistics. (Source: Morris, Heyl, and Hall 1973, p. 316.)

US lead production is useful in demonstrating the prudence of restriction of a life-cycle analysis to recognized modes of occurrence of the mineral commodity. Notice in Fig. 2.4 that prior to the exploitation of the lead–zinc deposits of the Viburnum area, the production time series showed a maximum sometime between 1925 and 1926. Had a logistic trend been fitted and extrapolated sometime after 1926 and prior to 1962 it would have continued the pattern of declining production since 1926, thereby missing completely the rejuvenation of lead production starting in 1962. The point to be made here is that the current lead–zinc resources of the region include a different mode of occurrence than that responsible for most production previous to 1962. Proper application and interpretation of trend analysis of the life cycle of lead in the US would have specified the extrapolation to reflect potential supply from only the conventional sources at that time. It would have resisted interpretation of the extrapolation as a forecast of potential supply from all lead resources. In the case of Hubbert's analysis of US crude oil, he specifically restricted interpretation, for he specified that crude oil in Alaska was not included. Perhaps, it should have been restricted further, to exclude crude oil from new OCS (outer-continental slope) areas, such as the offshore Atlantic. The future discovery of large resources in the Atlantic and California OCS areas could preclude the fulfilment of the trend in cumulative supply from conventional supply areas considered in aggregate.

The trend method is not useful for relatively young industries or regions, for in such cases there is not sufficient history to reliably define the life cycle. Use of trend analysis in such cases carries a very large margin of error. Of course, no method is reliable where data are meagre. An example of the difficulties that can arise in the use of a life-cycle model for a young industry is Lieberman's (1976) analysis of US production of U_3O_8. His best fit of a logistic curve to cumulative production yielded an estimate of $F(\infty)$ of 550 000 short tons (s.t.) of U_3O_8. Since cumulative production plus reserves in 1975 (p_t, $t = 1975$) amounted to 543 000 s.t., the value of 550 000 s.t. as $F(\infty)$ was not credible.

Although Lieberman suggests that any p_∞ from 500 000 to 800 000 would be consistent with the data, application of some of the traditional fitting techniques provides estimates much lower than the lower bound of that range. The logistic curve, fitted to production data by partial totals, selected three points, and least squares, provides estimates of p_∞ of 215 000, 270 000, and 194 000, respectively (Harris 1976). An iterative approach which selects the parameters of the logistic so as to provide the smallest standard error of the estimate provided an estimate for p_∞ of 290 000 s.t. Obviously, these values are meaningless as estimates of p_∞: with exception to the estimate of 290 000, they are less than cumulative production. Fitting of the Gompertz curve to the cumulative production time series provided a p_∞ of 297 400, a value in excess of cumulative production,

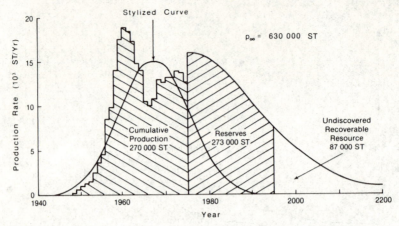

Fig. 2.5. A stylized first-derivative logistic curve compared to Lieberman's plot of U_3O_8 production and his postulated life cycle. (After Lieberman 1976.) (Copyright 1976 by The American Association for the Advancement of Science.)

but unacceptable as p_∞. While these values are meaningless as estimates of p_∞, they are consistent with the data.

If a production time series is assumed to conform to a first-derivative logistic curve, and if the parameters of this curve are estimated from the historical record, the curve most likely to emerge from analysis of the data on production would resemble that sketched on Fig. 2.5. The very rapid increase in production from 1948 to the late-1950s followed by a decline and levelling off would be reflected in the parameters estimated from the data. In other words, a fitted curve must reflect these same effects: a logistic curve which rises as rapidly and levels off as abruptly as do the data must fall in the same manner. Parameters cannot be obtained from historical data for a logistic curve which is not consistent with the data. Consequently, it is no surprise that objective fittings of the logistic curve indicate estimates of p_∞ which are approximately equal to cumulative production. While this result is unrealistic, it is compatible with the proposition that the life cycle is correctly represented by a first-derivative logistic curve and that the parameters of the curve can be estimated from the historical record. Obviously, in this case the compound proposition must be rejected because of additional knowledge which we possess about reserves.

Harris (1976) explored some alternate methods for fitting the logistic to the *discovery* time series employed by Lieberman. Fitting the logistic curve to discovery data by the method of selected three points provides an estimate of p_∞ very similar to that obtained by Lieberman (approximately 537 000 com-

pared to 534 000), but fitting by partial totals provided a much lower estimate of p_∞, approximately 396 000 s.t. While these estimates of p_∞ are closer to a believable level than those obtained from the production time series, they are still less than cumulative discoveries. Fitting the curve by an iterative method provided an estimate for p_∞ of approximately 550 000 s.t., a value just slightly larger than cumulative discoveries.

Fitting of a Gompertz curve to the discovery data by the method of partial totals provides an estimate of p_∞ of approximately 570 000 s.t. (Harris 1976). While this value is greater than cumulative discoveries, its margin of excess is small, approximately 30 000 s.t. What conclusions can be drawn from this exercise? Basically, the same conclusion made by Lieberman: undiscovered, recoverable resources of U_3O_8 cannot be estimated reliably through the life-cycle model. This conclusion is an obvious one because most of the estimates of p_∞ are less than cumulative discoveries. It is tempting to puzzle about how much greater than cumulative discoveries the estimate of p_∞ needs to be to lead to the opposite conclusion. If the estimated p_∞ were 10 per cent greater than cumulative discoveries, is it suddenly a credible estimate? The value selected by Lieberman is only a little more than 10 per cent greater. What if the estimated p_∞ were only 5 per cent greater or as much as 20 per cent? As indicated, differences in estimates of p_∞ as great or greater than 10 per cent of cumulative discoveries can be obtained simply by fitting the curve by a different method.

Let us turn to US bituminous and lignite coals, Hubbert (1974) shows the time series of Fig. 2.6.

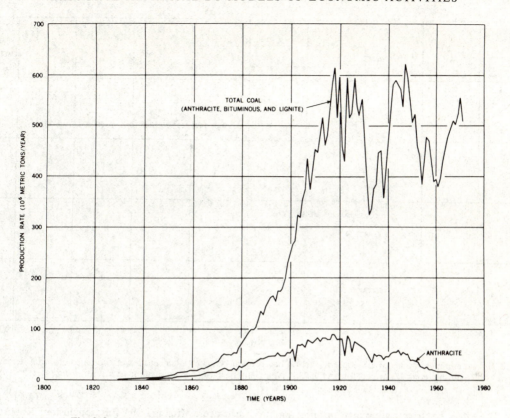

Fig. 2.6. United States production of coal and lignite. (Source: Hubbert 1974.)

Examination of such a time series as solely a trend phenomenon would lead to the suggestion that coal production may have approached its maximum around 1945 and that the total potential supply of bituminous coal and lignite would have been approximately equal to twice cumulative production to 1945. It is instructive to see how Hubbert treated coal resources. His approach was not a straight-forward analysis of the secular trend. Instead, he relied upon the work of Averitt (1969) to provide an estimate of US coal resources: 1486×10^9 tonnes. This quantity was taken to represent $p_\infty = F(\infty)$ and used along with past production to calculate the parameters of the implied logistic relationship. He then used this fitted function to project a complete cycle of US coal production (Fig. 2.7).

An interesting point to be made here is that, for reasons he did not elaborate upon, for coal Hubbert relied upon a source other than the trend mechanism to estimate coal resources in spite of the fact that the time series of production appeared to have peaked,

while for oil, he relied solely on the implication of trend. The use that Hubbert made of the derivative logistic after the fact to generate a future supply profile is of little relevance. For such a purpose, in the short run, econometric models would provide greater insight and would be more credible. For the long run, a supply profile is not credible to begin with; the total cumulative supply to the target horizon is a more realistic goal for long-term resource adequacy studies. A second interesting and important point is that the outlook for coal today belies the trend of Figs. 2.6 and 2.7. Similarly, estimates of potential supply to some target horizon based upon today's view of energy supply, domestically and world-wide, is very different from that which would be obtained by an extrapolated logistic that had been fitted to the past production series. The reasons for this change spring from our recently acquired view of energy resources: the oil embargo and its economic–political ramifications. This change provides two insights.

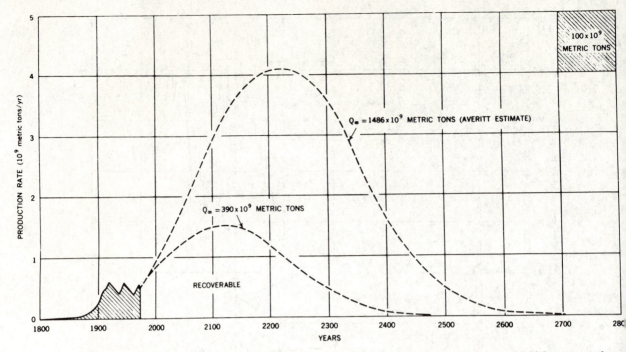

Fig. 2.7. Two complete cycles of US coal production based upon Averitt higher and lower estimates of initial resources of recoverable coal. (Source: Hubbert 1974.) *Note*: Hubbert's Q_∞ is equivalent to author's $F(\infty)$.

1. The effect of structural change in an economic system on mineral or energy resources;
2. Resources are defined within the economic system, and the quantity of resources of one kind is often dependent upon the quantity and cost of resources of a different kind.

Roberts and Torrens (1974) explored the concept of life cycle for nonferrous minerals. They correctly point out in the introduction to their paper that the fitting and extrapolation of S-shaped curves for resource prediction is based upon the assumption that the limit of the curves, which they called resources or ultimate reserves, is determined by present and past growth data. Roberts and Torrens (1974, p. 27) conclude

> It is plainly risky to extrapolate present trends in resource discovery and utilization, especially in the absence of a reliable estimate of the ultimate limit in reserves. Certainly, since extrapolations for the domestic oil life cycle in the U.S.A. yield widely differing values for Q_∞ depending on the model chosen to represent the curve...; such a procedure would have been quite unjustifiable for mineral resources where we are at an earlier stage in the life cycle.

The author wholeheartedly agrees with the above;

however, after making this conclusion, Roberts and Torrens suggest that a useful procedure is to take an independent appraisal of resources as $F(\infty)$ and then use a selected mathematical model of the life cycle to generate the profile of production that constitutes $F(\infty)$. The source of the independent estimate of $F(\infty)$ employed by them was the reserve prediction from McKelvey's (1960) reserve-abundance relationship. Since the focus in this book is the estimation of potential supply or endowment, the procedure advocated by Roberts and Torrens (1974) and demonstrated by Hubbert for coal of translating a stock measure into a profile of future annual production is only of passing interest. Furthermore, even if it were of primary interest, the procedure recommended by them is questionable, for as indicated in a subsequent section, McKelvey's reserve-abundance relationship is a highly dubious one and of questionable use for the appraisal of endowment or potential supply; consequently, creating a time profile of such an estimate is of questionable value.

To summarize, the projection of secular trends of metal production to infinity provides an estimate of potential supply, not mineral resources. However, the conditions for this potential supply are implicit to the analysis and are not stated explicitly. Even for the estimation of potential supply, trend extrapolation is useful only for very restricted conditions. These conditions include considerable production history and purposeful limiting of the scope of inference and interpretation to mineral from familiar modes of occurrence and from conventional supply areas. The method is more reliable the more limited the region, being useful and reasonably reliable for the deposit, but decreasing as the size of the region increases (a reflection of the magnitude of undiscovered deposits of familiar *and* of new modes of occurrence) and as modes of occurrence increase. The shorter the time horizon of the extrapolation, the more reliable the estimate. In fact, short- and moderate-term extrapolation of the production time series of a mature industry is robust. Long-term extrapolation as a basis of resource estimation is questionable because of the possibility for significant technological advance and changes in the economic structure of the specific industry and the economy in general.

The requirements on information and the strength of the assumptions required for application of implicit methods limit their usefulness for the appraisal of potential supply and metal endowment. These limitations have motivated the examination of alternative methods, methods that can be used for long-term evaluations and for contingency analyses for circumstances for which we have no economic history nor direct experience. These methods place much less stress upon moorings of economic structure and much greater stress upon the physical endowment of the earth. These are termed explicit methods and are the subject of a subsequent section.

2.4. A life-cycle model with price and technology

The notation adopted in § 2.3 referred to annual production as dp/dt. Conceptually, dp/dt was defined as a function of m economic variables

$$dp/dt = \gamma(e_1, e_2, \ldots, e_m).$$

Specification of each of the economic variables as a particular function of time was the first step to a more general forecasting relationship, one in which dp/dt was modelled as a single life cycle,

$$dp/dt = f(t)$$

and

$$p_t = F(t) = \int_0^t f(\tau) \, d\tau.$$

Thus, as demonstrated in § 2.3, p_∞, a quantity referred to by Hubbert (1969) as ultimate recoverable resources, can be computed as the asymptotic value of p_t, given the identification of an appropriate functional form for $f(t)$ or $F(t)$ and subsequent estimation of the unknown parameters.

The usual use of life-cycle models such as the Gompertz and logistic curves is to project them ahead, which reduces to evaluating $F(t)$ for some t in the future, $t = \infty$ being a special case. As stated in § 2.3, such a practice implies the continuation of the trends, which are present in the data base, of the m economic variables to the future time horizon. Since the individual trends are all orchestrated by a single time function (life-cycle model), it is impossible to know from the life-cycle model itself just what the states of the economic variables, such as technology and product price, are at the future time horizon.

Uri (1980) attempted to impose a structure on the life-cycle model for domestic crude oil so that the effect of changes in price and technology could be identified. Basically, Uri postulated that the asymptote of the logistic and the Gompertz is a function of price and technology. That is to say, ultimate recoverable resources are expanded by improved prices and technology.

Consider the logistic curve as a life-cycle model

$$p_t = p_\infty(1 + ae^{-bt})^{-1},$$

where p_∞, a, b are unknown parameters that must be estimated from time series data on cumulative production. The structure imposed by Uri is the specification of p_∞ as a function of price and technology

$$p_\infty = \sum_{i=0}^{k} \alpha_{1i} r_{t-i} + \alpha_2 \phi(t),$$

where $\phi(t) = 1/e^{(t-t_0)}$ = technical change, t_0 is the base year, r_{t-i} the price at time i periods prior to current period t, α_{1i} the coefficients of lagged price, and α_2 is the coefficient of technical change. Thus, this dynamic life-cycle model can be stated as follows (see § 2.8.1 for derivation)

$$p_t = \frac{\sum_{i=0}^{k} \alpha_{1i} r_{t-i} + \alpha_2 \phi(t)}{1 + ae^{-bt}}.$$

Such a specification is an explicit description of some of the parameters that define resources. Successful estimation of such a model would provide an indication of the long-run elasticity of resources to product price and technical change. Furthermore, it would allow the analyst to examine ultimately recoverable resources for various scenarios of prices.

The use of lagged prices in addition to current price reflects the fact that an observed increase in production may reflect, besides the profit maximization induced by current price, expanded productive capacity which was initiated during previous years, e.g. exploration and development programmes and production facilities. The modelling of technical change as a declining exponential is defended by Uri on the grounds there were no objective measures of efficiency improvements in drilling, enhanced recovery, etc. available and that he felt that the impact of improvements in the technology of drilling and production might soon exhaust itself.

Uri elected to estimate the first-derivative form of the dynamic logistic separately using annual production data and using annual discovery data

$$\frac{dp_t}{dt} = bp_t\left[1 - \frac{p_t}{\sum\limits_{i=0}^{k}\alpha_{1i}p_{t-i} + \alpha_2\phi(t)}\right].$$

Because of the nonlinear form of this equation, its unknown parameters were estimated by a maximum likelihood approach. The results of these estimations are the following equations

Discovery data [5]

$$\frac{ds_t}{dt} = 0.2041s_t\left[1 - \frac{s_t}{1.3620r_t + 1.4107r_{t-1} + {} + 1.0646r_{t-2} + 0.1722e^{-(t-t_0)}}\right],$$

Production data [5]

$$\frac{dp_t}{dt} = 0.4033p_t\left[1 - \frac{p_t}{1.3210r_t + 1.4040r_{t-1} + {} + 1.0719r_{t-2} + 0.2890e^{-(t-t_0)}}\right].$$

Since the denominator of these equations is $p_\infty = g(r_t, r_{t-1}, r_{t-2}, t)$, it can be used to estimate ultimate recoverable resources for selected price and technology scenarios. Uri assumed that the price of crude oil would not exceed US $45.43 per barrel (bbl) (Data Resources, Inc 1979). Using this value for r_t, r_{t-1}, r_{t-2}, we can compute the ultimate recoverable crude oil resources of the United States.

Discovery data

$$s_\infty = 1.3620(45.43) + 1.4107(45.43)$$
$$s_\infty = \quad 61.88 \quad + \quad 64.09$$
$$+ 1.0646(45.43) + 0.1722\,e^{-\infty}$$
$$+ \quad 48.36 \quad + 0 = 174.33 \times 10^9\ \text{bbl}.$$

Production data

$$p_\infty = 1.3210(45.43) + 1.4040(45.43)$$
$$p_\infty = \quad 60.01 \quad + \quad 63.78$$
$$+ 1.0719(45.43) + 0.2890\,e^{-\infty}$$
$$+ \quad 48.70 \quad + 0 = 172.49 \times 10^9\ \text{bbl}.$$

These quantities are very similar to the 170.6×10^9 barrels estimated by Hubbert (1969, p. 176).

Uri performed an identical analysis using the Gompertz equation as his basic life-cycle model

$$p_t = p_\infty a^{b^t}.$$

As with the logistic, p_∞ was specified to be a function of current price, lagged prices, and technology. p_∞ for the Gompertz was estimated to be, based upon discovery and production data, 180.73×10^9 bbl and 188.40×10^9 bbl, respectively. Notably, the best fit, as measured by the coefficient of determination ($R^2 = 0.9773$), was of the Gompertz to discovery data, giving p_∞ of 180.73×10^9 bbl.

Uri (1980) determined that the implicit price elasticity of production is 0.063 for the logistic model and 0.09 for the Gompertz. As noted by Uri these are somewhat smaller elasticities than the 0.20 estimated by MacAvoy and Pindyck (1975).

2.5. Discovery-rate models and oil resources (Hubbert) [6]

2.5.1. *Overview*

As described here, discovery-rate models employ the relationship of drilling yield to cumulative quantity of drilling as a basis for estimating the quantity of a mineral commodity that ultimately will be recoverable. As all mineral ground is explored, with respect to our conceptual framework and terminology, this quantity is equivalent to potential supply. However, the economics of this potential supply is not explicitly defined. Since discoveries do not in general equal production, in this section we will employ the symbol s_t to represent cumulative discoveries at time t; s_∞, the cumulative discoveries at $t = \infty$ is equal to $p(\infty)$, as defined for life-cycle models, and ps, the stock measure defined in Chapter 1, as potential supply.

This section describes the applications of a discovery-rate model by Hubbert (1969) to the estimation of ultimately recoverable crude oil of the US. Hubbert's (1969, 1974) application is used to introduce the concepts of discovery-rate models and as the premier case study. This is appropriate, because

Hubbert was the pioneer of this kind of model for resource analysis; furthermore, his application is by far the most extensive and most carefully done. Lieberman (1976) adopted Hubbert's methods for oil to analyse domestic uranium potential supply (§ 2.6).

Hubbert's initial motivation to construct a discovery-rate model was to refute the hypothesis by Zapp (1962) of constant yields to drilling. Hubbert's analysis of discovery rates showed that rates had not been constant and that it was unjustified to assume that the average yield on unexplored ground would equal the historical average. Subsequently, the discovery-rate model was employed by Hubbert to provide a second, independent, estimate of the quantity of crude oil that ultimately will be recovered in the United States. His first estimate was made using the derivative logistic curve as a life-model of production (see § 2.3).

2.5.2. Theory and data conformability

Define the cumulative quantity of recoverable oil that is discovered s as some function F of the cumulative footage of exploratory drilling h

$$s = F(h). \qquad (2.1)$$

Then $F(\infty)$ would represent the ultimate recoverable reserves s_∞. Since the earth is finite and oil deposits provide a sizeable target s_∞ can be approximated reasonably well by evaluating F at some finite footage $\tilde{h} < \infty$

$$F(\tilde{h}) \to F(\infty)$$
$$\to s_\infty. \qquad (2.2)$$

Hubbert's analysis of drilling data was motivated by the desire to estimate s_∞; therefore, he needed an approximation of F. However, the only data that were available were proved reserves of new discoveries, annual additions to and revisions of proved reserves of previous discoveries, and the footage of exploratory drilling. These data could not be used in the form in which they were reported. The problem with use of these data is that the proved reserves initially reported for a field represent only a fraction of the quantity of oil that ultimately will be realized as primary production. As the field is developed and produced, reserves are continually added by extensions of the boundary of the field and by revisions in the quantity producible from the field as new knowledge is gained about the reservoir and the economics of production. Over a long time span, say 30 years, the sum of cumulative production plus

remaining reserves may be several times the originally stated proved reserves. Thus, Hubbert developed a correction factor α which inflates reported reserves as a function of the time lapse (r) from initial discovery to the most recent reserve estimate

$$\alpha_r = \frac{1}{1 - e^{-0.076(r+1.503)}}, \qquad (2.3)$$

where r is the number of years lapsed since discovery of field and evaluation of its reserves. New fields $(r = 1)$ were multiplied by a large factor 5.8 while for old fields the correction factor was considerably smaller (for $r = 10$, $\alpha_{10} = 1.7$). Once corrections were made of the discovered reserves for each year, these data were considered as a discrete approximation of the time series of ds/dt. Similarly, the annual drilling footage data represent discrete approximations of dh/dt.

Hubbert aggregated across time the drilling data for units of 1×10^8 feet of drilling: $\Delta h = 1 \times 10^8$ ft. He then determined Δs, the discoveries made in the time period required to generate the increment of 1×10^8 ft of drilling. The ratio $\Delta s/\Delta h$ was plotted against the cumulative footage of drilling h as measured in units of 1×10^8 ft. Fig. 2.8, taken from Hubbert (1967), shows the plot of these data for cumulative drilling up to 15 units of 1×10^8 ft. Recall the objective, the identification of $F(h)$, and consider another function f as the derivative of F with respect to h

$$\frac{dF(h)}{dh} = f(h) = \frac{ds}{dh} \approx \frac{\Delta s}{\Delta h}. \qquad (2.4)$$

If we assume that Δs reflects no influences other than cumulative footage of drilling, hence depletion, then the plot of Fig. 2.8 could be considered to represent an empirical form $f(h)$. It follows that if the exact form of $f(h)$ could be identified, then $F(h)$ could be obtained simply by integration

$$F(h) = \int_0^h f(x)\, dx = s_h. \qquad (2.5)$$

Hubbert selected a simple exponential as the functional form of f

$$f(h) = Ke^{-Bh}. \qquad (2.6)$$

It follows, then, that $F(h)$ would be of the form

$$F(h) = \frac{K}{B} - \frac{Ke^{-Bh}}{B}$$

and

$$F(\infty) = \frac{K}{B} = s_\infty. \qquad (2.7)$$

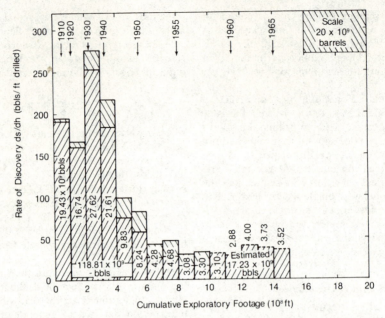

Fig. 2.8. Crude oil discoveries per foot of exploratory drilling versus cumulative exploratory footage in the United States, exclusive of Alaska, 1860–1967. (After Hubbert 1967.) (Reproduced, with permission, from *Bull. Am. Ass. of Petroleum Geologists*, **51**, Fig. 15, p. 2223.)

Visual examination of the plot of Fig. 2.8 raises questions concerning the suitability of an exponential model as the representation of these data. Furthermore, it is apparent that the empirical approximation of ds/dh may reflect in addition to the effects of physical depletion of resources a host of economic factors. But let us set these issues aside for the moment and consider them later, after we have examined the mechanical aspects of Hubbert's calculations.

2.5.3. *Estimation of parameters*

Hubbert's approach. Hubbert's method for estimating K and B was designed to assure two things.

(1) the area under the fitted curve to the last (ith) increment of drilling employed (h_i) is equal to the total quantity of oil discovered by that amount of drilling;

(2) the fitted curve is forced to pass through (ds/dh)$_i$, the rate of oil discovery at h_i the ith multiple of 10^8 feet of drilling.

Hubbert derives the following equation for the parameter B

$$B = \frac{\ln\left[K/(\mathrm{d}s/\mathrm{d}h)_i\right]}{h_i},$$

where i is the index of the last increment of 10^8 exploratory drilling footage. Thus, given a specified value for K, B could be computed. The procedure is to select arbitrarily a value for K, compute B, and then evaluate the integral of the resulting function to see if it equals s_i

$$s_i \stackrel{?}{=} K \int_0^{h_i} \mathrm{e}^{-Bh}\, \mathrm{d}h.$$

If this condition is not satisfied, a new value for K is selected and the procedure is repeated until the area under the fitted function approximates s_i to some selected degree of accuracy.

For example, suppose that 15×10^8 ft of drilling has been completed and that for the 15th increment of 10^8 ft, 35.2 bbl were discovered per foot, (ds/dh)$_{15}$ = 35.2. Suppose also that the cumulative quantity of oil discovered by 15×10^8 ft of drilling is 135.83×10^9 bbl. Substituting appropriately into Hubbert's formula for B we would have

$$B = \frac{\ln\,(K/35.2)}{15 \times 10^8}.$$

Now, suppose that we arbitrarily select 184.5 as our initial trial value for K. Carrying out the calculations we would find for this value of K that

$$B = \frac{\ln(184.5/35.2)}{15 \times 10^8} = 0.110440 \times 10^{-8}.$$

Employing the specified value for K and the computed value for B we could, according to Hubbert's method, compute the quantity of oil under this curve

$$184.5 \int_0^{15} e^{-0.110440 \times 10^{-8}h} \, dh$$

$$= 184.5 \left[\frac{1}{0.110440 \times 10^{-8}} - \frac{e^{-0.110440 \times 10^{-8}(15 \times 10^8)}}{0.110440 \times 10^{-8}} \right]$$

$$= 135.19 \times 10^9 \text{ bbl}.$$

This quantity is then compared to $s_{15} = 135.83 \times 10^9$, the quantity of oil actually discovered: s_{15} is slightly larger than the area under the fitted function ($135.83 \times 10^9 > 135.19 \times 10^9$). Selection of a slightly larger value for K will provide a closer match. Suppose that we set $K = 186$; calculations as demonstrated above would yield $B = 0.11098 \times 10^{-8}$, and

$$186 \int_0^{15} e^{-0.11098 \times 10^{-8}(h)} \, dh = 135.88 \times 10^9 \text{ bbl}.$$

While this quantity isn't equal to s_{15}, it is quite close, perhaps close enough. Once K and B have been determined, s_∞ is calculated very simply,

$$s_\infty = \frac{K}{B}.$$

In the foregoing example, we would have

$$s_\infty = \frac{186}{0.11098 \times 10^{-8}} = 167.6 \times 10^9 \text{ bbl} \approx 168 \times 10^9 \text{ bbl}.$$

This is the estimate of s_∞ given by Hubbert (1969). *Comment on Hubbert's method for estimating parameters.* The *great importance given to the last data* point in this procedure of fitting is obvious! In effect, the decreasing exponential curve is pivoted on this point and rotated to that position for which the area under the curve is equal to cumulative discoveries. All other data points are ignored in determining the shape of the curve. Statistically, such a procedure is a poor use of information. Even if by some unknown means it is known that the appropriate model is an exponential, preferred estimation procedures would determine its shape by the collective data, not one point. The fitting procedure adopted by Hubbert appears to be somewhat self-serving, and it is unstable with respect to the effect of subsequent data on the estimate of s_∞. The procedure is self-serving in that the fitted exponential always describes exactly what is known for the current cumulative drilling. This also assures that $s_\infty > s_i$. While the desire for a model possessing this feature is understandable, to fulfil this desire by a procedure that is relatively insensitive to the 'form' of the data is avoiding evidence and questions that would promote the search for an improved model. The most commonly used statistical estimators, such as least squares and maximum likelihood, do not carry such a guarantee, except when the model fits the data perfectly. Otherwise $\hat{s}_i$ may be greater or less than s_i; in fact, $\hat{s}_\infty$ may be less than s_i. Of course, the result that $\hat{s}_\infty < s_i$ would cause some concern about the selected model, as it should. It is interesting to note that a least-squares fit of an exponential to the data used by Hubbert yields the following estimates of the parameters

$$K = 213.053, \quad B = 0.159281 \times 10^{-8}.$$

Simple arithmetic (K/B) shows that $\hat{s}_\infty$ for the curve fit by the least squares procedure is 133.8×10^9 bbl, a quantity that is less than $s_{15} = 135.83 \times 10^9$. What does such a result mean? At the very least, it should raise questions about the suitability of the exponential model as a representation of these data and about the interpretation of these data.

Use of a fitted exponential when it is not in fact a good fit to the data must invoke some scepticism about the reliability of the predictions by the model. If the selected model is strongly indicated by theory, it may be accepted by critics even when the fit to available data is not a good one, but where theory is not the basis for the model, the entire responsibility for generating confidence in the selected model rests upon the suitability of the model as a representation of the data. If theory was the basis for selection of the exponential, one is forced to infer that Hubbert must have felt the case was so obvious and so strong that it required no defence or explanation, for none is given. More will be said about this later, but let us first proceed to demonstrate the instability created by the fitting procedure adopted by Hubbert.

It is highly instructive to apply Hubbert's calculations separately for each increment of 10^8 feet of exploratory drilling starting with the 5th and proceeding to the 15th. These calculations are identical to those demonstrated for $h = 15 \times 10^8$ ft. Such an exercise provides eleven estimates of s_∞. In effect, by doing this we are answering the question of 'what would Hubbert have estimated as s_∞ if he had made the estimate at the time that only 5×10^8 feet of exploratory drilling had been completed, or 6×10^8,

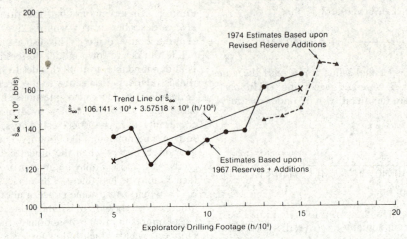

Fig. 2.9. Successive estimates of s_∞ by Hubbert's method as drilling is accumulated from 5×10^8 ft to 17×10^8 ft.

$7 \times 10^8, \ldots, 15 \times 10^8$ ft?' By computing successively $\hat{s}_\infty$ as cumulative drilling increased, we can examine the effect of new information on Hubbert's estimate of s_∞. The results of these calculations are shown in Fig. 2.9. The most striking and alarming feature of this figure is the strong trend in these estimates. Although there is some oscillation, the trend is strong to *higher estimates for* s_∞ as h increases. It is acknowledged that no estimation procedure will provide the same estimate as new data are acquired, but a preferred pattern would have shown oscillation around some central value, not a strong trend. In a comprehensive sense, the trend in s_∞ could be due to a number of things, but if we limit our focus to the estimation technique and the model for which the parameters are being estimated, the trend first must be attributed to the fact that the exponential is not an appropriate model for the data to which it is fit. Secondly, the procedure employed by Hubbert to fit the selected model translates the deviations of the data from the pattern of a true exponential into an upward trend in the estimates of s_∞.

Hubbert (1969) noted that the reversal in the decline of barrels discovered per foot deviated from the pattern of exponential decay; he attributed this deviation to be the result of (1) decreased amounts of drilling during the twelve-year period of 1955 to 1967, and (2) the discovery during this time of the large oil deposits offshore of Louisiana. Hubbert argued that during times of decreased exploration, such as during 1955 to 1967, only the better prospects are drilled and that this results, *ceteris paribus*,

in an increase in discoveries per foot of drilling over that expected. Even so, Hubbert believed that the principal reason for deviation from exponential decline of discovery rates was the discovery of the large oil deposits offshore of Louisiana. Both of these effects were considered by Hubbert to be intrinsically temporary, constituting only an episode in the long-term trend to declining discovery rates, a trend which he expressed by the fitted exponential relation.

Hubbert believes that the increased discovery rates for $h \geq 12 \times 10^8$ are anomalous and that future discoveries will be made at a rate that fulfils the promise of exponential decay. Luckily, Hubbert used the last of these data to estimate s_∞, in spite of his belief that they were not representative data. Had he estimated s_∞ from the data for $h = 11 \times 10^8$, the resulting s_∞ would have been less than the sum of cumulative production plus measured, indicated, and inferred *reserves* for the conterminous US, as estimated by the US Geological Survey (1975, pp. 28–9)

$$\hat{s}_\infty = 137.6 \times 10^9 < 151.2 \times 10^9 \text{ bbl.}$$

It is instructive to note that the estimates of s_∞ made for *all* values of h from 5 to 12×10^8 are considerably below the cumulative production plus total reserves, 151.2×10^9! The point to be made here is that it is the *departures* from the exponential decline—data that were considered by Hubbert to be anomalous—that keep the estimate of s_∞ by the procedure described by Hubbert from being less than cumulative production plus total reserves, a result

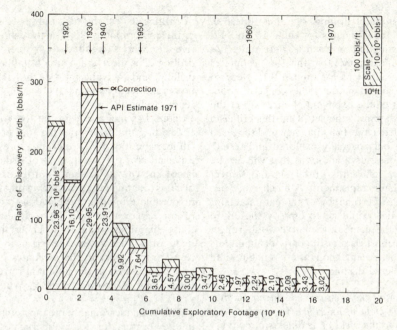

Fig. 2.10. Average discoveries of crude oil per foot for each 10^8 feet of exploratory drilling in the conterminous United States from 1860 to 1971. (After Hubbert 1974.)

that would be nonsense as a basis for inferring undiscovered resources.

As yet, no comment has been made concerning the dashed line of Fig. 2.9. Understanding the meaning of this line is expedited by recalling that the quantity of oil credited to exploratory drilling was approximated by multiplying the cumulative production plus known reserves of fields discovered in a given year by a correction factor α. The effect of multiplication by this factor is to inflate discovery data appropriately so that the data approximate the total oil that will ultimately be produced by the deposits found in a given year. The data of Fig. 2.8, data used by Hubbert to estimate s_∞, were corrected in this fashion prior to analysis reported in his 1967 paper. Later, in 1974, Hubbert updated the raw data for actual revisions and extensions reported since 1965, for which $h = 15 \times 10^8$ ft. He then expanded the revised data by newly computed factors. The result of this updating and revision is displayed in Fig. 2.10. Two observations are noteworthy.

1. Estimated additions to discoveries per foot of exploratory drilling for $h = 12, 13, 14$, and 15×10^8 ft that were made for the analysis leading to the 1967 paper have been considerably reduced. In other words, the revisions and extensions that were estimated to be forthcoming for the most recent drilling at that time were considerably overestimated. History, so far, has recorded considerably smaller revisions of and extensions to these reserves than were anticipated by Hubbert.

2. The estimated quantity of discoveries per foot of drilling for the units of drilling achieved since 1965, units 16 and 17, appear even more anomalous now than did units 12, 13, 14, and 15 in 1967.

The dashed line in Fig. 2.9 indicates the estimates of s_∞ that would have resulted from basing the estimate on the revised data for the 13th to 17th units of 10^8 ft of drilling. Based upon the updated and revised data, estimates of s_∞ continue the low level trend of estimates made from the initial data of Fig. 2.8 for units 7 to 12. Thus, for units 7–15, the resulting estimates of s_∞ would have been less than the sum of cumulative production through 1974 plus known reserves of all categories. In other words, if we ignore the last two units, 16 and 17, estimates of s_∞ are meaningless, as they are below that which is already known!

In view of Hubbert's overestimation in 1967 of the future additions to the reserves for what was at that time the recent units of drilling, one must question how reliable are the estimates for units 16 and 17. Are these overestimated as much as were units 12–15 in 1967? This fact alone, that the 1967 estimates of future reserve additions for units 12–15 were so much in error, should cause some concern about basing the fitting of the exponential curve upon the most unreliable datum of the set. That this criticism is valid follows from the fact that newly discovered fields have been only partially explored and tested. Thus, estimates of reserve additions that will accrue to these fields are inherently unreliable and subject to considerable later adjustment. A much more defensible approach to estimation of the parameters of the assumed model would be to employ the entire data; in this way the shape of the curve would reflect the much more robust data of the early drilling units as well as the most recent, though less reliable, data of the just-completed drilling.

2.5.4. *Calculation of the relative yield factor R: the ratio of the yield of undrilled, favourable sediments to the yield of sediments already drilled*

Perspective and method. One method of estimating the quantity of oil that may be present in favourable ground that has not yet been drilled is to determine the remaining volume of favourable sediments and then to multiply this volume by the barrels per cubic mile that these sediments are expected to yield. But, what yield factor should be employed? Appendix II of the report of the National Academy of Sciences (1975) documents some disagreement as to the relative yield of the undrilled ground. Will the undrilled ground be as productive as that already drilled? Most informed individuals agree that it probably will not be, but just how productive is a difficult question to answer. Hubbert professes to have computed the relative productivity to be 0.10; in other words the unexplored ground will yield approximately 10 per cent per unit of volume of that of the ground already drilled. Hubbert's estimate is based upon s_∞ and h, the quantity of drilling required to adequately test the undrilled favourable ground of the sedimentary basins of the conterminous US

$$R_i = \frac{\dfrac{F(\bar{h}) - F(h_i)}{(\bar{h} - h_i)C}}{\dfrac{F(h_i)}{h_i C}} = \frac{\dfrac{s_\infty - s_i}{\bar{h} - h_i}}{\dfrac{s_i}{h_i}},$$

where h_i is the ith unit of exploratory drilling, each unit representing 10^8 ft, $\bar{h}$ is 50×10^8 ft, the amount

of drilling to test the favourable sedimentary basins of the conterminous US, s_i is the estimate of cumulative discoveries credited to h_i feet of exploratory drilling, C is the average area of influence per foot of drilling, and R_i is the ratio of the yield of undrilled, favourable sediments to the yield of sediments already drilled.

Critique. As mentioned in the foregoing, estimation of $[ds/dh]_i$, the discoveries per foot of drilling for the ith increment of 10^8 ft of drilling, presents problems, especially for the recent units of drilling. Similarly s_i is not known with certainty. Furthermore, estimation of $\bar{h}$ is contingent upon the estimate of the total favourable ground and the average area of influence of an exploratory drill hole. Uncertainties about these quantities create some uncertainty in the estimate of R_i. However, the error in R_i that could result from errors in the estimates of $\bar{h}$ and s_i are minor compared to the potential for error in R_i due to the lack of knowledge of s_∞. What is the size of s_∞?

This is unquestionably the most uncertain quantity in the formula for R_i. Hubbert substitutes for this quantity his estimate of s_∞, 168×10^9 bbl, based upon drilling results for $h_{15} = 15 \times 10^8$ ft. As indicated in the previous discussion, Hubbert's method for estimating s_∞ is not without its problems; it follows that R_i must suffer from all of the weaknesses associated with $\hat{s}_\infty$ as well as those associated with s_i and h.

Let us examine how R_i should change with the progression of exploration of a finite region where ds/dh conforms to the Hubbert model. A computation formula for R_i can be derived by making the following substitutions in the equation for R_i,

$$s_\infty = \frac{K}{B}; \quad s_i = K\left(\frac{1}{B} - \frac{e^{-Bh_i}}{B}\right); \quad \bar{h} = 50 \times 10^8 \text{ ft.}$$

Simple algebraic manipulation yields for R_i

$$R_i = \left[\frac{K/B}{K\left(\dfrac{1}{B} - \dfrac{e^{-Bh_i}}{B}\right)} - 1.0 \right] \cdot \frac{h_i}{(50 \times 10^8 - h_i)}$$

or, more simply,

$$R_i = \left[\left(\frac{1}{1 - e^{-Bh_i}} - 1.0 \right) \cdot \left(\frac{h_i}{50 \times 10^8 - h_i} \right) \right].$$

Now, suppose for illustrative purposes that the real world were appropriately represented by Hubbert's equation

$$ds/dh = 186e^{-0.11098 \times 10^{-8}(h)}.$$

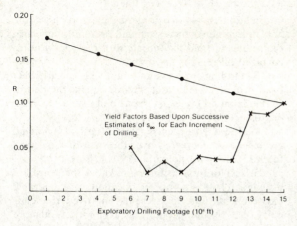

Yield Factors Based Upon Successive Estimates of s_∞ for Each Increment of Drilling.

Exploratory Drilling Footage (10^8 ft)

Fig. 2.11. Successive estimates of R by Hubbert's method compared to R derived from Hubbert's exponential model.

Using $B = 0.11098$ and the foregoing equation, R_i was computed for $h_i = 1, 4, 6, 9, 12,$ and 15×10^8 ft of exploratory drilling. For example, for 15×10^8 ft, we have

$$R_{15} = \left[\left(\frac{1}{1 - e^{-0.11098 \times 10^{-8}(15 \times 10^8)}} \right) - 1.0 \right] \times$$
$$\times \left(\frac{15 \times 10^8}{50 \times 10^8 - 15 \times 10^8} \right) = 0.1000.$$

Similarly, for $B = 0.11098$ and for $h_i = 1 \times 10^8$ ft, $R_i = 0.1739$.

Values of R_i that would prevail if the oil resources of the conterminous US were appropriately modelled by Hubbert's 1967 analysis are plotted in Fig. 2.11. A freehand, smooth curve drawn through these points shows a very slight curvilinearity.

There are three interesting results from this exercise *with respect to the model advocated by Hubbert which yielded* $\hat{s}_\infty \approx 168 \times 10^9$ bbl.

1. The behaviour of R demonstrates decreasing yields of remaining undrilled ground as drilling of the conterminous US progresses.
2. The *rate* of decay in R_i is very small ≈ 3.8 per cent per unit of drilling.
3. R has never been very high. After the first 10^8 feet of drilling, R was only approximately 17.4 per cent.

The lower graph of Fig. 2.11 shows the values of R_i associated with each of the estimates of s_∞ graphed in Fig. 2.10. As in exploring Hubbert's method for estimating s_∞, the appropriate perspective here is that we are in effect answering the question of what would have been Hubbert's estimate of R_i had he done his analysis when only 5×10^8, $6 \times 10^8, \ldots$, or 15×10^8 ft of drilling had been completed. The behaviour of the successive estimates of R as drilling progressed is quite anomalous when compared to the decay pattern of the 1967 model, based upon the estimate of B ($B = 0.11098$) for h_{15}. It is not expected that these estimates would exhibit a smooth profile, such as the pattern of the theoretical curve of R, for we are looking at *successive estimates*. However, it is a reasonable expectation that if any trend were to be present, it would be to lower values, not higher. Of course, since $\hat{s}_\infty$ is used to compute $\hat{R}_i$, the major reasons for this bizarre pattern are the same as those for the increasing trend in $\hat{s}_\infty$.

The points to be stressed here are:

1. The evidence that apparently so impressed the National Academy of Sciences (1975) for a low R is neither rigorous nor persuasive.
2. The NAS appears to have been inconsistent in that it rejected Hubbert's estimate of s_∞ as the quantity of undiscovered economically recoverable resources but at the same time accepted his arguments for R. Obviously, accepting Hubbert's R means acceptance of his estimate of s_∞.

2.5.5. *Conceptual issues with respect to* (ds/dh) *and its use*

In the foregoing critique of Hubbert's estimation procedures for s_∞ and R, the assumption of an exponential as the appropriate model of the relationship of ds/dh to h was identified as a critical assumption. The main focus of the discussion to this point was on the interaction of this assumed model with the estimation procedure. As indicated, this interaction appears to have imparted a rather strange character to resulting estimates of s_∞ and R. Let us now turn to a critique of the assumption, the exponential relationship.

Hubbert devotes no comment to justification of the exponential, encouraging the impression that it is demonstrated either by the data or by theory that the exponential model is appropriate. However, even a cursory examination of the data (Fig. 2.8) raises questions about the suitability of the exponential in terms of how well it fits the data. The deviations which obviously challenge the model are:

(1) the *increase* in ds/dh to a maximum at $h = 3 \times 10^8$ ft;
(2) the levelling off and even increase in ds/dh for $h > 9 \times 10^8$ ft.

The simple exponential model calls for the maximum of the function at $h = 0$ and for $f(h)$ to decrease not only monotonically thereafter, but at a constant rate.

Since the data do not make a convincing case for the exponential, we must turn to theory. But, what theory indicates the exponential as the appropriate model for ds/dh versus h? To the knowledge of the author, there is no theoretical foundation. True, there is the familiar exponential decline curve of reservoir production, but there is no bridge from that relationship to yields to exploration drilling.

A more useful argument is based upon statistical data which show that typically most of the known reserves of a region which has been well explored occur in a few large fields. Because of their size, these large fields often are among the first discoveries in a region. The operation of these two relationships in a region suggests that, *ceteris paribus*, the yields to cumulative exploration for that region would decrease with exploration drilling. Does this make the case for an exponential relationship of ds/dh versus h for the aggregate of regions in which drilling of the regions occurred at different times, hence different levels of h? No, not necessarily.

For the plot of ds/dh versus h to exhibit even a strictly monotonically decreasing pattern would require that all oil provinces be known at the onset of exploration, that explorationists could selectively identify the location of the large deposits in each province, that industry always possessed the ability to drill to whatever depths were required to locate the largest oil deposits, and that infrastructure and markets were compatible to the geography of the major deposits. Given these conditions, the plot of quantity of oil per foot against cumulative footage of drilling may exhibit a monotonically decreasing relationship, a relationship which may or may not be a simple exponential, depending upon relative frequencies of the various deposit sizes.

The conditions imposed to assure even a monotonically decreasing relationship are demanding, and they are even more so for an exponential. Did man exploit the oil resources under such conditions? Obviously not. If he had, the peak of discoveries per foot (Fig. 2.8) would have to occur with the first increment of drilling. Why didn't it? Among the many reasons are the following

1. The obvious, near-surface structural traps were drilled first, those marked by oil or gas seepage; these were not always the largest deposits;
2. Man's understanding of the habitat of oil was initially very limited, growing as exploration added

information on source materials, migration of oil, and entrapment. Increased understanding aided in the search for and identification of previously unrecognized oil regions and traps;
3. Drilling technology improved considerably from primitive cable tools limited to shallow depths to the diamond bit rotary capable of drilling to great depths;
4. There is evidence that the cost of drilling a given footage decreased over the span of time from the mid-1800s to the early-1970s [7];
5. Exploration technologies other than onshore drilling technology for the location of favourable environments and entrapments improved tremendously, e.g. seismic geophysical exploration, offshore drilling capability, and more recently 'bright spot' seismic analysis.

To the above list of factors that would influence the pattern of oil discovered per unit of drilling as drilling progressed must be added the growth in demand for oil products and other economic incentives (depletion allowances, crude prices, etc.). Simply stated, the effects of changing structure of the economy and new technologies (including scientific understanding and geologic information) are mixed with the effects of physical depletion in the graph of Fig. 2.8. Because of the aggregate of effects incorporated in these data, there is a danger of misinterpretation by not only Hubbert and his disciples but also by those who attempt to refute Hubbert's interpretation.

It is only natural that the neglect by Hubbert of the economic effects embodied in ds/dh versus h elicits economic arguments about the decline in ds/dh with h. A seemingly common initial reaction is to cite economic incentives for greater or lesser expenditures in exploration as major or sufficient reasons for lower or greater discoveries per foot. Conditions for an increased exploration activity are not sufficient of themselves for a decrease in yield per foot of drilling as drilling accumulates. The fact that drilling costs decrease, *ceteris paribus*, would encourage greater allocation of capital to exploration, but that alone does not make the case for a decline in barrels of oil discovered per foot of exploration drilling. To close such an argument *without* admitting to physical depletion requires the cost of drilling relative to the cost of other substitute exploration activities to decrease, causing substitution of drilling for other exploration activities. The extent of such substitution is not obvious, for at the same time that drilling costs decreased and drilling capabilities increased, our level of geological knowledge and the capability of predrilling exploration techniques also improved.

If the substitution effect is set aside, then an argument for a decline in yields to exploratory drilling without depletion must explain why firms would accept lower returns per foot of drilling. For, if deposits of comparable quality (including risk factors) were always available, drilling effort would be directed to their detection and, if they did exist, the yield per foot would be maintained. Firms would direct exploration to new regions containing the premium deposits. Lower drilling costs would simply mean a proportionately greater quantity of discovered oil. The motivation of the exploration firms to collect the economic rents of the premium deposits would hold the productivity of drilling as high as the quality of the remaining deposits would allow. Obviously, if there were a limited supply of large deposits and explorationists could preferentially drill them, any exploratory drilling would show decreasing returns.

Exploration decisions are complex and not easily described. While economic factors, such as crude oil prices, exploration costs, taxation rates, etc., all enter into the exploration decision, the expectation for the discovery of a giant deposit and the high risk of exploration for these deposits are major factors in the exploration decision.

Exploration firms look far and wide for environments having a reasonable likelihood of possessing the giant deposit, for its large size promises low unit costs and a very favourable cash flow for many years. As long as favourable environments for the giant deposits exist, or are thought to exist, exploration is directed to these environments and the identification of the deposits. Some of these giant deposits provide a large exploration target; consequently, it is argued by some that they are quickly recognized and drilled. This reasoning is employed by Drew (1975; personal communication) [8] to propose that a plot of ds/dh versus h should be a step function, maintaining an initial plateau until all of the giant deposits are found and then dropping to a low bench and maintaining this level while the more intense, lower risk exploration locates the small deposits (this intense exploration may be more responsive to price and cost considerations). The author finds no fault with this reasoning as a description of normative exploration behaviour; however, it is not an adequate description after the fact of the record of ds/dh versus h. For there was a marked change in level of geological understanding of the habitat of oil and in exploration

technology over the time period represented by these data. For these reasons, and others, ds/dh initially shows an increase to a peak, rather than an initial plateau.

While the foregoing description represents a simplistic description of exploration in general, the firm with a high aversion to risk may adopt quite a different exploration strategy than a firm that seeks to bear high risk for the expectation of greater return. As shown by Drew (1975), the intense drilling (cyclical drilling) that follows a major discovery (exploration play) finds less oil per well than does the ambient drilling (exploration in regions having no major deposit). However, the ambient drilling yields a smaller success ratio. Thus, risk-averse firms participate more heavily in cyclical drilling, seeking a greater assurance of a discovery and content with a smaller average quantity of oil per well drilled. Firms engaging in these two different kinds of exploration may respond differently to the changing economics of the petroleum industry. The cyclical drilling may be more responsive to change in economic incentives (crude prices, factor costs, taxation, etc.) than is the ambient drilling. Ambient drilling decisions are dominated by geostatistical aspects, the probability that a large deposit exists and that it can be detected. Product price and factor costs figure in because they affect the cash flow that feeds exploration, but this impact on ambient exploration decisions may not be so direct nor as great as it is on cyclical drilling.

The opportunity cost to US firms of regional, high-risk domestic exploration, the kind that locate new oil regions, increased because of the relatively higher probability for the discovery of giant oil fields in foreign countries. In addition, US firms were encouraged by the US government as well as foreign governments to undertake foreign exploration. The flight of high-risk capital to foreign exploration when combined with the decrease in drilling costs in the US may have resulted in a relatively larger amount of drilling of small-potential, but low-risk, targets by risk-averse exploration firms. Such a development could cause a decrease in ds/dh for largely economic reasons. Contributing to this effect would be the technological developments in drilling which were depth-favouring (Norgaard 1975).

How much effect would these economic factors have in overstating the physical depletion component? This question cannot be answered in quantitative terms from an analysis of ds/dh. Unravelling the effects that are folded into this data set by analysis of the data set alone is impossible. An answer to this question, if attainable, would derive from additional,

independent analysis of the architecture of exploration, economic incentives and risk factors, and the
endowment of the conterminous US in undiscovered
resources. While a quantitative statement of the size
of the economic component in drilling yields per foot
cannot be given, it does seem clear that the direction
of this effect is to overstate physical depletion as
interpreted from the plot of ds/dh versus h.

The use of ds/dh versus h as an indicator of
physical depletion must be called into question on
conceptual grounds, grounds which are related to the
economic issues discussed in the foregoing. Suppose
that we have an infinite resource of petroleum deposits and that the sizes of the deposits comprising
the resource were distributed randomly with depth.
If explorationists could selectively identify and drill
first the shallowest deposits, the quantity of oil found
per foot of drilling would show a decline with increasing footage of drilling. This decline would not
represent physical depletion and pending exhaustion,
only depletion of the shallow deposits. Of course,
our resources are not infinite, and exploration seeks
preferentially not just shallow deposits but also the
large deposits, so the effect of greater drilling depths
is included with other effects; nevertheless, there is
little doubt that the increase in drilling depths with
time tends to overstate the depletion effect.

There is another aspect of the use of ds/dh versus
h to represent depletion which is alarming and leads
to an overstatement of depletion, the practice of
combining drilling yields from different regions
which were drilled at different times and at different
depths to one aggregate representation, the plot of
ds/dh versus h employed by Hubbert. Even if exponential decline applies to a limited population for
given economics and technology, mixing the data on
drilling yields from *two or more populations which
were drilled at different periods of time, hence different
intervals of cumulative footage* h, *obviates any* a priori
conditions for an aggregate exponential. Even if the
exponential were appropriate as the model for ds/dh
versus h, it would apply in full rigour *only* for a given
province; or, if the province has more than one mode
of occurrence, it would apply only in full rigour for a
given *mode of occurrence within that province*. From a
purely mechanistic perspective, using the composite
data on ds/dh is in effect moving separate exponentials on to the h-axis of cumulative footage at different levels of h. Those arguments that could be raised
for an aggregate of exponentials also being exponential are destroyed when the data for each of the
exponentials is given an arbitrary starting point on
the h axis.

The Hubbert methodology should be restricted to
separate modes of occurrence within each province.
Such restriction would mean that a prediction of
aggregate s_∞ would consist of the sum of n separately
made estimates, $\hat{s}_\infty^{(i)}$, plus a quantity $\bar{s}$

$$\hat{s}_\infty = \sum_{i=1}^{n} \hat{s}_\infty^{(i)} + \bar{s}.$$

$\bar{s}$ represents the estimation of recoverable resources
in virgin or young petroleum provinces. $\bar{s}$ (the sum of
the estimates that it comprises) would have to be
made by methods other than those that are based
upon discovery rates, for the data requisite for such
analysis would not be available.

If Hubbert's methods are applied separately to
each major producing unit within a petroleum province, many criticisms of his discovery-rate model
due to aggregation of rates across time and depth
would be obviated. Used this way, Hubbert's
methods can be useful in the evaluation of potential
supply of producing regions.

2.5.6. *Conclusions*

Conclusions regarding the analysis of yields to drilling include

1. Theory permits only the hypothesis that for a
limited region and a given mode of occurrence, static
economics and technology, and full information, the
effects of exhaustion would yield a monotonically
decreasing relationship of ds/dh to h;

2. The simple exponential is only one of many
possible monotonically decreasing functions;

3. Knowing that economics and technology
have not been static emphasizes the need to restrict
the analysis at least to the oil province, better yet to
each of the modes of occurrence within the province.
Such restrictions decrease the impacts of changing
economics, technology, geologic information, and
varying depth with time, hence with h;

4. Data on ds/dh which represent all provinces
and changes in geologic understanding, economics,
and technology severely violate the conditions for a
monotonically decreasing function. There is no way
of knowing or theorizing as to the appropriate functional form for such data.

Even if each mode of occurrence in each province
were to possess an exponential functional relationship of ds/dh to h, since the provinces were explored
at different times and usually possessed oil reservoirs
at more than one depth, only a unique set of circumstances would cause the data aggregated across
all depths and provinces for the entire conterminous

US to exhibit an exponential pattern. It must follow that it is also dangerous to suppose that future data on ds/dh must conform to the assumed exponential, or even for that matter to a decreasing trend. Leasing of new areas, particularly if OCS leasing were on a large scale (accelerated rate), could create a new pattern of a sudden increase followed by a decline. Mixed with this pattern, of course, would be the effect of additional exploration activity in other regions. On the other hand, a more constrained leasing programme, one which parcelled out the premium blocks across a longer time interval could result in a moderate increase in ds/dh, an increase which could be held at a plateau for some finite, though indeterminate, amount of drilling.

If Hubbert's methods are applied separately to each major producing unit with a region, many of the faults of his discovery-rate model due to aggregation of rates across depth and time are removed, and his methods can be useful in the evaluation of potential supply of producing regions.

2.6. Economic issues of Lieberman's discovery-rate analysis of uranium

2.6.1. *A general description*

M. A. Lieberman (1976) concluded that our undiscovered, recoverable resources were approximately one-third of the estimates made at that time by ERDA. Specifically, Lieberman employed the methods demonstrated by Hubbert (1969) for oil to estimate the ultimately recoverable U_3O_8 in the United States. From this quantity, Lieberman determined that undiscovered resources of U_3O_8 recover-

able at a forward cost of US \$8/lb U_3O_8 were only 87 000 short tons (s.t.) of U_3O_8. He further compared his estimate, 1 134 000 s.t., of the total \$30 resources (cumulative production plus reserves plus undiscovered resources) with 3 720 000 s.t. of U_3O_8 which he attributed to the US Energy Research and Development Administration (ERDA): 'This very large discrepancy is a result of estimates of undiscovered resources which are not based on any objective procedures that I can discern...' The intent of this statement seems to have been to discredit the geologically-based estimates made by ERDA, because these estimates could not be described or documented by simple mathematical formulae or a logic algorithm and 'hard' data.

Unlike Hubbert, Lieberman based his analysis on discovery rates of a current dollar-cost category of discoveries (Hubbert employed a physical measure of discovery rate), as indicated in Fig. 2.12. This fact raises a host of economic and resource issues.

2.6.2. *Some economic issues*

Economic or physical depletion? Let us consider more carefully and comprehensively just what it is that we are or should be attempting to measure, estimate, or describe. A statement about our remaining undiscovered resources is a partial statement about resource depletion and scarcity of resources. Interact consumption requirements with known and unknown resources of some specified quality, and the stage is set for an appraisal of resource adequacy (scarcity). The demand side of the adequacy or scarcity issue is not explicitly considered here, only the potential for supply. The term scarcity is used loosely

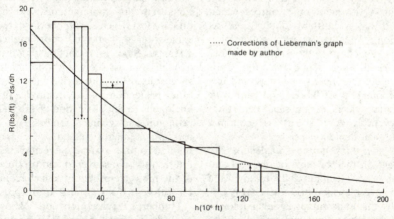

Fig. 2.12. Discovery rate of US \$8 per pound U_3O_8 compared to cumulative exploratory footage h drilled, on a linear scale. (After Lieberman 1976.) (Copyright 1976 by The American Association for the Advancement of Science.)

here to describe a relative state, demand conditions being equal or implicit to the analysis.

Suppose that the original endowment of a non-renewable energy resource were homogeneous with respect to quality. Any mining of this endowment and the utilization of its energy content would result in the depletion of the original endowment. Obviously, the end result of continued mining would be exhaustion of the resource. Use of the term depletion in this case is intuitive and unambiguous. Let us refer to this effect as physical depletion.

If we relax the condition of homogeneity with respect to quality and allow that man will selectively mine the highest-quality resources first, any mining will result in depletion of the original endowment, as it did for a homogeneous endowment; however, the degree of depletion would vary with quality classes of the endowment, decreasing with decreasing quality. The highest-quality classes could be totally exhausted in a small region while the lower-quality classes may exhibit no depletion.

Suppose that the two highest-quality classes of resources had been exhausted by time t_1 and that all mining by t_1 were of the third-quality class. Obviously, some physical depletion of the original endowment has taken place. Now, suppose that new technology and improved labour and capital productivity had lowered production costs so much that at t_1 the real cost of a unit of energy from the third-quality class of resources is the same as it was at t_0 from the first-quality class. In the same sense that a decrease in the average grade of mined ore indicates depletion of high-quality resources, an increase in the real cost of energy from that ore indicates increasing economic scarcity of resources. Let us refer to the diminishing of our endowment of resources which can be produced at a constant dollar cost as economic depletion. Note that whereas any mining results in physical depletion of the original endowment, it may not result in economic depletion. Conceptually, it is possible for new technology and improvements in productivity of labour and capital to offset the economic effects of physical depletion. Clearly, the relevant issue to society is economic depletion, not physical depletion *per se*.

Complications in measuring physical depletion. The foregoing comment on the concepts of physical and economic depletion was facilitated by taking as a known the original endowment of the energy resource. Obviously, this endowment is never known; consequently, at any given time, perception of the degree of depletion of the stock of high-quality resources is only as good as our estimate of the original endowment. Clearly, basing an assessment of physical depletion upon an estimate of s_∞ [9], the total recoverable resources, as inferred from economic data, is like shooting at a moving target, because economic data reflect technological advances and improvements in productivity as well as the advance of physical depletion.

Depletion in major metals. There can be little question that we have experienced marked physical depletion of high-grade resources of most major metals: the average grade of mined ore has dropped considerably since the early days of the industry. But, as shown by Barnett and Morse (1969), while average grades progressively decreased, the real cost of most metals declined. Improvements in the technology of exploration, mining, processing, and utilization of metal resources more than offset the decline in resource quality. In other words, there was no evidence of economic scarcity or economic depletion in most major metals.

While the results of the study by Barnett and Morse were encouraging, two developments since completion of their work threaten the continuance of trends in real costs of metals: (1) quadrupling of oil prices and (2) large increases in smelting costs due to measures to meet air quality standards.

Hubbert and Lieberman and depletion. Which depletion is at issue in the works of Hubbert and Lieberman? Economic or physical depletion? The answer to this question is not obvious. Hubbert's interpretation alludes to a physical depletion. The spirit of his analysis seems to be that economic factors such as product and factor prices simply are irrelevant if there are no deposits remaining to be found. At the extreme state of exhaustion of a resource, distinctions between economic and physical-quality depletion are lost. Even so, Hubbert's perception of future exhaustion is predicated upon implicit economic assessment. Since a production time series reflects the dynamics of markets and the technologies of resource discovery, production, processing, and utilization, projection of a life cycle of production is analogous to the projection of the trends of a host of economic and technical factors. But, since these factors are implicitly treated, we cannot discern their implied future states. Nevertheless, the resources inferred to be discovered and produced near the end of the life cycle probably reflect economic conditions far different from those that are presently known.

Hubbert's perception of exhaustion through analysis of discovery rates is conditional upon his estimation of future reserve additions. Future additions of reserves to known deposits clearly reflect future levels of product and factor prices and future advancements in technologies that influence oil recovery. Thus, estimation of these additions is an exercise in the projection of trends in economic and technologic factors. While this projection is made in a different manner than it is in the life-cycle model, it is similar in its implications: past and present trends in these factors will continue far into the future, and an estimate of s_∞ implies future levels of these factors which may differ considerably from those that are presently known.

Clearly, s_∞ estimated by Hubbert by either the life-cycle or discovery-rate models does not describe a resource of constant quality. In this respect, Hubbert speaks to economic depletion; however, the economic conditions of this depletion are not stated.

What about Lieberman's analysis of the life cycle of US $8 U_3O_8 resources? Rather than a physical measure of production and resources, as was used by Hubbert, Lieberman employs a forward cost measure. As with Hubbert's analysis, the time series of production contains resource dynamics; however, the analysis only of production quantities having a specified forward cost in current dollar value creates a distortion, for the effects of inflation alone would decrease the stock of US $8 resources and would alter the production of US $8 resources.

A note on inflation. Lieberman's claim that 'it has only been during the last few years that the inflationary correction has been of importance' is somewhat misleading when considered in the context of the analysis he made of reserves and production data. Even a low rate of cost inflation influences markedly the form of a time series of production or reserves quantities when these quantities are for a nonvariant cost level in current dollars and when this inflation persists for a long time.

When production data are for a given cost level in current dollars, inflation in costs causes a time series of production quantities at that cost level to be lower than it would be for a constant dollar cost level. Consider the hypothetical case in which costs and prices undergo a high rate of inflation for a number of years. If the rate of inflation were to be higher than the rate of growth in demand, production quantities at a specified cost in current dollars could show a declining trend even if the time series of production in physical units were increasing.

The presence of inflation effects in the discovery rates distorts the true effectiveness of exploration in finding new reserves. The rate of decline in discovery rates is overstated, for it reflects the decline in the purchasing power of the dollar for production factors in addition to the decline in effectiveness of exploration in finding new deposits. Consider the polar case in which we have an infinite resource at a constant depth. Discovery rates in this case would be constant. Further, assume that the amount of exploration drilling per year is constant and that we have had an annual rate of inflation in costs of 4 per cent. Then, although discovery rates measured in physical units are constant, rates based upon a specified, current dollar cost would decline at the rate of inflation, 4 per cent.

As indicated by Lieberman, the loss of US $8 reserves of U_3O_8 in 1974 was considerable, 77 000 short tons (s.t.). While losses of reserves in previous years were much less than the 1974 loss, those losses were significant. According to Weeb [10], inflation in labour and industrial commodities, the major cost components of mining and milling of uranium ores, makes a cost of US $8/lb U_3O_8 in January of 1969 inflate to a cost of US $12.80/lb U_3O_8 in January of 1975, implying an annual inflation rate of about 8 per cent. Weeb [10] estimates that adjustment for this inflation would increase reserves by a multiple of 2.5. In another study (John Klemenic [11], personal communication, July 1976), the average annual rate of loss of reserves for the seven years prior to 1974, the beginning of the very high inflation rates of recent years, was found to have been approximately 4 per cent. While this rate may not seem significant, continued inflation at this rate for a long period can result in a large loss of reserves and can significantly affect the data that were the basis of Lieberman's analysis.

2.6.3. *Two approaches to analysis*

Given that we must work with production at a specific cost in current dollars, there are two ways of handling the problem. One way is to remove from our production data the effects of increased productivity and inflation so that production quantities represent a constant quality of ore and to perform the analysis upon quantities of this constant quality. The other way is to adjust the data for the effects of inflation and future improvements in productivity so that the analysis is based upon quantities at a constant economic cost, rather than having a constant quality.

Analysis by either approach could achieve the same goal: commenting upon economic depletion. However, if analysis were to be performed upon resource and production data having a specified quality, it would be necessary to appraise, subsequent to the estimation of s_∞, the meaning of this estimate in economic terms.

Regardless of which approach is employed, three critical tasks are apparent.

1. Determining the effect of inflation in decreasing the quantities of US $8 ore reserves and US $8 production;
2. Adjusting for past and future improvements in productivity;
3. Selecting the multiplier (the ratio of the tonnage of undiscovered US $30 resources to US $8 resources) to be applied to the $\hat{s}_\infty$ for US $8 resources as a means of estimating s_∞ for resources recoverable at a forward cost of US $30.

2.6.4. *Productivity and inflation effects on discovery rates*

Suppose that at time t_1, the time required to accumulate 15 units of drilling, a plot is made of discovery rates and cumulative drilling footage. Curve A of Fig. 2.13 represents such a plot. This curve represents the net effect of improvements in productivity, inflation, and reserve additions due to development drilling to t_1. The information content of this idealized curve is analogous to the content of Lieberman's plot of discovery rates for US $8 U_3O_8 resources.

If it is our aim to comment on economic scarcity or economic depletion of uranium resources, then two adjustments to the discovery rates are in order. The first adjustment compensates for the attrition of quantities of reserves due to the inflation of costs:

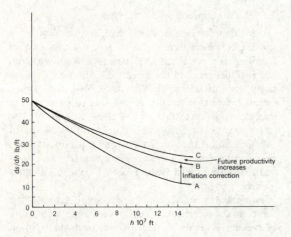

Fig. 2.13. Discovery rates and corrections for inflation and future productivity improvements.

inflation of costs causes some reserves of a given cost level in current US dollars to be moved to a higher cost category. Suppose in our fictitious case that inflation in costs resulted in an annual rate of loss of US $8 reserves of 4 per cent. Curve A represents this case. Correction of discovery data for this loss would produce Curve B.

One more correction is required. Curve B represents discoveries at a constant dollar cost and includes reserve additions due to development drilling and the benefits of productivity increases to t_1. Estimation of s_∞ requires that the inventory of resources which have not been produced by t_1 be further modified to include additions of resources which will be forthcoming from additional *development* drilling and from future improvements in productivity. In other words, future productivity improvements will result in the expansion of reserves of currently known deposits and this expansion must be accounted for in defining a curve to be used for the estimation of recoverable resources. Curve C is a curve that represents both adjustments, one for inflation and one for future productivity increases. Since productivity improvements would apply to all forward cost categories of resources, similar effects would be made on quantities of other cost categories: while the US $15 cost category would be diminished by moving some of these resources into the US $8 category, this category would be enlarged by some of the US $30 resources moving into the US $15 category. Similarly, some of the resources at forward costs higher than US $30 would become US $30 resources. Of course, the amounts added to a cost category of resources need not equal those removed.

If adjustments are not made to the discovery-rate data for future reserve additions, as in the manner described, the progression of economic depletion of US $8 resources is overstated. It follows that estimating the quantity of resources at a higher cost by ratioing up the inferred quantity of US $8 resources by a constant ratio which was based upon reserves in some previous time period will underestimate the higher cost resources.

Lieberman did not make adjustment of the data on discovery rates for future reserve additions or for the inflation of costs; consequently, his analysis is not a useful commentary upon economic depletion of the resource base of uranium deposits. What is the commentary about? Physical depletion? Perhaps, but it is not clear that the discovery data employed by Lieberman appropriately describes physical depletion either. For, the data on discovery rates reflect, on the one hand, the growth of reserves due to the decrease in cut-off grades caused by productivity improvements and, on the other hand, the loss of reserves due to the increase in cut-off grades caused by the inflation in costs. An overriding issue of Lieberman's analysis of discovery rates is the fact that reserve additions were treated as new discoveries instead of being attributed to the previous exploration drilling which resulted in discovery of the deposits. We will set this issue aside for a moment and assume that reserve additions had been treated appropriately. Then, if reserve additions due to productivity improvements had equalled reserve losses due to inflation of costs, data on discovery rates could be interpreted as describing the effectiveness of exploration in finding new deposits of a constant quality. Even for these idealized circumstances, estimation of s_∞ for an US $8 forward cost would require the assumption that in the future reserve additions due to productivity improvements would continue to equal reserve losses due to inflation. Furthermore, in order to comment upon economic depletion in terms of resources at real costs, it would be necessary to adjust an estimated s_∞ of a constant quality for the productivity effects.

Lieberman did not comment upon productivity effects, but he did comment upon the effect of inflation, dismissing it as inconsequential except in 1974, when 77 000 tons of US $8 reserves were lost due to inflation of costs. However, data indicate that the annual rate of reserve losses due to the inflation of costs has averaged about 4 per cent of reserves for the seven years prior to 1974.

2.6.5. An approximate adjustment of Lieberman's analysis for inflation effects

In a real situation, proper adjustment for inflation would be made by first determining from actual data on the deposits those quantities of ore lost due to inflation of costs; then, these quantities would be added to the discovery data. Although this adjustment could require considerable calculations, it is conceptually a straightforward analysis of data. While the examination and analysis of deposit data is the only really appropriate manner for adjusting for inflation, we will approximate the effect of the appropriate adjustment by adjusting the exponential which was fitted by Lieberman to the unadjusted data. But, let us first examine conceptually a basis for adjustment, given an idealized situation.

Assume that the unadjusted discovery data for U_3O_8 define an exponential relationship perfectly. In other words, the parameters of the function are

known with certainty. Furthermore, assume that inflation has caused a loss of $8 reserves at a constant rate of x per cent per year. Given these assumptions, making the appropriate adjustment of the data for inflation prior to fitting of the exponential would be equivalent to correcting the slope of the curve which had been fit to unadjusted data. The function representing adjusted data f^* could be determined by multiplying f, the function fitted to the unadjusted data, by another function ϕ

$$f^*(h) = f(h)\phi(h). \tag{2.8}$$

Let

$$\phi(h) = e^{rt(h)},$$

where r is the rate of loss of reserves, as a decimal fraction, $r = x/100$, and $t(h)$ is a function that associates a value of time with a value of cumulative footage of drilling. Then, given that f is a negative exponential, we have

$$f^*(h) = e^{rt(h)} \cdot Ke^{-\beta h}$$
$$f^*(h) = Ke^{rt(h)-\beta h}. \tag{2.9}$$

Suppose that

$$t(h) = \alpha h. \tag{2.10}$$

Then,

$$f^*(h) = Ke^{(\alpha r-\beta)h}. \tag{2.11}$$

It follows from eqns (2.5)–(2.7) that

$$F^*(\infty) = \frac{-K}{(\alpha r-\beta)} = s_\infty^*, \ \alpha r < \beta. \tag{2.12}$$

In other words, if we knew α, r, R, and β, then we could estimate recoverable resources simply by evaluating eqn (2.12).

Let's take Lieberman's exponential as $f(h)$

$$f(h) = 17.75\,e^{-0.0141\times10^{-6}h}.$$

By fitting a straight line to the plot of time, t, against cumulative footage, h (see Fig. 2.14), we have a rough estimate of α

$$\alpha = 0.1781\times10^{-6}\ \text{years/ft}.$$

Then,

$$\phi(h) = e^{-(0.1781\times10^{-6})rh}.$$

We assume that we have had, on average a 3 per cent rate of loss per year of US $8 reserves ($r = 0.03$). s_∞^*, the corrected estimate of s_∞, is estimated

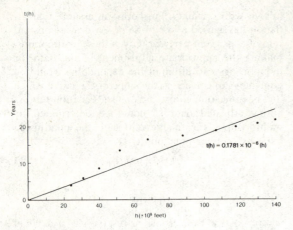

Fig. 2.14. Time $t(h)$ required to accumulate drilling footage h.

by substituting the values for α, r, R, and β into eqn (2.12).

$$s_\infty^* = \frac{-17.75}{[(0.1781)(0.03) - 0.0141] \times 10^{-6}}$$

$$\approx 2\,027\,000\,000/\text{lb U}_3\text{O}_8$$

$$\approx 1\,014\,000 \text{ s.t. U}_3\text{O}_8.$$

Thus, given the foregoing assumptions, adjustment for inflation would yield an estimate of approximately $1\,000\,000$ s.t. for recoverable resources of U_3O_8 instead of $630\,000$ s.t.

For a 4 per cent rate of loss of reserves due to inflation, the average rate for the seven years prior to 1974, our estimate of s_∞ for a constant dollar forward cost of US \$8 would be $1\,272\,000$ s.t. 'Ratioing up' this quantity with a multiplier of 1.8 provides an estimate for s_∞ for US \$30 reserves of $2\,290\,000$ s.t.

2.6.6. What adjustment for future reserve additions?

Even for the idealized circumstances in which discovery-rate data are perfectly represented by an exponential, adjusting the data for future reserve additions is not a simple analysis of data. Since this adjustment represents the result of future economic activities, the quantities to be added to discovery data cannot be estimated without employing some form of a model of the effect of development drilling and productivity. The model used by Hubbert multiplied discovery rates with a multiplier which decreased with the length of time from discovery to evaluation.

Simply for demonstration of ideas, let us suppose that for U_3O_8 the quantities of reserves to be added

to known discoveries can be approximated by multiplying the discovery rates by a value which increases exponentially with time [12]. Let this multiplier be $e^{\gamma t(h)}$, where γ is the rate of additions per year and $t(h)$ is a function which associates with cumulative footage h, the time required to achieve h. Then, discovery rates corrected for expected future reserve additions would be given by

$$ds/dh = e^{\gamma t(h)} \cdot Re^{-\beta h}. \qquad (2.13)$$

Alternatively,

$$ds/dh = Re^{\gamma t(h) - \beta h}. \qquad (2.14)$$

Suppose that $t(h) = \alpha h$, as was proposed in the demonstration of adjustment for inflation. Then,

$$ds/dh = Re^{(\gamma\alpha - \beta)h}. \qquad (2.15)$$

Eqn (2.15) is a functional representation of discovery rates which have been adjusted for the effects of future reserve additions, given that these additions can be appropriately modelled by multiplication of the factor $e^{\gamma\alpha h}$ with the discovery rate.

Putting eqns (2.12) and (2.15) together, we have a conceptual description for this simplified world of discovery rates which have been adjusted for inflation and for future reserve additions

$$ds/dh = Re^{(\alpha\gamma + \alpha r - \beta)h}. \qquad (2.16)$$

Given relationship (2.16), undiscovered, recoverable resources are approximated by

$$s_\infty^* = \frac{-R}{(\alpha\gamma + \alpha r - \beta)}. \qquad (2.17)$$

Let us take Lieberman's exponential as $Re^{-\beta h}$ and αr from our previous demonstrations of adjusting for inflation

$$s_\infty^* = \frac{-17.75}{[0.1781\gamma + (0.1781)(0.03) - 0.0141] \times 10^{-6}}. \qquad (2.18)$$

Thus, if we knew γ, the coefficient which adjusts discovery rates for future reserve additions and if we accepted the assumptions leading to (2.17), we could estimate s_∞^*. Even if γ were not known, if the total future additions were known and the assumptions leading to (2.17) were acceptable, γ could be roughly estimated, allowing estimation of s_∞^* by (2.18). For example, suppose it were given that the progression of mining, development drilling, and productivity improvements will add $50\,000$ s.t. of U_3O_8 to known deposits. Then, adjusted discoveries for 140.5×10^6 ft of drilling would be 593 000 s.t. (543 000 + 50 000) or 1 186 000 000 lb. Given the assumptions made for this simplified world, we can equate this quantity to the following expression

$$1\,186\,000\,000\,\text{lb} = \int_0^{140.5 \times 10^6} 17.75 e^{-\lambda h}\, dh$$

$$1\,186\,000\,000\,\text{lb} = \frac{17.75}{\lambda}[1 - e^{-\lambda(140.5 \times 10^6)}].$$

Solution of this equation yields $\lambda = 0.0123 \times 10^{-6}$. In this hypothetical solution, λ is the coefficient that would have resulted if the negative exponential had been fitted to corrected data.

Consider $-\lambda$ as the difference $\alpha\gamma - \beta$. If we take Lieberman's estimate of $\beta(0.0141 \times 10^{-6})$, we can solve for $\alpha\gamma$

$$-\lambda = \alpha\gamma - 0.0141 \times 10^{-6}.$$

Substituting for λ,

$$-0.0123 \times 10^{-6} = \alpha\gamma - 0.0141 \times 10^{-6}.$$

Therefore,

$$\alpha\gamma = 0.0018 \times 10^{-6}.$$

Take $\alpha = 0.1781 \times 10^{-6}$, as was done in the demonstration on inflation. Then

$$\gamma = 0.0101.$$

Substituting γ into (2.18), we obtain an estimate of s_∞^* for a US $8 forward cost in constant dollars of 1 275 000 s.t., and multiplying this quantity by 1.8, the ratio used by Lieberman, we would have an estimate for s_∞^* at a US $30 forward cost in constant dollars of 2 295 000 s.t. If we had used a 4 per cent rate of loss of reserves due to inflation, the estimate of s_∞^* for a $30 forward cost in constant dollars would have been 3 086 000 s.t.

What does this value mean? Nothing in an absolute sense. No significance can be attributed to γ, the adjustment coefficient for resource additions, for it is based upon an arbitrary selection of 50 000 s.t. as the sum of future additions to reserves. Furthermore, modelling future reserve additions simply by multiplying discovery rates by $e^{\gamma\alpha h}$ may be inappropriate. The only purpose served by this exercise is the demonstration of ideas.

Unfortunately, there is no way that λ can be determined from available data. Part of the difficulties in making a useful approximation of future reserve additions stems from the data available on reserve additions and from Lieberman's use of these

data. Given his use of the data, it is doubtful that any post-fitting adjustments can be made to his discovery-rate model for future reserve additions. Reasons for this skepticism are provided in the following section on data issues.

2.6.7. The ratio

Lieberman's approach to estimating undiscovered US $30 resources of U_3O_8 requires four numbers: s_∞ for US $8 resources, the ratio ρ of *undiscovered* US $30 *resources* to *undiscovered* US $8 *resources*, cumulative production and reserves of US $8 ore, and cumulative production and reserves of US $30 ore. While there are problems with the latter two numbers, as noted in previous sections, the greatest problems arise from the first two of these quantities. Obviously, Lieberman's estimate of undiscovered, recoverable US $30 resources can be no better than the first two of these four numbers. Previous sections of this book have explored Lieberman's estimation of s_∞ for US $8 resources. Comments in this section are restricted to ρ and its estimation.

Obviously, the true value of ρ is not known. Lieberman estimates ρ by the ratio of US $30 cumulative production and reserves to US $8 cumulative production and reserves. While this may seem, as Lieberman states, 'a prudent' thing to do, it in fact gives a highly questionable estimate. An important issue in this judgement regarding Lieberman's estimate of ρ is our incomplete information about the actual inventory of US $30 reserves. While our information about US $8 reserves is reasonably complete, it is quite incomplete for US $30 reserves. Consider this fact: the inventory of US $30 reserves reflects primarily the US $30 reserves associated with deposits that have US $8 reserves. In other words, many of the properties containing only US $30 reserves have not been considered in compiling the inventory of US $30 reserves. While the non-reporting of these reserves may seem like a less-than-responsible discharge of duty, it should be remembered that only recently has material producible at a forward cost of US $30 been considered to be of immediate interest as a resource. Firms have not thoroughly documented US $30 reserves in known deposits, particularly in those deposits which have no reserves at lower costs. In addition, the US Energy Research and Development Administration (ERDA) has devoted most of its efforts to improving the estimates of reserves at forward costs less than US $30.

An estimate of ρ derived from the ratio of US $30

reserves to US $8 reserves is suspect even if reporting of US $30 reserves were complete. Suppose that the distribution of grades in undiscovered deposits is the same as it is in discovered deposits and that grade is independent of depth to the deposits. The technologies and economics of exploration and the economics of mining indicate, generally, that the deposits at the surface and those at shallow depths are discovered and mined first. Reserves and production data would represent these deposits. As these deposits are depleted, additional exploration is directed to new areas and to greater depths in old areas. Simply having to explore for and mine deposits at progressively greater depths would make ρ greater at any given time than the ratio of US $30 reserves and production to US $8 reserves and production.

Consider a related issue: for any given depth, exploration is grade preferential, provided that ores are in radioactive equilibrium. For a given region and depth, the high-grade deposits discovered comprise a greater percentage of all high-grade deposits that exist than discovered deposits at some lower grade do of all deposits of the lower grade. And, as exploration is directed to ever greater depths, low-grade deposits become increasingly more difficult to locate because of the masking effect of deep cover on radioactivity. Thus, a ratio of low-grade reserves to high-grade reserves would understate the ratio of undiscovered low-grade resources to high-grade resources. In addition, there is the economic effect of depth. Increases in mining costs for deposits at greater depths would, *ceteris paribus*, result in a larger proportion of deposits having US $30 resources than would be the case for shallower deposits. All of these things combine to make the ratio of US $30 reserves plus production to US $8 reserves plus production an understatement of the ratio of undiscovered US $30 resources to undiscovered US $8 resources.

There are geological factors that challenge the ratio of US $30 reserves to US $8 reserves as an estimate of ρ. The geology of deposits constituting reserves has not been constant across time but has varied as new uranium resource regions were discovered or as new modes of occurrence within a given region were recognized. Depth to deposit may not be independent of grade, for within a given region, depth may be related to enrichment, oxidation, leaching, or reworking of deposits. Allowance must be made for the fact that undiscovered deposits may be different geologically in some respect from the heterogeneous set which comprises past production and current reserves; the proportion of undiscovered

resources recoverable at a forward cost of US $30 may differ from that of reserves plus production because of these geological factors.

Using the ratio of US $30 reserves plus production to US $8 reserves plus production as ρ amounts to making the assumption that deposits to be discovered in the future will be as rich (have as low forward production costs) as those which already are known or have been produced. This is a very strong assumption.

Everything considered, the choice made by Lieberman of the ratio to estimate s_∞ for a forward cost of US $30 is a difficult choice to defend. In a manner of speaking, instead of placing ERDA 'on trial' for advocating a larger ratio for undiscovered resources, Lieberman has put himself 'on trial' for not using a larger ratio.

2.6.8. *Summary*

Estimation of mineral or energy resources is a frustrating, difficult, and thankless task. No matter how the estimate is made, history will likely prove it to be in error. Every estimate should be *loosely* interpreted and *cautiously* employed. Proper perspective of mineral or energy resources requires the integration of two very different concepts. On the one hand, we have the concept of a fixed, non-renewable initial endowment as a heritage from previously operative earth processes. On the other hand, the utility of this endowment is totally dependent upon man's economic activities and technological capabilities. Resources of a mineral or energy come into being and are destroyed by dynamic economic processes.

It is unrealistic to believe that an appraisal by any method of the quantities of U_3O_8 present in unseen deposits which are supposed to have physical characteristics making them discoverable and economic to produce can be made with even modest reliability. Unfortunately those who employ resource numbers for policy decisions are sometimes so far removed from the process of appraisal that the basis for the estimates and their inherent uncertainties often are not recognized. The reading public as well as many persons involved in establishing policy often fail to differentiate between reserves and resources, let alone appreciating the reliability of various estimates of undiscovered resources. Most users of resource numbers lack motivation and training to appreciate the intimate relationship between the model and the estimate that it produces. The responsibility falls on the practitioners to explore and to comment upon such matters. The need for this increases with the increasing application of mathematical, statistical, and computer techniques. The quantitative methods which most of us employ to some degree often convey to the user of resource numbers an exaggeration of reliability.

On first appraisal, the exponential model of discovery rates seems to have interesting possibilities. However, there are no theoretical grounds for selecting the exponential or any other function as the proper model of discovery rates when discoveries are aggregated across regions, when the deposits of these regions occur at different depths, and when exploration in each region is in a different stage of advancement. The covariation of discovery rates and drilling footage could take on any form.

Lieberman's plot of discovery rates and cumulative footage does not represent accurately what it was intended to do: the effectiveness of exploration in finding new deposits. Annual additions of reserves to new deposits were incorrectly treated as discoveries and credited to the drilling in the year prior to that in which they were reported. Furthermore, it is widely recognized that some development drilling is reported by industry as exploration drilling.

An additional problem with discovery rates as used by Hubbert (1969) for oil and Lieberman (1976) for uranium arises from basing the rate on drilling footage. Even if the resource were infinite but contained in a region having a finite area, progressively drilling to greater depths would result in a decline in discoveries per foot as drilling accumulated. While circumstances of uranium resources differ from this hypothetical situation, the effect noted is present and imparts a negative bias to the estimate of undiscovered, recoverable resources.

Basing the analysis of undiscovered, recoverable resources of U_3O_8 on discovery rates of $8 reserves raises economic and data issues: (1) the effect of inflation on discovery rates; (2) the effect of improved productivity and future development drilling on discovery rates; and (3) the appropriate multiplier to be applied to undiscovered US $8 resources to infer the quantity of undiscovered US $30 resources. Contrary to Lieberman's claim, the inflation of costs has significantly eroded US $8 reserves from the very initiation of that category of reserves. Annual rates of losses of reserves due to inflation have averaged approximately 4 per cent for the seven years prior to 1974. The effect of inflation can be appreciated by considering the hypothetical situation in which the resource is infinite and a constant amount of exploration drilling is allocated each year. In this case, rates of discovery of reserves having a specified grade would be constant. But, if discovery rates were based upon reserves of a specified cost and if these costs were to inflate at an annual rate of 4 per cent, discovery rates would decline exponentially, as drilling progressed, at a rate equal to the rate of inflation.

Improvements in productivity would have an effect on discovery rates opposite to that of inflation. The manner in which inflation and productivity improvements should be treated varies, depending upon whether the immediate objective is to comment upon the effectiveness of exploration in finding new deposits having a constant economic quality (cost) or a constant physical quality (grade). Irrespective of which choice is made for the analysis of data, a comprehensive resource analysis ultimately requires the assessment of productivity improvements as well as physical depletion, for the issue of primary importance to society is the *economic* scarcity of uranium resources. Lieberman does not comment upon these issues.

Since undiscovered, recoverable US $30 resources are determined by ratioing up the estimate of undiscovered, recoverable US $8 resources, the result is subject to all of the aforementioned frailties plus uncertainty about the appropriate ratio. Conceptually, it is clear what this ratio should be: the ratio of *undiscovered* US $30 *resources* to *undiscovered* US $8 *resources*. Obviously, we do not know this ratio. While using, as Lieberman did, the ratio of US $30 reserves and production to US $8 reserves and production may appear to give a prudent estimate, this ratio probably understates considerably the undiscovered US $30 resources. The proportion of all undiscovered resources of U_3O_8 which are recoverable at a forward cost of US $30 most likely is considerably greater than is the proportion of reported reserves which are recoverable at US $30. An overriding issue in this judgement is that data on US $30 reserves were at the time of the analysis very incomplete (underreported); these data represent primarily the US $30 reserves in deposits having US $8 reserves. The US $30 reserves of many deposits having no US $8 reserves are not included in the inventory of US $30 reserves. Other issues spring from the fact that exploration has been progressively directed to targets at greater depth. The greater effectiveness of exploration in finding high-grade rather than low-grade deposits at increased depths and the increase in mining costs with depth imply a greater proportion of undiscovered resources in the US $30 forward cost category than is the case for current reserves and past production.

Several thoughts appear as an appropriate conclusion to this section. Any and all methods for the estimation of *unknown* resources must employ a model of some form of the endowment–exploration–production complex. Every model is a simplification to some degree of the real world and can be criticized in some regard. No method will provide *the* accurate estimate. Every estimate, whether determined mathematically or subjectively, is intrinsically uncertain. The increasing adoption of probabilistic methods for resource appraisal testifies to this reality.

2.7. A discovery-process model and the estimation of future oil and gas supply

2.7.1. *Perspective*

A report (US Geological Survey 1980), of the Interagency Oil and Gas Supply Project of the US Department of Interior and US Department of Energy—hereafter referred to as IOGSP—describes use of a discovery-process model as part of an impressive engineering cost-economic analysis of the future supply of oil and gas from the Permian Basin of West Texas and Southeastern New Mexico.

2.7.2. *The discovery-process model*

The discovery-process model employed in this study was proposed by Arps and Roberts (1958) and assumes that the probability for the next exploratory well finding a field of a given area is proportional to the ratio of the area of the field to the area of the basin. The model selected for the Permian Basin reflects this basic philosophy, but was modified to accommodate a basin having many productive horizons. The number of discoveries of size class i is specified to be a function of the number of exploratory wells w for the depth interval

$$F_{ij}(w) = F_{ij}(\infty)(1 - e^{-c_j \cdot a_{ij} \cdot w/b}),$$

where $F_{ij}(\infty)$ is the ultimate number of fields of the ith size class in the jth depth interval and c_j is the efficiency of exploration. For random drilling $c = 1$; the value used in an analysis is predicated on how much better or worse industry practice is in the jth depth interval as compared to random drilling. a_{ij} is the average areal extent of the fields in the ith size class and jth depth category and b is the area of basin. Twenty field-size classes were employed in the Permian Basin (see Table 2.3). The discovery-process model can be related to the conceptual framework of Chapter 1 by noting that $F_{ij}(\infty)$ is the

TABLE 2.3. *Comparison of the numbers of discoveries through 1974 with the number forecast, keyed on the pre-1961 discovery and exploratory drilling data in the 0–5000-foot depth interval.* (*Source*: US Geological Survey (1980), p. 29.)

Size class	Area (square miles)	Discoveries Actual	Discoveries Estimated	Discoveries Difference
1	0.13	211	200.1	10.9
2	0.14	84	66.0	18.0
3	0.16	84	84.7	−0.7
4	0.22	92	67.0	25.0
5	0.25	127	109.6	17.4
6	0.39	135	114.8	20.2
7	0.49	129	125.3	3.7
8	0.94	104	92.8	11.2
9	1.23	111	107.4	3.6
10	2.21	84	84.5	−0.5
11	4.24	75	82.9	−7.9
12	5.40	49	52.2	−3.2
13	8.30	35	33.3	1.7
14	18.19	19	18.2	0.8
15	40.42	14	14.0	0.0
16	49.19	16	16.0	0.0
17	67.20	9	9.0	0.0
18	81.75	6	6.0	0.0
19	129.88	2	2.0	0.0
20	40.25	1	1.0	0.0
Total		1387	1286.8	100.2

endowment of the jth depth interval of the basin in oil and gas fields of class i size. However, $F_{ij}(w)$ does not describe directly resources or potential supply because it is functionally related to $F_{ij}(\infty)$ by number of wells. The estimation of potential supply would require the association of costs to the fields discovered for a given number of exploration wells.

The use of this discovery-process model is contingent upon the estimation of its parameters, which are c_j and $F_{ij}(\infty)$. Two different procedures can be employed to estimate these parameters. One of these is the exterior specification of c_j on the basis of expert opinion or as a result of supplementary analysis, such as the comparison of historical drilling results to the results of a random drilling model. The other approach is to select, by iterative estimation, that pair of c_j and $F_{ij}(\infty)$ that gives the best fit to historical data.

The example provided by the IOGSP (US Geological Survey 1980, p. 23) specified c_j to be 2.0 and then proceeded to calculate $F_{ij}(\infty)$.

Given

> Average areal extent of fields = 2.2 mi^2
> Area of Permian Basin = 100 000 mi^2
> Size class 10: 1 520 000 to 3 040 000 bbl
> of oil equivalent
> Depth interval 1: 0–5000 ft
> Efficiency of exploration = 2.0
> Cumulative exploration wells through
> 1960 = 14 243
> Number of discoveries in size class 10
> and depth interval 1 through
> 1960 = 59.

Then,

$$59 = F_{10,1}(\infty)(1 - e^{-(2.0)(2.2)(14\,243)/100\,000}) \quad (2.19)$$

$$F_{10,1}(\infty) = 126.7.$$

Finally,

$$F_{10,1}(w) = 126.7(1 - e^{-(2.0)(2.2)(w)/100\,000}). \quad (2.20)$$

2.7.3. Predicted discoveries

A hindsight kind of analysis was used to demonstrate the credibility of estimates by this model. As indicated in this example, cumulative exploration drilling and discoveries through 1960 were employed to estimate $F_{10,1}(\infty)$. At the time of this analysis, both cumulative drilling and discoveries for 1974 were known. Thus, it was possible to substitute the 1974 number of exploration wells into eqn (2.20) and use this model to estimate the discoveries by 1974. For example, given the 25 055 exploratory wells drilled by the end of 1974, predicted discoveries for the 10th size class and depth interval 1 are 84.5 deposits

$$\hat{F}_{10,1}(25\,055) = 126.7(1 - e^{-(2.0)(2.2)(25\,055)/100\,000})$$

$$\hat{F}_{10,1}(25\,055) = 84.5.$$

Since by 1960, 59 fields had been discovered, this model forecasts 25.6 fields to be discovered between 1960 and 1974. Remarkably, 25 discoveries were made during this period. Table 2.3 compares estimates for the 20 size classes to actual discoveries. The accuracy of the model is remarkable. The forecasts for size classes 15 through 20 are perfect.

2.7.4. The estimation of potential supply

The discovery-process model describes, for a given depth interval and a given increment of drilling (number of exploration wells), a frequency distribution of discoveries by size class. By subtracting

known fields, a frequency distribution of incremental discoveries by size class can be associated with incremental drilling. But, since neither the costs of exploration drilling nor the costs of development and production are taken into account in making these estimates, the discovery-process model of itself does not estimate potential supply or resources. Clearly, the discovery-process model provides conditional estimates of discoveries: if a specified number of wells were to be drilled, the expected discoveries would be those estimated by the model. Estimation of potential supply requires an economic analysis of these discoveries.

The approach adopted by the IOGSP for computing potential supply was to construct the engineering and cost models necessary to ascribe exploration, development, and production costs to these discoveries and then to subject each discovery to a discounted cash-flow analysis, given a specified price and rate of return on capital. The fact that the discovery-process model is a saturated exponential with regard to the number of exploration wells means that the marginal physical product with respect to number of wells decreases as the cumulative number of wells increases. Consequently, for a specified price and rate of return, there must exist an optimum number of wells to be drilled, optimum in the sense that total marginal cost (inclusive of marginal costs of exploration, development, and production) equals marginal revenue.

The engineering and cost relations developed and employed to compute potential supply are listed in Table 2.4. The first column identifies the economic or engineering factor and the second column states the physical variable by which the factor is estimated. There are basically two kinds of relations in this table (1) relations which describe costs and (2) relations which ascribe physical parameters to discoveries. For example, relation 4, one of the latter of these kinds of relations, is used to categorize discoveries into either crude oil and associated-dissolved gas or nonassociated gas. Then, using relation 12, discoveries of crude oil and associated-dissolved gas are further categorized as either technically susceptible to primary techniques alone or technically susceptible to both primary and secondary techniques. Other relations in Table 2.4 ascribe additional physical parameters that are required to perform the economic analysis, such as recovery and production rate (decline curve). Once all discoveries have been given physical parameters, these parameters along with size class and depth interval are used

TABLE 2.4. *Engineering and cost relations used to compute potential supply*

Economic or engineering factor	Explanatory variable
1 Average exploratory well depth	Cumulative exploratory wells
2 Exploratory drilling and equipment costs	Well depth
3 Total exploration cost	Drilling and equipment costs
4 Ratio of oil fields to total fields	depth, size class
5 Ultimate oil recovery per field	depth, size class
6 Ultimate oil recovery per well from primary oil fields	depth, size class
7 Ultimate associated-dissolved gas recovery per oil well from primary fields	depth, size class
8 Ultimate oil recovery per well from secondary and pressure maintenance fields	depth, size class
9 Ultimate gas recovery per oil well from secondary and pressure maintenance fields	depth, size class
10 Ultimate nonassociated gas recovery per field	depth, size class
11 Ultimate nonassociated gas recovery per well	depth, size class
12 Ratio of primary oil fields to total oil fields	depth, size class
13 Cost of lease equipment per nonassociated gas development well	depth, size class
14 Development drilling and equipment costs per well	well depth
15 Cost of development of dry hole	well depth
16 Exponential oil well decline rates per year	depth, size class
17 Annual direct operating expenses for nonassociated gas wells	depth, size class
18 Lease equipment cost per well for primary oil production	well depth
19 Oil production decline curves, by size class and depth	time (years)
20 Per cent of expected ultimate gas recovery	per cent of expected ultimate oil recovery
21 Annual gas production, by size class and depth	time
22 Annual direct operating costs per producing oil well for primary recovery	well depth
23 Annual direct operating costs per producing oil well for secondary recovery	well depth

to ascribe various kinds of costs to the development and exploitation of these discoveries. For example,

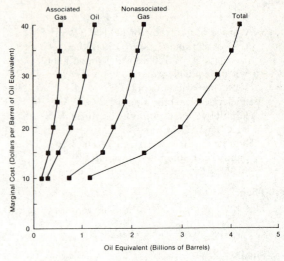

Fig. 2.15. Marginal cost of recoverable oil and gas resources from undiscovered deposits in the Permian Basin—15 per cent discounted cash-flow rate of return. (Source: US Geological Survey 1980, p. 45.)

relation 14 ascribes development and equipment costs to each development well; relation 22 ascribes direct operating costs to each producing well, given primary recovery.

Thus, by using relations of Table 2.4 each discovery can be given the physical parameters and costs necessary to perform a discounted cash flow analysis, which determines if, given the specified price and rate of return, the discovery can be produced economically.

The study group determined potential supply from currently undiscovered deposits for a specified price and rate of return by finding that level of drilling for which the positive surplus of present value from the various fields just offset the cost of exploration (US Geological Survey 1980, p. 40). Fig. 2.15 shows the marginal cost estimated by the study group for undiscovered oil and gas of the Permian Basin, given a rate of return of 15 per cent on capital.

2.8. Appendices

2.8.1. *Derivation of equation for first derivative logistic with price and technology variables*

Define the logistic model

$$p_t = p_\infty (1 + a e^{-bt})^{-1}. \qquad (2.21)$$

Then,

$$\frac{dp_t}{d_t} = \frac{-p_\infty(-abe^{-bt})}{(1+ae^{-bt})^2}. \quad (2.22)$$

But, note from (2.21) that

$$\left(\frac{p_\infty}{p_t}\right)^2 = (1+ae^{-bt})^2. \quad (2.23)$$

Then,

$$\frac{dp_t}{d_t} = \frac{-p_t^2(-abe^{-bt})}{p_\infty}. \quad (2.24)$$

Note that from eqn (2.21), we can write

$$\frac{p_\infty}{p_t} - 1 = ae^{-bt}. \quad (2.25)$$

Therefore,

$$\frac{dp_t}{dt} = \frac{bp_t^2(ae^{-bt})}{p_\infty} = \frac{bp_t^2\left(\frac{p_\infty}{p_t}-1\right)}{p_\infty}$$

$$= \frac{bp_t^2\left(\frac{p_\infty-p_t}{p_t}\right)}{p_\infty}, \quad (2.26)$$

$$\frac{dp_t}{d_t} = bp_t\left(1-\frac{p_t}{p_\infty}\right). \quad (2.27)$$

Now, define p_∞

$$p_\infty = \sum_{i=0}^{k}\alpha_{1i}r_{t-i} + \alpha_2\phi(t), \quad (2.28)$$

where r_{t-i} = product price i periods prior to current period t, α_{1i} are the coefficients of lagged price, $\phi(t)$ is a proxy for technology of production at time t, and α_2 is a coefficient of technology. Substituting eqn (2.28) in eqn (2.27) for p_∞,

$$\frac{dp_t}{d_t} = bp_t\left[1-\frac{p_t}{\sum_{i=0}^{k}\alpha_{1i}r_{t-i}+\alpha_2\phi(t)}\right]. \quad (2.29)$$

Eqn (2.29) is the form of the logistic defined by Uri (1980) to explicitly identify the effect of price and technology on the quantity of the mineral that is ultimately recoverable.

2.8.2. Demonstration of the effects of mixing drilling yields from two regions

Suppose that we have two populations of deposits, pI and pII and that the numbers of deposits and their size distributions of the two populations *are equal*. However, the deposits of pII *are twice as deep* as those of pI; this is the *only difference* in the two populations.

Let's suppose also that drilling costs and economic incentives are such that drilling on pI has pretty well ceased at a cumulative footage of 7×10^7 feet. Suppose that $(ds/dh)^I$ is described by the following exponential:

$$(ds/dh)^I = 100e^{-0.10\times10^{-7}h}.$$

Note that s_∞^I is 100×10^8 bbl of oil: $s_\infty^I = 100/(0.10\times10^{-7}) = 100\times10^8$ bbl. However, at the completion of 7×10^7 ft of drilling, only 47.865×10^8 bbl are attributed to discoveries (see Table 2.5). Now, suppose that at the completion of 7×10^7 ft on pI, a deep test exploratory well strikes a deposit in pII, and all drilling is transferred to targets of pII. Let us assume that it is then more economic to drill for targets of pII than those of pI until cumulative footage in pII = 7×10^7 ft.

If pII had been drilled first, its relationship of ds/dh to h would reflect the fact that resources of pII are equal to pI but at a depth twice as great as those of pI

$$(ds/dh)^{II} = 50e^{-0.10\times10^{-7}(h/2)}$$

or

$$(ds/dh)^{II} = 50e^{-0.05\times10^{-7}h}.$$

Of course, $s_\infty^{II} = 50/(0.05\times10^{-7}) = 1000\times10^7 = 100\times10^8$, the same as for pI: $s_\infty^I = s_\infty^{II}$. Obviously,

TABLE 2.5. ds/dh versus h for pI, pII, and pI+pII

h (10^7)	pI (10^7)	pII (10^7)	Combined (pI+pII) (10^7)
1	90.48		90.48
2	81.87		81.87
3	74.08		74.08
4	67.03		67.03
5	60.65		60.65
6	54.88		54.88
7	49.66		49.66
8		47.56	47.56
9		45.24	45.24
10		43.04	43.04
11		40.94	40.94
12		38.94	38.94
13		37.04	37.04
14		35.23	35.23
	478.65	287.99	766.64

$s_\infty^I + s_\infty^{II} = 200 \times 10^8$ bbl. The quantity of 14.0×10^7 ft is being used as an upper limit only because we wish to stop exploration at this point and to use the record to estimate $s_\infty^I + s_\infty^{II}$ under the assumption that we didn't know the underlying models but did have the data generated from them by 14.0×10^7 ft of drilling. In addition, in this simplistic model it is proposed that drilling on pII subsequent to its discovery would be more profitable than on pI until cumulative drilling on pII amounted to 7.0×10^7, an amount equal to that on pI but representing only one-half as much area. This simply reflects the fact that pII is twice as deep as pI. Obviously, other factors, such as greater lifting costs, and greater capital requirements would affect this trade-off; these are ignored in this hypothetical case.

Employing these models we would generate the combined data for ds/dh shown in column 4 of Table 2.5.

Data to be used in estimation of s_∞^{I+II} are $(\mathrm{d}s/\mathrm{d}h)^{I+II} = 35.2$ bbl/ft and $s_{14}^{I+II} = 766.64 \times 10^7$ bbl. Application of Hubbert's methods, as previously demonstrated, yields 136.4×10^8 bbl,

$$\hat{s}_\infty^{I+II} = 136.4 \times 10^8 \text{ bbl.}$$

Now, let's see what $\hat{s}_\infty^I + \hat{s}_\infty^{II}$ would have been if the yields to drilling of the two populations had been analysed separately by Hubbert's method. Based upon the data $(\mathrm{d}s/\mathrm{d}h)^I = 49.66$ bbl/ft, $s_7^I = 47.865 \times 10^8$ bbl, $(\mathrm{d}s/\mathrm{d}h)^{II} = 35.23$ bbl/ft, and $s_7^{II} = 287.99 \times 10^7$ bbl, application of Hubbert's method yields the following estimates

$$\hat{s}_\infty^I = 104.95 \times 10^8 \text{ bbl,}$$
$$\hat{s}_\infty^{II} = 110.40 \times 10^8 \text{ bbl,}$$
$$\hat{s}_\infty^I + \hat{s}_\infty^{II} = 215.35 \times 10^8 \text{ bbl.}$$

Thus, we find that *separate* analyses yield a quantity much closer to that known from the models

Known: $s_\infty^I + s_\infty^{II} = 200 \times 10^8$ bbl
$\hat{s}_\infty^{I+II} = 136.4 \times 10^8$ bbl
Estimates: $\hat{s}_\infty^I + \hat{s}_\infty^{II} = 215.35 \times 10^8$ bbl.

Actually, the fact that $\hat{s}_\infty^I + \hat{s}_\infty^{II}$ varies from 200×10^8 must be attributed to accuracy limitations of the hand calculator employed in the analysis. Such error is probably due to the heavy use of logarithm and exponential calculator functions. Of course, since in this contrived example these data were generated from exact exponential models, estimation of the parameters could have been done much more simply

by using only the first and last values of the two series

pI: $B = \ln (90.48/49.66)/6.0 \times 10^7$
$= 0.09998817528 \times 10^{-7}$
$K = 90.48/e^{-0.09998817528 \times 10^{-7}} = 99.995$
$\hat{s}_\infty = 100.01 \times 10^8$ bbl

pII: $B = \ln (47.56/35.23)/6.0 \times 10^7$
$= 0.0500156799 \times 10^{-7}$
$K = 47.56/e^{-0.0500156799 \times 10^{-7}} = 47.56$
$\hat{s}^{II} = 95.090 \times 10^8$
$\hat{s}_\infty^I + \hat{s}_\infty^{II} = 195.10 \times 10^8.$

This estimate of $s^I + s^{II}$ (195.10×10^8) is closer to 200×10^8 than that made by Hubbert's formula, probably because of the simpler numerical analysis.

References

Arps, J. J. and Roberts, T. G. (1958). Economics of drilling for Cretaceous oil on east flank of Denver–Julesburg Basin. *Am. Ass. petroleum Geol. Bull.* **42**(11), 2549–66.

Averitt, P. (1969). *Coal resources of the United States, Jan. 1, 1967*, Geological Survey Bulletin 1275. US Geological Survey, Washington, DC.

Barnett, H. J. and Morse, C. (1969). *Scarcity and growth*. The Johns Hopkins University Press, Baltimore, Maryland.

Brooks, D. B. (1976). Mineral supply as a stock. In *Economics of the mineral industries* (ed. W. A. Vogely), Chapter 2.5A, p. 127–207. AIME, New York.

Burrows, J. C. (1975). Econometric modelling of metal and mineral industries. In *Mineral materials modelling* (ed. W. A. Vogely), pp. 121–32. The Johns Hopkins University Press, Baltimore, Maryland.

Data Resources, Inc (1979). *Energy review: summer 1979*. Lexington, Massachusetts.

Drew, L. J. (1975). Linkage effects between deposit discovery and post-discovery exploratory drilling. *J. Res.* **3**(2), 169–79.

Harris, D. P. (1976). *The estimation of uranium resources by life-cycle or discovery-rate models—a critique*. Report prepared for US Energy Research and Development Administration, Grand Junction Office, Grand Junction, Colorado.

Hewett, D. F. (1929). Cycles in metal production. *Trans. AIME* **85**, 65–93.

Hubbert, M. K. (1965). National Academy of Sciences report on energy resources: reply (to discussion by John M. Ryan). *Am. Ass. petroleum Geol. Bull.* **49**(10), 1720–7.

—— (1967). Degree of advancement of petroleum exploration in United States. *Am. Ass. petroleum Geol. Bull.* **51**(11), 2207–27.

—— (1969). Energy resources. In *Resources and man* (A study and recommendations by the Committee on Resources and Man, National Academy of Sciences-National Research Council.) Chapter 8, pp. 157–242. W. H. Freeman & Company, San Francisco (for National Academy of Sciences).

—— (1974). *U.S. energy resources, a review as of 1972, Part I.* Background paper prepared at the request of Henry A. Jackson, Chairman, Committee on Interior and Insular Affairs, US Senate, 93rd Congress, 2nd Session, Committee Print Serial No. 93–40 (92–75). US Government Printing Office, Washington, DC.

Lieberman, M. A. (1976). United States uranium resources—an analysis of historical data. *Science* **192** (4238), 431–6.

MacAvoy, P. W. and Pindyck, R. S. (1975). *The economics of the natural gas shortage (1960–1980).* North-Holland, Amsterdam.

Mayer, L. S., Silverman, B., Zeger, S. L., and Bruce, A. G. (1979). *Modelling the rates of domestic crude oil discovery and production.* Resource Estimation and Validation Project, Depts. of Statistics and Geology, Princeton University, Princeton, New Jersey.

McKelvey, V. E. (1960). Relations of reserves of the elements to their crustal abundance. *Am. J. Sci.* **258-A** (Bradley volume), 234–41.

Morris, H. T., Heyl, A. V., and Hall, R. B. (1973). Lead. In *United States mineral resources* (ed. D. A. Brobst and W. P. Pratt), pp. 313–32. Geological Survey Prof. Paper 820, US Geological Survey, Washington, DC.

National Academy of Sciences (1975). Resources of fossil fuels. In *Mineral resources and the environment*, Chapter V, pp. 79–126. Committee on Mineral Resources and the Environment, National Academy of Sciences, Washington, DC.

Netschert, B. C. (1958). *The future supply of oil and gas.* The Johns Hopkins University Press, Baltimore, Maryland. (For Resources for the Future, Inc.)

—— and Landsberg, H. H. (1961). *The future supply of the major metals—a reconnaissance survey.* The Johns Hopkins University Press, Baltimore, Maryland. (For Resources for the Future, Inc.)

Norgaard, R. B. (1975). Resource scarcity and new technology in US petroleum development. *Natural Resources J.* **15**(2), 265–82.

Roberts, F. and Torrens, I. (1974). Analysis of the life cycle of non-ferrous minerals. *Resources Policy* **1**(1), (September 1974) 14–28.

Ryan, J. M. (1965). *Limitations of statistical methods for predicting petroleum and natural gas reserve and availability.* Preprint number SPE 1256, 40th Annual Fall Meeting of the Society of Petroleum Engineers of AIME, Denver, Colorado.

US Geological Survey (1975). *Geological estimates of undiscovered recoverable oil and gas resources in the United States.* Circular 725, US Geological Survey, Washington, DC.

—— (1980). *Future supply of oil and gas from the Permian basin of West Texas and Southeastern New Mexico.* Circular 828, US Geological Survey, Washington, DC.

Uri, N. D. (1980). Crude oil resource appraisal in the United States. *Energy J. (IAEE)* **1**(3), 65–74.

Weeks, L. G. (1959). Where will energy come from in 2059? *Petroleum Engr.* **31** A-24–A-31.

Zapp, A. D. (1962). *Future petroleum-producing capacity of the United States.* Bulletin 1142-H, US Geological Survey, Washington, DC.

Notes

1. Burrows (1975) does not identify this variable.
2. Harris, D. P. (1965). An application of multivariate statistical analysis to mineral exploration. Ph.D. dissertation, The Pennsylvania State University.
3. Zapp, A. D. (1961). World petroleum resources; domestic and world resources of fossil fuels, radioactive minerals, and geothermal energy. Unpublished preliminary reports prepared by members of the US Geological Survey for the Natural Resources Subcommittee of the Federal Council of Science and Technology.
4. Moore, C. L. (1965). Discussion on paper number SPE 1256 'Limitations of statistical methods for predicting petroleum and natural gas reserves and availability' by John M. Ryan. Presentation at the 40th Annual Fall Meeting of the Society of Petroleum Engineers of AIME, Denver, Colorado.
5. In accordance with notation established in Chapter 1, cumulative discoveries and cumulative production are represented by s_t and p_t, respectively.
6. § 2.5 is part of a larger manuscript that was prepared by the author under contract to the National Science Foundation during the summer of 1975.
7. According to Norgaard (1975), if deposit factors are held constant, the real price of wells decreased from 53 to 87 per cent from 1939 to 1968; new technology and inputs have been depth-favouring.
8. L. J. Drew, Office of Resource Analysis, US Geological Survey, Reston, Virginia.

9. As in the previous section, s_t represents cumulative discoveries at time t.

10. Weeb, H. (1976). Uranium supply—a producer's view. Paper presented at AIF Fuel Cycle Conference, Phoenix, Arizona.

11. John Klemenic, US Energy Research and Development Administration, Grand Junction Office, Grand Junction, Colorado.

12. The effect is to expand reserves of recently discovered deposits by large factors. The reserves of those deposits discovered progressively earlier are multiplied by factors that are progressively smaller by a constant percentage. This effect is similar in kind to that achieved by Hubbert's alpha factor.

3 QUANTITY–QUALITY RELATIONS (MODELS)

3.1. Perspective

This chapter could be entitled 'Tonnage–grade relations', for its subject matter generally is known by that name. However, the term tonnage–grade relations has been used variously to represent two very different classes of phenomena:

(1) the magnitude of an inventory of mineralized material for different levels of grade;
(2) the statistical properties of:
    (a) Tonnage of mineralized material per deposit and of average grade of mineralized material per deposit;
    (b) The expectation for grade per unit (deposit, etc.), given the size of the unit of mineralized material.

The first of these classes is the subject of this chapter. The title of this chapter was chosen to emphasize this fact. Assuming this goal has been achieved, the term tonnage–grade and quantity–quality will be used here interchangeably.

Tonnage–grade (grade–tonnage) relations of the quantity–quality type have been used to describe several different issues

(1) the relationship of the tonnage of ore reserves in an ore deposit to the cut-off grade of ore;
(2) the relationship of the tonnage of ore reserves having grades above specified cut-off grades to the average grade of all ore above the cut-off grades;
(3) the relationship of the total tonnage of ore reserves from a group of deposits to cut-off grades (same as 1, but for a set of deposits considered collectively);
(4) the relationship of the total tonnage of ore reserves from a group of deposits to average grade (same as 2, except for a set of deposits considered collectively);
(5) issues 3 and 4, but for resources, inclusive of reserves.

Chapter 3 examines contributions to the state of knowledge of these issues. In-depth comment with respect to ideas and issues largely will be deferred until some of the concepts have been established and until a historical perspective of the evolution of ideas

has been presented. This design is purposeful, for there seems to be some confusion as to what can or cannot be interpreted from a tonnage–grade relationship; consequently, it seems appropriate to examine the major contributions on this topic.

3.2. Lasky's initial treatise: a benchmark

Interest in tonnage–grade relations was sparked by a paper authored by S. G. Lasky (1950a) entitled 'How tonnage and grade relations help predict ore reserves'.

Lasky interprets the results of his analysis as follows:

> As a conclusion from the analysis presented herein and from related studies, it may be stated as a general principle that in many mineral deposits in which there is a graduation from relatively rich to relatively lean material, the tonnage increases at a constant geometric rate as the grade decreases. Or, as the tonnage increases, the mineral content of the cumulative tonnage decreases at a constant declining rate.

In reading this summary of Lasky's findings, the phrase 'increases at a constant geometric rate' should be emphasized. To appreciate fully the implication of this relationship consider the familiar compounding of interest

$$F_n = P\left(1 + \frac{r}{k}\right)^{kn}, \qquad (3.1)$$

where F_n is the future worth in year n, r is the nominal (annual) interest rate, P the principal (initial amount), k the number of compounding periods per year, and n is the number of years. For example, consider the case in which we have invested US\$100 in an account earning 10 per cent annually, but compounded twice per year, and we wish to know the value of our investment next year.

For this hypothetical situation, $n = 1$, $P = \text{US\$100}$, $k = 2$, and $r = 0.10$. Then,

$$F_1 = \text{US\$100}\left(1 + \frac{0.10}{2}\right)^{(2)(1)} = \text{US\$100}(1.05)^2$$

$$= \text{US\$100}(1.05)(1.05);$$

$$F_1 = (\text{US\$105})(1.05) = \text{US\$110.25}.$$

In this case, time is treated in discrete blocks. The *rate of increase* in the value of the investment P from one year to the next is 10.25 per cent, or 5 per cent per compounding period. In other words the value of the investment at the end of any compounding period is 5 per cent greater than it was in the previous period, but the value at the end of any year, which consists of two compounding periods, is 10.25 per cent greater than it was in the previous year. This is the concept of rate of increase. Suppose now, that the number of compounding periods per year becomes very large, approaching infinity; this is called continuous compounding. Mathematicians demonstrate that the appropriate way to calculate future value for the case of continuous compounding is as follows:

$$F_n = P \cdot e^{rn} \qquad (3.2)$$

Eqn (3.2) reflects the fact that the limit of $(1 + r/k)^{kn}$ as k approaches infinity is e^{rn}

$$\lim_{k \to \infty} \left[\left(1 + \frac{r}{k} \right)^{kn} \right] = e^{rn}.$$

Note, that if we take the natural logarithms of both sides of (3.2), we have the equation

$$\ln F_n = \ln P + r \cdot n \cdot \ln (e),$$

or, since $\ln (e) = 1.0$,

$$\ln F_n = \ln P + r \cdot n. \qquad (3.3)$$

This is a linear equation, and the plot of $\ln F_n$ against n would appear as a straight line, a line having an intercept of $\ln P$ and a slope of r. Eqn (3.3) is of the general form described by Lasky for the logarithm of the tonnage of ore as a function of average grade, except that the slope of the line is negative, which reflects his stated conclusions of a constant rate of decrease in average grade as tonnage increases.

As a graphic demonstration of negative exponential relations, consider the following equation: $y = 100(0.80)^X$. As X increases, y decreases geometrically, as indicated by Fig. 3.1, which exhibits a curvilinear relationship that is concave [1] to the origin. If we take common logarithms of each side of this equation, we obtain a linear equation

$$\log y = 2.0 - 0.09691\,X.$$

This is equivalent to showing that the plot of the logarithm of y against X (for y and X that are related exponentially) exhibits a straight line. This fact is demonstrated in Fig. 3.2, in which the scale for y is the base 10 log-scale while that for X is

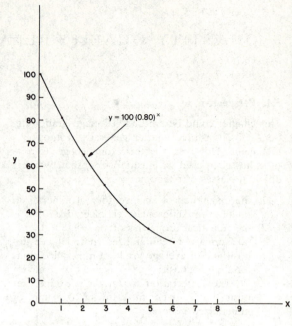

Fig. 3.1. A negative exponential relationship.

linear. The data for the plots of Figs. 3.1 and 3.2 were generated from the equation $y = 100(0.80)^X$, and are provided in Table 3.1.

Lasky demonstrated that the relationship of the logarithm of cumulative ore tonnage to average grade for each of the 10 major porphyry copper deposits known in the US at that time was of the

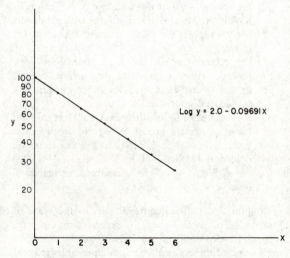

Fig. 3.2. A negative exponential relationship.

TABLE 3.1. *Data for an exponential relationship*

X	y
0	100.0
1	80.0
2	64.0
3	51.2
4	41.0
5	32.8
6	26.2

mathematical form

$$\bar{q} = K_1 - K_2 \log t, \qquad (3.4)$$

where $\bar{q}$ is the average grade, t the cumulative tonnage of ore, and K_1 and K_2 are constants. Alternatively, $\log t = K_1 - \bar{q}/K_2$. It follows that $\log t = K_1/K_2 - 1/(K_2)\bar{q}$. If we observe that K_1/K_2 and $1/K_2$ are simply two constants and designate $C_1 = K_1/K_2$ and $C_2 = 1/K_2$, we have for $\log t$

$$\log t = C_1 - C_2 \bar{q} \qquad (3.5)$$

or

$$t = 10^{C_1 - C_2 \bar{q}}. \qquad (3.6)$$

Thus, Lasky found the cumulative tonnage of ore to

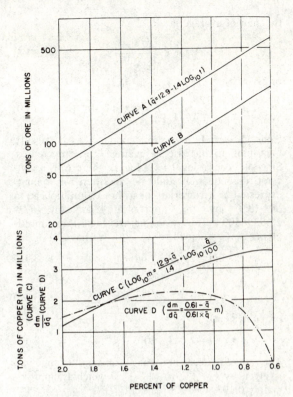

Fig. 3.4. Characteristics of hypothetical average porphyry copper deposit. Curve A, total material in the ground plotted against average grade; Curve B, total material plotted against cutoff grade; Curve C, copper content; Curve D, rate of addition of copper. (After Lasky 1950*a*.)

be related to average grade through an exponential relationship. As was demonstrated in Fig. 3.2, exponential relations are linear when the logarithm of the dependent variable (left-hand side of the equation—see eqn (3.5)) is plotted against the independent variable. Fig. 3.3 shows the tonnage-grade relations for each of the 10 porphyry copper deposits studied by Lasky and for the aggregate of the 10 deposits. Fig. 3.4 shows the relationship for a 'hypothetical average' of all 10 deposits. Based upon aggregated data for the 10 deposits, Lasky determined what he called the tonnage–grade relationship for the typical porphyry

$$\bar{q} = 12.9 - 1.4 \log t. \qquad (3.7)$$

The above relationship shows average grade to decrease as tonnage increases. By rearranging the terms of this equation, tonnage can be described as a

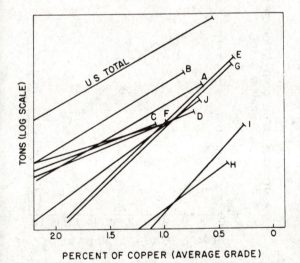

Fig. 3.3. Grade–tonnage relations and relative magnitude of ten American porphyry copper deposits. Groups A, B, C, D, F; J, E, G; and H, I are deposits with similar characteristics. Ordinate scale left off in order not to reveal identity of individual deposits. (After Lasky 1950*a*.)

function of average grade

$$\log t = \frac{12.9 - \bar{q}}{1.4}, \tag{3.8}$$

or

$$\log t = \frac{12.9}{1.4} - \frac{1}{1.4} \bar{q} = 9.2143 - 0.7143\bar{q}. \tag{3.9}$$

Eqns (3.8) and (3.9) show tonnage, as a base-10 logarithm, to increase as average grade decreases. Since in general $\log_x t = C \cdot \log_y t$, where C is a constant, this equation could be rewritten for tonnage expressed as a Naperian logarithm by multiplication of (3.9) by the appropriate constant, $C = 2.302585093$. Thus, using natural logarithms (multiplying by C, rounded to 2.3026), we have

$$\ln t = 21.22 - 1.645\bar{q}, \tag{3.10}$$

or

$$t = e^{21.22 - 1.645\bar{q}}, \tag{3.11}$$

or, equivalently,

$$t = 1.643 \times 10^9 e^{-1.645\bar{q}}. \tag{3.12}$$

The rate of increase in tonnage for a unit change in $\bar{q}$ is given by $e^{-1.645}$ (or $10^{-0.7143}$), which is approximately 0.193, or 19.3 per cent [2].

In his initial paper, Lasky examined in some form the first four issues of tonnage–grade relations that were cited at the beginning of this section; these are the relations of tonnage of ore reserves for the individual deposit and for the set of deposits to average grade and cut-off grade. Lasky did *no more* and *no less* than to examine the behaviour of logarithm of cumulative tonnage of ore and average grade of ore within an individual deposit or an aggregate of deposits as the cut-off grade is successively lowered.

3.3. Lasky on the appraisal of metal resources

In another paper entitled 'Mineral resource appraisal by the US. Geological Survey', Lasky (1950*b*) demonstrates that the tonnage–grade relations for such diverse deposits as the gold deposits in Juneau, Alaska, manganese in the Artillery Mountains of Arizona, the vanadium and phosphate deposits in the Phosphoria of Idaho and Wyoming, and the Falconbridge nickel deposits are exponential, each having different values for K_1 and K_2. Lasky (1950*b*) proposed that the tonnage–grade relationship determined *for the set* of porphyry copper deposits could be used to estimate *unknown copper resources*, the quantity of

metallized rock present in association with the known reserves but having concentrations well below economic cut-off grade at that time, which was approximately 0.65 per cent Cu. Specifically, he suggested that extrapolation of the relationship to average grades of 0.3 or 0.35 per cent would be reasonable. Thus, in this paper, Lasky *did* address the use of tonnage–grade relations for the appraisal of not just reserves but also of unknown mineral resources.

3.4. Musgrove's exposition of exponential relations

In 1965, Musgrove published an article entitled 'Lead: grade–tonnage relation'. The stated purpose of the investigation leading to this article was to see if, as had been suggested by Netschert and Landsberg (1961), lead reserves are anomalous in that they may not follow an exponential law. For 58 deposits or mineralized zones from 23 countries, Musgrove plotted cumulative tonnage of lead versus *cut-off* grade (Fig. 3.5). It should be noted that whereas Lasky

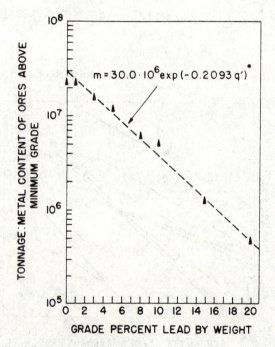

Fig. 3.5. Grade–tonnage relationship. (After Musgrove 1965.) *The equation [$m = 6.28 \times 10^6 \exp(-0.2093\,q')$] reported by Musgrove (1965, p. 251) does not appear to agree with his plot or with his description. The author has changed the equation to fit the plot and description, as noted on Fig. 3.5.

plotted cumulative ore tonnage against average grade, Musgrove plotted cumulative metal against cut-off grade. Musgrove concluded that lead is not anomalous, for it 'is characterized by the same sort of grade–tonnage relationship as are the other metals'

$$m = 6.28 \times 10^6 e^{-0.2093q'} \qquad (3.13)$$

where q' is the cut-off grade, and m the quantity of metal. He did, however, admit that for cut-off grades from zero to 1 per cent, there is a departure from the exponential law. He discounted this departure as being significant on the basis that even for a cut-off grade of zero, the data show 79.5 per cent of the quantity indicated by the fitted exponential relationship.

Later Musgrove (1971) published a paper entitled 'The distribution of metal resources (tests and implications of the exponential grade–size relation)'. This paper consists of three parts: the first part develops exponential theory and relations as they apply to grade and tonnage; the second part imparts to this relationship a third dimension, that of time, and examined some general economics in terms of the grade–tonnage relationship; and the third part examines fits of the exponential relationship to historical data for a number of metals.

Musgrove bases his development upon the assumption that the *density of resources* $r(q)$ at any grade q is *defined* by an *exponential* law

$$r(q) = \frac{A}{K} e^{-q/K}. \qquad (3.14)$$

It follows that the cumulative tonnage of ore $R(q)$ above a cut-off grade of q' is the integral of $r(q)$ for $q \lesssim q_{max}$

$$R(q') = \frac{A}{K} \int_{q'}^{q_{max}} e^{-q/k} \, dq = A(e^{-q'/K} - e^{-q_{max}/K}). \qquad (3.15)$$

Musgrove simplifies the expression for cumulative tonnage of ore above a cut-off grade by assuming that $e^{-q_{max}/K}$ approaches zero,

$$R(q') = A e^{-q'/K}. \qquad (3.16)$$

In this form $R(q') = Kr(q')$. In other words, the cumulative ore for grades of at least the cut-off grade is a constant multiple of the quantity of ore at that cut-off grade; this multiple K does not vary with the grade, but remains constant throughout the grade range.

The proposition of exponential grade size relations

as described by Musgrove implies the graphical representations of Fig. 3.6. If the logarithm of tonnage were plotted against cut-off or average grade, the curved lines of Fig. 3.6 would appear as straight lines, as demonstrated in the beginning of this section.

If tonnage and grade are statistically independent, then Musgrove's developments imply an exponential grade distribution. A grade distribution of this kind is not commonly observed in nature; more often a histogram showing the quantity of ore at specified grades or a histogram of grades of samples appears normal or lognormal, with a peak to the right of the origin. The effect of the grade distribution on the shape of the tonnage–grade relationship for the case of independence of deposit grade and tonnage will be examined further within this chapter. We here proceed to examine Musgrove's findings. Musgrove showed that for the exponential distribution, average grade and cut-off grade are related by a simple linear law

$$\bar{q} = q' + K. \qquad (3.17)$$

Therefore, the cumulative ore for a specific average grade can be determined from (3.16), the relationship for cut-off grade $R(q')$ by stating q' in terms of $\bar{q}$

$$R(\bar{q} - K) = A e^{-(\bar{q}-K)/K} = A e \cdot e^{-\bar{q}/K} = eR(\bar{q}). \qquad (3.18)$$

Thus, given function R, we have

Cumulative ore tonnage for cut-off grade q'
$$= R(q') = eR(\bar{q}),$$

where $\bar{q} = q' + K$.

An alternative representation, one compatible with Fig. 3.6, is to let concentration q represent an average grade or a cut-off grade and employ a new function $\bar{R}$ to describe cumulative ore tonnage when concentration is an average grade

For cut-off grade, cumulative ore tonnage $= R(q)$;

For average grade, cumulative ore
$$\text{tonnage } [3] = \bar{R}(q) = eR(q). \qquad (3.19)$$

After fitting exponential relations for cut-off and average grades and considering data issues, Musgrove (1971, p. 397) concludes that '... exponential relations appear to be even more widely applicable than was previously supposed'. Using grade or cut-off grade

$$\text{Tonnage density at grade } q: r(q) = \frac{A}{K} e^{-q/K}$$

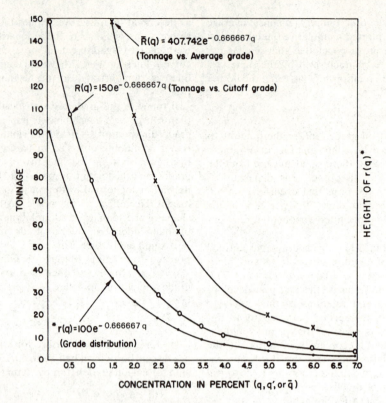

Fig. 3.6. Exponential grade–size relationships of Musgrove. *The function $r(q)$ is a density function; consequently, it cannot be plotted on the same ordinate axis as are $R(q)$ and $\bar{R}(q)$. The axis on right-handed side of the figure, height of $r(q)$, is for the plotting of $r(q)$.

Cumulative tonnage at cut-off grade: $R(q) = A e^{-q/K}$

Using average grade

  Cumulative tonnage: $\bar{R}(q) = e R(q) = e A e^{-q/K}$

Some examples of fitted exponential equations follow ($R(q)$ and $\bar{R}(q)$ describe cumulative ore tonnage as a function of cut-off and average grades, respectively) [4].

World copper resources (61 observations, beginning in 1935):

  $R(q) = (6.510 \times 10^9) e^{-0.720q}$

  $\bar{R}(q) = (16.89 \times 10^9) e^{-0.736q}$

World aluminium (bauxite):

  $R(q) = (75.62 \times 10^9) e^{-0.084q}$

  $\bar{R}(q) = (168.3 \times 10^9) e^{-0.127q}$

Thus, as indicated by the equation for $R(q)$ for aluminium, Musgrove's analysis implies $75.62 \times$ 10^9 tons of material as a source of aluminium, given a cut-off grade of zero per cent. The average grade for a cut-off grade of zero is 11.9 [5] per cent aluminium, giving 75.62×10^9 tons of ore and 9.0×10^9 tons of aluminium metal. Similarly, Musgrove's analysis indicates a world resource of 9.05×10^7 tons of copper contained in 6.51×10^9 tons of mineralized material having an average grade of 1.39 per cent copper for a cut-off grade of zero per cent.

3.5. Uranium reserves and resources: a departure from exponential relations

Ellis, Harris, and Van Wie (1975) examined the relationship of cumulative U_3O_8 reserves in New Mexico to average grade in a manner similar to that employed by Lasky for a set of porphyry copper deposits. However, in this case, the plot of the logarithm of cumulative tonnage of ore (current reserves and past production of U_3O_8 deposits in New Mexico) against average grade leaves some doubt

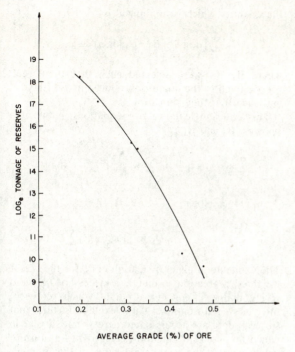

Fig. 3.7. Tonnage relationship for U_3O_8 reserves New
Mexico (Source: Ellis *et al.* 1975.)

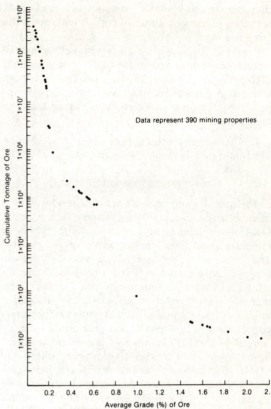

Data represent 390 mining properties

Fig. 3.8. Tonnage–average–grade relationship for Wyoming uranium properties (Source of data: personal
communication, 1976, US Energy Research and
Development Administration.)

about a straight line; rather the plot seems to exhibit
an overall curvilinear pattern that is convex to the
origin (see Fig. 3.7).

A much more striking departure from a straight
line is shown by the plot of the logarithm of cumulative ore tonnage against average grade for the
uranium properties of Wyoming (see Fig. 3.8). Thus,
plots for the same metal exhibit opposite curva-
tures, a result that seems confounding. However,
while these plots are for the same metal, the
tonnage–grade data represent two quite different
geographical regions (Wyoming and New Mexico)
and two different modes of occurrence of uranium.
In terms of the statistical nature of the data from the
two regions, the Wyoming deposits vary considerably
more in grade than do those of New Mexico. Whereas
the distribution of grades in New Mexico is narrow,
that for Wyoming is broad. As will be demonstrated
later in this chapter, there is a relationship between the
variation of grades and the form of the cumulative
tonnage–average grade relationship, given independence of deposit grade and tonnage.

3.6. Cargill, Root, and Bailey's use of production data

Cargill, Root, and Bailey (1980) employed quantity–
quality relations to estimate what they referred to as
resources of mercury for the United States, the
world, and selected mining districts. With respect to
terminology employed in this book, their estimates
are some mix of endowment and resources. The fact
that their method provides an estimate which is
defined by grade gives the estimate an endowment
character. However, as endowment this quantity is
incompletely defined, because neither minimum size
nor maximum depth to deposit is specified. Rather,
these values are whatever economics of exploration
and exploitation have allowed in the past. This indirect use of economics gives the estimate a resource

character. In this book the estimates by Cargill *et al.* are referred to as estimates of endowment, given the foregoing caveat.

Cargill *et al.* base their analysis upon records of annual production and grade. This is not without precedent, for Lasky (1950a, b) worked with both production records and reserves. However, the approach by Cargill *et al.* differs from that of Lasky in two respects

1. The way in which the time series of production and grade is used to construct quantity–quality data;
2. The form of the mathematical model.

The quantity and grade of material produced by a mine in a given year reflects, to some degree, decisions of the mine manager to maximize profits or minimize losses given current and expected product and factor prices; consequently, a time series of ore and associated grades exhibit fluctuations in the average grades of annual production. Lasky commented upon the effect of economics on production grades and demonstrated on a hypothetical porphyry copper deposit how production data could be *rearranged* so that (1) quantities of like grade are combined, irrespective of when they were produced and (2) the production is described in terms of decreasing grade. After this rearranging, cumulative average grade, as production grades are successively lowered, can be calculated. Cargill *et al.* (1980) did not perform this rearranging of data before computing cumulative average grade [6].

The mathematical model selected by Cargill *et al.* is log–log, instead of the log–linear relationship employed by Lasky,

$$\log \bar{q} = \beta_0 + \beta_1 \log t. \qquad (3.20)$$

Equivalently,

$$\bar{q} = At^{\beta_1}, \qquad (3.21)$$

where $\bar{q}$ is the average grade (absolute), t the cumulative quantity of mercury ore in 10^6 kg, and $A = 10^{\beta_0}$. For example, consider the equation estimated for the entire United States

$$\widehat{\log \bar{q}} = 0.674 - 0.670 \log t. \qquad (3.22)$$

Cargill *et al.* employed weighted regression to estimate the intercept and slope parameters of this equation. Instead of the usual least-squares criterion, which is the minimizing of the quantity

$$\sum_{i=1}^{n} (\log \bar{q}_i - \hat{\beta}_0 - \hat{\beta}_1 \log t_i)^2,$$

the quantity which is minimized is

$$\sum_{i=1}^{n} [(\log \bar{q}_i - \hat{\beta}_0 - \hat{\beta}_1 \log t_i)^2 w_i],$$

where the w_i were selected such that they were proportional to the quantity produced in the ith year and such that they sum to n.

This criterion leads to two equations in two unknowns, $\hat{\beta}_0$ and $\hat{\beta}_1$,

$$\sum_{i=1}^{n} w_i \cdot \log q_i = \hat{\beta}_0 \sum_{i=1}^{n} w_i + \hat{\beta}_1 \sum_{i=1}^{n} w_i \cdot \log t_i$$

$$\sum_{i=1}^{n} w_i \cdot \log q_i \cdot \log t_i$$

$$= \hat{\beta}_0 \sum_{i=1}^{n} w_i \cdot \log t_i + \hat{\beta}_1 \sum_{i=1}^{n} w_i (\log t_i)^2.$$

The explanation given by Cargill *et al.* for the use of weighted regression is that it is necessary to avoid giving undue importance to data which represent little new information. They explain further that since all data are accumulated across time, a year in which no actual production occurred has a nonzero value, namely the cumulative value of the previous year. Conventional regression gives that year's cumulative production the same weight as that of the previous year, but weighted regression, as applied by Cargill *et al.*, gives it a weight of zero, because it represents no new information.

The cumulative tonnage of mercury ore produced by 1977 is $17\,524.52 \times 10^6$ kg. Substitution of 17 524.52 into (3.22) gives $\widehat{\log \bar{q}} = -2.1692$, or $\hat{\bar{q}} = 0.68$ per cent Hg. This compares favourably with the actual average grade of 0.70 per cent Hg. Fig. 3.9 shows that this equation represents the data well [7].

The extrapolation of a quantity–quality relationship provides either an estimate of a stock of material for a specified average grade, or an estimate of average grade for a specified size of the stock. If the estimate of a quantity–quality relationship is to be subjected to even the most casual economic interpretation, the question arises naturally as to what production grade is implied by a particular average grade. Cargill *et al.* (1980, p. 508) derived the relationship between what they call average annual grade q' and cumulative average grade $\bar{q}$.

Define m as cumulative metal. Then,

$$m = \bar{q} \cdot t.$$

Alternatively,

$$\log m = \log \bar{q} + \log t.$$

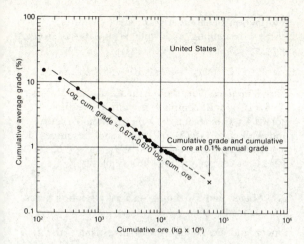

Fig. 3.9. US production–grade plot, 1850–1977 (Source: Cargill *et al* 1980). Note that the units of the ordinate of this graph describe grade as a percentage, while the fitted equation describes it in absolute terms. For example, given cumulative ore of 10^4 kg, the graph shows a cumulative grade of approximately 1 per cent, while the equation yields approximately 0.01 for cumulative grade.

Or, using (3.20), we can write

$$\log m = (\beta_0 + \beta_1 \log t) + \log t,$$
$$\log m = \beta_0 + (\beta_1 + 1) \log t. \qquad (3.23)$$

Now, define q', average annual grade at cumulative production t, as dm/dt. Then,

$$dm/dt = (\beta_1 + 1)\left(\frac{m}{t}\right).$$

But,

$$m/t = \bar{q} \quad \text{and} \quad dm/dt = q'.$$

Therefore,

$$q' = (\beta_1 + 1)\bar{q}. \qquad (3.24)$$

Suppose that it is desired to have an estimate of the endowment if average annual grades were to be as low as 0.1 per cent Hg. From (3.22), we have a value for $\hat{\beta}_1$ of -0.67. Using eqn (3.24), we find that an average annual grade (q') of 0.1 per cent Hg implies a cumulative average grade ($\bar{q}$) of 0.30 per cent Hg

$$\hat{\bar{q}} = \frac{q'}{(\hat{\beta}_1 + 1)} = \frac{0.001}{(-0.670 + 1)} = \frac{0.001}{0.33} = 0.00303.$$

Rewriting (3.22) and substituting $\hat{\bar{q}} = 0.00303$, we have an estimate of t for $\hat{\bar{q}} = 0.00303$,

$$\widehat{\log \bar{q}} = 0.674 - 0.670 \log t$$
$$\widehat{\log t} = \frac{0.674}{0.670} - \frac{\log \bar{q}}{0.670} = 1.0060$$
$$- 1.4925 \log \bar{q}$$

For

$$\hat{\bar{q}} = 0.00303, \widehat{\log \bar{q}} = -2.5186$$
$$\widehat{\log t} = 1.0060 - 1.4925(-2.5186)$$
$$= 1.0060 + 3.7590$$
$$\hat{t} = 10^{4.7650} \approx 58\,210(\times 10^6 \text{ kg}).$$

The initial endowment of mercury can be estimated as the product of $\hat{t}$ and $\hat{\bar{q}}$,

$$\hat{m} = (58\,210 \times 10^6 \text{ kg}) \cdot (0.00303)$$
$$= 176.38 \times 10^6 \text{ kg of Hg}.$$

The remaining (non-produced) mercury endowment as of 1977, given a minimum production grade of 0.1 per cent Hg, is estimated to be approximately 54×10^6 kg. This is the difference (rounded) of initial endowment of 176.38×10^6 kg and cumulative metal production in 1977 of 122.45×10^6 kg.

While the foregoing calculations effectively demonstrate concepts, it is important that it be understood that rewriting a regression equation of the form $\hat{y} = \hat{\beta}_0 + \hat{\beta}_1 x$ to $\hat{x} = (\hat{\beta}_0/\hat{\beta}_1) + (1/\hat{\beta}_1)y$ does not in general yield a least-squares estimate of x, as would the direct regression of x on y, giving $\hat{x} = \hat{\alpha}_0 + \hat{\alpha}_1 y$. In other words, generally, $\hat{\alpha}_0 \neq \hat{\beta}_0/\hat{\beta}_1$ and $\hat{\alpha}_1 \neq 1/\hat{\beta}_1$.

The only time that rewriting a regression equation yields a least-squares estimate is when the data are perfectly fitted by a linear model. The poorer the fit, the less the agreement betwen 'solved for' and least-squares estimates. When the data are not perfectly explained by a linear model and estimates of both x and y are required, the correct procedure is to perform two regressions: $\hat{x} = \hat{\alpha}_0 + \hat{\alpha}_1 y$ and $\hat{y} = \hat{\beta}_0 + \hat{\beta}_1 x$. In the foregoing, and in some subsequent demonstrations of concepts in this chapter, this procedure is not followed because (1) only one equation has been estimated and (2) the major objective here is the demonstration of concepts.

In a subsequent study, Cargill, Root, and Bailey (1981) subjected data on domestic copper production to the same analysis that they demonstrated on mercury. Fig. 3.10 shows copper tonnage and grade data. The most noticeable feature in this figure is the presence of two linear patterns having similar slope

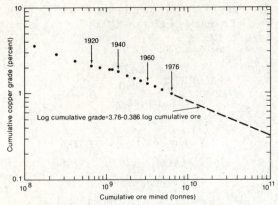

Fig. 3.10. Cumulative production–grade history of copper mining in the United States through 1976 (Source: Cargill *et al.* 1981.)

but different intercepts: (1) pre-1920 data and (2) post-1930 data. For estimation of the quantity–quality relationship, Cargill *et al.* employed data only from 1926 to 1976, arguing that adoption of improved metallurgical technology caused this change in pattern, which they referred to as a change in slope. Employing weighted regression, they estimated the relationship

$$\widehat{\log \bar{q}} = 3.76 - 0.386 \log t, \qquad (3.25)$$

where $\bar{q}$ is in per cent and t is in tonnes. Using this relationship, initial domestic copper endowment for a mining grade of 0.2 per cent Cu was estimated, as shown below, to be 328×10^6 tonnes of copper.

Using (3.24), we calculate $\hat{\bar{q}} = 0.326$ per cent Cu

$$\hat{\bar{q}} = \frac{q'}{(\hat{\beta}_1 + 1)} = \frac{0.2}{(-0.386 + 1)} = \frac{0.2}{0.614}$$

$$= 0.326 \text{ per cent.}$$

Substituting $\hat{\bar{q}}$ into (3.25), the magnitude of mineralized rock is estimated to be $100\,462 \times 10^6$ tonnes,

$$\log (0.326) = 3.76 - 0.386 \log t$$

$$\widehat{\log t} = \frac{3.76 - \log (0.326)}{0.386} = 11.002$$

$$\hat{t} \approx 100\,462 \times 10^6 \text{ tonnes.}$$

Multiplying t by $\bar{q}/100$ gives m, the quantity of initial endowment

$$m = t \cdot \bar{q}/100$$

$$\hat{m} = (100\,462 \times 10^6) \cdot (0.00326)$$

$$\approx 328 \times 10^6 \text{ tonnes copper.}$$

Subtraction of cumulative production through 1976 gives a remaining endowment of 270×10^6 tonnes copper

$$270 \times 10^6 = 328 \times 10^6 - 58 \times 10^6.$$

Cargill *et al.* convert their estimate to short tons (s.t.) (298×10^6) and compare it with the estimate reported by Cox, Schmidt, Vine, Kirkemo, Tourtelot, and Fleischer (1973) of conditional resources adjusted for production from 1973 to 1976, 254×10^6 s.t. of copper, noting their similarity.

3.7. Singer and DeYoung—a Lasky relation across deposits

Singer and DeYoung (1980) investigated the relationship of quantity to quality for a population of deposits of a metal. The procedure employed by them is analogous to the construction of a tonnage–grade curve for a deposit, except that grades are

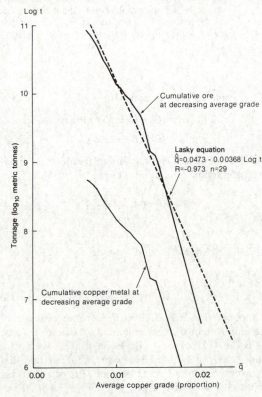

Fig. 3.11. Cumulative 'ore' tonnage and contained metal for 165 porphyry copper deposits and fitted Lasky equation (After Singer and De Young 1980).

analysed for entire deposits instead of mining blocks within a deposit. Imagine ranking a population of deposits by deposit average grade and subsequently computing cumulative tonnage of ore and metal as cut-off grade is lowered so that it is less than the average grade of the next richest deposit. This procedure is followed until the deposit with the lowest grade of the population has been added to the inventory of ore and metal. Then, for each data pair of cumulative ore and metal, an average grade is computed, in the same manner as was done by Lasky. Fig. 3.11 shows the plot of the logarithm of cumulative tonnage of ore against average grade for 165 copper porphyry deposits. This figure also shows the fitted quantity–quality relationship

$$\hat{q} = 0.0473 - 0.00368 \log t.$$

While the coefficient of correlation between $\bar{q}$ and $\log t$ is high (-0.973), suggesting a good fit of this Lasky relationship, the deviations from the linear model appear to be strongly non-random, reflecting nonlinearity in the tonnage grade data. On the basis of what appear to be auto-correlated residuals, examination of a nonlinear model for these data seems warranted. It is noteworthy that if the logarithm of cumulative tonnage had been plotted against the logarithm of average grade, as was done by Cargill et al. (1980), the nonlinear pattern exhibited in Fig. 3.11 would be considerably exaggerated, meaning that a log–log model would represent the data even less well.

3.8. Model structure

3.8.1. The influence of support

The exposition by Lasky (1950a) of the exponential relationship of cumulative tonnage to average grade and the generalization by Musgrove (1971) of exponential relations established an impression, one which still prevails, that all tonnage–grade relations are exponential. This exponential relation has become known as Lasky's law, a fact that is suggestive of its general and widespread acceptance. As suggested in the foregoing review of literature on tonnage–grade relations, such an uncritical acceptance is not appropriate. While some stocks of mineralized material do exhibit a Lasky relationship, others do not. In fact, the same metal may exhibit a Lasky relationship in one circumstance but some other relationship in another circumstance. Moreover, the shape of a tonnage–grade relation for a given ore deposit can be modified simply by chang-

ing the size of the mining block, the physical unit from which grade data derive (see DeYoung 1981, pp. 13–16 for further discussion on this point). Unfortunately, the influence of support—a term used by Matheron (1971) to refer to the physical unit upon which basic measurements or estimations are made—upon the shape of a tonnage–grade relation is not generally appreciated, or at times even recognized. It is important that it be understood that the shape of the tonnage–grade curve is reflective of the *variation* in grade and that variation in grade reflects the support for grade measurement (estimation) as well as the mode of occurrence.

The effect of support on grade variation is a special case of a more general law that is described by the Matheron–DeWijs variance–volume relation,

$$\sigma^2 = \gamma \ln\left(\frac{V}{v}\right), \qquad (3.26)$$

where σ^2 is the variance of grade, γ a coefficient of intrinsic variation, V the volume of the environment, and v is the volume of the physical unit upon which grade measurements (estimates) are made. Consistent with the focus of this chapter, V and v could be the volumes of the ore body and mining blocks, respectively. Thus, for a given ore body and hence a given γ and V, the variance of grade varies inversely with the size of the mining block. In terms of grade distributions, employing a large size of mining block results, *ceteris paribus*, in a distribution that is relatively narrow, while the converse is true for a small size of block.

Given the perspective that support is related to variance, let us examine the effect of variance on the shape of the tonnage–grade relation. In order to examine these issues more fully, a computer routine was designed that would generate the tonnage-average grade relationship for a lognormal distribution of grades having specified parameters when *grade and tonnage are statistically independent*. Since the location parameter, α (expectation of the logarithms of grades), is of little consequence in investigating *patterns* of relations, it was set at -1.00, and the logarithmic standard deviation was varied from 0.05 to 1.00, providing the tonnage-grade distributions of Figs. 3.12–3.16. Because of assumed independence of deposit tonnage and grade, it was not necessary to introduce a tonnage distribution in order to demonstrate the cumulative tonnage-average grade relationship for various shaped lognormal populations. Instead, the total quantity of material was taken to be one ton. For this reason,

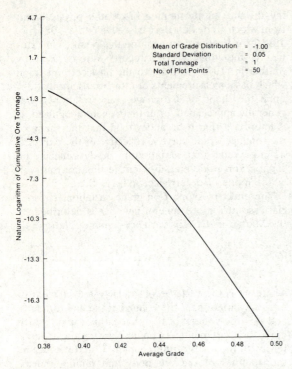

Fig. 3.12. Grade–tonnage relationship for a population in which deposit tonnage and grade are statistically independent and grades are lognormally distributed.

the maximum ordinate value on Figs. 3.12–3.16 is zero. This value is the logarithm of one, the total tonnage, and is associated with an average grade of $e^{\alpha + \sigma^2/2}$.

Another way of viewing Fig. 3.12 is that the ordinate values describe the logarithm of the fractions of the total tonnage of resources associated with average grades from the lognormal grade distribution having parameters $\alpha = -1.00$ and $\sigma = 0.05$. This total tonnage could be one ton or one billion tons. As long as tonnage and grade are statistically independent, the actual tonnage has no effect on the *shape* of the cumulative tonnage–average grade relationship.

Figs. 3.12–3.16 are highly instructive, for they demonstrate that, if tonnage and grade were statistically independent and grade were distributed lognormally, a wide range of different shaped tonnage–grade patterns could arise, depending upon the variance of the distribution. One of these patterns is exponential. It should be noted, however, that these statements apply only to the relationship of average grade to the logarithm of cumulative tonnage of ore.

Unlike the case described by Musgrove for an *exponential grade* distribution (assuming independence of deposit grade and tonnage), the cut-off grade relationship derived from a lognormal grade distribution *is not* a constant multiple of the average grade relationship, *nor* does it resemble the average grade relationship in general shape. The plot of the logarithm of cumulative tonnage against cut-off grade exhibits a distorted backwards ∫ pattern, while none of the patterns for average grade examined (Figs. 3.12–3.16) exhibit such a shape.

A priori reasoning would dictate the distorted backwards ∫ pattern for the cut-off grade relationship when grade by tonnage of material is distributed lognormally. If grade is distributed lognormally, it must follow that the cumulative tonnage of ore having grades *less* than a specified grade must exhibit a standard symmetric ∫ shape, for this distribution is nothing more nor less than the distribution function of the normal probability distribution

$$\frac{1}{\sigma\sqrt{2\pi}} \int_{-\infty}^{\ln q'} e^{-(\ln q - \alpha)^2/2\sigma^2} \, \mathrm{d}\ln q = F\!\left(\frac{\ln q' - \alpha}{\sigma}\right), \quad (3.27)$$

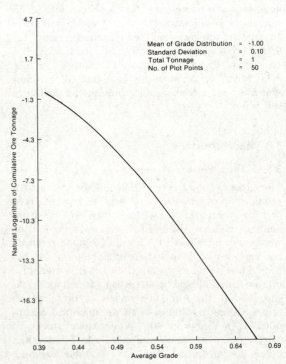

Fig. 3.13. Grade–tonnage relationship for a population in which deposit tonnage and grade are statistically independent and grades are lognormally distributed.

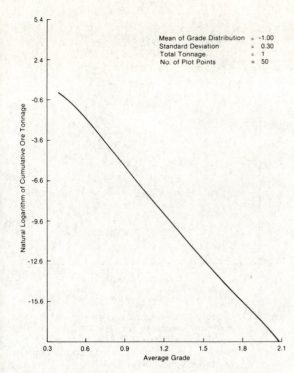

Mean of Grade Distribution = -1.00
Standard Deviation   = 0.30
Total Tonnage   = 1
No. of Plot Points   = 50

Fig. 3.14. Grade–tonnage relationship for a population in which deposit tonnage and grade are statistically independent and grades are lognormally distributed.

where $F[(\ln q' - \alpha)/\sigma]$ is the normal distribution function. It follows that the cumulative ore having q greater than q' must be $1 - F[(\ln q' - \alpha)/\sigma]$. Since $F[(\ln q' - \alpha)/\sigma]$ describes a standard symmetric ∫ curve, $1 - F[(\ln q' - \alpha)/\sigma]$ must describe a symmetric backwards ∫. Plotting the *logarithm* of tonnage for deposits having grades *above* cut-off grades against cut-off grade is plotting $\ln\{1 - F[(\ln q' - \alpha)/\sigma]\}$ against q', instead of $\ln q'$. Graphically, this effect is to compress $1 - F[(\ln q' - \alpha)/\sigma]$ differentially, the high values greater than the low values, and to do just the opposite for grades, shift the high values of grade relatively farther to the right than the low grades. The overall effect is a distortion of the backwards ∫. Nevertheless, it still exhibits the same number and kinds of curvature; although distorted, the pattern is nonlinear. Thus, the tonnage–average grade relationship does not resemble the tonnage-cut-off grade relationship when grades are distributed lognormally.

3.8.2. *The influence of correlation*

The influence of correlation arises when constructing a quantity–quality relationship for a population of physical units (deposits, blocks, etc.) in which the support is not constant. The foregoing section emphasized the influence of support on the shape of the tonnage–grade relationship. Given that support is not constant, and the issue of interest is model structure, the question arises naturally about the presence or absence of correlation between the size of the physical unit and its average grade and about the influence of this correlation on the shape of the tonnage–grade relationship. The correlation issue is especially relevant when a quantity–quality relation is being developed on a population of deposits and when each deposit is represented by a single tonnage and grade.

DeYoung (1981) employed computer simulation to investigate the effect of correlation between deposit size and grade on the Lasky relationship. In essence he postulated lognormal distributions for deposit size and deposit grade. Then, he varied the correlation between size and grade, and computed

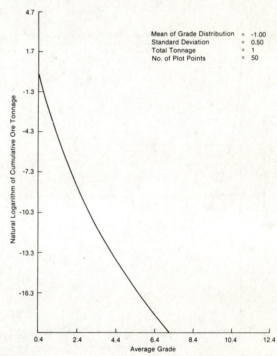

Mean of Grade Distribution = -1.00
Standard Deviation   = 0.50
Total Tonnage   = 1
No. of Plot Points   = 50

Fig. 3.15. Grade–tonnage relationship for a population in which deposit tonnage and grade are statistically independent and grades are lognormally distributed.

quantity–quality relations for each level of correlation. Fig. 3.17 shows the results of his simulation study. DeYoung concluded that the Lasky relation applies to all five plots and that inferences about the correlation between deposit size and grade cannot be made as a result of the agreement of a quantity–quality plot with a Lasky relationship (DeYoung 1981, p. 26). Visual examination of the quantity–quality plots for the various correlations evokes support for DeYoung's conclusions regarding the influence of correlation. The visual senses may be taxed a bit, however, in the judgement that the simulated data for $r = 0.5$ exhibit a Lasky, hence linear, pattern. If this plot were viewed in isolation by an empiricist, he might be inclined to explore a nonlinear relationship between average grade and the logarithm of cumulative tonnage, for it seems likely that residuals from a straight line fitted to these data would be auto-correlated, suggesting that a nonlinear relation may be in order. Even so, this is not relevant to the importance of DeYoung's main conclusion. For, when consideration is given to the fact that both support and γ, the measure of intrinsic

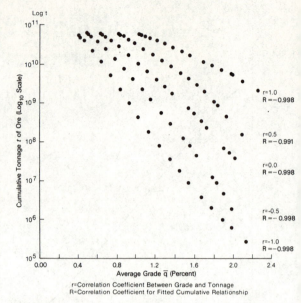

r=Correlation Coefficient Between Grade and Tonnage
R=Correlation Coefficient for Fitted Cumulative Relationship

Fig. 3.17. Plots of cumulative tonnage of ore and average grade of cumulative tonnage for five simulated populations having different correlations between grade and tonnage of individual deposits (After DeYoung 1981).

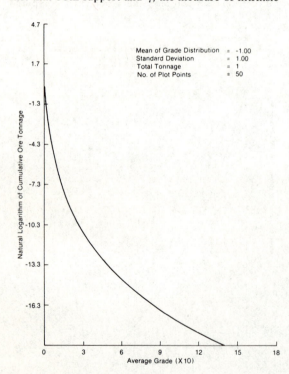

Mean of Grade Distribution	=	-1.00
Standard Deviation	=	1.00
Total Tonnage	=	1
No. of Plot Points	=	50

Fig. 3.16. Grade–tonnage relationship for a population in which deposit tonnage and grade are statistically independent and grades are lognormally distributed.

variation of grade, are reflected in the *shape* of an *empirically* determined quantity–quality plot, DeYoung's conclusion about the inability to make inference from the quantity–quality plot as to the correlation between deposit size and grade is very well taken.

DeYoung's analysis is important and particularly useful in removing some of the confusion about tonnage–grade relations. It is commonly believed that the negative slope of Lasky's relation implies a negative correlation between deposit size and grade. DeYoung's analysis demonstrates clearly that this is not so, for he obtained plots with a negative slope when the correlation between deposit size and grade is zero, +0.5, and +1.0.

3.8.3. *The need for a more general approach to model structure*

A point that emerges from some of the foregoing discussion on model structure and which needs emphasis is that the *exponential* tonnage–average grade relationship is a *special case* of tonnage–average grade relations of a more general formulation. The fact that the lognormal distribution of grades can give rise to exponential tonnage–grade relations is important, for the lognormal distribution appears to be an acceptable model for concentrations of some metals at various levels and in various volumes, ranging from element concentrations in geochemical samples to metal in blocks of an ore deposit. If deposit tonnage and grade are statistically independent, we might view the grade distribution as *the fundamental representation*, while the tonnage–grade relationship is auxiliary to it. If there is a dependency of deposit tonnage and grade, then the fundamental representation would require a dependent bivariate distribution of appropriate form.

It is also very important that a lognormal distribution of grades can give rise to a tonnage–average grade relationship that is non-exponential. As shown in § 3.8.1, given that grade and tonnage are statistically independent and grade is distributed lognormally, all that is required for a non-exponential tonnage–average grade relation is that the distribution of grades have a relatively small or relatively large variance. A model for tonnage–average grade relations must allow for exponential and non-exponential forms. From an applied perspective, the implication is that we should strive to identify the appropriate form rather than try to describe all relations as exponential by reasoning that all *departures reflect data* or *information anomalies*.

Suppose that we have an inventory for an aggregate of deposits of the tonnage of ore and the tonnage of metal in all ore with concentrations above specified cut-off grades. Such an inventory might be symbolically described by Table 3.2.

Symbolically, we could describe the tonnage of ore and metal as functions of the grade

$CT(q') = $ cumulative tonnage of ore

having grades above q'.

$CM(q') = $ cumulative tonnage of metal in ore

having grades above q'.

Similarly, since $\bar{q}_i = CM_i/CT_i$, $\bar{q}$ can be considered a function of the cut-off grade

$$\bar{q}(q') = \frac{CM(q')}{CT(q')}. \tag{3.28}$$

The tonnage–grade relationship being considered here associates $CT(q')$ with $\bar{q}(q')$ by function γ

$$CT(q') = \gamma[\bar{q}(q')]. \tag{3.29}$$

Relative to this symbolic representation, Lasky and Musgrove considered the function γ to be of a simple exponential form, or alternatively $\ln[\gamma(\bar{q}(q'))]$ to be of a linear form

$$\ln[\gamma(\bar{q}(q'))] = \ln[CT(q')] = K_0 + K_1\bar{q}(q'). \tag{3.30}$$

Let us describe a tonnage–grade model that is general, allowing for the use of cut-off grade as well as average grade and allowing for various shapes of cumulative tonnage. Let us represent the average grade measure as $u(q')$ and the cumulative tonnage measure as $\omega(q')$. Further, let us allow for the use in a tonnage–grade relationship of various transformations of $\omega(q')$ and $u(q')$ so that the relationship can take on various shapes. Then, a general tonnage–grade model might be represented as

$$\phi_0[\omega(q')] = K_0 + K_1\phi_1[u(q')] + K_2\phi_2[u(q')], \tag{3.31}$$

where ϕ_i are transformations, i.e. $\phi(X) = X^2$, $\ln X$, e^X, etc.

In terms of the general model described above,

TABLE 3.2. *Tonnage–grade quantities*

Cut-off grade	Cumulative tonnage of ore with grades above cut-off	Cumulative tonnage of metal in ore with grades above cut-off	Average grade of ore with grades above cut-off
q'_1	CT_1	CM_1	$\bar{q}_1 = CM_1/CT_1$
q'_2	CT_2	CM_2	$\bar{q}_2 = CM_2/CT_2$
.	.	.	.
.	.	.	.
.	.	.	.
q'_n	CT_n	CM_n	$\bar{q}_n = CM_n/CT_n$

selection of a second-degree parabola for the relationship of the logarithm of cumulative tonnage to average grade is equivalent to making the identifications,

$$\omega(q') = CT(q'),$$
$$u(q') = \bar{q}(q'),$$
$$\phi_0[\omega(q')] = \ln[CT(q')],$$
$$\phi_1[u(q')] = \bar{q}(q'),$$
$$\phi_2[u(q')] = [\bar{q}(q')]^2, \qquad (3.32)$$

and

$$\ln[CT(q')] = K_0 + K_1\bar{q}(q') + K_2[\bar{q}(q')]^2. \qquad (3.33)$$

In practice, the data upon which a cumulative tonnage–average grade model is quantified result from calculations like those represented symbolically in Table 3.2. The results of these calculations may be influenced by the support (volume) of the sample. If grades of ore were constant [9] within the deposit, then it would make no difference whether the data used to get $CT(q')$ and $\bar{q}(q')$ were tonnages and average grades of deposits or the mining blocks for all the deposits. However, this is never the case; consequently, support is an important issue in practical application. Where there is considerable variation in grade within the deposits, computing $CT(q')$ and $\bar{q}(q')$ using grades and tonnages of the deposits can give a different pattern than that using average grades and tonnages of mining blocks of the deposits. A different relationship could emerge for every different size of the basic data unit (block, deposit, etc.). Computing $CT(q')$ and $\bar{q}(q')$ on deposits instead of mining blocks is analogous to computing a tonnage–grade relationship on a distribution having a smaller variance of grade than that for blocks. Thus, if the plot of the logarithm of cumulative tonnage versus average grade for small mining blocks appears a straight line, the same plot for deposits, instead of mining blocks of the deposits, may be curvilinear.

Consider, for example, the quantity–quality plot (Fig. 3.18) by DeYoung (1981) for 267 copper deposits of mixed types (porphyry, massive sulphide, and stratabound) from various regions of the world. A Lasky relation represents these data very well. Now, consider the quantity–quality plot by Cargill *et al.* (1981) (Fig. 3.10) for domestic copper production. This log–log plot exhibits good linearity; consequently, Cargill *et al.*'s log–log equation was found to represent these data reasonably well. Note that this linear feature would be a nonlinear one if the log of

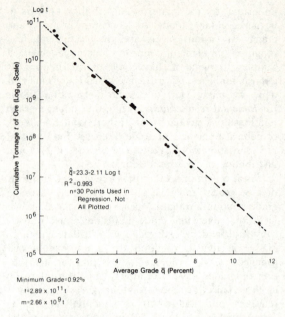

Fig. 3.18. Cumulative tonnage of ore and average grade of cumulative tonnage for 267 copper deposits. (Source of data: Singer, Cox, and Drew (1975). After De Young 1981.)

cumulative tonnage were plotted against average grade instead of the logarithm of average grade. In other words, a Lasky relation would be a poor representation of these data. It is interesting that Cargill *et al.* base their analyses on linear features in log–log plots and that such features, *ceteris paribus*, contradict an exponential relationship.

Consider also the quantity–quality plot (Fig. 3.11) by Singer and DeYoung (1980) for 165 porphyry copper deposits. Here, the Lasky relation is not as satisfying [10] a representation of the data as it is for the 265 copper deposits of Fig. 3.10. This is a bit perplexing since Lasky's own work on copper included a plot for the aggregate of 10 porphyry copper deposits. Granted, the populations are different. But, that isn't all that is different. Whereas Lasky aggregated production by grade class across deposits, Singer and DeYoung represented each deposit as a single tonnage of material having a single average grade [11]. Thus, the implied support by Singer and DeYoung is large compared to that implicit to Lasky's data or to the data used by Cargill *et al.* (1981). The point to be made here is that because of the large support implied by representing each deposit by one grade, variation in grade for the population of deposits is much less than it would have been if aggregation across deposits had been made of mining blocks for each of a number of grade classes. Thus, the convex pattern exhibited in the plot by Singer and DeYoung may be due, at least in part, to the use of deposit grades [11].

If a semi-log plot of quantity and quality data which had been derived by aggregation of mining blocks of ore across a population of deposits by grade classes is exponential, hence a straight line, then it must be true that the semi-log plot of quantity and quality data for these same deposits would be convex to the origin, if the quantity and quality data were derived by treating each deposit as a homogeneous quantity of ore having average grade [12].

If a semi-log plot of quantity and quality data based upon aggregation of mining blocks across deposits by grade is exponential, hence a straight line, then the semi-log plot of quantity and quality data for these same deposits but based upon much smaller blocks would be nonlinear, being concave to the origin.

In summary, the support for grade estimation is an important determinant of the shape of the quantity–quality plot and, therefore, of the appropriate mathematical model. Of course, all statements about the effect of support on the quantity–quality relation apply in full strength in a conditional sense, conditional upon the shape of the grade distribution. One, but not the only, expression of this shape is the variance of grade, which was shown earlier to be a function of γ, the measure of intrinsic variability, and the support of grade measurement. While it is true, as previously stated, that for the lognormal distribution the shape of the quantity–quality relation is determined solely by γ and the support, when considering more generally all grade distributions, other attributes of the distribution also may influence the shape of the quantity–quality relation. Stated simply, the quantity–quality relation is influenced by the shape of the grade distribution, and two of the determinants of this shape are γ and the support.

3.9. Issues in the use of quantity–quality relations for prediction

3.9.1. Perspective

§§ 3.9.2 and 3.9.3 consider two technical issues that arise when data on quantity and quality are used as a basis for prediction of quantities at lower grades or of grades associated with larger quantities.

1. The selection of the function (mathematical model) to be fitted to the data on tonnage and grade;
2. Limitations on the extrapolation of the fitted function.

These two issues must be dealt with regardless of whether the tonnage–grade relation represents the reserves of one deposit and is to be used to estimate quantities of ore or known subeconomic resources at lower grades, or whether it represents known resources of a region and is to be used to estimate undiscovered resources or endowment. However, the latter application involves a wider set of conceptual and empirical issues; consequently, § 3.9.4 deals with issues that are either relevant exclusively to the estimation of undiscovered resources or that take on quite a different complexity than they do in the analysis of a deposit. Problems in the application of quantity–quality relations to the estimation of undiscovered resources are separated into two classes: conceptual and application. These are examined in § 3.9.4 under the subheadings 'Conceptual consideration' and 'Problems in applications'. Under a further subheading, 'Estimation procedure based upon a composite inventory', the use of tonnage–grade relations as an integral part of a larger methodology to estimate undiscovered resources and endowment is examined. Finally, some selected comments are made on the application of quantity–quality relations by Cargill *et al.* (1980, 1981) to the estimation of undiscovered endowment.

3.9.2. Selection of the function to be fitted to tonnage–grade data

Estimation of subeconomic resources by a tonnage–grade relationship requires the extrapolation of a mathematical function which has been fitted to the tonnage–grade pattern. Obviously, the selection of the functional form influences the estimate of subeconomic resources. This influence derives from the different behaviour of various functions, each of which may be a reasonable fit to the data, over the extrapolation interval.

A simple linear equation can be employed quite extensively by making the appropriate transformations of the tonnage data. Consider the three patterns of $\ln t$ and $\bar{q}$ in Fig. 3.19.

Case 1 is the plot of the logarithm of tonnage when tonnage t and grade $\bar{q}$ are related by a simple *linear* relationship,

$$t = K_1 + K_2\bar{q}.$$

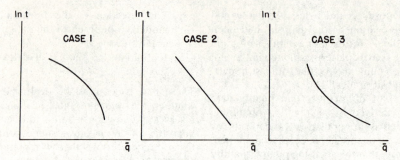

Fig. 3.19. Patterns that can be represented by a linear model.

Therefore, when a pattern such as that of Case 1 arises from the plot of $\ln t$ and $\bar{q}$, analysis can be made using t and $\bar{q}$ in a linear model.

Case 2 is the plot of a true exponential relationship betwen t and $\bar{q}$, $t = A \cdot e^{K_2\bar{q}}$. This is the Lasky relationship. For this case, analysis should employ a linear relationship between $\ln t$ and $\bar{q}$,

$$\ln t = K_1 + K_2\bar{q},$$

where $\ln A = K_1$.

Case 3 is the plot of data which define a nonlinear relationship between $\ln t$ and $\bar{q}$. There are two simple approaches to a linear model. One of these is to consider the data to define an exponential relationship betwen $\ln t$ and $\bar{q}$

$$\ln t = A \cdot e^{K_2\bar{q}}. \tag{3.34}$$

Then, by making a second logarithmic transformation, a linear equation is produced

$$\ln(\ln t) = K_1 + K_2\bar{q}, \tag{3.35}$$

where $\ln A = K_1$. The second approach is to consider the plot to represent a power relationship between t and $\bar{q}$

$$t = A\bar{q}^{K_2}, \quad K_2 < 0. \tag{3.36}$$

Taking logarithms of both sides, we have

$$\ln t = K_1 + K_2 \ln \bar{q}, \tag{3.37}$$

where $\ln A = K_1$ and $K_2 < 0$.

Of course, there are countless patterns that differ somewhat from those of these three cases. Nevertheless, these three cases will cover quite a few situations. Where a pattern does not fit either of these three cases, analysis may have to employ a more complex model.

3.9.3. *Determining the limit to extrapolation*

Let us represent the tonnage of material present in a deposit by the histogram in Fig. 3.20(a). The total

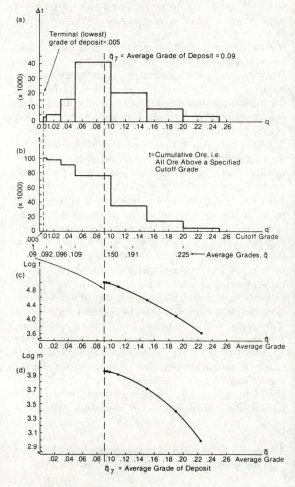

Fig. 3.20. (a) Histogram of grades by tonnage; (b) tonnage of ore having grades above cutoff grades; (c) quantity–quality (cumulative tonnage versus average grade) relation; (d) cumulative metal versus average grade.

ore in the deposit is the sum of the heights of the seven histogram bars. Fig. 3.20(b) shows the cumulative ore for these same cut-off grades. Fig. 3.20(b) exhibits an extra row of numbers under the cut-off grades of the abscissa; these numbers are the average grades associated with the cut-off grades. Fig. 3.20(c) shows that the quantity–quality plot consists of associating the logarithm of cumulative tonnages for selected cut-off grades (Fig. 3.20(b)) with the average grades for those same cut-off grades.

The purpose of this figure is to emphasize by a graphic demonstration that all of the ore in the deposit has been used to compute $\bar{q}_7$ and that this total ore is t_7. Therefore, the tonnage grade curve of Fig. 3.20(c) must terminate at $\bar{q}_7$ and t_7. Clearly, extrapolation to grades below $\bar{q}_7$ (average grade of the deposit) and tonnages greater than t_7 violates the material constraints of the deposit, as represented in Fig. 3.20(a).

Suppose that we compute the product for each of these seven pairs of average grade and cumulative tonnage of ore to give seven quantities of cumulative metal: $m = t \cdot \bar{q}$. The solid line of Fig. 3.20(d) shows these products plotted against average grade. Cumulative metal increases as average grade decreases to $\bar{q}_7$. Within this deposit, metal does not exist for average grades below $\bar{q}_7$.

Suppose quantity of material within a deposit is finite and that the distribution of grades within the deposit is described by a continuous distribution defined on the grade range of 0 to q_{max}. Then, it must be true that the cumulative amount of metal increases and approaches asymptotically the total metal in the deposit as average grade is lowered towards the average grade of the total deposit. This must be so because (1) the quantity of material is finite and (2) the last increments of material have grades that approach zero, meaning that the amount of metal which they contribute to the total approaches zero as the average grade approaches the average grade of the deposit. Consequently, the curve describing quantity of metal must become asymptotic as average grade approaches the terminal average grade, which implies that cut-off grade approaches zero. *Extrapolating the quantity–quality relationship beyond this terminal average grade* is equivalent to adding material with *negative grades*, hence negative metal. The cumulative metal–average grade curve produced by such an improper extrapolation— average grades below terminal average grade—must, therefore, possess a maximum of metal at the terminal average grade [13].

We can employ this fact to estimate the terminal value of average grade—the average grade of the deposit—for an empirically derived tonnage–grade relation. Specifically, the terminal value of average grade will be that grade for which cumulative metal achieves its maximum value.

Suppose that a tonnage–grade plot is well represented by a Lasky relationship. Here we will use the form $\ln t = f(\bar{q})$, rather than $\bar{q} = \phi(\ln t)$.

Specifically,

$$\ln t = \alpha_0 + \alpha_1 \bar{q},$$

where $\bar{q}$ is a proportion, not a percentage. Then, the logarithm of cumulative metal is defined as

$$\ln m = \ln t + \ln \bar{q} = \alpha_0 + \alpha_1 \bar{q} + \ln \bar{q}.$$

Taking the derivative of m with respect to average grade, we have

$$\left(\frac{1}{m}\right)\frac{dm}{d\bar{q}} = \alpha_1 + \frac{1}{\bar{q}},$$

$$\frac{dm}{d\bar{q}} = \alpha_1 m + \frac{m}{\bar{q}}.$$

Setting $dm/d\bar{q} = 0$, we have

$$\bar{q} = -\frac{1}{\alpha_1}. \tag{3.38}$$

Thus, the Lasky tonnage-grade relation cannot be extrapolated beyond $-1/\alpha_1$. Let us employ this fact to examine the terminal grade implied by the equation given by Lasky (1950a) for a hypothetical copper porphyry [14],

$$\widehat{\ln t} = 21.22 - 1.645.$$

From (3.38) we obtain a terminal grade of 0.61 per cent

$$\hat{\bar{q}} = -\frac{1.0}{(-1.645)} =$$

$$\hat{\bar{q}} \approx 0.61 \text{ per cent Cu [15].}$$

That this amount of copper is a maximum and is achieved at the average grade of 0.61 per cent Cu can be demonstrated by computing the amount of copper for grades of 0.60, 0.61, and 0.62 per cent,

$$m_{0.60} = (0.0060) \cdot e^{21.22-1.645(0.60)} = 3\,674\,781 \text{ s.t.,}$$

$$m_{0.61} = (0.0061) \cdot e^{21.22-1.645(0.61)} = 3\,675\,073 \text{ s.t.,}$$

$$m_{0.62} = (0.0062) \cdot e^{21.22-1.645(0.62)} = 3\,674\,376 \text{ s.t.}$$

The above argument and demonstration may offend the senses of the practising engineer, because in real life the amount of metal in a deposit never decreases as successively lower cut-off grades are established. Rather, the amount of metal either increases or becomes asymptotic as all of the material in the deposit is accounted for. This response is appropriate. Certainly, in the physical sense, the quantity of metal can never decrease. Furthermore, given that the physical constraints of the deposit or set of deposits are known, there can never be a need to estimate the total inventory of ore or the terminal average grade (average grade of that total stock).

Suppose, however, that tonnages and grades were available only for the high-grade portion of the stock and in the absence of complete data, one wishes to estimate the quantities and grades of associated lower-grade materials. One method for achieving this goal is to estimate the quantity–quality relationship from the high-grade data and then use the estimated model to describe the unknown part of the stock. In this case the physical constraints, e.g. terminal average grade or total amount of material, are not known. But, if the estimated quantity–quality model is the correct model for that stock of material, the terminal average grade and the total quantity of material can be estimated by finding that average grade for which cumulative metal is a maximum.

Alternatively, this same result—terminal grade of 0.61 per cent Cu—can be obtained by exploring the relationship between cut-off and average grade in the Lasky model

$$\hat{\bar{q}} = 12.9 - 1.4 \log t.$$

Or, in natural logarithms,

$$\hat{\bar{q}} = 12.9 - 1.4 \left(\frac{\ln t}{2.3026} \right),$$

$$\hat{\bar{q}} = 12.9 - 0.61 \ln t.$$

And, using the relationship betwen metal, tonnage, and average grade, we can write

$$\hat{m} = t \cdot \hat{\bar{q}} = 12.9\, t - (0.61)(t) \ln t.$$

Therefore,

$$\frac{d\hat{m}}{dt} = 12.9 - 0.61 \left(\ln t + \frac{t}{t} \right).$$

Or,

$$\frac{d\hat{m}}{dt} = 12.9 - 0.61 \ln t - 0.61.$$

Recognizing $(12.9 - 0.61 \ln t)$ as $\hat{\bar{q}}$ and letting q' be cut-off grade, we have

$$\frac{d\hat{m}}{dt} = \hat{q}' = \hat{\bar{q}} - 0.61.$$

Alternatively,

$$\hat{\bar{q}} = \hat{q}' + 0.61.$$

When $q' = 0$, $\hat{\bar{q}} = 0.61$. In other words, when all of the material in the deposit represented by this model has been included, the average grade is the same grade for which cumulative metal is a maximum.

In a real application, the terminal average grade indicated by the quantity–quality relationship may not agree with that computed from the actual blocks of ore. Since the quantity–quality relation is a fitted (estimated) *model*, the poorer the fit of the model, especially at the lower average grades, the greater the discrepancy between model and actual terminal average grades. Discrepancy can arise by misuse of the quantity–quality relation. For example, a tonnage and average grade inventory for mining is determined by specifying a cut-off grade greater than zero. It is improper to compare the average grade of this inventory with the terminal average grade computed from the quantity–quality relation for the condition of maximum metal, for this assumes a cut-off grade of zero.

Consider the case in which we have a tonnage–grade relation that is quadratic in average grade. As before, the terminal average grade can be determined by finding that average grade for which cumulative metal is a maximum. Given

$$\ln t = \alpha_0 + \alpha_1 \bar{q} + \alpha_2 \bar{q}^2,$$

then,

$$\ln m = \ln t + \ln \bar{q}$$

or,

$$\ln m = \alpha_0 + \alpha_1 \bar{q} + \alpha_2 \bar{q}^2 + \ln \bar{q}$$

and,

$$\left(\frac{1}{m} \right) \frac{dm}{d\bar{q}} = \alpha_1 + 2\alpha_2 \bar{q} + \frac{1}{q}.$$

Therefore,

$$\frac{dm}{d\bar{q}} = \alpha_1 m + 2\alpha_2 m\bar{q} + \frac{m}{\bar{q}}.$$

Setting $dm/d\bar{q} = 0$, we have

$$\frac{m}{\bar{q}} = -\alpha_1 m - 2m\alpha_2 \bar{q},$$

$$\frac{1}{\bar{q}} = -\alpha_1 - 2\alpha_2 q,$$

$$1 = -\alpha_1 \bar{q} - 2\alpha_2 \bar{q}^2.$$

Alternatively,

$$2\alpha_2 \bar{q}^2 + \alpha_1 \bar{q} + 1 = 0.$$

Finally,

$$\bar{q} = \frac{-\alpha_1 \pm \{\alpha_1^2 - 4(2\alpha_2)(1)\}^{\frac{1}{2}}}{2(2\alpha_2)}. \qquad (3.39)$$

This value for $\bar{q}$ is that value for which cumulative metal is a maximum, or stated differently but equivalently, it is the terminal average grade, a grade below which the tonnage–grade relation has no physical meaning [16].

As an example of the use of a quadratic relationship of $\ln t$ to $\bar{q}$, consider the grade–tonnage relationship estimated by Ellis *et al.* (1975) for uranium resources of New Mexico (see Fig. 3.7),

$$\widehat{\ln t} = 21.8424 - 4.74298\,\bar{q} - 27.9998\,\bar{q}^2. \qquad (3.40)$$

Employing (3.39), the terminal average grade is found to be 0.0978 per cent U_3O_8,

$$\hat{\bar{q}} = \frac{-(-4.74298)}{\pm[(-4.74298)^2 - (4)(2)(-27.9998)(1)]^{\frac{1}{2}}}{(2)(2)(-27.9998)}$$

$$\hat{\bar{q}} = \frac{4.74298 \pm 15.70014}{-111.9992}$$

$$\hat{\bar{q}} = 0.0978 \text{ per cent } U_3O_8.$$

When the relationship between $\ln t$ and $\bar{q}$ is quadratic the determination of the cut-off grade associated with an average grade is somewhat more complicated than it is for Lasky or log–log relations. Suppose, for example, that we have the relationship

$$\bar{q} = \alpha_0 + \alpha_1 \ln t + \alpha_2 (\ln t)^2. \qquad (3.41)$$

Then,

$$m = t \cdot \bar{q} = t[\alpha_0 + \alpha_1 \ln t + \alpha_2 (\ln t)^2]$$

and

$$\frac{dm}{dt} = \alpha_0 + \alpha_1(\ln t + 1) + \alpha_2\left(\frac{2\ln t}{t}(t) + (\ln t)^2\right)$$

$$\frac{dm}{dt} = \alpha_0 + \alpha_1 \ln t + \alpha_2(\ln t)^2 + \alpha_1 + 2\alpha_2 \ln t$$

$$\frac{dm}{dt} = \bar{q} + \alpha_1 + 2\alpha_2 \ln t.$$

Letting $dm/dt = q'$ cut-off grade,

$$q' = \bar{q} + \alpha_1 + 2\alpha_2 \ln t. \qquad (3.42)$$

As an example of the use of (3.42), let us suppose that the tonnage–grade data on New Mexico uranium also were represented by an equation defining average grade as a quadratic function of the logarithm of tonnage,

$$\hat{\bar{q}} = -2.8112 + 0.36645 \ln t - 0.01083(\ln t)^2 \qquad (3.43)$$

and

$$\widehat{\ln t} = 21.8424 - 4.74298\,\bar{q} - 27.9998\,\bar{q}^2. \qquad (3.44)$$

Suppose further that we wished to estimate the quantity of mineralized material at an average grade of 0.12 per cent U_3O_8 and to state the associated cut-off grade. Using (3.44) we estimate 1158×10^6 s.t. of mineralized material having an average grade of 0.12 per cent U_3O_8, giving approximately 1.4×10^6 s.t. of U_3O_8,

$$\widehat{\ln t} = 21.8424 - 4.74298(0.12) - 27.9998(0.12)^2;$$

$$\widehat{\ln t} = 20.87;$$

$$\hat{t} = 1158 \times 10^6 \text{ s.t.}$$

Using (3.42) and (3.43), we find that the cut-off grade of the material is 0.0344 per cent U_3O_8,

$$\hat{q}' = 0.12 + 0.36645 - 0.02166(20.87)$$

$$\hat{q}' = 0.12 + 0.36645 - 0.45204$$

$$\hat{q}' = 0.0344 \text{ per cent } U_3O_8.$$

3.9.4. *Estimation of endowment or resources of a region*

Conceptual consideration.

Consideration of the comments by Lovering (1969, p. 113) seems an effective introduction to conceptual issues of tonnage–grade relations [17]

> The essential point is that the A|G ratio applies only to certain individual deposits and not to ore deposits in general. It should not be used in estimating the unfound reserves of a region or a nation.

Lovering considers Lasky's work a major contribution to our understanding of tonnage–grade relations, but advocates that the relationship be restricted to the deposit. He severely criticizes Brook's (1967) suggestion that tonnage–grade relations be used in estimation of undiscovered resources. Of course, as pointed out earlier in this chapter, the suggestion that such relations could be useful in the estimation of undiscovered resources originated not with Brooks nor with Musgrove, but with Lasky (1950*b*) himself.

Lovering's argument is well presented and is documented by a life of astute observation of geology and mineral deposits; thus, it merits careful consideration. Basically, Lovering points out that for many kinds of metals, typical deposits appear to have distinct boundaries, with little or virtually no transition zone from ore to protore. For such deposits of metal, lowering cut-off grade past a certain level adds nothing to reserves until the cut-off grade approaches crustal abundance, and then tonnage increases precipitously. Lovering, in effect, reasons further that, if a tonnage–grade relationship is strictly bounded by grade for the deposit, then its use to infer subeconomic resources of a region by extrapolating a relationship that represents an aggregate of deposits cannot be justified. In other words, if the relationship defined on the deposit cannot be extrapolated to subeconomic grades, neither can a relationship that represents an aggregate of deposits.

There can be no doubt that Lovering's observations are accurate regarding characteristics of some kinds of deposits. Furthermore, given that his observations for certain kinds of metal deposits are accurate, then his argument against the extrapolation of a tonnage–grade relationship beyond some lower limiting grade must be accepted for the deposit, and in general for small areas for which space considerations, combined with exhaustive exploration, simply do not allow for the existence of additional deposits. However, contrary to Lovering's appeal, that which applies to the deposit or restricted area *need not* apply to the aggregate of deposits in a large region. As the size of the region increases and the degree of exploration is considerably less than physically exhaustive, Lovering's arguments, which are founded on the concept of a grade-bounded deposit, lose strength with respect to the resources of a region. For, at a point in time, allowance must be made for the possible existence of an inventory (set), possibly large, of undiscovered deposits. Furthermore, the limiting grade of each of the deposits of this set may be at a different level. If some deposits of this set, deposits that are yet unknown, have limiting grades below those of known, currently economic deposits, then conceptually, one must allow for the existence of a cumulative tonnage–average grade relationship for the region that may extend beyond the limiting grade of any specific deposit of the *known* set, or the limiting grade typical of the set of *known, economic* deposits. Argument in defence of extrapolation hinges primarily on the existence of undiscovered deposits having grades lower than the grades of known deposits. If the region is large and exploration is superficial, in theory, the geology permitting, allowance must be given for the possibility that such deposits exist. Given these conditions, the only binding argument against the existence of a tonnage–grade relationship for deposits with grades below grades of currently known deposits is that there are ore genesis–geochemical reasons why concentrations physically cannot occur below some 'limiting' grade *and* that *the limiting grade is known*.

On the other hand, so long as the volume of the region is finite and we are considering deposits of *one* kind only, a limiting grade greater than the crustal abundance of the region must exist if deposits have distinct boundaries that delineate them from the rock materials that 'house' them. This kind of an occurrence scheme depicts deposits as grade anomalies within a grade background, analogous to phenocrysts in a rock matrix, or a signal in a band of noise. The limiting grade for such a situation may be far above crustal abundance. A tonnage–average grade relationship that describes this set of deposits, irrespective of its shape, *must terminate* at the *average grade* of *the cumulative tonnage* of *the set of deposits*. At this grade, cumulative tonnage is the total tonnage of all deposits, not of the crustal material in the region. Extrapolation beyond this grade is not only meaningless, but deceptive. Thus, for a resource world of this kind, we arrive at a conclusion different from that of Lovering in that the tonnage–grade relationship potentially is useful and can be defended as a tool for the appraisal of mineral resources, but similar to that of Lovering in that extrapolation to crustal abundance is not appropriate.

Although it is the preferred practice in any resource appraisal to treat each mode of occurrence separately, there may be some value to also examining the concept of a tonnage–grade relationship across modes. The value of this exercise is that it may prevent the myopia that results from being overly occupied with reserves and resources from conventional, familar modes of occurrence of the metal. Such a relationship would be limited only by the crustal abundance of the region; at that grade, the tonnage of resources would be the tonnage of rock within the region.

It is this relationship that could be most easily misused. Suppose that the currently recognized and exploitable resources of a region derive from only two modes of occurrence. Data on past production and reserves provide approximations to some points at one end of this curve, and the total tonnage of the earth's crust and its crustal abundance provide an estimate of the terminal point on this curve (see Fig. 3.21). These quantities are referred to as estimates because crustal abundance is seldom determined separately for regions; usually an estimate of crustal abundance made for the entire continental crust is employed. Of course, with variation in the composition of the crust as it is, a region, especially a small one, may have a crustal abundance quite different from that of the entire continental crust. With regard to the tonnage–average grade relationship, data from

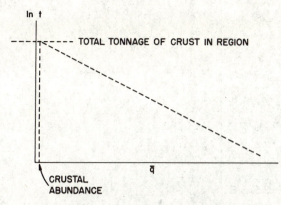

Fig. 3.21. Inference from the aggregate relationship.

past production and reserves are obviously reflective of the degree of exploration in the region. Thus, at a point in time, these data may be poor estimates. We will set data issues aside for a moment, assuming that these data are known, and examine issues regarding their use and misuse. Obviously, the motivation for such an exercise is the examination of resources at average grades much below that of current and past operations. There is nothing wrong with this motivation; however, the *service or disservice done by the exercise* is *dependent* upon *the interpretation of the results.* It is with respect to such an exercise that some of Lovering's comments are especially pertinent; namely, that the tonnage–grade relationship may not be smooth and continuous, but, instead, may be irregular with steep slopes at various grades. These slopes reflect transition from one deposit type to another at the high grades or from one rock type to another at low grades. Even so, the exercise has a value for grades well above those of common rock types and below average grades of current experience. If properly used, the value of it is that it motivates basic questions and broad thinking about resources. For example, if currently recognized and exploited modes of occurrence have finite boundaries, the implied large tonnages of resources at grades considerably below current grades either do not exist at all (meaning the curve may flatten in this region) or

1. There are deposits of current modes but lower grades yet to be discovered;
2. There exist deposits in the region in one or more unknown modes;
3. These implied resources exist in undiscovered deposits of known and unknown modes.

Recognition that these tonnages of resources *could* exist, hopefully, should motivate a turning to basic geoscience findings to substantiate or deny their existence. Such research cannot be anything but useful, particularly, since the natural tendency of man is to discount the unknown in favour of the implication of the known. For example, in the US, traditional resources of copper have been massive sulphide and porphyry deposits. Only recently has much consideration been given to the possibility of stratabound deposits, even though they have been known for years in Europe. Similarly, analyses of pelagic sediments of the oceans indicate that copper concentrations run as much as 100 times average crustal abundance in igneous rocks (Cloud 1969) and on average about 30 times crustal abundance. While mining of such low-grade material in its deposition sites presents formidable problems, recognition of this occurrence raises another possibility, the possibility that large, low-grade sedimentary deposits may have been formed by similar processes in the geologic past. As Cloud (1969) points out, the interesting prospect is that we could learn to locate these ancient environments in land-locked rocks and to apply large-scale mining operations. It is the potential for such resources that must be borne in mind when considering the long-term resource picture.

Singer and DeYoung (1980) explored the compatibility of current tonnage–grade data with the crustal abundance proposition. Table 3.3 presents their analyses on komatiite nickel, laterite nickel, small intrusive nickel, all types of nickel deposits, skarn copper, mafic volcanogenic copper, all types of copper deposits, porphyry molybdenum, and tactite tungsten. Note that two versions of a quantity–quality relationship have been estimated for each population,

$$\hat{\bar{q}} = a + b \cdot \log t,$$

$$\widehat{\log t} = c + d \cdot \bar{q}.$$

The first of these equations was evaluated at $t = 10^{18}$ tonnes, the quantity taken as the weight of the Earth's crust. The second equation was evaluated for $\bar{q}$, average grade, equal to the crustal abundance of the metal of interest. The estimated crustal grade and tonnage for a metal were multiplied to give the estimated quantity of metal in the Earth's crust. Table 3.3 shows these estimates: $E[\bar{Q}]$ at $t = 10^{18}$, $E[\log T]$ at crustal abundance, and $E[\log M]$ at crustal abundance. This exercise produced average grades less than zero and tonnages of material that are considerably less than the weight of the crust.

TABLE 3.3 *Cumulative tonnage–grade relationships and related calculations. (After Singer and DeYoung 1980.)*

Deposit type	Commodity	Number of deposits	Correlation† coefficient†	a (intercept)†	b (slope)	$E(\bar{Q})$ at log t = 18‡	c (intercept)	d (slope)	Crustal abundance§ ($\times 10^{-6}$)	$E(\log T)$ at crustal abundance	Cumulative 'ore' of sample (log)	$E(\log M)$ at crustal abundance	Cumulative metal of sample (log)
Komatiite	nickel	52	−0.898	0.110	−0.0104	−0.0771	10.2	−77.6	89	10.2	9.48	6.11	7.32
Laterite	nickel	54	−0.997	0.0489	−0.00361	−0.0160	13.5	−275.0	89	13.5	9.82	9.46	7.95
Small intrusive	nickel	50	−0.962	0.0514	−0.00539	−0.0457	9.38	−172.0	89	9.37	8.09	5.32	5.89
All deposits	nickel	156	−0.982	0.0882	−0.00757	−0.0481	11.6	−127.0	89	11.5	9.99	7.49	8.04
Skarn	copper	35	−0.997	0.129	−0.0138	−0.119	9.37	−72.0	63	9.37	8.53	5.17	6.63
Mafic volcanogenic	copper	37	−0.975	0.260	−0.0273	−0.232	9.44	−34.8	63	9.44	8.44	5.24	6.86
Felsic volcanogenic	copper	92	−0.983	0.283	−0.0298	−0.254	9.43	−32.3	63	9.43	8.91	5.23	7.15
Porphyry	copper	165	−0.973	0.0474	−0.00368	−0.0189	12.7	−257.0	63	12.7	10.9	8.50	8.74
All deposits	copper	395**	−0.950	0.194	−0.0180	−0.129	10.6	−50.2	63	10.6	10.9	6.40	8.76
Porphyry	molybdenum	34	−0.989	0.0157	−0.00147	−0.0108	10.6	−665.0	1.3	10.6	9.58	4.73	6.75
Tactite	tungsten	32	−0.979	0.0232	−0.00224	−0.0170	10.3	−428.0	1.3	10.3	8.10	4.29	5.78

t = tonnage of mineralized material ('ore'), m = contained metal, q = average grade of cumulated material, t and m in metric tonnes, $\bar{q} = a + b \cdot \log t$, $\log t = c + d \cdot \bar{q}$
† Musgrove (1971, p. 374) has observed that the use of ordinary least-squares regression is not entirely justified because the cumulated variable t results in the persistence of any errors in lower-grade observations. This violation of the assumption of the regression model obviates the use of significance tests on the correlation coefficient.
‡ Crustal tonnage of 10^{18} metric tonnes from Brinck (1971); $E(\bar{Q})$ is the mathematical expectation of the random variable $\bar{Q}$.
§ Lee and Yao (1970).
** Includes copper in 46 small intrusive nickel deposits and 20 komatiite nickel deposits.

TABLE 3.4. *Comparison of estimates from equations with crustal metal*

Metal	Estimated crustal metal (tonnes)	Crustal metal (tonnes)
Nickel (3 deposit types)	$10^{7.49}$	$10^{13.9}$
Copper (7 deposit types)	$10^{6.4}$	$10^{13.8}$
Molybdenum (1 deposit type)	$10^{4.73}$	$10^{12.1}$
Tungsten (1 deposit type)	$10^{4.29}$	$10^{12.0}$

Table 3.4 compares estimates of metal that result from the use of these equations with crustal abundance quantities. The quantity of metal estimated by the equations for each metal is much less than crustal metal. Furthermore, with the exception of laterite nickel deposits, more metal is contained in the sample of the deposits than was predicted by the equations for tonnages and grades at crustal abundance.

These results seem to indicate that the assumption of grade continuity, which is the cornerstone of crustal abundance models of endowment, may not be justified. Analogously, these findings seem to lend weight to the proposition by Skinner (1976) and to the discussion by Singer (1977) that the frequency (by tonnage) of grades in the crust is bimodal, rather than unimodal, where the first mode represents concentrations in silicate structures and the second mode (at higher grades) represents concentrations in sulphide and oxide ore minerals. Skinner's proposition springs from geochemical considerations, i.e. minimum concentrations required to form ore minerals (Harris and Skinner 1982). These inferences by Singer and DeYoung may indeed be correct; however, the empirical evidence for these inferences is no stronger than the underlying assumption that *all* deposits in the crust that have economic grades have been found. To the extent that this assumption is not true, the Lasky curve which shows tonnage as a function of grade would be shifted upward. Of course, such a shift would modify the estimates of metal in a direction such that they would compare more favourably with the quantity of crustal metal.

Problems in applications

Problems in the application of tonnage–grade relations fall into three main categories.

1. Selection of the proper model;
2. Given the proper model, estimation of its parameters from available data;
3. Identification of the limits of extrapolation.

Although these categories of problems were separated for discussion in previous sections, determination of a tonnage–grade relationship from available data on deposits and the extrapolation of the relationship for resource appraisal may be an exercise of frustration because of the need to resolve all of these problems solely by the examination of the tonnage and grade data. If the form of the tonnage–grade relationship were known, problems may be eased somewhat. In this regard, the evidence and argument presented earlier in this section that tonnage–average grade relations may not all follow the exponential model serves to compound problems in application, for it means that the basic form of the relationship must be identified either from the data, theoretical argument, or some other empirical study.

Musgrove (1971, pp. 404–5) found by examining the tonnage–grade curves for a given metal based upon data for two different points in time that these curves may shift or change slope, or both shift and change slope (see Fig. 3.22). He accounted for these shifts as follows (expressions in brackets have been modified to agree with notation employed in this section)

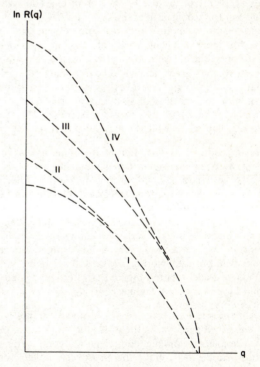

Fig. 3.22. Possible shifts in the grade–tonnage relation, as exploration proceeds. (After Musgrove 1971.)

Additions to known resources of ore may occur in three distinct, idealized ways. Continued exploration may simply identify and make available material whose existence is already implied by an exponential distribution: $R(G)$ $[R(q)]$ then shifts from position I to position II in Figure 8 [3.22]. This process might be characteristic of a single deposit in which *all* the ore of a given grade is found before *any* ore of lower grade is mined. ... If instead new ore is found at all grades in the proportions already prevailing, $R(G)$ $[R(q)]$ shifts outward to position III: ... The distribution might shift in this way when exploration is extended to new districts similar to those already exploited at the same range of grades. Finally, proportionately more new ore may be found at some grades than at others, so that the slope of the function changes. ... The line is therefore shown shifting to position IV.

The foregoing discussion by Musgrove identifies clearly the changes that can take place and the difficulty of determining from production and reserves data where we are at a given time along the tonnage–grade curve that depicts total economic resources, except for small regions which have been exhaustively explored. Since incomplete exploration may mean that neither the slope nor the position of the relationship can be established accurately, the existence of incomplete exploration creates significant problems in the use of the tonnage–grade relationship for resource appraisal.

When exploration is known to have been exhaustive for deposits having grades above some specified level, then the relationship can be fitted to the data down to that grade level and extrapolated to estimate subeconomic resources; however, when this condition is unsatisfied, such an approach is not feasible. There are two ways of handling this dilemma, neither of which is without its problems.

1. Estimate independently the quantity of resources in *undiscovered* deposits having *economic grades* and add this inventory to that for *known deposits*, generating a tonnage–grade relationship for the *composite inventory*;
2. Employ a mixed model, a time-dependent, tonnage–grade model. Model the known inventory of deposits as a detection process operating upon an unknown physical world, a world described by a tonnage–grade relationship or its alternative statement, a distribution of grades.

A time-dependent, tonnage-grade model has not yet been developed, so nothing at this time can be provided as an example, and, given the complexities, little can be said about the prospects of such an approach. The following subsection elaborates on the first alternative, the use of a composite inventory.

Estimation procedure based upon a composite inventory

The term composite inventory refers to a stock of material by grade in which the quantity of material at a specific grade is inclusive of past production, known resources, and estimates of unknown resources. In other words, the time shift in the tonnage–grade curve described by Musgrove (1971) as due to subsequent discoveries is compensated for by estimating this stock (undiscovered economic resources) and adding this to the known stock. Since this section deals with the use of quantity–quality relations to estimate undiscovered resources, the question arises naturally as to why and how estimation of the undiscovered stock is made prior to fitting a function to the composite stock. So to speak, it must appear that in order to use the quantity–quality model, we must estimate the very thing for which the model is to be used to estimate—undiscovered resources. This appearance is partially correct. The appropriate perspective here is that the estimation of undiscovered resources is decomposed into two tasks

1. The estimation of undiscovered *economic* resources;
2. The estimation of *subeconomic* resources.

There is some appeal to the proposition that estimation of undiscovered subeconomic resources is far more difficult than the estimation of yet undiscovered deposits having familiar (economic) sizes and grades. Geologists are reluctant, perhaps for good reason, to estimate the number of deposits (and their tonnage and grade characteristics) occurring in a region for grades considerably lower than those that constitute current exploration targets (Harris 1973), because they have had little experience with subeconomic deposits. On the other hand, for regions that have received some exploration and for which some deposits are known, an expert geologist may have strong impressions of the number of economic deposits that occur in the region and have not been discovered. In other words, if geoscience can estimate any resource measure, it is the additional deposits of a known kind and having economic sizes and grades that exist in a region, particularly if for that region there has been exploration and exploitation sufficient to provide a data base of deposit characteristics and the identification of relations of deposits to geological features.

Suppose that the assumption is made that the undiscovered deposits will be very similar in terms of size and grade as the deposits that have been found. Furthermore, suppose that the region is large enough and has received exploration and development sufficient to provide considerable data on tonnages and grades. Then, the geologist's task could be reduced to estimating *only the number* of undiscovered deposits having economic sizes and grades. Once these had been estimated, the tonnages and grades which they represent would be obtained from the statistical data on known deposits and would be added to the known inventory. Subsequently, the cumulative tonnage and average grade curve could be recomputed, based upon this complete (known plus unknown for economic grades) inventory. The way in which this composite inventory would be determined would depend upon the support implied by known data. If the support of the known data were mining blocks, then an additional distribution would be required; namely, the distribution of block grades for a typical deposit. The estimated composite inventory would represent the quantity and quality for the total number of deposits in that region that have familiar grades and sizes, i.e. like those already known. A quantity–quality model could be fitted to this composite inventory. Then, the quantity of subeconomic material and its grade could be estimated by extrapolation of the fitted model and by the analysis of the resulting estimates.

Resource appraisal by alternative one is demonstrated by a subjective probability appraisal of the U₃O₈ resources of New Mexico (Ellis *et al.* 1975). Although the only example available of this alternative employed subjective probabilities for the assessment of unknown economic resources, other methods that could be employed include those of multivariate statistical inference and geologic analogy; these methods are discussed elsewhere in this book.

Selected comments on the quantity–quality analysis by Cargill et al.

The quantity–quality model and analysis by Cargill *et al.* (1980, 1981) have been described in § 3.6. Additional comments are provided here because

1. The use by Cargill *et al.* of the quantity–quality relation is, as they describe it, for the estimation of undiscovered usable resources,
2. The model and data analysis differ somewhat from those of Lasky.

§ 3.6 commented on the fact that Cargill *et al.* construct the cumulative tonnage cumulative-average grade data from a time series and do not follow the approach of Lasky (1950a) of grouping productions of like grade. This seems to be an illogical procedure

for the construction of a quantity–quality relationship, which by historical precedent and accepted usage is the description of a physical stock. In fairness to Cargill *et al.*, this anomaly is in part a result of the classification by the author of this book of their model as a quantity–quality relationship. A reading of their work discloses that their preferred model would relate cumulative production to cumulative effort. In the absence of data on effort, cumulative average grade is used as its proxy. Given their preferred model form and philosophical approach, the decision to not group quantities of like grade is consistent. The difficulty in accepting this procedure stems from the equating of cumulative average grade with cumulative effort. Even if the assumption is made that richest deposits are found first, these two measures may be related in a complex fashion. Of course, the fact that richest grades are not always produced first compounds things. Furthermore, adverse economics prompts high grading, which, *ceteris paribus*, violates the orderly decline of grade. These facts seem to argue for the reordering of productions by grade and the modelling of the quantity–quality relation of the stock instead of treating it as a quantity–effort relationship.

While the foregoing comments seem justified by the concepts involved, there are two pragmatic issues that make reordering of productions somewhat less strongly indicated. One of these is that when annual production derives from a number of mines, proper analysis would require reordering of grades by mine prior to aggregation. Often these data are not available. Reordering of the *aggregated* series is at best a poor second-best procedure. The second pragmatic reason is that when there has been a large fall in grades over the production history and when a quantity–quality relation is fitted *only to* the low-grade portion of the data, the influence of grade aberrations of earlier years at relatively high grades is of little consequence, because the cumulative average for the low-grade portion may be unaffected by reordering production at the earlier high grades.

On the other hand, in some cases, reordering may facilitate analysis of otherwise questionable data. Consider Table 3.5 and Fig. 3.23, which are the data and plot, respectively, employed by Cargill *et al.* (1980) for the Monte Amiata District of Italy. Table 3.5 shows production for each five-year interval ascribed to the median (central) year. Cargill *et al.* (1980, p. 505) did not fit a quantity–quality relationship to these data, commenting that 'The use of these historical data to make a resource estimate for Italy is not reasonable...' [18]. Table 3.6 and Fig. 3.24

TABLE 3.5. *Monte Amiata District, Italy, mercury production in 5-year periods; cumulative data beginning with opening of Siele Mine in 1872. (Source: Cargill et al. 1980.)*

Year	Ore treated (kg×10⁶)	Hg production (kg×10⁶)	5-year average grade per cent	Cumulative ore (kg×10⁶)	Cumulative Hg (kg×10⁶)	Cumulative grade per cent
1850	3.85	0.02	0.63			
1855	11.02	0.05	0.42			
1860	41.21	0.14	0.33	(Starting with 1872–7 period)		
1865	26.02	0.11	0.42			
1870	28.57	0.15	0.54			
1875	11.59	0.37	3.19	11.59	0.37	3.19
1880	16.39	0.74	4.51	27.98	1.11	3.97
1885	36.25	1.17	3.22	64.23	2.28	3.55
1890	64.62	1.78	2.76	128.85	4.06	3.15
1895	79.94	1.11	1.39	208.79	5.17	2.48
1900	165.33	1.18	0.71	374.12	6.35	1.70
1905	336.51	1.79	0.53	710.63	8.14	1.15
1910	453.26	4.26	0.94	1163.89	12.40	1.07
1915	585.57	4.84	0.83	1749.46	17.24	0.99
1920†	198.79	3.13	1.57	1948.25	20.37	1.05
1925	873.16	6.60	0.76	2821.41	26.97	0.96
1930	736.08	6.07	0.83	3557.49	33.04	0.93
1935	319.52	4.40	1.38	3877.01	37.44	0.97
1940	846.27	11.59	1.37	4723.28	49.03	1.04
1945	390.24	5.43	1.39	5113.52	54.46	1.07
1950	734.36	8.40	1.14	5847.88	62.86	1.08
1955	1327.87	9.80	0.74	7175.75	72.66	1.01
1960	1394.46	9.31	0.67	8570.21	81.97	0.96
1965	1459.20	9.32	0.64	10,029.41	91.29	0.91
1970	1606.88	7.96	0.50	11,636.29	99.25	0.86

† Although the Idria mine was producing mercury from 1919 to 1944 under control of Italy, these production records have been credited to Idria and removed from the Monte Amiata records.

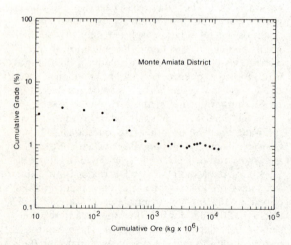

Fig. 3.23. Monte Amiata district, Italy; production–grade plot, 1872–1972 (Source: Cargill *et al.* 1980.)

are the reordered data and plot, respectively, of the five-year production groupings. Note the more orderly pattern. Table 3.7 shows log–log quantity–quality relations estimated by weighted regression, as described by Cargill *et al.*, using all of the data and using two subsets of the data. Following the procedure described by Cargill *et al.* which uses only the linear part of the quantity–quality plot (see Fig. 3.23), we would select the last equation of Table 3.7 as the preferred quantity–quality relation

$$\widehat{\log \bar{q}} = -0.72920 - 0.32828 \log t. \quad (3.45)$$

Let us specify 0.1 per cent Hg as the production grade of interest. From (3.24), we compute 0.149 per cent as the average grade associated with the mining grade,

$$\hat{\bar{q}} = \frac{q'}{(\hat{\beta}+1)} = \frac{0.1 \text{ per cent}}{0.67172} \approx 0.149 \text{ per cent.} \quad (3.46)$$

TABLE 3.6. *Production of the Monte Amiata mercury district (data reordered by declining grade). (Source of data: Cargill et al. 1980.)*

Year	Ore treated (kg×10^6)	Hg production (kg×10^6)	5-year average grade per cent	Cumulative ore (kg×10^6)	Cumulative Hg (kg×10^6)	Cumulative grade per cent
1880	16.39	0.74	4.51	16.39	0.74	4.51
1885	36.25	1.17	3.22	52.64	1.91	3.63
1875	11.59	0.37	3.19	64.23	2.28	3.55
1890	64.62	1.78	2.76	128.85	4.06	3.15
1920	198.79	3.13	1.57	327.64	7.19	2.19
1895	79.94	1.11	1.39	407.58	8.30	2.04
1945	390.24	5.43	1.39	797.82	13.73	1.72
1935	319.52	4.40	1.38	1117.34	18.13	1.62
1940	846.27	11.59	1.37	1963.61	29.72	1.51
1950	734.36	8.40	1.14	2697.97	38.12	1.41
1910	453.26	4.26	0.94	3151.23	42.38	1.34
1915	585.57	4.84	0.83	3736.80	47.22	1.26
1930	736.08	6.07	0.83	4472.88	53.29	1.19
1925	873.16	6.60	0.76	5346.04	59.89	1.12
1955	1327.87	9.80	0.74	6673.91	69.69	1.04
1900	165.33	1.18	0.71	6839.24	70.87	1.04
1960	1394.46	9.31	0.67	8233.70	80.18	0.97
1965	1459.20	9.32	0.64	9692.90	89.50	0.92
1850	3.85	0.02	0.63	9696.75	89.52	0.92
1870	28.57	0.15	0.54	9725.32	89.67	0.92
1905	336.51	1.79	0.53	10061.83	91.46	0.91
1970	1606.88	7.96	0.50	11668.71	99.42	0.85
1855	11.02	0.05	0.42	11679.73	99.47	0.85
1865	26.02	0.11	0.42	11705.75	99.58	0.85
1860	41.21	0.14	0.33	11746.96	99.72	0.85

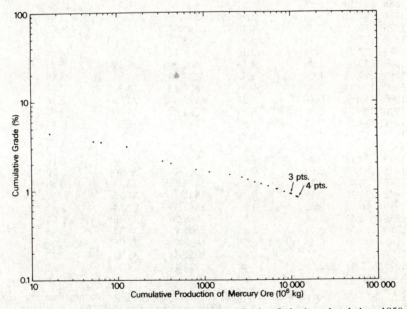

Fig. 3.24. Quantity–quality data for the Monte Amiata mercury district, Italy (reordered data 1850 to 1975—5-year intervals, 25 points). (Source of data: Cargill *et al.* 1980.)

TABLE 3.7. *Quantity–quality relations for the Monte Amiata District, Italy†* (*data reordered by declining grade*)

1. For all 25 observations:

$$\widehat{\log \bar{q}} = -0.93384 - 0.27499 \log t.$$

2. Leaving out the 1850, 1855, 1860, 1865, and 1870 observations (which are low-grade, appearing near the end of the reordered data) 20 observations:

$$\widehat{\log \bar{q}} = -0.93487 - 0.27467 \log t.$$

3. Leaving out the first 8 observations: 1880, 1885, 1875, 1890, 1920, 1895, 1945, 1935:

$$\widehat{\log \bar{q}} = -0.72920 - 0.32828 \log t$$

$\bar{q} =$ cumulative average grade. $t =$ cumulative ore in 10^6 kg. $\log \bar{q} = \alpha + \beta \log t.$
† The parameters of these equations were estimated using weighted regression, as described by Cargill *et al.* (1980).

Again, following Cargill *et al.*, the cumulative quantity of ore associated with this average grade is $2\,453\,000 \times 10^6$ kg,

$$\widehat{\log t} = \frac{\log(0.00149) + 0.72920}{-0.32828} = \frac{-2.09761}{-0.32828} = 6.3897,$$

$$\hat{t} = 2\,453\,000 \times 10^6 \text{ kg}.$$

(All quantity data analysed were stated in terms of 10^6 kg.) Therefore, this relation estimates 3655×10^6 kg of mercury ($2\,453\,000 \times 10^6$ kg $\times 0.00149$) for a mining grade of 0.1 per cent. Table 3.5 shows that this quantity is approximately 37 times cumulative mercury production by the close of 1975.

As a second example of analysis with and without reordering of grades, consider the New Almaden Mine of California. Table 3.8 presents the data employed by Cargill *et al.* and Fig. 3.25 shows the plot of the data of Table 3.8, except for data points for years

TABLE 3.8. *New Almaden Mine, California, mercury-production data in 5-year periods.* (*Source: Cargill* et al. *1980.*)

Year	Ore treated (kg×10^6)	Hg production (kg×10^6)	5-year average grade per cent	Cumulative ore (kg×10^6)	Cumulative Hg (kg×10^6)	Cumulative grade per cent
1850	6.56	2.14	32.62	6.56	2.14	32.62
1855	21.86	4.89	22.37	28.42	7.03	24.74
1860	18.25	3.59	19.67	46.67	10.62	22.76
1865	54.10	6.15	11.37	100.77	16.77	16.64
1870	54.21	3.24	5.98	154.98	20.01	12.91
1875	40.89	2.75	6.73	195.87	22.76	11.62
1880	117.48	3.93	3.35	313.35	26.69	8.52
1885	172.83	3.74	2.16	486.18	30.43	6.26
1890	123.81	1.96	1.58	609.99	32.39	5.31
1895	117.61	1.08	0.92	727.60	33.47	4.60
1900	159.83	0.87	0.54	887.43	34.34	3.87
1905	151.64	0.56	0.37	1039.07	34.90	3.36
1910	185.73	0.90	0.49	1224.80	35.80	2.92
1915	54.49	0.53	0.97	1279.29	36.33	2.84
1920	57.41	0.41	0.71	1336.70	36.74	2.75
1925†	—	—	—	1336.70	36.74	2.75
1930	30.13	0.20	0.66	1366.83	36.94	2.70
1935	0.95	0.02	2.11	1367.78	36.96	2.70
1940	70.49	0.18	0.26	1438.27	37.14	2.58
1945	124.10	0.19	0.15	1562.37	37.33	2.39
1950	0.72	0.01	1.39	1563.09	37.34	2.39
1955	3.11	0.06	1.93	1566.20	37.40	2.39
1960	24.33	0.11	0.45	1590.53	37.51	2.36
1965	42.91	0.25	0.58	1633.44	37.76	2.31
1970	77.60	0.27	0.35	1711.04	38.03	2.22
1975	12.40	0.06	0.48	1723.44	38.09	2.21

† At the New Almaden mine, according to US Bureau of Mines records, there was no primary mine production from 1926 to 1932 and from 1934 to 1936.

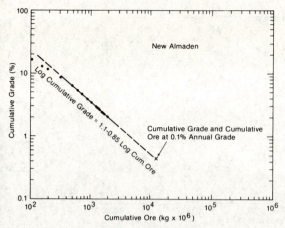

Fig. 3.25. New Almaden, California; production–grade plot, 1850–1976. (Source: Cargill *et al.* 1980.)

1850, 1855, and 1860, which are not plotted. They used only the data from 1875–1975 for fitting of the log–log relation—this is 20 observations because

there was no production for 1925 [19],

$$\widehat{\log \bar{q}} = 1.1 - 0.85 \log t. \qquad (3.47)$$

Table 3.9 provides the data reordered by grade, and Fig. 3.26 is a plot of all reordered data (1850–1975). Table 3.10 shows the log–log equations obtained by using weighted regression as described by Cargill *et al.* (1980) but for different sets of data. The equation for 20 points is based upon the same raw observations as used by Cargill *et al.* to estimate eqn (3.47); however, these raw observations were reordered prior to estimation of the quantity–quality relationship. This equation (eqn 2 of Table 3.10) describes approximately $14\,440 \times 10^6$ kg of material having an average grade of 0.442 per cent, given a cut-off of 0.1 per cent. This amounts to 63.82×10^6 kg of mercury. The equation estimated by Cargill *et al.* gives 7140×10^6 kg of material having an average grade of 0.667 per cent, giving 47.62×10^6 kg of mercury.

Table 3.10 shows that when three more observations are dropped and the remaining 17 observations are subjected to analysis, the equation that

TABLE 3.9. *Production of the New Almaden mercury mine (data reordered by declining grade).* (*Source of data: Cargill* et al. *1980.*)

Year	Ore treated (kg×10⁶)	Hg production (kg×10⁶)	5-year average grade per cent	Cumulative ore (kg×10⁶)	Cumulative Hg (kg×10⁶)	Cumulative grade per cent
1850	6.56	2.14	32.62	6.56	2.14	32.62
1855	21.86	4.89	22.37	28.42	7.03	24.74
1860	18.25	3.59	19.67	46.67	10.62	22.76
1865	54.10	6.15	11.37	100.77	16.77	16.64
1875	40.89	2.75	6.73	141.66	19.52	13.78
1870	54.21	3.24	5.98	195.87	22.76	11.62
1880	117.48	3.93	3.35	313.35	26.69	8.52
1885	172.83	3.74	2.16	486.18	30.43	6.26
1935	0.95	0.02	2.11	487.13	30.45	6.25
1955	3.11	0.06	1.93	490.24	30.51	6.22
1890	123.81	1.96	1.58	614.05	32.47	5.29
1950	0.72	0.01	1.39	614.77	32.48	5.28
1915	54.49	0.53	0.97	669.26	33.01	4.93
1895	117.61	1.08	0.92	786.87	34.09	4.33
1920	57.41	0.41	0.71	844.28	34.50	4.09
1930	30.13	0.20	0.66	874.41	34.70	3.97
1965	42.91	0.25	0.58	917.32	34.95	3.81
1900	159.83	0.87	0.54	1077.15	35.82	3.33
1910	185.73	0.90	0.49	1262.88	36.72	2.91
1975	12.40	0.06	0.48	1275.28	36.78	2.88
1960	24.33	0.11	0.45	1299.61	36.89	2.84
1905	151.64	0.56	0.37	1451.25	37.45	2.58
1970	77.60	0.27	0.35	1528.85	37.72	2.47
1940	70.49	0.18	0.26	1599.34	37.90	2.37
1945	124.10	0.19	0.15	1723.44	38.09	2.21

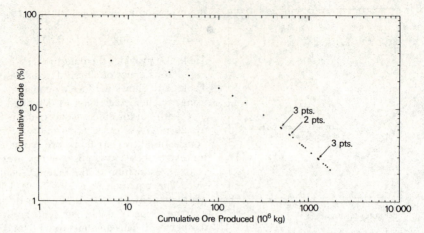

Fig. 3.26. Quantity–quality data for the New Almaden Mine, California (reordered data 1850 to 1975—5-year intervals, 25 points). (Source of data: Cargill *et al.* 1980.)

results is very close to that estimated by Cargill *et al.* This is a demonstration of the point made earlier that if production has occurred over a wide range of grades and if only the data for low average grades are used to fit the equation, reordering of the grades in the high-grade portion has little effect. Of course, this does not answer the question of whether all data or just part of the data should be used.

TABLE 3.10. *New Almaden Mine, California. Regression†of average grade against cumulative ore production*

1. For all data (25 observations):
$$\widehat{\log \bar{q}} = 0.527 - 0.660 \log t.$$

2. For 20 observations, leaving out 1850, 1855, 1860, 1865, 1870:
$$\widehat{\log \bar{q}} = 0.865 - 0.774 \log t.$$

3. For 19 observations, leaving out 1875, and above deletions:
$$\widehat{\log \bar{q}} = 0.949 - 0.801 \log t.$$

4. For 18 observations, leaving out 1880 and above deletions:
$$\widehat{\log \bar{q}} = 1.020 - 0.825 \log t.$$

5. For 17 observations, leaving out 1885 and above deletions:
$$\widehat{\log \bar{q}} = 1.096 - 0.843 \log t.$$

Cargill, *et al.*
$$\widehat{\log \bar{q}} = 1.1 - 0.85 \log t$$

$\bar{q}$ = average grade. t = cumulative ore in 10^6 kg.
† Weighted regression, as described by Cargill *et al.* (1980).

The choice of using all or part of the tonnage and grade data must reflect two primary considerations:

1. The intended use of the quantity–quality relation;
2. The completeness of the data.

Suppose that the intended use of the relation were to predict the quantity of unknown resources at average grades below those of the data. Suppose also that, for the higher grades for which quantity data are available, the data were believed to be complete; in other words, there are no undiscovered deposits in the regions having these high grades. Then, there might be some appeal to using only the tonnage–grade data for the lower average grades, particularly if there is a strong nonlinear pattern in the semi-log plot of these data. The argument here is that for the estimation of unknown resources at average grades below available data, provided these average grades are above the terminal average grade, it is more important to have a good fitting curve for the lower average grades than it is to have a good fit to all of the data.

As a means of clarifying and illustrating the foregoing comments, consider Fig. 3.11, the quantity–quality plot by Singer and DeYoung (1980) of 165 copper porhyry deposits. This figure also shows a Lasky curve that has been fitted to these data. If the purpose of fitting this Lasky curve were for the estimation of unknown resources at average grades below those of the data and if the data were believed to be complete, the use of the fitted Lasky relation for this purpose would cause some concern about the departure of the data from the fitted model for low average grades, those closest to the average grades for which estimates of quantity would be made. This concern would be increased by the fact that there is a high density of points in this region of low average grades. Given the assumptions about those data made here for the purpose of exposition of concepts and issues, the alternative demonstrated by Cargill *et al.* (1980) of fitting the quantity–quality model only to data for the lower average grades appears superior to fitting the Lasky relation to the entire tonnage and grade data. Of course, this superiority reflects the nonlinear pattern of the tonnage–grade plot of Fig. 3.11. If a nonlinear model had been fitted to these data, the appeal of using only part of the data perhaps would have been lessened considerably. Even so, it probably is true generally that fitting a model to the entire data will sacrifice to some degree the goodness of fit at the lower average grades. This fact must be weighed against additional information present in the complete data.

The foregoing statements are conditional upon the completeness of tonnage data for the grade range selected. If the data are not complete, i.e. there remain in the region undiscovered deposits having grades similar to those represented in the tonnage–grade data, then, no model will provide good estimates. Nevertheless, given incompleteness of data, there is some appeal to the possibility that a model which has been fitted to all of the data will provide better estimates than one which has been fitted to only the low-grade part. Critical in this appeal is the fact that typically exploration has been more effective in finding the high-grade deposits than it has the low-grade ones. In practice, deposits having marginally economic grades are the least well represented in the tonnage–grade data.

References

Agterberg, F. P. and Divi, S. R. (1978). A statistical model for the distribution of copper, lead, and zinc in the Canadian Appalachian region. *Econ. Geol.* **73,** 230–45.

Brinck, J. W. (1971). MIMIC, The prediction of mineral resources and long-term price trends in the non-ferrous metal mining industry is no longer utopian. *Eurospectra* **X**(2), 46–56.

Brooks, D. B. (1967). The lead–zinc anomaly. *Trans. Soc. mining Engs* **238,** 129–36.

Cargill, S. M., Root, D. H., and Bailey, E. H. (1980). Resource estimation from historical data: mercury, a test case. *J. Int. Ass. Math. Geol.* **12**(5), 489–522.

——, ——, and —— (1981). Estimating usable resources from historical industry data. *Econ. Geol.* **76,** 1081–95.

Cloud, P. (1969). Mineral resources from the sea. In *Resources and man* (A study and recommendations by the Committee on Resources and Man, National Academy of Sciences—National Research Council, Chapter 7, pp. 135–55. W. H. Freeman & Company, San Francisco. (For National Academy of Sciences.)

Cox, D. P., Schmidt, R. G., Vine, J. D., Kirkemo, H., Tourtelot, E. B., and Fleischer, M. (1973). Copper. In *United States Mineral Resources, Professional Paper 820* (ed. D. A. Brobst and W. P. Pratt), pp. 163–90. US Geological Survey, Washington, DC.

DeYoung, J. H., Jr. (1981). The Lasky cumulative tonnage–grade relationship—a re-examination. *Econ. Geol.* **76,** 1067–80.

Ellis, J. R., Harris, D. P., and Van Wie, N. H. (1975). *A subjective probability appraisal of uranium resources in the state of New Mexico.* Open File Report GJO-110(76). US Energy Research and Development Administration, Grand Junction, Colorado.

Harris, D. P. (1973). A subjective probability appraisal of metal endowment of Northern Sonora, Mexico. *Econ. Geol.* **68**(2), 222–42.

——, and Skinner, B. J. (1982). The assessment of long-term supplies of minerals. In *Explorations in natural resource economics* (ed. V. K. Smith and J. V. Krutilla), pp. 247–326. The Johns Hopkins University Press, Baltimore (for Resources for the Future, Inc).

Lasky, S. G. (1950*a*). How tonnage and grade relations help predict ore reserves. *Eng. Mining J.* **151**(4), 81–5.

—— (1950*b*). Mineral resource appraisal by the US Geological Survey. *Colorado School of Mines Quart.* **45**(1A), 1–27.

Lee, T. and Yao, C. (1970). Abundance of chemical elements in the earth's crust and its major tectonic units. *Internat. Geol. Rev.* **12**(7), 778–86.

Lovering, T. S. (1969). Mineral resources from the land. In *Resources and man* (A study and recommendations by the Committee on Resources and Man, National Academy of Sciences—National Research Council), Chapter 6, pp. 109–34. W. H. Freeman & Company, San Francisco. (For National Academy of Sciences.)

Matheron, G. (1971). *The theory of regionalized variables and its applications.* Les Cahiers du Centre de Morphalogie Mathematique de Fontainebleau, no. 5.

Musgrove, P. A. (1965). Lead: grade–tonnage relation. *Mining Mag.* **112**(4), 249–51.

—— (1971). The distribution of metal resources

(tests and implications of the exponential grade-size relation). *Proc. Council Econom. AIME*, pp. 349–417. AIME, New York.

Netschert, B. C. and Landsberg, H. H. (1961). *The future supply of the major metals—a reconnaissance survey*. The Johns Hopkins University Press, Baltimore, Maryland. (For Resources for the Future, Inc.)

Singer, D. A. (1977). Long-term adequacy of metal resources. *Resources Policy* **3**(2), 127–33.

—— Cox, D. P., and Drew, L. J. (1975). *Grade and tonnage relationships among copper deposits, professional paper 907-A*, pp. A-1–A-11. US Geological Survey, Washington, DC.

—— and DeYoung, J. H., Jr. (1980). What can grade–tonnage relations really tell us? In *Ressources minérales—mineral resources* (ed. Claude Guilleman and Philippe Lagny), pp. 91–101, 26th CGI, Bur. Recherches Géol. et Minières Mém. 106, Orleans, France.

Skinner, B. J. (1976). A second iron age ahead? *Am. Scientist* **64**(3), 258–69.

Notes

1. Concave as viewed from the origin.
2. Lasky's paper interprets his equation to show an increase in tonnage of approximately 18 per cent for a one-unit change in average grade.
3. Let $Ae \cdot e^{-\bar{q}/K} = A'e^{-\bar{q}/K}$. Then this function is of the same form as R, except that it involves $\bar{q}$ and has a different constant. Let us refer to $A'e^{-\bar{q}/K}$ as $\bar{\mathbf{R}}(\bar{\mathbf{q}})$. Substituting in $\bar{R}$ for $\bar{q}$, we have $\bar{\mathbf{R}}(q'+K) = A'e^{-q'/K-K/K} = e^{-1}\bar{R}(q') = (A'/e)e^{-q'/K} = \mathbf{Ae}^{-q'/K} = \mathbf{R}(q')$. Thus, for concentration q, $e^{-1}\bar{\mathbf{R}}(q) = R(q)$; alternatively, $\bar{R}(q) = eR(q)$.
4. The parameters of R and $\bar{R}$ were estimated separately from the data; consequently, A' of R is not necessarily identical to eA of R, nor is the estimate of K for R identical to that of $\bar{R}$, as the theory specifies.
5. $\bar{q} = q' + K \Rightarrow \bar{q} = 0 + 1/0.084 = 11.9$ per cent.
6. Except where required to avoid ambiguity, the qualifying adjective (cumulative) of average grade will not be used hereafter in this chapter.
7. The data for 1850, 1855, and 1860, which are the first three observations, are not included in this plot.
8. Note that the units of the ordinate of Fig. 3.9 describe grade as a percentage while the fitted equation describes it in absolute terms. For example, given cumulative ore of 10^4 kg, the graph shows a cumulative grade of approximately 1 per cent, while the equation yields approximately 0.01 for cumulative grade.
9. Of course, grades cannot be constant for sample sizes at atomic levels unless $\bar{q} = 0$ or 100 per cent. See

Agterberg and Divi (1978) and DeYoung (1981) for further comment on this topic.

10. The deviations from the fitted Lasky relation exhibit nonrandom features because of the nonlinearity of the data plot.
11. Here it should be recognized that Singer and DeYoung could not have aggregated ore by mining blocks across this entire population of 165 deposits because the requisite grade data by mining blocks are not available. DeYoung (1981) does comment on the effect on the cumulative tonnage–average grade relation of grouping deposits by grade class prior to construction of the tonnage and grade data.
12. These arguments assume that deposit tonnage and grade are statistically independent.
13. It is assumed in this conceptual development that the deposit is delimited from the surrounding rock by some combination of spatial, structural, or mineralogical features. Otherwise, lowering cut-off grade to zero would include all crustal material.
14. This equation is a restatement of Lasky's equation ($\bar{q} = 12.9 - 1.4 \log t$) to define the natural logarithm of cumulative tonnage as a function of average grade.
15. DeYoung (1981, p. 22) also determined the terminal average grade, which he refers to as G_{mm}, for Lasky's model: $G_{mm} = -b \log_{10} e$, where b is the coefficient of $\log t$ in Lasky's equation for porphyry copper; $G_{mm} = 1.4 \cdot (0.43) = 0.61$ per cent.
16. DeYoung (1981, pp. 22–4) demonstrates the physically impossible results that are obtained when extrapolation is made beyond the terminal average grade, which is referred to by DeYoung as the minimum average grade.
17. A/G ratio stands for the ratio of the arithmetic mean to the geometric mean, which refers to the exponential tonnage–grade relationship: an arithmetic increase in grade induces a geometric increase in tonnage of ore.
18. Cargill et al. did not plot the first five intervals (5-year) of data. Had they done so, the quantity-quality plot would have been even less appealing, for the very low grades of early years were followed by high grades.
19. There is some confusion here, for Cargill et al. state in a footnote to Table 3.8, referenced to the year 1925, that there was no production in years 1926–32 and 1934–6. If this were so, the production for 1930 (1928–32) should be zero. But production reported for 1930 is not zero; rather, production reported for 1925 is zero. Either the years identified in the footnote are in error, or the productions assigned in Table 3.8 to the years in question are in error. While the year of assignment of production may be important in the analysis by Cargill et al., it is not important when productions are reordered by grade; as long as the actual quantities and grades are correct, it is irrelevant when they occurred or to what year they are assigned. The analysis here reported is based upon the assumption that the productions and their grades are correct.

4 DETERMINISTIC GEOLOGICAL METHODS

4.1. Introduction

In an article entitled 'Mineral resource estimates and public policy', McKelvey (1973) provides a brief review of methods for 'quantifying the undiscovered'. In this review, he introduces his 'abundance–reserve relationship' by a statement of the inadequacies of the 'rate methods' (trend extrapolation).

> Even the goal of such projections, namely, the prediction of ultimate production, is not a useful one. Not only is it impossible to predict the quantitative effects of man's future activities but the concept implies that the activities of the past are a part of an inexorable process with only one possible outcome. Far more useful, in my opinion, are estimates of the amounts of various kinds of materials that are in the ground in various environments; such estimates establish targets for both the explorer and the technologist, and they give us a basis for choosing among alternative ways of meeting our needs for mineral supplies.

While the author does not necessarily concur with all aspects of McKelvey's appraisal of the rate methods, as demonstrated in the previous chapter, McKelvey's statement of the motivation to explore alternative methods, methods that approach resources from their physical side, establishes an appropriate perspective for the contents of this chapter.

The methods and models described in this chapter are non-probabilistic and employ some measure or relationship that is physical or chemical, at least in part. As indicated in the quotation from McKelvey, the motivation for these methods is to estimate resources by relations and measures that are largely independent of economics and technology. As will become apparent during the reading of this section, it is one thing to identify a physical or chemical relationship of mineral resources, but it is quite a different thing to *use* that relationship to *appraise* mineral resources without resorting to the use of some data which are economic. Mineral reserves, resources, and production *are economic entities.* Relations observed in or quantified on such data *are not free from economic influences.*

4.2. Crustal abundance

A basic reference for metal concentration that is independent of economic influence is crustal abundance. It is not surprising that in broad speculation about resources attention turns to this ultimate measure of endowment.

As an example, let us look at copper from a reserves, resources, and crustal abundance perspective. The concentration of copper in the crust of the US has been estimated to be 50 g/tonne (Erickson 1973). This is equivalent to a concentration of about 0.005 per cent. This concentration, when combined with the quantity of rock in the crust of the earth within the US to one kilometre of depth, implies approximately 1356 billion short tons of copper as an estimate of total copper abundance. This is a staggering quantity. Compare this quantity with reserves of 83 000 000 short tons and other resources—the sum of the estimated hypothetical, speculative, and conditional resources—of about 400 000 000 tons (Cox, Schmidt, Vine, Kirkemo, Tourtelot, and Fleischer 1973).

It is easy to become complacent about resources if one examines only crustal abundance measures of metal. However, making allowance for the economics of discovery and extraction undermines this perception of cornucopiance. For this quantity (crustal abundance) of copper to be a reserve would require prices of metal and the mining and extractive technologies that would make it possible to extract it from the average rock of the crust at a profit. Of course, we are far from such a circumstance; currently, economically mineable deposits must be of a grade approximately 100 times that of crustal abundance. Nevertheless, crustal abundance helps us to broaden our perspective and to view reserves of a metal as a dynamic entity, a quantity that can be increased, within limits, by raising prices or lowering costs or both. In addition, it provokes the question: if we have approximately 400 000 000 tons of economic resources at 0.5 per cent copper and 2700 times that quantity at 0.005 per cent, what would be our resources at a grade of 0.15 or 0.05 per cent? Can we count on deposits occurring at these grades? If so, how many and of what size? Answers to these questions are vital in the appraisal of resources, for, even if there existed a smooth, continuous relationship between total metal availability and grade down to concentrations at the level of crustal abundance, little could be said as to the economic importance of deposits of low grades, such as 0.10 per cent Cu, unless something is also said about the tonnage of metal or ore in these deposits. The usefulness of inference motivated by crustal abundance is one thing if, as the grade of deposits decreases, there is, on average, a geometric increase in the tonnage of ore and quite another if there is no relationship between tonnage of ore in a deposit and its grade. In the latter case, the lower-grade deposits would contain proportionately smaller amounts of metal, necessitating extremely high prices for their economic exploitation.

4.3. The abundance–reserve relationship

A method for making rough estimates of recoverable reserves of metals from crustal abundance data was suggested by McKelvey (1960). McKelvey plotted recoverable reserves in the US for various metals against their crustal abundance and proposed that there was a general relationship (see Fig. 4.1)

$$R = A \times 10^k \qquad (4.1)$$

where k is a number from 9 to 10, A is the crustal abundance in per cent, and R is tons of currently mineable domestic reserves of metal. In essence, this relationship states that the more abundant the ele-

ment in the earth's crust, the greater are the recoverable reserves of that element.

Examination of McKelvey's plot, however, shows a very wide scatter, even though data are plotted in logarithms, a practice which normally tends to reduce the magnitude of variation as appraised by visual inspection of such a plot. As demonstrated by McKelvey, to include all points between parallel lines requires the exponent K to vary from 6 to 10, a factor of 10 000. Obviously, the relationship between abundance and recoverable reserves when examined across all metals is a very weak one. By restricting the set of elements to those that form the chief constituents of their ores and have been sought the longest and most intensely, the scatter is considerably reduced. It is upon this set of elements that McKelvey's abundance–reserve equation is predicated.

Erickson (1973), observing that the current reserves of lead were 2.7 times that indicated by McKelvey's relationship, standardized the relationship on lead, modifying it appropriately to describe reserves in tonnes instead of short tons and for grade in parts per million instead of per cent (2.45×10^6 instead of 2.7×10^{10}) (Fig. 4.2) [1].

$$R = 2.45 \times A \times 10^6 \qquad (4.2)$$

where A is the crustal abundance in parts per million and R is tonnes of recoverable metal resources.

Since this equation was standardized on lead, the relationship describes for all other metals some part

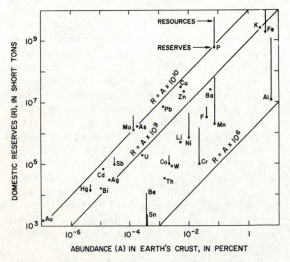

Fig. 4.1. Domestic reserves of elements compared to their abundance in the earth's crust. Tonnage of ore mineable now is shown by a dot; tonnage of lower-grade ores whose exploitation depends upon future technological advances or higher prices is shown by a bar. (After McKelvey 1960.)

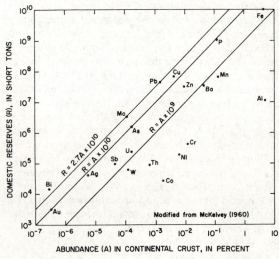

Fig. 4.2. Domestic reserves of elements compared to their abundance in the earth's crust. (After Erickson 1973.)

of potentially recoverable resources instead of reserves, because it includes materials not yet known.

While it may be remarkable that any relationship at all can be demonstrated empirically, such a relationship, even if reliable, is of limited value in resource evaluation. First of all, the fact that the relationship is based upon reserves at a point in time defeats the purpose of using crustal abundance as a basis for resource prediction, for reserves are a function of economics and technology, variables that change with time. The reserve–abundance equation relates these time-dependent variables to a measure that is time-invariant, but space-variant. It is questionable that the resulting relationship is as useful as direct analysis and extrapolation of the time patterns of reserves and production alone, as represented by the work of Hubbert (1969), a method that is disparaged by McKelvey (1973). A more useful crustal abundance relationship would describe for a given metal how variation in the reserves of geographic areas is related to spatial variation in crustal abundance and the degree to which the crust has been tested.

Secondly, the relationship of crustal abundance to reserves, when viewed across all metals, exhibits a wide scatter of points, not a well-defined pattern. Even when this data set is restricted for what appear to be well-argued reasons, McKelvey allows that the coefficient in the equation can be anywhere from 9 to 10, a whole order of magnitude of variation.

In view of the possible degree of error in the equation, the generalization by Erickson of the McKelvey equation to predict resources instead of reserves hardly seems warranted. Erickson's equation predicts the *economically recoverable resources* of a given metal by the degree to which the crustal abundance equation *underestimates lead reserves*. Such a standardization ascribes to lead a rather elevated importance. The multiplier in eqn (4.2) is the ratio of known reserves of lead to the reserves predicted by McKelvey's equation. Use of Erickson's equation to predict economically recoverable resources multiplies the reserves prediction of McKelvey's equation by this factor.

McKelvey and Erickson were aware of these issues, stating that the reserve–abundance equation should be interpreted as only a rough approximation or guide, that it demonstrates, in general, the more abundant the element, the greater the reserves of that element. As a resource appraisal method the reserve–abundance relationship fails to meet the objective implied by McKelvey in his criticism of the rate methods, the freeing of the appraisal from economic–political factors. The chief merit of McKelvey's study and equation has been to expand and stimulate our thinking about crustal abundance, reserves, and resources.

4.4. Estimation by analogy

4.4.1. *Perspective*

Analogy methods represent the traditional and conventional approaches to the appraisal of resources. In reality, these methods generally estimate unknown economic resources, given current economics and technologies of exploration and exploitation. Occasionally, estimates will include unknown subeconomic resources. The procedure has the weight of tradition and the certification of reasonableness; namely, the comparison of the region of interest to regions known to be endowed with deposits. This comparison may be based only upon a density measure of mineralization (per unit length, area, or volume), or it may include a comparison of the geological environments of the two areas.

The inability of man to observe mineral resources directly without costly, closely spaced drilling or excavation encouraged long ago the use of geological features that had been observed to be associated with known deposits as a guide to the search for new, unknown deposits. The science of ore genesis and the art–science of exploration are predicated upon the association of geological features with deposits. From these features, the geologist infers the prior operation of geological processes that were responsible for the geology and the emplacement of the mineral deposits. A set of processes that have interacted over some specific geological time interval is loosely referred to as a geological environment. Earth scientists have observed that within generally defined geological environments, certain geological associations are reasonable indicators of 'favourable ground' for the occurrence of a mineral deposit. These same geological associations outside of the environment in which they were recognized and defined may not have the same reliability as a guide to mineral deposits. This taxonomic approach to the geology–mineral deposit phenomenon has given rise to labelling of environments by deposit type; for example, the porphyry, massive copper sulphide, and stratabound environments of copper deposits, or the 'roll'-type uranium-deposit environment.

Since geology has a geographic reference, specific environments have an apparent geography. The geographic zone of one or more environments may become known as a metallogenic province, which is simply the recognition that favourable environments and metal deposits of a specific kind do occur in this generally defined region, while they are not known, or at least not known to occur as frequently, in surrounding regions.

Analogy methods vary with the conditions of appraisal, e.g. direct information on deposits, geological information, and proximity to a recognized favourable geological environment or metallogenic province. If resources are being appraised within a mining district, both spatial (room) considerations and the nature of high-level geological information (geochemical or geophysical anomalies, or alteration zones), if available, may be useful in the appraisal. Appraisal of resources within a metallogenic province may consider density relations, the presence of generally favourable macrofeatures, such as an igneous intrusive in contact with favourable host rocks, and the degree to which the ground is untested. Appraisal of a region not known to be in a favourable environment may proceed in several steps: an appraisal of its general geology, the comparison of this geological setting to known favourable environments, and the association of some density measure, a measure based upon the occurrence of mineral deposits in seemingly similar environments. The least reliable appraisal results when so little geological information is present that specific geological comparisons cannot be made. The only recourse is the application of a density measure representative of a composite of favourable and less favourable environments.

4.4.2. Simple density

The first notable description of a basis for inference by mineral density was proposed by Nolan (1950, p. 604): ... 'If mineralization has occurred fairly uniformly throughout a major geologic province, it is safe to conclude, if large enough areas are involved, that a comparable number of mining districts of various sizes may be expected in that part of the province covered by younger rocks as is found in explored areas.'

Nolan (1950) found that 'the areal distribution of nearly 300 mining districts revealed no recognizable correlations with major geologic features within the province, such as would suggest a specific nonuniform control of ore deposits to form districts.' Nolan (1950) also found that the 'number of districts in the four states was approximately proportional to the area of the states ...'. He concluded that 'a roughly constant total amount of ore material has

been introduced per unit area by the process of mineralization, and that in addition, the quantitative distribution of this ore material in separate districts has also been relatively constant.'

The implication of his proposition and findings is that the expectation for mining districts in the areas covered by post-ore sediments is equal to the density measure of districts in the exposed areas.

Nolan's finding of no recognizable correlation in the distribution of the districts and major geological features is startling in view of subsequent studies. But, since no identification is given of the geological features nor of the manner by which the correlation was investigated, little can be said critically and authoritatively regarding this observation.

4.4.3. Compound density

The basis for the compound scheme is essentially the same as it is for the simple, except that the process of inference is more indirect and requires several steps of reasoning.

One or more areas are selected to form a control

TABLE 4.1. *The density method*

Control area analysis

Geologic subdivision (Conditions)	Quantity of endowment	Area or volume	Density measure
G_1	E_1	A_1^C	$D_1 = E_1/A_1^C$
G_2	E_2	A_2^C	$D_2 = E_2/A_2^C$
G_3	E_3	A_3^C	$D_3 = E_3/A_3^C$
$\vdots$	$\vdots$	$\vdots$	$\vdots$
G_i	E_i	A_i^C	$D_i = E_i/A_i^C$
$\vdots$	$\vdots$	$\vdots$	$\vdots$
G_N	E_N	A_N^C	$D_N = E_N/A_N^C$

Analysis of study area(s)

Geologic subdivision	Area or volume	Potential (undiscovered resources)
G_1	A_1^S	$A_1^S D_1$
G_2	A_2^S	$A_2^S D_2$
G_3	A_3^S	$A_3^S D_3$
$\vdots$	$\vdots$	$\vdots$
G_i	A_i^S	$A_i^S D_i$
$\vdots$		
G_N	A_N^S	$A_N^S D_N$

$$\text{Total estimated potential} = \sum_{i=1}^{N} A_i^S D_i$$

area. This control area is subdivided on the basis of geological characteristics or deposit types, or both. For each subdivision, one or more measures of density are computed.

The study area is examined with respect to the geological criteria used to subdivide the control area, and it is subdivided accordingly. The number of units in each subdivision of the study area are multiplied by the appropriate density measures, giving the endowment of each subdivision. If desired, the endowments of the subdivisions can be summed to give an endowment of the total area. The scheme in general is summarized by Table 4.1.

This procedure may be compounded by computing several density measures for each subdivision, each measure representing different modes of occurrence: for example, number of vein deposits, number of porphyry deposits, and the number of placer deposits in a given environment.

4.4.4. Some examples of the methodology and criticisms

General reference

Examples of resource appraisals by geological analogy include the use of analogy by Lowell (1970) for copper resources, Weeks (1950, 1965) and Hendricks (1965) for oil, and Oison and Overstreet (1964) for world thorium resources. Lowell (1970, p. 70) describes a form of analogy.

> A crude approximation may be possible if one compares the number of known deposits in each district with the percentage of the district in which the preore surface has been prospected. The area prospected ordinarily would include the preore outcrop plus that portion of the area of postore cover which has been adequately tested by drilling. On this basis, one could make the following approximations assuming present mining grades: in the Southwest area approximately 30 deposits have been found in 30% of the total preore surface which has been prospected, leaving 70 deposits undiscovered. In Chile and Peru, approximately 12 deposits have been found in the 50% of the mineral belt which has been prospected, leaving 12 undiscovered deposits. In British Columbia, 13 deposits have been found, but only 10–15% of the preore surface has been explored, so that 100 deposits may remain to be found.

Resource estimates of Professional Paper 820

In 1973, the US Geological Survey published the impressive *United States Mineral Resources, Professional Paper 820* (Brobst and Pratt 1973). This work provides not only a comprehensive review of the geology and geochemistry of the major deposits and modes of occurrence for a wide range of minerals

(including fuels and rock), but also a brief review of the history of each industry and estimates of reserves and resources. While the methods employed by the many scientists who contributed to this publication vary in their details, the basic means for estimation of undiscovered resources was that of analogy of the region being appraised to well-known producing regions. The National Academy of Sciences (1975, p. 136) referred to the approach which was employed by the US Geological Survey as 'experienced judgment' and described it as follows:

> Depending upon the degree of geological knowledge in the areas involved, such appraisal can be made as follows:
> 1. *In known copper provinces*, the potential for discovery of new copper resources can be assessed for each geologic type of deposit known, or expectable, in the province:
>   (a) as to the number of discoveries to be made, according to the degree of exploration of the geologically favorable environments and to the density of mineralization in known mineral districts and belts, and
>   (b) as to size of new deposits according to tonnage and grade distribution of known deposits in the province.
> 2. *In new copper provinces*, newly recognized because of a recent discovery, e.g., Australasian Island Arcs, Central America and Central Iran porphyry copper provinces, the potential can be assessed by comparison with geologically similar known provinces where the largest known deposits of the same geologic type are similar in size and geology to the recent discovery in the new provinces.
> 3. *In potentially future copper provinces*, which are regions considered geologically favorable for the occurrence of copper deposits, because of geological similarity with known provinces. The provinces can be assessed simply by comparison with an average of geologically similar copper provinces, using statistics of the deposit population in similar areas. The Pacific Belt of Far Eastern Siberia, the eastern side of the Ural Mountains, and parts of North Africa may be considered future provinces. [Reproduced with permission from *Mineral resources and the environment*, National Academy Press, Washington, DC, 1975]

The NURE methodology

The method employed by the US Energy Research and Development Administration (ERDA) [2] to estimate the magnitude of undiscovered uranium resources, referred to by ERDA as potential resources, is a formalized version of geological analogy. ERDA employed the following equation,

$$PR = N \cdot F \cdot U \cdot T, \qquad (4.3)$$

where *PR* are potential resources for a stated forward cost level, e.g. US \$30/lb U_3O_8; N is the magnitude of favourable ground in terms of area, volume, or length, whichever unit is indicated by the mode of occurrence; F is geological favourability, as a decimal fraction; U is the fraction of N that remains unexplored; and T is the density of mineralization, i.e. lbs. of U_3O_8 per unit of N. In the NURE methodology, factors N and U are determined from the area being appraised, with due regard to the fact that the magnitude of N reflects the comparison of the geology of the control area with that of the study area. In other words, N is determined by the extent of the favourable geology in the study area. Of course, what constitutes favourable geology in the study area is reflective of the geology of the known resource regions (the control areas). F denotes how favourable the geology that supports N is as compared to the geology of the control region. T is determined from the control area, although in practice it sometimes is modified when the study and control areas differ in some important factors thought to influence the density of mineralization. Fig. 4.3 [3] shows schematically how the elements of appraisal by ERDA would be carried out and combined. In Fig. 4.3 Basin A is the control area that is being used as the basis for appraisal. The left of Fig. 4.3 shows a comparison of the control and study areas on selected geological factors. This comparison is the basis for the estimation of F, relative geological favourability. In Fig. 4.3, this geological comparison is loosely made and is strictly qualitative. An attempt later was made by ERDA to formalize this comparison by computing an index of similarity between the control and study areas. Table 4.2 is a list of the geological factors that entered into the computation of this index. However, as applied by ERDA geologists, the magnitude of factor F usually was a judgement call, with consideration given to not just the index of similarity but to all available geological evidence.

As a demonstration of the ERDA methodology, Hetland (1979, p. 233) presented a case study of the estimation of U_3O_8 potential resources for the

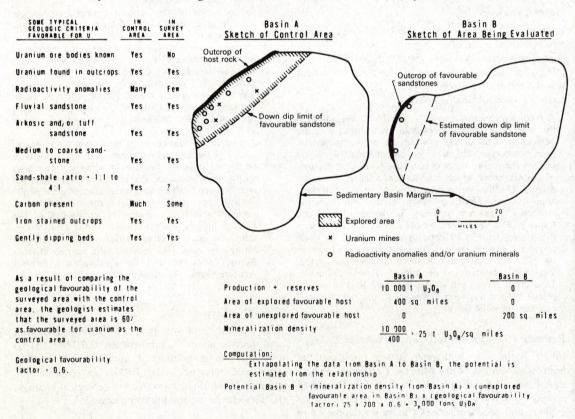

Fig. 4.3. A simplified example illustrating the principle of estimating potential uranium resources. (Source: Hetland 1979.)

TABLE 4.2. *Derivation of favourability factors based on ranking of favourability criteria.* (*Source*: *Curry 1978, pp. 24–8.*) [*Reproduced with permission from* Concepts of uranium resources and producibility, *National Academy Press, Washington, DC, 1978*)

Sandstone-type deposits	Scores	
Criterion-scale	Control area	Area to be evaluated
1. Depositional environment of potential host rocks, 0–20	20	20
Fluvial: coalesced alluvial fans		
Fluvial: stream channel and flood plains		
Marginal marine: deltaic, lagoonal, barrier bar		
Lacustrine and marine		
Aeolian and glacial		
In general, order is from most favourable to least favourable; however, highest score in area being appraised would be for whichever environment is most important in geologically similar area with important deposits.		
2. Lithology of potential host rocks		
A. Composition 0–10	10	10
0 is least favourable and 10 is most favourable sedimentary rock based on comparison with similar geological environments with important deposits.		
B. Sand–shale ratios 0–15	15	10
0 is least favourable and 15 is most favourable ratio based on comparison with similar geological environments with important deposits.		
C. Sandstone thickness 0–15	15	10
0 is least favourable and 15 is most favourable thickness based on comparison with similar geological environments with important deposits.		
D. Grain sizes 0–15	15	15
0 is least favourable and 15 is most favourable grain size based on comparison with similar geological environments with important deposits.		
E. Favourable permeability relationships 0–15	15	10
Score on basis of comparison with similar geological environments with important deposits.		
F. Reductant 0–40	40	40
Score high for abundant reductant (carbonaceous trash or H_2S) and low for little or no reductant.		
G. Tuffaceous content in overlying or interbedded sediments 0–30 (pre-erosion)	30	30
Score high for abundant, altered or unaltered, tuffs and low for tuffaceous content minor or absent.		
3. Source area of host rocks 0–20	20	20
Score high for predominately granitic rocks and low for no granitic rocks in provenance.		
4. Alteration		
A. Anomalous iron–staining (limonite–haematite)		
(1) Outcrops 0–20	20	20
0 is no anomalous iron-staining in outcrops and 20 is abundant anomalous iron-staining in outcrops based on comparison with similar geological environments with important deposits.		
(2) At depth 0–20	20	20
0 is potential host sediment completely		

TABLE 4.2 Continued

Sandstone-type deposits	Scores	
Criterion-scale	Control area	Area to be evaluated
oxidized or oxidized to great apparent depths and 20 is potential host sediments oxidized at outcrops and to shallow depths only.		
(3) Bleaching 0–20 Score on basis of importance in similar geological environments with deposits.	0	0
(4) Calcification 0–15 Score on basis of importance in similar geological environments with deposits.	15	12
B. Reduced beds (bleaching) in thick red bed sequences 0–20 Score on basis of importance in similar geological environments with deposits.	0	0
C. Pyrite content in unoxidized zone 0–15 Score on basis of abundance in area being appraised relative to abundance in similar geological environments with important deposits.	15	15
5. Structure		
A. Dip of beds 0–25 Score high for gentle dips and low for steep dips.	25	25
B. Significant unconformity or erosional surface subjacent or superjacent to section containing favourable host rocks 0–25 Score high for widespread unconformity or erosional surface and low for no unconformity or erosional surface.	25	25
C. Structural terraces or flattening of dip 0–25 Score on basis of importance in similar geological environments with deposits.	0	0
D. Faulting or graben structures 0–20 Score on basis of importance in similar geological environments with deposits.	0	0
6. Regional tectonic environments 0–20 Intracratonic basins on forelands of foldbelts Intrafoldbelt basins Geosynclinal margins Continental platforms Shields Geosynclines Order is from most favourable to least favourable; however, certain exceptions exist as in the Texas Coastal Plain where the most important regional environment is a geosynclinal margin. Also in the Rocky Mountain Province, the most important environment for Tertiary deposits is intrafoldbelt basins. In area being appraised, score highest for environment that is most important in geologically similar areas with important deposits.	20	20
7. Age of potential host rocks 0–20 Triassic, Jurassic, Tertiary Cretaceous Permian Pennsylvanian	20	20

TABLE 4.2 Continued

Sandstone-type deposits	Scores	
Criterion-scale	Control area	Area to be evaluated

    Other
    Order is from most favourable to least favourable;
    however, exceptions include Black Hills (Cretaceous),
    Anadarko Basin (Permian), etc. In area being
    appraised, score highest for host rock age that is
    most important in similar geological environments
    with important deposits.

8. Geophysical surveys		
A. Ground and air radiometric surveys 0–50	50	30
Score high for numerous strong anomalies; score low for no anomalies.		
B. Radiometric anomalies in oil and water wells 0–40	0	0
See 8A		
C. Random surveys 0–10	0	0
See 8A		
9. Geochemical surveys		
A. U in waters 0–30	0	0
See 8A		
B. U in potential host rocks 0–20	0	0
See 8A		
C. U in soils 0–10	0	0
See 8A		
Total score for geological, geophysical, and geochemical criteria	390	352
10. Character of mineralization		
A. Persistence of mineralization 0–30	30	25
High score for demonstrated significant lateral and/or vertical continuity; low score for uranium mineralization restricted to shallow depths or to small pod-like occurrences.		
B. Distribution patterns 0–25	25	20
Score high for known deposits in established or inferred trends or other predictable patterns; score low for no recognized trends.		
11. U deposits†		
A. Size (Reserves + production; enter appropriate Roman numeral in scoring column)		
large deposits, >5,000 tons U_3O_8 (I)	I	III
medium deposits, 1,000–5,000 tons U_3O_8 (II)		
occurrences & small deposits <1,000 tons U_3O_8 (III)		
mineral occurrences (IV)		
no mineral occurrences (V)		

† These criteria are not to be given numerical values; however, the relative size and the distribution of deposits in the area being appraised should be considered as a basis for adjusting the favourability factor derived by scoring geological, geochemical, and geophysical criteria in items 1 through 9.

Monument Hill–Box Creek area of the Southern Powder River basin of Wyoming [4].

1. Delineation of favorable ground (N)—The altered ground is the favorable ground, and is defined by the dashed line in Fig. 3 [4.4]. The portion of the line used, which is considered to represent approximately the farthest subsurface advance of the solution front, extends through the Monument Hill and Box Creek localities from the vicinity of its intersection with the two contacts of the Wasatch with pre-Wasatch (Fort Union) sedimentary rock on the west and south. The total length of solution front represented by this line is 67 miles of which segments aggregating 20 miles were used in the determination of the mineralization factor. Thus, N equals 47 linear miles of solution front.

2. Assignment of geologic favorability factor (F)—The Monument Hill–Box Creek area was assigned a favorability factor of 50 percent. Thus, the 47 miles of solution front being evaluated are considered to be 50 percent as favorable as the 20 miles of developed front used in the determination of the mineralization factor.

3. The unexplored portions (U) of the 47 linear miles of solution front being evaluated amounts to 40 percent. This is an approximation based on knowledge of uranium exploration activities in the area.

4. Mineralization factor (T)—A factor of 1,950 tons

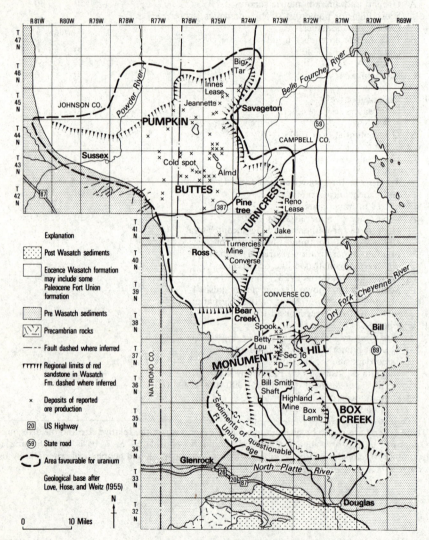

Fig. 4.4. Potential uranium resources in the Southern Powder River Basin, Wyoming. (Source: Hetland 1979.)

U_3O_8 per linear mile of roll front was determined by dividing the sum of production plus reserves (at $8 per pound U_3O_8) associated with a fully developed portion of the solution front by the length of that portion of the front.

Thus, by substituting these factors in the equation, potential is estimated to be 18,330 tons of U_3O_8: $Potential = N \times F \times U \times T = 47 \times 0.50 \times 0.40 \times 1,950 = 18,330$ tons U_3O_8.

The appraisal, as described thus far, has produced a quantity of U_3O_8. What does this quantity represent? Is it endowment, resources, or potential supply? Since the mineralization factor T is based upon the sum of cumulative production and reserves at a currently relevant forward cost, the estimate appears more like potential supply than an endowment or resources. However, the price that might elicit this supply is not clearly defined. This price cannot be the forward cost measure, because as defined by ERDA, even for undiscovered deposits, this cost neglects some costs, the most significant ones being the required return on invested capital and taxes.

For the purpose of examining more fully the ERDA methodology, let us set the price versus forward cost issue aside and take as a given that the objective is to describe the magnitude of potential supply for various levels of forward cost. In order to achieve this objective, some further analysis is necessary. First of all, the quantity of U_3O_8 estimated by the basic resource equation is relevant for the base forward cost only if conditions affecting costs of U_3O_8 production are equal in the control and study areas. To the extent that they are not equal, the quantity of U_3O_8 must be adjusted accordingly. This same adjustment must be reflected in resource estimates for all forward costs. The procedure followed by ERDA was to first estimate cut-off grades for each of several posited forward costs, using the following relationship

$$q' = \frac{\left(\begin{array}{c}\text{cost of mining, hauling,}\\ \text{royalty, and milling}\end{array}\right) \Big/ (\text{ton of ore})}{(\text{chosen cost/lb } U_3O_8) \times (\text{mill recovery}) \times (20)}$$

$$(4.4)$$

where q' is the cut-off grade. Consider, for example, the resource appraisal performed by ERDA on the East Chaco Canyon area of the San Juan Basin of New Mexico. Analogy of the East Chaco Canyon area to two segments of the Grant's mineral belt (see Fig. 4.5) provided an estimate of base potential of

52 000 tons of U_3O_8,

$$PR = N \cdot F \cdot U \cdot T$$
$$= (797) \cdot (0.3) \cdot (0.95) \cdot (230)$$
$$= 52\,243 \approx 52\,000.$$

The quantity, 52 000 s.t. U_3O_8, was considered to overstate the US $15-forward-cost potential for the East Chaco Canyon area because depths to these hypothetical deposits were expected to range from 3000 to 5000 feet, while the deposits in the control areas averaged about 1000 feet (US Department of Energy [5], p. H-12). The sum of costs of mining, hauling, and milling and royalty were estimated for the potential deposits of East Chaco Canyon. These costs, along with milling recovery, were used to compute cut-off grades for three forward costs [5, p. H-14].

q' (cut-off grade) (per cent U_3O_8)	Selected forward cost (US $/lb U_3O_8)
0.13	15
0.06	30
0.04	50

In order to complete the resource analysis, we need to estimate (1) the quantity of mineralized material and (2) average grades for each of these cut-off grades. Of course, since the estimated resources consist of inferred deposits, information on deposit sizes and grade distributions are not available. In totally virgin areas, the only thing that can be done to complete the economic analysis is to employ the mineral inventory of the control region on the assumption that if the study area is geologically similar, the grade distribution of the inferred deposits on average will be similar to the grade distribution of the mineral inventory.

Fig. 4.6 shows the relationship of average grade to cut-off grade and the cumulative distribution of ore by cut-off grade for Ambrosia Lake, New Mexico. These relations were used for the economic analysis of potential resources of East Chaco Canyon. The first step in the analysis is the computation of the total inventory, i.e. the total tonnage of U_3O_8 in the deposit. Suppose that for the reference case we have the 52 000 tons of U_3O_8 (the base potential computed by geological analogy), given a cut-off grade of 0.09 per cent U_3O_8. Entering Fig. 4.6 with a 0.09 per cent cut-off grade, we find from the inventory curve that 48 per cent of the inventory of the Ambrosia Lake district occurs in material having grades

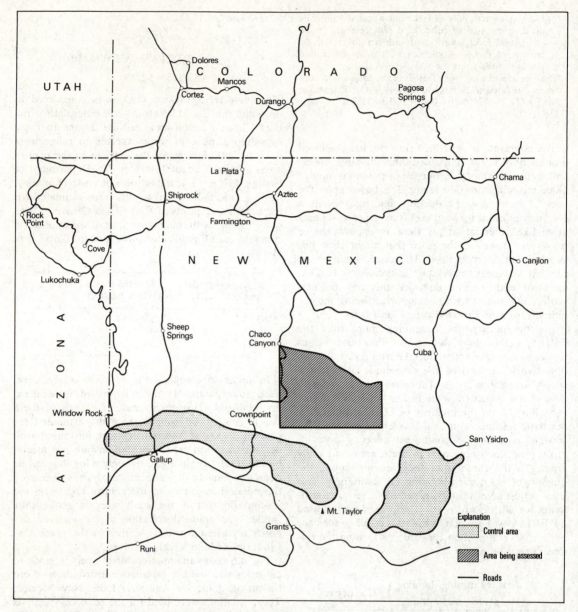

Fig. 4.5. Example of uranium potential resource estimations, East Chaco Canyon, San Juan Basin, New Mexico. (After US Department of Energy [5], p. H–11.)

above this cut-off; therefore, the total tonnage of uranium in East Chaco Canyon is estimated to be 108 000 tons of U_3O_8: $52\,000 \div 0.48 \approx 108\,000$. By projecting the cut-off grade of 0.09 per cent on to the average grade curve, we estimate the average grade of ore for the material having grades above the cut-off grade of 0.09 per cent U_3O_8 to be 0.18 per cent U_3O_8. Consequently, the amount of ore with grades above the cut-off grade of 0.09 per cent is approximately 29 000 000 tons: $29\,000\,000 \approx$

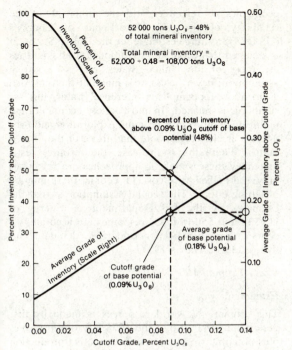

Fig. 4.6. Distribution of uranium inventory by grade, Ambrosia Lake, New Mexico. (Source: US Department of Energy [5], p. H–15.)

$52\,000 \div 0.0018$. Similar analyses were carried out for three forward costs (US Department of Energy [5], p. H-14).

Forward cost (US $/lb U_3O_8)	Tons of ore	Average grade (per cent U_3O_8)	Tons of U_3O_8 (rounded)
15	16 000 000	0.24	38 000
30	48 000 000	0.14	67 000
50	81 000 000	0.10	81 000

The final step in the economic analysis by ERDA is the estimation of the capital (physical plant) requirements necessary to develop and exploit the resources. If the sum of these expenditures on capital per lb U_3O_8 and the estimated operating costs is less than the specified forward cost, then these quantities of U_3O_8 were considered as potential resources.

Criticisms of the method of analogy.

The first point to be emphasized is that analogy methods generally estimate unknown *economic* re-

sources of *known* modes of occurrence. Of course, these estimates are valuable, because they are credible and refer to the metal that could be forthcoming under current economics and technologies of exploration and exploitation. However, they are deficient for the longer time frame, for economics and technology (technology includes our level of science) change, creating resources not accounted for by traditional methods of analogy.

Obviously, there are limitations to the 'experienced judgement' method—basically limitations on data and on the level of the science of ore genesis. The criticisms by the National Academy of Sciences (1975, p. 136) reflect these limitations.

> The 'experienced judgment' method cannot reasonably take into account the potential of regions of unknown geology, such as parts of Antarctica or the sand and laterite covered regions of Central Australia.
>
> . . . .
>
> The 'experienced judgment' method cannot account for completely unconventional resources, such as manganese nodules, for which we lack experience. What the experienced judgment estimate suggests, therefore, is that a very significant fraction of the world's recoverable copper resources will be found in deposits of the kind with which we are already familiar. [Reproduced with permission from *Mineral resources and the environment*, National Academy Press, Washington, DC, 1975.]

Of course, every method of appraisal faces limitations of data and theory, so the 'experienced judgement' method, or the method of analogies in general, is not unique in this regard. However, it is useful to stress, as did the National Academy of Sciences, the fact that we find what we are trained to look for, so that the occurrence of metal resources in one or more modes that are different from the familiar or conventional modes may be totally overlooked because of our bounded intelligence. Furthermore, there is much that we do not understand about the occurrence of deposits in familiar modes. Guild (1971, p. 70) states this fact well.

> The uneven distribution of ores in the crust is well known; the reasons for it are not. Among the fundamental problems are: Do the concentrations in certain areas (as, for example, of copper in the southwestern United States) result from original inhomogeneities or because favorable conditions for ore genesis prevailed? Were the metals derived directly from the mantle or have multistage processes reworked the crustal material to form ores? To what extent do magmas constitute the immediate sources of metals: Why are some ores (for example, nickel sulfides, stratiform chromite, and titanium in anorthosite) largely restricted to older Precambrian rocks, whereas others (such as porphyry copper and molybdenum, antimony, and mercury) are, with few exceptions, of Mesozoic or Tertiary Age? Answers to

these and other questions are not immediately forthcoming, of course, but documentation of the facts may help to provide them.

Guild (1971) also describes the new evidences for the association of plate tectonics with metallogeny and suggests that geologic analogy, including plate tectonics, should be used on a broad basis to identify new metal provinces.

4.5. World uranium resource estimates

4.5.1. *Perspective*

During the mid- and late-1970s, there was great concern about the adequacy of world uranium resources to meet projected requirements. Cumulative commitments [6] as high as 6 708 000 (Jacoby [7]) and 21 000 000 (Duret, Phillips, Veeder, Wolfe, and Williams [8]) s.t. of U_3O_8 had been projected for years 2000 and 2020, respectively. These projected commitments were being compared to US $30 reasonably assured resources of 2 500 000 s.t. of U_3O_8 and estimated additional resources of 2 100 000 s.t. U_3O_8 (Wright 1977). The large numerical differences between resource estimates and projected commitments were interpreted by some as a harbinger of future shortages and a reason for questioning the contribution that nuclear power could make to future energy requirements: specifically, some advocated that the indicated scarcity of uranium resources dictated a de-emphasis on nuclear power.

At the height of the concern about uranium resource adequacy, this author was requested to provide estimates of world uranium resources to a Nonproliferation Alternative Systems Assessment Program/International Nuclear Fuel Cycle Evaluation (NASAP/INFCE) conference on nuclear power (Harris [9]). The following section is a reproduction, with some minor modifications, of part of a paper (pp. 25–38) presented at that conference and describes estimates of world potential supply of U_3O_8 for US $30 and $50/lb by three different methods.

(1) expansion of reserves to potential supply, using the US ratio for the world;
(2) simple analogy, using a mineral density of a control area;
(3) integrative approach: normalizing for exploration, followed by reserve expansion and adjustment for economic and geological factors.

The making of these estimates by the three methods listed above requires two assumptions, one about the economics of resources and the other about the reliability of the US Department of Energy's (US DOE) resource estimate for the United States. It is assumed that economic conditions for all countries are those of the United States. This is a strong assumption; nevertheless, it is made at the outset so as to allow for simplistic inference. Later, this assumption is relaxed. In most cases, economic and political conditions for uranium exploration and production are less favourable than those of the United States. Where this is the case, the resources estimated by these simplistic approaches are resources only at a higher price/cost. Of course, there may be offsetting effects. The second assumption is that the estimates by the US Department of Energy of US $30 and $50/lb U_3O_8 resources are accurate. Of course, there has been considerable debate about this issue (see Harris 1977).

4.5.2. *Estimation*

Estimate 1

This estimate of world resources is made by first determining the ratio of the 1978 US total (reserves plus potential) resources plus cumulative production (initial resources) to the 1975 reasonable reserves reported by the Organization for Economic Cooperation and Development/International Atomic Energy Agency (OECD/IAEA) (1975). The assumption is made that this ratio is an expectation for other regions. The decision to employ the 1975 data was made because the more recently provided data by Wright (1977) updated to 1977 the reasonably assured reserves and estimated additional resources for the United States and Canada, but not for the rest of

TABLE 4.3. *World† uranium reserves (US $15/lb U_3O_8). (Source: OECD/IAEA 1975.)*

Region	Quantity (1000 s.t. U_3O_8)
United States	416
Canada‡, Australia, Western Europe	582.7
Rest of world§	406
Total	1404.7

† Exclusive of Communist countries.
‡ Canada's reserves are computed with reference to price, while US reserves are computed with reference to forward cost. IAEA employs an approximation to full costs, except that exploration costs are not included.
§ Restricted to Algeria, Argentina, Brazil, Central African Republic, Gabon, India, Japan, Korea, Mexico, Niger, South Africa, Southwest Africa, and Zaire.

the world. It was deemed desirable to have as consistent a set of data as possible. Similarly, the 1975 estimated additional resources were not used because the effort to make estimates of this class of resources was highly varied among countries, some not estimating it at all for US $30/lb U_3O_8. For this reason, only US $15/lb (1975) U_3O_8 reasonably assured reserves were employed, as summarized in Table 4.3. Two ratios were formed, one for each forward cost level.

$$r_1 = \frac{\left(\begin{array}{c} \text{Total US \$30/lb } U_3O_8 \text{ (\$1978)} \\ \text{resources} + \text{cumulative production} \end{array}\right)}{\left(\begin{array}{c} \text{US \$15/lb } U_3O_8 \text{ (\$1975)} \\ \text{reasonably assured reserves} \end{array}\right)},$$

$$r_2 = \frac{\left(\begin{array}{c} \text{Total US \$50/lb } U_3O_8 \text{ (\$1978)} \\ \text{resources} + \text{cumulative production} \end{array}\right)}{\left(\begin{array}{c} \text{US \$15/lb } U_3O_8 \text{ (\$1975)} \\ \text{reasonably assured reserves} \end{array}\right)}.$$

US cumulative production through 1975 is 282 400 short tons (s.t.) U_3O_8. Combining this quantity with the US $15 resources, we have 628 400 s.t. of U_3O_8 as the initial known US $15 resource.

Table 4.4 shows the US $30 and $50 reserves and potential as of 1 January 1978. The sum of US $50 reserves and potential is 4 365 000 s.t. of U_3O_8. Adding to this quantity the cumulative US production (313 100 s.t. of U_3O_8) to 1 January 1978, we have 4 678 100 s.t. U_3O_8 as the *initial* US $50 resource. A similar combining of numbers gives 3 568 100 s.t. of U_3O_8 as the *initial* US $30 resource of U_3O_8, based upon a 1978 dollar.

The ratio of 1978 US $30 total *initial* resources to 1975 US $15 reserves is 8.58, and for US $50, the ratio is 11.25 ($r_1 = 8.58$ and $r_2 = 11.25$). The numbers in Table 4.5 have been derived by applying these ratios (8.58 and 11.25) to the 1975 US $15 reserves (Table 4.3). Subtracting world cumulative production from the calculated values, we have estimates of 11 400 000 s.t. and 15 200 000 s.t. of U_3O_8 as the world's US $30 and $50/lb U_3O_8 resources, respectively (see Table 4.5).

This approach does *not* assume that all regions are equally endowed in uranium, only that the relationship of high-cost resources to low-cost resources is the same for all regions as it is for the United States. Other assumptions made in this approach are that (1) exploration has advanced to the same level in all producing countries as it has in the United States, and (2) countries that had no US $15/lb U_3O_8 (1975) reserves in 1975 have no resources at all, not even at higher costs. By virtue of these assumptions, this method of inference appears to considerably underestimate world resources. To assume that all producing countries are equally well explored certainly is contrary to fact. In some countries of South Africa and South America exploration has just begun. Note, for example, the small amount of exploration and developmental drilling in countries other than the United States, Canada, and Australia: in 1974 US drilling amounted to 6.7×10^6 m, which is 93 per cent of total world drilling (7.2×10^6 m). Even in Australia, where over the past few years very large resources have been identified, the country is only partially explored as compared to the United States. The second assumption is even stronger and a greater distortion of reality than the first. Uranium is ubiquitous; uranium deposits are formed in a wide range of geological environments. Given this fact, it

TABLE 4.4. *Comparison of US uranium resources (1 January 1977 to 1 January 1978)*

| US $/lb U_3O_8 Cost category | Reserve | | Potential | | | | | |
| | | | Probable | | Possible | | Speculative | |
	1/1/77	1/1/78	1/1/77	1/1/78	1/1/77	1/1/78	1/1/77	1/1/78
US $15	410	370	585	540	490	490	190	165
US $15–$30 Increment	270	320	505	475	630	645	290	250
US $30	680	690	1090	1015	1120	1135	480	415
US $30–$50 Increment	160	200	280	380	300	380	60	150
$ 50	840	890	1370	1395	1420	1515	540	565

Source: Hetland, D. L., Chief of Potential Resources Branch, Resources Division, US Department of Energy, Grand Junction Office, Grand Junction, Colorado. Materials presented at a seminar on the NURE programme, 10 May 1978.

TABLE 4.5. *World resources of U_3O_8—Estimate 1 (expansion using US resources and potential)*

Region	Initial[†] resources (1000 s.t. U_3O_8)	
	US \$30[‡]/lb U_3O_8	US \$50[‡]/lb U_3O_8[§]
United States	3569.3	4678.1
Canada, Australia,		
Western Europe	4999.6	6555.4
Rest of world[§§]	3483.5	4567.5
Total	12 052.4	15 801.0
Cumulative production	650.3[*]	650.3[*]
Remaining resources	11 402.1	15 150.7

† Cumulative production plus remaining resources.
‡ 1978 US dollar.
§ Estimates made by dividing 1975 \$15 reserves by the ratio of US 1975 \$15 reserves + 1975 cumulative production to US 1978 \$50 reserves and potential plus cumulative production.
§§ Restricted to countries having reserves or estimated additional resources, see footnote 3 of Table 4.3.
* Personal communication, July, 1978, John Patterson, US Department of Energy, Washington, DC.

simply is extremely unlikely that the large crustal blocks of the Earth which now have no reported reserves and resources, such as in South America, are actually barren of uranium deposits. *The current geographic distribution of reported uranium reserves and resources in the more industrial countries and the lack of such in the lesser developed countries (LDC) represents more the historical development of markets for uranium in these countries and their politically favourable conditions for exploration and investment than the geographical distribution of uranium endowment.*

What about the initial assumption that the relationship of high-cost resources to low-cost resources is the same for all countries as it is for the United States? The effect of this assumption is difficult to evaluate. This appears to be a strong assumption in the sense that some 94.4 percent (Chenoweth [10] of US 1978 cumulative production derived from sandstone deposits, while for the world, this percentage is smaller. Similarly, most US reserves are in sandstone deposits, while only approximately 35 per cent of the world's 1975 reasonably assured reserves are in sandstone deposits. There is no reason *a priori* for the US ratio to apply to other countries in which uranium occurs more in non-sandstone environments, e.g. the Rossing deposit of South-west Africa in granite or the Ranger and Jabiluka deposits of

Australia which occur in metamorphic host rocks beneath an unconformity. However, it is impossible to say whether making such an assumption overstates or understates the resources that are so estimated. At present, we do not know enough about the quality distribution of non-sandstone resources to evaluate even the direction of bias which may result from employing this assumption, let alone the magnitude of the bias.

Estimate 2

This approach employs the concept of mineral density, which has a tradition established by French scholars (Blondel and Ventura 1954, 1956; Blondel, Ventura, and Callot 1961) in the 1950s and more recently by Griffiths (1969, 1978) in his unit regional value measure. Basically, the French considered the value of mineral production per unit area of developed regions an expectation for undeveloped regions. The approach employed here is similar. The proposition is as follows:

> For regions large enough to have a wide variety of geologic environments, it is reasonable to assume that they have an equal amount of uranium per unit of area or volume.

While it is easy to cite examples of a local area which possesses primarily one environment and which, at this time at least, does not appear favourable to the occurrence of uranium deposits, if we deal only with very large regions, this proposition has considerable strength. It is further strengthened by the fact that the more we know about uranium occurrence, the longer grows the list of favourable geological environments. It should be noted, however, that even if the amount of uranium were constant, the economic value of this endowment may vary, for deposits of one region may be fewer but of higher grade or larger size than those of another region. Additionally, as discussed under the previous section, economic conditions may be more or less favourable. Thus, while the uranium endowments of large regions may be similar, their resources can vary considerably because of economic conditions of the region and the deposit characteristics.

Application of geographical analogy presents yet another problem: the representativeness of the region used for the analogy. In this book, the United States is used. As a region to be used for a basis of geographic analogy for resource estimation, it is not particularly large. Therefore, the question of its representativeness arises. Is it more or less endowed than the average region of a similar size? By virtue of the dominance of sandstone deposits, it does not appear to be a representative sample in terms of variety in uranium environments. Even so, such nonrepresentativeness of geological environment does not make the case for it being anomalously endowed with uranium deposits. At present, it is Australia that promises to be the 'Saudi Arabia' of uranium producers. It could very well be that as exploration progresses in other regions, the United States will be shown to be average in terms of its uranium endowment and resources.

Estimate 2 is made by employing the assumption that the United States is a reasonable standard for inference. Thus, the sum of cumulative production and total estimated resources is divided by the land area of the United States. This density measure is then multiplied by the land areas of the other regions, yielding the quantities of Table 4.6. As expected, these quantities are much larger than those obtained by Estimate 1: 20 900 000 and 27 700 000 s.t. of U_3O_8 at US $30 and $50/lb U_3O_8, respectively, compared to 11 400 000 and 15 200 000 s.t. of U_3O_8. Part of this increase is due to the use of the US uranium density, but part is due to the fact that all non-Communist regions were included, as contrasted to Estimate 1 which included only those regions with known US $15/lb U_3O_8 (US $1975) reasonably assured reserves. Of course, the caveat offered in the previous section for Estimate 1 to the effect that economic, political, terrain, and climatic conditions may combine to give these inferred resources a higher cost than those used in inference also applies here. More will be said about this later.

Estimate 3

This approach combines exploration, geographic analogy, and crude economic adjustment to estimate world resources. The first step is to determine a base resource; then this base is subsequently adjusted. The base is determined by employing the proposition that it is incorrect to expand US $15 ($1975) to $50 ($1978) total resources without first adjusting for the different intensities of exploration among the regions. Therefore, the base quantity of US $15 (1975)

TABLE 4.6. *World resources of U_3O_8—Estimate 2 (by geographic analogy)*

Region	Area (mi^2)	Initial† resources (1000 s.t. U_3O_8)	
		US $30§/lb U_3O_8	US $50§/lb U_3O_8
United States	3 615 122	3569.3	4678.1
Canada, Australia, Western Europe	8 609 766	8497.8	11 141.0
Rest of world‡	9 651 700	9526.2	12 489.3
Total	21 876 588	21 593.3	28 308.4
Cumulative production		650.3	650.3
Remaining resources		20 943.0	27 658.1

† Cumulative production plus remaining resources.
‡ Excludes Communist countries, but includes countries with and without known reserves or additional resources.
§ 1978 US dollar.

reserves for each region is determined by normalizing on the intensity of exploration in the United States. In order to really compute the base resource in this fashion, we need the cumulative amount of exploration for each region. This information is not available. Therefore, the assumption is made that the exploration effort by region in 1977 is proportionate to the cumulative effort by region. Unfortunately, 1977 exploration data by region are not available either, but Duval (1977, pp. 116 and 122) has provided estimates.

> The additional information to which we have access is only fragmentary, and mostly unofficial, but I do not think a figure of $400 million or perhaps $420 million/year would differ much from the true one . . . the geographical distribution of the +$400 million is approximately as follows: US—50%; Canada, Australia, Western Europe—30%; rest of the world—20%.

These percentages appear in column 2 of Table 4.7. Columns 3, 4, and 5 show the normalization of exploration per square mile to the US level. Column 6 shows the US $15 ($1975) reserves, and column 7 shows the base US $15 ($1975) reserve when all regions are assumed to be as thoroughly explored as is the United States. For the moment, consider relative favourability to be 1.0 for all regions. Then, columns 10 and 11 show the US $30 ($1978) and $50 ($1978) resources by region. The world US $30 and $50 base resources are 83 628 000 and 109 652 000 s.t. U_3O_8, respectively.

These large numbers result from some very strong assumptions about endowment, exploration, economics, and politics. Realities with regard to some of these factors require considerable adjustments. A hint of the magnitude of some of these adjustments is given by Hansen (1976, pp. 23 and 25):

> It has been established that 15% of the land surface of

the earth has been explored for uranium. It might be safe to guess that an additional 20% is probably geologically uninteresting at present, about 10% would present serious logistical problems with presently known surface exploration and mining methods, perhaps 15% more is urban or agricultural land which would present special problems in exploration and mining, and perhaps 15% is politically uninteresting. The remaining 25% is probably geologically interesting, politically and environmentally available, and logistically accessible. The remainder, including the areas already explored, may eventually be the target of further exploration effort and new discoveries.

Let us take Hansen's 25 per cent of the land surface as a reasonable identification of that part which may contribute to uranium supply in the future. However, since our world is exclusive of the Communist countries, we have already excluded most of the politically uninteresting regions. Therefore, let us propose that 30 per cent of the remaining non Communist world is the potential supply region. Multiplication of this factor by the base resource gives 25 000 000 s.t. and 33 000 000 s.t. as our estimates of US $30 ($1978) and $50 ($1978) world resources of U_3O_8.

Nothing has been said about differentials among the regions. These differentials could result from more or less geological endowment or more or less severe economics of exploration and production. There simply is not at present enough information on each of these factors to make individual adjustments. Everything considered collectively, it seems reasonable to consider the combined region of Canada, Australia, and Western Europe to be similar in overall favourability to the United States, the standard of reference. True, Western Europe may be geologically less well endowed and less receptive to exploration and production, but balancing this is the extremely rich endowment of Australia.

The rest of the world is a mixed bag, and a bit worrisome with respect to potential uranium supply.

TABLE 4.7. *World resources of U_3O_8—Estimate 3 worksheet*

Region	E Exploration (per cent of total)	A Area ($\times 10^6$ mi²)	E/A ($\times 10^{-6}$)	X (Normalized E/A)	R US $15 reserves (1975)	R/X	F Relative favourability	$y = \dfrac{R \cdot F}{X}$	US $30/lb U_3O_8 (y) (8.58)	$50/lb U_3O_8 (y) (11.25)
United States	50	3.6	13.9	1.0	416.0	416.0	1.0	416.0	3569.3	4680.0
Canada, Australia, Western Europe	30	8.6	3.5	0.25	582.7	2330.8	1.0	2330.8	19 998.3	26 221.5
Rest of World	20	25.0	0.8	0.058	406.0	7000.0	1.0	7000.0	60 060.0	78 750.0
							0.5	3500.0	30 030.0	39 375.0
							0.2	1400.0	12 012.0	15 750.0

While it may be reasonable to expect this very large region to have a uranium *endowment* per square mile similar to that of the United States, it may not be reasonable to ascribe to it the same density of resources or potential supply for a specified economic reference. Dahlkamp (1977, pp. 131–2) provides some insights.

> In contrast, those countries where there has been very little or no exploration effort in the past still offer excellent opportunities for the discovery of outcropping deposits. However, most such countries are located in latitudes where geographical obstacles make exploration difficult. Primitive infrastructures hamper vital logistic operations and, added to this, the thick surficial covers of certain climatic zones restrict the applicability of standard techniques. Such zones are found in: (a) the tropics, where lateritic soils up to 100 m in thickness support dense vegetation; (b) the arctic and subarctic, where glacial deposits have built up to a thickness of 100 m or more and the field season is not more than 3–4 months, therefore limiting the productivity of the work; and (c) the moderate latitudes, in which soil formations and detrital scree of up to several meter thickness are encountered.

Some of these factors may have been accounted for in Hansen's reduction of the earth's surface to 25 per cent. It is difficult to know what additional adjustment is necessary for adverse climates, terrain, and infrastructure conditions. Basically, this inference assumes that all of the 30 per cent of the earth's crust deemed as favourable is comparable to the United States, not in endowment but in its receptiveness and amenability (economically and physically) to uranium exploration. To the extent that this assumption is too strong, the estimates of 25 and 33 million s.t. U_3O_8 should be diminished.

An important adjustment still remains. While the spirit of accounting for the inequality of exploration before expanding reserves to resources is appropriate, the method of accounting, normalizing on US exploration, basically assumes that returns to a unit of exploration activity are constant during the history of reserve development. The decline in the US of the quantity of uranium found per foot of drilling suggests that returns have not been constant. There is a problem here of overinterpretation, however, because drilling footages used in this computation have included both exploration and development drilling. Even so, normalizing on US exploration undoubtedly overstates the base resource of other regions. So, we are caught between two opposing facts and effects: failure to account for inequality of exploration in the ratioing of reserves to resources understates resources, but normalizing on US exploration for those

TABLE 4.8. *World resources of U_3O_8—Estimate 3 (using world exploration and US reserves-to-potential relationship)*

Favourability factor for rest of world†	Initial resources (1000 s.t. U_3O_8)	
	US $30/lb U_3O_8‡	US $50/lb U_3O_8‡
0.2	11 000	14 000
0.5	16 000	21 000
1.0	25 000	33 000

† Excludes Communist countries, but includes all countries except United States, Canada, Australia, Western Europe, and Yugoslavia. A favourability factor of 1.0 was used for United States, Canada, Australia, and Western Europe. See Table 4.7 for details.
‡ 1978 US dollar.

regions which are relatively little explored tends to overstate the resources of those regions. There is little point in attempting to refine an adjustment because of the crudeness of the estimates used for exploration effort. Somewhat arbitrarily, an adjustment of 0.5 is selected to account for the sum effect of this adjustment bias and the unresolved differentials for the rest of the world. Making this adjustment for the rest of the world results in estimates of approximately 15 and 20×10^6 s.t. as the world's total US $30 and $50 potential supply of U_3O_8.

Table 4.8 shows three estimates of resources for the US $30 and $50/lb U_3O_8 cost levels, one estimate for each of three levels of favourability of the rest of the world. A favourability of 1.0 means that no additional adjustment is necessary.

4.5.3. *Summary of total resource estimate*

Table 4.9 presents all of the estimates for comparison. Not surprisingly, we have quite a range of estimates. At our current level of information, it is impossible to know what number to use. Even so, it

TABLE 4.9. *Estimates of world uranium resources (1000 s.t. U_3O_8)*

	Estimate				
	1	2	3†		
Favourability of rest of world	—	—	(1.0)	(0.5)	(0.2)
US $30/lb U_3O_8 ($1978)	11 000	21 000	24 000	15 000	10 000
US $50/lb U_3O_8 ($1978)	15 000	28 000	32 000	20 000	13 000

† These are rounded, after subtracting cumulative production.

is the author's opinion (nothing more) that 11 000 000 and 15 000 000 s.t. U_3O_8 are, because of the assumptions of the method by which they were derived, too low. Similarly, because of the assumption of equal density made in obtaining Estimate 2, the 21 000 000 and the 28 000 000 s.t. of U_3O_8 are probably too high. Therefore, as a very gross estimate, 15 000 000 s.t. and 20 000 000 s.t. of U_3O_8 are selected as reasonable estimates for world US $30 and $50/lb U_3O_8 resources.

4.5.4. An international assessment by experts

Shortly after making the foregoing simplistic estimates of world resources and potential supply, the author learned of a joint effort by the Nuclear Energy Agency (NEA) of OECD with the International Atomic Energy Agency (IAEA) to make an international evaluation of world uranium potential. Since these estimates and those of the author, as described in the foregoing sections, were made independently, they afford an opportunity to compare subjective and disaggregated geological estimates with those made by cruder methods of inference without the benefit of geological evaluation by region. For this reason these estimates are briefly described in § 4.5.4.

The objective of the NEA/IAEA effort was to estimate what it referred to as speculative uranium resources recoverable at a cost of US $130/kg U (approximately US $50/lb U_3O_8—$1977). Speculative resources were defined as resources not included in Reasonably Assured Resources [11, 13] (RAR) or Estimated Additional Resources (EAR) [12, 13]. In preparation for this assessment, members of the NEA/IAEA steering group and consultants engaged by NEA and IAEA compiled data on the following items for each of 185 countries [13].

> General geography—including the area, population, climate, terrain, communications, means of access to different areas and, when available, a brief summary of the laws which would be pertinent to an exploration program.
> Geology in relation to potentially favorable uranium-bearing areas.
> Past exploration.
> Uranium occurrences, resources, and past production.
> Present status of exploration.
> Potential for new discoveries.

On the basis of information on these items, the NEA/IAEA steering group, by consensus, placed each country into one of six categories of potential for speculative resources: low, moderate, moderate-to-high, high, high-to-very high, and very high. Furthermore, based upon known resource regions, a

TABLE 4.10. *Speculative resources listed by continent.* (*Source:* [13], p.vi.)

Continent	Number of countries	Speculative resources (million tonnes of U)
Africa	51	1.2–4.0
America, North	3	2.1–3.6
America, South and Central	41	0.7–1.9
Asia and Far East†	41	0.2–1.0
Australia and Oceania	18	2.0–3.0
Western Europe	22	0.3–1.3
Subtotal	176	6.5–14.8
Eastern Europe USSR, Peoples Republic of China	9 —	3.3–7.3‡ —
Total	185	9.8–22.1

† Excluding Peoples Republic of China and the eastern part of USSR.
‡ The potential shown here is 'Estimated total potential plus production'.

range of tonnages of uranium was identified for each of these categories, thereby allowing the group to ascribe a range of speculative resources to each of the 185 countries. Speculative resources for aggregates of the 185 countries were obtained by summing the end-points of the ranges. Table 4.10 reports speculative resources by continent, as estimated by the NEA/IAEA steering group.

Given these estimates for speculative resources, an estimate of world potential supply can be obtained by computing the sum of RAR, EAR, and speculative resources. RAR and EAR were estimated (OECD/IAEA 1977) in 1977 to be 2 190 000 and 2 100 000 tonnes of U, respectively. Thus, potential supply of uranium for the non-Communist countries of the world at a cost of US $130/kg U is estimated to be within the range of 10.79 and 19.09 million tonnes [14]. Converting these quantities to short tons of U_3O_8, gives a range (rounded) of $14-25 \times 10^6$ s.t. of U_3O_8 at a cost of US $50/lb U_3O_8.

4.5.5. Some criticisms and speculations [15]

As estimates of world potential supply, the numbers resulting from simplistic inferences must be accorded proper qualifications. By virtue of the neglect of countries with no reported reserves, the estimate of potential supply by reserve expansion only seems predisposed to be an obviously conservatively biased estimate and should be rejected. This might indeed be the case, but it must be remembered that two very important assumptions were made in order to use the simplistic approach: the estimate of US $50 potential supply by US DOE is accurate and the ratio of US $50 potential supply to US $15 reserve for the US applies to other countries. To the extent that these assumptions are violated and the two measures are too large, the neglect of regions having no US $15 reserves is offset to some degree and the estimate of 15 000 000 tons by this approach becomes a more possible state of nature. Even if the estimate by US DOE of US $50 potential supply were an unbiased estimate, the probability distribution for US potential supply must be very broad, implying a significant probability for quantities smaller than 4 365 000 tons of U_3O_8. Thus, it must follow that there is a significant probability for US $50 world potential supply being less than 15 000 000 tons of U_3O_8. At this time, there is no way of knowing how this uncertainty is to be traded off against the potential of the neglected unexplored regions. Similarly, since we have only one observation of the ratio of US $50 potential supply to US $15 reserves, that for the United States, we must acknowledge that there is a probability for this ratio in other countries being less than or greater than this measure, but at present we are ignorant of the statistical properties of this measure and can say very little about the probability for specific ratios. Thus, the quantity of 50 000 000 tons of U_3O_8 should not be interpreted as an absolute lower bound.

Similarly, it can be argued that to the extent that the estimate of US $50 potential supply for the US is too low because of the resource area neglected in the NURE programme, the estimate of world potential supply by the density approach may be too low. Contributing to this possibility is the possibility that the uranium density of the United States is a conservatively biased estimate of world density. But, even if the US density measure is unbiased, to the extent that there is a probability for US $50 potential supply for the US being greater than the 4 365 000 tons of U_3O_8, there is a probability, *ceteris paribus*, for the world potential supply of U_3O_8 exceeding the 28 000 000 tons, as estimated by this approach. Therefore, the nature of the simplistic analysis dictates that while the two numbers (15 000 000 and 28 000 000) constitute a range, it is a range very loosely defined and of largely unknown statistical properties.

The fact that the independent study by NEA/IAEA produced a similar range (14×10^6–25×10^6) seems to lend weight to the usefulness of potential supply estimates in the general range of 14 to 28×10^6 tons of U_3O_8. But, it must remain true that little is known about the statistical properties of this range.

The inability to construct a firm and certain analytical basis for the estimation of potential supply from undiscovered deposits very likely elicits the response of 'so what', 'what has been accomplished?' 'what does it really mean?' These are proper responses. The reply must be that it does not mean very much with regard to current and near-future supply issues, and, for sure, it must qualify as a highly speculative adventure in resource analysis. Actually, the chief useful purpose that it serves is to suggest that we should not be overly intimidated by the projections of future requirements for uranium. For one thing, such projections of requirements are themselves speculative and may not be realized as the world economies balance growth and life styles against all social costs of energy production and consumption— witness the recent projections for the United States (Clark and Reynolds 1978). Furthermore, viewing projected requirements against currently known reserves is clearly 'stacking the deck' for an exaggerated view of resource inadequacy.

While there may be a number of valid reasons for discounting the role of nuclear power in supplying future energy requirements, the lack of resources does not seem to be one of them. The persuasion is strong that there are sufficient uranium resources to satisfy projected world requirements well into the twenty-first century with once through nuclear technologies to the extent that the general economics and politics of nuclear power warrant the nuclear option. This statement may seem strong given the admitted qualifications about world potential supply. But, perhaps it is not, given proper appreciation of the strengths as well as weaknesses of the potential supply analysis.

The strength of the analysis lies in the fact that we are dealing with large blocks of continental crust and with the world in general. The geological ubiquity of uranium gives promise for its widespread geographic distribution and its presence in many relatively unexplored regions. This provides strength to the use of simplistic inference, for local areas that have low endowments are balanced by rich areas. The major weakness in the analysis is in describing how much of the implied endowments might be discoverable and producible at various costs (prices). Economic, political, and infrastructure conditions are imposed by man and are difficult to assess and predict. Some of this potential supply will be produced at costs considerably less than US $50, but it is easily possible that some of it, from the economically harsh and politically difficult regions, may qualify for potential supply only at higher costs, perhaps as high as US $75 to $100/lb U_3O_8.

The presence of such weakness does detract from the credibility of the potential supply estimates, as such. However, it is important to distinguish between a limited potential supply deriving from an implied small endowment of uranium deposits having high or intermediate grades, and a limited potential supply for a stated cost (price). The former state, which has been suggested by advocates of limited uranium resources, holds little promise except pending exhaustion and substitution of other energy sources. The latter may imply a large endowment and a supply potential which, while limited at current prices and costs, is responsive to economic incentives and favourable mineral policy. When considering world potential supply this distinction is very important, because currently adverse conditions in some of the resource regions may be modified by future political–economic developments within those regions, thereby increasing potential supply beyond currently perceived levels for a given economic reference. This distinction is particularly important in view of the small part that uranium plays in the total cost of nuclear power. For very long-term policy assessment and planning, it is more important to have a proper perspective of the abundance of uranium resources even if the cost analysis is very loose, than to have a highly credible cost analysis on only a small part of the resources, hence an exaggeration of resource limitations.

4.6. Composite deterministic models

Composite models, in contrast with the aggregate perspective of the economic models, can be viewed as 'build-up' types of models, models in which the component elements of the phenomena of metal resources are modeled separately, but combined for analysis. The obvious motivation of this approach to modelling is twofold.

1. Decomposition encourages greater care and, hopefully, accuracy in stating limitations, or the lack thereof, of the physical system.
2. It provides a basis for behavioural modelling of economic activities, which allows the analysis of extraordinary economic conditions, conditions for which the historical record provides no experience. Such capability makes possible contingency-types of analyses which are useful in policy evaluation.

As a means of expressing aggregate economic rela-tions, such as supply or potential supply, composite models can be no better than the linkages between their components. In this regard, there may be a price to be paid for the greater flexibility of the 'build-up' type of model.

Estimation of metal resources via composite models is accomplished by integrating two major models: metal endowment and economics. Each of these may be further decomposed, depending upon the objective of the resource analysis.

Metal endowment: number of deposits, tonnage per deposit, grade given tonnage, depth of cover, thickness, type of mineralogy, mode of occurrence, etc.

Economics: exploration, development, mining, infrastructure, risk, market constraints, etc.

An appraisal of metal resources requires the interaction of both of these major models. As indicated in the conceptual framework on resources, metal endowment is not equivalent to resources [16]. Metal endowment m is purely a physical concept by definition, although it has economic implications. No statement is made explicitly as to technology, prices, or costs. When referring to a specific region, the ith region, instead of the entire crust, the symbol m_i is employed [17].

Given the specification of the minimum levels of deposit characteristics, every area has a fixed metal endowment, an endowment that is immutable with time or economic pursuits of man. Although a unique endowment exists, it may be relatively unknown to man, depending upon the degree to which the earth has been tested by exploration drilling. Only when sampling has been done at a density guaranteed to detect the metal occurrences that comprise metal endowment can knowledge of a specific endowment become perfect. In practice, only three of the many characteristics of deposits, other than mode of occurrence, are generally used to define metal endowment: tonnage, grade, and depth of burial. Sometimes only tonnage and grade will be used.

In practice, it seems to be useful to model endowment and economics separately and then to interact them through computer simulation to provide the appraisal of resources under specified economic conditions. Resource adequacy appraisals made by geological methods do not yield forecasts of the time profile of Q_i^S (production), as do the aggregate econometric [18] models of Chapter 2. Rather, they estimate a stock of metal as a subset of endowment;

this has *not* been created by the cumulation of projected annual flows of supply Q_t^S, as is done by the economic models; therefore industrial structure is not an explicit factor in the generation by these methods of potential supply. The metal endowment is translated to potential supply by representing industry by a giant firm that possesses cost and efficiency characteristics of some typical firm. Such a model is analogous to the behaviour of a perfectly competitive industry.

Of course, a resource appraisal by a compound model is no more definitive and reliable than the credibility of the endowment model and the practicality in terms of costs and efficiency of the exploration and exploitation models. In a way, the geological and the aggregate econometric models can be viewed as approaching the appraisal of metal resources from opposite directions—the physical and the economic. Aggregate econometric models employ relations that reflect market responses to provide data on Q_t^S and Q_t^D (demand), while geological models are founded on the physical characteristics of the Earth and the translation of these characteristics to potential supply. Resource-adequacy judgements are made by comparing potential supply to cumulative requirements. While aggregate econometric models require extrapolation across time of economic variables, geological methods place the primary burden upon the geoscientist to infer from geology of a region the number of metal occurrences and their physical characteristics. The issues of estimation are different, but the *need for a model* to facilitate estimation is similar.

A metal endowment *model* describes the relationship of metal occurrence to some physical feature, e.g. geology, geochemical concentration, geophysical responses, or metal or deposit density per unit area or volume. These relations may have been defined on an area that has been well explored (a control area) and extrapolated to the region of interest.

The economic submodel of a composite model describes the activities involved in metal production, the transformation of metal endowment to potential supply. For example, the exploration and exploitation of metal deposits are expressed in terms of cost and efficiency in such a manner that these activities can interact with the metal endowment model to provide an appraisal of metal resources for specified economic conditions and technologies.

Depending upon the forms and complexities of the metal endowment and economic models, which together constitute the composite model, they may be interacted through mathematical analysis, or through computer simulation. Computer simulation is especially useful if metal endowment has been described probabilistically.

Probabilistic models of metal endowment and subsequent computer simulation are appropriate when not only the expectation for metal resources but the variance is of interest, or stated differently, when it is desired to know the distribution of the possible states of resources and the likelihood (probability) of each state. Those methods or techniques that relate probabilistically some feature of the physical system—the Earth—to metal endowment are loosely referred to as geostatistics. The following chapters describe a conceptual framework for geostatistical models of endowment and examine applications of geostatistics to the appraisal of metal resources.

References

Blondel, F. and Ventura, E. (1954). Estimation de la valeur de la production miniere mondiale en 1950. *Annls. Mines Carbur.* **143**(X), 25–81.

—— and —— (1956). Structure de la distribution des produits mineraux dans le Monde; 1953. *Annls. Mines Carbur.* **145**(XI) 2–91.

——, —— and Callot, F. (1961). Valeur de la production miniere mondiale in 1958; sa repartition geographique et son evolution. *Anals. Mines Carbur.* **246,** 13–108.

Brobst, D. A. and Pratt, W. P. (Eds.) (1973). *United States mineral resources, Geological Survey Professional Paper 820* (ed. D. A. Brobst and W. P. Pratt). US Geological Survey, Washington, DC.

Clark, G. R. and Reynolds, A. W. (1978). Uranium market—domestic and foreign requirements. In *Proc. Uranium Industry Seminar. Oct. 17–18.* Grand Junction Office, US Department of Energy, Grand Junction, Colorado.

Cox, D. P., Schmidt, R. G., Vine, J. D., Kirkemo, H., Tourtelot, E. B., and Fleischer, M. (1973). Copper. In *United States mineral resources, Geological Survey Professional Paper 820* (ed. D. A. Brobst and W. P. Pratt), pp. 163–90. US Geological Survey, Washington, DC.

Curry, D. L. (1978). Estimation of potential uranium resources. In *Workshop on concepts of uranium resources and producibility*, pp. 13–34. National Academy of Sciences, Washington, DC.

Dahlkamp, F. J. (1977). Uranium exploration techniques—their applicability and limitations. In *Uranium supply and demand*, pp. 130–41. Mining Journal Books Ltd (for Uranium Inst.), Edenbridge, Kent.

Duval, B. C. (1977). The changing picture of uranium exploration. In *Uranium supply and demand*, pp. 110–29. Mining Journal Books Ltd (for Uranium Inst.), Edenbridge, Kent.

Erickson, R. L. (1973). Crustal abundance of elements, and mineral reserves and resources. In *United States Mineral Resources, Geological Survey Professional Paper 820* (ed D. A. Brobst and W. P. Pratt), pp. 21–5. US Geological Survey, Washington, DC.

Griffiths, J. C. (1969). *The unit regional-value concept and its application to Kansas.* Special Publication No. 38, Kansas State Geological Survey, University of Kansas, Lawrence, Kansas.

—— (1978). Mineral resource assessment using the unit regional value concept. *J. Int. Ass. Math. Geol.* **10**(5), 441–72.

Guild, P. W. (1971). Metallogeny: a key to exploration. *Mining Engng.* **23**(1), 69–72.

Hansen, M. (1976). Trends in uranium supply. *Int. Atom. Energy Agency Bull.* **18**, 16–27.

Harris, D. P. (1977). Undiscovered uranium resources and potential supply: a non-technical description of methods for estimation and comment on estimates made by US ERDA, Lieberman, and the European School (Brinck and PAU). Part VI. *Mineral endowment, resources, and potential supply: theory, methods for appraisal, and case studies.* MINRESCO, Tucson, Arizona.

—— (1979). World uranium resources. *Ann. Rev. Energy* **4**, 403–32.

Hendricks, T. A. (1965). *Resources of oil, gas, and natural gas liquids in the U.S. and the world, Circular 522.* US Geological Survey, Washington, DC.

Hetland, D. L. (1979). Estimation of undiscovered uranium resources by US ERDA. In *Evaluation of uranium resources*, pp. 231–50. Proceedings of an Advisory Group Meeting, International Atomic Energy Agency, Vienna.

Hubbert, M. K. (1969). Energy resources. In *Resources and man*, (A study and recommendations by the Committee on Resources and Man, National Academy of Sciences–National Research Council), Chapter 8, pp. 157–242. W. H. Freeman & Company, San Francisco. (For National Academy of Sciences.)

Love, J. D., Hose, R. K., and Weitz, J. L. (1955). Geologic map of Wyoming. US Geological Survey, Washington, DC.

Lowell, J. D. (1970). Cooper resources. *Mining Engng* **22**, 67–73.

McKelvey, V. E. (1960). Relations of reserves of the elements to their crustal abundance. *Am. J. Sci.* **258-A** (Bradley volume), 234–41.

—— (1973). Mineral resource estimates and public policy. In *United States mineral resources, Geological Survey Professional Paper 820* (ed. D. A. Brobst and W. P. Pratt), pp. 9–19. US Geological Survey, Washington, DC.

National Academy of Sciences (1975). Resources of copper. In *Mineral resources and the environment*, Chapter VI, pp. 127–83. Committee on Mineral Resources and the Environment, National Academy of Sciences, Washington, DC.

Nolan, T. B. (1950). The search for new mining districts. *Econ. Geol.* **45**(7), 601–8.

Olson, J. C. and Overstreet, W. C. (1964). *Geologic distribution and resources of thorium, Bulletin 1204.* US Geological Survey, Washington, DC.

Organization for Economic Cooperation and Development/International Atomic Energy Agency (OECD/IAEA) (1975). *Uranium—resources, production, and demand.* Joint Report by OECD Nuclear Energy Agency and International Atomic Energy Agency. OECD, Paris, France.

—— (1977). *Uranium—resources, production and demand.* Joint Report by OECD Nuclear Energy Agency and International Atomic Energy Agency. OECD, Paris, France.

—— (1978). *Report on the International Uranium Resources Evaluation Project, Phase I.* A Report by the Joint Steering Group on Uranium Resources of the OECD Nuclear Energy Agency and the International Atomic Energy Agency. IAEA, Vienna.

Weeks, L. G. (1950). Concerning estimates of potential oil reserves. *Am. Ass. Petroleum Geologists Bull.*, **34**(10), 1947–53.

—— (1965). World offshore petroleum resources. *Am. Ass. Petroleum Geologists Bull.* **49**(10), 1680–93.

Wright, R. J. (1977). Foreign uranium developments. In *Proc. Uranium Industry Seminar, Oct. 26–27*, pp. 237–68. Grand Junction Office, US Department of Energy, Grand Junction, Colorado.

Notes

1. Erickson's relationship defines R in tonnes, but Fig. 4.2 is in English units.
2. This administration later was dissolved and its functions were conveyed to the US Department of Energy.
3. In this figure the term 'survey area' is equivalent to study area.

4. Solution front or 'roll'-type deposits predominate in the state of Wyoming. The deposits result from the gradual encroachment of uraniferous oxidizing solutions into unoxidized permeable sandstone. Uranium is deposited in many sites along a sinuous interface between the altered and unaltered ground and is generally recognized by the resulting haematitic and/or limonitic colouration of the sandstone (Hetland 1979, p. 235).

5. US Department of Energy (1979). Uranium resource assessment manual. Grand Junction, Colorado.

6. A commitment is the sum of annual requirements required to satisfy the remaining life of the reactor, given an initial life expectancy of 30 years.

7. Jacoby, H. D. (1977). Uranium dependence and the proliferation problem. Center for International Studies, Massachusetts Institute of Technology, Cambridge, Massachusetts.

8. Duret, M. F., Phillips, G. J. Veeder, J. I., Wolfe, W. A., and Williams, R. M. (1977). The contribution of nuclear power to world energy supply—1975 to 2000. Paper presented at World Energy Conference, Istanbul, Turkey.

9. Harris, D. P. (1978). World uranium resources and potential supply. Paper presented at the NASAP/INFCE Summer Study, Aspen, Colorado.

10. Chenoweth, W. L. (1978). Introduction to geology of uranium deposits. Materials presented at a seminar on the NURE programme. US DOE, Grand Junction, Colorado.

11. Reasonably Assured Resources refers to uranium that occurs in known mineral deposits of such size, grade, and configuration that it could be recovered within the given production cost ranges with currently proven mining and processing technology. Estimates of tonnage and grade are based upon specific sample data and measurements of the deposits and on knowledge of deposit characteristics.

12. Estimated Additional Resources refers to uranium in addition to Reasonably Assured Resources that is expected to occur, mostly on the basis of direct geological evidence, in (1) extensions of well-explored deposits; (2) little-explored deposits; and (3) undiscovered deposits believed to exist along a well-defined geological trend with known deposits.

13. Report on the International Uranium Resources Evaluation Project, Phase 1 (1978). A report by the joint steering group on uranium resources of the OECD Nuclear Energy Agency and the International Atomic Energy Agency, Vienna, pp. 473–4.

14. Potential supply range in millions of tonnes = $(4.10+2.19+2.10)$ to $(14.8+2.19+2.10) = 10.79$ to 19.09. Potential supply = RAR + EAR + Speculative (Table 4.10).

15. § 4.5.5 is reproduced with minor modifications from Harris (1979, pp. 427–29). (Reproduced, with Permission, from the *Annual Review of Energy*, **4**. Copyright © 1979 by Annual Reviews, Inc.)

16. $m = \sum_D Z(r_j)$, where D is a subset of RB ($RB = D \cup \bar{D}$) such that for $r_j \in D$ requires that $\kappa_{j,l} \geq \kappa'_l$, $l = 1, 2, \ldots NCM$; $NCM \leq NC$. Otherwise, $r_j \in \bar{D}$. $D = \{r_1, r_2, \ldots, r_{NMM}\}$, where NMM is the number of metal occurrences for which $\kappa_{j,l} \geq \kappa'_l$, $l = 1, 2, \ldots, NCM$. $\kappa_{j,l}$, $l = 1, \ldots, NCM$, are the NCM physical characteristics of the jth metal occurrences; and κ'_l, $l = 1, \ldots, NCM$, are the minimum levels of the NCM characteristics selected for classification of an occurrence as endowment. RB represents the set (collection) of all metal occurrences in the region; thus, D is the subset of occurrences meeting the specified physical requirements.

17. $m_i = \sum_{D_i} Z(r_{ij})$, where $D_i = \{r_{i1}, \ldots, r_{i,NMM}\}$.

18. Here, the models of Chapter 2 are referred to as aggregate econometric models so as to differentiate them from the models of exploration and exploitation which are collectively referred to as an economic model and which, together with an endowment model, constitute the composite model.

5 GEOSTATISTICAL MODELS OF METAL ENDOWMENT—A CONCEPTUAL FRAMEWORK

5.1. The evolution of geostatistical models

The approaches which have been taken in the geostatistical modelling of metal endowment are highly varied, both in purpose and in mathematical structure. Early models reflect the desire to subject regional exploration to the analytics of operations research; consequently, these models view resources through the phenomenon of the mine or mining district, abstracted from its geological foundations to its frequency of occurrence within some unit of area. The primary objective of these models was the description of the unknown *economic* deposits of a relatively unexplored area, for these were the current exploration targets. No attempt was made to infer to the extent of *unknown subeconomic* resources. More recent studies have been designed specifically for metal-resource analysis; consequently, they seek to appraise both *unknown economic and subeconomic resources*. The orientation and scope of the early models have been modified to provide also for the assessment of subeconomic metal resources in regions having a long history of metal production, for the metal resources in unknown subeconomic deposits of these traditionally producing regions may be considerable, perhaps greater than the unknown economic and subeconomic resources in many of the relatively unexplored regions.

Estimation of either unknown economic or unknown subeconomic metal resources is a difficult and frustrating task. However, of these two kinds, the subeconomic resources constitute a far greater problem than do those that are economic. Estimation of these resources is highly dependent upon the assumed model of metal endowment, hence metal-resource estimates by different scientists can vary widely, even if the economic framework for appraisal is the same. Since the endowment model is so critical to the resource appraisal, major emphasis in this book is given to the endowment models.

This chapter explores a conceptual framework for geostatistical models of endowment. In this chapter symbolic description is used liberally as a means of communications and as a basis for some mathematical description and manipulation. For the reader who does not wish to pursue the concepts in the detail of this chapter but wishes an overview of the concepts, a simplified summary is provided in § 5.7.

5.2. Conditions for a probabilistic model for metal endowment

Suppose that we partition a region into NS subregions and define by a common set of criteria a set of metallizations for each of the NS subregions

$$D = D_1 \cup D_2 \cup \ldots \cup D_{KS} \cup D_{KS+1} \cup \ldots \cup D_{NS}. \quad (5.1)$$

Suppose that although all NS subsets exist, our knowledge of metal endowment is limited to KS subsets. Let us designate D_0 as the union of subsets for which metal endowment, m, is known.

$$D_0 = D_1 \cup D_2 \cup \ldots \cup D_{KS}, \; m_i \text{ is known}$$
$$\text{for all } D_i \in D_0. \quad (5.2)$$

Obviously, $D = D_0 \cup \bar{D}_0$, where $\bar{D}_0$ means 'not D_0'. Now, suppose that it is desired to estimate the metal endowment of D_i, the set of metallizations for the ith subregion, one of the subregions for which metallizations are not known ($D_i \in \bar{D}_0$). If metal endowment for each of the KS regions for which metallizations are known were equal, there would be no reason to employ as an estimate of the metal endowment of the ith region anything other than this constant value of each region in D_0. However, where there is a great variation in endowment for $D_i \in D_0$, the statistical properties of the estimate for $D_i \in \bar{D}_0$ become of special interest. One way of expressing uncertainty of the estimate is by a probability distribution for endowment. An approximation to such a distribution would be the relative frequency distribution of the metal endowments of the KS regions of D_0. For such an approach to be appropriate and to yield reliable estimates, there would need to be some assurance that m is randomly distributed in the KS regions of D_0. Any persistent patterns in the geography of endowment may create suspicion about the reliability of such an estimation.

Empirical evidence suggests distinctive nonrandom features in the geography of metal endowment. It must be admitted, however, that this conclusion is predicated upon a pattern created by the interaction of man's economic pursuits with a basic endowment; consequently, the non-random character may be exaggerated. Nevertheless, the motivation of experience is strong—strong enough to raise doubt about the random hypothesis, at least for many metals. This doubt is increased by geological science, which demonstrates that, at least for tonnages and grades near those characteristic of economic deposits, complex earth processes are required to create the accumulations of metals.

In fact, the approach to the science of ore-deposit genesis, like all physical sciences, stresses physical laws, in this case laws or relations of earth processes that *cause* ore deposits. The perspective of geoscience is the explanation of a mineral deposit as a resultant of earth processes. Emphasis on cause-and-effect relations translates in model terms to a deterministic model. A deterministic view of the world hardly seems compatible with principles of probability and statistical inference. This apparent incompatibility often is exaggerated by the perspective of the geologist with regard to probability; namely, that probability relates only to repetitive phenomena, such as tossing a coin so many times and observing the fraction of the total times in which a head occurred. The geologist may view a deposit as a single and unique event, not as the outcome of an experiment that can be repeated; hence, to the geologist, probability may not appear as an appropriate description of the occurrence of a mineral deposit or of mineral resources. In order to demonstrate the usefulness and appropriateness of probability models in mineral-resource analysis, let us begin with a deterministic model of metal endowment and demonstrate the basis for the probabilistic approach.

5.3. Geostatistical theory of metal endowment

The following postulate seems a reasonable one as a foundation upon which one could conceptualize, one that would be acceptable to many geologists

$$m = \phi(\rho_1, \rho_2, \ldots, \rho_n), \qquad (5.3)$$

where m is the metal endowment, ϕ the function, and ρ_j the jth earth process. Earth processes refer to activities such as the intrusion of a magmatic body into host rocks of the earth's crust; they do not refer to the geologic features that result from the activity, such as granite rock. This postulate supports a *deterministic model*, implying that if for the area in question

we knew the earth processes that had transpired and if we knew the function ϕ, we could describe with certainty its metal endowment. Of course, we are far from having this complete an understanding of the earth and its processes. Although earth science has contributed much to a knowledge of the formation of ore deposits, we do not yet know for *certain* even the *identity* of the *processes*, the ρs, let alone the form of the function ϕ. We do know that geological features caused by the earth processes have been useful in locating mineral deposits. For simplicity, let us represent this as follows.

Let

$$g_i = \alpha_i(\rho_1, \rho_2, \ldots, \rho_n), \qquad (5.4)$$

where g_i is the jth geologic feature and $i = 1, 2, \ldots, p$. Under very rigid assumptions, it can be demonstrated that from (5.3) and (5.4) it can be deduced that metal endowment can be written as a function of geological features (those not familiar with matrix algebra may skip to (5.13)),

$$m = \lambda(g_1, g_2, \ldots, g_p). \qquad (5.5)$$

Suppose for demonstration that each of the p equations of (5.4) is linear or can be made linear by the appropriate transformation

$$g_1 = a_{11}\beta_1(\rho_1) + a_{12}\beta_2(\rho_2) + \ldots + a_{1n}\beta_n(\rho_n)$$
$$g_2 = a_{21}\beta_1(\rho_1) + a_{22}\beta_2(\rho_2) + \ldots + a_{2n}\beta_n(\rho_n)$$
$$\cdots \cdots \cdots \cdots \cdots \cdots \qquad (5.6)$$
$$g_p = a_{p1}\beta_1(\rho_1) + a_{p2}\beta_2(\rho_2) + \ldots + a_{pn}\beta_n(\rho_n),$$

where $\beta_j(\rho_j)$ is some transformation function of the jth earth process; for example, $\beta_j(\rho_j)$ may be ρ_j^2, $\sqrt{\rho_j}$, ρ_j, etc. In matrix form (5.6) can be rewritten as a simple equation

$$G = AX, \qquad (5.7)$$

where G is a p by 1 column vector, the ith element of which is g_i, A is a p by n matrix of coefficients, the ijth element of which is $[a_{ij}]$, and X is an n by 1 column vector, the jth element of which is $[x_j] = \beta_j(\rho_j)$.

Suppose that $p = n$ and that the elements of X are linearly independent. This is equivalent to stating that the rank r of matrix A is equal to n: $r = n$. Under these conditions, A has a nonsingular determinant and possesses an inverse A^{-1}. Given (5.7) and these stated conditions, we can solve for X

$$G = AX$$
$$A^{-1}G = A^{-1}AX \qquad (5.8)$$
$$A^{-1}G = X$$

Let $[c_{ij}]$ represent the ijth element of A^{-1}. Then from (5.8), we can write

$$\beta_1(\rho_1) = c_{11}g_1 + c_{12}g_2 + \ldots + c_{1n}g_n$$
$$\beta_2(\rho_2) = c_{21}g_2 + c_{22}g_2 + \ldots + c_{2n}g_n$$
$$\cdots \cdots \cdots \cdots \cdots \cdots$$
$$\beta_n(\rho_n) = c_{n1}g_2 + c_{n2}g_n + \ldots + c_{nn}g_n. \qquad (5.9)$$

From (5.9), we can write

$$\rho_j = \beta_j^{-1}(c_{j1}g_1 + c_{j2}g_2 + \ldots + c_{jn}g_n) \qquad (5.10)$$

or, alternatively

$$\rho_j = \alpha_j^{-1}(g_1, g_2, \ldots, g_n). \qquad (5.11)$$

Having defined the jth process as a function of the n geological features, metal endowment can be rewritten as a function of the geological measurements (the arguments of the α functions have been dropped for notational simplicity)

$$m = \phi(\alpha_1^{-1}, \alpha_2^{-1}, \ldots, \alpha_n^{-1}) \qquad (5.12)$$

or, equivalently,

$$m = \lambda(g_1, g_2, \ldots, g_n). \qquad (5.13)$$

Thus, if the assumptions were met, if we knew all of the ρs and gs, and if we knew the function forms ϕ, and α_j for all j, a *deterministic model* could be constructed in which *metal endowment is a function of geological features*. Let's suppose that all of these conditions hold except that λ is not known and that some of the geological features are imperfectly known. In such a case, it would be necessary to assume a functional form and to estimate its parameters from data on metal occurrence and the geological features

$$\hat{m} = \lambda_0(\hat{g}_1, \hat{g}_2, \ldots, \hat{g}_D; g_{D+1}, \ldots, g_n) + e, \qquad (5.14)$$

where $\hat{m}$ is the estimate of m generated by the assumed functional form and its estimated parameters, λ_0 is the assumed functional form, $\hat{g}_i$ are the imperfectly known geological variables, $i = 1, 2, \ldots, D$, e is the error in estimation of m by $\hat{m}$ due to assumed functional form and measurement error in the gs. g_i are the perfectly known geological variables, $i = D+1, \ldots, n$. Lack of knowledge of the true relationship, λ, and errors in the data would impart error to our predictions and justify adopting a probabilistic model for decision-making. Seldom are all of the geological features observable; consequently, an additional error, an error of specification,

is imparted to the estimating equation because of the missing variables

$$\hat{m} = \lambda_0(\hat{g}_1, \hat{g}_2, \ldots, \hat{g}_D) + e + \omega \qquad (5.15)$$

where ω is the error in the estimation of m by $\hat{m}$ due to the missing variables.

Our real circumstances with respect to knowledge of a quantitative model of metal endowment are worse than those just described. For example, even if we knew the identity of the earth processes and the functional forms ($\phi; \alpha_j, j = 1, 2, \ldots, n$) but instead of p equalling n, p were greater than n, or the geological features were not independent, we could not write (5.13) directly via deductive reasoning from (5.3) and (5.4), for there would be no unique solution. On these grounds alone, we would be forced to adopt a much weaker proposition, one in which geological features are associated with metal endowment not by a unique deterministic function but by probabilistic relationships. Actually, we do not know the form of any of the functions; our measurable geological features are correlated; and p generally is not equal to n. In short, our lack of knowledge is so great that it is fruitless to speculate about mathematical relationships that would lead to an equation in which metal endowment is a well defined *deterministic* mathematical function of *geological features*. We simply do not yet know enough to formulate such a quantitative model. Then, what was the point of the exercise? Precisely this: one can begin with a *deterministic* conceptual model in which metal endowment is defined as a function of earth processes as a basic premise, one which would appeal to earth scientists; yet, because of lack of information and meagre knowledge of relationships, one could justify the adoption of a conditional probability model as a practical decision-making tool. The model must be formulated to express as well as possible the geological theory of ore formation, but its quantification by necessity must be based upon laws of *statistically related phenomena*.

The effect of this lack of information on decision-making and evaluation is that one area that looks identical to a mineral-rich area, as examined across a *subset* of size D of the gs may have little or no metallization. Thus, the metal endowment of an area, conditional upon the gs, should be considered as a random variable M, a variable that is continuous, meaning that it can take on an infinite number of values, and for which the likelihood of it having a value between two limits, m_1 and m_2 ($m_2 > m_1$), is appropriately stated in terms of probability

$$P(m_1 \leq M \leq m_2 \mid g_1, g_2, \ldots, g_D)$$

$$= \int_{m_1}^{m_2} f(m \mid g_1, g_2, \ldots, g_D) \, dm. \quad (5.16)$$

Let us designate G_D as the vector (set) of geological variables. Then the above relationship can be written more simply

$$P(m_1 \leq M \leq m_2 \mid G_D) = \int_{m_1}^{m_2} f(m \mid G_D) \, dm, \quad (5.17)$$

where $f(m \mid G_D)$ is the probability density function. The expression (function) $f(m \mid G_D)$ is here referred to as the basic geostatistical model of metal endowment.

Eqn (5.17) states the essence of geostatistical theory for metal endowment: namely, that so far as our knowledge is concerned, unknown metal endowment is most appropriately stated in terms of probability.

5.4. Taxonomy of models

Although particulars of most geostatistical models make each of them unique in some respect, two contrasting kinds of models can be recognized: deposit models and crustal-abundance models. The latter model may also be referred to as the element distribution. Even though the objectives of these two models may be the same—the appraisal of metal endowment—their routes to achieving the objective are markedly different.

Generally speaking, a complete deposit model first estimates the endowment of a region in unknown economic deposits and then employs some auxiliary relationship, such as a grade–cumulative tonnage of ore relationship, as a means of assessing the magnitude of unknown subeconomic deposits. This relationship may have been determined solely upon the inventory of known deposits, or it may also reflect the grades and tonnages of unknown, but anticipated, economic deposits.

The crustal-abundance model is predicated upon the appropriate description of the statistical distribution of the concentration of an element in the earth's crust, generally, with reference to small volumes, the volumes of geochemical samples. Most models employed have assumed this distribution to be lognormal, having as its mean the crustal abundance of the element. The endowment of a region in metal in concentrations and accumulations of the order of economic deposits is inferred from the element distribution by adjusting the variance of the element distribution to reflect the distribution of the element in larger volumes, the volumes of ore deposits. Thus, the deposit models employ man's experience with economic deposits, the anomalies of metal concentration and accumulation, as a basis for inference to unknown economic and subeconomic deposits, while the geochemical models infer from the opposite direction, starting with the ultimate deposit of metal, the earth's crust, and attempting to infer from this ultimate to the anomalous occurrences, the economic and subeconomic ore deposits. Each has its advantages, disadvantages, and problems.

5.5. Geostatistical deposit models

5.5.1. The basic model

The function $f(m \mid G_D)$, the metal endowment model, serves as a reference to which various submodels can be related. For appraisal by deposit models, greater utility may be obtained by stating $f(m \mid G_D)$ in terms of its component models, models more directly expressive of the phenomenon of the deposit. This can be accomplished by considering m, metal endowment, to be the result of three more elementary phenomena, the number of deposits and the tonnage and grade of a deposit. In other words, the random variable M is a function of the three random variables N, T, and Q

$$M = \theta(N, T, Q) = N \cdot T \cdot Q, \quad (5.18)$$

where N is the number of deposits, T the deposit tonnage, and Q the deposit grade (proportion, not percentage).

Let us designate the probability density functions for N, T, and Q, respectively, as h, j, and k [1]

$$h(n \mid q, G_D), j(t \mid q, G_D), k(q \mid G_D). \quad (5.19)$$

Then, y, a probability density for the joint occurrence of N, T, and Q, can be defined in terms of these three functions

$$y(n, t, q \mid G_D) = h(n \mid q, G_D) \cdot j(t \mid q, G_D) \cdot k(q \mid G_D). \quad (5.20)$$

By definition, $M = N \cdot T \cdot Q$, or $N = M/(T \cdot Q)$. Through change of variable the function $f(m \mid G_D)$ can be derived from relationship (5.20) (for mathematical details, see § 5.8),

$$f(m \mid G_D) = \int_T \int_Q y\left(\frac{m}{t \cdot q}, t, q \mid G_D\right) \cdot \frac{dq\, dt}{t \cdot q}.$$

(5.21)

Alternatively, (5.21) can be rewritten in terms of the three component models, h, j, and k

$$f(m \mid G_D) = \int_T \int_Q \left\{ h\left(\frac{m}{t \cdot q} \mid q, G_D\right) \cdot j(t \mid q, G_D) \times \right.$$
$$\left. \times k(q \mid G_D) \right\} \cdot \frac{dq\, dt}{t \cdot q}. \quad (5.22)$$

This is the basic deposit model [2]; it shows how phenomena of deposits relate to the measurement of metal endowment, m.

The formulation of the probability for number of deposits in this basic model to be conditional upon q and G_D is to allow for the possibility that as the grade of deposits decreases, the frequency of deposits increases. This is the more general formulation and includes the special case in which number of deposits is independent of grade.

The describing of the probability for tonnage as dependent upon grade is purposeful. For a given mode of occurrence, tonnage and grade may be statistically independent, as shown for copper deposits by Singer, Cox, and Drew (1975), but when viewed *across modes*, there may be an inverse relationship [3].

The various deposit models that have thus far been developed can be viewed as being related to this basic model in one or more of the following ways.

1. They represent specific conditions imposed on geological information;

2. They are a form of one or two of the submodels: j, h, or k;

3. They describe the dependency of some form of the submodels to each other, or of the function f to one or more of the submodels. For example, the correlation, or lack thereof, between average grade and tonnage of ore per deposit, or the relationship between cumulative tonnage of metal or ore and cut-off grade of ore for the aggregate of deposits.

5.5.2. Metal density

Metal density measures of a region that has been well explored are sometimes used as an expectation for the endowment of another, unexplored, region (Blondel and Ventura 1954, 1956; Blondel, Ventura, and Callot 1961; Lowell 1970). To see how this measure relates to the general model, let's suppose

that there is a joint probability density function $u(G_D)$, a function that describes the probability for the joint occurrence of the D geological variables. Then, $\bar{m}$, the expectation for M, is defined from the general model

$$\bar{m} = \int_M \int_{G_D} m \cdot f(m \mid G_D) \cdot u(G_D)\, dG_D\, dm.$$

(5.23)

As indicated, the effects of geology on metal density are ignored. Furthermore, a statistic $\bar{m}$ is used to represent the statistical distribution of M.

5.5.3. Multivariate models

Models labeled multivariate geostatistical are designed to estimate for the ith region $f_i(m \mid G_D)$ or $\bar{h}_i(n \mid G_D)$:

$$\bar{h}_i(n \mid G_D) = \int_Q h_i(n \mid q, G_D) \cdot k_i(q \mid G_D)\, dq.$$

(5.24)

The basic scheme employed has been to estimate one or the other of these relations on a well-explored region and to use this relationship to infer m or n for a relatively unexplored region by evaluating the function on the geology observed for the unexplored region.

Models of the multivariate type have been developed by Harris (1966, 1968), Agterberg (1971), Sinclair and Woodsworth (1970), De Geoffroy and Wignall (1971), Kelly and Sheriff (1969), Agterberg and Cabilio (1969), and Singer [4].

5.5.4. Spatial models

Spatial models for number of mines (Slichter, Dixon, and Myer 1962), mining districts (Allais 1957), and deposits or land sections (Wilmot, Hazen, and Wertz [5]) can be viewed as approximations to the submodel $h(n \mid q, G_D)$ for the special case in which grade and geology are ignored (integrated out)

$$N(n) = \int_Q \int_{*G_D} h(n \mid q, G_D) \cdot k(q \mid G_D) \cdot u(G_D)\, dG_D\, d_q$$

(5.25)

where $N(n)$ represents spatial models, e.g. the negative exponential, the negative binomial, and the Poisson and $*G_D$ represents the domain of G_D. These models ignore the effect of both geology and grade on the probability for number of deposits.

5.5.5. Trend models

Suppose that we postulate that there is a region of interest which contains subregions and that this region is two-dimensional with respect to the reference scheme for the subregions; then, each of the subregions can be referenced by two coordinates, x and y. Let us postulate that there exists for each subregion a distribution for metal endowment, $f_{xy}(m \mid G_D)$, and a distribution for geology, $u_{xy}(G_D)$. Then, from our general model, we can define for each set of coordinates an expected value for M

$$\bar{m}_{xy} = \int_M \int_{G_D} m \cdot f_{xy}(m \mid G_D) \cdot u_{xy}(G_D) \, dG_D \, dm.$$
$$(5.26)$$

In the general case, as x and y take on various values, $\bar{m}_{xy}$ changes, as f_{xy} or u_{xy} change. Thus, metal endowment in general $\bar{m}$ could be considered as some function w of x, y, a function unique to the region,

$$\bar{m} = w(x, y).$$

This is the trend model. The unit-regional value concept developed by Griffiths (1969) for the Kansas Geological Survey is a model of this kind, except that the variable of interest is not metal endowment but a composite V of metals, nonmetals, and fuels aggregated by a price vector. Agterberg and Cabilio (1969), Agterberg (1971), and Singer [4] also have employed trend models.

5.5.6. Composite multivariate and trend models

Suppose that our perspective is similar to that described for the trend model, except that we do not integrate across the geology

$$\bar{m}_{x,y,G_D} = \int_M m \cdot f_{xy}(m \mid G_D) \, dm. \qquad (5.27)$$

This expected value, $\bar{m}_{x,y,G_D}$, varies with both the coordinates of location and the geology. Let's suppose that this variation is of such nature that it can be described by function c,

$$\bar{m} = c(x, y, G_D). \qquad (5.28)$$

Models of this kind have been developed by Singer [4] and Agterberg (1971).

5.6. The crustal-abundance (element distribution) model

5.6.1. Concepts and theory

The crustal-abundance geostatistical (CAG) model can be related conceptually to the probabilistic description of metal endowment by setting the vector of deposit requirements appropriately; e.g. the minimum level of concentration near zero. Setting the minimum grade requirements near zero implies that all of the earth's crust to a specified depth contributes to metal endowment. In this situation, it becomes necessary and convenient to consider all rock of the earth's crust to some minable depth as metallized material of interest.

The CAG approach to estimating the endowment E of a region is to multiply the weight W of the crust within the region by a probability p and an average grade $\bar{q}$

$$E = W \cdot p \cdot \bar{q}. \qquad (5.29)$$

The term, crustal abundance geostatistical (CAG) derives from the fact that p is defined by either a single or bivariate probability density distribution or function for which one or more of its parameters are linked directly or indirectly to a measure of crustal abundance, e.g. the Clarke. The average grade $\bar{q}$ is computed from this same distribution for a specified cut-off grade. While eqn (5.29) conveys the gist of the CAG approach, the equation varies in details with the probability model selected and the degree to which economics are built into the model. For example, the probability model specified by Drew (1977) is bivariate (grade and tonnage). Therefore, p can be determined only if both cut-off grade and minimum tonnage are specified. Drew accomplishes this by relating cost of production to tonnage and grade and specifying the maximum production cost of interest. Of course, in this case, $\bar{q}$ also is computed on that part of the two-dimensional space that is truncated by the cost function.

With the exception of the model developed by Drew (1977), crustal-abundance models have not allowed for mineral deposits having intrinsic sizes or morphologies. Instead, size has been either a discretionary variable, the value of which is specified by the modeller, or it has been ignored (integrated out). The general conceptual description which follows reflects the theme of the European School in which size affects endowment but is specified by the modeller.

Suppose that the crustal material of a region is divided into N blocks, each being of size t, where $t = W/N$ and W is the weight of the crustal material. Letting n_i be the number of blocks having grades that fall within the interval $q_i + \Delta q$, the relative frequency, r_i, of these grades for blocks of size $t = W/N$ is simply n_i/N.

If concentration of the element of interest is randomly distributed throughout the region, the probability for a crustal block, drawn at random, having a grade which lies within the interval $q_i + \Delta q$ is approximated by the relative frequency r_i when Δq approaches zero.

$$P(q_i \leq Q \leq q_i + \Delta q \mid t) \approx r_i = n_i/N \quad (5.30)$$

and

$$P(Q \geq q_i \mid t) \approx \sum_{j=i}^{NI} r_j, \quad (5.31)$$

where NI is the number of grade intervals. The average grade, $\bar{q}_{q_i \mid t}$, of all blocks having grades of at least q_i and having size t is approximated by

$$\bar{q}_{q_i \mid t} \approx \sum_{j=i}^{NI} n_j \cdot \left(\frac{q_j + (q_j + \Delta q)}{2} \right) \bigg/ \sum_{j=i}^{NI} n_j$$

$$= \sum_{j=i}^{NI} \frac{r_j \left(\frac{q_j + (q_j + \Delta q)}{2} \right)}{\sum_{j=i}^{NI} r_j}. \quad (5.32)$$

Clearly, as Δq approaches zero and NI infinity, this quantity approaches the true average grade of the truncated population.

A CAG model of the European School computes the mineral endowment, $E_{q_i \mid t}$, conditional upon block size t and cut-off grade q_i, by obtaining the product of W, $P(Q \geq q_i \mid t)$, and $\bar{q}_{q_i \mid t}$

$$E_{q_i \mid t} = W \cdot P(Q \geq q_i \mid t) \cdot \bar{q}_{q_i \mid t}. \quad (5.33)$$

Alternatively,

$$E_{q_i \mid t} = N \cdot t \cdot P(Q \geq q_i \mid t) \cdot \bar{q}_{q_i \mid t}. \quad (5.34)$$

Eqn (5.34) is highly instructive of the crustal-abundance approach of the European School (Brinck 1967) to estimating endowment. First, given that W is known, or measurable, and that t is set by the modeller, endowment is predicated upon the relative frequencies of block grades. The product $N \cdot t \cdot P(Q \geq q_i \mid t)$ defines that quantity of crustal material that contributes to endowment. The multiplication of this quantity by its average grade $\bar{q}_{q_i \mid t}$ converts this stock of mineralized matter to quantity of metal $E_{q_i \mid t}$.

Let us represent the relative frequencies r_i by probability density function $\lambda(q \mid t)$,

$$\lambda(q \mid t), \quad 0 \leq q \leq q_{max}$$

$$0, \quad \text{otherwise}.$$

Then, defining cut-off grade to be q' instead of q_i we have

$$P(Q \geq q' \mid t) = \int_{q'}^{q_{max}} \lambda(q \mid t) \, dq \quad (5.35)$$

and

$$\bar{q}_{q' \mid t} = \int_{q'}^{q_{max}} q \cdot \frac{\lambda(q \mid t)}{\int_{q'}^{q_{max}} \lambda(q \mid t) \, dq} \, dq. \quad (5.36)$$

Finally, the basic crustal-abundance model can be written

$$E_{q' \mid t} = N \cdot t \cdot \left\{ \int_{q'}^{q_{max}} \lambda(q \mid t) \, dq \right\} \times$$

$$\left\{ \int_{q'}^{q_{max}} q \cdot \lambda(q \mid t) \, dq \bigg/ \int_{q'}^{q_{max}} \lambda(q \mid t) \, dq \right\}. \quad (5.37)$$

Equivalently,

$$E_{q' \mid t} = N \cdot t \cdot \int_{q'}^{q_{max}} q \cdot \lambda(q \mid t) \, dq. \quad (5.38)$$

Eqn (5.38) shows the appeal of CAG models: namely, once $\lambda(q \mid t)$ has been estimated, it is a relatively simple matter to estimate endowment for specified subeconomic grades.

It is especially noteworthy to those who are examining CAG models for the first time that *endowment is not described probabilistically*. Use of $\lambda(q \mid t)$ to obtain a fraction to convert crustal material to endowment material denies its subsequent use to describe the probabilistic nature of that endowment. Of course, even a *total* convert to the crustal abundance approach would not advocate that an *estimate* of endowment using a crustal-abundance model is a certain quantity. Since $\lambda(q \mid t)$ must itself be estimated prior to estimating endowment, the estimate is imperfectly known because of uncertainty in the estimated parameters of $\lambda(q \mid t)$. But, while $E_{q' \mid t}$ is uncertain, this uncertainty is not directly definable from the crustal abundance model, for it is only a reflection of error in statistical estimation of parameters.

While $\lambda(q \mid t)$ is the objective of the CAG approach, as the approach was first demonstrated, it is not sought directly. The procedure is to estimate $\lambda(q \mid t_0)$, the distribution of grades in geochemical samples from the region of interest, and then to estimate $\lambda(q \mid t)$ from $\lambda(q \mid t_0)$

$$\lambda(q \mid t) = \pi[\lambda(q \mid t_0), t] \quad (5.39)$$

where π is a transformation function. The computations for quantity and average grade of resources can be made with respect to any value for t. The details of this adjustment vary with the mathematical form of the crustal-abundance model. Consider, for example, the adjustment for the lognormal distribution, which is, perhaps, the most popular of the crustal-abundance models. In the initial application, and whenever possible, the parameters of the lognormal model, μ and σ_v^2, are estimated from geochemical data

$$\hat{\mu} = \frac{1}{n} \sum_{i=1}^{n} \ln q_i,$$
$$\hat{\sigma}_v^2 = \frac{\sum (\ln q_i - \ln \mu)^2}{n-1}.$$
(5.40)

Once σ_v^2 and μ have been estimated, they are used to estimate α, a measure of absolute variation, using the DeWijs–Matheron relationship

$$\hat{\alpha} = \frac{\hat{\sigma}_v^2}{\ln\left(\dfrac{V}{v}\right)}$$
(5.41)

where $\hat{\sigma}_v^2$ is the estimated variance for geochemical samples of volume v in an environment of volume V. Or alternatively,

$$\hat{\alpha} = \frac{\hat{\sigma}_v^2}{3 \ln\left(\dfrac{D}{d}\right)},$$
(5.42)

where D, d are linear equivalents of volumes V and v, respectively. Having an estimate of α provides a means for estimating the variance for any size deposit (volume v')

$$\hat{\sigma}_{v'}^2 = \hat{\alpha} 3 \ln\left(\frac{D}{d'}\right),$$
(5.43)

where d' is the linear equivalent of volume v'.

The persistence of the lognormal form for concentrations of an element in volumes of various sizes is a critical issue, for the basic scheme of this approach is to estimate the quantity of metal resources in deposit-sized concentrations from the statistical properties of concentrations in geochemical samples. The case for the lognormal distribution as a metal-resource model will be considered shortly, but now that the general idea of CAG models has been established, let us explore the broad question of the relationship between $\lambda(q \mid t)$ and $f(m \mid G_D)$, the basic model developed in § 5.3, 'Geostatistical theory of

metal endowment'. A brief exploration of this question is an effective way of commenting on differences in the approaches of deposit models and CAG models.

First, let us restate $*j$ and $*k$ so that grade is conditional upon tonnage instead of tonnage conditional upon grade. This is possible because for any dependent events, A and B, there are two ways of describing the relationship between the events,

$$P(A, B) = P(A \mid B) \cdot P(B)$$

or

$$P(A, B) = P(B \mid A) \cdot P(A).$$

While the engineer, because of his production bent, finds it natural to describe tonnage as conditional upon grade, from the point of view of probability theory, either statement is equally valid. Let $*\tilde{j}$ and $*\tilde{k}$ be these restated densities. Then, we can define

$$f(m \mid G_D) = \int_T \int_Q h\left(\frac{m}{t \cdot q} \,\Big|\, q, G_D\right) \times$$
$$\times *\tilde{j}(q \mid t, G_D) \cdot *\tilde{k}(t \mid G_D) \frac{1}{t} \frac{1}{q} \, dq \, dt. \quad (5.44)$$

Now, suppose that, for a specified t, the probability that the random variable T falls within the interval $t + \Delta t$ is 1.0 as Δt approaches zero. Then, we may define a special form of the endowment model, one conditional upon t,

$$*f(m \mid t) = \int_{*G_D} \int_Q \int_T h\left(\frac{m}{t \cdot q} \,\Big|\, q, G_D\right) \times$$
$$\times *\tilde{j}(q \mid t, G_D) \cdot u(G_D) \cdot \frac{1}{t} \cdot \frac{1}{q} \, dt \, dq \, dG_D. \quad (5.45)$$

Of course, (5.45) integrates out and hence removes geology as a conditioning variable. The p.d.f. $\lambda(q \mid t)$ is related to $*f(m \mid t)$ by

$$P(M \geq m \mid t) = \int_m^\infty *f(m \mid t) \, dm. \quad (5.46)$$

But, given that t is specified—has a probability of 1.0—it must also be true that

$$P(M \geq m \mid t) = P(Q \cdot t \geq q \cdot t \mid t) = P(Q \geq q \mid t). \quad (5.47)$$

But,

$$P(Q \geq q' \mid t) \quad \text{is} \quad \int_{q'}^{q_{max}} \lambda(q \mid t) \, dq. \quad (5.48)$$

Therefore,

$$\int_{m'=q'\cdot t}^{m_{max}=q_{max}\cdot t} \lambda\left(\frac{m}{t}\bigg|\, t\right)\frac{dm}{t} = \int_{m'}^{m_{max}} {}^*f(m\,|\,t)\,dm.$$

$$(5.49)$$

Eqn (5.49) demonstrates the conceptual linkage between $\lambda(q\,|\,t)$ and ${}^*f(m\,|\,t)$, the latter being a special form of $f(m\,|\,G_D)$. Now, let us examine the lognormal distribution as a CAG model.

5.6.2. *The case for the lognormal distribution*

In 1954, L. Ahrens published his provocative paper entitled 'The lognormal distribution of the elements' and, in so doing, set the stage for professional argument, discussion, and in general, interest in the statistical distribution of element concentrations that continued for years. Professional journals reflect the considerable impact of his paper upon the profession of geochemistry. This impact, which varied from concurrence with his findings and propositions to indignation, was generated not by his finding that the lognormal distribution fitted well the histograms of element concentrations of empirical observations, but from his proposition of the lognormal distribution as a fundamental law of geochemistry (Ahrens 1953, p. 1148):

> 'The concentration of an element is lognormally distributed in a specific igneous rock.' [Reprinted with permission from *Nature*, **172**(4390), 1148. Copyright © 1953 Macmillan Journals Limited.]

He added to this so-called 'fundamental law,' what he designated as the second geochemical law concerning the nature of the distribution of the concentration of an element (Ahrens 1954, p. 69):

> 'The abundance of an element in an igneous rock is always greater than its most prevalent concentration; the difference may be immeasurably small or very large and is determined solely by the magnitude of the dispersion of its concentration.'

The proposition of a lognormal law was challenged by Chayes (1954) on two counts.

1. That the statistical procedures employed by Ahrens were inadequate,
2. That on conceptual grounds it is clear that the abundant elements cannot exhibit the positive skew characteristic of the lognormal distribution while it is clear that the low-abundance elements will exhibit such a pattern.

Miller and Goldberg (1955) similarly challenged Ahren's proposition by pointing out that clearly some elements appear to be normally distributed and that elements in geochemical universes may not all be distributed according to the lognormal or any single distribution form. They postulated that the statistical distribution of an element is a function of four independent factors.

1. Chemical environment of formation or deposition;
2. The nature and number of elements involved in the rock type or mineral suits;
3. Geologic time considerations;
4. The reversibility or irreversibility of the chemical reactions.

Aubrey (1955) challenged the lognormal proposition of Ahrens by showing that in a two-component system, if the distribution of one element is positively skewed, that of the other component must by necessity be negatively skewed. He admitted that when the number of components is greater than two, the result is not so clear-cut, but he suggested that at least one of the constituents will demonstrate a certain amount of negative skewness in its distribution. Aubrey argued further that many minor elements will follow major constituents in failing to obey the lognormal distribution.

Vistelius (1960, pp. 10–11) described two conceptual schemes by which positively-skewed distributions could arise. He describes the first scheme.

> Let us have a concentration, X, which may be regarded as the sum of a large number of impulses, $Z_1, Z_2, \ldots, Z_n$. The impulses are mutually independent and act in the order of their subscripts. Let the increase produced by the impulse Z_v be assumed to be directly proportional to Z_v and to the concentration X. The concentration X_v results from the action of $v-1$ of the preceding impulses. In this case
>
> $$X_{v+1} - X_v = kZ_vX_v, \qquad (5.50)$$
>
> and hence
>
> $$Z_1 + \ldots + Z_n = \frac{1}{k}\sum_1^n \frac{X_{v+1} - X_v}{X_v}.$$
>
> If this process is discontinuous [continuous] [6],
>
> $$w = \frac{1}{k}\int_{X_1}^{X_2}\frac{dt}{g(t)} \qquad (5.51)$$
>
> and w will be normally distributed, so that we shall have a lognormal distribution. It is obvious .... that we shall get a lognormal distribution only when $g(t)$ is a simple linear function, i.e. $g(t) = at$. In other cases we shall have various functions which would be very troublesome to use in normal distributions.

Vistelius (1960, p. 11) describes the second scheme.

> The geochemical process at every separate moment gives a concentration of the elements in conditions of the central-limit theorem (Cramer, 1946). In the course of time the mean values of the deposited concentrations increase. At the same time the values of variances also increase. The variability of the mean values and variances have a linear positive correlation as an approximate estimate of their relations. In other words, the probability density, $f(x)$, is $f(x) = \sum_i p_i f_i(x)$, where $f_i(x)$ is normal density, p_i is the function of weight of summarized densities and i is the stage of the geochemical process in the order of time . . . .
>
> . . . .
>
> The principal difference of the last scheme from lognormal is the following: the frequency distribution functions for one separate stage of the geochemical process are normal. The frequency distribution functions for all joint products of the geochemical process have a positive skewness (we called these distributions 'joint distributions').

Vistelius referred to the distributions at a given point in time as the local distribution. He demonstrated the normality of the local distribution by dividing a piece of a biotite granodiorite rock weighing 1 kg into smaller samples, each weighing 5 g. The P_2O_5 content of each sample was determined with great care, and Vistelius found the distribution of P_2O_5 to be normal.

As a means of examining the nature of the joint distributions, Vistelius constructed a histogram of Na_2O obtained for 4788 analyses of igneous rocks. This distribution exhibited great skewness. The Na_2O in 200 samples of the basalts of the world was analysed in a similar manner. Vistelius found, consistent with the implication of scheme 2, that the distribution of Na_2O was also positively skewed, as it was for Na_2O in all rocks, but the skewness is smaller for Na_2O in the basalts. Vistelius (1960, p. 12) concluded

> All rocks of the world are a collection of results of a very wide range of stages of the geochemical process. Their joint distribution is very skew. All of the basalts of the world are also a collection of the results of the range of stages of the geochemical process, but their range of the geochemical process is narrower than the range of those of all rocks.

The pervasiveness of the lognormal distribution in the distribution of grades in ore deposits supports this theory, for an ore under current economics and technology requires a manyfold concentration over ordinary crustal abundance, which implies many stages of the geochemical process. Hence, according to the theory of Vistelius, the distributions of grades of ore should exhibit considerable positive skewness, particularly for those metals of low crustal abundance.

Although many arguments were marshalled to challenge the lornormal distribution as a geochemical *law*, data do demonstrate that the concentrations of some elements are distributed lognormally. Setting aside the proposition of the lognormal distribution as a geochemical law, evidence is supportive of the weaker proposition that the lognormal distribution is a useful description of a very wide range of mineral-resource phenomena. Not only does this distribution describe well the distribution of some elements in igneous rocks, but it has been found to describe well the frequency of grades of an element in an ore deposit. Especially pertinent to the use of the lognormal distribution as a resources model are the findings of Brinck (1967) and Coulomb (1959). Brinck analysed the concentrations of copper, lead, and zinc found in a regional geochemical survey of the Oslo region of Norway and used these data to estimate parameters of the lognormal distribution of each of these metals; the lognormal model was then employed as a resources model. Coulomb (1959, as summarized in Brinck 1967) found the lognormal distribution to describe uranium in several granitic areas studied, and he demonstrated that division of such areas into panels resulted in lognormal uranium distributions for each panel.

Shifting our attention from the geochemical sample to the deposit level, we find that ore reserves have been found to be lognormally distributed (Patterson [7]; DeWijs 1951; Krige [8]; Sichel 1952). Krige (1952) found the lognormal distribution to describe well the gold values of the Basal Reef in the Orange Free State Goldfield.

In a recent study by Singer *et al.* (1975), data were assembled for 267 copper deposits. These data included historical production plus estimated reserves. Distributions for copper grade were constructed for all 267 deposits and separately for porphyry, stratabound, and massive sulphide deposits. Copper grades were weighted by cumulative production and reserves. They found that with the exception of the southwestern Pacific porphyry deposits, the lognormal distribution was superior to the normal distribution as a model for grade and for tonnage of ore per deposit.

From an even more aggregate perspective, that of the distribution of value per mine for a region, the lognormal distribution has been found to be appropriate (Slichter *et al.* 1962). Slichter *et al.* found that the distribution of value per mine was lognormal for each of the following cases.

(1) 3145 mines of all types in the Western US;
(2) 285 mines in the Basin and Range Area;
(3) 1259 mines in the southwestern USA.

In addition, when the 1259 mines in the southwestern USA were classified by metal (copper, gold, and silver) he found that value per mine for each metal was lognormally distributed. Similarly, Allais (1957) found the value across metals and across the mines contained in the mining district to follow the lognormal distribution for each of three regions: western US, North Africa, and France.

According to the National Academy of Sciences (1975), 'the French school of geostatisticians headed by Matheron has shown that, in a general manner, ore deposits over large areas tend to have grade distributions, which, when plotted in logarithms on the abscissae against the tonnage plotted on the ordinate, yield a normal Gaussian bell-shaped curve'.

Griffiths and Singer (1973) found that the size of uranium deposits, as measured by the length of the deposits, is lognormally distributed for deposits for each of the three regions they examined: Shirley Basin, Gas Hills, and Ambrosia Lake. Similarly, they found that the value per mine for 200 of the orebodies of the Ambrosia Lake region is lognormally distributed, when the frequency distribution is examined by the chi-square tests or by moment values.

Brink (1967, p. 8) summarizes the case for the lognormal distribution as a resources model.

Such lognormal distributions have been found for many, if not all elements. The lognormality appears to be fairly independent of the size of the sampled environment and is found in all stages of mineral exploration from regional prospection with a very wide sampling grid, through systematic and detailed prospection to the measurement of ore reserves, with everdecreasing size of grid.

While the evidence is not overwhelming in terms of quantity, what evidence there is on the distribution properties of concentrations of metal is more supportive of the lognormal proposition than it is negative. Thus, for many mineral-resource phenomena, the lognormal distribution does appear to be a useful model.

5.7. Simplified summary of concepts

Let D_j be defined as the jth subset of the NS subsets that comprise the universal set D. Suppose that D represents the earth's crust, being the set of all metal occurrences in the crust. D_j, a subset of D, is the set of metal occurrences in the jth subregion of the earth's crust. Suppose also that although NS regions exist, our knowledge of metal endowment (sum of the quantity of metal in a set of metal occurrences) is restricted to KS regions. Let us designate D_0 as the collection (union) of the KS subsets for which metal occurrences and metal endowment m are known. Now, suppose that it is desired to estimate the metal endowment of one of the regions for which metal occurrences are not known. If metal endowment for each of the KS regions for which endowment is known were equal, there would be no reason to employ as an estimate of the unknown metal endowment anything other than this constant value of m for the KS subsets in D_0. However, where there is a great variation in m for each of the KS subsets in D_0, the statistical properties of the estimate of m for the unknown region become of special interest. One way of expressing uncertainty of the estimate is by a probability distribution for endowment. An approximation to such a distribution would be the relative frequency distribution of the metal endowments of the KS regions represented by D_0. For such an approach to be appropriate and to yield reliable estimates, there would need to be some assurance that m, the metal endowment, is randomly distributed in the KS regions represented by D_0. Any persistent patterns in the geography of endowment may create suspicion about the reliability of such an estimation.

Empirical evidence suggests distinctive nonrandom features in the geography of metal endowment. It must be admitted, however, that this conclusion is predicated upon a pattern created by the interaction of man's economic pursuits with a basic endowment; consequently, the nonrandom character may be exaggerated. Nevertheless, the motivation of experience is strong—strong enough to raise doubt about the random hypotheses, at least for many metals. This doubt is increased by geological science, which demonstrates that, at least for tonnage and grade near those characteristic of economic deposits, complex earth processes are required to create the accumulations of metals.

One way of accounting for geographical variation in metal endowment is to partition D_0 into subsets, a subset for each of a selected number of earth processes, and then to construct a probability (frequency) distribution for each subset. Inference to a D_i not in D_0 would require identifying the subset to which it belongs by virtue of the earth processes that have transpired in its history. However, these earth processes are not directly observable. We generally have only indirect evidence, geological features, by which to infer the prior existence of specific earth processes in some prior geological time period. Because of our incomplete understanding of the geology–ore deposit relationship, substituting geological observation for the earth processes causes error in our assessment; this error is compounded by errors in geological observation and interpretation and the unavailability of complete geological information on all earth processes. Consequently, given the geology of a region, its metal endowment can be considered a random variable, a measure that can take on any of a range of values. In other words, for decision-making and appraisal, it is appropriate to refer to metal endowment of a region in terms of probability. In probability language the metal endowment of a region is a random variable M. Given the geology of the region, there is a probability for M being greater than a specified endowment m_1, but less than m_2

$$P(m_1 < M < m_2 \mid G_D) = \int_{m_1}^{m_2} f(m \mid G_D)\,dm,$$

where G_D represents the set of D geological variables. The function $f(m \mid G_D)$ is the conditional probability density function. $f(m \mid G_D)$ is referred to here as the basic geostatistical model of metal endowment.

A class of models that describes various aspects of metal deposits probabilistically is referred to as deposit models, a subset of geostatistical models. These models simulate man's experience and view metal endowment of a region in terms of numbers of deposits having specified tonnage and grade characteristics. This is in effect decomposing $f(m \mid G_D)$ into three submodels, one for number, one for tonnage, and one for grade

$$h(n \mid q, G_D), j(t \mid q, G_D), k(q \mid G_D),$$

where n is the number of deposits, t the deposit tonnage, and q the deposit grade. Both the probabilities for number of deposits and for deposit tonnage are considered to be conditional upon grade and geology. But, the probability for grade is defined to be conditional upon only geology.

Spatial probability models, such as the Poisson, which have been used to describe the number of mining districts are considered to be a form of h, in which the effect of geology and grade are ignored (integrated out). Multivariate geostatistical models have been employed to represent forms of $f(m \mid G_D)$

and $h(n \mid G_D)$. Trend models examine the expectation (averages) of f or h or some function of them, such as value, with respect to their geographical pattern of variation.

Crustal-abundance geostatistical (CAG) models focus upon the statistical distribution of metal concentrations in geochemical samples (rock, stream, sediment) taken from the area of interest. This statistical distribution, $\lambda(q \mid t)$, can be considered as a special form of the metal-endowment model, $f(m \mid G_D)$, in which the size and grade limitations that define metal endowment are lowered to include all crustal material; the geology is ignored (in other words integrated out); and all deposits are of the same size t.

The basic scheme in the CAG approach is to first define $\lambda(q \mid t_0)$ for the area of interest from geochemical data (size of observational or measurement unit is t_0) and then to modify it to describe the probability for metal endowment occurring in concentrations and accumulations typical of economic deposits (size $= t$),

$$\lambda(q \mid t) = \pi[\lambda(q \mid t_0), t],$$

where π is a transformation function.

Reasoning from geochemical evidence and principles suggests that for some metals, particularly the least abundant, this distribution will have a large positive skewness. Specifically, the more geochemical stages of concentration that have sequentially affected the geochemical environment of the metal, the larger the skew. Thus, theory would dictate that the distribution of grades in an ore deposit would commonly, but not always, be highly skewed. Empirical evidence supports this theory and suggests that for some metals, element concentrations measured in sizes ranging from geochemical volumes to ore deposits appear to be well described by the lognormal distribution. Applications have employed either the lognormal distribution, or its discrete approximation, the logbinomial, as the model by which inference is made to metal endowment and resources.

5.8. Appendix: Derivation of the probability density for metal, m, from the densities for n, t, and q

Let the probability density functions for number of mines n, tonnage of ore t, and grade of ore q, be h, j, and k, respectively,

$$h(n \mid q, G_D), \quad j(t \mid q, G_D), \quad \text{and} \quad k(q \mid G_D). \tag{5.52}$$

Then, y, the probability density function for the joint occurrence of n, t, and q is defined

$$y(n, t, q \mid G_D) = h(n \mid q, G_D) \cdot j(t \mid q, G_D) \cdot k(q \mid G_D). \tag{5.53}$$

Now, define three new variables, M_1, M_2, and M_3 such that

$$\begin{aligned} M_1 &= N \cdot T \cdot Q \\ M_2 &= T \\ M_3 &= Q. \end{aligned} \tag{5.54}$$

Therefore, $N = M_1/(M_2 M_3)$, $T = M_2$, and $Q = M_3$. The joint probability density function for the new variables is given by

$$f(m_1, m_2, m_3 \mid G_D) = y\left(\frac{m_1}{m_2 \cdot m_3}, m_2, m_3 \mid G_D\right) |J|, \tag{5.55}$$

where $|J|$ is the Jacobian of the transformation,

$$|J| = \begin{vmatrix} \dfrac{\partial n}{\partial m_1} & \dfrac{\partial n}{\partial m_2} & \dfrac{\partial n}{\partial m_3} \\ \dfrac{\partial t}{\partial m_1} & \dfrac{\partial t}{\partial m_2} & \dfrac{\partial t}{\partial m_3} \\ \dfrac{\partial q}{\partial m_1} & \dfrac{\partial q}{\partial m_2} & \dfrac{\partial q}{\partial m_3} \end{vmatrix}$$

$$= \begin{vmatrix} \dfrac{1}{m_2 m_3} & -\dfrac{m_1}{m_2^2 m_3} & -\dfrac{m_1}{m_2 m_3^2} \\ 0 & 1 & 0 \\ 0 & 0 & 1 \end{vmatrix} = \dfrac{1}{m_2 m_3}. \tag{5.56}$$

Therefore,

$$f(m_1, m_2, m_3 \mid G_D) = y\left(\frac{m_1}{m_2 \cdot m_3}, m_2, m_3 \mid G_D\right) \times$$
$$\times \left(\frac{1}{m_2 \cdot m_3}\right),$$

$$\begin{aligned} & m_1 \in M_1 \\ & m_2 \in M_2 = 0, \text{ otherwise.} \\ & m_3 \in M_3 \end{aligned} \tag{5.57}$$

Finally, the marginal probability density for m_1 is derived from (5.57) by integration

$$f \cdot (m_1 \mid G_D) =$$
$$\int_{M_2} \int_{M_3} y\left(\frac{m_1}{m_2 \cdot m_3}, m_2, m_3 \mid G_D\right) \frac{dm_2\, dm_3}{m_2 \cdot m_3}.$$

Or, resubstituting for M_2 and M_3 and letting M_1 be metal M and f its density, we have

$$f(m \mid G_D) = \int_T \int_Q y\left(\frac{m}{t \cdot q}, t, q \mid G_D\right) \frac{dq\, dt}{t \cdot q}.$$

References

Agterberg, F. P. (1971). A probability index for detecting favourable geological environments. *Can. Inst. Mining Met.* **10**, 82–91.

—— and Cabilio, P., (1969). Two-stage least squares model for the relationship between mappable geological variables. *J. Int. Ass. Math. Geol.* **1**(2), 137–53.

Ahrens, L. H. (1953). A fundamental law of geochemistry. *Nature* **172**(4390), 1148.

—— (1954). The lognormal distribution of the elements. *Geochim. cosmochim. Acta* **5**, 49–73.

Allais, M. (1957). Method of appraising economic prospects of mining exploration over large territories: Algerian Sahara case study. *Management Sci.* **3**(4), 285–347.

Aubrey, K. V. (1955). Frequency-distributions of elements in igneous rocks. *Geoch. cosmochim. Acta* **8**, 83–89.

Blondel, F. and Ventura, E. (1954). Estimation de la valeur de la production miniere mondiale en 1950. *Anns. Mines Carbur., Paris* **143**(X), 25–81.

—— and —— (1956). Structure de la distribution des produits mineraux dans le Monde; 1953. *Anns. Mines Carbur., Paris* **145**(XI), 2–91.

——, —— and Callot, F. (1961). Valeur de la production miniere mondiale in 1958; sa repartition geographique et son evolution. *Anns. Mines Carbur., Paris* **246**, 13–108.

Brinck, J. W. (1967). Note on the distribution and predictability of mineral resources. *Euratom 3461*, Brussels.

Chayes, F. (1954). The lognormal distribution of elements: a discussion. *Geochim. cosmochim. Acta* **6**(2/3), 119–21.

Coulomb, R. (1959). Contribution à la géochimie de l'uranium dans les granites intrusifs. *Rapport C. E. A.*, no. 1173.

Cramer, H. (1946). *Mathematical methods of statistics.* Princeton Mathematical Series, no. 9, Princeton University Press, Princeton, N.J.

DeGeoffroy, J. and Wignall, T. K. (1971). A probabilistic appraisal of mineral resources in a portion of the Grenville Province of the Canadian Shield. *Econ. Geol.* **66**(3), 466–79.

DeWijs, H. J. (1951). Statistics of ore distribution, Part I. *J. R. Netherlands Geol. Min. Soc.* November, 1951.

Drew, M. W. (1977). U. S. uranium deposits—a geostatistical model. *Resources Policy* 3(1), 60–70.

Griffiths, J. C. (1969). *The unit regional-value concept and its application to Kansas.* Special Publication No. 38, Kansas State Geological Survey. University of Kansas, Lawrence, Kansas.

—— and Singer, D. A. (1973). Size, shape, and arrangement of some uranium ore bodies. *11th Int. Symp. Computer Applications in the Minerals Industry,* Vol. 1, pp. B82–B112. College of Mines, University of Arizona, Tucson, Arizona.

Harris, D. P. (1966). A probability model of mineral wealth. *Trans. SME* June 1966, pp. 199–216.

—— (1968). Alaska's base and precious metals resources: A probabilistic regional appraisal. *Mineral resources of northern Alaska,* MIRL Report No. 16, pp. 189–224. Mineral Industries Research Laboratory, University of Alaska.

Kelly, A. M. and Sheriff, W. J. (1969). A statistical examination of the metallic mineral resources of British Columbia. *Proc. Symp. Decision-Making Mineral Ind,* pp. 221–43. University of British Columbia.

Krige, D. G. (1952). A statistical analysis of some of the borehole values in the Orange Free State Goldfield. *J. chem. metallurg. mining Soc. South Africa* 53(2), 47–64.

Lowell, J. D. (1970). Copper resources. *Mining Eng.* 22, 67–73.

Miller, R. L. and Goldberg, E. D. (1955). The normal distribution in geochemistry. *Geochim. cosmochim. Acta.* 8, 53–62.

National Academy of Sciences (1975). Resources of copper. In *Mineral resources and the environment,* Chapter VI, pp. 127–83. Committee on Mineral Resources and the Environment, National Academy of Science, Washington, DC.

Sichel, H. S. (1952). New methods in the statistical evaluation of mine sampling data. *Trans. Mining Metallurgy, Lond.,* March, 1952.

Sinclair, A. J. and Woodsworth, G. L. (1970). Multiple regression as a method of estimating exploration potential in an area near Terrace, B. C. *Econ. Geol.* 65(8), 998–1003.

Singer, D. A., Cox, D. P., and Drew, L. J. (1975). *Grade and tonnage relationships among copper deposits, Professional Paper 907-A,* pp. A-1–A-11. US Geological Survey, Washington, DC.

Slichter, L. B., Dixon, W. J., and Myer, G. H. (1962). Statistics as a guide to prospecting. *Proc. Symp. Mathematical and Computer Applications in Mining and Exploration,* pp. F1-1–F1-27. College of Mines, University of Arizona, Tucson, Arizona.

Vistelius, A. B. (1960). The skew frequency distributions and the fundamental law of geochemistry. *J. Geol.* 68, 1–22.

Notes

1. Technically, N is a discrete variable and h is a probability function, not a density function; however, to simplify the notation and operations necessary to elucidate concepts, N is considered continuous and h integrable.
2. This model is considered to apply to each of the P modes of occurrence of a metal, separately; that is, for the ith mode there is a unique $f_i(m \mid G_D)$, $i = 1, 2, \ldots, P$. However, where information does not allow for the specification of separate models, a general model for all known modes may be necessary. For simplicity of notation differentiation of the model for separate modes has been suppressed.
3. The case in which tonnage and grade are statistically independent is a special case of this general formulation.
4. Singer, D. A. (1972). Multivariate statistical analysis of the unit regional value of mineral resources. Unpublished Ph.D. dissertation, The Pennsylvania State University.
5. Wilmot, R. C., Hazen, S. W., Jr., and Wertz, J. B. (1966). Some aspects of the distributions of gold, silver, copper, zinc, and lead deposits of the Basin and Range Province in Southwest United States. Paper presented at the 6th Annual Int. Symp. on Computers and Operations Research held at The Pennsylvania State University.
6. The word in brackets is the author's interpretation.
7. Patterson, J. A. (1963). Domestic uranium reserves. Paper presented at National Western Minerals Conference, Denver, Colorado.
8. Krige, D. G. (1951). A statistical approach to some mine valuation and allied problems on the Witwatersrand. MS thesis, University of Witwatersrand.

6 A MULTIVARIATE MODEL FOR WEALTH (A VALUE AGGREGATE OF METALS)

6.1. Perspective and theory

Metal endowment was described in the conceptual section probabilistically by $f(m \mid G_D)$ [see eqns (5.17) and (5.22)]. In the most careful statement of theory, $f(m \mid G_D)$ is defined for the ith mode of occurrence of the metal in the jth region: $f_{ij}(m \mid G_D)$. For notational simplicity, the function will not be subscripted on region and mode. Unless otherwise stated such a specification is to be understood. It was specifically stated in the development of $f(m \mid G_D)$ that it referred to a single metal. Let us add a subscript k to represent the kth metal,

$$f_k(m_k \mid G_D), \quad k = 1, 2, 3, 4, \ldots, r. \qquad (6.1)$$

Suppose that there is a set of weights (constants) that represents some common aspect of these five metals: $\{p_1, p_2, \ldots, p_r\}$. Multiplication of m_k by p_k would create a new measure v_k. The probability distribution for the new random variable, $V_k = M_k \cdot p_k$, can be derived from the probability distribution for M_k, given $f_k(m_k \mid G_D)$ and $m_k = v_k/p_k$. By transformation of variable, we have

$$P(v_k'' < V_k < v_k' \mid G_D) = \int_{v''}^{v'} f_k\left(\frac{v_k}{p_k} \,\middle|\, G_D\right) \frac{dv_k}{p_k}. \qquad (6.2)$$

For simplicity of notation, let us specify a new density function, $f_k^v(v_k \mid G_D)$, allowing the functional form of f_k^v to express the particulars of the transformation.

$$f_k^v(v_k \mid G_D)\,dv_k \to f_k\left(\frac{v_k}{p_k} \,\middle|\, G_D\right)\frac{dv_k}{p_k}. \qquad (6.3)$$

For the case in which the weight p_k is a price of m_k, (6.2) is referred to as a model of the wealth of the region in the kth metal.

Suppose for simplicity, that we assume the occurrence of any one of r metals to be statistically independent of the other metals. Then, we could describe the joint occurrence of the value of the r metals by the product of their probability-density functions

$$f^v(v_1, v_2, \ldots, v_r \mid G_D)$$
$$= f_1^v(v_1 \mid G_D) \cdot f_2^v(v_2 \mid G_D) \cdot \ldots \cdot f_r^v(v_r \mid G_D). \qquad (6.4)$$

Now, let us propose a new variable w which is the sum of the r values

$$w = \sum_{k=1}^{r} v_k. \qquad (6.5)$$

By making a transformation of variable, we can determine from (6.4) a probability density function for w (see § 6.7)

$$f^w(w \mid G_D). \qquad (6.6)$$

Thus, we could refer to the probability for the random variable W, mineral wealth, being between two levels, w_1 and w_2, as

$$P(w_1 < W < w_2 \mid G_D) = \int_{w_1}^{w_2} f^w(w \mid G_D)\,dw. \qquad (6.7)$$

The occurrences of some metals appear to be correlated, a prime example being the common occurrence of zinc in sphalerite with lead in galena. Thus, for certain suites of metals, the assumption of statistical independence of the occurrence of the metals may be contrary to reality. Even if this were so, the existence of a mineral-wealth probability-density function (6.7) is not obviated, for (6.7) also could be derived for the case of dependency between metals. However, the presence of correlation would require the probability-density functions for any one metal to be defined as conditional upon the other metals. For example, for the first metal we would have

$$f_1^v(v_1 \mid G_D; v_2, \ldots, v_r). \qquad (6.8)$$

Given this form of an endowment model, the probability density for the joint occurrence of the values of the r metals would take the form

$$f^v(v_1, v_2, \ldots, v_r \mid G_D)$$
$$= f_1^v(v_1 \mid G_D; v_2, \ldots, v_r) \cdot f_2^v(v_2 \mid G_D; v_3, \ldots, v_r) \cdot \ldots$$

$$\ldots \cdot f_{r-1}^v(v_{r-1} \mid G_D, v_r) \cdot f_r^v(v_r \mid G_D). \qquad (6.9)$$

A transformation of variable ($W = V_1 + V_2 + \ldots + V_r$) could be made on (6.9) in a straightforward fashion using $f^v(v_1, v_2, \ldots, v_r \mid G_D)$, as is described in § 6.7.

The relationship of (6.9) is actually more representative of nature, *given our perspective* of *endowment as being comprised of metal in deposits* (anomalous concentrations) *of ore minerals*. The complications in the estimation of the endowment of a specific metal that arise from the correlations among metals were not specified in the conceptual framework for metal endowment. Lack of this specification is defended by several arguments.

1. The need to keep the model simple to stress the macrorelations.
2. The conceptual development dealt with the endowment of only one metal for the situation in which information on the occurrence of any other metal would not be available.
3. So long as only one metal is of interest and appraisal is predicated upon geology, the fact that a prediction of a quantity m_k implies, on average, a quantity of m_{k+i} is immaterial with respect to the prediction $\hat{m}_k$.

These arguments justify the treatment of m_k as a separate quantity; nevertheless, when considering the estimation of an *aggregate* of metals, these estimates must be consistent with the correlations between the metals. Such a model conceptually would be of the form of (6.9).

In practice, models of the wealth of an aggregate of metals have not evolved by the convolution of models of specific metals. In fact, the only probability models for mineral wealth so far have approached the description of the probabilities for w directly by selecting a functional form and estimating its parameters.

6.2. The Harris model

6.2.1. *The basic proposition*

The initial effort in the design of a multivariate probability model for mineral wealth was that of Harris ([1], 1966a). The basic proposition was that the probability for mineral wealth is conditional upon four geological variables

$$P(w_1 < W < w_2 \mid x_1, x_2, x_3, x_4)$$
$$= \int_{w_1}^{w_2} f^w(w \mid x_1, x_2, x_3, x_4)\,dw, \quad (6.10)$$

where x_1 is the age and type of rock, x_2 the rock fracturing, x_3 the structural forms, and x_4 the age of igneous activity and contact relations.

The design of this model, as with any multivariate model of endowment, was intended to reflect good geological theory. Thus, such a statistical model is also a geological model, a model which reflects certain characteristics of deposit occurrence in the region for which the model is constructed. In this case, the region was comprised of southern, central, and southeastern Arizona and southwestern New Mexico. Model design by necessity must also reflect the level of geological information that is available. In this case, the data on these four variables were derived from reconnaissance geological maps of a scale of 1 : 250 000.

6.2.2. *The geological model*

Age and type of rock. If one considers ore formation in a geological province typified by veins and porphyries, the relevant source of metal is the magma. It seems consistent then to propose that for these modes of occurrence the frequency of occurrence of metal deposits is greatest in those rocks associated with the igneous rocks or in the igneous rocks themselves. A prospector given the choice of exploring a sequence of rocks that is totally sedimentary and not associated with an igneous intrusive or of exploring an igneous rock would not hesitate to choose the latter. For example, one would have a much greater chance of success in looking for a deposit of chromite in a basic igneous body than in a sequence of sandstone and shale. For certain other metals, such as lead and zinc, it may be the joint occurrence of igneous intrusives and chemically favourable sedimentary rocks that is important.

Rock fracturing. The intricate vein deposits of Butte, Montana, that occupy fissures and fault zones of the granodiorite stock testify to the importance of rock fracturing in controlling the deposition of these ores. Fractures serve as channels through which the gaseous and liquid emanations of the igneous body traverse. They often provide the opening that is filled by the minerals deposited by the fluids and gases emanating from the intrusive and by the chemical interaction of these emanations with the host rock. Whether the deposit is formed by replacement or by cavity filling, a well-fractured rock aids in its formation.

Age of igneous activity and contact relations. Obviously, this variable is related to the rock-type variable; however, there is a difference in favourability for ore formation between the occurrence of a body of pre-Cambrian granite over which a sequence of sedimentary rocks had been deposited and the intrusion of a Laramide igneous stock into that sequence of sedimentary rocks. It is the latter phenomenon that this factor describes. The contact metamorphic and metasomatic deposits of lead, zinc, copper, tungsten, manganese, and other metals are justification enough for this measure.

Structural forms. Although gross structural forms may not relate directly to the immediate localization of the orebody, they are very important features at the reconnaissance level of exploration. The presence of a structural lineament, which is in general a zone of weakness in the Earth's crust, within a certain area makes it more attractive as a potential ore producer. Igneous intrusives that are at depths and may not yet be exposed by erosion may have intruded along this lineament. Structural highs such as domes and large anticlinal folds are also important. A domed area may be the reflection of an underlying igneous stock. An anticline, if folded tightly, may serve as a localizing agent, as indicated by the famous saddle reefs of Bendigo, Australia. In the larger sense, structural highs reflect tectonic activity that transpired during past geological periods; this previous tectonic activity enhances the likelihood of ore occurring in such an area. Regional faults create zones of weakness along which igneous bodies can move, and they may facilitate ore deposition.

6.2.3. *Usable variables*

Geology in the form of these four variables cannot be expressed directly in quantitative form. However, it is possible to get a reflection of them through the construction of crude, less meaningful variables that can be quantified. These variables are valued as counts, percentages of area, and lengths of geological features that are present in a cell (geographic subdivision of the region). Obviously, as defined, any one of them considered separately may not appear to have much relationship to the occurrence of ore, but several of them, each measuring a different thing, may define one or more of the conceptual variables. Thus

$$g_1 = a_{11}\ x_1 + a_{12}\ x_2 + a_{13}\ x_3 + a_{14}\ x_4$$
$$g_2 = a_{21}\ x_2 + a_{22}\ x_2 + a_{23}\ x_3 + a_{24}\ x_4 \quad (6.11)$$
$$\cdots\cdots\cdots\cdots\cdots$$
$$g_{26} = a_{26,1} x_1 + a_{26,2} x_2 + a_{26,3} x_3 + a_{26,4} x_4$$

where x_i, $i = 1, 2, 3, 4$ are the theoretical variables, and g_j, $j = 1, 2, \ldots, 26$ are the measurement variables. Now, for any one of the g variables, the coefficients for some of the xs may be zero such that g_j may be a function of as few as one x_i. The conceptual variables and the variables created to measure them are defined as follows (the definition of the measurement variables was constructed specifically for the geology of southern, central, and southeastern Arizona and southwestern New Mexico and may be somewhat different for another area).

Age and type of rock $= x_1$

$g_1 =$ Per cent of cell consisting of pre-Tertiary sedimentary rocks

$g_2 =$ Per cent of cell consisting of pre-Cambrian igneous intrusive rocks (includes diabase)

$g_3 =$ Per cent of cell consisting of Laramide and Nevadan igneous intrusive rocks (includes injection gneiss and contact schists)

$g_4 =$ Per cent of cell consisting of igneous extrusive rocks

$g_5 =$ Per cent of cell consisting of pre-Cambrian metamorphic rocks undifferentiated

Rock fracturing $= x_2$

$g_6 =$ Number of high angle faults, 0–8 miles in length

$g_7 =$ Number of high angle faults, greater than 8 miles in length

$g_8 =$ Number of thrust faults, 0–8 miles in length

$g_9 =$ Number of thrust faults, greater than 8 miles in length

$g_{12} =$ Number of high angle fault intersections

$g_{13} =$ Number of low–high angle fault intersections

$g_{24} =$ Number of igneous dikes

Structural forms $= x_3$

$g_{10} =$ Number of anticlines, 0–8 miles in length

$g_{11} =$ Number of anticlines, greater than 8 miles in length

$g_{25} =$ Distance from northeast-trending structural lineament as measured normal to the trace

$g_{26} =$ Distance from northwest structural lineament as measured normal to the trace

Age of igneous activity and contact relations $= x_4$

$g_{14} =$ Length of the contact of Laramide and Nevadan intrusive rocks with sedimentary rocks

$g_{15} =$ Number of exposures of the above contact

$g_{16} =$ Length of the contact of Laramide and Nevadan igneous intrusive rocks with pre-Cambrian igneous intrusive rocks

$g_{17} =$ Number of exposures of the above contact

$g_{18} =$ Length of the contact of Laramide and Nevadan igneous intrusive rocks with pre-Cambrian metamorphic rocks

$g_{19} =$ Number of exposures of the above contact

$g_{20} =$ Length of the contact of Laramide igneous intrusive rocks with Cretaceous igneous intrusive rocks

$g_{21} =$ Number of exposures of the above contact

$g_{22} =$ Length of the contact of pre-Cambrian igneous intrusive rocks with pre-Cambrian metamorphic rocks

$g_{23} =$ Number of exposures of the above contact

The region upon which this model was quantified (control area) was subdivided into 20-mile square cells, and the measurements were recorded for each of the 26 measurement variables for each of these cells, giving an expression of the geology of each cell.

6.2.4. *The value measure*

The aggregate mineral-wealth model of § 6.1 was derived from r endowment models, one model for each of the r metals. This study considers wealth to be comprised by five metals ($r = 5$): copper, lead, zinc, silver, and gold. Thus, conceptually, the desired model of mineral wealth would be derived from the endowment models of each of these metals. Of course, the endowment models are unknown to us; consequently, this means of defining the mineral-wealth model is not feasible. We must assume some functional form for the aggregate wealth model and attempt to quantify the model from available data. A discussion of the *form* of the model is taken up in a later section. Regardless of this form, so long as the model relates to mineral wealth as an aggregate of endowments, we are faced with the realities of our data. *Our data do not define endowment, as the term was defined in* § 1.2.1. Our data on the control area are limited to time series of production by mining district, and even that data series terminated in 1957, the last year that such data were published by the US Bureau of Mines.

The measurement of value for each cell was obtained by summing the quantity (weight) of production for the metals that were produced in each district in the cell over the history of the district and then weighting these quantities by a price vector reflecting the average price in US dollars for each of the metals for 1963: gold, $35.00 per oz; silver, $1.30 per oz; lead, $0.14 per lb; zinc, $0.13 per lb; and copper, $0.30 per lb.

Metal prices in 1963 were used as weights, chiefly because a mining company evaluates mineral deposits in terms of the economics of that day. Faced with current costs and prices, a gross-value term is most meaningful as a measure of mineral wealth

when it is constructed with current prices. Another reason for the use of one set of prices is the length of time over which the inception of production for mining districts has occurred, beginning in the late-nineteenth century and extending to the middle of the twentieth century. If the prices that prevailed during each year of production are used, a quantity of production for one district may have quite a different value than that same quantity of production from another district that produced over a different time period.

An objection to the use of current prices is that it glosses over the effect that price changes have had on the quantity of metal produced. If current economic conditions had prevailed since the middle-nineteenth century, a different production pattern would most probably have occurred; however, it is difficult to assess exactly what effect this would have had on the amount of metal that was eventually produced from a mine or mining district. The impact of present mining and ore-processing technology would have had as great or greater an effect on the volume of ore mined than the mere imposing of current prices; however, one cannot separate these two factors, for they are to a certain extent interrelated.

Present-day technology would very likely have caused more metal to have been mined. The large-scale, low-cost mining methods make it possible to mine ores that were uneconomic in the past. A greater production could have been realized by the sweetening of these associated low-grade ores with high-grade materials. There would have been less ore left in the ground, ore that now is uneconomic to recover because of the cost of reopening the mines. The more efficient recovery of metals by the smelters would have resulted in the payment to the mine owner for more metal content.

On the other hand, with the present high cost of labour, many of the very small high-grade deposits with no fringe of low-grade ores may not have supplied their metal, for this type of mining would still have to be done by hand methods, and the present cost of labour would have made much of this mining uneconomic. Any one or two of these mines would have little effect on total production, but all of them combined cannot be ignored.

Obviously, a value measure for the jth metal v_j obtained by the methods described constitutes the value of cumulative production, to 1957, not the value of metal endowment. Similarly, the aggregate measure w constitutes the aggregated value, wealth, of cumulative supply.

An effort was made to expand the measure of

value beyond the value of aggregate supply by including the economic and subeconomic reserves of
known districts. Published reserve figures were not
used, in recognition of the fact that mines commonly
quote reserves equal to only a few years' production
and that these reserve figures seldom reflect the
totality of known economic reserves, let alone the
known, but subeconomic, resources. The procedure
employed in this study was to estimate the economic
and subeconomic resources of a district from its time
series of production by employing the assumption
that the production life cycle of a district conforms to
a bell-shaped curve, as demonstrated by Fig. 6.1.
Estimation by this method requires identification of
where in this postulated cycle the district was by
1957 and then estimating the quantity of resources
implied for completion of the cycle. Thus, a plot was
made for each major district of the time series of its
production aggregated to a value measure using
1963 prices for the five metals, as demonstrated in
Fig. 6.2. In order to emphasize the overall trend, the
erratic and short-term cyclical effects were smoothed
out by applying three successive three-year moving

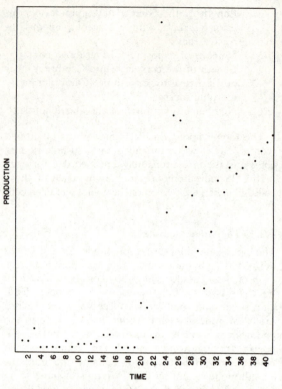

Fig. 6.2. Graph of raw production data (Source: Harris [1].)

averages. Fig. 6.3 shows the effects of this smoothing
of the raw data of Fig. 6.2. The smoothed time series
was examined to determine its progression on the
bell-shaped life cycle. The value of cumulative production to 1957 was multiplied by a factor that
represented the inverse of the fractional completion
of the time series on the bell-shaped life cycle, or, it
was determined by fitting a logistic curve to the
cumulative production series and evaluating the
function at ∞. For example, the smoothed time series
of Fig. 6.3 was interpreted to suggest that approximately one-half of the cycle had been completed.
Thus, the mineral wealth of this district was estimated by multiplying cumulative production by a
factor of two.

Each mining district which was active during one
of the years of 1955, 1956, and 1957 was appraised
in the fashion described. The measure of wealth that
resulted was allocated to cells on the basis of the
area of the district lying in a cell. The mineral wealth
of a cell was determined by summing that mineral
wealth imparted to it by each district that was totally

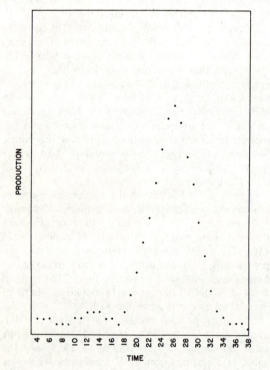

Fig. 6.1. Moving average (three successive three-year averages) graph of an exhausted mining district
(Source: Harris [1].)

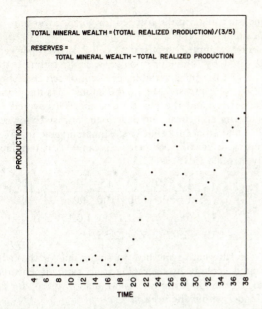

TOTAL MINERAL WEALTH = (TOTAL REALIZED PRODUCTION)/(3/5)

RESERVES =
        TOTAL MINERAL WEALTH − TOTAL REALIZED PRODUCTION

Fig. 6.3. Graph of smoothed series using three successive three-year moving averages (Source: Harris [1].)

or in part contained within the boundaries of the cell. It was this measure of mineral wealth that was examined statistically with respect to the geological variables.

6.2.5. *Incomplete geological information*

The question of what to do with cells that are totally or mostly covered by alluvium arises in the construction of a multivariate model, for alluvial covering implies partial observation of variables, a condition that is not allowed in the application of conventional multivariate techniques. There are four treatments of the alluvium issue.

1. Delete from the data base those cells having alluvium.
2. Specify the model as a model of potential supply and use alluvium as a proxy for the effect of exploration.
3. Include alluvium as a variable and then purge its effects from the model.
4. Estimate the covered geology and use the exposed plus covered geology as the basis for the analysis.

The initial study by Harris [1] employed the second, third, and fourth treatments while, in a later study (1968), treatments 1 and 4 were employed.

Treatment 1 is the *proper* treatment of alluvial cover from the purely statistical point of view and needs little comment in this regard, for multivariate models *do not allow* for incomplete observation. However, it may carry a liability from a purely pragmatic point of view, for there may be in a region very few cells having no alluvial cover. Furthermore, using cells with no alluvium may introduce a geological bias, for resistance to erosion reflects geology.

Treatments 2 and 3 include alluvial cover as a geological variable in the multivariate model. The basic argument for this approach might be that the objective of the analysis is a predictive model for the value of *potential supply*, not endowment. Therefore, since the presence of alluvial cover precludes complete surface exploration and has a direct impact on the mineral wealth realized or to be realized for the cell, it should be treated explicitly as a variable in the multivariate model. In other words, the measure of mineral wealth for a cell should reflect the presence of alluvial cover. By including cover as a variable the mineral wealth and geology are compatible, for alluvium covers mineral deposits as well as it does the geology. Evaluation of the potential supply of an unknown cell partially covered by alluvium would proceed by evaluating the multivariate model on the cell's geology. This would provide an estimate of potential supply, given the alluvium covering on the cell. Appraisal of the effects of removing the cover could be made by adjusting this estimate, as is described in § 6.2.6.

Treatment 4 carries the obvious statistical complication of basing an estimate upon an estimate; nevertheless, considering both the statistical and practical issues, this treatment is probably the most desirable of the four. The geology of the covered portion of a cell probably is estimated most accurately by a geoscientist who has a considerable first-hand field experience in the region and employs his experience and science to interpret the covered geology. However, it may be that such an individual is not available or that time and resources do not allow for this approach. Given this situation, the geology may be estimated by statistical procedures.

1. Direct expansion;
2. Direct expansion smoothed by a weighted average;
3. Trend analysis.

Direct expansion would simply inflate the exposed geology of the cell to represent 100 per cent exposure,

$$\hat{g}_{ijk} = \frac{g'_{ijk}}{(100 - C_{ij})} \cdot 100, \qquad (6.12)$$

where g'_{ijk} is the kth geological measurement of the ijth cell, $\hat{g}_{ijk}$ is the estimate of g_{ijk} made by direct expansion, and C_{ij} is the per cent cover of the ijth cell. Obviously, this estimation procedure requires that some part, small though it may be, of the cell is not covered by alluvium. The chief virtue of this procedure is its ease and simplicity. Other than the fact that it cannot be used on totally covered cells, a drawback of this estimate is that the smaller the exposed area, the greater the chance that it is not representative of the cell and that geology inferred from the exposure may be in contrast (not compatible) to the geology of adjacent cells.

A modified version of expansion would be to consider the geology of adjacent cells with the exposed geology of the cell to estimate the covered geology

$$\hat{g}^*_{ijk} = g'_{ijk} + \left\{ \frac{4g'_{ijk}}{(100-C_{ij})} + \frac{g'_{i-1,j,k}}{(100-C_{i-1,j})} \right.$$
$$+ \frac{g'_{i+1,j,k}}{(100-C_{i+1,j})} + \frac{g'_{i,j-1,k}}{(100-C_{i,j-1})}$$
$$\left. + \frac{g'_{i,j+1,k}}{(100-C_{i,j+1})} \right\} \left(\frac{C_{ij}}{N} \right), \qquad (6.13)$$

where N is the sum of weights used in averaging, which varies from cell to cell, depending upon the number of cells in contact with the ijth cell. The maximum value for N is 8 and the minimum is 4 (in which this equation produces the same estimate as direct expansion). $\hat{g}^*_{ijk}$ is the smoothed estimate by inflation and averaging, and g'_{ijk} is the kth geological

1,3	1,4	1,5
	$C_{1,4} = 50$	
	$g'_{1,4,3} = 10$	
2,3	2,4	2,5
$C_{2,3} = 10$	$C_{2,4} = 20$	$C_{2,5} = 70$
$g'_{2,3,3} = 0$	$g'_{2,4,3} = 10$	$g'_{2,5,3} = 5$
3,3	3,4	3,5
	$C_{3,4} = 0$	
	$g'_{3,4,3} = 15$	

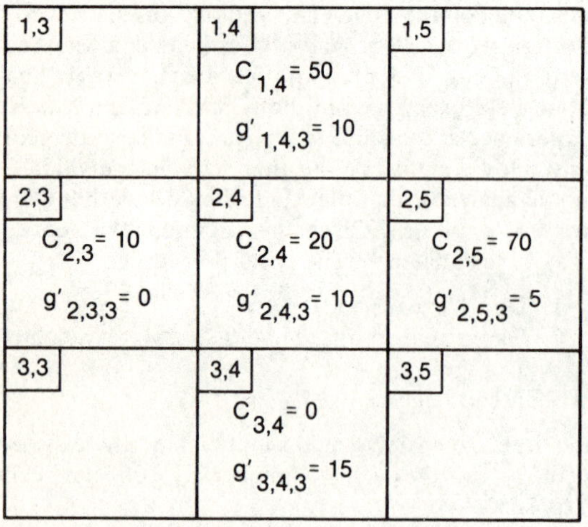

Fig. 6.4. Map of cells, showing cell coordinates and values for C_{ij} and g'_{ij3}.

measurement on the ijth cell for which cover may be present.

For example, suppose that cell 2, 4 is 20 per cent covered by alluvium and we wish to estimate the value of the third variable, per cent of cell consisting of igneous intrusive. Fig. 6.4 demonstrates the physical setting and the per cent of the cell covered by alluvium and consisting of igneous intrusives for cell 2, 4 and adjacent cells. The estimated value for $\hat{g}_{2,4,3}$ representing 100 per cent exposure, as determined by formula (6.13) is 12.55

$$\hat{g}^*_{2,4,3} = 10 + \left\{ \frac{(4)(10)}{80} + \frac{10}{50} + \frac{15}{100} + \frac{0}{90} + \frac{5}{30} \right\} \cdot \left(\frac{20}{8} \right)$$
$$\hat{g}^*_{2,4,3} = 10 + (0.5 + 0.2 + 0.15 + 0 + 0.17)(2.5)$$
$$\hat{g}^*_{2,4,3} = 10 + (1.02)(2.5) = 12.55.$$

An alternative method to smoothing of the estimated geology by averaging is to estimate covered geology by performing a trend analysis on $\hat{g}_{ijk}$ for all i and j within the area,

$$\hat{g}^{**}_{ijk} = g'_{ijk} + \hat{g}^T_{ijk} \cdot (C_{ij}/100), \qquad (6.14)$$

where $\hat{g}^T_{ijk} = Z(i, j)$ and $Z(i, j)$ is a trend equation. $\hat{g}^T_{ijk}$ would represent a smoothing of $\hat{g}_{ijk}$, based upon the overall pattern of $\hat{g}_{ijk}$ in the entire area. Such a value is similar to that obtained by contouring of $\hat{g}_{ijk}$ using broad contour intervals. However, estimation of the covered portion of g_{ijk} by this approach is recommended only for the special case in which the geological variables are statistically independent. Separate (individual) estimation for each correlated variable does not guarantee that the estimated values of each variable will be consistent with the relationship between variables. For the general case, that of correlated geological variables, this procedure can be employed by first making a transformation to a set of independent variables. A commonly used transformation is that of factor analysis (principal components). This procedure was also examined by Harris [1]. We shall not examine the methods of factor analysis here, for it is a rather complex method of multivariate statistical analysis designed to address very specific questions. An exposition with a demonstration is provided by Harris (1966b) and Klovan (1968). Standard references include Harmon (1962) and Cattell (1965). For our purposes here, consider factor analysis as a means of expressing the information of D correlated geological measurements as D new, uncorrelated measurements s_k (factor scores), $k = 1, 2, \ldots, D$. Rather than describing the geology of each cell by the original measurements, it would be described by D factor scores. Since these factor scores would be uncorrelated, each s_k could be independently described by a trend surface,

$$s_k^T = Z_k(i, j). \qquad (6.15)$$

s_k^T is smoothed s_k. After the trend values for each factor have been determined for each cell (provided that as many factors were extracted as variables), this trend analysis can be followed by a second transformation, yielding the smoothed estimates of the geological variables.

As a means to understanding this procedure, consider factor analysis to have produced D factor equations. The kth factor equation defines the kth factor score for the ijth cell as a function of the expanded but nonsmoothed geological variables,

$$s_{ijk} = a_{1k}\hat{g}_{ij1} + a_{2k}\hat{g}_{ij2} + \ldots + a_{Dk}\hat{g}_{ijD},$$
$$k = 1, 2, \ldots, D. \quad (6.16)$$

Factor analysis yields the constants a_{ik}, $i = 1, 2, \ldots, D$, for each of the D factors. Having a knowledge of these constants allows the calculation of a factor score by substituting into the equation the values of the expanded geological variables. Then, the factor scores are smoothed by trend analysis, yielding s_{ijk}^T.

The question to be answered is what are the values of the geological variables implied by the set of trended D factor scores. This can be answered by equating the smoothed values of the factor scores to the sum of unknown geological variables times the known coefficients

$$s_{ij1}^T = a_{11}\hat{g}_{ij1}^T + a_{2r}\hat{g}_{ij2}^T + \ldots + a_{D1}g_{ijD}^T$$
$$s_{ij2}^T = a_{12}\hat{g}_{ij1}^T + a_{22}\hat{g}_{ij2}^T + \ldots + a_{D2}\hat{g}_{ijD}^T \quad (6.17)$$
$$\cdots \cdots \cdots \cdots \cdots$$
$$s_{ijD}^T = a_{1D}\hat{g}_{ij1}^T + a_{2D}\hat{g}_{ij2}^T + \ldots + a_{DD}\hat{g}_{ijD}^T.$$

Thus, we have D equations in D unknowns (the smoothed geological variables $\hat{g}_{ijk}^T$). In matrix notation, we have

$$S_{ij}^T = AG_{ij}^T. \qquad (6.18)$$

Then, $G_{ij}^T = A^{-1}S_{ij}^T$, giving the trended (smoothed) values of the D expanded geological variables, $\hat{g}_{ijk}^T$, $k = 1, 2, \ldots, D$. Finally, the estimated geology $\hat{g}_{ijk}^{**}$ for the ijth cell is determined by combining this expanded and smoothed estimate $\hat{g}_{ijk}^T$ with the geology actually observed g_{ijk}',

$$\hat{g}_{ijk}^{**} = g_{ijk}' + \hat{g}_{ijk}^T \cdot (C_{ij}/100).$$

A virtue of the procedure is that it can be used to provide estimated geology of cells that are completely covered by alluvium. Obviously, the geology of such a cell is the geology obtained from the trend analysis and subsequent retransformation $\hat{g}_{ijk}^T$, for g_{ijk}' is zero.

Harris [1] applied orthogonal polynomial trend surfaces to geological factors (factor scores of orthogonal factors) that had been expanded to represent 100 per cent exposed geological factors. Then, these smoothed, estimated factors were used in the mineral-wealth model.

6.2.6. The use of the expanded information

Obviously, the motivation behind estimating 100 per cent exposed geology for a cell is to 'look underneath the cover', to estimate the mineral wealth that may have been realized if all geology were exposed. Although the motivation is clear, the procedure is not. Two approaches could be employed.

1. Quantify the mineral wealth upon exposed geology only and inflate estimates by the factor of $(100 - C_{ij})/100$, provided that $C_{ij} \neq 100$.

$$\hat{w}_{ij} = \theta(g_{ij1}', \ldots, g_{ijD}') \bigg/ \left(\frac{100 - C_{ij}}{100}\right), \quad (6.19)$$

where $\hat{w}_{ij}$ is an estimate of the expectation of mineral wealth for the ijth cell.

2. Consider C_{ij} as another geological variable, quantifying the relationship of mineral wealth to the D geological variables and C_{ij} and then purging the effects of C_{ij} by setting it to zero and evaluating the equation on the expanded geological variables.

Relationship

$$\bar{w}_{ij} = \theta_C(g_{ij1}', \ldots, g_{ijD}', C_{ij}), \qquad (6.20)$$

Estimate

$$\hat{w}_{ij} = \theta(\tilde{g}_{ij1}, \ldots, \tilde{g}_{ijD}, 0.0), \qquad (6.21)$$

where $\tilde{g}_{ijk}$ is an estimate of 100 per cent geology, either $\hat{g}_{ijk}$, $\hat{g}_{ijk}^*$, or $\hat{g}_{ijk}^{**}$.

The first approach makes the assumption that for a given geology, on average, the potential of an area is proportional to the exposed geology. The second approach makes no such simplistic assumption, as cover is a variable in the equation. The effect of setting cover to zero and using the estimated values of 100 per cent exposed geology depends upon the parameters of the equation, the importance of alluvium as an impedance to exploration, and the new geological information introduced by $\tilde{g}_{ijk}$, the estimate of 100 per cent exposed geology. Estimating the covered geology may provide additional geological information which results in an estimate of mineral wealth that is more definitive. Obviously, whether or not this eventuates depends upon the means of estimating the covered geology.

The foregoing comments refer to (6.19) and (6.20), which are equations that define an expectation for mineral wealth, but they also are relevant to probabilistic descriptions of mineral wealth of the form of (6.6). However, the effects of incomplete geology on the probability for W are not so intuitive as they are for eqns (6.19) and (6.20), for these effects alter the probability space upon which the probability for a specified mineral wealth w is defined.

6.2.7. Relating probability, mineral wealth, and geology

General. The development thus far has defined the geological measurement variables and identified information problems with respect to a conceptual model

$$f^w(w \mid G_D). \tag{6.22}$$

Of course, we do not know the form of the model or its parameters. Thus, we shall have to assume a form and estimate its parameters from data. The approach employed by Harris to quantify (6.22) was to partition the mineral-wealth variable into six intervals of mineral wealth (Table 6.1) and to describe membership of a cell in each wealth group as a function of the geology of the cell.

The procedure followed was to classify each of the 243 cells of Arizona and New Mexico into one of the wealth classes, based upon value of cumulative production of the five metals and inferred resources of the producing districts within the cell. Then, multiple discriminant analysis was employed to investigate the differences of the geology of the cells within the various groups. A set of equations (discriminant equations) was determined that described the influence of geology upon cell membership in these groups. Evaluation of an unknown cell, unknown in that the class to which it belongs is not known, is made by computing its discriminant scores from its geology and the discriminant equations. Bayesian classifica-

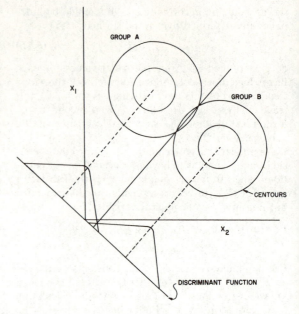

Fig. 6.5. Schematic representation of discriminant analysis.

tion analysis was employed to compute from the discriminant scores a probability for the unknown cell belonging to each of the six wealth classes.

Although the mathematics of multiple discriminant and Bayesian classification analysis may appear complex and cumbersome, the concepts are simple. To demonstrate the concepts we shall turn to a simple case in which there are only two groups of cells and two variables. Fig. 6.5 demonstrates the discriminant problem. Imagine that you plot all cells of the two groups (groups A and B) in a two-variable space, based upon the measurements for each cell of the two features (variables). Suppose also that the frequency of occurrence of cells in a given unit of area of this two-variable space were contoured. Such a procedure performed on a large number of cells could produce the lines of equal frequency drawn in Fig. 6.5, labelled centours. These centours represent two-dimensional probability distributions for each of the two populations. At the bottom of Fig. 6.5 is a reflection of a cross-section through these centours, giving typical univariate frequency curves in the selected plane of the cross-section across the two-variable space. The typical discriminant problem is the case where some cells of group A lie in the same position in the two-variable space as do cells from group B. In other words, the tails of the implied

TABLE 6.1. *Classes of mineral wealth*

Interval index	Range of wealth (US $)
1	0 to 10 000
2	10 000 to 100 000
3	100 000 to 1 000 000
4	1 000 000 to 10 000 000
5	10 000 000 to 100 000 000
6	100 000 000 to 5 000 000 000

frequency distributions overlap. The objective of discriminant analysis is to determine that linear combination of the two variables that provides the maximum accuracy in describing membership in the two populations. The auxiliary line, drawn perpendicular to the line separating the two groups, represents a discriminant function. Evaluating the equation of such a line on the variables of a cell, assigns to the cell a position on this line. The discriminant score may clearly indicate that the cell belongs to one group; however, where the areas of overlap are large, the group membership may not be clear. A decision of group membership must reflect not only the position of the discriminant score relative to the means of the two distributions, but also the dispersion (variances) of the distributions. If we make the assumption that the discriminant scores are normally distributed, then a probability for group membership can be computed, given the means and variances of the discriminant scores of the two populations.

Simple discriminant and probability analysis. In order to demonstrate these ideas, we shall not worry at this point how the discriminant equation is determined; rather, we will assume that the analysis has been performed on a two-variable, two-population universe yielding the discriminant equation

$$\text{disc}_i = (1) \cdot X_{1i} - (0.54) \cdot X_{2i}, \quad (6.23)$$

where disc_i is the discriminant score for the ith cell and X_{1i}, X_{2i} are the values of measurement variables for the ith cell. Thus, for any cell, a discriminant score can be obtained by substituting into (6.23) its measurements. Suppose that such an evaluation is made for each of the four cells in group 1 and the four cells in group 2, yielding the results of Table 6.2. From the data of Table 6.2, we can compute a mean discriminant score and variance for each group

$$\overline{\text{disc}_1} = -1.020 \qquad \overline{\text{disc}_2} = 1.020$$
$$\hat{\sigma}^2_{D1} = 0.556 \qquad \hat{\sigma}^2_{D2} = 1.695$$
$$\hat{\sigma}_{D1} = 0.746 \qquad \hat{\sigma}_{D2} = 1.302.$$

TABLE 6.2. *Discriminant scores of cells within groups*

Group 1	Group 2
-1.00	2.54
-0.54	0.46
-2.08	-0.46
-0.46	1.54

Now, suppose that we are presented with the raw variable scores (measurements) of an unknown ($X_1 = 1.0$; $X_2 = 2.0$); that is, we do not know to which population (1 or 2) this individual belongs. However, since we have his raw scores and a discriminant equation, we can compute his discriminant score and compare it to the means of the scores of each of the two groups in discriminant space

$$\text{disc}_i = 1(1.0) - 0.54(2) = 1 - 1.08 = -0.08. \quad (6.24)$$

The means of the two groups in discriminant space were calculated to be -1.02 for group 1 and $+1.02$ for group 2. By visual comparison, we might conclude that the unknown belongs to group 1. In some cases, the score of the unknown may not lead to a clear conclusion. In order to be better able to describe objectively the uncertainty associated with the classification of an unknown, the discriminant analysis is combined with probability theory and Bayes' rule.

Before demonstrating this rule, we need an additional concept, the probability for group membership irrespective of the status of the variables X_1 and X_2.

Let us refer to this as a marginal probability for membership. Suppose that $f(h, x_1, x_2)$ represent the joint probability distribution for group membership and the conditions of X_1 and X_2; then, $f_h(h)$ is the marginal probability distribution for h (membership in group h)

$$f_h(h) = \int_{X_2} \int_{X_1} f(h, x_1 x_2) \, dx_1 \, dx_2. \quad (6.25)$$

If we ignore geology, our estimate of the probability that a cell selected at random will belong to a selected wealth group is the marginal probability of membership in the wealth group, but, if we have observed certain geological conditions in the unknown cell, how does this affect the probability that the cell of unknown membership belongs to a specific wealth group? If geology is related to mineral wealth, we would expect that knowledge of a cell's geology would improve our estimate of the probabilities of group membership. Bayes' rule is a means of computing the probability of group membership, given the observed geology.

To simplify the demonstration of the mechanics of Bayes' rule, let's suppose that X_1 and X_2 are discrete, binary variables, then the marginal probability for group membership would be defined

$$f_h(h) = \sum_{X_1=0}^{1} \sum_{X_2=0}^{1} f(h, x_1, x_2).$$

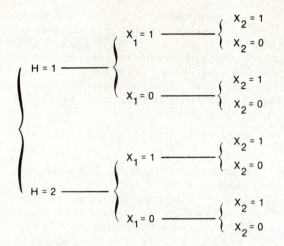

Fig. 6.6. Hypothetical event space. (The joint probability tree of Fig. 6.7 is associated with this event tree.)

Further, as in our example, let's suppose that there are only two groups, or hypotheses $H = 1, 2$. Then, our event space could be drawn as a tree diagram, as shown in Fig. 6.6.

Now, suppose that we know that event $X_1 = 1$ and $X_2 = 0$ has occurred. Then we also know that we are at one of two points in Fig. 6.7, those marked by an asterisk. In other words, either the event, $X_1 = 1$ and $X_2 = 0$, has occurred and $H = 1$, or $X_1 = 1$, $X_2 = 0$, and $H = 2$. The probability, given $X_1 = 1$ and $X_2 = 0$, for $H = 1$ and $H = 2$ can be computed by Bayes' rule.

$$P(H = 1 \mid X_1 = 1; X_2 = 0)$$
$$= \frac{\{P(X_1 = 1, X_2 = 0 \mid H = 1) \cdot P(H = 1)\} \div}{\div \{P(X_1 = 1, X_2 = 0 \mid H = 1) \cdot P(H = 1) + \\ + P(X_1 = 1, X_2 = 0 \mid H = 2) \cdot P(H = 2)\}}$$

$$P(H = 2 \mid X_1 = 1; X_2 = 0)$$
$$= \frac{\{P(X_1 = 1, X_2 = 0 \mid H = 2) \cdot P(H = 2)\} \div}{\div \{P(X_1 = 1, X_2 = 0 \mid H = 2) \cdot P(H = 2) + \\ + P(X_1 = 1, X_2 = 0 \mid H = 1) \cdot P(H = 1)\}}.$$

$$(6.26)$$

Use of probability theory and Bayes' rule to convert the discriminant score to probability requires knowledge of the marginal probabilities of group membership, which in (6.26) are labelled $P(H = 1)$ and $P(H = 2)$. In the absence of this information, the relative frequencies of cells in each group could be employed as estimates of the marginal probabilities. For such a practice to be good procedure requires that the data submitted to discriminant analysis represent a random sampling of the mixed population.

Referring back to the data of Table 6.2, we have four cells in each group. If these data represented a random sampling of the mixed population, then the marginal probability for membership in group 1 is equal to that for group 2: $P(H = 1) = P(H = 2) = 0.5$. Thus, employing Bayes' rule for this example, we would write the probability that given the discriminant score of the ith unknown it belongs to group 1 as

$$P(H = 1 \mid \mathrm{DISC}_i = -0.08)$$
$$= \frac{\{P(\mathrm{DISC}_i = -0.08 \mid H = 1) \cdot P(H = 1)\} \div}{\div \{P(\mathrm{DISC}_i = -0.08 \mid H = 1) \cdot P(H = 1) + \\ + P(\mathrm{DISC}_i = -0.08 \mid H = 2) \cdot P(H = 2)\}}.$$

$$(6.27)$$

Using $P(H = 1) = 0.5 = P(H = 2)$, we have

$$P(H = 1 \mid \mathrm{DISC}_i = -0.08)$$
$$= \frac{\{P(\mathrm{DISC}_i = -0.08 \mid H = 1) \cdot (0.5)\} \div}{\div \{P(\mathrm{DISC}_i = -0.08 \mid H = 1) \cdot (0.5) + \\ + P(\mathrm{DISC}_i = -0.08 \mid H = 2) \cdot (0.5)\}}.$$

$$(6.28)$$

But, before the probabilities for $H = 1$, given $\mathrm{DISC}_i = -0.08$, can be computed, we must obtain $P(\mathrm{DISC}_i = -0.08 \mid H = 1)$ and $P(\mathrm{DISC}_i = -0.08 \mid H = 2)$. Simply stated, the probability can be viewed as answers to the question: if we assume that the unknown belongs to group 1, what is the probability that it would have the discriminant score of -0.08? The second probability is an answer to a similar question with respect to group 2.

By making the assumption that discriminant scores of each group are normally distributed, each population having means and variances equal to the means and variances of the discriminant scores of the data submitted to discriminant analysis (Table 6.2), we can estimate these probabilities from the standard normal probability distribution. Although areas could be used, the computer routine employed by Harris, adapted from Cooley and Lohnes (1962), employed the ordinate value of the density function.

$$P(\mathrm{DISC}_i = \mathrm{disc}_i \mid H = 1)$$
$$= \frac{\exp\left(-\tfrac{1}{2}[(\mathrm{disc}_i - \overline{\mathrm{disc}_1})/\hat{\sigma}_{D1}]^2\right)}{\hat{\sigma}_{D1}\sqrt{(2\pi)}} \quad (6.29)$$

and

$$P(\mathrm{DISC}_i = \mathrm{disc}_i \mid H = 2)$$
$$= \frac{\exp\left(-\tfrac{1}{2}[(\mathrm{disc}_i - \overline{\mathrm{disc}_2})/\hat{\sigma}_{D2}]^2\right)}{\hat{\sigma}_{D2}\sqrt{(2\pi)}}. \quad (6.30)$$

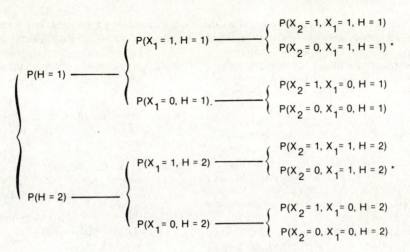

Fig. 6.7. Hypothetical joint probability tree.

Let us look at an example: we found from analysis of the data of Table 6.2 that $\overline{disc_1} = -1.02$, $\hat{\sigma}_{D1} = 0.74565$; $\overline{disc_2} = 1.02$, $\hat{\sigma}_{D2} = 1.302$. These are estimates of the parameters of two normal distributions. We also found a discriminant score of -0.08 for the ith unknown, $DISC_i = -0.08$. Substitution of these quantities into (6.29) and (6.30) gives

$$P(DISC_i = -0.08 \mid H = 1)$$
$$= \frac{\exp\left(-\tfrac{1}{2}[(-0.08-(-1.02))/0.746]^2\right)}{0.746\sqrt{(2\pi)}} = 0.2418,$$

$$P(DISC_i = -0.08 \mid H = 2)$$
$$= \frac{\exp\left(-\tfrac{1}{2}[(-0.08-1.02)/1.302]^2\right)}{1.302\sqrt{(2\pi)}} = 0.2144.$$

Finally, by substituting these probabilities into (6.28), the probability for $H = 1$, given the discriminant score of -0.08, can be computed

$$P(H = 1 \mid DISC_i = -0.08)$$
$$= \frac{(0.2418)(0.5)}{(0.2418)(0.5) + (0.2144)(0.5)} = 0.5300$$

and

$$P(H = 2 \mid DISC_i = -0.08) = 1 - 0.5300 = 0.4700.$$

The method employed by Harris to relate probability to mineral wealth and geology, in its simplest form, can be summarized as follows.

1. Identify a control area, a well-explored region.

2. Classify the cells of the region into value groups.

3. Compute the discriminant function, a linear equation that describes the differences of the geology of the cells in each group.

4. Estimate the mean and variance of the distribution of the discriminant scores of the populations of each group from the means and variances of the discriminant scores of the cells classified in the groups and submitted to discriminant analysis.

5. Estimate marginal probabilities for group membership in the mixed population. In the case of random sampling of the mixed population, these may be the relative frequencies of cells classified into the value groups.

6. Combine the marginal probabilities for group membership with the probability for the computed discriminant score, given group membership, by Bayes' rule to yield the probability for group membership, given the discriminant score.

The evaluation of an unexplored cell, or a cell of another region, would be done as follows.

1. Substitute the geological measurements into the discriminant equation, producing a discriminant score for the unknown cell,

2. Substitute the discriminant score into the normal probability equations for each group,

3. Combine these probabilities with the marginal probabilities in Bayes' rule to yield the probabilities for group membership, given the computed discriminant score.

The foregoing demonstration was reduced to the simplest case, a two-variable, two-group universe. A universe of several variables and two groups introduces no complications in the probability analysis over the simplest case, because the several variables are combined through the discriminant equation to yield one discriminant score per cell. Naturally, computations required to obtain the discriminant score used in the probability analysis are increased by increasing the variables. Increasing the number of groups as well as variables obviously increases the computations in the probability analysis, but these computations are simple and straightforward as long as only one discriminant function is computed and employed.

A universe consisting of several variables on several groups may not be completely described by one discriminant function. Whenever the number of groups exceeds two, one must consider the necessity of employing more than one discriminant function. The maximum possible number of discriminant functions is the lesser of two numbers: the number of variables or one less than the number of groups. The appropriate number to use can only be determined by statistical analysis and is the number of equations that are statistically significant at some selected level of significance. The general case of discriminant analysis allows for more than one equation; this is referred to as multiple discriminant analysis and is described in the following section.

6.2.8. Multiple-discriminant and Bayesian probability analysis

Before examining the statistical relations of multiple-discriminant analysis, let us clarify notation, for some of the symbols that were employed in § 6.2.7 have a different meaning in this section. First of all there are NG groups represented in our sample and NG populations in the universe. Multiple discriminant analysis yields r discriminant functions. Since there are r discriminant functions, r discriminant scores (disc_{ij}, $j = 1, 2, \ldots, r$) can be computed for the ith individual by evaluating the r functions on the geological variables that constitute them. Averaging the discriminant scores of the jth function on the N_h cells of the hth group gives a mean discriminant score of the jth function for the hth group; this mean is referred to as $\overline{\text{disc}}_{hj}$. Since there are r discriminant functions, there are r of these means. These r means for the hth group are referred to by the vector $\overline{\text{DISC}}_h$

$$\overline{\text{DISC}}_h = [\overline{\text{disc}}_{h1}, \overline{\text{disc}}_{h2}, \ldots, \overline{\text{disc}}_{hr}]. \quad (6.31)$$

The following notation is employed to describe the various vectors of multiple-discriminant analysis.

DISC_i = a vector of r discriminant scores for the ith cell.

$\overline{\text{DISC}}_h$ = a vector of r mean discriminant scores (a centroid) for the hth group, $h = 1, 2, \ldots, NG$.

$'\text{DISC}_i$ = a random vector for the ith individual. Note: DISC_i is a specific vector, a realization of $'\text{DISC}_i$. $\quad (6.32)$

DIF_{ih} = the vector of the differences $(\text{DISC}_i - \overline{\text{DISC}}_h)$ for the ith cell and hth group:

$$\text{DIF}_{ih}^{\text{T}} = [\text{disc}_{i1} - \overline{\text{disc}}_{h1}, \text{disc}_{i2} - \overline{\text{disc}}_{h2}, \ldots$$
$$\ldots, \text{disc}_{ir} - \overline{\text{disc}}_{hr}].$$

Instead of having a variance for each of the NG groups as we did in simple discriminant analysis, we have a variance–covariance matrix, D_h, $h = 1, 2, \ldots, NG$. The diagonal of D_h consists of the variances of the r discriminant scores across the cells of the hth group. Each of these NG matrices is an $r \times r$ matrix. Let us refer to the pqth element of the hth matrix D_h by the notation $[d_{pq}]$. Then, $[d_{pq}]$ can be defined in terms of discriminant scores

$$[d_{pq}] = \left[\sum_{i=1}^{N_h} \sum_{j=1}^{N_h} \text{disc}_{ip} \cdot \text{disc}_{jq} - \frac{\sum_{i=1}^{N_h} \text{disc}_{ip} \sum_{j=1}^{N_h} \text{disc}_{jq}}{N_h} \right] / N_h,$$

$$(6.33)$$

where N_h is the number of cells in the hth group and disc_{ip}, disc_{jq} is the score of the pth and qth functions for the ith and jth individuals, respectively, of the hth group.

Using the terms defined above, we can define the square of a standardized score for the ith individual for the hth group as

$$x_{ih}^2 = \text{DIF}_{ih}^{\text{T}} D_h^{-1} \text{DIF}_{ih}, \quad (6.34)$$

where D_h^{-1} is the inverse of the dispersion matrix of the hth group, x_{ih}^2 is a scalar for the ith individual and hth group, and $\text{DIF}_{ih}^{\text{T}}$ is the transpose of DIF_{ih}.

Now, we can define the probability for membership in the hth group, given the vector of discriminant scores, DISC_i, for the ith individual in the NG-

population universe, as

$$P(H = h \mid {}'DISC_i = DISC_i)$$

$$= \frac{\left[\frac{1}{|D_h|^{\frac{1}{2}}} \exp\left(\frac{-x_{ih}^2}{2}\right)\right] \cdot P(H = h)}{\sum_{k=1}^{NG} \left[\frac{1}{|D_k|^{\frac{1}{2}}} \exp\left(\frac{-x_{ik}^2}{2}\right) \cdot P(H = k)\right]}, \quad (6.35)$$

where ${}'DISC_i$ is the random vector and $DISC_i$ is a specific vector. Note that the expression in the brackets is of the same form as (6.29) for a two-group, two-variable universe. However, the scalar of (6.35), x_{ih}^2, in the simplest case does not require vector and matrix operations.

Once the matrix and vector operations have been performed to yield x_{ih}^2, the probability analysis is identical to that previously described for the two-group, single-discriminant function, case. The complexity of the probability analysis derives primarily from the necessity of matrix and vector operations leading to the scalar x_{ih}^2. The following numerical example for a three-variable, three-population universe serves to demonstrate these calculations.

Suppose that we have postulated a three-group, four-variable universe, gathered the data on the cells of a control area, classified the cells into the three groups, and submitted these data to multiple-discriminant analysis, which yielded the following results.

Discriminant equations

$$disc_{i1} = 5x_{i1} + 10x_{i2} - 20x_{i3} - 15x_{i4} \quad (6.36)$$
$$disc_{i2} = 20x_{i1} - 10x_{i2} + 5x_{i3} + 10x_{i4}$$

Centroids (three groups)

Equation	$\overline{DISC_1}$	$\overline{DISC_2}$	$\overline{DISC_3}$
1	−53	−52	−61 (6.37)
2	36	33	30

Inverse dispersion matrices

$$D_1^{-1} = \begin{bmatrix} 0.146 & 0.097 \\ 0.097 & 0.368 \end{bmatrix}, \quad D_2^{-1} = \begin{bmatrix} 0.133 & 0.078 \\ 0.078 & 0.156 \end{bmatrix},$$

$$D_3^{-1} = \begin{bmatrix} 0.0396 & -0.00784 \\ -0.00784 & 0.00819 \end{bmatrix} \quad (6.38)$$

Determinants of dispersion matrices

$$|D_1| = 22.564 \quad |D_2| = 68.194 \quad |D_3| = 3804.306$$

and

$$|D_1|^{\frac{1}{2}} = 4.750 \quad |D_2|^{\frac{1}{2}} = 8.258 \quad |D_3|^{\frac{1}{2}} = 61.679$$

$$(6.39)$$

Suppose that we are presented with an unexplored cell, the ith cell, for which value-class membership is unknown. Examination of the geology of the ith cell in terms of the four measurement variables reveals

$$X_{i1} = 1.0, \quad X_{i2} = 2.5, \quad X_{i3} = 2.0, \quad X_{i4} = 3.0.$$

On the basis of the values of the measurement variables and the statistical relations determined on the control area, we can estimate the probability that the cell belongs to each of the three value groups. The first step in this estimation is the calculation of the discriminant scores by evaluating the two discriminant equations on the geology of the unexplored cell

$$disc_{i1} = 5(1.0) + 10(2.5) - 20(2.0) - 15(3.0) = -55$$

$$(6.40)$$

$$disc_{i2} = 20(1.0) - 10(2.5) + 5(2.0) + 10(3.0) = 35.$$

Next, using these discriminant scores and the centroids of each group, the vector DIF_{ih}^T can be computed for each of the value groups

$$DIF_{i1}^T = [-55 - (-53), 35 - 36] = [-2, -1]$$
$$DIF_{i2}^T = [-55 - (-52), 35 - 33] = [-3, 2] \quad (6.41)$$
$$DIF_{i3}^T = [-55 - (-61), 35 - 30] = [6, 5].$$

Using the vectors, DIF_{ih} and D_h^{-1}, $h = 1, 2, 3$, we can compute the scalars x_{ih}^2

$$x_{ih}^2 = DIF_{ih}^T D_h^{-1} DIF_{ih}, \quad h = 1, 2, 3. \quad (6.42)$$

Thus, for $h = 1$,

$$x_{i1}^2 = [-2, -1] \cdot \begin{bmatrix} 0.146 & 0.097 \\ 0.097 & 0.368 \end{bmatrix} \cdot \begin{bmatrix} -2 \\ -1 \end{bmatrix}$$

$$(6.43)$$

$$x_{i1}^2 = [-0.389, -0.562] \begin{bmatrix} -2 \\ -1 \end{bmatrix}$$

$$x_{i1}^2 = 1.34.$$

For $h = 2$,

$$x_{i2}^2 = [-3, 2] \begin{bmatrix} 0.133 & 0.078 \\ 0.078 & 0.156 \end{bmatrix} \begin{bmatrix} -3 \\ 2 \end{bmatrix}$$

$$(6.44)$$

$$x_{i2}^2 = [-0.243, 0.078] \begin{bmatrix} -3 \\ 2 \end{bmatrix}$$

$$x_{i2}^2 = 0.885$$

and, for $h = 3$,

$$x_{i3}^2 = [6, 5] \begin{bmatrix} 0.0396 & -0.00784 \\ -0.00784 & 0.00819 \end{bmatrix} \begin{bmatrix} 6 \\ 5 \end{bmatrix}$$

$$(6.45)$$

$$x_{i3}^2 = [0.1984, -0.00609] \begin{bmatrix} 6 \\ 5 \end{bmatrix}$$

$$x_{i3}^2 = 1.160.$$

With the scalars x_{ih}^2 we can compute, for $h = 1, 2, 3$,

$$P({}^r\text{DISC}_i = \text{DISC}_i \mid H = 1)$$

$$= \frac{\dfrac{\exp\left(\dfrac{-1.34}{2}\right)}{4.750\sqrt{(2\pi)}}}{\dfrac{\exp\left(\dfrac{-1.34}{2}\right)}{4.750\sqrt{(2\pi)}} + \dfrac{\exp\left(\dfrac{-0.885}{2}\right)}{8.258\sqrt{(2\pi)}} + \dfrac{\exp\left(\dfrac{-1.160}{2}\right)}{61.679\sqrt{(2\pi)}}}$$

$$= \frac{0.0430}{0.0430 + 0.0310 + 0.00362}. \qquad (6.46)$$

where $\text{DISC}_i = [-55, 35]$, the discriminant scores from the two discriminant functions for the ith cell. Finally,

$$P({}^r\text{DISC}_i = \text{DISC}_i \mid H = 1) = 0.5540.$$

Similarly, for $H = 2$ and $H = 3$, we have

$$P({}^r\text{DISC}_i = \text{DISC}_i \mid H = 2) = \frac{0.0311}{0.07762}$$
$$= 0.3994 \qquad (6.47)$$

$$P({}^r\text{DISC}_i = \text{DISC}_i \mid H = 3) = \frac{0.00362}{0.07762}$$
$$= 0.0466. \qquad (6.48)$$

Before the probabilities for group membership can be computed, we need estimates of marginal probabilities for group membership (independent of geology), $P(H = 1)$, $P(H = 2)$, $P(H = 3)$. Suppose that these probabilities are not known but that we use the relative frequency of membership of cells of the control area in the value classes. Say, that these relative frequencies are 0.5, 0.3, and 0.2,

$$P(H = 1) = 0.5$$
$$P(H = 2) = 0.3 \qquad (6.49)$$
$$P(H = 3) = 0.2.$$

Then, the probabilities for membership in each of the three groups can be calculated using Bayes' rule

$$P(H = 1 \mid {}^r\text{DISC}_i = \text{DISC}_i)$$

$$= \frac{(0.554)(0.5)}{(0.554)(0.5) + (0.3994)(0.3) + (0.0466)(0.2)}$$

$$= \frac{0.2770}{0.40614} = 0.682$$

$$P(H = 2 \mid {}^r\text{DISC}_i = \text{DISC}_i)$$

$$= \frac{(0.3994)(0.3)}{(0.554)(0.5) + (0.3994)(0.3) + (0.0466)(0.2)}$$

$$= \frac{0.1198}{0.40614} = 0.295$$

$$P(H = 3 \mid {}^r\text{DISC}_i = \text{DISC}_i)$$

$$= \frac{(0.0466)(0.2)}{(0.554)(0.5) + (0.3994)(0.3) + (0.0466)(0.2)}$$

$$= \frac{0.0093}{0.40614} = 0.0229. \qquad (6.50)$$

6.2.9. A word on discriminant analysis

The multivariate statistical procedure with which scientists and engineers are most familiar is that of simple and multiple regression, or in terms often employed, the least-square fitting of curves, planes, or hypersurfaces. In a simplistic sense, the regression procedure seeks an answer to the question: Given the status of the explanatory variables, what is the expectation for the dependent variable? In other words, on the assumption that an unknown belongs to the same population as the sample upon which the regression equation was determined, the basic question addressed by regression is the *size* of the *dependent variable* in response to the explanatory variables.

Multiple discriminant analysis addresses a more basic question than does regression: Given the characteristics of an unknown, to which population does it belong? There is no dependent variable in discriminant analysis; hence the correlation of the size of a dependent variable with respect to explanatory variables is never examined directly.

Although discriminant analysis neither requires or employs a dependent variable for the computation of the discriminant equation and associated matrices, there must exist some criterion independent of the measurement variables for classification of the cells of the control area. This criterion need not be a quantitative measure, but such a criterion must be observable for the cells of the control area. Discriminant analysis is predicated upon the assumption that the classification of the cells of the control area by the independent criterion is known. Given this classification by the criterion, discriminant analysis compares the levels of measurement variables of the cells in each of the groups to see if the cells of the groups are different, viewed solely in terms of the measurement variables. This can be viewed as a multivariate test for the differences between means of the measurement variables (geology) of the groups. If geology, as measured on the cells, has no relationship to mineral occurrence, then there would be no statistically significant difference in the levels of the measurement variables of the value groups.

The theory of discriminant analysis is summarized

in § 6.7.2, and a simple numerical example demonstrates the mathematical calculations. This example yields the discriminant equation employed in (6.23) to demonstrate the probability analysis for a simple discriminant analysis. The mathematical development is basically a summary of the development of Bryan (1951), except for the section on determining the number of significant discriminant equations, which is after Cooley and Lohnes (1962).

Basic to discriminant analysis are two variance matrices: the between (among)-groups variance matrix and the pooled-within-groups variance matrix. These variance matrices reflect the variance and covariance of the discriminant scores of the cells of the various groups. Discriminant analysis can be viewed as selecting the coefficients of the discriminant functions that maximize the ratio of the variance between groups relative to the pooled-within-groups variance. In other words, the equation or equations maximize the separation of the groups so that classification of unknowns can be achieved with a minimum of error, given the measurement variables and the classification of cells of the control area.

The importance of the assumption that the discriminant scores for each group are normally distributed is demonstrated in the probability analysis, where the normal probability equation was used to compute ordinate values. Values computed in this fashion provide an accurate picture of the world only if the discriminant scores are normally distributed. Departures from normality imply probabilities that may be biased estimates of those of the actual populations. Obviously, if the measurement variables themselves are normally distributed, discriminant scores shall be normally distributed, for the discriminant score is simply a linear combination of normally distributed variates. The approach followed by Harris was to transform the raw measurements to forms that were more normally distributed; however, even after transformation, few of the variables could be considered to be normally distributed. It was suggested by Cooley and Lohnes (1962) that the departure of measurement from normality might not be serious when probability analysis is based upon discriminant scores. This suggestion rests on the argument that since a discriminant score is a linear combination, it is basically a sum, and probability theory shows, through the Central Limit Theorem, that sums, like averages, in the limit approach a normal distribution as the size of the sample (items in the sum) approaches infinity. Strictly speaking, the sum or average envisioned in the Central Limit Theorem is based upon a random sample of size n of a single variate, not a sample of size one of n variates; consequently, the Central Limit Theorem does not in the strict sense apply to a discriminant score. However, there is still an intuitive appeal to the argument that a sum of responses of a number of variates, particularly if these responses are similarly scaled, would tend to balance out highs and lows and be more normally distributed than the individual measurements.

In the case of Harris's study, the normality assumption may have been reasonably well met because the transformation of the raw measurements was followed by a transformation to factor scores, and it was upon factor scores that the discriminant analysis was performed. Since factor scores are also linear combinations, the discriminant scores which were used in the probability analysis were linear combinations of linear combinations, which, if the argument presented above has any merit, should yield a distribution of discriminant scores for a group that approximates a normal distribution.

6.2.10. *The analysis*

Variables

The analysis performed by Harris was based upon factor scores. Factor analysis was used in this study merely to create a set of orthogonal (statistically independent) variables. This particular use of factor analysis is often referred to as principal-components analysis [2]. Such analysis neither adds nor subtracts information when as many factors are extracted as variables, as was the case in this study; information is merely rearranged. This simplistic use of factor analysis does not warrant, in this report, delving into its theory or mechanics, particularly since Harris found in subsequent analysis that the use of factor scores added little to the overall analysis over what was obtained by simple transformations of the geological variables, such as $\log(g)$ instead of g. Therefore, consider such analysis to have produced a new representation of the information in the original measurement variables, an arrangement that in effect gives statistically independent variables, which is one of the assumptions of multivariate techniques.

The first analysis performed by Harris, as explained below, was a regression of mineral wealth on the factor scores. The purpose of this analysis was to select a subset of the factors to be employed in the multiple-discriminant analysis. The use of regression analysis for this purpose is not required nor necessarily best practice. Variables can be eliminated directly by the manipulation of the discriminant analysis. Provided that a discriminant model is the appropriate one, this latter approach to variable elimination is preferable, for the most important variables in regression may not be the most important in multiple-discriminant analysis. However, in experiments performed on the two approaches, Harris found that the variable selections are often very similar.

It is appropriate to point out that if the objective of the analysis of wealth and geology were to yield directly an estimate of mineral wealth, instead of a probability, regression analysis might be the appropriate model, as was the case in subsequent studies by Agterberg, Chung, Fabbri, Kelly, and Springer (1972) and Sinclair and Woodsworth (1970).

Correlation and regression of value-plus-reserves on factor scores

The logarithmic transformation, $z = \log(\text{values} + \text{reserves} + 10)$, term was regressed on the 26 factor scores generated for each of the cells. The multiple correlation coefficient for value as a linear function of all 26 factor scores was 0.7462. Note that this coefficient is higher than that obtained for value (plus reserves) as a function of the 26 transformed variables, which was 0.7207, and that both of these coefficients are higher than those for the value term without reserves regressed upon either the transformed or the raw variables.

A computer programme with a parsimony option was used to eliminate those factor scores that were least important. The elimination by parsimony is accomplished by eliminating that variable first for which the ratio of $b_i^2/S_{b_i}^2$ is the smallest in the entire set of b^2/S_b^2 at that stage, where b_i is the least-squares estimate of the true regression coefficient of X_i and $S_{b_i}^2$ is its sample variance.

Factor scores were eliminated by parsimony until the resulting regression equation consisted of terms for which the partial correlation coefficients were significant at the 0.01 level. Note that the partial correlation test is valid in this case because the factor scores are uncorrelated. Nineteen of the 26 variables (factors) were eliminated, leaving a regression equation in which value plus reserves is a function of seven factors. The multiple correlation coefficient was reduced from 0.7462 to 0.7099. This coefficient is significant at the 0.001 level. The relationship of the transformed estimate of value to the seven factor scores is

$$\overset{\scriptscriptstyle (0.03205)\quad(0.05056)\quad(0.05034)}{\hat{w} = 3.04370 - 0.31300 F_1 + 0.31191 F_2 + 0.12474 F_3 +}$$

$$\overset{(0.21644)\quad(0.32261)\quad(0.43258)\quad(0.81527)}{+ 0.48427 F_{11} + 0.69372 F_{15} + 1.3393 F_{17} - 2.97480 F_{20}}$$

$$(6.51)$$

where the fraction of explained variance $= 0.504$ and the numbers in parentheses above the coefficients are the standard errors of the coefficients.

Examination of this regression equation reveals that some of the later factors to be extracted are those that were important in explaining the variation in mineral wealth. The eigenvalue associated with a factor extracted by the principal-components method when divided by the number of variables loaded on the factors gives an expression of the fraction of variance in the original variables that is explained by that factor. The eigenvalues decrease with each successive factor extracted, the twentieth factor explaining only 0.9 per cent of the variance in the *geological* variables. Yet, when the factor scores were eliminated by parsimony down to the very last one, the twentieth factor is third from the last variable to be discarded. So, although this factor accounts for only 0.9 per cent of the variance in common to the transformed geological variables, that particular part of the variance that it does represent is more important to mineral wealth than the variance in the geological variables explained by some of the earlier extracted factors, such as the third factor which represents 12 per cent of the variance in the geological variables.

Multiple-discriminant analysis

A multiple-discriminant analysis was performed on the factor scores for the cells of the six value groups. The five discriminant equations produced by the analysis are

$$\begin{aligned} \text{disc}_1 = {}& 0.04598 F_1 - 0.19703 F_2 - 0.01024 F_3 \\ & - 0.11605 F_{11} - 0.05574 F_{15} \\ & - 0.54545 F_{17} + 0.80340 F_{20} \end{aligned}$$

$$\begin{aligned} \text{disc}_2 = {}& 0.06164 F_1 + 0.00979 F_2 + 0.02268 F_3 \\ & + 0.18943 F_{11} - 0.91669 F_{15} \\ & - 0.20857 F_{17} - 0.27540 F_{20} \end{aligned}$$

$$\begin{aligned} \text{disc}_3 = {}& 0.00958 F_1 - 0.02142 F_2 + 0.04478 F_3 \\ & + 0.23492 F_{11} + 0.04844 F_{15} \qquad (6.52) \\ & - 0.57415 F_{17} + 0.78119 F_{20} \end{aligned}$$

$$\begin{aligned} \text{disc}_4 = {}& 0.00660 F_1 + 0.02761 F_2 + 0.01562 F_3 \\ & + 0.39830 F_{11} - 0.02137 F_{15} \\ & - 0.55010 F_{17} + 0.83330 F_{20} \end{aligned}$$

$$\begin{aligned} \text{disc}_5 = {}& 0.02423 F_1 + 0.03262 F_2 - 0.20870 F_3 \\ & + 0.25400 F_{11} - 0.02490 F_{15} \\ & + 0.19171 F_{17} + 0.92353 F_{20}. \end{aligned}$$

The Wilks' lambda criterion which is a measure of the discriminating power of the battery of discriminant functions is 0.694. An approximation to an 'F' test outlined by Rao (1952, pp. 258–72) tests the significance of the battery of the discriminant functions. This statistic tests the null hypothesis that there is no difference between centroids of the groups. Applying this test to the lambda value computed for this analysis indicates that the null hypothesis is rejected at the 0.001 level,

Computed 'F' value = 2.523
Test F_{974}^{35} value [3] = 1.92.

In other words, the chance of producing group differences as large as those found in this analysis by drawing six random samples from a seven-dimensional multivariate distribution is less than one in one thousand. Thus, we conclude that in this case the multiple-discriminant model can distinguish between cells of the selected value classes on the basis of their profile of factor scores.

By virtue of the discriminant equations, any cell can be defined by a set of discriminant scores by substituting into the equations its factor scores. This model compares the vector of discriminant scores for a cell to the centroid for each group, computes the measures of deviation from the centroids (Table 6.3) weighted by the group dispersions, and compares the densities of all of the groups. Probabilities are generated for a cell with a given discriminant score vector belonging to each of the six value groups as shown in Table 6.4.

One simple appraisal of the model is to compare the way in which it classifies the cells with the original classification, which was the input to multiple-discriminant analysis. This is analogous to examining the residuals or deviations from a least-squares fit of a straight line. In order to evaluate its accuracy in general terms, let us adopt as a decision rule the placing of a cell in a particular value group on the basis of the group for which probability of membership is the highest. With this in mind, let us look at those cells within Arizona and New Mexico

which are the giants of mineral wealth, those that belong to group six, US 100×10^6 to US 5×10^9. If we were to find that many cells which we know belong in this group are misclassified by the model it would be quite serious, for these are the real prizes. In scoring these results let us give each cell properly classified, a score of five points; missed by one group, four points; and so on.

There were 11 cells of the 243 that belong to this class according to production to present and the resource estimate. The probabilities generated by the above model for those 11 cells are shown in Table 6.5. As indicated in this table, 2 of the 11 cells have been seriously misclassified and one has been missed by one group.

The model can misclassify in another way: that is, it can generate the highest probability of class membership for group 6 when according to the value of production and reserves, the cell belongs to some other group. This occurred in two instances, as shown in Table 6.6.

These might be misclassifications by the model, but it is also possible that they are rich cells whose wealth has not yet been discovered. Although the preclassification of the first cell is in group 1, the profile of discriminant scores was found by this model to be more like the centroid of group 6. The second cell is a minor producer, but according to the geology of that area, it may still possess considerable mineral wealth. Both of these areas are specified by this model as good prospects, the first being the better because of its higher probability. Examination of the physical location of these cells shows the first one to be adjacent to a cell whose value of production places it in group 6. The geology of the two areas is very similar, and it was observed that although the misclassified cell had no production, it did have many prospects, indicating that the cell also had looked very good to the prospectors.

If we count misclassifications of both kinds as errors, the score on the giants is 47 out of a possible of 65 which is about 72 per cent. If misclassifications of the first kind only are counted as errors, then the

TABLE 6.3. *Means of the factor scores for each of the six groups.* (*Source: Harris 1966a.*)

Group	F_1	F_2	F_3	F_{11}	F_{15}	F_{17}	F_{20}
1	1.7009689	−0.9468770	−0.00920685	−0.0653160	−0.0165484	−0.0402529	0.0122068
2	0.2113750	1.1221450	0.0176700	0.1073431	−0.1088994	0.5522012	0.2513777
3	0.9879116	0.3444892	0.8070332	0.2121936	0.0529680	0.1455740	0.0162496
4	0.4406714	2.4914990	1.0984813	0.0942023	0.556450	−0.0279618	−0.0192523
5	−0.6105853	2.5779811	0.3853253	−0.0598912	−0.1606488	0.1630147	−0.1063800
6	3.539790	1.8324645	−0.5756845	0.1638973	0.4009391	−0.0091164	−0.0896555

TABLE 6.4. *Probabilities of group membership. (Source: Harris 1966a.)*

Cell identification	Group 1	Group 2	Group 3	Group 4	Group 5	Group 6
a	0.7584	0.0313	0.1360	0.0668	0.0075	0.0000
b	0.7105	0.0006	0.2128	0.0137	0.0623	0.0001
c	0.5858	0.0001	0.0841	0.2859	0.0440	0.0000
d	0.7733	0.0001	0.2179	0.0083	0.0005	0.0000
e	0.5788	0.0020	0.4017	0.0160	0.0016	0.0000
f	0.8705	0.0413	0.0865	0.0017	0.0000	0.0000
g	0.7196	0.0956	0.1846	0.0002	0.0000	0.0000
h	0.8592	0.0674	0.0609	0.0124	0.0000	0.0001
i	0.8123	0.0747	0.0722	0.0274	0.0122	0.0012
j	0.2311	0.0163	0.6386	0.0068	0.1073	0.0000
k	0.8133	0.0362	0.1224	0.0120	0.0149	0.0011
l	0.4653	0.0003	0.5342	0.0002	0.0000	0.0000
m	0.7127	0.0502	0.2367	0.0004	0.0000	0.0000
n	0.8551	0.0797	0.0462	0.0149	0.0039	0.0002
o	0.0694	0.6767	0.2227	0.0129	0.0182	0.0000
p	0.0001	0.0000	0.0003	0.0013	0.0000	0.9983
q	0.8710	0.0319	0.0283	0.0394	0.0056	0.0238
r	0.9419	0.0035	0.0209	0.0334	0.0003	0.0000
s	0.7970	0.0029	0.0764	0.1087	0.0150	0.0000
t	0.8821	0.0034	0.1029	0.0078	0.0039	0.0000
u	0.6692	0.2435	0.0859	0.0013	0.0000	0.0000
v	0.8790	0.0306	0.0849	0.0055	0.0000	0.0000
w	0.8859	0.0014	0.1117	0.0010	0.0000	0.0000
x	0.1369	0.7926	0.0547	0.0157	0.0001	0.0000
y	0.0001	0.0000	0.0001	0.0018	0.0000	0.9980
z	0.9034	0.0146	0.0283	0.0406	0.0047	0.0084

accuracy increases to 80 per cent. These results are quite encouraging considering the crudeness of the variables that entered into the analysis.

A similar analysis of the cells in group 1, the group with 0–US $10 000 production demonstrated an ac-curacy of about 82 per cent of the possible score (counting errors of both kinds). In absolute terms, ignoring how far the cells are misclassified and there-fore scoring a point for only those cells that are correctly classified, about 70 per cent of the cells that

TABLE 6.5. *Classification analysis—group 6. (Source: Harris 1966a.)*

Value of cell (in billions of US dollars)	Probability of membership in group 6	Group with highest probability of membership if other than 6	Probability of membership in other group	Score
1.43	0.998			5
1.97	0.998			5
2.28	0.319	1	0.36	0
2.91	0.976			5
0.15	0.454			5
0.46	0.987			5
4.78	0.334			5
0.13	0.335	1	0.40	0
0.14	1.000			5
0.84	0.829			5
0.61	0.339	4	0.44	3

TABLE 6.6. *Cells misclassified into group 6.* (*Source: Harris 1966a.*)

Value (US $)	Probability of membership in group 6	Preclassification	Probability of membership in preclassification group	Score
0	0.799	1	0.13	0
445 000	0.539	3	0.06	3

belonged in group 1 were allotted to that group by the above model. Those classified as belonging to a higher group may be areas that deserve further exploration. These are listed in Table 6.7.

Thus, on the basis of geology, this model would appear to be able to place a cell in its value group with a fair degree of accuracy and to point to those cells which may have undiscovered mineral values. Furthermore, the degree of uncertainty of the classification is explicit in the probabilities of membership for each group. It is this last aspect of the analysis that is of particular interest. This then constitutes a model of mineral wealth in which probabilities are a function of geology and, indirectly, of value.

6.2.11. *Test of the model on Utah*

As a test of his mineral-wealth model, Harris [1] designated the western part of Utah, an area consisting of 144 cells (20 miles square), as a study area. Obviously, some of the cells in this region have produced large quantities of metal. This fact makes possible a test of the model quantified on the control area, for if the probability model of mineral wealth is

indeed useful, it should by virtue of the geological measurements, ascribe to those cells in Utah that are known to have produced large quantities of metal a high probability for membership in one of the large value groups. The scheme for this test was to record values for the measurement variables for each of the 144 cells in Utah. Then, the discriminant functions developed on the control area (Arizona and New Mexico) were evaluated on these measurements to provide discriminant scores for the cells. A probability analysis was performed using the results of the discriminant analysis. In this way, probabilities for membership in each of the value groups were computed for each of the 144 cells.

For evaluation of the performance of the probability model, the perspective of an explorationist seeking to select a subset of cells for further exploration was adopted. The assumption was made that cells having mineral wealth of value classes 1, 2, and 3 would be of no interest to an explorationist, while those having values of groups 4, 5, or 6 would warrant further exploration. This is equivalent to assuming that only cells believed to possess mineral wealth in excess of US $1 000 000 (1963 prices) warrant further exploration.

TABLE 6.7. *Misclassification of group 1.* (*Source: Harris 1966a.*)

Actual value of production	Probability of membership in group 1	Group with highest probability of membership if other than 6	Probability of membership in other group	Value range of group for which probability of membership is highest (US$)
840	0.231	3	0.639	100 000– 1 000 000
0	0.465	3	0.534	100 000– 1 000 000
0	0.130	6	0.797	100 000 000–5 000 000 000
0	0.215	5	0.742	10 000 000– 100 000 000
0	0.399	4	0.596	1 000 000– 10 000 000
0	0.366	4	0.534	1 000 000– 10 000 000
807	0.036	3	0.964	100 000– 1 000 000
0	0.005	4	0.805	1 000 000– 10 000 000
0	0.267	5	0.625	10 000 000– 100 000 000
0	0.110	3	0.361	100 000– 1 000 000
0	0.006	3	0.994	100 000– 1 000 000
0	0.026	4	0.749	1 000 000– 10 000 000

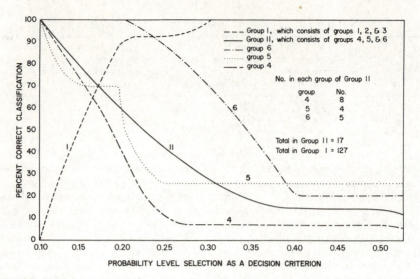

Fig. 6.8. Analysis of skimming as a function of the decision criterion (Source: Harris [1].)

The number of the 144 cells actually retained for further exploration varies with the decision rule. For example, the decision rule of retaining for further exploration any cell having a probability of 0.20 or greater for membership in group II (groups 4, 5, 6) retains 19 of the 144 cells in Utah. The 19 cells selected were identified by their known mineral production as follows: all five cells in the area with a value of US $100 000 000+; two of the four cells with a value of US $10 million to 100 million; three of the eight cells with a value of US $1 million to 10 million; and nine cells with a value of less than US $1 million (these are cells that should have been eliminated from the second stage of exploration) (see Fig. 6.8).

Raising the probability criterion results in the retention of fewer cells with a value of less than US $1 million, but only at the expense of losing some of those of high value. Conversely, lowering the criterion results in the retention of more of the cells with high value but at the cost of retaining more cells with a value of less than US $1 million. The task of the explorationist would be the selection of the optimum decision criterion, that is, selecting that level which balances the greater certainty of retaining the high value cells in the second stage by lowering the criterion against the increased exploration cost in the second stage caused by lowering the criterion (exploring more cells). This is much like standard hypothesis testing in which for a given sample size the probability of a Type I error cannot be decreased without increasing the probability of Type II error.

This emphasizes the importance stressed by Allais (1957) of beginning with a large area and performing an efficient and careful skimming of a large number of cells so as to be sure of retaining those few cells of large value.

Cells in group 6, the largest value group, vary more in their geology with respect to those cells in group I than do the cells in groups 4 or 5, for at any probability level (decision criterion) above 0.10, there is a higher per cent correct classification of group 6 than of group 4, and, for a decision criterion from 0.10 to 0.39, there is a higher per cent correct classification of group 6 than for group 5. Such a result must be pleasing to the geoscientist, for it supports the usefulness of geology in mineral exploration.

Overall, the test on Utah indicated that the probability model performed reasonably well in differentiating between cells having large and small values on the basis of geology, but it does not do nearly so well in differentiating between cells of adjacent value groups. The geology, as reflected by the measurement variables of this study, does not vary greatly between cells of adjacent value groups.

6.3. A model of the conditional expectation for mineral wealth

6.3.1. *Theory*

In § 6.2.1, it was shown that a probability model for the aggregate value of two or more metals,

$f^w(w \mid G_D)$, could be derived from the probability distributions of the endowments of r metals: $f_k(m_k \mid G_D)$, $k = 1, 2, \ldots, r$. Given $f^w(w \mid G_D)$, and an observed vector of geology, G_D^0, we can describe the expectation for mineral wealth $\bar{w}_{G\beta}$

$$\bar{w}_{G\beta} = \int_w w \cdot f^w(w \mid G_D^0) \, dw. \qquad (6.53)$$

Of course, this expectation varies as the geology varies. For a different set of geological conditions G_D' the expectation in general would be different

$$\bar{w}_{G_b'} = \int_w w \cdot f^w(w \mid G_D') \, dw \neq \bar{w}_{G\beta}. \qquad (6.54)$$

Let θ be a function that explains the relationship between the expectation for W and geology

$$\bar{w} = \theta(G_D). \qquad (6.55)$$

Relationship (6.55) here is referred to as a mineral-wealth equation. Relative to our probability model, this equation describes that mineral wealth which on average is associated with a particular realization of geology.

Of course, since $f^w(w \mid G_D)$ is not known, $\theta(G_D)$ cannot be derived as was done in theory. Consequently, $\theta(G_D)$ is generally sought directly. As with models for metal endowment, we do not know the identity of all of the geological variables or the functional form θ. Theory and judgement serve only as guides to the identity of the variables and the appropriate functional form. The usual means of quantification of a mineral-wealth equation is through the application of multiple regression analysis to observations on the mineral wealth and geology of cells of a control area. Given the quantification of the equation and the geology observed on a cell of unknown wealth, the cell's wealth is estimated by substituting the geology of the unknown into the mineral-wealth equation.

6.3.2. The mineral-wealth equation for Terrace, British Columbia

A. J. Sinclair and G. J. Woodsworth (1970, p. 998) developed a mineral-wealth equation for an area near Terrace, British Columbia. They advocated that multivariate techniques would provide a much more useful tool for the appraisal of 'mineral potential' if

1. more confined study areas were chosen; especially if an area were defined as a major mining camp; i.e. the order of hundreds to a few thousand square miles, and
2. value estimates of arbitrarily chosen cells were based on data for a single type of deposit.

Accordingly, they reduced the size of the cells to 4 miles square, instead of the 20 miles square used by Harris (1966a), and restricted the modes of occurrence to only one, vein deposits, but allowed that metals occurring in this mode could include copper, lead, zinc, and precious metals. For each of the 4×4 mile cells, estimates of total tonnage, grade, and dollar value in 1969 US dollars were made. In addition, measurements for 12 geological variables were made (Table 6.8).

Woodsworth and Sinclair designated two different control areas

1. Control area 1, designed to include most of the known deposits and a cross-section of the geology of the total area, consisted of 35 cells;
2. Control area 2, consisted exclusively of those cells (28) containing known deposits.

They concluded from their study that a control area consisting exclusively of cells with known deposits was a poor design of a control area, as no statistically significant correlation between wealth and geology, as they had measured it, could be quantified. On the other hand, regression analysis on the cells of control area 1 yielded statistically significant results

$$\sin^{-1}(\hat{w}/10^6)^{\frac{1}{2}} = -0.0329 - 0.0649 g_{12} + 0.2472 g_5$$
$$+ 0.2505 g_6 - 0.3080 g_{11} - 0.0326 g_7$$
$$+ 0.0317 g_8 - 0.0404 g_{10}, \qquad (6.56)$$

where $R^2 = 0.473$ and g_i is the ith transformed geological variable. The transformations used are shown in Table 6.8. Sinclair and Woodsworth (1970, p. 1003) concluded that analysis of control area 1, the area made up of cells with and without mines, had provided useful relations.

1. Multiple regression analysis of general geological variables provides a useful means of separating and combining those variables that correlate with various measures of value in arbitrarily chosen cells.
2. Evaluation of results of multiple regression studies must not be confined to a purely statistical approach. Subjective geological analysis of the results is imperative.
3. In the Terrace area, cells that seem to offer the best potential for relatively large tonnage, low-grade, lead–zinc vein deposits are those underlain by Bowser Group in the north-east part of the study area.
4. Potential for high-grade, low-tonnage deposits near Terrace is greatest in the area of east–west re-entrants at the contact between plutonic rocks and Hazelton Group.
5. It is probable that multiple regression studies as described here could be refined considerably if more detailed geological information were available. As

TABLE 6.8. *Cell variables and transforms used by Sinclair and Woodsworth (1970)*

Variable		Transform
	Value	
Y_1	Tonnage	$\arcsin (Y_1/10^5)^{\frac{1}{2}}$
Y_2	Average dollars per ton	$\arcsin (Y_2/100)^{\frac{1}{2}}$
Y_3	Total dollar value	$\arcsin (Y_3/10^6)^{\frac{1}{2}}$
	Geological	
X_1	Total length of major fracture zones	$\arcsin (X_1/10)^{\frac{1}{2}}$
X_2	Distance—cell centre to nearest major fracture	$\log_{10} (X_2)$
X_3	Percentage plutonic rocks	$\arcsin (X_3/100)^{\frac{1}{2}}$
X_4	Percentage Paleozoic rocks	$\arcsin (X_4/100)^{\frac{1}{2}}$
X_5	Percentage Hazelton Group	$\arcsin (X_5/1000)^{\frac{1}{2}}$
X_6	Percentage Bowser Group	$\arcsin (X_6/1000)^{\frac{1}{2}}$
X_7	Distance—cell centre to nearest Paleozoic rock	$(X_7+85)^{\frac{1}{2}}$
X_8	Distance—cell centre to nearest Hazelton Group	$(X_8+85)^{\frac{1}{2}}$
X_9	Distance—cell centre to nearest Bowser Group	$\log_{10} (X_9+85)$
X_{10}	Distance—cell centre to nearest plutonic rock	$(X_{10}-\bar{X}_{10})/25.95$
X_{11}	Length of igneous contact	$\arcsin (X_{11}/100)$
X_{12}	Distance—cell centre to nearest point on axis of east–west re-entrants	$\log_{10} (X_{12})$

Lengths and distances measured in miles.
If $X_i = 0$ prior to transform, X_i was set equal to 0.001.

with any method of examining 'Exploration priorities' there are problems that must be recognized; these include the following: (a) subjective analysis of results, (b) some highly significant statistical correlations may alter or obscure correlations, (d) a linear model may not be appropriate, and (e) there are serious restrictions on the kind of variables that can be quantified and included in a multiple regression analysis. Despite these limitations the method appears to offer much practical potential.

6.4. A probabilistic appraisal of the mineral wealth of a portion of the Grenville Province of the Canadian Shield

6.4.1. *Procedure*

De Geoffroy and Wignall (1971) employed the relations of geology to mineral wealth of a control area to appraise the mineral wealth of a study area in a manner similar to the procedure used by Harris [1]. Besides obvious differences in the regions of the two studies, the probability analysis performed by De Geoffroy and Wignall was different from that employed by Harris in that they employed a Bayesian classification analysis directly, bypassing the multiple-discriminant analysis. This is referred to as a generalized Bayesian classification procedure.

The control area selected by De Geoffroy and Wignall consisted of 21 100 square miles in south-

eastern Ontario. This area was divided into 211 cells of $100\,\text{mi}^2$ each (10 miles square). Commercial deposits of metals and nonmetals are present in this region: iron, copper (nickel), lead (zinc), molybdenum (uranium), gold, columbium (uranium), mica, fluorite, feldspar, apatite, sulfur (pyrite), talc, graphite, actinolite, nepheline, and corundum. By far the most abundant deposits are those of iron, followed by mica, copper, lead, molybdenum, and fluorite, the least abundant being corundum. Table 6.9 lists the geological measurement variables.

TABLE 6.9. *List of geological variables*

† g_1	Percentage of cell area underlain by carbonate meta-sediments
g_2	Percentage of cell area underlain by siliceous meta-sediments and/or meta-volcanics
† g_3	Percentage of cell area underlain by basic and ultrabasic intrusives
† g_4	Percentage of cell area underlain by syenite intrusives
† g_5	Percentage of cell area underlain by Paleozoic and/or basement complex
g_6	Number of fault intersections within cell
g_7	Length of faults within cell area
g_8	Number of fold axes within cell
† g_9	Number of mineral occurrences and prospects within cell

† Variable is statistically significant.

De Geoffroy and Wignall subjected the data from the control area to regression analysis to identify those geological variables that have a statistically significant relationship to mineral wealth, yielding the regression equation

$$\widehat{\ln w} = -4.43 + 0.0041 g_1 + 0.3464 \ln (1 + g_3)$$
$$+ 1.0027 \ln (1 + g_4) - 0.3146 \ln (1 + g_5)$$
$$+ 0.0069 g_9.$$

This regression equation was found to be significant at the 0.1 per cent level, i.e. there is less than 1 chance in 1000 that a relationship this strong could result from a random sample drawn from a population in which there is no relationship between the geological variables and mineral wealth.

6.4.2. *Probability analysis*

Having identified a set of geological variables, De Geoffroy and Wignall constructed a Bayesian probability model by identifying two groups of cells: group 1, consisting of 30 cells having wealth of at least US $2 000 000; and group 2, consisting of 13 cells having wealth of less than US $2 000 000. They then calculated the means of the five geological variables for cells of each group and applied the Hotelling T^2-test to see if the two vectors of means, one vector for each group, were significantly different; the result was that the differences in the geology of the two groups were statistically significant at the 0.1 per cent level, justifying the construction of a Bayesian probability model for the evaluation of cells of unknown wealth.

The probability model constructed by De Geoffroy and Wignall is similar to that constructed by Harris, except that there was not the intermediate step of multiple-discriminant analysis, hence no need for the transformation to discriminant scores. Instead, the Bayesian probability model employed directly the dispersion matrices of the five geological variables identified by regression analysis as the basis for computing the conditional probability

$$P(G_i \mid H = h) = \frac{\dfrac{\exp\left(-\tfrac{1}{2}[\mathrm{DIF}_i^T D_h^{-1} \mathrm{DIF}_i]\right)}{|D_h|^{\frac{1}{2}}}}{\displaystyle\sum_{k=1}^{NG} \dfrac{\exp\left(-\tfrac{1}{2}[\mathrm{DIF}_i^T D_k^{-1} \mathrm{DIF}_i]\right)}{|D_k|^{\frac{1}{2}}}} \quad (6.57)$$

where $\mathrm{DIF}_i = [G_i - \bar{G}_1, G_i - \bar{G}_2]$, G_i is the vector of five geological variables on the ith individual, $\bar{G}_1, \bar{G}_2$ are vectors of means of the five geological variables for groups 1 and 2, respectively, D_h is the dispersion matrix of the geological variables for the hth group, h is a realization of H, and $NG = 2$.

The probability for membership of the ith individual in the hth group was computed according to Bayes' rule

$$P(H = h \mid G_i) = \frac{P(G_i \mid H = h) \cdot P(H = h)}{\displaystyle\sum_{k=1}^{2} [P(G_i \mid H = k) \cdot P(H = k)]}.$$
$$(6.58)$$

For $P(H = h)$, De Geoffroy employed the relative frequency of success and failure in exploration in the control area over the last 80 years: $P(H = 1) = 0.138$ and $P(H = 2) = 0.862$.

A cell from the study area would be evaluated by observing its geology, G_i, and substituting it in (6.57) to compute $P(G_i \mid H = 1)$ and $P(G_i \mid H = 2)$. These probabilities were then combined with $P(H = 1)$ and $P(H = 2)$ to give the discrete probabilities $P(H = 1 \mid G_i)$ and $P(H = 2 \mid G_i)$, according to (6.58).

Probability analysis was performed on 170 cells, each of $100 \, \mathrm{mi}^2$, in a $17\,000 \, \mathrm{mi}^2$ portion of the Grenville Province. This analysis led to the selection of 11 cells of high merit. De Geoffroy and Wignall estimated that these cells contained US $425 800 000 of mineral wealth. They compared this estimate with US $382 500 000, an estimate based upon an occurrence model (methods of Chapter 7), concluding that 'The probabilistic method is more realistic than that based upon the occurrence model, because it takes into account local geological factors rather than assuming uniform conditions throughout the area.'

6.5. The models of Agterberg

F. P. Agterberg of the Geological Survey of Canada has constructed multivariate models that relate geological variables to some aspect of mineral occurrence. In these models he provides excellent discussion and treatment for a number of information and statistical problems. Some of these models have dealt in some manner with mineral wealth, but mineral wealth was used mainly as an index of favourability or as a basis for an occurrence model; consequently, Agterberg's work is discussed in the section on multivariate occurrence models.

6.6. Some issues about mineral-wealth models

An obvious issue about mineral-wealth models is that they aggregate across not only two or more metals, but also across tonnage and grade characteristics. Thus, in themselves, such models provide estimates that are not *directly* amenable to further economic analysis, such as the interaction of exploration and exploitation simulation models for the generation of potential supply for various economic or technological conditions. In order to perform such analysis, the wealth estimates must be decomposed to implied numbers of deposits of each metal and tonnages and grades for each metal, such as was done by Harris (1968) in an economic evaluation of the potential supply of base and precious metals from the Seward peninsula of Alaska. Such analysis requires that an auxiliary set of data on deposit characteristics within the control area be constructed and that these data be related to mineral wealth. Obviously, the assumption must be made that a predicted mineral wealth for a cell of the study area implies the same deposit characteristics as exist in the control area. The implications of such an assumption are unclear when several metals are involved, particularly if some of these metals occur in more than one mode, each mode having quite different deposit characteristics.

The complications imposed for subsequent economic analysis by mineral wealth are compounded when the objective of the appraisal is to estimate subeconomic resources. It is clear that if the economic and terrain conditions of the study and control areas are similar, the mineral wealth estimated for a cell of the study area reflects only *economic resources that one would expect* to be *discovered* and *produced*, in other words *potential supply*. Clearly, in the models herein examined, the probability for the discovery of additional deposits in the *control areas* is high, even for current economic conditions. It is equally clear that the inventory of discovered deposits is truncated at the economic cut-off grade at the time of the analysis, or more correctly, the time of the gathering of the data for analysis.

Estimation of metal endowment would require (1) an adjustment of the appraised wealth to include metal in undiscovered deposits and (2) an auxiliary model for inference to endowments of the metals having subeconomic grades. An auxiliary model that seemingly may be useful for this inference is the cumulative tonnage–average grade relationship. Argument is presented in the chapter on quantity–quality (tonnage–grade) relations for limiting the use of such relations to not only individual metals, but to specific modes of occurrence of a metal. These arguments are relevant here, meaning that even if the multivariate model is for wealth aggregated across several metals, estimation of metal endowment would require (1) decomposition of estimated wealth

to quantities of the various metals and (2) auxiliary analysis, based upon tonnage and grade relations for not only each metal, but for each mode of occurrence. If economic analysis is to be performed on this endowment to estimate mineral resources or potential supply, then additional models are necessary, models of number of deposits, deposit size and grade, and exploration and exploitation models. Obviously, the fewer the metals and modes of occurrence represented in this aggregate of value, the fewer the assumptions that are necessary and the more credible the appraisal.

One issue regarding geological variables, that of incomplete information, was discussed previously in this chapter; consequently, nothing more will be said here regarding it. However, there are other issues than this one that concern geological variables. One of these issues is the definition of the variable. Most geology is reported in qualitative terms. Use of geological information, as commonly reported, requires construction of some quantitative measure that reflects some aspect of the information. In the models reviewed in this chapter, these measurement variables typically took the form of counts, lengths, and areas. For some kinds of geological information these variable forms may not be the best form. Having performed a number of multivariate studies, the author is of the opinion that an area of cell that consists of a specific rock type is not the best measurement variable. Reasons for this conclusion are

1. As long as this measurement variable ignores the relative location within the cell of this rock outcrop, it is not so much the quantity of the exposure as whether or not it is present in combination with other rock types, e.g. limestone with granodiorite.

2. In some cases, e.g. igneous intrusive, larger amounts of a rock type within a cell may be favourable only to a point, past which larger amounts decrease the expectation for mineral wealth.

A cell having 100 per cent of its area consisting of igneous intrusive in some environments may have, on average, less potential than one having 50 per cent igneous intrusive, for the cell with 50 per cent may contain an igneous sedimentary contact. In this case, a linear measurement, such as per cent of area consisting of a specific rock type, introduces geological information in a manner that is not compatible with the regression or discriminant analyses, for the coefficients of the variables must remain fixed and do not vary with the percentage. The objective in the design of a geological variable must be to express the geological information in a manner that the variation in the level of the variable is compatible with the mechanics of the multivariate model and the theory of the geological model. Thus, in the case of the per cent of cell comprised by an igneous intrusive, perhaps the variable should be of the form of $g = [100 - \gamma(K - X)]$, where X is per cent of the cell area comprised by the igneous intrusive, K is some constant, and γ is a function. Suppose that $\gamma = |K - X|$, then $g = 100 - |K - X|$. The maximum value of g would be 100 and would occur when $K = X$. If the value of 50 per cent were selected for K, the maximum value for g would occur when $X = 50$ per cent, and the value for g for $X = 25$ per cent would be equal to the value of g for $X = 75$ per cent, making the transformation symmetric around $X = K = 50$ per cent. Such a measure would allow the coefficient to ascribe to this variable an increase in numerical value for g for X up to 50 per cent, which would be compatible with theory in that the cell with 50 per cent X may, on average, have a greater exposed contact zone, hence be more favourable for mineral wealth than if 75 per cent of its area consisted of the igneous intrusive. Obviously, the functional form of $|K - X|$ is symmetric, a property that may not be preferred for some conditions. There is some appeal to the argument that for vein deposits 25 per cent of the cell area consisting of an igneous intrusive is better than 75 per cent, for a condition of 25 per cent allows for the presence of the intrusive beneath other rocks in the cell, a condition that could favour the formation of replacement, fracture-filling, and contact types of deposits. The 25 per cent level may imply greater potential than 75 per cent for these types of deposits; furthermore, a level of 75 per cent may be correlated to a greater erosion depth, a condition which may have destroyed deposits either in the upper reaches of the intrusive or in the overlying rocks.

Reason 1, above, suggests that it may be good procedure to form variables that represent combinations of conditions. One way of doing this is to use products of variables: $g_i \times g_j$. A binary scheme may be desirable for some variables. For example, if an igneous intrusive is present and in contact with a limestone, the measurement variable representing this interaction would have a value of one, but a value of zero when only the intrusive or only the limestone is present.

In way of a highly critical comment with respect to multivariate models, the reader may recall the finding of Sinclair and Woodsworth (1970) that when mineral wealth was regressed against the geology of only those cells containing producing mines, the resulting wealth equation was not statistically significant. Similar results were observed with regards to discriminant analysis, namely that although the differences between the means of the geology of the value groups were statistically significant, they were less so when the classification excluded barren cells. These observations can be interpreted as suggesting that the broad, low-level geology, as expressed in these studies by the measurement variables, is primarily effective in differentiating between cells with significant mineralization and those without, in other words, favourable versus unfavourable environments. Given the set of mineralized cells, the set of measurements employed are not highly effective in explaining the *size* of mineralization. This is not necessarily saying that geology in general is not useful in explaining size of mineralization, though such could be the case. Rather, the level of geological information employed and introduced by the measurement variables of the models herein examined may not be very effective in explaining the size of the mineral accumulation.

Suppose that the above assessment is correct. This would carry three implications.

1. A simple (two-group) discriminant analysis is more appropriate than a regression analysis.
2. For many of the variables, a binary representation may not only be adequate, but in some cases more appropriate.
3. Techniques other than discriminant and regression analysis may better treat the combinatorial and hierarchical relations between geological variables.

Implications 1 and 2 have already been discussed. Implication 3 arises from the fact that there is a special kind of dependency among some geological features, that which derives from the chronology of earth processes. For example, a limestone unit must exist before it can be intruded, and the intrusive must have taken place before hydrothermal alteration or radial fracturing from the intrusive force could have been formed. An added feature of a hierarchical scheme would be that it would not require that all geological features be observed as do the multivariate models. On the other hand, hierarchical models have their liabilities, such as the problem of dealing with large numbers of combinations, the difficulty in quantification, and the generally more unwieldy relations as compared with those of regression and discriminant equations.

Arguments in favour of multivariate models must

include their relative simplicity, widespread recognition (in terms of the statistical techniques), the ability to analyse a large set of measurements simultaneously, the fact that they can express in a simple format the major effects of a large set of variables in a manner that can be subjected to statistical tests of significance, and their versatility with respect to variable forms and kinds of relations (this is especially true of regression models).

6.7. Appendix

6.7.1. *Derivation of the aggregate mineral-wealth probability distribution*

Let $f_h^v(v_h \mid G_D)$, $h = 1, 2, \ldots, r$ be the probability density function for value v of the hth metal. With the assumption that v_h is statistically independent of v_l for all $l \neq h$, the probability density function for the joint occurrence of the vs is given by

$$f^v(v_1, v_2, \ldots, v_r \mid G_D)$$
$$= f_1^v(v_1 \mid G_D) \cdot f_2^v(v_2 \mid G_D) \cdot \ldots$$
$$\ldots \cdot f_r^v(v_r \mid G_D), \quad \{v_1, v_2, \ldots, v_r\} \in \beta^v,$$
$$= 0, \quad \text{otherwise}, \qquad (6.59)$$

where $\beta^v = r$th dimensional probability space for v_is. Let us define r new variables by r transformation functions that map β^v into β^w

$$W_1 = V_1 + V_2 + \ldots + V_r$$
$$W_2 = V_2$$
$$\cdot \ \cdot \ \cdot \ \cdot$$
$$W_r = V_r.$$

Then,

$$V_1 = W_1 - V_2 - \ldots - V_r$$
$$V_2 = W_2$$
$$\cdot \ \cdot \ \cdot \ \cdot$$
$$V_r = W_r.$$

The joint probability density function (p.d.f.) for the new variables is defined on the new space β^w as

$$f^w(w_1, w_2, \ldots, w_r \mid G_D)$$
$$= f^v(w_1 - w_2 - \ldots - w_r, w_2, \ldots, w_r \mid G_D) \, |J|,$$
$$\{w_1, w_2, \ldots, w_r\} \in \beta^w,$$
$$= 0, \quad \text{otherwise}, \qquad (6.60)$$

where $|J|$ is the Jacobian of the transformation. But

$$|J| = \begin{vmatrix} \dfrac{\partial v_1}{\partial w_1} & \dfrac{\partial v_1}{\partial w_2} & \cdots & \dfrac{\partial v_1}{\partial w_r} \\ \cdots\cdots\cdots\cdots\cdots \\ \dfrac{\partial v_r}{\partial w_1} & \cdots\cdots\cdots & \dfrac{\partial v_r}{\partial w_r} \end{vmatrix} = \begin{vmatrix} 1 & -1 & \cdots\cdots\cdots & -1 \\ 0 & 1 & -1 & \cdots & -1 \\ \cdots\cdots\cdots\cdots\cdots \\ 0 & 0 & \cdots\cdots\cdots & 1 \end{vmatrix} = 1.$$
$$(6.61)$$

Therefore, since $|J| = 1$, we have

$$f^w(w_1, w_2, \ldots, w_r \mid G_D)$$
$$= f^v(w_1 - w_2 - \ldots - w_r, w_2, \ldots, w_r \mid G_D),$$
$$\{w_1, w_2, \ldots, w_r\} \in \beta^w$$
$$= 0, \quad \text{otherwise}.$$

By substituting for $W_2, \ldots, W_r$ and integrating over $V_2, \ldots, V_r$ we obtain the p.d.f. for w_1,

$$f_1^w(w_1 \mid G_D)$$
$$= \int_{V_r} \int_{V_{r-1}} \cdots \int_{V_2} f^v(w_1 - v_2 - \ldots$$
$$\ldots - v_r, v_2, \ldots, v_r \mid G_D) \, dv_2 \ldots dv_{r-1} \, dv_r,$$
$$w_1 \in \beta^w, \qquad (6.62)$$
$$f_1^w(w_1 \mid G_D) = 0, \quad \text{otherwise}.$$

Since there is only one w in (6.62), w_1, and by definition w_1 represents aggregate value, the subscript can be suppressed, giving the probability density of eqn (6.6), $f^w(w \mid G_D)$.

6.7.2. *Discriminant analysis*

Theory (after Bryan 1951; Cooley and Lohnes 1962)

Assume for simplicity a model of only two variables and two groups plus some exogenous criterion of classification [4]:

$$X_{1ig}, \quad X_{2ig},$$

where $i = 1, 2, \ldots, N$, $g = 1, 2, \ldots, KG$ (in this case, 2), N is the total number of individuals, N_g is the number of individuals in the gth group, and KG is the number of groups.

Define a variable

$$Y_{ig} = v_1 X_{1ig} + v_2 X_{2ig}, \qquad (6.63)$$

where the v_i are coefficients to be determined such that $\lambda = \phi/\gamma$ is a maximum, ϕ is the among-groups sums of squares of Y_g, and γ is the within-groups sums of squares of Y_g,

$$\gamma = \sum_g^{KG} \sum_i^{N_g} (Y_{ig} - \bar{Y}_g)^2$$
$$\phi = \sum_g^{KG} N_g \bar{Y}_g^2.$$

Since v_i are not known, Y_{ig} cannot be known. Only X_{1ig}, X_{2ig} are known.

$$\bar{Y}_g = \frac{1}{N_g} \sum_i^{N_g} (v_1 X_{1ig} + v_2 X_{2ig})$$
$$= \frac{V_1}{N_g} \sum_i^{N_g} X_{1ig} + \frac{V_2}{N_g} \sum_i^{N_g} X_{2ig} \qquad (6.64)$$

or

$$\bar{Y}_g = v_1 \bar{X}_{1g} + v_2 \bar{X}_{2g} \qquad (6.65)$$

and

$$\bar{Y}_g^2 = v_1^2 \bar{X}_{1g}^2 + v_2^2 \bar{X}_{2g}^2 + 2v_1 v_2 \bar{X}_{1g} \bar{X}_{2g}. \qquad (6.66)$$

Looking momentarily at ϕ only, for the case of 2 groups

$$\phi = \sum_{g=1}^{KG} N_g \bar{Y}_g^2 \qquad (6.67)$$

$$\phi = N_1(v_1^2 \bar{X}_{11}^2 + v_2^2 \bar{X}_{21}^2 + 2v_1 v_2 \bar{X}_{11} \bar{X}_{21}) + \\ + N_2(v_1^2 \bar{X}_{12}^2 + v_2^2 \bar{X}_{22}^2 + 2v_1 v_2 \bar{X}_{12} \bar{X}_{22}).$$

We define a matrix $A_{(2,2)}$ an element of which is

$$\{a_{jk}\} = \sum_g^{KG} N_g \bar{X}_{jg} \bar{X}_{kg};$$

then

$$A = \begin{bmatrix} N_1 \bar{X}_{11}^2 + N_2 \bar{X}_{12}^2 & N_1 \bar{X}_{11} \bar{X}_{21} + N_2 \bar{X}_{12} \bar{X}_{22} \\ N_1 \bar{X}_{21} \bar{X}_{11} + N_2 \bar{X}_{22} \bar{X}_{12} & N_1 \bar{X}_{21}^2 + N_2 \bar{X}_{22}^2 \end{bmatrix}. \qquad (6.68)$$

Also write a column vector, V

$$\begin{vmatrix} v_1 \\ v_2 \end{vmatrix}.$$

Then $\phi = V'AV$. This is an equivalent expression to (6.67).

In a similar manner, let us define a matrix $W_{(2,2)}$, an element of which is

$$\{w_{jk}\} = \sum_g^{KG} \sum_i^{N_g} (X_{jig} - \bar{X}_{jg})(X_{kig} - \bar{X}_{kg}). \qquad (6.69)$$

Then

$$\gamma = V'WV. \qquad (6.70)$$

Now we can write

$$\lambda = \frac{V'AV}{V'WV} = \frac{\phi}{\gamma}. \qquad (6.71)$$

For a given set of data A and W are determined; V is not. To maximize λ requires selecting the V which gives the maximum size of the numerator relative to the denominator.

V is determined by taking partial derivatives of λ relative to the v_i and setting

$$\frac{\partial \lambda}{\partial v_j} = 0.$$

This results in a system of equations

$$(V'WV)(AV) - (V'AV)(WV) = 0. \qquad (6.72)$$

Dividing through by $V'WV$, which is a constant, we get

$$AV - \left(\frac{V'AV}{V'WV}\right)(WV) = 0.$$

But λ was defined as $V'AV/V'WV$. Thus, we can write

$$AV - \lambda WV = (A - \lambda W)V = 0$$

and, by defining $R = W^{-1}A$, we finally have

$$(R - \lambda I)V = 0. \qquad (6.73)$$

For the case of 2 variables, this could be written as

$$(r_{11} - \lambda)V_1 + V_2 r_{12} = 0$$
$$r_{21} V_1 + (r_{22} - \lambda)V_2 = 0.$$

The values of λ which satisfy this condition are determined from

$$|R - \lambda I| = 0, \qquad (6.74)$$

or, for 2 variables,

$$\begin{vmatrix} r_{11} - \lambda & r_{12} \\ r_{21} & r_{22} - \lambda \end{vmatrix} = 0;$$

this determinant yields a polynomial in λ:

$$\lambda^2 - (r_{11} + r_{22})\lambda + r_{11} r_{22} - r_{21} r_{12}. \qquad (6.75)$$

For each root (eigenvalue) of the characteristic equation, there is an eigenvector. This eigenvector consists of the coefficients, v_1 and v_2, of a discriminant function,

$$Y_{i1} = \text{disc}_{i1} = v_1 X_{1i} + v_2 X_{2i}, \qquad (6.76)$$

where disc_{i1} is the discriminant score for the ith individual on the first discriminant equation. The number (maximum) of discriminants is given by the lesser of two numbers: $KG - 1$, one less than the number of groups; or m, the number of variables.

The eigenvalues can be employed to 'test the discriminating' power of the set of discriminants by computing the Wilks' Lambda criterion.

$$\Lambda = \prod_{i=2}^{r} \left(\frac{1}{1 + \lambda_i}\right). \qquad (6.77)$$

Rao (1952, pp. 258–72) proposes that the distribution of Λ can be approximated by the F distribution

$$F_{BS+2k}^{2\sigma} = \left(\frac{1 - \Lambda^{1/S}}{\Lambda^{\frac{1}{3}}}\right)\left(\frac{mS + 2k}{2\sigma}\right), \qquad (6.78)$$

where r is the number of discriminants, m the number of variables, KG the number of groups,

$q = KG - 1$, and (2σ) and $(BS + 2k)$ are degrees of freedom for numerator and denominator, respectively, of the F ratio.

$$k = -(mq - 2)/4$$
$$\sigma = mq/2$$
$$B = (N - 1) - (m + q + 1)/2$$
$$S = \{(m^2 q^2 - 4)/(m^2 + q^2 - 5)\}^{\frac{1}{2}}.$$

Although $ND = \min(KG - 1, m)$ discriminants might be computed, only r may be statistically significant.

The number of significant discriminants is determined by employing the χ^2 distribution to test the significance of the residual variance after extracting from the total explained variance that amount due to each function (Rao 1952, pp. 370–8).

Define

$$Z_p = (N - 0.5(KG + NV) \ln(1.0 + \lambda_p))$$
$$DF_p = KG + NV - 2P, \quad (6.79)$$

where Z_p is the variance explained or due the pth discriminant, DF_p is the degrees of freedom, KG the number of groups, NV the number of variables, p the index of eigenvalues, N the number of individuals, and λ_p is the pth eigenvalue. Then compute Z'_p and DF'_p by cumulating Z_p and DF_p upward. For example,

p	Z_p	DF_p	Z'_p	DF'_p
1	240	28	480	100
2	120	26	240	72
3	80	24	120	46
4	40	22	40	22

$$(6.80)$$

Z'_p is compared to χ^2 for $n = DF'_p$ and δ is a specified significance level,

$Z'_p > \chi^{2(n)}_\delta \rightarrow$ there exists at least one more significant equation (the $p + 1$ discriminant is significant).   (6.81)

Transform to the discriminant space.
1. Compute $C_{(r,KG)}$

$$C_{(r,KG)} = V'_{(r,NV)} \cdot \tilde{X}_{(NV,KG)}, \quad (6.82)$$

where

$C_{(r,KG)}$ is the matrix of centroids in reduced space,

i.e.

$$C_{11} = V_1 \bar{X}_{11} + V_2 \bar{X}_{21} + \ldots + V_{NV} \bar{X}_{NV,1}$$
$$C_{12} = V_1 \bar{X}_{12} + V_2 \bar{X}_{22} + \ldots + V_{NV} \bar{X}_{NV,2}$$
$$\ldots \ldots \ldots \ldots \ldots \ldots \ldots \ldots$$

and

$\bar{X}$ is the matrix of means, a vector (set) for each group.

Where in the variable space there are as many means as variables, in the discriminant space there are as many means as discriminant functions.

$$\left. \begin{array}{c} \bar{X}_{11} \\ \bar{X}_{21} \\ \cdot \\ \cdot \\ \bar{X}_{NV,1} \end{array} \right)$$

Means of raw variables $\underline{\text{Transformation}}$

$$\left(\begin{array}{ll} C_{11} & \text{Discriminant scores} \\ C_{21} & \text{from functions} \\ \cdot & \text{evaluated at the} \\ \cdot & \text{means of the raw} \\ C_{r1} & \text{variables.} \end{array} \right.$$

where $r < NV$.

2. Compute $D^{(g)}_{(r,r)}$, the dispersion matrix in the reduced (discriminant) space $g = 1, 2, \ldots, KG$,

$$D^{(g)}_{(r,r)} = V'_{(r,NV)} \cdot DD^{(g)}_{(NV,NV)} \cdot V_{(NV,r)}, \quad (6.83)$$

where $DD^{(g)}_{(NV,NV)}$ is the dispersion matrix in the variable space for the gth group.

Numerical example

	Group 1		Group 2	
X_{11}	X_{21}	X_{12}	X_{22}
-1	0	2	-1
0	1	1	1
-1	2	-1	-1
-1	-1	1	-1
$\overline{-3}$	$\overline{2}$	$\overline{3}$	$\overline{-2}$

$\bar{X}_{11} = -0.75$ $\bar{\bar{X}}_1 = 0$
$\bar{X}_{12} = +0.75$ $\bar{\bar{X}}_2 = 0$
$\bar{X}_{21} = 0.5$ $N = 8$
$\bar{X}_{22} = -0.5$ $N_1 = 4$
              $N_2 = 4$

I. Let us now form matrix A, relationship (6.68),

$$A = \begin{bmatrix} 4(-0.75)^2 + 4(0.75)^2 & 4(-0.75)(0.5) + 4(0.75)(-0.5) \\ 4(0.5)(-0.75) + 4(-0.5)(+0.75) & 4(0.5)^2 + 4(-0.5)^2 \end{bmatrix}$$

$$= \begin{bmatrix} 4.5 & -3.0 \\ -3.0 & 2 \end{bmatrix}.$$

II. Now, let us calculate the elements of W. From (6.69), we have that

$$w_{11} = \sum_{g=1}^{2} \sum_{i=1}^{4} (X_{1ig} - \bar{X}_{1g})(X_{1ig} - \bar{X}_{1g}).$$

(1) w_{11}:

$$w_{11} = \sum_i (X_{1i1} - \bar{X}_{11})(X_{1i1} - \bar{X}_{11}) +$$
$$+ \sum_i (X_{1i2} - \bar{X}_{12})(X_{1i2} - \bar{X}_{12})$$

or

$$w_{11} = \sum_i^{N_1} (X_{1i1} - \bar{X}_{11})^2 +$$
$$+ \sum_i^{N_2} (X_{1i2} - \bar{X}_{12})^2 = N_1 S_{11}^2 + N_2 S_{12}^2.$$

Calculation of $N_1 S_{11}^2$ and $N_2 S_{12}^2$ for w_{11} gives

$$N_1 S_{11}^2 = (-1 + 0.75)^2 + (0.75)^2 +$$
$$+ (-1 + 0.75)^2 + (-1 + 0.75)^2.$$
$$N_1 S_{11}^2 = 0.0625 + 0.5625 + 0.0625 + 0.0625 = 0.75$$
$$N_2 S_{12}^2 = (1.5625 + 0.0625 + 3.0625 + 0.0625) = 4.75$$
$$w_{11} = 0.75 + 4.75 = 5.50.$$

(2) $w_{12} = \sum_i (X_{1i1} - \bar{X}_{11})(X_{2i1} - \bar{X}_{21}) +$
$$+ \sum_i (X_{1i2} - \bar{X}_{12})(X_{2i2} - \bar{X}_{22})$$

$$w_{12} = N_1 COV_1 + N_2 COV_2$$
$$N_1 COV_1 = (-0.25)(-0.5) + (0.75)(0.5) +$$
$$+ (-0.25)(1.5) + (-0.25)(-1.5)$$
$$= 0.125 + 0.375 - 0.375 + 0.375$$
$$= 0.500$$
$$N_2 COV_2 = (1.25)(-0.5) + (0.25)(1.5) +$$
$$+ (-1.75)(-0.5) + (0.25)(-0.5)$$
$$= 0.500$$
$$w_{12} = 1.0 = N_1 COV_1 + N_2 COV_2$$
$$= 0.500 + 0.500 = 1.0.$$

(3) $w_{21} = 1.0.$

(4) $w_{22} = \sum_i (X_{2i1} - \bar{X}_{21})(X_{2i1} - \bar{X}_{21}) +$
$$+ \sum_i (X_{2i2} - \bar{X}_{22})(X_{2i2} - \bar{X}_{22})$$

$$w_{22} = N_1 S_{21}^2 + N_2 S_{22}^2$$
$$N_1 S_{21}^2 = (-0.5)^2 + (1 - 0.5)^2 +$$
$$+ (2 - 0.5)^2 + (-1 - 0.5)^2$$
$$N_1 S_{21}^2 = +0.25 + 0.25 + 2.25 + 2.25$$
$$N_1 S_{21}^2 = 5.0$$
$$N_2 S_{22}^2 = 0.25 + 2.25 + 0.25 + 0.25 = 3.0$$
$$w_{22} = 3.0 + 5.0 = 8.0.$$

(5) Thus, $W = \begin{bmatrix} 5.5 & 1.0 \\ 1.0 & 8.0 \end{bmatrix}.$

III. Calculate λ from (6.71).

Let $V = \begin{bmatrix} v_1 \\ v_2 \end{bmatrix}$, then $V' = [v_1 \quad v_2]$, and

$$V'W = [v_1 \quad v_2] \begin{bmatrix} 5.5 & 1.0 \\ 1.0 & 8.0 \end{bmatrix} = [5.5v_1 + v_2 \quad v_1 + 8v_2]$$

and

$$V'WV = [5.5v_1 + v_2 \quad v_1 + 8v_2] \begin{bmatrix} v_1 \\ v_2 \end{bmatrix}$$
$$= 5.5v_1^2 + v_1v_2 + v_1v_2 + 8v_2^2$$
$$V'WV = 5.5v_1^2 + 2v_1v_2 + 8v_2^2.$$

Further,

$$V'A = [4.5v_1 - 3v_2 \quad -3v_1 + 2v_2]$$
$$V'AV = 4.5v_1^2 - 3v_1v_2 - 3v_1v_2 + 2v_2^2.$$

Finally,

$$\lambda = \frac{V'AV}{V'WV} = \frac{4.5v_1^2 - 6v_1v_2 + 2v_2^2}{5.5v_1^2 + 2v_1v_2 + 8v_2^2}; \quad \lambda I = \begin{bmatrix} \lambda & 0 \\ 0 & \lambda \end{bmatrix}.$$

IV. Calculate W^{-1} (6.72). Given $W = \begin{bmatrix} 5.5 & 1 \\ 1 & 8 \end{bmatrix}$,

form matrix of determinants of cofactors

$$A_{ij} = \begin{bmatrix} 8 & -1 \\ -1 & 5.5 \end{bmatrix}.$$

Form transpose of A_{ij}; $A_{ij}^T = \begin{bmatrix} 8 & -1 \\ -1 & 5.5 \end{bmatrix}$,

$$W^{-1} = \frac{A_{ij}^T}{|W|}; \quad |W| = 44.0 - 1 = 43.$$

Thus, $W^{-1} = \begin{bmatrix} \dfrac{8}{43} & -\dfrac{1}{43} \\[2mm] -\dfrac{1}{43} & \dfrac{5.5}{43} \end{bmatrix}$.

V. Form product $W^{-1}A$.

$R = W^{-1}A = \begin{bmatrix} 8/43 & -1/43 \\ -1/43 & 5.5/43 \end{bmatrix}\begin{bmatrix} 4.5 & -3 \\ -3 & 2 \end{bmatrix}$

$= \dfrac{1}{43}\begin{bmatrix} 36+3=39 & -24-2=-26 \\ -4.5-16.5=-21 & 3+11=14 \end{bmatrix}$

$R = \begin{bmatrix} \dfrac{39}{43} & -\dfrac{26}{43} \\[2mm] -\dfrac{21}{43} & \dfrac{14}{43} \end{bmatrix}$.

VI. Determine $R - \lambda I$ (6.73).

$R - \lambda I = \begin{bmatrix} 39/43 - \lambda & -26/43 \\ -21/43 & 14/43 - \lambda \end{bmatrix}$.

VII. Take determinant of $R - \lambda I$ (6.74).

$|R - \lambda I| = \lambda^2 - \dfrac{39}{43}\lambda - \dfrac{14}{43}\lambda + \dfrac{(39)(14)}{(43)^2} - \dfrac{(-21)(-26)}{(43)^2}$

$= \lambda^2 - \dfrac{53}{43}\lambda + \dfrac{546}{(43)^2} - \dfrac{546}{(43)^2} = \lambda^2 - 1.2326\lambda$.

VIII. Determine roots of characteristic eqn (6.75). Set $\lambda^2 - 1.2326\lambda = 0$

$$\lambda_1 = 1.2326; \quad \lambda_2 = 0.$$

IX. Solve for v_1 and v_2 for largest root λ_1.

$\left.\begin{array}{l} (0.90698 - \lambda_1)v_1 - 0.60465v_2 = 0 \\ -0.48837v_1 + (0.32558 - \lambda_1)v_2 = 0 \end{array}\right\} \to [R - \lambda I][V] = 0$

$\begin{array}{l} -0.32558v_1 - 0.60465v_2 = 0 \\ -0.48837v_1 - 0.90698v_2 = 0. \end{array}$ (6.84)

Equating the above two equations and letting $v_1 = 1$,

$$v_2 = -0.53846 \approx -0.54.$$

The vs are not unique; any multiple will satisfy eqn (6.84),

$$v_1 = k, \quad v_2 = -0.54k.$$

A single discriminant equation converts this two-dimensional (in general n-dimensional) problem into one that is one-dimensional. In the original problem, individuals from two populations are compared on the basis of two variables X_1 and X_2. By evaluating the discriminant equation at X_1 and X_2, each indi-

vidual can be described by one discriminant score instead of the two raw variables: For example, the discriminant score for the first individual of group 1 on the first and only discriminant function would be calculated

$$\overset{(v_1)}{\downarrow} \qquad \overset{(v_2)}{\downarrow}$$
$$\mathrm{disc}_{11} = 1.0(X_{111}) - 0.54(X_{211})$$
$$= 1(-1) - 0.54(0) = -1.0. \qquad (6.85)$$

Similarly, the discriminant scores for all individuals in each group can be computed.

	Group 1	Group 2	
disc_{11}	-1.0	2.54	
disc_{21}	-0.54	0.46	(6.86)
disc_{31}	-2.08	-0.46	
disc_{41}	-0.46	1.54	

individual $\rightsquigarrow$ $\leftsquigarrow$ function

The mean discriminant score for each group and each function (here we have only one) can be calculated by the traditional approach,

$$\overline{\mathrm{disc}_{11}} = \tfrac{1}{4}\sum_{i=1}^{4} \mathrm{disc}_{i1} \qquad \overline{\mathrm{disc}_{21}} = \tfrac{1}{4}\sum_{i=1}^{4} \mathrm{disc}_{i1}. \quad (6.87)$$

Alternatively, the means in discriminant space can be calculated by evaluating the equation at the means of each of the variables for each group (this is possible because the discriminant equation is linear).

$$\overline{\mathrm{disc}_{11}} = (1)(\bar{X}_{11}) - (0.54)(\bar{X}_{21})$$
$$= 1(-0.75) - 0.54(0.5) = \underline{-1.02}$$
$$\overline{\mathrm{disc}_{21}} = (1)(\bar{X}_{12}) - (0.54)(\bar{X}_{22})$$
$$= 1(0.75) - 0.54(-0.5) = \underline{1.02}. \qquad (6.88)$$

The most straightforward way to calculate the standard deviation of the discriminant score for each group is to apply the traditional formula to the discriminant scores of the individuals in the groups,

$$\hat{\sigma}^2_{Dh} = \left[\sum_{i=1}^{N_h} (\mathrm{disc}_{ih})^2 - N_h(\overline{\mathrm{disc}_h})^2\right] \Big/ (N_h - 1). \quad (6.89)$$

Note: This is the special case of eqn (6.33) in which there is only one discriminant function.

In our numeric example, $h = 1, 2$ and $N_1 = N_2 = 4$. Substituting these values and the statistics calculated from the data of (6.86) into (6.89), the variances of the two groups can be calculated,

$$\hat{\sigma}_{D1}^2 = [5.8296 - 4(1.0404)]/3 = 0.556$$
$$\hat{\sigma}_{D1} = \sqrt{0.556} = 0.746$$
$$\hat{\sigma}_{D2}^2 = [9.2464 - 4(1.0404)]/3 = 1.695$$
$$\hat{\sigma}_{D2} = \sqrt{1.6949} = 1.302.$$

This completes the transformation from the raw variable space to the discriminant space.

References

Agterberg, F. P., Chung, C. F., Fabbri, A. G., Kelly, A. M., and Springer, J. S. (1972). *Geomathematical evaluation of copper and zinc potential of the Abitibi Area, Ontario and Quebec.* Geological Survey Canada Paper 71-41.

Allais, M. (1957). Method of appraising economic prospects of mining exploration over large territories: Algerian Sahara case study. *Management Sci.* **3**(4), 285–347.

Bryan, J. C. (1951). The generalized discriminant function: mathematical foundation and computational routine. *Harvard Educat. Rev.* **21**(2), 90–5.

Cattell, R. B. (1965). Factor analysis: introduction to essentials. *Biometrics* **21**(1), 190–215; (2), 405–435.

Cooley, W. W. and Lohnes, P. R. (1962). *Multivariate procedures for the behavioural sciences.* John Wiley & Sons, New York.

De Geoffroy, J. and Wignall, T. K. (1971). A probabilistic appraisal of mineral resources in a portion of the Grenville Province of the Canadian Shield. *Econ. Geol.* **66**(3), 466–79.

Harmon, H. H. (1962). *Modern factor analysis* (2nd Impression). University of Illinois Press, Chicago.

Harris, D. P. (1966a). A probability model of mineral wealth. *Trans. SME* June 1966, pp. 199–216.

—— (1966b). Factor analysis—a tool for quantitative studies in mineral exploration. *Proc. 6th Int. Symp. on Computers and Operations Research in the Mineral Industries*, pp. GG1–GG37. Mineral Industries Experiment Station Special Publication 2-65, The Pennsylvania State University, University Park.

—— (1968). Alaska's base and precious metals resources: a probabilistic regional appraisal. *Mineral resources of Northern Alaska*, pp. 189–224. MIRL Report No. 16, Mineral Industries Research Laboratory, University of Alaska.

Klovan, J. E. (1968). Selection of target areas by factor analysis. *Proc. Symp. Decision-Making in Mineral Exploration*, pp. 19–27, Vancouver, British Columbia.

Rao, C. R. (1952). *Advanced statistical methods in biometric research.* John Wiley & Sons, New York.

Sinclair, A. J. and Woodsworth, G. L. (1970). Multiple regression as a method of estimating exploration potential in an area near Terrace, B.C. *Econ. Geol.* **65**(8), 998–1003.

Notes

1. Harris, D. P. (1965). An application of multivariate statistical analysis to mineral exploration, Ph.D. dissertation, The Pennsylvania State University.
2. Principal-components analysis is the special case of factor analysis in which communalities of one are employed, which, in simple terms, implies that all information present in the geological variables will be present in the factors.
3. The numbers on F, 35 and 974, are the degrees of freedom for the numerator and denominator, respectively, for the F distribution statistic.
4. In this derivation X_1 and X_2 are assumed to have means of zero in the mixed population (consisting of N_g groups).

7 OCCURRENCE MODELS

7.1. Perspective on occurrence models

The term 'occurrence model' has been used (Harris 1967) to refer to models that describe the probability for some discrete form of a metal accumulation, usually a mine or mining district. Occurrence models that have been investigated include both univariate models, which describe the unconditional distribution of the unit of metallization, and multivariate models, which describe the probability for the occurrence of the unit of metallization conditional upon the status of a set of geological variables. The univariate models are often referred to as spatial models, and the conditional-probability models have been referred to as multivariate geostatistical (MG) models. These labels shall be employed similarly in the following discussions.

Occurrence models can be related to the conceptualization of the geostatistical deposit models by identifying the spatial models as some form of $N(n)$ and the MG models as a form of $\tilde{h}(n \mid G_D)$. (See eqns (5.24) and (5.25).)

7.2. Spatial models

The search for a probabilistic law to explain the distribution of mineral deposits has consisted of two parts.

(1) relating properties of known functions to characteristics of the habitat of deposits to see if the mathematical underpinnings (assumptions) were consistent with the physical model;
(2) fitting mathematical functions to empirical data on the distribution of some unit that reflects the occurrence of a mineral deposit (mine, mining district, etc).

The hope in the fitting of mathematical functions was that such an exercise would discover a relationship that fits the data so well that it could be accepted as the mathematical law of the spatial distribution of mineral deposits.

A probability function possesses one or more constants that must be known before it can be used in prediction; these constants are known as parameters, and their estimation from data constitutes the fitting of the function.

7.2.1. *Concepts of fitting of functions*

Fitting of a function implies the assumption that it (the function) is the law that explains the phenomenon. Given this assumption, the task is merely one of computing from the data the statistics that estimate the parameters.

There are several kinds of estimators of the parameters of a function (population), e.g. least squares, maximum likelihood, moments, and minimum χ^2. Computation of the maximum likelihood estimator will be demonstrated on a negative exponential function. The exponential probability density is

$$f(t) = \alpha e^{-\alpha t}, \quad 0 \le t \le \infty. \qquad (7.1)$$

Examination of (7.1) shows this probability density function (p.d.f.) to be completely defined by the parameter α. In order to fit this distribution, an estimator for α first must be determined. Then, the appropriate statistic can be calculated from sample data.

Suppose that we have selected a random sample of size n of observations on t: $t_1, t_2, \ldots, t_n$ and that we wish to fit the exponential function of (7.1) to these observed values. To do so, we must first determine what measure made on our sample is a good estimator for the parameter α. Suppose that we decide to use a maximum likelihood estimator because this class of estimators are efficient, consistent, and sufficient (if the parameter has a sufficient estimator). How do we determine the maximum likelihood estimator $\hat{\alpha}$ of α for our function? First, a likelihood function must be defined.

The likelihood function L of this random sample is written as $L(\hat{\alpha}; t_1, t_2, \ldots, t_n) = f(t_1; \hat{\alpha}) \cdot f(t_2; \hat{\alpha}) \ldots f(t_n; \hat{\alpha})$. In terms of the exponential p.d.f., the likelihood function can be written

$$L(\hat{\alpha}; t_1, t_2, \ldots, t_n) = (\hat{\alpha} e^{-\hat{\alpha} t_1}) \cdot (\hat{\alpha} e^{-\hat{\alpha} t_2}) \ldots (\hat{\alpha} e^{-\hat{\alpha} t_n})$$
$$L(\hat{\alpha}; t_1, t_2, \ldots, t_n) = \hat{\alpha}^n e^{-\hat{\alpha} \sum_{i=1}^{n} t_i}. \qquad (7.2)$$

Since this expression is in product form, greater facility in the solution of the expression for the maximum likelihood estimator is obtained from the logarithmic form of the likelihood function

$$\ln[L(\hat{\alpha}; t_1, t_2, \ldots, t_n)] = n \ln \hat{\alpha} - \hat{\alpha} \sum_{i=1}^{n} t_i. \qquad (7.3)$$

The derivative with respect to α of this logarithmic likelihood function yields

$$\frac{d\{\ln[L(\hat{\alpha}; t_1, t_2, \ldots, t_n)]\}}{d\hat{\alpha}} = \frac{n}{\hat{\alpha}} - \sum_{i=1}^{n} t_i. \quad (7.4)$$

By setting this derivative equal to zero, we have the maximum likelihood estimator for α,

$$\frac{n}{\hat{\alpha}} = \sum_{i=1}^{n} t_i \quad (7.5)$$

or

$$\frac{1}{\hat{\alpha}} = \frac{1}{n} \sum_{i=1}^{n} t_i = \bar{t} \quad (7.6)$$

$$\hat{\alpha} = \frac{1}{\bar{t}}. \quad (7.7)$$

Thus, fitting the exponential consists of estimating the parameter α by relationship (7.7), yielding

$$\hat{\alpha} e^{-\hat{\alpha}t}, \quad 0 \leq t \leq \infty,$$

where $\hat{\alpha}$ is the estimated parameter. A graphic demonstration of this function is provided by Fig. 7.1.

7.2.2. Allais's study

The classic study of spatial models is that of Maurice Allais (1957). The French were interested in appraising the value to them of the Algerian Sahara. One possible source of value in this area was the undiscovered mineral deposits that it might contain. Allais was asked to perform a study of the economic merits of conducting mineral exploration in the Algerian Sahara. This study could have been performed in the traditional way in which subjective, qualitative statements are made about the favourability of an area for the occurrence of deposits. Unfortunately, terms such as favourable and unfavourable, although conveying a meaning, do not state in a quantitative sense what the economic consequences might be of conducting an exploration programme. Allais could have gone a step further and attempted to estimate the most likely number of deposits to occur in the area and the expected tonnage and grade per deposit, based upon intuition and experience. These expectations could have been combined, giving the total amount of metal. Or, an analysis could have been performed in other units of occurrence, such as mines or mining districts. By employing expectations for size and grade of occurrences and for price of contained metal these mines could have been converted to value per mine. Then, by applying an expected cost per ton to the tonnage of each mine, a gross estimate might have been obtained of the quantity of metal that could be economically produced from the area and of the expected net value of resource development. In other words, the expectations of the important aspects of the problem could be combined to give an estimate of the merits of exploration. This, of course, would yield just one estimate of profitability.

The obvious weakness of this approach is that it gives the estimate derived by manipulation of the expectations an exaggerated reliability. Being singular, it carries with it no additional information as to the certainty or uncertainty about this particular estimate. In other words, faced with the very meagre amount of information present at that time on the Algerian Sahara, rather than the value of the Algerian Sahara being adequately represented by one number, the expected value, there really exists a probability distribution of values which represent the outcome of exploring the Sahara.

If this expectation of profitability of exploring the region were negative, the obvious conclusion would be to not conduct exploration in the Algerian Sahara. A more interesting question is the following. If the value were slightly positive, would it be rational to conduct exploration of the Sahara? The answer to this by no means is simple in a comprehensive sense; to answer it, one must have more information about possible outcomes other than the expected one. In other words, it would be desirable to know something about the distribution of value instead of merely the expectation.

Consider the case where the expected outcome would be a profit of, say, two million dollars, but one hundred million dollars is required to earn this two million. It may be that if the risk is sizeable, one would not wish to gamble US $100 000 000 just to earn an *additional* US $2 000 000. Those individuals who have participated in mineral exploration are very much aware of the many uncertainties in the outcome of an exploration venture; indeed, given the expected outcome of say two million dollars, the

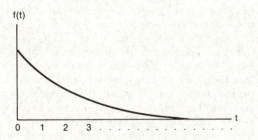

Fig. 7.1. Exponential distribution.

probability may be fairly high that the outcome would be a net loss. How an individual or government might react to undertaking such a venture depends somewhat upon their response to risk, which in turn reflects their financial resources and how serious it would be to sustain the loss. The point to be made here is that to make a rational decision, an expectation alone is not enough. There should be some information as to the uncertainty of the estimate or, said differently, there is a need for information about the *probability distribution* for the outcome.

In his study of the Algerian Sahara, Allais found that the expectation of net gain is 50×10^9 French francs; however, having conducted this study in a probability framework he was able to provide other interesting information, such as the probability for a net gain is 35 per cent and probability for losing 20×10^9 French francs is 65 per cent. Thus, the risk involved in this exploration is high.

The feature of the Allais paper that makes it a classic is that it is the first attempt by anyone to appraise the economic merits of exploration of a large region within a probability framework such that the outcome could be stated in terms of probability, indicating the associated risk. This kind of information cannot be arrived at by the combining of expectations of the events to yield net gain or loss. To obtain this information, each of the events that combine must be modelled probabilistically and their interaction accounted for explicitly. Naturally one of these events, a very important one, is the number of occurrences.

Attention on occurrence models focused first on the probability that some elementary zone, here a cell, would contain 1, 2, 3, or, in general, n mining districts. In order to be able to compute these probabilities, Allais took what seemed to be a reasonable approach; in the absence of information on the Sahara itself he examined other areas that had been well explored. A basic assumption implicit in this procedure is that these areas had received sufficient exploration that the number of mining districts known to occur would be a reasonable approximation to the number of mining districts that *actually exist* in these areas. The objective in examining these data was to search for a mathematical law that describes the distribution of mining districts. Given identification of this law, it could then be employed to make inference to the probability for the occurrence of mining districts in the Sahara. One of the 'control areas' examined by Allais was the western part of the United States. This area was subdivided into cells of

a 100 km^2, and the number of cells that had no mining districts was recorded simply by counting those in which mining districts did not occur. Similarly a count was made of all the cells with one mining district, two mining districts, and so on. In this way, a frequency distribution of cells containing stated numbers of mines was generated for the American West. This same procedure was performed on the other areas that he selected for examination. Allais tested known mathematical laws to see if any of them could provide a reasonable description of the observed phenomenon, and in all cases in which the distribution of mining districts was examined, he found that the Poisson distribution was an excellent fit to the observed data,

$$p(n) = \frac{\mu^{-n} e^{\mu}}{n!}, \quad n = 0, 1, 2, \dots.$$

7.2.3. *Fitting the Poisson*

Fitting the Poisson distribution to data of the selected areas consists mainly of estimating the parameter μ. Given the numerical value of μ, which is to be estimated from the data, the Poisson equation generates the probability for n mining districts occurring in each of the cells of the area. Thus, multiplication of this probability times the total number of cells in the area gives the number of cells in the entire area having n districts. The theoretical number of cells having n districts then can be compared to the observed number of cells having n districts. In this way, the goodness of fit can be visually estimated.

A more rigorous examination of the goodness of fit of a theoretical distribution to data is to compute the chi-square (χ^2) statistic from the observed frequencies and frequencies of the theoretical distribution (in this case the Poisson) and compare the computed χ^2 statistic to a statistic selected from the χ^2 probability distribution. Table 7.1 is an example of the estimation of the Poisson parameter μ and the calculation of the theoretical frequencies of the Poisson distribution using tabled values of the Poisson function. In addition, the χ^2 (goodness of fit) is calculated and a demonstration is given of the use of the χ^2 probability distribution to test the hypothesis that the observed data are Poisson. In this example, the hypothesis of no difference between the observed data and the Poisson distribution cannot be rejected at the 5 per cent significance level; therefore, we must conclude that the data could have come from a Poisson population, or, equivalently, we conclude

TABLE 7.1. *Fitting the Poisson*

$$p(n) = \frac{\mu^n e^{-\mu}}{n!}$$

n (Number of mines)	$Z(n)$ Number of cells with n	$r(n)$ Relative frequency	$(n) \cdot (r(n))$	$p(n)$	$r(n) - p(n)$	$\dfrac{(r(n) - p(n))^2}{p(n)}$
0	20	0.20	0.00	0.1705	0.0295	0.004600
1	30	0.30	0.30	0.2963	0.0037	0.000046
2	20	0.20	0.40	0.2628	−0.0628	0.015000
3	15	0.15	0.45	0.1584	−0.0084	0.000450
4	10	0.10	0.40	0.0729	0.0271	0.010100
5+	5	0.05	0.25	0.0389	0.0111	0.003200
	100	1.00	1.80	0.9998		$\chi_0^2 = 0.033396 \times 100 = 3.34$

$$\hat{\mu} = \sum_{n=0}^{\infty} n \cdot Z(n) = 180/100 = 1.80$$

Table values only for $\mu_L = 1.5$ and $\mu_U = 2.0$.

$$p(n) = p(n \mid \mu_L) + (p(n \mid \mu_U) - p(n \mid \mu_L))((\hat{\mu} - \mu_L)/(\mu_U - \mu_L)).$$

For $n = 0$, $p(0) = 0.2231 + (0.1353 - 0.2231)((1.8 - 1.5)/(2.0 - 1.5))$
$$p(0) = 0.2231 + (-0.0878)(0.6) = 0.2231 - 0.0526 = 0.1705$$

$$\chi_0^2 = \sum_{n=0}^{S} \frac{[Z(n) - (100)(p(n))]^2}{100 P(n)}$$

$$= 100 \sum_{n=0}^{S} \frac{(r(n) - p(n))^2}{P(n)}$$

$$\chi_0^2 = 0.033396 \times 100 = \underline{3.34}$$

$H_0 =$ No difference between observed and Poisson probabilities. Probability level (significance level) = 5 per cent or 0.05. Degrees of freedom (d.f.) = Number of classes − (number of constraints + number of parameters). In this example, there is one parameter μ and one constraint, the forced agreement of $\sum_{n=0}^{5} r(n)$ and $\sum_{n=0}^{5} p(n)$.

d.f. $= 6 - (1 + 1) = 4$; $\chi_{0.95,4}^2 = 9.488$; $\chi_0^2 < \chi_{0.95,4}^2 \rightarrow$ accept hypothesis of no difference $\rightarrow$ Poisson.

that the Poisson is an acceptable model. An alternative to calculation of the probabilities $p(n)$ by interpolation of tabled values of the Poisson function is to calculate them directly from the formula for the Poisson. Such calculation yields the probabilities 0.1653, 0.2975, 0.2678, 0.1607, 0.0723, and 0.0364. χ^2 for these probabilities is 4.09, instead of 3.34, as obtained by interpolation.

7.2.4. *Implications of the Poisson*

The fact that the Poisson distribution was a good fit to the distribution of cells having the stated numbers of deposits in each of the areas was itself an interesting conclusion when examined in light of the conditions necessary to generate a Poisson distribution.

Specifically these are as follows. First, the probability that the event of interest, in this case number of mining districts, can occur in any one of the cells is small. Second, this probability is constant across the cells; in other words, no one cell has a higher probability than any of the other cells for possessing n mining districts. Third, the probability of a compound event, that is, two mining districts occurring in any given cell, is extremely small. Condition 2, that of uniform probability across all of the cells, is often referred to by labelling the Poisson distribution as a random occurrence model. In other words it precludes any differential probability in an *a priori* sense for one cell over another cell. In terms of characteristics common to mineral deposits, this would mean that there would be no clustering of deposits, at least in terms of the units in which the phenomena were observed (in this case, mining districts). Allais' study suggests that for mining districts, the distribution appears to be Poisson, implying that the generating mechanism for mining districts is a random process; there is no significant clustering or nonrandom character in the occurrence of mining districts in the areas investigated. In terms of interest to an explorationist, if cell 25, say, had a mining district, this would not change the probability that cell 24, which would be adjacent to it, would have a mining district. Furthermore, cell 25 would not be a good place to look for another mining district; exploration should be directed to cells with no known districts.

7.2.5. Distributions for mines

Allais's research on the Algerian Sahara fostered interest by mining companies as well as by academicians in occurrence models. Since exploration firms are interested in finding a deposit that will result in a mine, subsequent studies examined the distribution of mines rather than mining districts. The desirability of the mining district as the basic observation variable for occurrence was questioned because of the vague conditions that define a district. If the mining district corresponded strictly to a physical–chemical phenomenon, such as metallization, then it would make a great deal of sense as a random variable for a probability law. In many cases this happens, but in some cases the distribution represents not only metallization in the area but local political boundaries or topographic features. In short, it may be a mix of the physical occurrence of metal and cultural, economic, and political factors. Be that as it may, replacing the mining district as the observation variable may be substituting a new set of problems for a set of less serious ones. The mine as a unit isn't altogether ideal either, because the mine really represents a resolution of a great number of features, including (besides occurrence of metallization) economic and physical characteristics which influence mining design. Thus, one metallization feature may give rise to more than one mine, which may introduce clustering phenomena. We will return to some generalizations about the shortcomings of the mine or the mining district as observational units and about the way that their characteristics influence the probability distributions, but first we will take a look at the developments that took place in searching for a probability law for the distribution of mines.

7.2.6. Slichter's work

The success of the 'fitting' approach depends not only upon the selection of the correct function but upon selection of an appropriate sample. Because of the uneven distribution of exploration, selecting an appropriate sample may be a very difficult task. For example, how can one know how much area, especially barren area, to include in the sample? It was this question that led Slichter, Dixon, and Myer (1962) to defining a new characteristic that could be used in fitting the mathematical distribution functions, a characteristic that is independent of the number of barren cells, hence independent of the size-of-area decision.

The study by Slichter et al. examined the statistical distribution of mines for several different areas: western US, a portion of the Basin and Range Area (using the data of Nolan), southwestern US (using Burnham's data), western US (based upon Bear Creek Mining Company's data), and finally the data on the pre-Cambrian area of Ontario. This study also examined, for some of the areas, data on value of the major metals produced by the mines and the distribution of mines for various value classes.

Slichter et al. first investigated an obvious dilemma in fitting a distribution to the numbers of mines in a given area, that of defining boundaries of the area. Often the boundaries are positioned quite arbitrarily; yet this decision affects the adequacy of fit of the mathematical law under investigation. In other words, merely by enlarging or shrinking the area appropriately, the number of cells with zero mines can be modified by the researcher. Naturally, this would affect the 'goodness of fit' of a theoretical distribution. Recognizing subjectivity in the drawing of boundaries, they proposed a different approach. Instead of using the mean number of mines per cell for the area of interest, they suggested using statistics based upon some other characteristic of the cells of the area. Obviously this other characteristic should be independent of the total number of cells if the boundary problem is not to influence the fit of the distribution. Slichter et al. proposed that the parameter of a distribution that is being investigated be based upon a characteristic of only those cells that contain at least one mine; specifically, this characteristic was the ratio of the total number of mines to the number of cells with at least one mine. Estimating the parameter of a probability distribution from this characteristic is, in effect, estimating the parameter of a *truncated* distribution, a distribution truncated at a value of 1 for the random variable.

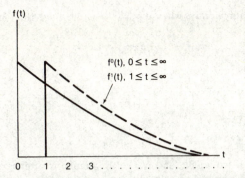

f(t)

$f^0(t)$, $0 \leq t \leq \infty$

$f^1(t)$, $1 \leq t \leq \infty$

0 1 2 3 . . . . t

Fig. 7.2. Exponential and associated truncated exponential distributions.

To demonstrate the concept behind the fitting of a truncated distribution, the maximum likelihood estimator based upon number of cells having at least one mine will here be derived on a simple exponential distribution

$$f(t) = \alpha e^{-\alpha t}, \quad 0 \leq t \leq \infty.$$

The basic approach is visualized in Fig. 7.2.

Although the solid line portrays the function desired $f^0(t)$, Slichter et al. proposed estimation of the parameters of the function described by the dashed line, $f^1(t)$, as a means to defining $f^0(t)$, the reason being that the domain of this function is truncated at $t = 1$. This truncation is necessary because the objective was to be able to fit the function to frequency data on only those cells having one or more mines. The functions $f^1(t)$ and $f^0(t)$ are related by

$$f^1(t) = f^0(t) \Big/ \int_1^\infty f^0(t)\, dt, \quad 1 \leq t \leq \infty. \quad (7.8)$$

If the parameters of $f^1(t)$ can be estimated by consideration of only nonzero content cells, then the desired function, $f^0(t)$, $0 \leq t \leq \infty$ can be obtained simply by multiplication of $f^1(t)$ by a constant,

$$f^0(t) = f^1(t) \cdot \int_1^\infty f^0(t)\, dt, \quad 0 \leq t \leq \infty. \quad (7.9)$$

Substituting the exponential for $f^0(t)$ in (7.8), we have

$$f^1(t) = \frac{\alpha e^{-\alpha t}}{\int_1^\infty \alpha e^{-\alpha t}\, dt}, \quad 1 \leq t \leq \infty. \quad (7.10)$$

Examine the denominator of (7.10)

$$\int_1^\infty \alpha e^{-\alpha t}\, dt = -e^{-\alpha t}\Big|_1^\infty = 0 - (-e^{-\alpha}) = e^{-\alpha}. \quad (7.11)$$

Thus,

$$f^1(t) = \frac{\alpha e^{-\alpha t}}{e^{-\alpha}}, \quad 1 \leq t \leq \infty. \quad (7.12)$$

Now, calculate μ_1, the mean of $f^1(t)$

$$\mu_1 = E[t] = \int_1^\infty \frac{(t)(\alpha e^{-\alpha t})}{e^{-\alpha}}\, dt$$

$$= \frac{1}{e^{-\alpha}} \int_1^\infty (t)(\alpha e^{-\alpha t})\, dt. \quad (7.13)$$

μ_1 can be determined by using the formula for integrating by parts. Let $u = t$ and $dv = \alpha e^{-\alpha t}\, dt$, then using the relationship of $\int u\, dv = uv - \int v\, du$, we have

$$e^{-\alpha}\mu_1 = e^{-\alpha} \int u\, dv = t(-e^{-\alpha t}) - \int_1^\infty -e^{-\alpha t}\, dt$$

$$= -te^{-\alpha t} - \frac{e^{-\alpha t}}{\alpha}\Big|_1^\infty$$

$$= -\infty e^{-\alpha \infty} - \frac{e^{-\alpha \infty}}{\alpha} - \left(-e^{-\alpha} - \frac{e^{-\alpha}}{\alpha}\right)$$

$$= -e^{-\alpha \infty}\left(\infty + \frac{1}{\alpha}\right) - \left(-e^{-\alpha} - \frac{e^{-\alpha}}{\alpha}\right)$$

$$= -e^{-\alpha \infty}\left(\infty + \frac{1}{\alpha}\right) - e^{-\alpha}\left(-1 - \frac{1}{\alpha}\right)$$

$$e^{-\alpha} \int u\, dv = -e^{-\alpha}\left(-1 - \frac{1}{\alpha}\right).$$

Finally,

$$\mu_1 = \int u\, dv = -\left(-1 - \frac{1}{\alpha}\right) = \frac{1}{\alpha} + 1$$

or

$$\mu_1 - 1 = \frac{1}{\alpha}.$$

Let us examine next the derivation of a maximum likelihood estimator for α, the parameter of the truncated distribution, $f^1(t)$, $1 < t < \infty$. Suppose that we have drawn a sample of size n from a truncated population, one for which the event $t = 0$ is not recognized: $t'_1, \ldots, t'_n$; $1 \leq t_i$, $i = 1, 2, \ldots, n$. Denoting the maximum likelihood estimator for this distribution as $\hat{\alpha}$ and employing (7.12), we can write the likelihood function for $\hat{\alpha}$, given our sample of size n,

$$L(\hat{\alpha}; t'_1, t'_2, \ldots, t'_n) =$$

$$\frac{(\hat{\alpha})^n \exp\left(-\hat{\alpha} \sum_{i=1}^n t'_i\right)}{e^{-n\hat{\alpha}}}, \quad 1 < t' < \infty. \quad (7.14)$$

It follows that

$$\ln[L(\hat{\alpha}; t_1', \ldots, t_n')] = n \ln \hat{\alpha} - \hat{\alpha} \sum_{i=1}^{n} t_i' + n\hat{\alpha}$$

$$(7.15)$$

and

$$\frac{d\{\ln[L(\hat{\alpha}; t_1', \ldots, t_n')]\}}{d\hat{\alpha}} = \frac{n}{\hat{\alpha}} - \sum_{i=1}^{n} t_i' + n. \quad (7.16)$$

Setting the derivative equal to zero, and solving for $\hat{\alpha}$, we have

$$\frac{n}{\hat{\alpha}} = \sum_{i=1}^{n} t_i' - n$$

Rearranging terms, we have

$$\frac{1}{\hat{\alpha}} = \left(\sum_{i=1}^{n} t_i'/n\right) - 1,$$

or

$$\frac{1}{\hat{\alpha}} = \bar{t}' - 1, \quad (7.17)$$

and

$$\hat{\alpha} = \frac{1}{\bar{t}' - 1}.$$

Recalling that $\bar{t}'$ is the average of the sample from the truncated population, we can interpret (7.17) to mean that the maximum likelihood estimator (7.12) is one over the quantity defined by the mean of the truncated sample minus 1.0

$$\hat{f}^1(t) = \left[\frac{\exp\left(-\dfrac{t}{(\bar{t}'-1)}\right)}{\bar{t}'-1}\right] \Big/ \left[\exp\left(-\frac{1}{(\bar{t}'-1)}\right)\right].$$

$$(7.18)$$

From relationship (7.8) we have a relationship which allows us to define $f^0(t)$ from $f^1(t)$,

$$f^0(t) = f^1(t) \cdot \int_1^{\infty} f^0(t)\,dt, \quad 0 \le t \le \infty.$$

In terms of our maximum likelihood estimator,

$$\hat{f}^0(t) = \left\{\left[\frac{\exp\left(-\dfrac{t}{(\bar{t}'-1)}\right)}{(\bar{t}'-1)}\right] \Big/ \left[\exp\left(-\frac{1}{(\bar{t}'-1)}\right)\right]\right\}$$
$$\cdot \left[\exp\left(-\frac{1}{(\bar{t}'-1)}\right)\right].$$

Therefore,

$$\hat{f}^0(t) = \frac{\exp\left(-\dfrac{t}{(\bar{t}'-1)}\right)}{(\bar{t}'-1)}, \quad 0 \le t \le \infty. \quad (7.19)$$

Equivalently, when $\alpha = 1/(\bar{t}'-1)$, we have the familiar form

$$\hat{f}^0(t) = \hat{\alpha} e^{-\hat{\alpha}t},$$

where

$$\hat{\mu} = E[t] = \frac{1}{\hat{\alpha}} = \bar{t}' - 1 \quad (7.20)$$

or

$$\hat{\mu} + 1 = \bar{t}'.$$

If we let N_m and N_w be the number of mines and the number of cells with at least one mine, respectively, we have $\bar{t}' = N_m/N_w$, or $\hat{\mu} + 1 = N_m/N_w$.

As an example, consider the data on the Basin and Range: 154 mines and 357 cells (1000 km^2), giving 0.431 as the average number of mines per cell. However, there are only 107 cells with at least one mine, giving $N_m/N_w = 1.439$. Thus, the mean of the implied complete (non-truncated) exponential distribution, by (7.20) is $1.439 - 1 = 0.439$. Slichter et al. (1962) show 0.439. Similarly, for cells of 250 km^2, there are 154 mines in 3213 cells, giving $\mu_0 = 0.0479$. Since 149 cells have at least one mine and there are 154 mines, $N_m/N_w = 1.03355$, implying a mean of 0.03355. Slichter et al. show 0.0336 for the exponential distribution.

Slichter et al. derived estimators for the parameters of the truncated populations for each of three distributions: exponential, Poisson, and logarithmic. The formulas for these distributions and their parameters follow.

Let N_m be the total number of mines, n the number of mines, $Z_0(n)$ the number of cells with n mines observed from the data, and N_w the number of cells with at least one mine. Then,

$$q = \frac{N_m}{N_w}. \quad (7.21)$$

Poisson distribution ($f_1^1(n)$).

$$f_1^1(n) = \frac{\mu_1^n e^{-\mu_1}}{n!}; \quad \mu_1 = q(1 - e^{-\mu_1}). \quad (7.22)$$

Exponential distribution ($f_2^1(n)$).

$$f_2^1(n) = 10^{-n\alpha}(1 - 10^{-\alpha}),$$

where

$$(7.23)$$

$$q^{-1} = 1 - 10^{-\alpha},$$
$$\alpha = -\log_{10}(1 - q^{-1}),$$
$$\mu_2 = q - 1.$$

$$(7.23a)$$

TABLE 7.2. *Total number of cells Z'_j.* (*Source*: Slichter et al. *1962*)

Area	Data	Function		
		Poisson (Z'_1)	Exponential (Z'_2)	Logarithmic (Z'_3)
Western USA (cells of 1000 km^2)	2620	1159	1959	785
Basin and Range (cells of 1000 km^2) (copper)	357	198	351	107
Southwest USA (cells of 10 000 km^2)	307	217	370	141

Logarithmic distribution.

$$f_3^1(n) = [-n \log_e (1-\beta)]^{-1} \beta^n, \quad n \geq 1$$

$$\mu_3 = q = [-(1-\beta) \log_e (1-\beta)]^{-1} \beta \qquad (7.24)$$

$$\beta = q[-(1-\beta) \log_e (1-\beta)].$$

Thus, we see that the parameter of each of the distributions is calculated from a knowledge of the observed characteristic, q, of the data.

Given the estimated parameters, Slichter *et al.* transformed $f_j^1(t)$ to $f_j^0(t)$ and computed the number of barren cells $(Z_j(0))$ required to satisfy the full population for the jth probability function [1]

$$Z_j(0) = \left[\sum_{i=1}^{n} Z_0(i) \bigg/ \int_1^{\infty} f_j^0(t) \, dt \right] - \sum_{i=1}^{n} Z_0(i), \qquad (7.25)$$

where j represents the function, $j = 1, 2, 3$. Naturally, this number varied for each distribution. Similarly the quantity $Z_j(0) + \sum_{i=1}^{n} Z_0(i) = Z'_j$, the total number of cells, varied for each distribution (see Table 7.2).

Table 7.3 details the calculations made by Slichter *et al.* (1962) on the data for mines in the western United States. Notice that in this table there are columns under the headings of Poisson, exponential, and logarithmic.

The first column under each of the distributions has at the head of it, $Z_1(n)$ for the Poisson, $Z_2(n)$ for the exponential, and $Z_3(n)$ for the logarithmic. The column in each case is a revised frequency of cells distribution. In other words, the original data have been modified appropriately for each of the functional forms, giving to each function the number of zero cells that it required.

Once the parameter of a distribution has been estimated, the expectation of the distribution μ is either known directly from the parameter, as is the case for the Poisson, or it can be calculated from the parameter. For example, for $q = 1.669$, we have from eqn (7.23) that α, the parameter of the exponential distribution is estimated from the equation $\alpha = -\log_{10}(1 - q^{-1}) = 0.3971$. But, the expectation for number of mines from an exponential distribution with $\alpha = 0.3971$ is computed from (7.23a) as $\mu = q - 1 = 1.669 - 1 = 0.669$. These means show the expected number of mines per cell based upon the characteristics of each distribution. The mean of each of these distributions, then, can be compared with the mean of the data, the average number of mines per cell. Such a comparison in the case of the work done by Slichter *et al.* (1962) showed that the mean of the exponential distribution (0.669) agreed much more closely [2] with the mean of the data (0.500) than did that of the Poisson (1.130). This is true for several different cell sizes, specifically cell sizes of 1000 km^2, 250 km^2, and 111 km^2. This type of manipulation of the data and the distributions was performed by Slichter *et al.* upon all of the other data sets and also for certain subpopulations based upon value of the mines in the data sets. In all cases they concluded that the exponential distribution was a much better fit to the data than were the other distributions when evaluated by comparison of the mean of the implied distribution to the mean number of mines per cell of the observed data and by the comparison of the probabilities for one or more mines for each of the distributions to the proportion containing one or more mines based upon the revised data set. The Poisson in all cases appeared to be a much inferior fit to the revised data set. This is tantamount to concluding that a random process is not the best model to assume as a generating process for mines, which is in contradiction to the conclusion of Allais with regard to the distribution of *mining districts.*

Slichter (1960), in his paper on the need of a new philosophy of prospecting, which was a 1960 Jackling lecture, states that finding the exponential to be a better fit than the Poisson distribution has important implications, for the exponential distribution implies that the chance for one or more additional mines

TABLE 7.3. *Calculations of Slichter et al.* (*1962*). *Mines in western US* (*E. Wisser*)

Observed data		Poisson			Exponential			Logarithmic		
n	$Z_0(n)$ $r_0(n)$	$Z_1(n)$	$r_1(n)$	$f_1(n)$	$Z_2(n)$	$r_2(n)$	$f_2(n)$	$Z_3(n)$	$r_3(n)$	$f_3(n)$
0	1835 0.700	374	0.3227	0.3230	1174	0.5993	0.5993	—	—	—
1	486 0.1855	486	0.4193	0.3650	486	0.2481	0.2401	486	0.6191	0.6408
2	177 0.06755	177	0.1527	0.2062	177	0.09035	0.09618	177	0.2255	0.1986
3	61 0.02330	61	0.05263	0.0777	61	0.03114	0.03855	61	0.0777	0.0821
4	32 0.01220	32	0.02761	0.0219	32	0.01633	0.01544	32	0.0408	0.0382
5	17 0.00649	17	0.001467	0.00496	17	0.008678	0.006195	17	0.0217	0.0189
6	5 0.00191	5	0.000431	0.000934	5	0.002552	0.002483	5	0.0064	0.0098
7	4 0.00153	4	0.000345	0.000151	4	0.002042	0.000995	4	0.0051	0.0052

	Data	Poisson	Exponential	Logarithmic
Total cells	2620	1159	1959	785
N_w	785	785	785	785
N_m	1310	1310	1310	1310
μ	0.500	1.130	0.669	1.67

$\alpha = 0.3971$, $\beta = 0.64$.

μ = The expected number of mines per cell for a particular probability function
$Z_0(n)$ = Number of cells observed to have n mines.
$r_0(n)$ = Proportion of all cells observed to have n mines.
$Z_1(n), Z_2(n), Z_3(n)$ = Revised data: the number of cells with n mines when the number of empty cells is restricted to that called for by the Poisson, exponential, and logarithmic distributions, respectively, based upon the calculation of the parameter from q.
$r_1(n), r_2(n), r_3(n)$ = The proportion of the cells having n mines based upon the revised data $Z_1(n)$, $Z_2(n)$, $Z_3(n)$.
$f_1(n), f_2(n), f_3(n)$ = The theoretical probabilities for n mines for the Poisson, exponential, and logarithmic probability distributions, respectively, based upon the parameter as calculated from q.

existing in any one cell is independent of the number already known to exist. If the Poisson distribution had been found to have been the best fit to the data, the implication would have been that for a cell in which mines are already known to occur, in a narrow sense, there is less chance of finding another mine in that cell than in other cells with no known mines. Thus, one should look in other cells. Notice that the exponential distribution conforms to the old adage of the prospector: search for new mines where mines are already known. This implies, of course, that the probability of discovery is higher in areas of known occurrence than in areas of unknown occurrence. For a given region, it is not clear in general whether or not this is true or just apparent. Such a result could arise from the fact that in areas of known mineral occurrence the information is higher, facilitating the *discovery* of additional deposits.

It may not be that the conclusion of Allais concerning the distribution of mining districts is in contradiction to that of Slichter regarding the distribution of mines. When an igneous body intrudes into an area of favourable host rock and mineralizes a section of the rock, this zone of mineralizing (metallization) is the ideal physical unit representative of the metallizing process. It could be that the mining district is a better representation of this unit than is the mine, and as suggested by Allais' work, this unit may be distributed according to the Poisson distribution. It is not inconsistent with such a condition that if one were to examine the distribution of some smaller unit of observation, such as a mine, bearing in mind that there might be several mines located upon this one zone of metallization, the distribution may not be Poisson, primarily because mines would cluster within the metallization unit. Such clustering would violate one of the assumptions of the Poisson distribution, that of a random process. In the case of mines within mining districts, if cells were smaller than the mining districts in which the mines were counted, there would tend to be a clustering of the mines; for in an area where one mine is known to occur, the probability would be much higher that the cell adjacent to it would contain a mine than some cell somewhat removed. In other words, it may be consistent for mining districts to be Poisson distributed and, at the same time, for some subdivision of the mining district, like a mine, to be exponentially distributed.

7.2.7. Clustering and the negative binomial

This clustering effect identified by Slichter *et al.* (1962) was the primary interest of Wilmot, Drew, and Hazen [3] in their study for the US Bureau of Mines of the distribution of gold and silver deposits in Arizona and south-western New Mexico. In their work they examined the fit of the negative binomial distribution to the distribution of mines

$$f(n) = q^{-k} \frac{(k+n-1)!}{n!(k-1)!} \left(\frac{p}{q}\right)^n, \qquad (7.26)$$

where $q = 1 + p$ and k is the clustering parameter. Moment estimates for p and k are

$$k = \frac{\bar{X}^2}{S^2 - \bar{X}} \qquad (7.27)$$

$$p = \frac{S^2 - \bar{X}}{\bar{X}}, \qquad (7.28)$$

where $\bar{X}$ is the mean of sample and S^2 the variance of sample.

For an area of 112 600 square miles in Arizona and New Mexico, a grid was constructed, defining cells, and the number of cells having $1, 2, \ldots, n$ mines was recorded. For a 10×10 mile grid size, there were 1126 cells. From the data for this grid, the parameters of the negative binomial were estimated by the method of moments, giving the results

$$f(n) = 6.9291^{-0.1424} \frac{(0.1424 + n - 1)}{n!(0.1424 - 1)} \left(\frac{5.9291}{6.9291}\right)^n. \qquad (7.29)$$

By evaluating f at 0, we see that the probability for a cell selected at random from this area having 0 mines is approximately 0.759.

As indicated in the equation for the negative binomial, two parameters must be estimated from the data to fit this distribution; one of them is k and the other one is p. q is $1 + p$. Examining the parameter k, it can be seen that if the variance and the mean of the sample are equal, the parameter k is equal to infinity. This is the special case in which the negative binomial degenerates to the Poisson distribution, namely where the variance and the mean are equal. Equality of variance and of the mean then is typical

of the random process underlying the Poisson distribution. Where this randomness does not prevail but instead there is a clustering in the data, the standard deviation exceeds the mean and the negative binomial is a more appropriate fit to the data than is the Poisson. Any distribution that would contain a long tail, in other words, one that is highly skewed, will have a standard deviation larger than the mean, and the k parameter will be less than infinity. Table 7.4 is an example of fitting the negative binomial to a hypothetical set of data by the method of moments. Thus, having estimates of the parameters, probabilities for various numbers of mines can be calculated by evaluating the negative binomial function appropriately

$$P(N = 0) = 0.044108 \frac{(4.2257 + 0.0 - 1)!}{0!(4.2277 - 1)!} (0.52222)^0$$

$$= 0.044$$

$$P(N = 1) = 0.044108 \frac{(4.2257)!}{1!(3.2257)!} (0.52222)^1$$

$$= 0.097$$

$$P(N = 2) = 0.044108 \frac{(5.2257)!}{2!(3.2257)!} (0.52222)^2$$

$$= \left[\frac{5.2257}{2} (0.52222)\right] [P(N = 1)]$$

$$= 0.133$$

and, generally,

$$P(N = n) = 0.044108 \frac{(4.2257 + n - 1)!}{n!(3.2257)!} (0.52222)^n.$$

Table 7.5 shows the probabilities and the theoretical frequencies computed from the fitted negative binomial and the observed frequencies. A goodness-of-fit test may be performed using the observed frequencies $(N_0(n))$ and frequencies from the fitted distribution $(f(n) \cdot 100)$ in a manner similar to that demonstrated on the Poisson.

In the study by Wilmot *et al.* [3] it was found in general that the negative binomial was a much more acceptable fit to the number of mines than was the Poisson. They also found by varying the cell sizes that larger cells produced higher ks and therefore a distribution that tended to be better fitted by the Poisson than the distribution for cells of small size. In general, the larger the cell size, the higher the k and the better the fit by the Poisson, but even for large cell sizes, such as 1600 mi^2, the negative binomial was distinctly a superior fit to the data. The

TABLE 7.4. *Fitting the negative binomial*

$$P(N=n)=f(n)=q^{-k}\frac{(k+n-1)!}{n!\,(k-1)!}\left(\frac{p}{q}\right)^n$$

$$=\frac{(k+n-1)!}{n!\,(k-1)!}\left(\frac{p^n}{q^{k+n}}\right)$$

$$p=\frac{S^2-\bar{n}}{\bar{n}}\qquad\qquad k=\frac{\bar{n}^2}{S^2-\bar{n}}$$

$$q=1+p$$

Number of mines n	Number of cells $N_0(n)$	$n\cdot N_0(n)$	n^2	$n^2\cdot N_0(n)$
0	5	0	0	5
1	10	10	1	10
2	15	30	4	60
3	20	60	9	180
4	10	40	16	160
5	5	25	25	125
6	3	18	36	108
7	2	14	49	98
8	10	80	64	640
9	15	135	81	1215
10	5	50	100	500
$\sum N_0(n)=100$		$\sum n\cdot N_0(n)=462$		$\sum n^2\cdot N_0(n)=3101$

$$\bar{n}=\frac{\sum n\cdot N_0(n)}{\sum N_0(n)}=\frac{462}{100}=4.62.$$

$$S^2=\frac{1}{n}\sum n^2 f(n)-\bar{n}^2=\frac{3101}{100}-(4.62)^2$$
$$=31.01-21.34=9.67.$$

$$p=\frac{9.67-4.62}{4.62}=\frac{5.05}{4.62}=1.093.\quad k=\frac{(4.62)^2}{9.67-4.62}=\frac{21.34}{5.05}=4.2257.$$

$$q=1+1.093=2.093.\quad \frac{p}{q}=\frac{1.093}{2.093}=0.52222.\quad q^{-k}=\left(\frac{1}{q}\right)^k=0.044108.$$

results of the study by Slichter *et al.* (1962) and also by Wilmot *et al.* [3] appeared to be quite strong evidence for the rejection of the Poisson as a reasonable model for the distribution of mines. This, of course, does not negate the Poisson as the pertinent law for mining districts, only for mines. As indicated in previous comments, these two conclusions may not be in contradiction, since the mine may be a subdivision of the true unit of metallization, a unit more closely approximated by the mining district than the mine.

7.2.8. *Issues regarding spatial models*

Considerable discussion has already been given to one of the issues, that of the appropriate unit of observation. Conceptually, it is clear that it should be the deposit, not the mine, for a mine is an economic unit. Mining districts as a unit of observation do not suffer from this fault as much as does the mine. On the other hand, mining districts are often delineated by political or topographical features. Furthermore, they may include *more* than one *deposit*. Data that are commonly available usually are for either the mine or the mining district. To define mineral occurrence in terms of deposits rather than mines or mining districts would require working with primary data on the physical features of mineralized areas. These data generally are not available to the public; consequently, most studies of areas of any large size are forced to use data on mines or mining districts. Thus, unless a special effort is made, data upon which spatial distributions are defined are not of the preferred form.

So long as studies on spatial distributions are

TABLE 7.5. *Negative binomial probabilities and theoretical and observed frequencies.*

n	$f(n) = P(N = n)$		Theoretical frequencies $f(n) \cdot 100$	Observed frequencies $N_0(n)$
0	0.044108		4	5
1	0.097335		10	10
2	0.132812		13	15
3	0.143932		14	20
4	0.135779		14	10
5	0.116651		12	5
6	0.093668		9	3
7	0.071456		7	2
8	0.052362		5	10
9	0.037145		4	15
10	0.025655	$\sum_{x=0}^{10} f(n) = 0.950903$	3	5
11	0.017326		95	100
12	0.011480			
13	0.007483	$\sum_{x=0}^{13} f(n) = 0.987192$		

restricted to a noisy unit of observation (mines and mining districts) it is expecting a great deal of them to define a universal law of statistical distribution.

From a practical application point of view, the motivation for examining the statistical distribution of a unit of metallization includes

1. Inference to the area upon which the distribution was fitted;
2. Identification of the mathematical form of the law and its use to establish exploration philosophy;
3. Inference from a control area to the study area.

For application 1 to be effective, it is necessary to have a knowledge of, and a belief in, a statistical distribution analogue of the metallizing process. Given this knowledge or the assumption of such knowledge, it would be used in the following manner. A statistical documentation (histogram) of all known metallization would be made and such documentation would be compared to the form (shape) of the known (assumed) distribution. If the documentation of the cells in the region shows too many barren cells or too few cells having 2 (in general n) deposits, with respect to the known mathematical law, then the implication is that additional deposits remain in the region.

Application 2 is less demanding in terms of knowledge or assumptions and is typified by Slichter's

(1960) interpretation of the meaning of the negative exponential as a spatial model: the number of mines already known to exist in a cell does not affect the probability for an additional mine. The exploration philosophy motivated by such interpretation is to search for mines where mines already exist. Similarly, the Poisson as a model for metallization would dictate the philosophy that the probability for one or more mines in a given cell is independent of the number of mines in the adjacent cell. However, inasmuch as the best-fitting mathematical form has been shown to be sensitive to the unit of observation and to cell size, there seems to be little justification for predicating exploration philosophy on a statistical model. Such philosophy is best motivated by direct exploration experience.

Application 3 raises issues of an additional dimension, for it requires inference from one region to another via spatial models of the statistical nature of the occurrence of metal deposits. These issues exist even if the 'true' spatial model were known. Of course, they are compounded if the 'true' spatial model is not known and an assumed model is employed.

Suppose that the form of the spatial model for number of deposits were known and that use of a spatial model as a basis for inference to the probability for number of deposits of an unexplored area is the objective. Inference would consist of estimation of the parameters of the spatial model from a selected control area and then the use of this quantified model on the unexplored area. To examine the issues, let us recall the conceptual description of the model for number of deposits: $h(n \mid q, G_D)$. This description states that the probability for n deposits is conditional upon grade and geology. A spatial model for number of deposits unconditional upon grade and geology requires the ignoring of the relationship between grade and frequency of deposits and geology and frequency of deposits. This is apparent from the necessity of integrating out of $h(n \mid q, G_D)$ both q and G_D

$$N(n) = \int_Q \int_{G_D} h(n \mid q, G_D) \cdot k(q \mid G_D) \cdot u(G_D) \, dG_D \, dq.$$

(7.30)

It is obvious that for $N(n)$, determined on the control area, area i, to be an *accurate* statement of the probability for n deposits in area j, $h(n \mid q, G_D)$, $k(q \mid G_D)$, and $u(G_D)$ must be the same for each area. Suppose that h represents deposits of only one mode of occurrence (deposit type) of metal, then we might feel it acceptable to assume that the relationship of q to n and the relationship of n and q to G_D is invariant with geography. This is equivalent to stating that $N_i(n)$ provides accurate estimates of $N_j(n)$ only if $u_i(G_D) = u_j(G_D)$. To the extent that $u_i(G_D) \neq u_j(G_D)$ and that other assumptions are violated, $N_i(n)$ will not be an accurate statement of $N_j(n)$.

Striving for *accuracy* in a statistical estimate is striving for the unattainable, even for phenomena less complex than metal resources. Statistical theory examines estimators relative to more attainable 'yardsticks', such as bias and efficiency. The fact that $u_i(G_D) \neq u_j(G_D)$ does not necessarily imply that estimates by $N_i(n)$ will be biased estimates of $N_j(n)$. If, on average, $N_i(n) = N_j(n)$, the condition for an unbiased estimator is satisfied. However, if there is evidence of strong regional trends in geology, $u_i(G_D)$ may differ from $u_j(G_D)$ in a consistent manner, which would, *ceteris paribus*, give the variation of $N_i(n)$ with respect to $N_j(n)$ a consistent pattern, hence a bias in $N_i(n)$ as an estimator of $N_j(n)$.

Geographical trends in geology are more often present than they are absent, as evidenced by the use of trend analysis by explorationists and geoscientists in the interpretation of geological, geochemical, and geophysical data.

Setting aside the issues of geological continuity and proper unit of observation, *estimating the model N(n) solely from available 'hard' data on area i* most assuredly creates a biased estimator unless area i is of such small size that it has been exhaustively explored or that 'room' considerations simply do not allow for additional deposits. For large areas, this bias exists and derives from man's basic economic motivation

(1) easy-to-find deposits of high grade are usually located first;
(2) easy-to-find low-grade and buried high-grade deposits are discovered as the economics and technologies of exploration and exploitation and the market dictate.

The implications of these effects is that the data on deposit occurrence are truncated on grade and biased in terms of frequency of deposit occurrence by incomplete exploration and discovery even above the grade of truncation. The fact that the data are truncated on grade increases the bias due to incomplete exploration and discovery.

Slichter's fitting of truncated distributions can be viewed as an effort to compensate for the bias of incomplete discovery. Of course compensation by this approach may be only partial, for it treats the effect of incomplete discovery on only the frequency of cells having zero deposits. Only when the *effect* of incomplete discovery on the frequencies (probabilities) is *proportional to the frequencies* for each number class is Slichter's approach sufficient. Of course, the less explored the region and the stronger the relationship between number of deposits and grade, the less likely that such a simplistic compensation is sufficient.

What about a relationship between grade and number of deposits? Is there one, or is number of deposits statistically independent of grade? To my knowledge, this relationship has not been investigated by the analysis of data. Investigations of grade relations have examined the covariation of tonnage of ore with grade. Specification of $h(n \mid q, G_D)$ such that n is conditional upon grade was predicated upon conceptual considerations, not upon data analysis.

It is generally agreed that ore deposits, particularly those having high-grade ores, are a resultant of many sequences of earth processes, each of which causes enrichment of some zones and depletion of others. The proposition that high-grade deposits represent a rare event because of the combinations of sequential enrichment–depletion appeals to intuition. The converse of this relationship is equally appealing; namely, that very low-grade deposits represent combinations of processes that are more likely to transpire because of their relative simplicity. If complexity translates to low frequency and simplicity to relatively high frequency, then probability for a specified number of deposits varies inversely with grade; hence it may be appropriate to specify a probability model for number of deposits as conditional upon grade as well as geology. Although attention in the past has focused upon the relationship of grade and tonnage, perhaps it is time to examine the statistical relationship between number of deposits and grade, particularly since good arguments have been raised for the statistical independence of grade and tonnage on a deposit basis. For copper deposits of a given type, data support the thrust of such arguments.

Spatial models which are fitted to data from a well-explored region and which are used for the appraisal of an unexplored region do not of themselves provide much insight as to the quantity of subeconomic resources, for the parameters of such models were estimated from *production data*. Obviously these data contain little explicit information about subeconomic resources. When the economic conditions of the relatively unexplored region are much less favourable than they are for the control region, the resources implied by a spatial model which was quantified on data of the control region are in excess of economic resources at that time, and, therefore, these resources do include some subeconomic resources of that region. To estimate comprehensively the number of deposits comprising subeconomic resources, an auxiliary relationship is required, such as the correlation (relationship) between grade and number of deposits.

As is true for most models for resource appraisal, the greater the specificity of the model, the less likely that constraints on the physical system will be unknowingly violated by inference from spatial models. Thus, it is better to use a separate model for not only each metal but for each mode of occurrence of that metal.

7.3. Multivariate models

7.3.1. Theory

The conceptual framework for geostatistical deposit models defined the probability distribution for number of deposits as being conditional upon grade q and geology G_D

$$h(n \mid q, G_D). \qquad (7.31)$$

By integrating out the effects of grade on the probability for n deposits, we have a new probability density for n, conditional upon geology only

$$\bar{h}(n \mid G_D) = \int_Q h(n \mid q, G_D) \cdot k(q) \, dq, \qquad (7.32)$$

where $k(q)$ is the probability density for grade q.

Now, suppose that we compute the expectation for the random variable N from $\bar{h}(n \mid G_D)$

$$n_{G_D} = \int_N n \cdot \bar{h}(n \mid G_D) \, dn. \qquad (7.33)$$

Eqn (7.33) expresses the concept that only for observed geology G_D is the expectation of $\bar{h}(n \mid G_D)$ a computable value. Let $n_{G_D^0}$ represent the expectation for a specific geology G_D^0. In general, this value would be different for geology G_D^0 than for G_D'

$$\bar{n}_{G_D^0} \neq \bar{n}_{G_D'}. \qquad (7.34)$$

In this sense, we can describe $\bar{n}$, generally, as a function of geology

$$\bar{n} = R(G_D). \qquad (7.35)$$

The multivariate models for number of deposits that have been constructed have been of the form of either (7.32) or (7.35)

$$\bar{h}(n \mid G_D),$$
$$\bar{n} = R(G_D).$$

The second of these models for number of deposits we will refer to as a number equation.

7.3.2. A number equation

The first number equation was developed by Agterberg and Cabilio (1969) to describe the gold occurrence in the Greenbelt of western Quebec as a function of lithologic variables. The control area consisted of 7232 square miles. This region was divided into 113 cells, each cell 8 miles square. In this area, 444 gold occurrences had been recorded, giving an average of 3.929 occurrences per cell. A gold occurrence was defined as a 'place where the element gold occurs in a relatively high concentration, usually in one or more quartz veins' (Agterberg and Cabilio 1969, p. 4). Only 67 of these occurrences were gold mines; these mines occurred in 20 of the 113 cells.

For each of the 113 cells, observations were made on the number of gold occurrences and the percentage of the cell area comprised by each of the following six rock types.

1. Granite rocks, granite gneisses, felsic rocks;
2. Mafic rocks;
3. Ultramafic rocks;

4. Early Pre-Cambrian sedimentary rocks;
5. Rhyolitic and pyroclastic rocks;
6. Mafic lavas.

Because of the fact that these variables add to 100 per cent, one of them was eliminated, the reason being that they comprise a dependent set and would yield a singular variance–covariance matrix, a matrix that could not be inverted—inverting is a numerical operation required for the estimation of the regression coefficients (the constants in the number equation).

Agterberg and Cabilio found via regression analysis and analysis of variance that the fraction of the total variance in the number of gold occurrences explained by the five geological variables was statistically significant at the 0.01 per cent level. In other words, the likelihood that a relationship as strong as the one apparent in the data would be present in a sample drawn at random from a multivariate population in which there is no relationship between geology and number of gold occurrences is less than one in 10 000.

Agterberg and Cabilio found that there were patterns in the deviations of the regression estimates from observed values. This is equivalent to the statement in statistical terminology that auto-correlation was present in the residuals, or that the expectation for number of gold occurrences for a *given* geology, G_B^0, $B < D$, varied in a consistent manner over the region. Reasons for auto-correlated residuals include the fact that one or more $(D - B)$ important variables have been left out of the equation, variables that explain the patterns (trends) in the residuals and that information is incomplete either for geology or for number of occurrences. An obvious reason for incomplete information is the unequal allocation of exploration and geological mapping, which in turn reflect economic motivation, difficulty of access to various regions, and political influences.

Agterberg and Cabilio chose to represent the missing variables and information effects (geology, exploration effort, etc.) by proxy variables, the coordinates of location (x, y). Their reasoning was that the number of deposits in a cell is the sum of two effects: the regional trend and the local geology

$$\bar{n} = \bar{n}_T + \bar{n}_L, \qquad (7.36)$$

where $\bar{n}_T$, $\bar{n}_L$ are the expected trend and local geology contributions to number $\bar{n}$ of trend and local geology, respectively.

$$\bar{n}_T = R_T(x, y) \qquad (7.37)$$

$$\bar{n}_L = R_L(G_D). \qquad (7.38)$$

Or, alternatively,

$$R(G_D) = R_T(x, y) + R_L(G_B), \qquad (7.39)$$

where x, y are coordinates of location and $B < D$. One approach to defining $R(G_D)$ would be to first compute $\hat{R}_T(x, y)$, then regress the residuals, $n_{x,y} - \hat{R}(x, y)$, on G_B to estimate $R_L(G_B)$. Together, $\hat{R}_T(x, y)$ and $\hat{R}_L(G_D)$ provide the estimate $\hat{R}(G_D)$. Thus, evaluation of an unknown cell would require two calculations.

Agterberg and Cabilio (1969) demonstrate mathematically that the two-stage process is equivalent to the estimate obtained by regressing number of gold occurrences simultaneously on the geological variables and the coordinates of locations

$$\hat{n} = \hat{R}(G_B, \theta(x, y)) \rightarrow \hat{R}(G_D), \qquad (7.40)$$

where $\theta(x, y)$ is a set of polynomial terms in x and y and $B < D$. More specifically, a linear number equation of (7.40) would have the following form

$$\hat{n} = a_0 + a_1 g_1 + \ldots + a_B g_B + c_1 x + d_1 y + \ldots + c_n x^n +$$
$$+ d_n y^n + \ldots + e_1 xy + \ldots + e_m x^m y^m, \quad (7.41)$$

where the as, bs, cs, ds and es are coefficients to be estimated by regression analysis.

Cabilio and Agterberg found that a cubic trend surface alone explained 63 per cent of the variance in number of gold occurrences; the local geology and regional geology combined explained 53 per cent; the local geology alone explained 10 per cent; and trend combined with local geology explained the most variance, 68 per cent.

7.3.3. *A probability model for number of copper deposits for the Abitibi Area, Ontario and Quebec*

Agterberg, Chung, Fabbri, Kelly, and Springer (1972), employed a rather novel approach to estimating a probability model of the form of (7.32)

$$\bar{h}(n \mid G_D).$$

As Harris [4] did in his mineral-wealth model, Agterberg et al. divided the Abitibi Area into square cells; however, the size of these cells was considerably smaller than that employed by Harris (10 × 10 km compared to 20 × 20 miles), allowing for greater specificity of the relationship of mineral occurrence to geology. A second modification of the scheme employed by Harris [4] was that separate regions, each consisting of contiguous cells, were not identified as control and study areas, rather a single region, the Abitibi Area, was considered to comprise both the study and control areas. In general, the mineralized, non-contiguous, cells constituted the control area, the remaining cells comprised the study area, the cells to be evaluated. A third modification (improvement) on the methods employed by Harris was the construction of combination variables (products) from the basic measurement variables, the purpose being to represent the important geological interactions as variables, such as an igneous intrusive with host rocks, etc. The basic measurement variables are listed in Table 7.6. These 10 variables were augmented by their combinations, giving a total of 55 geological variables.

For each cell, the sum of produced copper and reserves of copper metal across all deposits in the cell constituted the dependent variable, the variable to be related to the geological variables. Control cells were selected by virtue of their copper mineralization: only those cells having large deposits, giving 27 cells.

Large deposits were considered to be those whose total production plus reserves exceeded 1000 tons of copper metal. The dependent variable for a cell consisted of the logarithm of the sum of total production and reserves of all large mines within the cell.

A stepwise regression analysis was performed on the control cells, relating quantity of metal to the geological variables. Analysis showed that all of the 11 most important geological variables were product variables, emphasizing the importance of geological interactions to the occurrence of metal deposits. The first five most important variables and their regression coefficients are listed in Table 7.7, in descending order of importance.

The regression equation determined on the control cells was considered to estimate $y_i = \theta_i \cdot \bar{m}$, where θ_i is the probability for the ith cell having a deposit and $\bar{m}$ is the average quantity of metal per cell. With

TABLE 7.6. *Measurement variables for Archean geology*

1. Per cent of the cell consisting of granitic rocks (acid intrusions and gneisses)
2. Per cent of the cell consisting of mafic intrusions (gabbros and diorites)
3. Ultramafics
4. Acid volcanics (rhyolites and pyroclastics)
5. Mafic volcanics
6. Archean sedimentary rocks
7. Metamorphic rocks of sedimentary origin
8. Approximate total length of layered iron formations per cell
9. Average Bouguer anomaly per cell
10. Regional aeromagnetic anomaly at cell centre

TABLE 7.7. *The five most important variables for copper potential*

Rank	Name of variable	Regression coefficient
1	Acid volcanics × mafic volcanics	0.00045
2	Granite rocks × acid volcanics	0.00147
3	Acid volcanics × sediments	0.00182
4	Acid volcanics × iron formations	−0.00334
5	Acid volcanics × aeromagnetics	−0.01958

this perspective, if $\bar{m}$ were known, division of y_i by $\bar{m}$ would yield θ_i. The authors (Agterberg *et al.* 1972) recognized that dividing by the average metal per cell for control cells would underestimate θ_i for cells of the study area in general, for the control cells all possessed, by definition, one or more large deposits. As a means for compensating for this bias, the authors identified a composite control area as including the control cells and all other cells in the *restricted regions* around the control cells, making a total of 145 cells, still only a fraction of the total of 644 cells in the Abitibi Area.

Adjustment was effected by estimating y_i for each of the 145 cells of the control area using the regression equation. Each of these 145 estimates was divided by the average metal per cell for the composite control area, and these quotients were summed and compared to the number of control cells (24)

$$\text{Relationship:} \quad \sum_{i=1}^{145} y_i = \bar{m} \sum_{i=1}^{145} \theta_i. \quad (7.42)$$

Therefore,

$$\sum_{i=1}^{145} y_i \Big/ \bar{m} = \sum_{i=1}^{145} \theta_i. \quad (7.43)$$

Then,

$$A = \sum_{i=1}^{145} \theta_i \Big/ 24, \quad (7.44)$$

where A is an adjustment factor. Thus, the average metal per cell used to isolate θ_i from y_i was $A \cdot \bar{m}$, where $\bar{m}$ is the mean metal per control cell

$$\theta_i = y_i \Big/ (\bar{m}/A) = \frac{y_i \cdot A}{\bar{m}} \quad (7.45)$$

Agterberg *et al.* (1972) found that $A = 1.35$.

An approximation of θ_i for each of the remaining 499 cells, the cells of unknown metal potential, was determined by computing y_i for each of them by the regression equation and dividing by $(\bar{m}/A)$. The authors described θ_i as only approximations to the true probability

$$\hat{\theta}_i \approx P_i(N \geq 1 \mid G_D^0). \qquad (7.46)$$

The next step in the probability analysis was to designate a group of 16 cells (a region of 40×40 km) as the size of the reference area for a probability distribution. For each contiguous group of 16 cells, the average of the $\hat{\theta}_{ij}$ was computed

$$\bar{\hat{\theta}}_i = \frac{1}{16} \sum_{j=1}^{16} \hat{\theta}_{ij}, \quad i = 1, 2, \ldots, 40. \qquad (7.47)$$

$\bar{\hat{\theta}}_i$ was interpreted as the parameter of a binomial probability distribution

$$b_i(x; n = 16, p = \bar{\hat{\theta}}_i) = \binom{16}{x}(\bar{\hat{\theta}}_i)^x(1 - \bar{\hat{\theta}}_i)^{n-x}. \qquad (7.48)$$

This binomial probability distribution defines for reference region i the probability for x cells having one or more large copper deposits. Since most of the control cells upon which the regression analysis was performed had only one large deposit, this probability is also essentially the probability that the 16-cell region contains x large copper deposits.

In order to translate their probability analysis into an estimate of copper potential, the authors examined the distribution of copper per control cell, finding that the quantity ranged from 1084 to 1 179 000 tons, an average being 140 000 tons. The expected tonnage of copper per reference region was computed

$$\bar{\hat{m}}_i = 140\,000 \sum_{j=1}^{16} \hat{\theta}_{ij}.$$

Obviously, this occurrence model, like the wealth model by Harris [4] describes and estimates economic resources only, for data on the control cells were truncated at economic cut-off grades. Furthermore, the description of economic resources is probably biased on the low side, for it is doubtful that exploration of the control area or control cells, even for economic deposits, had been exhaustive. The authors were aware of these limitations, and others of a geological and statistical nature, as demonstrated from the following lengthy but very relevant quotations taken from their publication (Agterberg *et al.* 1972, pp. 34–7).

The formation of a mineral deposit at a given place was, in general, determined by many physical and chemical factors and conditions most of which are unknown. In order to reconstruct the processes, which resulted in a specific deposit, the geologist is forced to work with limited data for a complex three-dimensional assemblage of rocks preserved after the metallogenic processes had ended. The changes that took place in the course of time cannot be studied directly.

It is possible to map three-dimensionally the geological setting of large orebodies which are being mined out. The surrounding areas of mines also may be well-known because of extensive drilling. By a detailed interpretation of the setting of deposits, much can be said about provenance, processes and favorable conditions. This has led to guidelines for prospecting where the objective is to locate features elsewhere in the country indicating that favorable conditions may have existed. Features to look for may include certain types of faults and folds, other structures, rock types with specific properties such as porosity and permeability, contacts or other associations between two or more different types of rock, etc.

The method used in this paper is different. We could not make use of the many detailed relationships derived from the setting of specific deposits, mainly because most features listed above are rather specialized and unknown almost everywhere over a large region. Instead of this, our data base contains very limited facts available for most 10×10 km cells in the region. Consequently, the statistical results will not allow us to assess the probability that a specific type of deposit was formed at a given place which could, for example, be a good target for drilling.

Finally, one of the more severe limitations of the approach is the uncertainty regarding the completeness of information on the occurrence of mineral deposits. For copper, the data consisted of total production of all mines to the end of 1968 and reserves estimated at that time. Total reserves . . . for copper amount to thirty percent of total estimated tonnage. They are largely for proven reserves. It is likely that these numbers would increase significantly when possible reserves could be considered. Estimates of possible reserves can best be attained in well-explored areas, usually in the vicinity of known deposits, where the geology is well-documented. Fair estimates could perhaps be gathered through the Delphi method.

The two problems of lack of completeness of data on large copper deposits and variations in intensity of exploration are closely interrelated. Intensity of exploration is the result of factors such as abundance and types of outcrops, type and emphasis of exploration activity and amount of interpretation on the basis of local geology and geophysical and/or geochemical surveys. The latter factor includes number and types of drillholes per cell. Abundant information is in existence for these factors but it is widely scattered over many different sources and not of a standard form. Moreover, much information used for exploration in the past was lost or is still kept confidential. These factors were not considered in a direct manner by us. Use of the Delphi method has already been suggested as one method to obtain estimates of possible reserves in or near the control cells. Another possibility is historical studies of the type undertaken by Harris [4] who plotted annual production against time for mining areas, estimating final totals on the assumption that trends of the past can be extrapolated into the future.

A limitation is that the models can only predict the distribution of mineralization in two dimensions. The third dimension, depth, can be considered in the well-explored parts of the area. It is then necessary to perform a detailed study of the geometrical configuration in three dimensions of all large deposits and the geology of their immediate environment and to attempt systematic statistical extrapolations in three-dimensional space for the control cells and cells adjacent to them. This would improve the results presented in this report which are based on generalized and restricted measures for total amount of copper and zinc per control cell.

7.4. A compound probability model for number of deposits

7.4.1. Theory

A probability density distribution for $N \geq 1$, given the geology G_D can be derived from our basic geostatistical model [5]

$$P(N \geq 1 \mid G_D) = \int_{0.5}^{\infty} \int_Q h(n \mid q, G_D) \cdot k(q) \, dq \, dn$$

$$= 1 - H(0 \mid G_D), \quad (7.49)$$

where $H(0 \mid G_D)$ is the distribution function for n, the number of deposits, i.e. it defines the probability for number of deposits being less than or equal to zero, given G_D. $H(0 \mid G_D)$ can also be viewed as a special form of $\bar{h}(n \mid G_D)$

$$H(0 \mid G_D) = 1 - \int_{0.5}^{\infty} \bar{h}(n \mid G_D) \, dn. \quad (7.50)$$

A second probability distribution $N(n)$ was defined in the section on spatial models as a spatial probability model for number of deposits

$$N(n) = \int_{*G_D} \int_Q h(n \mid q, G_D) \cdot k(q) \cdot u(G_D) \, dq \, dG_D \quad (7.51)$$

where $*G_D$ represents the domain of the geological variables.

Let us define a new form of $N(n)$ for the number of deposits on a restricted range for number of deposits

$$\phi(n \mid n \geq 1) = N(n)/[1 - N(0)], \quad 1 \leq n. \quad (7.52)$$

Now, we can define the probability for n deposits as

a compound probability

$$P(N = n \mid G_D) = P(N \geq 1 \mid G_D) \cdot P(N = n \mid N \geq 1), \quad (7.53)$$

$$P(N = n \mid G_D) = [1 - H(0 \mid G_D)] \cdot \phi(n \mid n \geq 1). \quad (7.54)$$

The probability defined by (7.54) is not in general equal to that computed from $\bar{h}(n \mid G_D)$

$$\bar{h}(n \mid G_D) \neq [1 - H(0 \mid G_D)] \cdot \phi(n \mid n \geq 1). \quad (7.55)$$

The reason for this non-equality is that the effects of G_D on probability for number of deposits n for $n > 0$ was integrated out in the formulation of $N(n)$. However, on average, over all values of G_D, the probabilities defined by $\bar{h}(n \mid G_D)$ and by $[1 - H(0 \mid G_D)] \cdot \phi(n \mid n \geq 1)$ are equal. The pertinent question is, 'Why would one employ $[1 - H(0 \mid G_D)] \cdot \phi(n \mid n \geq 1)$ when a more definitive probability can be obtained from $\bar{h}(n \mid G_D)$?' The answer to this question is that none of these relations is known, and geological information is expressed by measured variables. Given certain limitations on the level of geological information, the compound probability model of (7.54) may be appropriate.

For example, suppose that the set of D geological variables is defined in such a way that the information content of the variables modifies *only* the probability for *one or more* deposits. In other words, the variables contain information that relates only to differentiation of 'barren ground' (no deposits) from 'fertile ground' (one or more deposits). Furthermore, let us assume that, given 'fertile ground', the number of deposits is a random variable N having a value greater than zero; the specific values of N in the domain of numbers greater than zero are independent of the geological variables and are distributed according to a known univariate probability law.

Let us designate the measurement variables restricted in this way as g_i', $i = 1, 2, \ldots, D$. And, let us represent the probability for $N \geq 1$, given G_D', as $1 - H(0 \mid G_D')$,

$$P(N \geq 1 \mid G_D') = 1 - H(0 \mid G_D') \quad (7.56)$$

$$P(N = 0 \mid G_D') = H(0 \mid G_D'). \quad (7.57)$$

Thus, eqns (7.56), (7.57), and (7.52) taken together define a probability model for number of deposits for N ranging over all non-negative integers

$$P(N = n \mid G_D') = [1 - H(0 \mid G_D')] \cdot \phi(n \mid n > 1), \quad n > 0,$$

$$P(N = 0 \mid G_D') = H(0 \mid G_D'). \quad (7.58)$$

This model combines geology in the form of a conditional probability law with purely stochastic properties of a spatial distribution. As stated, such a wedding requires that the geological variables be defined in such a way that they provide information only on barren versus fertile ground. Although $\bar{h}(n \mid G_D)$ may represent the definitive and desired model, practical problems of estimation and application may dictate a compound model which employs $H(0 \mid G'_D)$ and $\phi(n \mid n \geq 1)$.

7.4.2. *Application possibilities*

In Chapter 6, the suggestion was made that the information content of the crude measurements of geological features, such as those made from geological maps by Harris [4] and by Sinclair and Woodsworth (1970), may be useful primarily in the discrimination of fertile land—contains one or more deposits—and barren land. To the extent that this postulation is correct, the use of a compound probability model for number of deposits is appealing. For example, a multiple-discriminant model which discriminates between barren and fertile ground could be developed on a control area. Then, this estimated model could be employed in conjunction with Bayesian probability analysis, to estimate the probability that an unknown (unexplored) cell contains one or more deposits. In other words, this model would compute, based upon the unknown-cells geology, the probability represented by $1 - H(0 \mid G'_D)$.

Suppose that statistical analysis of only those cells of the control area having one or more deposits is made and a univariate function, like the negative binomial, is fitted to these truncated data, following the example of Slichter *et al.* (1962). This fitted function, when truncated at zero, could be used to estimate for an unknown cell the probability that it has n deposits, given that it is known to have at least one deposit.

Thus, by combining a discriminant and Bayesian probability model with a truncated spatial model, in this hypothetical case a negative binomial, the probability, given the measured geology, that the unknown cell has n deposits can be computed

$$P(N = n \mid G'_D) = \begin{bmatrix} \text{Probability from multiple-} \\ \text{discriminant and Bayesian} \\ \text{probability model} \end{bmatrix} \times$$

$$\times \begin{bmatrix} \text{Probability from} \\ \text{truncated negative} \\ \text{binomial} \end{bmatrix},$$

$$P(N = n \mid G'_D) = P(N \geq 1 \mid G'_D) \times P(N = n \mid n \geq 1).$$

Another possibility of applying a compound model is to employ a geologist to analyse the geology of the unknown cell and to estimate subjectively the probability that the cell contains one or more deposits. In other words, the geologist replaces the multivariate geostatistical model. This subjective probability could then be multiplied by the probability computed by the truncated spatial model, which in this hypothetical case is a negative binomial.

The use of geologists for the estimation of probabilities is discussed at great length in Chapters 13, 14, and 15.

References

Agterberg, F. P. and Cabilio, P. (1969). Two-stage least squares model for the relationship between mappable geological variables. *J. Int. Ass. Math. Geol.* **1**(2), 137–53.

—— Chung, C. F., Fabbri, A. G., Kelly, A. M., and Springer, J. S. (1972). *Geomathematical evaluation of copper and zinc potential of the Abitibi Area, Ontario and Quebec.* Geol. Survey Canada, Paper 71–41.

Allais, M. (1957). Method of appraising economic prospects of mining exploration over large territories: Algerian Sahara case study. *Management Sci.* **3** (4), 285–347.

Harris, D. P. (1967). Operations research and regional mineral exploration. *Trans. SME*, December, 1967, 450–9.

Sinclair, A. J. and Woodsworth, G. L. (1970). Multiple regression as a method of estimating exploration potential in an area near Terrace, B.C. *Econ. Geol.* **65**(8), 998–1003.

Slichter, L. B. (1960). The need of a new philosophy of prospecting. *Mining Eng.* June 1960, 570–5.

——, Dixon, W. J., and Myer, G. H. (1962). Statistics as a guide to prospecting. *Mathematical and Computer Applications in Mining and Exploration, Symposium Proceedings*, pp. F1-1–F1-27. College of Mines, University of Arizona, Tucson, Arizona.

Notes

1. If $f_j^0(t)$ is continuous, the integral in (7.25) should range from 0.5 to ∞.
2. Slichter *et al.* (1962) report 0.699 instead of 0.669. This discrepancy appears to be a typographical error.
3. Wilmot, R. C., Drew, L. J., and Hazen, S. W., Jr.

(1968). Distribution of gold and silver production in Arizona and southwestern New Mexico. Unpublished report on investigations, US Bureau of Mines.

4. Harris, D. P. (1965). An application of multivariate statistical analysis to mineral exploration. Ph.D. dissertation, The Pennsylvania State University.

5. The lower range of the integral is 0.5 instead of 1.0 because a continuous function h is being used to represent a discrete random variable, number of deposits. $N = 1$ is represented by the range 0.5–1.5.

8 THE CRUSTAL ABUNDANCE GEOSTATISTICAL (CAG) APPROACH OF BRINCK

8.1. Relationship to geostatistical theory

Chapter 5 showed how $y(q)$, the probability density for crustal grade is related to the model for metal endowment $f(m \mid G_D)$. $y(q)$ is of central interest in the geochemical element approach to the estimation of metal endowment. The entire procedure as described by Brinck (1967a, 1974) is based upon a probability distribution for grades in deposits of a specified tonnage t, of mineralized rock. Brinck (1967a,b, 1974) has employed both the lognormal and logbinomial probability laws as $y(q)$.

Many of the basic ideas advanced and developed by Brinck derive from the works of DeWijs (1951, 1953). Consequently, it seems that the appropriate place to begin a study of these methods is the works of DeWijs.

8.2. The geostatistical relations of DeWijs—a foundation

DeWijs, a Dutch mining engineer–statistician, sought to describe and analyse the assemblage of ore grades in mining blocks of an underground mine working, such as a drift, by a statistical distribution. The ore deposit on which he demonstrated his initial ideas was the Pulacayo mine of Bolivia. This deposit consisted essentially of a sphalerite–quartz vein, which at the 446 metre level had been exposed by a drift of 240 m and had been sampled at 2-m intervals. Since the sampling interval was constant, each sample had equal weight, making the average grade simply the arithmetic mean of the samples.

By designating 10 grade classes with a constant interval of 4 per cent, the frequency distribution of Table 8.1 was developed. Fig. 8.1, a histogram of frequencies and grades, shows a non-symmetric, discrete distribution skewed to the right. At this point, all that has been accomplished is to describe the physical system and the transition to a statistical description, the histogram, of some feature of that system, grade.

A common motivation in examining statistical distributions of empirical data is to search for a mathematical law that describes the statistical dis-

tribution. For, given identification of the law, the information conveyed by a graph is contained in a mathematical formula. Benefits of the mathematical formula are its concise expression, its ease of manipulation, and the possibility for extension to related issues of interest.

TABLE 8.1. *Frequency distribution of zinc assays—Pulacayo mine. (Source: DeWijs 1951.)*

Grade (per cent Zn)	Number of samples
0–4	2
4–8	18
8–12	27
12–16	24
16–20	15
20–4	13
24–8	9
28–32	5
32–6	3
36–40	2
40–4	0

DeWijs explains briefly that his choice of a mathematical relationship was predicated upon consideration of the variation in grades and a simple assumption about the propagation of variation, the result being a binomial equation. DeWijs's reasoning goes something like the following: Consider an orebody with a definable boundary and known total tonnage of ore T and average grade $\bar{Q}$. This orebody can be divided into two halves of equal tonnage $T/2$ but differing grades. The grade of the richer half can be represented by $\bar{Q}(1+d)$ and the leaner half by $\bar{Q}(1-d)$.

$$T\bar{Q} \begin{cases} \left(\dfrac{T}{2}\bar{Q}\right)(1+d) \\[2ex] \left(\dfrac{T}{2}\bar{Q}\right)(1-d). \end{cases}$$

Obviously, the two halves together have an average

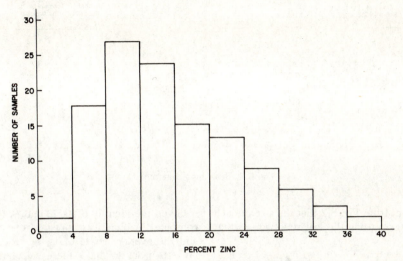

Fig. 8.1. Histogram of observed frequency distribution of zinc assays—Pulacayo. (After DeWijs 1951.)

grade of $\bar{Q}$, which preserves the initial condition

$$\bar{Q} = \frac{\left(\frac{T}{2}\right)(\bar{Q})(1+d) + \left(\frac{T}{2}\right)(\bar{Q})(1-d)}{2\left(\frac{T}{2}\right)}$$

$$= \frac{\bar{Q} + d\bar{Q} + \bar{Q} - d\bar{Q}}{2} = \frac{2\bar{Q}}{2} = \bar{Q}. \qquad (8.1)$$

Each of these two halves similarly can be divided into a leaner and richer part, making a total of four blocks.

$$\frac{T}{2}(1+d)\bar{Q} - \begin{cases} \dfrac{\left[\dfrac{T}{2}(1+d)\bar{Q}\right]}{2}(1+d) \\[3mm] \dfrac{\left[\dfrac{T}{2}(1+d)\bar{Q}\right]}{2}(1-d) \end{cases}$$

$$\frac{T}{2}(1-d)\bar{Q} - \begin{cases} \dfrac{\left[\dfrac{T}{2}(1-d)\bar{Q}\right]}{2}(1+d) \\[3mm] \dfrac{\left[\dfrac{T}{2}(1-d)\bar{Q}\right]}{2}(1-d). \end{cases}$$

This splitting process can be represented in a branching diagram (Fig. 8.2).

Let us look at a simple hypothetical numerical example, an iron deposit of 10 000 000 tons having an average grade of 30 per cent. Suppose that the enrichment factor d for this deposit is 0.10. Then, we would have the branch diagram of Fig. 8.3.

Thus, this hypothetical deposit having a total tonnage of 10 000 000 tons at 30 per cent Fe consists of four blocks, each of 2 500 000 tons having grades of 36.3, 29.7, 29.7, and 24.3 per cent iron.

If we examine only the grades that are developed by the splitting process in Fig. 8.2, it is easily seen that the grades correspond to $\bar{Q}$ times the terms of a binomial expansion (Table 8.2). In general, any grade is described by

$$\text{Grade} = \bar{Q}(1+d)^{\beta-k}(1-d)^{k}, \qquad (8.2)$$

where β is the highest order of subdivision and $k = 0, 1, \ldots, \beta$. Thus, for $\beta = 2$, as in the last row of Fig. 8.2, we have terms and conditions shown in Table 8.3.

The number of blocks of a grade of $\bar{Q}(1+d)^{\beta-k}(1-d)^{k}$ is given by the term

$$C_{k}^{\beta} = \frac{\beta!}{(\beta-k)!\,k!}. \qquad (8.3)$$

This relationship can be demonstrated by again referring to the last row of Fig. 8.2, in which $\beta = 2$. We see in the diagram that there are two blocks of grade $\bar{Q}(1+d)(1-d)$. From Table 8.3, we have that for these grades, $\beta - k = 1$ and $k = 1$. Substituting into eqn (8.3) we have $C_{k}^{\beta} = C_{1}^{2} = 2!/\{(2-1)!\,(1)!\} = 2$.

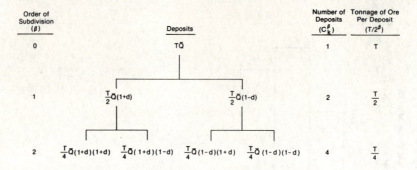

Fig. 8.2. Branching diagram.

It is also apparent from Fig. 8.2 that the size of each block is $T/2^\beta$ (again using the last row, we see that $4 = 2^2$).

Summarizing we have

Grade $= \bar{Q}(1+d)^{\beta-k}(1-d)^k$,

Frequency of grade for specified β and $k = C_k^\beta$,

$$(8.4)$$

Tonnage per block for specified $\beta = \dfrac{T}{2^\beta}$, (8.5)

Total tonnage of deposit $= T = \dfrac{T}{2^\beta} \displaystyle\sum_{k=0}^{\beta} C_k^\beta$, (8.6)

Total metal in deposit $= M = T \cdot \bar{Q}$

$$= \frac{T}{2^\beta} \bar{Q} \sum_{k=0}^{\beta} C_k^\beta (1+d)^{\beta-k}(1-d)^k. \quad (8.7)$$

Given the identity of $\bar{Q}$, d, and β, it is possible to compute the quantity of ore $t_{q'}$ above cut-off grade q' and the average grade of $t_{q'}$, $\bar{q}_{q'}$ from the binomial law. In order to make these calculations, it is first necessary to compute k', the value of k associated with the cut-off grade of q'. This is easily done by employing (8.2), the description of grade. Since $\bar{Q}$, β, and d would be known and q' is specified, k' can be solved for directly

$$q' = \bar{Q}(1+d)^{\beta-k'}(1-d)^{k'}$$

$$\ln q' = \ln \bar{Q} + (\beta - k') \ln (1+d) + k' \ln (1-d)$$

$$\ln q' = \ln \bar{Q} + \beta \ln (1+d) - k' \ln (1+d) + k' \ln (1-d)$$

$$k'[\ln (1+d) - \ln (1-d)] = \beta \ln (1+d) - \ln q' + \ln \bar{Q}$$

$$k' = \frac{[\beta \ln (1+d) - \ln q' + \ln \bar{Q}]}{[\ln (1+d) - \ln (1-d)]}. \quad (8.8)$$

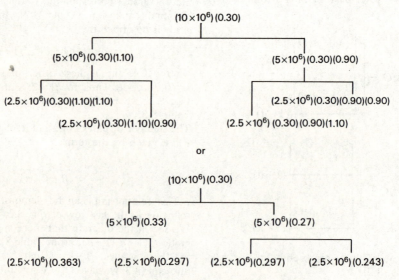

Fig. 8.3. Numerical example of branching diagram.

TABLE 8.2. *Description of grades by binomial*

Order (β)	Grades	Expansion
0	$\bar{Q}$	$\bar{Q}[(1+d)+(1-d)]^0$
1	$\bar{Q}(1+d), \bar{Q}(1-d)$	$\bar{Q}[(1+d)+(1-d)]^1$
2	$\bar{Q}(1+d)^2, 2\bar{Q}(1+d)(1-d), \bar{Q}(1-d)^2$	$\bar{Q}[(1+d)+(1-d)]^2$

Then, having k', the $t_{q'}$ and $\bar{q}_{q'}$ are calculated

$$t_{q'} = \frac{T}{2^\beta} \sum_{k=0}^{k'} C_k^\beta, \quad (8.9)$$

$$\bar{q}_{q'} = \frac{\bar{Q} \cdot \sum_{k=0}^{k'} C_k^\beta (1+d)^{\beta-k}(1-d)^k}{\sum_{k=0}^{k'} C_k^\beta}. \quad (8.10)$$

Before these mathematical relations can be employed, it is necessary to estimate the parameters $\bar{Q}$, d, T, and β. $\bar{Q}$ the average grade can be estimated directly from the samples. In the case of equally spaced and independent samples the arithmetic mean is an unbiased estimate of $\bar{Q}$. It is usually assumed that T is known, but in reality, the bounds of the deposit are not well known. In the case of the Pulacayo mine, according to the description of De-Wijs, T was reasonably well known. Thus, under the best of conditions there are two unknown parameters, β and d.

The procedure described by DeWijs for the estimation of β is straightforward. Estimation employs the fact that the number of samples (grades) must be equal to 2^β: $N = 2^\beta$; therefore $\beta = \ln N/\ln 2$. In the example of Pulacayo, the number of samples is 118; therefore, $\beta = \ln(118)/\ln(2) = 6.883$. To simplify calculations, DeWijs employed the nearest integer value $k = 7$ (for fractional values of k, the binomial expansion becomes an infinite series).

The appropriate estimator for d from the assay values is not so obvious. DeWijs derived an estimator by considering any pair of adjacent assays, V_i and V_{i+1}, to be from a single block of ore. Based upon these assays, the block has an average grade $\bar{q}_i = \frac{1}{2}(V_i + V_{i+1})$. This block, having an average grade of $\bar{q}_i$, can be considered to be divisible into two parts of equal size, one part enriched by d and the other

TABLE 8.3. *Effects of index k on grade description*

Grade	Binomial expression		k	$\beta-k$
$\bar{Q}(1+d)^2$	$= \bar{Q}(1+d)^2(1-d)^0$		0	2
$\bar{Q}(1+d)(1-d)$	$= \bar{Q}(1+d)^1(1-d)^1$		1	1
$\bar{Q}(1-d)^2$	$= \bar{Q}(1+d)^0(1-d)^2$		2	0

impoverished by d

$$V_i = \bar{q}_i(1+d) \quad (8.11)$$
$$V_{i+1} = \bar{q}_i(1-d). \quad (8.12)$$

Substituting the definition of $\bar{q}_i$ into (8.11) and (8.12), we have the following definitions for assays V_i and V_{i+1}

$$V_i = \left(\frac{V_i + V_{i+1}}{2}\right)(1+d), \quad (8.13)$$

$$V_{i+1} = \left(\frac{V_i + V_{i+1}}{2}\right)(1-d). \quad (8.14)$$

Let us now define a difference $\Delta V_i = V_i - V_{i+1}$. From eqns (8.13) and (8.14) we can write

$$\Delta V_1 = \left(\frac{V_1 + V_2}{2}\right)(1+d) - \left(\frac{V_1 + V_2}{2}\right)(1-d)$$
$$\vdots$$
$$\Delta V_i = \left(\frac{V_i + V_{i+1}}{2}\right)(1+d) - \left(\frac{V_i + V_{i+1}}{2}\right)(1-d)$$
$$\Delta V_{i+1} = \left(\frac{V_{i+1} + V_{i+2}}{2}\right)(1+d) - \left(\frac{V_{i+1} + V_{i+2}}{2}\right)(1-d)$$
$$\vdots$$
$$\Delta V_{n-1} = \left(\frac{V_{n-1} + V_n}{2}\right)(1+d) - \left(\frac{V_{n-1} + V_n}{2}\right)(1-d). \quad (8.15)$$

Then, the sum of the ΔV_i ($i = 1, 2, \ldots, n-1$) is defined as

$$\sum_{i=1}^{n-1} \Delta V_i = \left(\frac{V_1}{2}\right)(1+d) + \left(\frac{V_2}{2}\right)(1+d) - \left(\frac{V_1}{2}\right)(1-d) -$$
$$- \left(\frac{V_2}{2}\right)(1-d) + \left(\frac{V_2}{2}\right)(1+d) + \left(\frac{V_3}{2}\right)(1+d) -$$
$$- \left(\frac{V_2}{2}\right)(1-d) - \left(\frac{V_3}{2}\right)(1-d) \ldots$$
$$\ldots \left(\frac{V_{n-2}}{2}\right)(1+d) + \left(\frac{V_{n-1}}{2}\right)(1+d) - \left(\frac{V_{n-2}}{2}\right)(1-d) -$$
$$- \left(\frac{V_{n-1}}{2}\right)(1-d) + \left(\frac{V_{n-1}}{2}\right)(1+d) +$$
$$+ \left(\frac{V_n}{2}\right)(1+d) - \left(\frac{V_{n-1}}{2}\right)(1-d) - \left(\frac{V_n}{2}\right)(1-d). \quad (8.16)$$

Or,

$$\sum_{i=1}^{n-1} \Delta V_i = \left(\frac{V_1}{2}\right)(1+d) + V_2(1+d) + \dots$$

$$\dots + V_{n-1}(1+d) + \left(\frac{V_n}{2}\right)(1+d) -$$

$$-\left(\frac{V_1}{2}\right)(1-d) - V_2(1-d) - \dots$$

$$\dots - V_{n-1}(1-d) - \left(\frac{V_n}{2}\right)(1-d).$$

And

$$\sum_{i=1}^{n-1} \Delta V_i = \frac{V_1}{2} + \frac{V_1}{2}d + V_2 + V_2 d + \dots$$

$$\dots + V_{n-1} + V_{n-1}d + \frac{V_n}{2} + \frac{V_n}{2}d -$$

$$- \frac{V_1}{2} + \frac{V_1}{2}d - V_2 + V_2 d - \dots$$

$$\dots - V_{n-1} + V_{n-1}d - \frac{V_n}{2} + \frac{V_n}{2}d.$$

Gathering terms, we have

$$\sum_{i=1}^{n-1} \Delta V_i = V_1 d + 2V_2 d + \dots + 2V_{n-1}d + V_n d,$$

(8.17)

or

$$\sum_{i=1}^{n-1} \Delta V_i = 2d\left[\left(\sum_{i=2}^{n-1} V_i\right) + \left(\frac{V_1 + V_n}{2}\right)\right]. \quad (8.18)$$

Therefore,

$$d = \frac{\displaystyle\sum_{i=1}^{n-1} \Delta V_i}{2\left[\left(\displaystyle\sum_{i=2}^{n-1} V_i\right) + \left(\dfrac{V_1 + V_n}{2}\right)\right]}. \quad (8.19)$$

The denominator can be rewritten

$$2\left[\left(\sum_{i=2}^{n-1} V_i\right) + \frac{V_1 + V_n}{2}\right] = 2\left[\sum_{i=1}^{n} V_i - \left(\frac{V_1 + V_n}{2}\right)\right]$$

$$= \left(2\sum_{i=1}^{n} V_i\right) - (V_1 + V_n). \quad (8.20)$$

Furthermore, $\sum_{i=1}^{n} V_i$ can be recognized as $n\bar{Q}$; consequently, we can rewrite (8.20) in terms of $\bar{Q}$

$$d = \frac{\displaystyle\sum_{i=1}^{n-1} \Delta V_i}{2n\bar{Q} - (V_1 + V_n)}. \quad (8.21)$$

This last equation defines the estimator for d given by DeWijs (1951). DeWijs provides the following illustration.

Suppose we have a set of five consecutive sample assays (in percent)

5.4   10.8   3.3   6.8   3.7.

The mean of the assays is 6.0: $\hat{Q} = \sum V_i/n = 30/5 = 6.0$.
This set of five assays produces four differences (in absolute values)

5.4   7.5   3.5   3.1.

The sum of these differences is 19.5: $\sum_{i=1}^{4} \Delta V_i = 19.5$.
Obviously, $V_1 = 5.4$ and $V_n = V_5 = 3.7$. Therefore, using these data and eqn (8.21) we can compute d

$$d = \frac{19.5}{(2)(5)(6) - (5.4 + 3.7)}$$

$$= \frac{19.5}{60 - 9.1} = \frac{19.5}{50.9} \approx 0.383 \text{ per cent.}$$

For the Pulacayo zinc vein, DeWijs found $\hat{Q} = 15.61$ per cent, $\hat{\beta} = 7$, and $\hat{d} = 0.205$. Using these estimates and the relations (8.2) and (8.3), DeWijs computed theoretical frequencies for the grades of the Pulacayo vein (Table 8.4).

DeWijs did not stop with the fitting of a binomial to the assay values. He observed that although the empirical histogram of grades as well as the fitted binomial were skewed, by plotting frequencies of grades against the logarithm of grade, a symmetric distribution resulted. Because of this symmetry and the fact that the normal distribution is convenient

TABLE 8.4. *The binomial model of the Pulacayo vein. (Source: DeWijs 1951.)*

Number of blocks (samples)	Grade (per cent Zn)	
1	$\bar{Q}(1+d)^7(1-d)^0$	$= 57.59$
7	$\bar{Q}(1+d)^6(1-d)$	$= 37.99$
21	$\bar{Q}(1+d)^5(1-d)^2$	$= 25.07$
35	$\bar{Q}(1+d)^4(1-d)^3$	$= 16.54$
35	$\bar{Q}(1+d)^3(1-d)^4$	$= 10.91$
21	$\bar{Q}(1+d)^2(1-d)^5$	$= 7.20$
7	$\bar{Q}(1+d)(1-d)^6$	$= 4.75$
1	$\bar{Q}(1+d)^0(1-d)^7$	$= 3.13$
128		$\bar{Q} = 15.61$

and easy to work with, particularly with regard to subsequent statistical operations, DeWijs fitted the normal distribution to the logbinomial, using the relations

$$e^\gamma = \bar{Q}(1+d)^{\beta/2}(1-d)^{\beta/2}, \qquad (8.22)$$

$$\sigma = 1/2\sqrt{\beta} \ln\left(\frac{1+d}{1-d}\right), \qquad (8.23)$$

where γ and σ are the parameters of the lognormal model. Table 8.5 demonstrates the close fit of the lognormal model to the distribution of grades in the Pulacayo vein.

TABLE 8.5. *Theoretical and observed frequencies. (Source: DeWijs 1951.)*

Per cent zinc	Theoretical frequency	Observed frequency
0–4	1.54	2
4–8	18.52	18
8–12	29.07	27
12–16	24.50	24
16–20	16.73	15
20–4	10.55	13
24–8	6.48	9
28–32	3.96	5
32–6	2.43	3
36–40	1.53	2

Thus, DeWijs (1951) provided the basic models and relations that later were employed by Brinck, with the exception that DeWijs developed them as models of ore reserves, not resources:

1. The logbinomial distribution as a mathematical model of the ore-generating processes of the Earth;
2. The relationship of the logbinomial to a lognormal distribution. Furthermore, DeWijs raised the possibility that the lognormal distribution is a suitable model of the ore-generating processes of the Earth.

If we judge the impact of the exposition by De-Wijs of the logbinomial by the appearance of papers that pursued his name, it was minor at that time. Reasons for this undoubtedly must include resistance of the profession at that time to statistical and mathematical treatment of sample data from ore deposits. Another reason may be equally important—the appearance of professional papers on the appropriateness of the lognormal distribution for

the analysis of samples from orebodies (Krige 1952) and for geochemical data (Ahrens 1953, 1954, 1957; Aubrey 1955; Miller and Goldberg 1955). The fitting of the lognormal in these studies was not done by first fitting the logbinomial, as was done by De-Wijs, but by direct estimation of its parameters γ and σ from sample data

$$\hat{\gamma} = \sum_{i=1}^{n} \ln X_i/n \qquad (8.24)$$

$$\hat{\sigma} = \left\{\frac{\sum_{i=1}^{n}(\ln X_i - \gamma)^2}{n-1}\right\}^{\frac{1}{2}}. \qquad (8.25)$$

While to DeWijs the lognormal distribution was of incidental interest, it soon thereafter became the object of keen interest and, in the case of geochemical data, the subject of spirited contention as a *geochemical law*—a proposition made by Ahrens (1953).

Vistelius (1960) provided a definitive criticism of the lognormal distribution as a geochemical law, demonstrating that the lognormal distribution can be expected to adequately describe geochemical measures that reflect the joint occurrence of a number of events, such as concentration of an element across mixed environments, or a sequential modification of grade by interrelated earth processes, such as processes required to concentrate an element into an ore deposit. On the other hand, he pointed out that some geochemical measures may be better described by another distribution form, such as the normal law.

8.3. The extensions made by Brinck

8.3.1. *Perspective*

Given the historical setting and trend of scientific interest in statistical representation of geochemical measures, it is fitting that Brinck's first papers on the appraisal of mineral resources employed the lognormal distribution as a resource model.

Brinck's motivation was inference to the resources of a metal in a region from geochemical samples taken in that region. For such inference to be accepted, it must be performed by a model that not only describes adequately the statistical distribution properties of that metal in geochemical sample-sized quantities of the Earth's crust, but can also be adjusted appropriately so that the information obtained from the geochemical samples applies to concentrations of metal in accumulations the size of minable ore deposits. In other words, the model must be based upon an acceptable means of generalizing from metal concentrations of very small quantities of rock material to metal concentrations in ore, quantities of material having economic concentrations and accumulations.

To the geologist, who thinks of an ore deposit as a rare event, one which results from the complex interaction of a number of earth processes, generalizing by a statistical model from metal concentrations taken from small quantities of soil or, at best, rock outcrop to this rarity of nature, the ore deposit, may be rather presumptive, if not heretical. Nevertheless, because of the utility of being able to make such inference, the model demands consideration as a resource appraisal tool. A central issue is the assumptions required for such generalization and the degree to which they violate the 'science' of ore genesis as man understands it. Can these assumptions be tolerated in light of the benefits from a general resource appraisal model?

As a springboard to generalization, Brinck cites the reserve–abundance relationship advocated by McKelvey (1960) as quantitative evidence of a general relationship between crustal abundance and quantity of ore reserves. Actually, Brinck's approach neither is saved nor stands condemned by McKelvey's work, which is probably good, for the so-called abundance–reserve relationship of McKelvey is somewhat dubious [1]. McKelvey sought to demonstrate that when ore reserves at a point in time are plotted against crustal abundance for the elements, there is a usable relationship; in other words, the more abundant an element, the larger the ore reserves. Brinck's method does not require such a relationship: The credibility of his method is not dependent upon whether or not the reserves of an abundant metal are greater than those of a scarce one. The critical relationship in Brinck's approach is whether a high average concentration of a *given* metal in one region means more reserves in that region than in another region where the average concentration is lower. The geologist's response to the meaning of a relatively high geochemical concentration would be, 'That depends upon the rocks and the geological environment.' This underscores the critical assumption in the approach used by Brinck; namely, *high concentration of a given metal implies, irrespective of geology, the accumulation of large quantities of that metal into deposits.* As the size of the area under study increases, the more acceptable this assumption becomes, because the larger the area, the more likely it is that many host rocks and geological environments are represented within the

area; therefore, the more likely it is that a high concentration in geochemical samples implies a relatively large accumulation of metal in anomalous concentrations somewhere within the large region.

The question is, do these higher concentrations occur in deposit sizes or geochemical sample sizes? Before hazarding a guess as to the answer to this question, a geologist would want to examine the spatial distribution of these samples to see if high concentrations occur in groups, giving hint to a contiguous body of high concentrations, a possible orebody. Here, again, the method employed by Brinck, the lognormal distribution and the estimation of its parameters from geochemical data, assumes that there is no significant pattern in the spatial distribution of geochemical concentrations for, if there were, the variance of the lognormal distribution could not be estimated by employing traditional methods, as used by Brinck. Yet, the method provides for the inference to high concentrations in deposit-sized accumulations of ore from concentrations of the element in geochemical-size samples. This is done by the assumption that a statistic, the variance of the lognormal distribution, can be modified appropriately to describe resources occurring in any specified size of deposit. Such modification is based upon (1) a measure called the coefficient of mineralizability; (2) the influence of the geochemical sample; and (3) the size of the environment (area of study). Details will be provided later.

To capture the essence of Brinck's approach, it is necessary to free our traditional thinking about ore as an anomaly of metal concentration occurring in a mineralogic ensemble associated with structured geological processes and to view ore as just another rock, albeit an unusual one, that contributes geochemical information. Alternatively, all rock is considered as potential ore, deposits that are customarily mined being different only by virtue of their size or by their high concentrations.

8.3.2. *Basis for a probabilistic model*

With this perspective—that ore is rock and rock is ore—in mind, consider partitioning the continental earth's crust into equal-sized blocks, say 2.5 km on a side. Suppose also that the amount of metal in each block is known and can be expressed as a concentration q

$$q = \text{(quantity of metal/quantity of material).}$$
$$\quad \text{in block} \qquad \text{in block}$$

The number of these blocks in the environment is determined simply by dividing the volume of the environment (earth's crust) by the volume of a block

$$n = \frac{VE}{VB} = \frac{375 \times 10^6 \text{ km}^3}{15.625 \text{ km}^3} = 240 \times 10^5. \quad (8.26)$$

Taking the weight of the continental earth's crust to a depth of 2.5 km to be 1×10^{18} tonnes implies that each block weighs approximately 4.17×10^{10} tonnes.

Suppose that for each of the 240×10^5 blocks the concentration of that block in copper is known: q_i, $i = 1, 2, \ldots, 240 \times 10^5$. It would be possible to set up NC classes of grade and to count the number of blocks having grades falling within each grade class. This procedure is identical to that followed by De-Wijs in the Pulacayo zinc deposit, and would result in a histogram of grades like that of Fig. 8.1; the frequency of grades in the jth class being f_j, $j = 1, 2, \ldots, NC$. Obviously, $\sum_{j=1}^{NC} f_j = 240 \times 10^5$. If the distribution of grades of copper in these blocks were lognormal, this histogram would be skewed, to the right, like that of Fig. 8.1.

From the set of frequencies, relative frequencies can be computed

$$RF_j = f_j/240 \times 10^5. \quad (8.27)$$

Since $N = 240 \times 10^5$ represents the entire population, these relative frequencies are the probabilities for concentrations of copper in the discrete grade classes specified

$$\tilde{P}_j = RF_j = \frac{f_j}{240 \times 10^5}, \quad j = 1, 2, \ldots, NC. \quad (8.28)$$

But, concentration of an element is a continuous measure, for it can take on any value; consequently, the NC probabilities $\tilde{P}_j$ are discrete approximations to the true probabilities P_j

$$\tilde{P}_j \approx P_j = P(q_j'' \leq Q \leq q_j'), \quad (8.29)$$

where q_j'' and q_j' are the lower and upper grades, respectively, of the jth grade class and Q is a random variable.

8.3.3. Use of the normal probability law for estimation of tonnages

Suppose that the true distribution is lognormal; i.e. the plot of the logarithm of grades describes a normal distribution

$$P_j = P(q_j'' \leq Q \leq q_j') =$$
$$= \frac{1}{\sigma\sqrt{2\pi}} \int_{\ln q_j''}^{\ln q_j'} \exp\left(\frac{-\frac{1}{2}(\ln q - \gamma)^2}{\sigma^2}\right) d \ln q. \quad (8.30)$$

The probabilities for each of the grade classes as well as any specified grade interval could be computed if the parameters γ and σ were known or if estimates of them were available. Since in this hypothetical case our sample consists of the entire population, the entire set of blocks of 15.625 km³ in the continental Earth's crust, these parameters could be computed from our data

$$\gamma = \sum_{i=1}^{240 \times 10^5} \ln q_i/240 \times 10^5, \quad (8.31)$$

$$\sigma = \left\{\frac{\sum_{i=1}^{240 \times 10^5} (\ln q_i - \gamma)^2}{240 \times 10^5}\right\}^{\frac{1}{2}}. \quad (8.32)$$

Given knowledge of γ and σ, the normal probability distribution could be employed in a straightforward way to calculate probability; this probability would represent that fraction of the total 240×10^5 blocks of 15.625 km³ that would have a concentration of metal falling within the interval of q' and q'', or since this is the entire population, it represents that fraction of the earth's crust to a depth of 2.5 km. For example, suppose that data on the concentration of copper in each of the 240×10^5 blocks were available and that formulas (8.31) and (8.32) had been employed, yielding

$$\gamma = -4.9618 \Rightarrow e^\gamma = 0.007 \text{ per cent,}$$
$$\sigma = 0.5193. \quad (8.33)$$

Suppose that it is desired to know that fraction of the total number of blocks having grades greater than 0.007 per cent but less than 0.02 per cent. This can be determined directly from the normal distribution, provided that we transform the grades to a logarithmic scale

$$\ln (0.02) = -3.9120. \quad (8.34)$$

As indicated by the shaded area of Fig. 8.4, the desired fraction is that probability from a normal distribution—having a mean of -4.9618 and a standard deviation of 0.5193—between the mean value and the value of -3.9120.

This probability can be determined by calculating the standardized normal variate z and comparing it to tabled values of z and associated probabilities. For example,

$$z = \frac{-3.9120 - \ln (0.007)}{0.5193} = \frac{-3.9120 - (-4.9618)}{0.5193}$$
$$= \frac{1.0498}{0.5193} = 2.02. \quad (8.35)$$

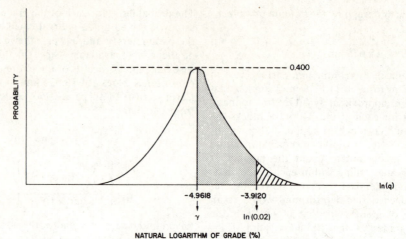

NATURAL LOGARITHM OF GRADE (%)

Fig. 8.4. Lognormal probability distribution.

From standardized unit normal tables we find that the probability associated with $Z = 2.02$ is 0.4783

$$P(-4.9618 \leq Z \leq -3.9120) = 0.4783.$$

Now, in this contrived example, each block is of equal size; therefore, if we ignore variation in lithology and assume that each block is also of equal weight, the quantity of rock of the continental earth's crust having grades between 0.02 and 0.007 per cent is proportional to the number of blocks having grades within this interval

$$t_{q''-q'} = K \cdot n_{q''-q'}, \tag{8.36}$$

where $t_{q''-q'}$ and $n_{q''-q'}$ are the tonnage of rock and number of blocks, respectively, having grades within the interval of $[q'' - q']$ and K is the constant of proportionality, which in this case is the weight per block. Suppose that we divide each side of (8.36) by n, the total number of blocks

$$\frac{t_{q''-q'}}{n} = \frac{K \cdot n_{q''-q'}}{n} \tag{8.37}$$

or

$$\frac{t_{q''-q'}}{n \cdot K} = \frac{n_{q''-q'}}{n}. \tag{8.38}$$

Suppose that this proportionality factor (average tons/block) is equal for all grade classes. Then, the total tonnage T is the product of the total number of blocks n and K, $T = n \cdot K$. Substitution of T for $n \cdot K$ into (8.38) gives

$$\frac{t_{q''-q'}}{T} = \frac{n_{q''-q'}}{n}. \tag{8.39}$$

And $n_{q''-q'}/n$ has been shown to be the discrete approximation of $P(q'' \leq Q \leq q')$; thus,

$$\frac{t_{q''-q'}}{T} = P(q'' \leq Q \leq q'). \tag{8.40}$$

Finally,

$$t_{q''-q'} = T \cdot P(q'' \leq Q \leq q'). \tag{8.41}$$

This is the relationship employed by Brinck to estimate quantity of mineralized rock; it can be written in terms of the probability function

$$t_{q''-q'} = \frac{T}{\sigma(2\pi)^{\frac{1}{2}}} \int_{\ln q''}^{\ln q'} \exp\left(-\frac{1}{2}\left(\frac{\ln q - \gamma}{\sigma}\right)^2\right) d\ln q. \tag{8.42}$$

Provided that grades are distributed lognormally, and given γ and σ, or reliable estimates thereof, the tonnage of rock containing concentrations between q'' and q' is determined by a straightforward use of the standardized unit normal probability tables. For example, from (8.35) we have for our hypothetical example that 47.831 per cent of the blocks have copper concentrations between 0.02 and 0.007 per cent; blocks having these grades would be contained in approximately 4.78×10^{17} tonnes of metallized rock.

In the case where it is desired to know the estimate of the quantity of rock having grades of at least q', we have

$$t_{q'+} = \frac{T}{\sigma(2\pi)^{\frac{1}{2}}} \int_{\ln q'}^{\infty} \exp\left(-\frac{1}{2}\left(\frac{\ln q - \gamma}{\sigma}\right)^2\right) d\ln q. \tag{8.43}$$

Employing our hypothetical example, we find that quantity of metallized rock having grades of at least 0.02 per cent is approximately 2.2×10^{16} tonnes:

$$t_{0.02\%+} \approx (1 \times 10^{18})(0.5000 - 0.4783).$$

8.4. Estimation of average grade

The foregoing equations demonstrate the calculation of tonnage of metallized rock. How does one calculate the amount of metal in rock having the specified grades? Conceptually, such a calculation is trivial, for it requires only the multiplication of $(t_{q''-q'})(\bar{q}_{q''-q'})$, where $\bar{q}_{q''-q'}$ is the *average* grade of metallized rock having grades between q'' and q'

$$m_{q''-q'} = (t_{q''-q'}) \cdot (\bar{q}_{q''-q'}). \qquad (8.44)$$

The problem in making this calculation is obtaining the *arithmetic average* grade of a *truncated* distribution in which the variate is in logarithms.

Let us approach the problem a step at a time, beginning with a review of the calculation of the average (expectation) of a distribution. If X is a continuous random variable having a probability density function (p.d.f.) of $f(x)$, ($f(x) \, dx$ describes the distribution of probability for X), then the arithmetic mean of the distribution, $\bar{x}$ is known as the expectation of X and is calculated

$$\bar{x} = E[X] = \int_a^b x \cdot f(x) \, dx, \quad a \le x \le b. \quad (8.45)$$

As an example, we take the simple case in which the probability for X is a constant (this is known as a rectangular (uniform) distribution)

$$\begin{aligned} f(x) &= 1, \quad 0 \le x \le 1, \\ f(x) &= 0, \quad \text{otherwise.} \end{aligned} \qquad (8.46)$$

Then, from (8.43), we have

$$\bar{x} = E[X] = \int_0^1 x \cdot (1) \, dx = \frac{x^2}{2} \bigg|_0^1 = \frac{1}{2}. \quad (8.47)$$

This calculation confirms what is known intuitively, that in the case of a rectangular distribution over the interval of $(0, 1)$, the mean would be $\frac{1}{2}$ of the interval: $1.0/2 = \frac{1}{2} = \bar{x}$.

For a second example, take the case in which X is a continuous variable having the p.d.f. of $x^3/4$

$$\begin{aligned} f(x) &= \frac{x^3}{4}, \quad 0 \le x \le 2, \\ f(x) &= 0, \quad \text{otherwise.} \end{aligned} \qquad (8.48)$$

Trivially,

$$\frac{1}{4} \int_0^2 x^3 \, dX = \left(\frac{1}{4}\right)\left(\frac{x^4}{4}\right) \bigg|_0^2 = \frac{16}{16} = 1.0,$$

as is required for a p.d.f.

$$\bar{x} = E[X] = \int_0^2 x \cdot \frac{x^3}{4} \, dx = \int_0^2 \frac{x^4}{4} \, dx = \frac{x^5}{20} \bigg|_0^2 = \frac{32}{20} = 1.6.$$
$$(8.49)$$

Next, examine the calculation of the mean of a truncated distribution. Suppose that we have the same p.d.f. as in the foregoing example (8.48), but, in this case we wish to know the expectation for X when X is greater than 1. We observe first that the sum of the probabilities described by the above p.d.f. on the interval of $(1.0, 2.0)$ must be less than 1.0, for the domain of the function is over a larger interval $(0, 2.0)$. The operation of expectation as defined by (8.45) requires that the value of the integral of the p.d.f. over the interval of interest must be 1.0. Consequently, before performing the expectation operation, the p.d.f. must be modified so that the integral over the truncated distribution, the interval $(1.0, 2.0)$ is 1.0. This modification will in effect inflate the probabilities over the specified interval so that the value of the integral is 1.0, as desired. In essence, we need to determine a number less than 1.0 by which to divide the p.d.f. to create this inflation. This number is obviously the value of the integral of the p.d.f. over the interval of $(1.0, 2.0)$

$$\tilde{f}(x) = f(x)/K, \qquad (8.50)$$

where

$$K = \int_{1.0}^{2.0} f(x) \, dx. \qquad (8.51)$$

$$\tilde{f}(x) = \frac{f(x)}{\int_{1.0}^{2.0} f(x) \, dx}, \quad 1.0 \le x \le 2.0. \quad (8.52)$$

Employing $x^3/4$ as $f(x)$, $0 \le x \le 2.0$, we have

$$\tilde{f}(x) = \frac{x^3/4}{1/4 \int_{1.0}^{2.0} x^3 \, dx}, \quad 1.0 \le x \le 2.0. \quad (8.53)$$

Taking the denominator separately, we have

$$\frac{1}{4} \int_{1.0}^{2.0} x^3 \, dx = \frac{x^4}{16} \bigg|_{1.0}^{2.0} = 1.0 - \frac{1}{16} = \frac{15}{16}. \quad (8.54)$$

Thus,

$$\tilde{f}(x) = \frac{x^3/4}{15/16} = \frac{4x^3}{15}, \quad 1.0 \le x \le 2.0$$

$$f(x) = 0, \quad \text{otherwise.} \tag{8.55}$$

Let us check $\tilde{f}(x)$ to see if it sums to 1.0 over its domain.

$$\frac{4}{15} \int_{1.0}^{2.0} x^3 \, dX = \left(\frac{4}{15}\right) \frac{x^4}{4} \Big|_{1.0}^{2.0} = \frac{x^4}{15} \Big|_{1.0}^{2.0}$$

$$= \frac{16}{15} - \frac{1}{15} = \frac{15}{15} = 1.0. \tag{8.56}$$

The foregoing demonstrates all of the concepts involved in the calculation of the mean (expectation) of a truncated probability distribution; however, the lognormal distribution is somewhat more difficult to work with than the simple, contrived distributions employed to demonstrate the ideas and computations. Let us now turn to the derivation of an expression for the average grade of a truncated lognormal distribution of grades.

To facilitate the calculation of this expectation and to simplify notation, make the substitution

$$z = \ln q, \tag{8.57}$$

and

$$e^z = q$$

$$\frac{d \ln q}{dz} = 1 \Rightarrow d \ln q = dz. \tag{8.58}$$

Then,

$$E[Q] = \frac{\dfrac{1}{\sigma(2\pi)^{\frac{1}{2}}} \displaystyle\int_{z''=\ln q''}^{z'=\ln q'} e^z \cdot \exp\left(-\frac{1}{2}\left(\frac{z-\gamma}{\sigma}\right)^2\right) dz}{\dfrac{1}{\sigma(2\pi)^{\frac{1}{2}}} \displaystyle\int_{z''=\ln q''}^{z'=\ln q'} \exp\left(-\frac{1}{2}\left(\frac{z-\gamma}{\sigma}\right)^2\right) dz}$$

$$= \bar{q}_{q''-q'}. \tag{8.59}$$

Designate the product of the exponential terms in the numerator as $f(z)$:

$$f(z) = e^z \cdot \exp\left(-\frac{1}{2}\left(\frac{z-\gamma}{\sigma}\right)^2\right) \tag{8.60}$$

or

$$f(z) = \exp\left(-\frac{1}{2}\left[\frac{z^2}{\sigma^2} - \frac{2z\gamma}{\sigma^2} + \frac{\gamma^2}{\sigma^2} - \frac{2\sigma^2 z}{\sigma^2}\right]\right)$$

Completing the square, we have for $f(z)$

$$f(z) = \exp\left(-\frac{1}{2}\left[\frac{z^2}{\sigma^2} - \frac{2(\gamma+\sigma^2)z}{\sigma^2} + \frac{(\gamma+\sigma^2)^2}{\sigma^2} - \frac{(\gamma+\sigma^2)^2}{\sigma^2} + \frac{\gamma^2}{\sigma^2}\right]\right)$$

$$f(z) = \exp\left(-\frac{1}{2}\left[\frac{z-(\gamma+\sigma^2)}{\sigma}\right]^2\right) \times$$

$$\times \exp\left(+\frac{1}{2}\left(\frac{\gamma+\sigma^2}{\sigma}\right)^2 - \frac{\gamma^2}{2\sigma^2}\right)$$

$$f(z) = \exp\left(-\frac{1}{2}\left[\frac{z-(\gamma+\sigma^2)}{\sigma}\right]^2\right) \times$$

$$\times \exp\left(\frac{1}{2}\left[\frac{\gamma^2+2\gamma^2+\sigma^4}{\sigma^2}\right] - \frac{\gamma^2}{2\sigma^2}\right)$$

$$f(z) = \exp\left(-\frac{1}{2}\left[\frac{z-(\gamma+\sigma^2)}{\sigma}\right]^2\right) \cdot \exp\left(\gamma+\sigma^2/2\right). \tag{8.61}$$

Obviously, the last term $e^{\gamma+\sigma^2/2}$, does not depend upon z, thus, we can rewrite (8.59)

$$\bar{q}_{q''-q'} =$$

$$\frac{\dfrac{\exp(\gamma+\sigma^2/2)}{\sigma(2\pi)^{\frac{1}{2}}} \displaystyle\int_{z''}^{z'} \exp\left(-\frac{1}{2}\left[\frac{z-(\gamma+\sigma^2)}{\sigma}\right]^2\right) dz}{\dfrac{1}{\sigma(2\pi)^{\frac{1}{2}}} \displaystyle\int_{z''}^{z'} \exp\left(-\frac{1}{2}\left(\frac{z-\gamma}{\sigma}\right)^2\right) dz}. \tag{8.62}$$

Resubstituting $z = \ln q$, we have

$$\bar{q}_{q''-q'} =$$

$$= \frac{\dfrac{\exp(\gamma+\sigma^2/2)}{\sigma(2\pi)^{\frac{1}{2}}} \displaystyle\int_{\ln q''}^{\ln q'} \exp\left(-\frac{1}{2}\left[\frac{\ln q-(\gamma+\sigma^2)}{\sigma}\right]^2\right) d\ln q}{\dfrac{1}{\sigma(2\pi)^{\frac{1}{2}}} \displaystyle\int_{\ln q''}^{\ln q'} \exp\left(-\frac{1}{2}\left[\frac{\ln q-\gamma}{\sigma}\right]^2\right) d\ln q} \tag{8.63}$$

Examination of the numerator of the above expression reveals it to be the product of a constant K and a probability from a normal p.d.f. having a mean of $\gamma+\sigma^2$ and a variance of σ^2, while the denominator is a probability from a normal p.d.f. having a mean of γ and variance of σ^2. Therefore, let us rewrite (8.63) in a simpler notation

$$\bar{q}_{q''-q'} = K \cdot \left\{ \frac{P[\ln q'' \le \ln Q \le \ln q' \mid N(\gamma+\sigma^2, \sigma^2)]}{P[\ln q'' \le \ln Q \le \ln q' \mid N(\gamma, \sigma^2)]} \right\}. \tag{8.64}$$

The expression in the numerator signifies the probability for Q falling within the interval of (q'', q') given that the distribution is normal, having a mean of $\gamma + \sigma^2$ and variance of σ^2. The denominator signifies a similar probability except that the normal distribution has a mean of γ. Thus, given a knowledge of γ and σ, or reliable estimates thereof, the average of grades that are distributed lognormally can be determined simply by multiplying a constant times the ratio of two probabilities obtainable from a table of probabilities for the standardized unit normal distribution.

8.5. Example of calculations of tonnages and average grades using the lognormal distribution

As an example of these calculations, let us return to our fictitious problem of determining the average concentration of copper in rock of the earth's crust having concentrations falling within the interval of (0.007, 0.02). These grades were specified as being distributed according to a lognormal distribution having a mean of $\ln(0.007)$ and variance of $(0.5193)^2$: $N(-4.9618, 0.26967)$.

Recall that the ratio of probabilities was multiplied by a constant,

$$e^{\gamma + \sigma^2/2} = \gamma e^{\sigma^2/2}.$$

For $e^\gamma = 0.007$ and $\sigma^2 = 0.26967$, we have that

$$(0.007)e^{\sigma^2/2} = (0.007)e^{0.13484} = \underline{0.00801}.$$

Next, compute the standardized normal variates for the numerator of (8.61)

$$z' = \frac{\ln q' - (\gamma + \sigma^2)}{\sigma} = \frac{\ln(0.02) - (\gamma + 0.26967)}{0.5193}$$

$$= \frac{-3.9120 - (-4.9618 + 0.26967)}{0.5193}$$

$$z' = \frac{-3.9120 + 4.69213}{0.5193} = \frac{0.78011}{0.5193} = 1.502 \approx 1.50$$

and

$$z'' = \frac{\ln q'' - (\gamma + \sigma^2)}{\sigma} = \frac{\gamma - (\gamma + 0.26967)}{0.5193}$$

$$z'' = \frac{-0.26967}{0.5193} = -0.519 \approx -0.52.$$

Thus, we can rewrite the numerator in terms of standardized scores

$$P(-0.52 \leq Z \leq 1.50) \qquad (8.65)$$

Now we do the same for the denominator

$$z' = \frac{\ln q' - \gamma}{\sigma} = \frac{\ln(0.02) - (-4.9618)}{0.5193}$$

$$= \frac{-3.9120 + 4.9618}{0.5193} = 2.02, \text{ and}$$

$$z'' = \frac{\ln q'' - \gamma}{\sigma} = \frac{\ln(0.007) - (-4.9618)}{0.5193} = 0.$$

Thus, for the denominator the probability can be rewritten

$$P(0 \leq Z \leq 2.02). \qquad (8.66)$$

Now, both probabilities are in terms of standardized scores for a standard unit normal distribution having a mean of 0 and a variance of 1: $N(0, 1)$. Since both probabilities can be obtained from the same normal distribution, our notation can be simplified

$$\bar{q}_{q''-q'} = (0.00801) \left\{ \frac{P(-0.52 \leq Z \leq 1.50)}{P(0 \leq Z \leq 2.02)} \right\}. \qquad (8.67)$$

In the foregoing demonstration of the use of normal probability tables, we determined that $P(0 \leq Z \leq 2.02) = 0.4783$. All that remains is to determine the probability in the numerator. It is important to remember that tabled probabilities for the normal probability distribution always refer to a distribution having a mean of zero and a variance of 1.0. Since we computed standardized scores, our expressions for probabilities are compatible with these tables. Examination of the numerator shows that the lower value, the one for z'', is less than zero, the mean of the standard unit normal p.d.f. while the value for z' is greater. To obtain the appropriate probability from the normal distribution tables, the numerator must be decomposed to two probabilities

$$P(-0.52 \leq Z \leq 1.50) = P(Z \leq 1.50) -$$
$$- P(Z \leq -0.52). \qquad (8.68)$$

Since these probabilities are described by a normal probability distribution, we can define them as values of the normal distribution function F

$$P(-0.52 \leq Z \leq 1.50) = F(1.50) - F(-0.52). \qquad (8.69)$$

Or, employing the symmetry of the normal distribution,

$$P(-0.52 \leq Z \leq 1.50) = F(1.50) - [1 - F(0.52)], \tag{8.70}$$

$$P(-0.52 \leq Z \leq 1.50) = F(1.50) + F(0.52) - 1. \tag{8.71}$$

Tabled values for the normal distribution function F can be consulted for the probabilities $F(1.50) = 0.9332$ and $F(0.52) = 0.6985$. Therefore, from (8.71), we have

$$P(-0.52 \leq Z \leq 1.50) = 0.9332 + 0.6985 - 1$$

$$= 0.6317. \tag{8.72}$$

All that remains now for the calculation of $\bar{q}_{0.007-0.02}$ is just arithmetic

$$\bar{q}_{0.007-0.02} = 0.00801 \left\{ \frac{0.6317}{0.4783} \right\} = 0.0106 \text{ per cent.} \tag{8.73}$$

Thus, combining this result with a previous result, we can state that there are 4.7831×10^{17} tonnes of rock having concentrations between 0.007 and 0.02 per cent copper. The average grade of this material is 0.0106 per cent copper, implying that resources of copper in ore having grades within this grade interval are $4.7831 \times 10^{17} \times 0.000106 = 5.07 \times 10^{13}$ tonnes of copper.

As an additional demonstration of the method, consider the more typical question: How much ore and how much copper do we have with concentrations of at least 0.02 per cent copper? There is nothing new required to answer this question, so long as the probability tables are correctly used. From eqns (8.43) and (8.59) we have

$$t_{0.02+} = \frac{T}{\sigma(2\pi)^{\frac{1}{2}}} \int_{\ln(0.02)}^{\infty} \exp\left(-\frac{1}{2}\left(\frac{\ln q - \gamma}{\sigma}\right)^2\right) d \ln q,$$

$$\bar{q}_{0.02+} = \gamma \exp(\sigma^2/2) \times$$

$$\times \left\{ \frac{\dfrac{1}{\sigma(2\pi)^{\frac{1}{2}}} \displaystyle\int_{\ln(0.02)}^{\infty} \exp\left(-\frac{1}{2}\left[\frac{\ln q - (\gamma + \sigma^2)}{\sigma}\right]^2\right) d \ln q}{\dfrac{1}{\sigma(2\pi)^{\frac{1}{2}}} \displaystyle\int_{\ln(0.02)}^{\infty} \exp\left(-\frac{1}{2}\left[\frac{\ln q - \gamma}{\sigma}\right]^2\right) d \ln q} \right\},$$

$$m_{0.02+} = (t_{0.02+}) \cdot (\bar{q}_{0.02+}),$$

$$t_{0.02+} = T \cdot P(0.02 \leq Q \leq \infty),$$

or

$$t_{0.02+} = T \cdot P(\ln(0.02) \leq \ln Q \leq \infty)$$

$$= T \cdot P(-3.9120 \leq Q < \infty). \tag{8.74}$$

In terms of the standardized variate Z we have

$$t_{0.02+} = T \cdot P(2.02 \leq Z \leq \infty).$$

And, in terms of the normal distribution function, we have

$$t_{0.02+} = T \cdot [F(\infty) - F(2.02)] = T[1 - F(2.02)]$$

$$= T(1 - 0.9783) = \underline{0.0217T}$$

Again, taking $T = 1 \times 10^{18}$, we have that there are approximately 2.17×10^{16} tonnes of rock in the continental earth's crust to a depth of 2.5 km having concentrations of at least 0.02 per cent copper.

Let us calculate the average grade of this material

$$\bar{q}_{0.02+} = (0.00801) \times$$

$$\times \left\{ \frac{P[\ln(0.02) \leq \ln Q \leq \infty \mid N(\gamma + \sigma^2, \sigma^2)]}{P[\ln(0.02) \leq \ln Q \leq \infty \mid N(\gamma, \sigma^2)]} \right\}$$

$$\bar{q}_{0.02+} = (0.00801) \times$$

$$\times \left\{ \frac{P[-3.9120 \leq \ln Q \leq \infty \mid N(\gamma + \sigma^2, \sigma^2)]}{P[-3.9120 \leq \ln Q \leq \infty \mid N(\gamma, \sigma^2)]} \right\}.$$

Transforming to standard scores, we have

$$\bar{q}_{0.02+} = (0.00801) \left\{ \frac{P(1.50 \leq Z \leq \infty)}{P(2.02 \leq Z \leq \infty)} \right\}.$$

Then,

$$\bar{q}_{0.02+} = (0.00801) \left\{ \frac{F(\infty) - F(1.50)}{F(\infty) - F(2.02)} \right\}.$$

From the tables for $Z = 1.50$ and 2.02, we obtain the probabilities of 0.9332 and 0.9783, respectively. Consequently, we have that

$$\bar{q}_{0.02+} = (0.00801) \left\{ \frac{1 - 0.9332}{1 - 0.9783} \right\}$$

$$= (0.00801) \left\{ \frac{0.0668}{0.0217} \right\} = 0.025 \text{ per cent.}$$

Finally, we can compute the amount of copper metal

$$m_{0.02+} = (t_{0.02+})(\bar{q}_{0.02+}) = (2.17 \times 10^{16})(0.00025)$$

$$= 5.43 \times 10^{12} \text{ tonnes of copper.}$$

Thus, 5.43×10^{12} tonnes of copper are inferred to be present in rock having concentrations of at least 0.02 per cent copper. This copper is contained in 2.17×10^{16} tonnes of rock having an average grade of 0.025 per cent copper.

8.6. Importance of block (deposit) size

Once the analysis has been completed and resources are stated in numerical terms, as demonstrated above, there is a danger that the appropriate perspective of the estimates, in terms of what they represent, will become forgotten, or at best vague. While the analyst may have understood, the user of the analysis may not have ever understood, for proper perspective requires that the assumptions made in order to perform this broad, general inference be understood. For example, the lognormal distribution that served as the basis of this inference, in the example here employed, applies only to the case in which the earth's crust is divided into equal-sized blocks, blocks of 15.625 km³. While the actual size employed is important because of its effect on quantity of resources at a specified cut-off grade, size also is important in a more general way. The appraisal made pertains *only* to blocks (deposits) of *that size*, not to blocks of other sizes.

Would the resources having grades of at least 0.02 per cent copper be the same if blocks of 1 km² served as the basis of the histogram and the associated lognormal distribution? No! One only need appeal to intuition for the realization that the larger the size of the blocks, the smaller is that fraction (probability) of all the blocks which contain average concentrations significantly higher or lower than the average concentration of the Earth's crust, the limiting case being one block that constitutes the crust and has a concentration equal to crustal abundance. In this limiting case, the probability for a concentration higher than crustal abundance is zero, since there is only one block. In terms of properties of a lognormal distribution, the dispersion (variance) of the distribution (range of grade) decreases as block size increases. The upshot of this exposition is that the distribution applies only to the physical conditions imposed for its generation. The distribution developed in this example, as it stands (unmodified), cannot be used to estimate resources of copper in deposits of 100 000 000 tonnes, for it was developed as a frequency distribution for blocks of 15.625 km³, or 4.17×10^{10} tonnes; similarly, it cannot be used to make estimates about resources of copper in blocks that are 5 m on a side (volume of 125 m³). The critical point here is that the appraisal of resources by these methods refers to some specific size of deposit. Appraisal of resources in deposits of a size different from the unit (line, area, or volume) upon which the concentration was measured requires another distribution. This fact was critical to Brinck's objective of estimating resources of economic deposits from geochemical data. Obviously, one way of overcoming the problem is to obtain the metal concentration for volumes of the crust of the desired

size, but such a procedure usually is not acceptable, given the economics of close-spaced geochemical sampling on a regional scale. Furthermore, the utility of the method is significantly reduced if it is necessary to remeasure concentration and analyse the data for a new distribution for every deposit size of interest. What was needed was a way of modifying mathematically the distribution determined from concentrations representing one volume to a distribution of the desired volume.

The ideas and relations necessary for modification of the distribution of one sample size to another had been developed. One of the ideas comes from classical statistics, and the other from the work of DeWijs. Classical statistics has shown that the expectation of X is μ, and that an unbiased estimate for μ is $\bar{x}$, the mean of the sample

$$\hat{\mu} = \bar{x} = \sum_{i=1}^{n} x_i / n.$$

In other words, although any one sample of size n may not yield an $\bar{x}$ exactly equal to μ, on average $\bar{x}$ does give μ. Similarly, classical statistics has shown that if one were to take an infinite number of samples of size n from a normal p.d.f. and form the relative frequency distribution of all $\bar{x}$s, this distribution would be normal, as is the distribution of X; however the spread or dispersion of the distribution, which is reflected in σ, would be less. In fact, there is a mathematical relationship of the standard deviation for X, σ_X^2, to that for $\bar{X}$, $\sigma_{\bar{X}}^2$.

$$\sigma_{\bar{X}}^2 = \frac{\sigma_X^2}{n}.$$

What this means is that from a sample of size n, one can compute an estimate of μ and σ and, therefore, make probability statements about X. Furthermore since the expectations of X and of $\bar{X}$ are both the same, μ, and $\sigma_{\bar{X}} = \sigma_X / \sqrt{n}$, from the same sample one can estimate $\sigma_{\bar{X}}$ and make probability statements about the average of a measure over a set of individuals. At first glance, this looks like it may be useful in analysing the resources in blocks of a size different from the unit of observation; it can, but only in part. That the expectations of X and $\bar{X}$ are μ is useful directly, but $\sigma_{\bar{X}} = \sigma_X / \sqrt{n}$ is useful only because it is analogous to our problem with resources. For example, suppose that we have the heights of 50 male students and compute the following statistics from our sample

$$\hat{\mu} = \bar{X} = 5.9 \text{ ft},$$

$$\hat{\sigma} = 0.25 \text{ ft}.$$

Since heights of students are found to be normally distributed, we can use these statistics as estimates of the population parameters and make probability statements about the random variable; for example, the probability that an individual drawn at random would have a height of 6 feet or more is 0.3446,

$$Z = \frac{6.0 - 5.9}{0.25} = \frac{0.1}{0.25} = 0.4, \text{ and}$$

$$P(6.0 \le H \le \infty \,|\, N[5.9, (0.25)^2])$$
$$= P[0.4 \le Z \le \infty \,|\, N(0, 1)] = 1 - F(0.4).$$

From tables, we have $F(0.4) = 0.6554$. Therefore,

$$P(6.0 \le H \le \infty) = P(0.4 \le Z \le \infty)$$
$$= 1 - 0.6554 = 0.3446.$$

Now, suppose that we wished to know the probability that the *mean height of a sample of 49* students would be 6.0 ft or more. Our theory, as indicated in the foregoing section, states that we can use 5.9 as our estimate of the mean of the distribution of average heights and that we can compute a standard deviation for this distribution from the estimate of the standard deviation of the height of individuals

$$\hat{\sigma}_{\bar{x}} = \frac{\hat{\sigma}_x}{\sqrt{n}} = \frac{0.25}{\sqrt{49}} = \frac{0.25}{7} = 0.0357.$$

Thus, we can now compute the standard score for the mean height and determine the desired probability

$$Z = \frac{6.0 - 5.9}{0.0357} = \frac{0.1}{0.0357} = 2.8, \text{ and}$$

$$P(6 \le \bar{H} \le \infty) = P(2.8 \le Z \le \infty) = 1 - F(2.8)$$
$$P(6 \le \bar{H} \le \infty) = 1.00000 - 0.99744 = 0.00256.$$

While there was a sizeable probability 0.3446 for the height of an individual being 6 ft or more, we see that the probability for a group of 49 individuals having a mean height of at least 6 ft is very small. This illustrates an effect analogous to the postulated decrease in frequency of extreme (high or low) concentrations with increased block size, for which an appeal earlier was made to intuition.

DeWijs (1953) demonstrates this effect with the assays from the Pulacayo mine and his logbinomial model for the frequencies of grades. As demonstrated in a previous section which reviewed the logbinomial model, the size of the blocks dictated by the model is determined by $\beta = \ln n / \ln 2$, where n is the number of assays or blocks. Thus, given the

parameter d, the frequencies for grades in any size block can be determined by calculating the β associated with that block size. So long as the blocks are homothetic to the deposit, β is determined by

$$n = \frac{T}{t},$$

where T, t are the tonnage of deposit and block, respectively;

$$\beta = \frac{\ln n}{\ln 2} = \frac{\ln \left(\dfrac{T}{t} \right)}{\ln 2} = \frac{\ln T - \ln t}{\ln 2}. \tag{8.75}$$

The 118 assays of the Pulacayo vein were taken at equal intervals, 2 metres. It was from these 118 samples that $\hat{Q}$, β, and d were estimated as

$$\beta = 7,$$
$$d = 0.205,$$
$$\hat{Q} = 15.61 \text{ per cent.}$$

According to DeWijs, the practice at the Pulacayo mine was to divide the vein into blocks of about 5000 tons each, measuring 40 m along strike by 30 m in height by 1.3 m in depth. Since the samples were spaced at 2-m intervals, the grade of each block was the mean of 20 (equals 40/2) assays. The number of these blocks, $n = 118/20 = 5.9$; therefore $\beta = 2.561$; $\hat{Q}$ and d are the same as originally calculated, 15.61 per cent and 0.205, respectively. Employing the binomial formula DeWijs determined the lowest and highest grades occurring in these blocks. He did the same for blocks of 50 samples each. These values are summarized in Table 8.6.

This table demonstrates how, according to the theoretical binomial model, the dispersion of metal concentration decreases with block size. DeWijs fitted the normal distribution to the logbinomial model for the 20- and 50-sample block sizes and illustrated the results in Fig. 8.5. Besides the decrease in dispersion with block size, there is a

TABLE 8.6. *Theoretical range of assays—Pulacayo vein.* (*Source: DeWijs 1953.*)

Unit	Range (per cent Zn)	$\Delta q = q_{max} - q_{min}$
Individual assays	3.22–56.35	53.13
Blocks of 20 samples	8.68–23.72	15.04
Blocks of 50 samples	11.75–19.14	7.39
Total deposit	15.61–15.61	0.00

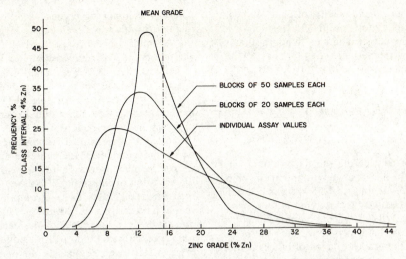

Fig. 8.5. Grade distributions and block size. (After DeWijs 1953.)

marked tendency towards symmetry as block size increases.

8.7. The variance–volume relationship of DeWijs

While studying the variance of gold assays in the Witwatersrand, DeWijs developed what was later called the 'DeWijsian scheme' by Matheron (1971); this is a mathematical statement of the relationship between block size and variance of grade for a given size of environment (deposit) containing the blocks:

$$\sigma^2 = \alpha \ln (V), \qquad (8.76)$$

where V is volume of the block and α is a coefficient unique to the deposit or environment that reflects that character of dispersion. α is independent of the unit or scale of observation. α is referred to variously as the coefficient of mineralizability or absolute dispersion. By plotting variance against block size for a given deposit, α can be estimated as the slope of the line.

The relationship of (8.76) was generalized to describe variance for varying environment as well as sample size. The concept here is that it is not just the absolute size of the unit of observation (sample) that is important, but its size relative to its environment. For example, the unit of observation might be assays (samples) within a panel (environment), or a panel within a block,

$$\sigma^2 = \alpha \ln (V/v), \qquad (8.77)$$

where V is the environment and v is the unit of observation.

Thus, if σ^2 had been estimated from sample data, both V and v would be known. Consequently, α could be solved for directly, $\alpha = \sigma^2/\ln (V/v)$.

α is an intrinsic value and does not vary with the scale of observation or support; it is a constant. Consequently, given α, the variance for some combination of V and v different from that of the sampling process can be computed simply by substituting them into eqn. (8.77).

For example, suppose that 100 samples have been taken on a square grid, each sample representing 8 ft^3 ($2' \times 2' \times 2'$), that the size of the environment (in this case a deposit) is 1000 ft^3 ($10' \times 10' \times 10'$), and that the variance of grade σ^2 has been estimated from the 100 samples to be 1.2. With this information, α can be calculated

$$\alpha = \frac{1.2}{\ln \left(\dfrac{1000}{8}\right)} = \frac{1.2}{\ln (125)} = \frac{1.2}{4.828} = \underline{0.2486}.$$

Knowing α and σ^2 for V and v, it is now possible to compute the variance for any other set of V and v that may be of interest. For example, suppose for this same deposit it is desired to know the variance for blocks of 27 ft^3 ($3' \times 3' \times 3'$). This variance would be calculated as

$$\sigma^2 = 0.2486 \ln \left(\frac{1000}{27}\right) = \underline{(0.2486)(3.612) = 0.8979},$$

$$\sigma = 0.9476.$$

Notice that the variance for the volume of 8 ft^3 is approximately a third larger (1.2 compared to

0.8979) than that for the volume of 27 ft³, indicating a smaller probability for extreme grades, high or low, occurring in the larger volume. Suppose that one wished to know the variance for blocks of 8 ft³ in a larger environment, say 4096 ft³ (16 ft × 16 ft × 16 ft) instead of 1000

$$\sigma^2 = 0.2485 \ln\left(\frac{4096}{8}\right) = (0.2485)(6.2383) = 1.5504,$$

$$\sigma = \underline{1.2452}.$$

The effect of considering the 8 ft³ volume as the unit reference in the larger environment of 4096 ft³ is to increase the variance to 1.5504 from 1.2, implying a higher probability for extreme grades.

Thus, the 'DeWijsian scheme' combined with the result from classical statistics concerning the mean—the average of the grades of a set of blocks in which the grade of each block is the average of a set of samples is the same as the average of all samples—provides a way for estimating the resources for a block of a size different from that of the original analysis. The critical step is the calculation of the new variance; this is done according to the DeWijsian scheme (8.77).

Before we can review Brinck's calculations, we need one more result, the generalization of the relationship of variance to volume described by DeWijs to volumes of differing geometry. The formula developed by DeWijs applies only when the geometry of the unit of inference and that of the environment are similar.

8.8. The Matheron–DeWijs formula for differing shapes of environment and deposit

8.8.1. *Perspective*

When the objective of the resource study is the estimation for a large area (environment), say of a state, of metal resources that exist in accumulations typical of economically exploitable deposits, the geometry of the unit of inference (deposit) and the environment may not be the same. Typically, the depth of the environment relative to its areal extent is much smaller than that of the deposit. If we let a be the size of the largest dimension of the environment, b the next largest, and c the smallest, then c/b for the environment is very small, much smaller than the same ratio for the deposit. The relationship of DeWijs does not allow for calculation of the variance for a deposit different in geometry from that employed in constructing the regional frequency distribution. What is needed is a formula for the var-

iance of volumes of bodies of differing geometry. Such a formula was developed as a generalization of the formula of DeWijs, and it is called the Matheron–DeWijs relationship.

This Matheron–DeWijs relationship was established by Matheron (1971) through his general theory for regionalized variables. Classical statistical methods are based upon the assumption that all observations correspond to random samples and that the value of the sampled response for one observation is independent of the value on any other observation. In other words, there is no spatial pattern in the variation of the response. Although grade of ore in some deposits fits these assumptions, in general, spatial patterns in the distribution of grade within an ore deposit are the rule, not the exception. Matheron's geostatistical theory of regionalized variables extends statistical methods to the analysis of spatial patterns in this variation. Analysis is done through a device called a variogram, which in simple terms shows how variation between samples varies with the distance (spatial separation) between them. For the case of random variation, as assumed for classical statistical analysis, there would be no systematic relationship of variation to distance. In this case, the average value of the variogram is the variance.

8.8.2. *The variogram*

In order to convey the concept of the variogram, let's take a hypothetical set of data and calculate the experimental variogram. Suppose that a vein deposit has been divided into 9 equally-sized blocks and the grade of each block has been determined by sampling. For example, suppose that sampling along a vein provided the grades

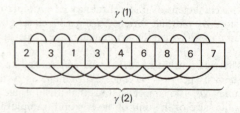

From these data, eight points on the variogram could be calculated

$$\gamma(1) = [(2-3)^2 + (3-1)^2 + (1-3)^2 + (3-4)^2$$
$$+ (4-6)^2 + (6-8)^2 + (8-6)^2 + (6-7)^2]/8.0,$$

$$\gamma(1) = \frac{1+4+4+1+4+4+4+1}{8.0} = \frac{23}{8.0} = \underline{2.9};$$

$\gamma(2) = [(2-1)^2 + (3-3)^2 + (1-4)^2 + (3-6)^2 +$
$\qquad + (4-8)^2 + (6-6)^2 + (8-7)^2]/7.0,$

$\gamma(2) = \dfrac{1+0+9+9+16+0+1}{7.0} = \dfrac{36}{7.0} = \underline{5.1};$

$\gamma(3) = [(2-3)^2 + (3-4)^2 + (1-6)^2 + (3-8)^2 +$
$\qquad + (4-6)^2 + (6-7)^2]/6.0,$

$\gamma(3) = \dfrac{1+1+25+25+4+1}{6.0} = \dfrac{57}{6.0} = \underline{9.5};$

$\gamma(4) = [(2-4)^2 + (3-6)^2 + (1-8)^2 + (3-6)^2 +$
$\qquad + (4-7)^2]/5.0,$

$\gamma(4) = \dfrac{4+9+49+9+9}{5.0} = \dfrac{80}{5.0} = \underline{16.0};$

$\gamma(5) = [(2-6)^2 + (3-8)^2 + (1-6)^2 +$
$\qquad + (3-7)^2]/4.0,$

$\gamma(5) = \dfrac{16+25+25+16}{4.0} = \dfrac{82}{4.0} = \underline{20.5};$

$\gamma(6) = \dfrac{[(2-8)^2 + (3-6)^2 + (1-7)^2]}{3.0} = \dfrac{36+9+36}{3.0}$

$\gamma(6) = \dfrac{81}{3.0} = \underline{27.0};$

$\gamma(7) = \dfrac{[(2-6)^2 + (3-7)^2]}{2.0} = \dfrac{16+16}{2.0} = \dfrac{32}{2.0} = \underline{16.0};$

$\gamma(8) = \dfrac{(2-7)^2}{1.0} = \underline{25.0}.$

The variogram of these data is plotted in Fig. 8.6. As indicated by the graph, variation in grades of blocks increases with the distance between blocks, at least to a separation of six blocks.

A formula that describes the calculations of the empirical variogram of Fig. 8.6 is,

$$\gamma(d) = \left\{ \sum_{i=1}^{N-d} (z_i - z_{i+d})^2 \right\} \Big/ (N-d),$$
$$d = 1, 2, \ldots, N-1, \quad (8.78)$$

where d is the number of block lengths, z_i, z_{i+d} the grades of the ith and $i+d$th blocks, respectively, and N the number of blocks. Obviously, the actual distance involved is the product of d with the length of a block: $d \times L$.

Although the above equation and example describe how the variogram of samples on a vein is calculated from sample data, variograms in the theory of regionalized variables are generally described in terms of functions and integrals. Let us look at the simplest case, the calculation of the variogram of grades on a line. Let the grade at point x be $f(x)$; then we have the relationship

$$2\gamma(h) = \frac{1}{(L-h)} \int_0^{L-h} [f(x) - f(x+h)]^2 \, dx. \quad (8.79)$$

In order to understand why $2\gamma(h)$ is used in eqn (8.79), we need to examine the expansion

$$[f(x) - f(x+h)]^2 = [f(x)]^2 - 2f(x)f(x+h) + [f(x+h)]^2.$$

Therefore

$$2\gamma(h) = \frac{1}{(L-h)} \int_0^{L-h} [f(x)]^2 \, dx -$$
$$- \frac{2}{(L-h)} \int_0^{L-h} f(x)f(x+h) \, dx +$$
$$+ \frac{1}{(L-h)} \int_0^{L-h} [f(x+h)]^2 \, dx. \quad (8.80)$$

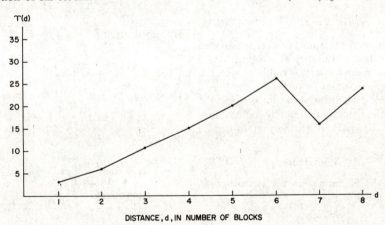

Fig. 8.6. Variogram.

Let us make a change of variable for the last integral in (8.80), $z = x + h$. Then

$$x = z - h,$$

$$\frac{dx}{dz} = 1$$

$$dx = dz.$$

For $x = 0$, $z = h$; for $x = L - h$, $z = L$. And we have the following expression for the last integral in (8.80)

$$\frac{1}{L-h} \int_h^L [f(z)]^2 \, dz. \qquad (8.81)$$

This integral looks just like the first integral, with the exception that it is taken over the interval (h, L) instead of $(0, L-h)$.

In the theory of regionalized variables, as developed by Matheron (1971), $f(x)$ is the realization of a random function. The realization at point x may be a different function than at $x+h$. The function itself is never known; consequently, we must think in terms of expectations of the random function when viewing these two integrals. It is in this sense that the two integrals are the same. Thus, eqn (8.80) can be simplified

$$2\gamma(h) = 2S^2 - 2C, \qquad (8.82)$$

where

$$S^2 = \frac{1}{L-h} \int_h^L [f(z)]^2 \, dz$$

$$= \frac{1}{L-h} \int_0^{L-h} [f(x)]^2 \, dx, \text{ and} \qquad (8.83)$$

$$C = \frac{1}{L-h} \int_0^{L-h} f(x)f(x+h) \, dx. \qquad (8.84)$$

Obviously,

$$\gamma(h) = S^2 - C. \qquad (8.85)$$

Thus, the variogram is the sum effect of a variance and a covariance. But, covariance C is defined for a given h only; any other value of h yields, in general, a different numerical value. In other words, C is a function of h while S^2 is invariant to h. Accordingly, let us designate the quantity defined by the relationship of (8.84) as $K(h)$. Then, the variogram can be defined as

$$\gamma(h) = S^2 - K(h). \qquad (8.86)$$

The measure $K(h)$ is known as the covariogram. Notice that, for $h = 0$,

$$K(0) = \frac{1}{L} \int_0^L [f(x)]^2 \, dx. \qquad (8.87)$$

Thus, the value of $K(0)$ is the same as S^2. Therefore, the variogram can be written in terms of the covariogram,

$$\gamma(h) = K(0) - K(h). \qquad (8.88)$$

For samples taken in two directions, the concept is the same, but the calculations are more complex, as they must provide for the additional dimension

$$\gamma(h) = \frac{1}{A} \int_0^{L-h} \int_0^{W-h} [f(x_1, x_2) - \\ - f(x_1+h, x_2+h)]^2 \, dx_1 \, dx_2, \qquad (8.89)$$

where $A = (L-h) \cdot (W-h)$ and x_1, x_2 are the coordinates of location in 2-space. And, for samples in a three-dimensional scheme, the variogram is described as

$$\gamma(h) = \frac{1}{V} \int_0^{L-h} \int_0^{W-h} \int_0^{T-h} [f(x_1, x_2, x_3) - \\ - f(x_1+h, x_2+h, x_3+h)]^2 \, dx_1 \, dx_2, \, dx_3, \qquad (8.90)$$

where x_1, x_2, x_3 are the coordinates of location in 3-space;

$$V = (L-h) \cdot (W-h) \cdot (T-h). \qquad (8.91)$$

The following are examples of variogram derivations from functional forms for a line and area.

Variogram calculation for grades on a line. Let

$$q = f(x) = x^2, \quad 0 \le x \le 2. \qquad (8.92)$$

Then

$$2\gamma(h) = \frac{1}{2-h} \int_0^{2-h} [f(x) - f(x+h)]^2 \, dx,$$

$$\gamma(h) = \frac{1}{4-2h} \int_0^{2-h} [f(x) - f(x+h)]^2 \, dx.$$

By substitution

$$\gamma(h) = \frac{1}{4-2h} \int_0^{2-h} [x^2 - (x+h)^2]^2 \, dx.$$

Expanding $[x^2 - (x+h)^2]^2$, we have

$$[x^2 - (x^2 + 2xh + h^2)]^2 = 4x^2h^2 + 4xh^3 + h^4.$$

Therefore,

$$\gamma(h) = \frac{1}{4-2h} \int_0^{2-h} (4x^2h^2 + 4xh^3 + h^4) \, dx$$

$$\gamma(h) = \frac{1}{4-2h} \left(\frac{4x^3h^2}{3} + \frac{4x^2h^3}{2} + xh^4 \right) \Big|_0^{2-h}$$

$$\gamma(h) = \tfrac{8}{3}h^2 - \tfrac{2}{3}h^3 + \tfrac{1}{6}h^4. \qquad (8.93)$$

Grades in a two-dimensional scheme.

$$q = f(x_1, x_2) = 2x_1 + 3x_2, \quad 0 \le x_1 \le 2; \, 0 \le x_2 \le 3, \tag{8.94}$$

$$2\gamma(h) = \frac{1}{(2-h)(3-h)} \int_0^{3-h} \int_0^{2-h} [(2x_1 + 3x_2) - \\ -(2(x_1+h) + 3(x_2+h))]^2 \, dx_1 \, dx_2.$$

Expanding the term within the brackets, we have

$$[(2x_1 + 3x_2) - [2(x_1+h) + 3(x_2+h)]]^2 = (2x_1 + 3x_2)^2 - \\ -2(x_1 + 3x_2)(2x_1 + 3x_2 + 5h) + (2x_1 + 3x_2 + 5h)^2$$

$$= (4x_1^2 + 12x_1x_2 + 9x_2^2) - \\ -2(4x_1^2 + 9x_2^2 + 12x_1x_2 + 10x_1h + 15x_2h) \\ +(4x_1^2 + 9x_2^2 + 12x_1x_2 + 20x_1h + 30x_2h + 25h^2).$$

All terms on the right-hand side of the equation cancel except for one, $25h^2$. Therefore, we have

$$2\gamma(h) = \frac{1}{(2-h)(3-h)} \int_0^{3-h} \int_0^{2-h} 25h^2 \, dx_1 \, dx_2$$

$$2\gamma(h) = \frac{1}{(2-h)(3-h)} \int_0^{3-h} 25h^2 x_1 \, dx_2 \Big|_0^{2-h}$$

$$2\gamma(h) = \frac{1}{(3-h)} \int_0^{3-h} 25h^2 \, dx_2 = \frac{1}{3-h}(25(3-h)h^2)$$

$$\gamma(h) = 12.5h^2. \tag{8.95}$$

Thus, if, for a deposit, the function describing the distribution of grade $f(x)$ were known, calculation of the variogram would be no more than a problem in calculus. In a real world, this function is *never* known!

Rather than attempt to estimate the function, the perspective in geostatistics is to calculate the empirical variogram from sample data and to compare this variogram with known mathematical models, models for which statistical relationships have been determined.

Given the identification of the appropriate model, geostatistical relationships found to apply to the model are used to facilitate analysis, such as the computation of variances for the measure of interest (sample, panel, or blocks), or to obtain the estimator of average grade that has minimum variance (Kriging). Schematic variograms of various models and a calculated DeWijsian variogram are shown in Fig. 8.7. Note the variogram for the random model; this describes the case of classical statistics, in which samples are independent; there is no consistent pattern of variation between samples with distance between samples.

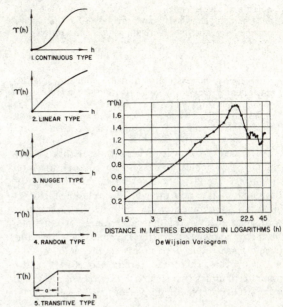

Fig. 8.7. Schematic variograms. (Source: Blais and Carlier 1968.)

8.8.3. *The DeWijsian variogram*

The DeWijsian variogram is of primary interest here. This variogram describes a phenomenon with an *infinite variance*! At first glance, it is not apparent how infinite variance could be an appropriate model for the distribution of grades; in this regard, consider the comment of Matheron (1971).

> Many phenomena have an almost unlimited capacity of dispersion, and cannot be properly described by attributing to them a finite a priori variance: this assertion is perhaps surprising, but we have to realize that nature is setting a sort of trap here. When samples v are taken from a field V, we get a histogram from which it is always possible to calculate a variance which takes thus a perfectly definite value. But this experimental variance is in fact a function $\sigma^2(v/V)$ of the support v and the field V. In particular, it increases as the field increases. If the samples of size v have a finite a priori variance, this should appear as the limit of the experimental variance $\sigma^2(v/V)$ in an infinite V.

Matheron (1971) elaborates upon the gold concentration of the Rand of South Africa as an example of a phenomenon having an infinite variance.

> It was in this way that the South African School (D. G. Krige, etc. . . .), starting from hundreds of thousands of samples drawn from the large orebody of the Rand, have been able to calculate the variance of these samples in

larger and larger panels, then in the entire concession, and then in the whole Rand orebody: thus they have obtained an experimental relationship of the form

$$\sigma^2(v/V) = \alpha \log (V/v).$$

The variance increases in accordance with this logarithmic rule (the DeWijs formula) right up to the last experimental point, for which the ratio of V/v is about ten thousand million. It can be concluded, beyond any doubt, that in this case, an a priori finite variance does not exist.

As stated previously, Matheron's theory of regionalized variables addresses the general situation in which there is spatial pattern in the variation of the phenomenon and provides the relationships that allow the computation of statistics or estimators through the device of the variogram. For example, Matheron shows that for the case in which the samples, v_i, are reduced to points in the field V, $V = v_1 \cup v_2 \cup v_3 \cup \cdots \cup v_n$, the variance, $\sigma^2(O/V)$ of the punctual samples (values at the points) within V can be written in terms of the variogram

$$\sigma^2(O/V) = \frac{1}{V^2} \int_V dx \int_V \gamma(x-y)\, dy, \quad (8.96)$$

where $\sigma^2(O/V)$ represents the variance of the point values that comprise V, $\gamma(x-y)$ is the variogram for the distance represented by $x-y$, and x, y represent locations of the points v_i. Thus, this variance is the mean value of the variogram over the entire domain V as x and y sweep V separately.

When v_i represents volumes, not points, and $V = v_1 \cup v_2 \cup v_3 \cup \ldots \cup v_n$, Matheron shows that the variance of v, the volume of the sample, within the field V also can be defined in terms of the variogram

$$\sigma^2(v/V) = \frac{1}{V^2} \int_{X_3} \int_{X_2} \int_{X_1} dx_1\, dx_2\, dx_3 \times$$

$$\times \int_{Y_3} \int_{Y_2} \int_{Y_1} \gamma(x_1-y_1, x_2-y_2, x_3-y_3)\, dy_1\, dy_2\, dy_3 -$$

$$-\frac{1}{v^2} \int_{X_3} \int_{X_2} \int_{X_1} dx_1\, dx_2\, dx_3 \times$$

$$\times \int_{Y_3} \int_{Y_2} \int_{Y_1} \gamma(x_1-y_1, x_2-y_2, x_3-y_3)\, dy_1\, dy_2\, dy_3,$$

$$(8.97)$$

where x_1, x_2, x_3 and y_1, y_2, y_3 for the first line of (8.97) are coordinates of location within V; and for the second line, x_1, x_2, x_3 and y_1, y_2, y_3 are coordinates of location within v.

Using vector notation, we can rewrite $\sigma^2(v/V)$ in a simpler notation

$$\sigma^2(v/V) = \frac{1}{V^2} \int_V dx \int_V \gamma(x-y)\, dy -$$

$$-\frac{1}{v^2} \int_v dx \int_v \gamma(x-y)\, dy. \quad (8.98)$$

Alternatively, using (8.97) we may define $\sigma^2(v/V)$ in terms of variances of points within volumes V and v

$$\sigma^2(v/V) = \sigma^2(O/V) - \sigma^2(O/v). \quad (8.99)$$

The DeWijsian variogram is defined by the intrinsic function (Matheron 1971)

$$\gamma(h) = 3\alpha \log h. \quad (8.100)$$

If we substitute $x-y = h$, we have $\gamma(x-y) = 3\alpha \log |x-y|$. Furthermore, if we substitute $3\alpha \log |x-y|$ for $\gamma(x-y)$ in (8.98), we have

$$\sigma^2(v/V) = 3\alpha \left[\frac{1}{V^2} \int_V dx \int_V \log |x-y|\, dy \right.$$

$$\left. -\frac{1}{v^2} \int_v dx \int_v \log |x-y|\, dy \right]. \quad (8.101)$$

Matheron defines the function

$$F(V) = \frac{1}{V^2} \int_V dx \int_V \log |x-y|\, dy. \quad (8.102)$$

Rewriting (8.101) using $F(V)$ and $F(v)$, we have

$$\sigma^2(v/V) = 3\alpha [F(V) - F(v)]. \quad (8.103)$$

Matheron next proposes that if two volumes, V and V', provide the same value for $F(V)$, these volumes are said to be equivalent

$$F(V') = F(V) \Rightarrow \text{volumes } V' \text{ and } V \text{ are equivalent.}$$

He then shows that, for a line segment of length l,

$$F(l) = \log l - \tfrac{3}{2}. \quad (8.104)$$

The term 'linear equivalent' is given to the length d of a line segment giving the same value for F as does the volume v; d is said to be the linear equivalent of v. Thus, for the volumes v and V, there are linear equivalents

$$F(v) = \log d - \tfrac{3}{2},$$

$$F(V) = \log D - \tfrac{3}{2}. \quad (8.105)$$

Substituting these volumes for $F(v)$ and $F(V)$ into

(8.103), we have

$$\sigma^2(v/V) = 3\alpha[F(V) - F(v)] \qquad (8.106)$$

$$= 3\alpha[(\log D - \tfrac{3}{2}) - (\log d - \tfrac{3}{2})]$$

$$= 3\alpha(\log D - \log d). \qquad (8.107)$$

Finally,

$$\sigma^2(v/V) = 3\alpha \log (D/d). \qquad (8.108)$$

When v and V are geometrically similar and each can be described as an equivalent cubic body,

$$V = D^3, \quad D = V^{\frac{1}{3}}, \qquad (8.109)$$

$$v = d^3, \quad d = v^{\frac{1}{3}}. \qquad (8.110)$$

Then, by substitution into (8.108), we have the original formula of DeWijs

$$\sigma^2(v/V) = 3\alpha \log [(V/v)^{\frac{1}{3}}] \qquad (8.111)$$

$$= 3 \cdot \alpha \cdot (\tfrac{1}{3}) \log [V/v]$$

$$= \alpha \log [V/v]. \qquad (8.112)$$

Thus, the formula of DeWijs is for the special case of a phenomenon characterized by infinite variance, and in which the volume of the sample and the field are homothetic (having the same geometry). The generalized formula by Matheron allows for the calculation of variance when the geometry of the sample and field are not the same by the use of the linear equivalent of the volume.

As an aid to the use of the Matheron–DeWijs formula, Matheron (1971) provides graphs for the determination of the linear equivalent of a volume of a specified shape. The shape of a volume is described by ratios of the lengths of its three sides: b/a, c/b, $a \geq b \geq c$. However, Matheron provides what he describes as an excellent approximation of linear equivalent D

$$D = a + b + 0.7c.$$

8.9. Application—an exercise in statistical inference

8.9.1. *Procedure recapitulated*

The basic scheme of resource appraisal by this method is to take a set of rock or sediment samples from the area of interest and to determine the concentration of the metal(s) of interest in each sample. From these data, estimates of the parameters (γ, σ_s) of the lognormal distribution of sample concentration (grade) are made. Then, the coefficient of

mineralizability α is estimated using the estimate of σ_s determined from the geochemical samples, the average volume of influence of the samples v_s, and the volume of the total area sampled V, the environment. Using the graphs or formulae provided by Matheron, the linear equivalent d_s of the volume of the samples and that of the environment D_s are calculated. These quantities are combined according to (8.108) to give α. Now, suppose that it is desired to know the endowment of a metal occurring in a volume typical of currently economic deposits v_d. Before this can be calculated, the standard deviation for grades in volumes of this size must be determined. This is done by virtue of α and the linear equivalents of v_d and V

$$\sigma_d = \left[3\alpha \ln \left(\frac{D}{d_d} \right) \right]^{\frac{1}{2}},$$

where σ_d is the standard deviation of volumes of deposit size and d_d, D are the linear equivalents of the deposit volume v_d and the environment V, respectively.

8.9.2. *Demonstration on Oslo*

Brinck demonstrated the method on the Oslo region (environment) of Norway. This region consisted of 19 200 km^2, from which 146 geochemical samples were taken. Each sample was considered to represent 15 km^2. Using this information, linear equivalents of the sample d_s and of the environment D were calculated:

$$d_s = 7.75 \text{ km},$$

$$D = 380 \text{ km}.$$

From the 146 samples, estimates of γ and σ_s for copper were made [2]

$$\text{crustal abundance} = 89 \times 10^{-6} \Rightarrow e^{\gamma}$$

$$\gamma = \ln (0.0089) = -4.7217,$$

$$\hat{\sigma}_s = 0.6119.$$

Thus, using d_s, D, and $\hat{\sigma}_s$, α was estimated by relationship (8.108)

$$\hat{\alpha} = 0.0376.$$

Now suppose that we wished to know the quantity of rock in the Oslo region with copper accumulations similar in size and concentration to the typical deposit, 1.7 per cent Cu and 65×10^6 tons of ore, as determined by Brinck, based upon data available in 1967. Brinck takes the dimensional parameters given by Bateman (1950) as a description of the shape of the typical deposit, and with this shape and the typical tonnage (65×10^6) tons, he calculates the linear equivalent of the typical deposit

$$d_d = 1.2 \text{ km.}$$

This quantity, with α and D as already calculated, was used to compute σ_d, the standard deviation of grades in accumulations like the *typical deposit*

$$\hat{\sigma}_d = \left[(0.0376)3 \ln \left(\frac{380}{1.2} \right) \right]^{\frac{1}{2}}$$

$$\hat{\sigma}_d = \underline{0.8053}.$$

Now, the endowment in terms of total metallized rock in the Oslo region having accumulations of this size and grades of at least 1.7 per cent Cu is determined by evaluating the normal probability distribution for a probability and by multiplying the probability by the tonnage of rock (T) in the Oslo region:

$$t_{1.7+} = \frac{T}{(0.8053)(2\pi)^{\frac{1}{2}}} \times$$

$$\times \int_{\ln(1.7)}^{\infty} \exp \left(-\frac{[-4.7217 - \ln q]^2}{2(0.8053)^2} \right) \mathrm{d} \ln q,$$

$$t_{1.7+} = \frac{T}{2.9 \times 10^{10}},$$

where T is the tonnage of rock in the environment, here, the Oslo region. Taking $T = 6.25 \times 10^{13}$, we have $t_{1.7+} = 2.4 \times 10^3$ tonnes of metallized rock. Thus, the copper endowment of Oslo in deposits of at least 1.7 per cent Cu, as estimated, is negligible. The quantity of metal contained in $t_{1.7+}$ could be determined by calculating the average grade for $t_{1.7+}$ by substituting $\hat{\gamma}$ and $\hat{\sigma}$ in relationship (8.63) and then forming the product of the two quantities, $t_{1.7+}$ and $\bar{q}_{1.7+}/(100)$.

8.9.3. *The case of no usable geochemical data*

As demonstrated in the foregoing example of the Oslo region of Norway, the estimation of metal resources by the approach described by Brinck requires estimation of γ and σ_s from geochemical samples from the environment of interest. Statistics from the geochemical data and the geometry and size of the environment and deposit of interest are used to estimate resources of the element of interest in deposits of ore of the quantity of the deposit of interest and having grades falling within the interval specified.

Criticism of the assumptions implicit in this approach will be presented later. The utility of this method for the appraisal of resources here will be examined, with the assumption that the method is acceptable. Obviously, the utility of this approach is diminished by the need for geochemical samples of the environment. Regions for which *reliable* and *usable* data of this kind are available are generally very small. Experience has shown that available data often are neither randomly nor systematically taken from even small regions. Seldom, if ever, do we have a usable set of geochemical data for a region the size of a state, let alone a nation.

In order to employ the concepts of the element distribution for the appraisal of metal resources where geochemical data are not available, Brinck describes an alternative method for the estimation of the parameters of the element distribution for the environment specified, a method based upon cumulative production and known reserves of the metal. The critical assumptions are

1. The sum of all past production of ore and known ore reserves represent the *totality* of material in the environment; all deposits with grades above the economic cut-off grade have been discovered.
2. The parameter of location [3] γ of the element distribution is *known*.
3. The sum of all ore reserves and cumulative production of ore was derived from deposits of some *typical, constant size* in terms of tonnage of ore.
4. The concentration of metal in deposits of the typical size is distributed lognormally, having a mean [4] of γ and variance of σ_d^2.
5. $\sigma_{d'}^2 = 3\alpha \ln (d/d')$, where d' is a different size than d.

For the time being, let us accept these assumptions and work through the logic and calculations.

Given the foregoing assumptions, reason dictates that the inventory of cumulative production and reserves t represents some part of the total environment. Specifically, it represents that part of the environment having grades of at least q', the cut-off grade of the typical, current mining operation. If this quantity t is divided by the quantity of material in the environment T, the resulting fraction represents the fraction of the environment having grades of at least q'. If the concentration of the metal in deposits typical of those that comprise t is distributed lognormally, then t/T must be $P (\ln q' \leq \ln Q \leq \infty)$:

$$\frac{t}{T} = P (\ln q' \leq \ln Q \leq \infty \mid N(\gamma, \sigma_d^2)) = p.$$

Given that p is a probability from a normal distribution and given that γ, the mean of this distribution, is known, σ_d can be estimated simply by obtaining from the tabled probabilities the standardized score associated with p and then solving directly for σ_d

$$\frac{t}{T} = p \Rightarrow z.$$

By definition,

$$z = \frac{\ln q - \gamma}{\sigma_d}.$$

Therefore,

$$\sigma_d = \frac{\ln q - \gamma}{z}.$$

As an example, let us examine Brinck's estimation of σ_d for copper. Brinck takes 70 parts per million as the crustal abundance for copper [5]

$$e^{\hat{\gamma}} = 70 \times 10^{-6}.$$

The weight of the continental Earth's crust to a depth of 2.5 km is taken to be 1×10^{18} tonnes. On the basis of cumulative production and reserves data, Brinck uses 1.7 per cent for $\bar{q}$ and $(219 \times 10^6)/0.017$ for m, the amount of copper metal either produced or present in ore. With these data, the following calculations were made (Brinck 1967a, p. 15)

$$p = \frac{(219 \times 10^6/0.017)}{1 \times 10^{18}}$$

$$p = \frac{1}{7.75 \times 10^7} \Rightarrow z = 5.55,$$

$$\hat{\sigma}_d = \frac{\ln(0.017) - \ln(0.00007)}{5.55} = \underline{0.9886}.$$

And, from the size and dimensions of the environment and the typical deposit, the coefficient of absolute variation α is estimated

$$\hat{\alpha} = (0.9886)^2/3 \ln(D/d) = 0.0329.$$

Using $\hat{\gamma}$ and $\hat{\sigma}_d$, Brinck calculates the probability for the occurrence of copper, in concentrations of at least 1.7 per cent and in quantities of ore of the typical deposit 65×10^6 tons, to be 9.35×10^{-8}. Taking the weight of the earth's crust to be 1×10^{18} tonnes, the endowment in terms of metallized rock in deposits of this kind is calculated to be

$$t_{1.7+} = (9.35 \times 10^{-8}) \cdot (1 \times 10^{18}) = 9.35 \times 10^{10} \text{ tonnes.}$$

The average grade of this endowment can be esti-

mated using relationship (8.63) to be 2.34 per cent Cu. Thus, the world's endowment in copper is estimated to be 2.2×10^9 tonnes

$$m_{1.7+} = (9.35 \times 10^{10}) \cdot (0.0234) = 2.2 \times 10^9 \text{ tonnes.}$$

This quantity is approximately twice the sum of identified, hypothetical, and speculative reserves (Cox, Schmidt, Vine, Kirkemo, Tourtelot, and Fleischer 1973). If the typical reserve were of a grade of 0.6 instead of 1.7 per cent, but of the same ore tonnage 65×10^6, the copper metal endowment would increase considerably, to 10×10^{10} tonnes. Thus, the endowment estimate is very sensitive to the characteristics of the typical reserve.

In the conceptual description, the element distribution approach was developed from a histogram for grades in blocks of equal size. This is the assumption behind the lognormal element distribution, as employed by Brinck. Of course, real data on copper deposits show a distribution of sizes, a distribution that is often lognormal. Thus, for implementation of the element distribution it is necessary to represent this distribution by a single, typical size. Obviously, our concept of the typical size is defined from production and reserves, quantities that change with time as additional discoveries are made and in particular, as new modes of occurrence are recognized.

It is important to note that while the use of geochemical samples from a region allows an estimate by the element distribution method that is relatively free from the influence of time-related phenomena, estimates of endowment for large regions using the inventory of known reserves and cumulative production provides a 'mixed bag', an estimate based upon a model of *element concentrations* but quantified on the basis of *economic data*.

As an additional example, consider the estimate of the endowment of the world in zinc made by Brinck's (1967a, p. 19) method: for a typical deposit of 4.3 per cent zinc and 10×10^6 tonnes of ore, the world endowment in zinc is estimated to be 2.24×10^{10} tonnes of rock having an average grade of 5.9 per cent zinc, implying 1.32×10^9 tonnes of zinc. This quantity is virtually the same as the estimate of zinc in identified and undiscovered ore made by conventional methods, 1.3×10^9 short tons (s.t.) (Wedow, Kilsgaard, Heyl, and Hall 1973). Such an agreement is not necessarily desirable, for time has shown man's appraisal of metal resources by conventional methods to be conservative, even for known modes of occurrences and restricted regions. The element distribution model represents all environments, some of which are known and some of which we may not yet recognize, for the world. Given the definition of what the element distribution represents, it is reasonable to expect from it larger endowment estimates than those made by conventional geological analysis.

8.10. A comparison of methods—New Mexico uranium

A study by Ellis, Harris, and Van Wie (1975) describes the appraisal of uranium endowment by subjective probabilities (see Chapter 13) and extrapolation of a quantity–quality relationship. This same study also estimated the U_3O_8 endowment of New Mexico by Brinck's CAG method. The results of these appraisals are described here as a further inquiry of Brinck's methodology and a comparison of estimates by that methodology with those of a more conventional approach, geological inference.

    Estimation by Brinck's CAG method is described below.

Environment. State of New Mexico to a depth of 1 mile.

$T = 1.5 \times 10^{15}$ s.t., the weight of the environment.

Crustal abundance $= 3 \times 10^{-6}$.

Typical deposit.

Geometric mean deposit size $= 1827.3$ s.t. of ore.

Geometric mean grade of deposit

$$= 0.128 \text{ per cent } U = 1280 \times 10^{-6}.$$

Total known reserves plus cumulative production $=$ 130 889 462 s.t. of ore at an average grade of 0.1368 per cent U.

Calculations [6].

$$p = \frac{1.31 \times 10^8}{1.50 \times 10^{15}} = 8.73 \times 10^{-8}.$$

$p = 8.73 \times 10^{-8}$ implies $Z = 5.223$, the standard normal variate.

$$\hat{\sigma} = \frac{\ln(1280) - \ln(3)}{5.223} = 1.16.$$

Endowment of New Mexico in U which occurs in deposits of the typical size but having grades of at least 0.085 per cent uranium (0.10 per cent U_3O_8)

$$Z = \frac{\ln(850) - \ln(3)}{1.16} = \frac{5.6466}{1.16} = 4.87.$$

From the normal distribution, we have that $Z = 4.87$, implying that $p = 5.62 \times 10^{-7}$.

Endowment in terms of ore

$$= (5.62 \times 10^{-7})(1.5 \times 10^{15})$$
$$= 8.43 \times 10^8 \text{ s.t.}$$

    The study by Ellis *et al.* (1975) subdivided the State of New Mexico into 62 cells. Then, after studying the geology of a cell, a geologist provided probabilities for number of deposits, tonnage per deposit, and grade given tonnage of deposit. These probability distributions were combined by Monte Carlo methods to provide an expected inventory by average grade—quantity–quality relation—of potential resources. These quantity–quality estimates for potential resources were merged with quantity–quality data for reserves and cumulative production to produce composite (potential and known) quantity–quality data. A mathematical relation was fitted to these data to yield a quantity–quality (cumulative tonnage–average grade) relation.

    Extrapolation of the grade–tonnage relationship provided an estimate of the quantity of ore having grades of at least 0.10 per cent U_3O_8 as approximately 609 000 000 tons (Ellis *et al.* 1975). Thus, the estimate by the deposit methodology is more conservative than that of the element distribution. Conceptually, this is as one would expect, for the element distribution is based upon a measure that reflects the occurrence of a given metal in *all modes* of occurrence, while the deposit method relates only to *recognized* modes of occurrence. For example, in New Mexico, known modes of occurrence do not include uranium in igneous rocks, but crustal abundance reflects the occurrence of metal in all rocks.

    The disparity between estimates of these two methods of appraisals is significant for endowment estimated to exist in deposits having *very low grades.* As indicated in the description of the New Mexico study, the extrapolation of the grade–tonnage relationship estimates declining quantities of metallized rock in grade classes below the 0.10–0.15 per cent U_3O_8 class. This implies an underlying population having a modal grade greater than 0.10 per cent U_3O_8. In the case of the element distribution, tonnages of ore increase with a decrease in grade until that grade of interest is below that of crustal abundance, 0.0003 per cent U. For example, the quantity of metallized rock having grades of at least 0.01 per cent U_3O_8 (0.00848 per cent U) is estimated to be 3×10^{12} s.t., having an average grade of 0.0147 per cent U_3O_8, implying 4.41×10^8 s.t. of U_3O_8. Compare this to 3.76×10^9 s.t. of ore and 1.44×10^6 s.t. of U_3O_8 estimated by the deposit approach.

While in theory, estimates from element distribution methods should be optimistic relative to estimates by deposit methods, in practice this may not always be the case, as suggested by comparison of the estimates of the endowment of the world in zinc made by Brinck's (1967a, p. 19) method to that made by the US Geological Survey (Wedow et al. 1973) using traditional methods; these are virtually the same. A possible reason for this inconsistency is that the estimate of one of the parameters γ reflects the totality of metal occurrence. Yet, when σ and α are estimated not from geochemical samples, but from the inventory of reserves and cumulative production, they reflect time-related phenomena.

8.11. The logbinomial model

Brinck followed his work on the lognormal distribution with the development of the logbinomial, a discrete approximation to the lognormal. As indicated in the beginning of this chapter, the logbinomial was first described as a model of the reserves of an ore deposit by DeWijs (1951, 1953). Brinck (1967b, 1974) generalized the model to describe resources

$$m = \frac{T}{2^\beta} \cdot \bar{Q} \cdot \sum_{k=0}^{\beta} [(1+d)^{\beta-k}(1-d)k],$$
(8.113)

where T is the weight of the environment, $\bar{Q}$ the average grade of the environment, d and β are parameters to be estimated from the data on mineral occurrences, and m is the tonnage of metal. The parameters d, β, and $\bar{Q}$ define the model. Given $\bar{Q}$ and d, a specific grade q' is defined by β and K: $q' = \bar{Q}(1+d)^{\beta-k}(1-d)k$; similarly, the tonnage of rock associated with q' is defined by $(T/2^\beta) \times (C_k^\beta)$.

Conceptually, apart from its discrete nature and the particulars of the estimation of its parameters, the logbinomial conveys the same information as does the lognormal. When fitted to a given set of data on metal concentrations, this logbinomial describes frequencies of concentrations for deposits of equal size, a size defined by $T/2^\beta$. However, the discrete logbinomial is more easily manipulated numerically on the computer than is the continuous lognormal. It is especially more useful in playing the 'if' game, the exploration of various scenarios of endowment, for it can be manipulated to give tonnages and number of deposits by varying β. Brinck

(1971) expressed a preference for the logbinomial over the lognormal on theoretical as well as practical grounds. As pointed out first by DeWijs (1951, 1953) and later by Brinck (1974), the parameters of each model can be expressed in terms of those of the other model.

8.12. Issues of the CAG approach of Brinck

8.12.1. Continuity of grade distribution

Continuity is not only the most apparent issue of the CAG approach, as described by Brinck, but also the most critical issue with regard to its application. Some discussion of the continuity issue was provided in the chapter on quantity–quality relations, Chapter 3. Comments in that chapter also are relevant to the CAG approach.

Given appropriate estimates of γ and σ, estimates of mineral endowment at subeconomic grades are predicated upon the assumption that there is a smooth transition within the earth's crust from high to low grades. In Brinck's approach this transition is described by the lognormal probability model, or its discrete analogue, the logbinomial. The basic issue is whether concentration of metal in a region is described by one smooth and continuous distribution or whether there is a set of distributions, one for each mode of occurrence. If one were to employ a single-population model when really there are several different populations, the result probably would be the ascribing of incorrect characteristics (tonnage and average grade per deposit) to the unknown resources, for the tonnage and average grade of ore per deposit may be very different for each subpopulation. By employing a single population model, one is likely to ascribe to the inferred deposits those characteristics observed from known resources. If endowment of a metal for grades considerably below grades of known deposits is estimated via a single population CAG model when indeed there are several subpopulations, there is a considerable risk of overestimating endowment that will be available to us at low grades. The reasoning for this overestimation is that we would interpret this estimate in terms of known deposits, or at best, in terms of deposit characteristics inferred from tonnage–grade relations based upon known resources, while in fact some of this inferred endowment may exist in new, unfamiliar modes of occurrence, modes for which tonnage, average grade, depth, geometry, mineralogy, density, etc. are quite different from those of known resources, or different from characteristics inferred by extrapolations of relations observed from data on known resources. The comparison of methods on the estimation of endowment of U_3O_8 in New Mexico demonstrated the implications of the single-population model. In this comparison, it was found that endowment estimates by the two methods were similar for economic and marginally economic grades, but very different for subeconomic grades: the CAG model inferred great tonnages in these low-grade intervals, while the deposit approach inferred considerable endowment only in marginally economic grade intervals. In essence, the deposit approach implies that deposits of the recognized modes of occurrence in New Mexico do not frequently occur as very low-grade masses; rather, the genesis of the typical deposits is such that if these deposits are formed, typically their grades are far above crustal abundance. The deposit approach would allow that if additional endowment exists in New Mexico in deposits having very low average grades, these deposits represent different, currently unrecognized, modes of occurrence for that region. On the other hand, the CAG approach does not recognize modes of occurrence. Endowment in terms of quantity of mineralized rock in a constant grade interval continues to increase as the relationship is extrapolated to crustal abundance.

One danger in using a CAG model is that since the concept of mode of occurrence is not explicit to the model, those who use its estimates may ascribe to the endowment inferred for subeconomic grades those characteristics observed on known deposits, overlooking the possibility that some of the inferred endowment may be present in deposits of unfamiliar modes, hence deposits of very different characteristics.

8.12.2. Tonnage–grade relations and Brinck's calculations

Considerable care was taken in the examination of the concepts underlying the crustal abundance geostatistical approach to emphasize that use of the lognormal (logbinomial) distribution model, as outlined by Brinck, implies a constant size of deposit (block). For a given size of deposit, endowment for specified grade intervals is computed simply by using normal probability relations. Naturally, as the grade is decreased, the total rock and metal increases until the specified grades approach crustal abundance. However, for a given size of deposit, the quantity of metal *per deposit* decreases as the specified grade is lowered. This is a natural consequence of lowering the concentration of the typical deposit while keeping the quantity of ore constant. Obviously, such a result has significant implications to the resource value of the endowment.

In his resource appraisals, Brinck manipulates both grade and size of deposit to investigate the interaction of exploration and exploitation with these characteristics. It is important in interpretation of his work that the reader realizes that such manipulation implies that *all metal* occurs in *deposits* of *that specified size*. A proper perspective would be: suppose that all metal occurs in deposits of size *t*, what would our resources be? Or, what are our resources if grade is lowered to *q*, given that all deposits have *t* tonnes of ore?

Throughout his work, Brinck employs an inverse relationship of tonnage size and average grade. He justifies such an approach by citing deposits that are known to be of the size and grade specified. Here, considerable caution should be exercised to not equate a rare occurrence with an expectation, for tonnage per deposit for a given mode is often lognormally distributed, meaning that occasionally very large tonnages occur even though the mean or most likely tonnage is much smaller.

Analysis of data on size and grade of copper deposits suggests that for a given mode of occurrence, grade and tonnage per deposit may be independent (Singer, Cox, and Drew 1975), but across modes there may be a weak correlation. If this indeed is the case, then increasing deposit size as grade is lowered implies that analysis is *transcending modes of occurrence*. In other words, accepting an endowment estimate made by adjusting the variance for larger deposit size as grade is lowered to subeconomic grades *requires acceptance* of *the proposition that* the *endowment includes metal in multiple modes, some of which currently may not be recognized.*

8.12.3. Estimation of parameters from production and reserves data

Let us set aside issues involving the use of an element distribution for resource appraisal and examine estimation of parameters of the distribution. Estimation of γ and σ for the lognormal distribution from geochemical data is a rather straightforward statistical procedure, as it requires calculation of the weighted mean of the logarithms of the grades and the logarithmic variance from sample data. Additionally, conditional upon the proper recognition of the area of influence of the samples, estimation of α is also a straightforward use of the Matheron–DeWijs relationship.

While parameter estimation from geochemical data is straightforward, estimation of the parameters from what Brinck refers to as the reference distribution (production and reserves) is anything but straightforward. Accurate estimates by this procedure would require rather unrealistic conditions.

1. For the region serving as the data base, all deposits (*across all modes*) having grades of at least the cut-off grade *are known*.
2. From the distribution of tonnages and grades on known deposits, it is possible to select that tonnage and grade that represent the typical deposit.
3. The parameter γ [7] of the lognormal distribution for the region is reasonably estimated by one of the commonly accepted measures of crustal abundance.

The assumption for the region, which in some of Brinck's studies has been the world, that all endowment to some selected grade is known obviously is contrary to fact. It is a near certainty that even for currently recognized modes of occurrence in current supply areas endowment exists in undiscovered deposits. Add to this the endowment in new, forthcoming supply areas and even for currently known modes condition 1 certainly is not satisfied. Endowment existing in unknown modes of occurrence challenges further this assumption.

Suppose, for example, that $\gamma = -4.00$, $T = 1 \times 10^{12}$, and $t = 2 \times 10^{10}$ for $\ln q = -2.00$. Then our estimate of σ is 0.7843.

$$p = \frac{2 \times 10^{10}}{1 \times 10^{12}} = 0.02 \rightarrow Z_{0.48} = 2.05,$$

$$\hat{\sigma} = \frac{-2.00 - (-4.00)}{Z_{0.48}} = \frac{2.00}{2.05} \approx 0.98,$$

where $\hat{\sigma}$ is the estimate of the logarithmic variance, given the volume of the typical deposit and the environment. But, suppose that our estimate of t for $\ln q = -2.00$ is too low by an order of magnitude

$$p = \frac{2 \times 10^{11}}{1 \times 10^{12}} = 0.20 \rightarrow Z_{0.30} = 0.84,$$

$$\hat{\sigma} = \frac{-2.00 - (-4.00)}{Z_{0.30}} = \frac{2.00}{0.84} = 2.38.$$

Thus, an estimate of σ based upon production and reserves from large regions, regions which contain considerable undiscovered economic resources, may be considerably underestimated by the reference distribution approach. It is very possible that production plus reserves underestimates endowment for a specified q by a factor of 10. Underestimation of σ has the effect of understating our endowment in the high- and low-grade intervals. Furthermore, if σ is underestimated, then so is α, the measure of absolute dispersion. Obviously extension variances computed from α for deposits of specified sizes would also be underestimated.

Conceptually, it is not clear that median grade should be used in the estimation of σ by the reference distribution approach. Brinck refers to the median tonnage and grade of a deposit. His use of the term median is equivalent to the customary use of the term geometric mean. Suppose for argument that we knew total endowment for grades of at least q and that there were no correlation between grade and deposit tonnage. In this special case, *it is clear* that the *proper* estimate of σ would require the use of the *cut-off grade q'*, not the geometric average of grades above cut-off grade q. However, in reality, we may have a less complete inventory of the deposits having grades near cut-off grade. Such deposits may make up only a small part of the known production and reserves; consequently, they would not be representative of the total endowment of grades near cut-off. Furthermore, in application, Brinck increases the size of deposit as grade is lowered, and the extension variance must reflect this change in deposit size. Perhaps some grade above cut-off should be employed in this situation. But, should this grade necessarily be the geometric mean?

As a way of exploring some of these issues, a computer program was developed to simulate the estimation of the standard deviation by the reference distribution (production plus reserves) method described by Brinck. In this simulation, metal endowment consisted of metal deposits from 10 subpopulations (modes of occurrence). Each subpopulation was described by a distribution of grade, a distribution of tonnage per deposit, and the total quantity of the Earth's crust comprised by the deposits of each of these subpopulations (see Table 8.7). Tonnage and grade per deposit were considered to be statistically independent.

The endowment of these 10 modes of occurrence can be expressed by two composite distributions, one for grade and one for tonnage of deposit.

Composite grade distribution

$$\gamma = -5.1549,$$
$$\sigma = 1.25.$$

TABLE 8.7. *Subpopulations (modes of occurrence) of the simulated metal endowment*

Mode of occurrence	Grade distribution		Tonnage/deposit distribution		Quantity of Rock (tons)
	γ	σ	γ	σ	
1	−1.442	0.132	7.617	0.690	16.380×10^8
2	−1.640	0.303	6.354	0.828	15.038×10^9
3	−2.233	0.162	8.369	0.565	56.444×10^9
4	−3.300	0.500	8.200	0.500	50.000×10^{15}
5	−4.100	1.000	7.100	0.500	19.000×10^{16}
6	−5.200	0.920	7.500	0.570	56.000×10^{16}
7	−6.200	1.000	8.000	0.500	15.000×10^{16}
8	−7.000	0.500	7.300	0.500	50.000×10^{15}
9	−8.070	0.160	5.700	0.700	56.000×10^9
10	−10.140	0.300	8.646	0.830	17.000×10^9

Composite tonnage per deposit

$\gamma = 7.5$,

$\sigma = 0.635$.

Total tonnage of crust $\approx 1.0 \times 10^{18}$ tons.

Each of these composite distributions is lognormal. Figs. 8.8–8.11 show the shapes of the subpopulations and of their composites.

The basic scheme of the simulator was to select a cut-off grade and to generate by sampling of these

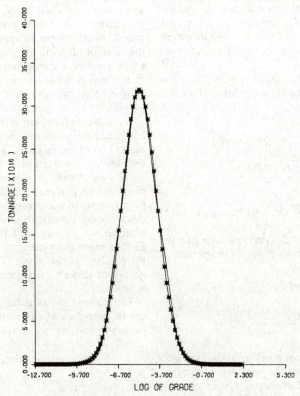

Fig. 8.8. Reference distribution of deposit grade and composite approximation.

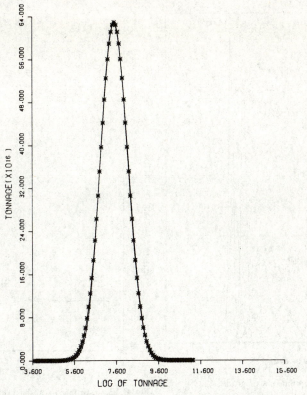

Fig. 8.9. Reference and composite approximation distribution of deposit tonnage.

subpopulations an inventory of deposits, each deposit in the inventory being represented by an average grade and tonnage. The number of deposits, n_j, of the jth population (mode of occurrence) present in the inventory was made proportional to the ratio of the quantity of rock represented by the jth population t_j to the average size $\bar{r}_j$ of deposits of the jth population

$$n_j = k\left(\frac{t_j}{\bar{r}_j}\right),$$

where k is a constant of proportionality, t_j is the total tonnage of the earth's crust represented by the jth mode, and $\bar{r}_j$ is the average tonnage per deposit for the jth mode.

For a given cut-off grade q', Brinck's method for estimating the parameters was simulated on the inventory of deposits having grades above q'. In this simulation, σ was estimated by using the cut-off grade, the arithmetic average grade, and the weighted geometrical mean exhibit a bizarre pattern and tion experiment are shown in Figs. 8.12–8.14. The

results obtained from the arithmetic mean and the cut-off grade are essentially the same, both providing a reasonably good estimate of σ for inventories generated across the entire range of cut-off grades. However, the estimates obtained by using the weighted geometrical mean exhibit a bizarre pattern and provide good estimates only for inventories of deposits for high cut-off grades. Overall, this experiment suggests that using the geometrical mean (Brinck's median) and the methods demonstrated by Brinck, provides a poor estimate of σ. However, in actual application, we would be operating on inventories associated with high cut-off grades, so the estimates obtained using the geometrical mean may be acceptable for the grade range of our current experience. On the basis of this experiment, however, the arithmetic mean grade may be a better statistic if we have complete knowledge of the endowment for grades above cut-off grade. Further analysis is required to test the effects of incomplete information.

In the applications demonstrated by Brinck in

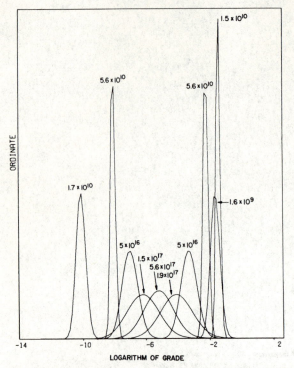

Fig. 8.10. Subpopulations of grade.

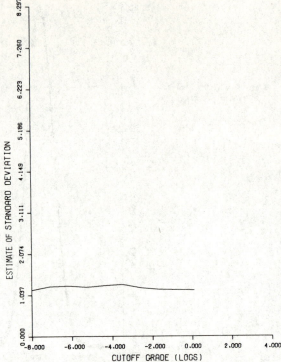

Fig. 8.12. Estimated standard deviation versus grade (standard deviation estimated using cut-off grade).

which the parameters of the lognormal distribution were estimated through the reference distribution, a measure of crustal abundance for the continental earth's crust was employed as the estimate of e^γ. Assuming that this measure is appropriate for the entire continental crust, is it the appropriate measure for a smaller region, say the crust within a state, or nation? How different are measures of crustal abundance on smaller regions? And, how much does the variation of crustal abundance by region or metallographic province affect the appraised resources? These are basic questions that need further exploration and study.

8.12.4. *Crustal abundance and geology*

Let us turn to the case in which geochemical sampling has been completed on the region of interest. Conditional upon the relevance of the assumptions of continuity, one method of appraisal would be to employ the geochemical-element distribution, based upon the estimates of its parameters made from the

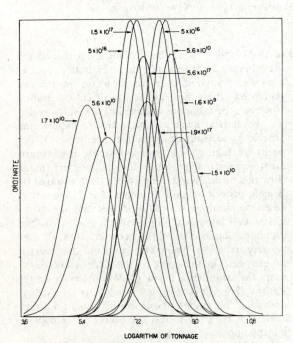

Fig. 8.11. Subpopulations of tonnage per deposit.

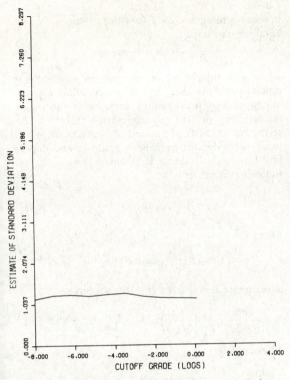

Fig. 8.13. Estimated standard deviation versus grade (standard deviation estimated using mean grade).

of grades as a model of endowment. Most of Brinck's economic analysis has been made using the logbinomial model

$$m = \frac{T}{2^\beta} \cdot \bar{Q} \cdot \sum_{k=0}^{\beta} [(1+d)^{\beta-k}(1-d)^k],$$

(8.114)

where m is the tonnage of metal endowment, T is the weight of the environment (Earth's crust to some specified depth in the region of interest), $\bar{Q}$ is the average grade (as a decimal fraction) of environment (crustal abundance), and d and β are parameters that must be estimated for a given metal. d reflects the tendency of a metal to occur in high-grade accumulations and was labelled by Brinck as the 'mineralizability' of an element.

The quantity 2^β is the number of deposits in the environment, and the expression $\bar{Q}(1+d)^{\beta-k}(1-d)^k$, $k = 0, 1, \ldots, \beta$ represents a distribution of grades of deposits (blocks), each of size $T/2^\beta$.

survey data. But, what about the situation in which geological and/or geophysical data are available? Even if one were a strong advocate of the CAG approach, to use the geochemical data alone, ignoring the geophysics and geology would seem to deny a more comprehensive analysis in favour of the manipulatability and apparent simplicity of the univariate element distribution.

If there truly is a correlation of geologic features to metal occurrence, as postulated in the theory of metal endowment, then, availability of such data begs a more comprehensive, multivariate type of model, one which includes geological, geophysical, and geochemical measurements. Obviously, much research is needed in this area of resource modelling.

8.13. The economic model

8.13.1. *Overview and recapitulation*

The foregoing subsections described Brinck's use of both the lognormal and the logbinomial distributions

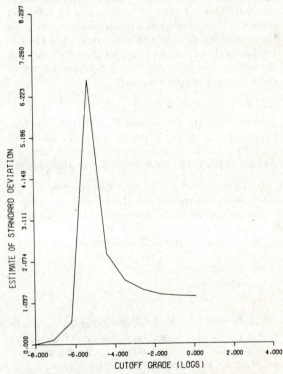

Fig. 8.14. Estimated standard deviation versus grade (standard deviation estimated using weighted geometric mean grade).

Once the parameters β and k have been determined, given $\bar{Q}$ and T, the endowment model is specified, and the quantity of metal occurring in blocks of size $T/2^\beta$ and having a specified grade can be determined by selecting the combinations of $[(1+d)^{\beta-k}(1-d)^k\bar{Q}]$ giving that grade. Since β, d, and $\bar{Q}$ are fixed once the model is quantified, identifying grades of interest requires identifying the levels of k that produces those grades. It can be seen that this model describes an endowment in which all deposits are of one size $T/2^\beta$. The perspective of this model is quite different from that of most other resource models. Here, a deposit is any size of partition of the crust that is of interest; the grade of a deposit is the average grade of a block in an environment in which metal is distributed randomly. Given this philosophy and the resulting structure of the endowment model, deposit size is a variable which must be specified. A proper perspective of this model is that deposit size reflects economics of scale of exploration and production and the long-term price of the metal. Thus, the function of Brinck's economic model is to compute the costs of potential supply for various sizes of deposits; and, since changing size of deposit changes the distribution of grade, this economic analysis also reflects the interaction of deposit size and grade on the economics of supply. Brinck considered the potential supply of a metal to reflect the endowment of the region and three cost factors: exploration cost, capital cost, and operating cost.

8.13.2. *The cost model*

Costing procedure. Production costs are calculated by Brinck (1972) on a US dollars-per-pound-of-metal basis by performing a discounted cash flow analysis on each deposit. The basic inputs to this analysis are

(a) the exploration cost per tonne of rock;
(b) the operating cost per short ton;
(c) the capital costs per short ton of handling capacity;
(d) the cost of capital (discount rate);
(e) the mining life of the deposit;
(f) deposit tonnage;
(g) deposit grade;
(h) deposit shape.

Brinck (1972, p. 8) postulated that the discount rate ϕ for the discounted cash flow analysis is determined by the interest on bonds i_b, the marginal tax on profits π, the minimum after tax return on equity i_e, and the risk capital ratio r

$$\phi = [(i_e \cdot r)/(1-\pi)] + i_b(1-r). \quad (8.115)$$

Capital cost. Brinck describes capital costs of uranium production as a function of the daily ore-handling capacity

$$y_1 = 2.1e^{11.11775 - 0.35757\ln\nu}, \quad (8.116)$$

where y_1 is the capital cost of uranium production in dollars per daily short ton of ore-handling capacity and ν is daily ore handling capacity in short tons. Relationship (8.116) can be restated (8.119) to describe capital costs per pound of uranium (cap) as a function of deposit tonnage t, grade q, and deposit life l by substituting $t/365l$ for ν and using the following equivalent

$$y_1 = 2000(cap)(q)(t)\Big/\frac{t}{365l}. \quad (8.117)$$

Then,

$$cap\Big/\frac{t}{365l} = y_1/(2000q \cdot t).$$

Substituting for y_1 from (8.116), we have

$$\frac{cap}{(t/365l)} = t^{-1}\left(\frac{2.1}{2000}\right)q^{-1}e^{11.11775 - 0.35757\ln(t/365l)}.$$

Alternatively,

$$\frac{cap}{(t/365l)} = (t^{-1})(1.05\times10^{-3})\times$$
$$\times e^{11.11775 - 0.35757\ln(t/365l) - \ln q}. \quad (8.118)$$

Finally,

$$cap = \left(\frac{1.05\times10^{-3}}{365l}\right)\times$$
$$\times e^{11.11775 - 0.35757\ln(t/365l) - \ln q}. \quad (8.119)$$

Eqn (8.119) expresses capital cost in dollars per pound of uranium for the production of a deposit of size t, mining life of l, and deposit grade of q. Suppose that $\nu = 1102 = t/365l$, $q = 0.005$, and $l = 16$. Substituting these values in (8.119) gives the result that $cap = $ US \$0.20/lb uranium.

Operating cost. Operating costs, which include mining, milling, and marketing costs, were described by Brinck as a function of daily ore-handling capacity ν

$$y_2 = (1.0)e^{3.90197 - 0.23856\ln\nu}, \quad (8.120)$$

where y_2 is the operating cost in US dollars per ton of ore and ν is the daily ore-handling capacity in short tons. Operating costs per pound of uranium op can be described in terms of y_2

$$op = y_2/2000q$$

or

$$op = 0.5 \times 10^{-3} e^{3.90197 - 0.23856 \ln(t/365l) - \ln q}. \tag{8.121}$$

Assuming a life of 16 years and a discount rate of 10 per cent, a discounted total cost per pound of uranium c can be computed from (8.119) and (8.121)

$$c = cap + \frac{1}{t \cdot q} \int_0^{16} \frac{t \cdot q}{16} \, ope^{-0.10x} \, dx. \tag{8.122}$$

More specifically, from (8.119) and (8.121), we have

$$c = \frac{(1.05 \times 10^{-3}) e^{11.11757 - 0.35757 \ln(t/5840) - \ln q}}{5840} +$$

$$+ \left[\int_0^{16} \left(\frac{t \cdot q}{16} \right) \cdot (0.5 \times 10^{-3}) \times \right.$$

$$\left. \times e^{3.90197 - 0.23856 \ln(t/5840) - \ln q - 0.10x} \, dx \right] \bigg/ t \cdot q. \tag{8.123}$$

Let $v = 1102$ tons/day ($t = 6\,435\,680$ s.t.; $l = 16$), and $q = 0.005$ (0.5 per cent). Substituting in (8.123) appropriately and performing the mathematical operations indicated, we have

$$c = \$0.20 + \$0.474 \approx \text{US } \$0.67/\text{lb U}.$$

Exploration cost. Brinck's basic premise is that exploration cost is a function of the chance for discovering a deposit of the specified tonnage and grade in its geologic environment and that this chance is directly proportional to the number of deposits with the specified characteristics that are present in the environment.

Essentially, Brinck first estimates e_0, the exploration cost for a reference deposit, one representative of those deposits which constitute known reserves. Additionally, n_0, the number of reference deposits in the environment, is estimated. Then, e_1, the exploration cost for a deposit having specified characteristics, is estimated as

$$e_1 = e_0 \cdot (\lambda_0/\lambda_1) \cdot (n_0/n_1)^{2/3}, \tag{8.124}$$

where e_0, e_1 are the exploration cost per ton of rock of the reference deposit and the deposit being evaluated, respectively; λ_0, λ_1 are the linear equivalents of the reference deposit and the deposit being evaluated, respectively, and n_0, n_1 are the number of deposits in the geologic environment of the reference deposit and the deposit being evaluated, respectively.

Linear equivalents are a form of description of deposit size and shape. For a deposit having a shape such that the lengths of its axes are in the relationship of $L_1 > L_2 > L_3$, the linear equivalent of the deposit is approximately $\lambda = L_1 + L_2 + L_3$ (Brinck 1972, p. 8).

Brinck estimated that in 1971, the typical uranium deposit had a grade of 0.185 per cent U (0.218 per cent U_3O_8) and contained 4.00×10^3 tonnes of uranium. He calculated that the linear equivalent of this deposit is 666.5 m and that there are 43 of these deposits in the environment. Finally, he estimated that the exploration cost per tonne of ore for this reference deposit is US $3.84. This cost is equivalent to US $1.11/lb uranium or US $0.94/lb U_3O_8.

Suppose that it is desired to estimate the cost for the discovery of a deposit of 1 800 000 tonnes of ore having a grade of 0.11 per cent uranium, a shape described by $L_1/L_2 = 0.5$ and $L_2/L_3 = 0.1$, and a linear equivalent of 465 metres. Before Brinck's exploration cost equation can be used to estimate the cost of discovering such a deposit, the number of these deposits in the environment must be estimated. From Brinck (1972), we have the relations

$$\text{Number of deposits} = \binom{\beta}{k}, \tag{8.125}$$

$$\text{Size of deposit} = T/2^{\beta}, \tag{8.126}$$

$$\text{Average grade of deposit} = \bar{Q}(1+d)^{\beta-k}(1-d)^k, \tag{8.127}$$

where T is the weight of Earth's crust and $\bar{Q}$ is crustal abundance as a decimal fraction.

Let $\bar{Q} = 0.000003$, $T = 1 \times 10^{18}$ tonnes, and $d = 0.2003$. The first step is to solve for β from (8.126) by employing the fact that the deposit tonnage is 1 800 000 tonnes.

$$1\,800\,000 = \frac{1 \times 10^{18}}{2^{\beta}}$$

$$\beta = \ln\left(\frac{1 \times 10^{18}}{1\,800\,000}\right) \bigg/ \ln 2 \tag{8.128}$$

$$= 27.0432/0.6931 = 39.02.$$

Let us take 39 as the nearest integer approximation of β. Given that $\beta = 39$, k can be calculated from (8.127) by using the average grade of the deposit, (0.11 per cent), $\bar{Q} = 0.000003$, and $d = 0.2003$.

$$0.0011 = 0.000003(1.2003)^{39-k}(0.7997)^k$$

$$\ln(0.0011/0.000003) = (39 - k) \ln(1.2003) +$$

$$+ (k) \ln(0.7997)$$

$$-1.2158 = (-k)(0.1826) + (k)(-0.2235)$$

$$-1.2158 = -0.4061k$$

$$k = 2.99 \approx 3. \tag{8.129}$$

Then, for $\beta = 39$ and $k = 3$, the number of deposits n_1 having the specified tonnage and grade is calculated from (8.125)

$$n_1 = \binom{39}{3} = \frac{39!}{(36!) \cdot (3!)} = 9139. \qquad (8.130)$$

Finally, the exploration cost per tonne of ore is calculated from (8.124) by substituting the calculated values appropriately

$$e_1 = e_0 \cdot (\lambda_0/\lambda_1) \cdot (n_0/n_1)^{\frac{2}{3}}$$

$$e_1 = \$3.84 \left(\frac{666.5}{465.0}\right)(43/9139)^{\frac{2}{3}}$$

$$= (\$3.84)(1.43)(0.028)$$

$$e_1 = 0.15/\text{tonne} = \text{US } \$0.06/\text{lb uranium}. \qquad (8.131)$$

8.13.3. *Comment on the exploration model*

The example calculations in § 8.13.2 (*Exploration cost*) show a very low cost per pound of uranium for the discovery of a deposit of the specified characteristics (1 800 000 tonnes with a grade of 0.11 per cent uranium). Of course, the total cost of discovering these 9139 deposits is considerable, approximately US $2.4 billion. As is apparent from the above calculation, this low cost is due to the great number of such deposits (9139), as compared to the number of reference deposits that are in the Earth's crust (43), and the proposition that exploration costs are proportional to the frequency of occurrence. It

follows from the nature of Brinck's model that the number of low-grade deposits increases rapidly as grade of deposit is decreased, hence, according to Brinck's postulate, the probability for discovery for such deposits is high. This causes the cost per pound of uranium discovered to drop to very low levels as grade is decreased, as is indicated in the above example.

Brinck's exploration model does not service the dynamics of efficiency of search and exploration cost. In essence, the model is predicated on the assumption that all deposits of a specific size, shape, and grade are discovered at the cost described by the exploration cost equation. Because of the structure of this exploration model, there are considerable economies in the exploration for smaller lower-grade deposits. For example, the amount of uranium in 9139 deposits each of 1 800 000 tonnes of ore and a grade of 0.11 per cent uranium is approximately 105 times that in deposits each of which has 2 162 000 tonnes of ore and a grade of 0.185 per cent uranium, but the cost of discovery of the lower-grade deposits is only about six times that of the higher-grade deposits.

8.13.4. *Long-term metal price*

Brinck (1972, p. 6) proposes that the historical average price of some major non-ferrous metals, such as copper, lead, and gold can be estimated within 25 per cent of the true price by the following equation

$$pr = (e^{8.96637 - 25.5688d})/(\bar{Q} \times 10^6), \qquad (8.132)$$

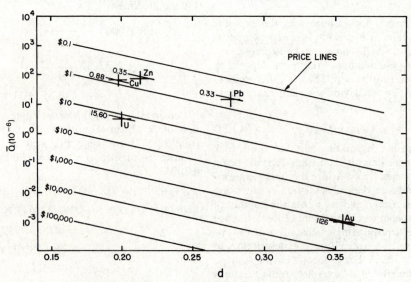

Fig. 8.15. Long-term metal prices. (Source: Brinck 1972.)

where *pr* is in US $/kg. For example, the long-term price of uranium is US $15.59/kg.

Given $\bar{Q} = 0.000003$ and $d = 0.2003$,

$$pr = 46.76 \times 10^{-6}/0.000003$$

$$pr = 15.59 \text{ kg uranium} = \text{US } \$7.08/\text{lb uranium}$$

$$= \text{US } \$8.35/\text{lb } U_3O_8.$$

The coefficients of eqn (8.132) were estimated by nonlinear regression analysis; this analysis indicated a coefficient of multiple determination of 0.99801. Fig. 8.15 taken from Brinck (1972) shows the predicted price lines and the actual prices (1971). Brinck observed that the prices of metals with the largest average size of ore deposits, like copper, appear to be underestimated, whereas the prices of lead and zinc which have smaller ore deposits appear to be overestimated.

8.14. Brinck's analysis of resources and potential supply

Subsequent to his demonstration of the lognormal model, Brinck adopted the logbinomial as an endow-ment model, and his later work employed the log-binomial in the economic analysis of metal resources and potential supply.

To facilitate the use of the logbinomial model, a computer program called IRIS was developed (De-Wolde and Brinck 1970), which manipulated the parameters of the model to describe combinations of deposit size and grade that give the same quantity of metal. Output from IRIS is plotted in such a manner that it shows the interrelationships of grade, metal, and cost of resources (see Fig. 8.16). This plot is known as the IRIS diagram. The vertical and hori-zontal scales of Fig. 8.16 are grade and quantity of copper endowment of the world, respectively. The upward sloping, slightly convex curves are the IRIS lines. These are lines of equal metal for combinations of grade and quantity of metallized rock. The U-shaped curves are constant-cost curves, which rep-resent exploration and exploitation costs for deposits having the size and grade characteristics indicated by the diagram. Costs were computed in accordance with the exploration-, capital-, and operating-cost relations in § 8.13.2.

Each IRIS line terminates at an intersection with a

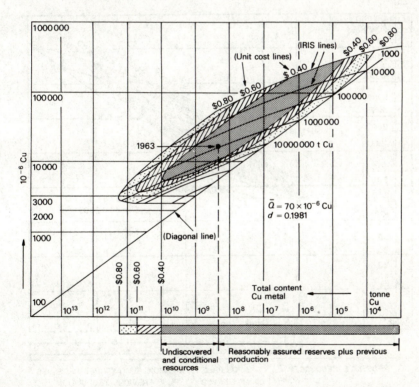

Fig. 8.16. World resources of copper. (From article 'MIMIC') by J. W. Brinck in *Eurospectra*. **X,** no. 2, June 1971.)

vertical line, a line which represents a quantity of metal. Projecting this point of termination to the vertical scale indicates the highest grade formed in the logbinomial expansion that gives that quantity of metal indicated on the horizontal scale. For example, the endowment in deposits having a grade of 4.1 per cent copper is approximately 10^6 tons of copper metal. There is only one deposit of this grade and size: tonnage of ore $= 24.4 \times 10^6$ tonnes at 4.1 per cent copper. For the same endowment of metal, but for an average grade of 2.82 per cent, there are 10 deposits, each having a size of 35.5×10^6 tons of ore (National Academy of Sciences 1975, pp. 137–9). In order to understand how these quantities and relationships are presented in the IRIS diagram, start with a potential supply of 1×10^6 tonnes; this quantity is located on the horizontal scale. Project this quantity upward along the vertical line to its intersection with the diagonal line. This intersection also is the intersection of an IRIS line of constant metal content of 1×10^6 tonnes of copper. Follow the IRIS line of 1×10^6 tonnes of copper to the left (sliding down the line) to its intersection with the vertical line

of 10^7. Then, project this intersection onto the vertical scale, the grade axis in parts per million (10^{-6}); this shows that the average grade of the deposits constituting the endowment of 1×10^7 tonnes of copper is 2.82 per cent copper. Each of these deposits contain 1×10^6 tonnes of copper. The number of these deposits is determined as

$$n = \frac{\text{tonnage of metal on abscissa}}{\text{tonnage for IRIS line}}$$

$$n = \frac{1 \times 10^7}{1 \times 10^6} = 10.$$

Thus, there are ten depostis of grade 2.82 per cent copper and each consisting of 35.5×10^6 tonnes of ore

$$35.5 \times 10^6 = \frac{1 \times 10^6}{0.0282}.$$

Of course, the total world copper endowment in deposits having a grade of 2.82 per cent and a size of 35.5×10^6 tonnes is 1×10^7 tonnes.

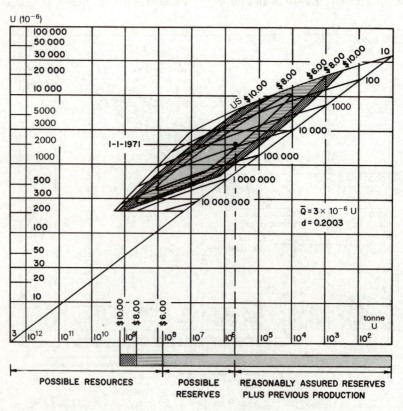

Fig. 8.17. World resource of uranium in the earth's crust to a depth of 2.5 km. (Source: J. W. Brinck 1971.)

One additional kind of information is plotted on the IRIS diagram, the cost at which the endowment is potential supply. In the example just provided, the intersection of the IRIS line 1×10^6 with 1×10^7 falls on the cost contour of $0.40/lb copper. Thus, according to Brinck's (1971) analysis, the cost at which this endowment constitutes potential supply is US $0.40/lb.

By locating the lower left-hand (toward the origin of the axes) extension of the shaded area and projecting this extremum to the horizontal axis, we find the maximum potential supply of copper at a cost (price) of US $0.40/lb copper ($1 \times 10^{10}$ tonnes) would occur if deposits contain approximately 4.7×10^6 tonnes of metal and have a grade of approximately 0.55 per cent copper. Similarly, Fig. 8.16 shows Brinck's estimation of the potential supply for costs per pound of copper of US $0.60 and US $0.80.

Fig. 8.17 is a graphic representation of Brinck's analysis by the program IRIS of world uranium resources. This analysis indicates that for the world the potential supply of uranium at a cost (price) in 1971 dollars of $6.00/lb U_3O_8 is 80×10^6 tonnes. At a price of US $10.00/lb U_3O_8, potential supply is approximately 1.5×10^9 tonnes [8].

References

Ahrens, L. H. (1953). A fundamental law of geochemistry. *Nature* **172** (4390), 1148.

—— (1954). The lognormal distribution of the elements. *Geochim. Cosmochim. Acta* **5,** 49–73; **6,** 121–31.

—— (1957). Lognormal-type distributions-III. *Geochim. Cosmochim. Acta* **11,** 205–12.

Aubrey, K. V. (1955). Frequency-distributions of elements in igneous rocks. *Geochim. Cosmochim. Acta* **8,** 83–9.

Bateman, A. (1950). *Economic mineral deposits.* John Wiley & Sons, New York.

Blais, R. A. and Carlier, P. A. (1968). *Applications of geostatistics in ore evaluation.* Canadian Institute of Mining and Metallurgy (CIM) Special Volume No. 9.

Brinck, J. W. (1967a). Note on the distribution and predictability of mineral resources. *Euratom 3461,* Brussels.

—— (1967b). Calculating the world's uranium resources. *Euratom Bull.* **VI,** (4).

—— (1971). MIMIC. *Eurospectra,* v. X, no. 2, Brussels.

—— (1972). Prediction of mineral resources and long-term price trends in the nonferrous metal mining industry. In *Section 4-Mineral deposits, twenty-fourth session International Geological Congress, Montreal* pp. 3–15. 24th International Geological Congress, Ottawa, Canada.

—— (1974). *The geochemical distribution of uranium as a primary criterion for the formation of ore deposits.* International Atomic Energy Agency, Symposium on the Formation of Uranium Deposits.

Cox, D. P., Schmidt, R. G., Vine, J. D., Kirkemo, H., Tourtelot, E. B., and Fleischer, M. (1973). Copper. In *United States mineral resources, Prof. Paper 820* (ed. D. A. Brobst and W. P. Pratt), pp. 163–90. US Geological Survey, Washington, DC.

DeWijs, H. J. (1951). Statistics of ore distribution, Part I. *J. R. Netherlands Geol. Min. Soc.,* Nov. 1951.

—— (1953). Statistics of ore distribution, Part II. *J. R. Netherlands Geol. Min. Soc.,* Jan. 1953.

DeWolde, H. I. and Brinck, J. W. (1970). The estimation of mineral resources by the computer program IRIS. *Euratom 4607e.* Joint Nuclear Research Centre, Ispra Establishment-Italy.

Ellis, J. R., Harris, D. P., and Van Wie, N. H. (1975). *A subjective probability appraisal of uranium resources in the State of New Mexico.* Open File Report GJO-110(76). US Energy Research and Development Adminstration, Grand Junction, Colorado.

Krige, D. G. (1952). A statistical analysis of some of the borehole values in the Orange Free State Goldfield. *J. Chem. Metallurg. Mining Soc. S. Afr.,* **53**(2), 47–64.

Matheron, G. (1971). *The theory of regionalized variables and its applications.* Les Cahiers du Centre de Morphalogie Mathematique di Fontainebleau, no. 5.

McKelvey, V. E. (1960). Relations of reserves of the elements to their crustal abundance. *Am. J. Sci.* **258-A** (Bradley volume), 234–41.

Miller, R. L. and Goldberg, E. D. (1955). The normal distribution in geochemistry. *Geochim. Cosmochim. Acta* **8,** 53–62.

National Academy of Sciences (1975). *Mineral resources and the environment,* pp. 137–9. Committee on Mineral Resources and the Environment, National Academy of Sciences, Washington, DC.

Singer, D. A., Cox, D. P., and Drew, L. J. (1975). *Grade and tonnage relationships among copper deposits, Professional Paper 907-A,* pp. A1–A11. US Geological Survey, Washington, DC.

Vistelius, A. B. (1960). The skew frequency distributions and the fundamental law of geochemistry. *J. Geol.* **68,** 1–22.

Wedow, H., Jr., Kilsgaard, T. H., Heyl, A. V., and Hall, R. B. (1973). Zinc. In *United States mineral resources, Professional Paper 820* (ed. D. A. Brobst and W. P. Pratt), pp. 697–722. US Geological Survey, Washington, DC.

Notes

1. See discussion of McKelvey's abundance–reserve equation in Chapter 4 'Deterministic geological methods'.

2. In this example grade is a percentage; therefore $\gamma = \ln\{(89/10^6) \times 100\}$.

3. This is the expectation of the logarithm of grade.

4. Mean (expectation) of logarithms of the population of grades.

5. In this example grade is a proportion.

6. In this example, the variate of the lognormal distribution is element concentration in parts per million (10^{-6}).

7. γ is the expectation for $\ln q$ where q is grade.

8. This quantity was not specifically reported by Brinck; it is an approximate quantity which was interpreted visually from the IRIS diagram.

9 UNIVARIATE LOGNORMAL CRUSTAL ABUNDANCE GEOSTATISTICAL MODELS OF MINERAL ENDOWMENT

9.1. Perspective and scope

The previous chapter documented the initial contribution of Brinck (1967) to the use of a lognormal crustal abundance geostatistical (CAG) model of mineral endowment. Brinck's later work replaced the lognormal model by a logbinomial distribution. In addition, by linking the logbinomial model to exploration and exploitation cost models, Brinck (1972) extended his work to the estimation of mineral resources and potential supply. Prompted by the desire to model costs more precisely, Drew (1977) replaced Brinck's logbinomial model by an independent bivariate distribution of deposit grade and tonnage. This model, referred to as the PAU model, constitutes a major departure from the initial crustal abundance concept of a univariate distribution of the concentration of an element, the concept identified by Ahrens (1953) and employed by Brinck in the development of his models. This departure by Drew (1977) raises questions that require considerable probing. Consequently, while historical sequence calls for examination of the PAU model in this chapter, that examination is deferred to Chapter 10, allowing examination in this chapter of models that are closely related to the basic theme demonstrated by Brinck.

9.2. The analysis by Agterberg and Divi of the mineral endowment of the Canadian Appalachian Region

9.2.1. General description of approach

Agterberg and Divi (1978) employed a lognormal model to represent separately the parent distributions of copper, lead, and zinc in the Canadian Appalachian Region. They employed the basic axiom of CAG models for the estimation of endowment

$$E_{q'} = \rho_{q'} \cdot W \cdot \bar{q}_{q'}, \qquad (9.1)$$

where W is the weight of crustal material in the region, q' is the cut-off grade,

$$\rho_{q'} = P(Q \geq q') = \int_{q'}^{\infty} \lambda(q) \, dq, \qquad (9.2)$$

$\lambda(q)$ is the probability density function for crustal grades, and $\bar{q}_{q'}$ is the average grade, given cut-off grade q'. Thus, $R_{q'}$, the amount of mineralized material in a region given a cut-off grade q', is defined by W, q', and $\lambda(q)$

$$R_{q'} = W \cdot \int_{q'}^{\infty} \lambda(q) \, dq.$$

And, given $R_{q'}$, endowment $E_{q'}$ is determined by $\bar{q}_{q'}$

$$E_{q'} = R_{q'} \cdot \bar{q}_{q'}. \qquad (9.3)$$

Agterberg and Divi selected the lognormal distribution for $\lambda(q)$. Their approach to estimation of the unknown parameters was similar to that of Brinck (1967) in that, given the lack of geochemical sample data, they employed the inventory of cumulative production and reserves in the estimation of the unknown parameters of the lognormal distribution. However, their approach differs from Brinck's in two important regards

1. Crustal abundance is equated to mean crustal grade, instead of modal crustal grade.
2. σ, the logarithmic standard deviation and a parameter of the lognormal distribution, was estimated only after explicitly analysing how estimates of σ vary with cut-off grade.

With respect to the second of these differences, Agterberg and Divi reasoned that $R_{q'}$ is better known for high values of q' than for low ones. Therefore, they based their estimate of σ upon the pattern of variation in estimates of σ with cut-off grades. In contrast, Brinck selected a single cut-off grade, that 'typical' of the current operations, and employed the associated measure of R to estimate σ.

9.2.2. Specific relations

Consider the proposition

$$P(Q > q) = P(X > x) = \frac{1}{\sigma(2\pi)^{\frac{1}{2}}} \int_{x}^{\infty} \exp\left(-\frac{(t-\mu)^2}{2\sigma^2}\right) dt, \qquad (9.4)$$

where $x = \ln q$, and μ and σ^2, the parameters of the normal distribution, are the mean and variance of x. Then, since X is normally distributed, having parameters of μ and σ, $Z = x - \mu/\sigma$ is normally distributed having parameters of 0 and 1: $Z \sim N(0, 1)$.

From lognormal theory, the expectation for Q is defined as

$$E[Q] = e^{\mu + \sigma^2/2}. \tag{9.5}$$

Suppose that we equate crustal abundance to $E[Q]$, the expected value for crustal grade. Let us designate the logarithm of crustal abundance as A

$$A = \ln\{E[Q]\} = \ln[\text{crustal abundance}].$$

Then from (9.5),

$$A = \ln\{E[Q]\} = \mu + \sigma^2/2 \tag{9.6}$$

and

$$\mu = A - \sigma^2/2. \tag{9.7}$$

Since by definition the standardized variable $Z = (x - \mu)/\sigma$, it follows that

$$\sigma Z = x - \mu. \tag{9.8}$$

Substituting the definition of μ from (9.7) into (9.8), we have

$$\sigma Z = x - A + \sigma^2/2. \tag{9.9}$$

Rewriting (9.9),

$$\frac{\sigma^2}{2} - \sigma Z = A - x$$

and

$$\sigma^2 - 2\sigma Z = 2A - 2x. \tag{9.10}$$

Completing the square of (9.10),

$$Z^2 + \sigma^2 - 2\sigma Z = Z^2 + 2A - 2x$$

or

$$(Z - \sigma)^2 = Z^2 + 2A - 2x. \tag{9.11}$$

Agterberg and Divi (1978) provide the following solutions to (9.11)

$$\sigma = Z - (Z^2 + 2A - 2x)^{\frac{1}{2}}, \quad \text{for } Z > \sigma \tag{9.12}$$

and

$$\sigma = Z + (Z^2 + 2A - 2x)^{\frac{1}{2}}, \quad \text{for } Z \leq \sigma. \tag{9.13}$$

Given that an acceptable measure of crustal abundance is available, and given a specified cut-off grade, eqns (9.12) and (9.13) show the unknown σ to be a function of the standard score Z. Thus, if a value for Z can be estimated, eqns (9.12) and (9.13) can be employed to provide an estimate of σ. And, given $\hat{\sigma}$ and A, μ is estimated by eqn (9.7). Clearly,

the estimation of σ depends critically upon the existence of an estimate of Z. Therefore, let us examine the means for obtaining such an estimate.

Since Z is a standardized score for the normal probability distribution, it is related to a probability. The procedure employed by Agterberg and Divi is the same as that demonstrated by Brinck (1967), namely to identify a cut-off grade q' and the value for $R_{q'}$, (cumulative production plus reserves), given q'. Then,

$$P(Q \geq q') \approx \frac{R_{q'}}{W} \Rightarrow Z_{q'}. \tag{9.14}$$

$Z_{q'}$ can be determined by consulting normal probability tables or by use of the complementary error function, erfc (Agterberg and Divi 1978, p. 239). Fig. 9.1 is a graph of this function. Then, given q', $Z_{q'}$, and A, the lognormal parameters σ and μ are estimated from eqns (9.7), (9.12), and (9.13).

9.2.3. Estimates

Agterberg and Divi developed crustal-abundance models for copper, lead, and zinc. Only their model for copper is described here. The data consisted of cumulative production, reserves, and average grade for 127 copper deposits in the Canadian Appalachian Region.

The tonnages and grades of the 127 copper deposits were processed to provide the first two columns of Table 9.1. The grades of column (1) are cut-off grades ($q'_i, i = 1, 2, \ldots, 7$). Column (2) states the quantity of known mineralized material ($R_{q'_i}$) for each of the 7 cut-off grades. Agterberg and Divi calculated the weight of the earth's crust in this region to a depth of 200 metres to be 0.1954×10^{15} tonnes (Agterberg and Divi 1978, p. 238). Thus, by dividing $R_{q'_i}$ by this quantity, the probabilities of column (3) are obtained. These probabilities were evaluated by the erfc function to give Z values for each cut-off grade. For example, the probability for cut-off grade of 5.0 per cent is approximately

$$\frac{R_{5.0}}{W} = \frac{0.198 \times 10^6}{0.1954 \times 10^{15}} = 1.013 \times 10^{-9} \approx 1.0 \times 10^{-9}.$$

For this probability, the erfc function gives a Z value of 6.0.

Agterberg and Divi took 63×10^{-6} (Tan and Chi-Lung, 1965) as the crustal abundance of copper. An estimate of the standard deviation for a cut-off grade of 5 per cent—the first estimate in Table 9.1—is obtained by substituting $\ln(63)$ for A, $\ln(50\,000)$ for

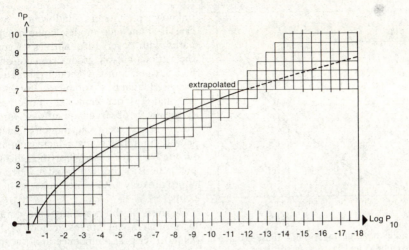

Fig. 9.1. The complimentary error function (erfc). (Source: Brinck 1967.)

x (5 per cent $= 50\,000 \times 10^{-6}$), and 6.0 for Z in eqn (9.12)

$$\hat{\sigma} = 6.0 - [36 + 2 \ln (63) - 2 \ln (50\,000)]^{\frac{1}{2}}$$

$$\hat{\sigma} = 6.0 - (36 + 8.2863 - 21.6396)$$

$$\hat{\sigma} = 6.0 - 4.76 = 1.24 \, [1].$$

Employing $\hat{\sigma} = 1.24$ and $A = \ln (63)$, μ is estimated by equation (9.7) to be [2]

$$\hat{\mu} = 4.1431 - (1.24)^2/2$$

$$\hat{\mu} = 4.1431 - 0.7688 = \underline{3.3743}.$$

Column (4) of Table 9.1 shows the estimates of σ for each of seven different cut-off grades. Agterberg and Divi reasoned that the estimates for σ were

similar for cut-off grades 1, 2, 3, and 5.0 per cent; consequently, the average of the four estimates was selected as the preferred estimate $\hat{\sigma} = 1.236$. Given $\hat{\sigma} = 1.236$, from eqn (9.7) we calculate [2] that $\hat{\mu} = 3.3793$. Thus, employing the approach of Agterberg and Divi, the parameters of the crustal-abundance geostatistical copper model for the Canadian Appalachian Region are

$$W = 0.1954 \times 10^{15} \text{ tonnes,}$$

$$\hat{\mu} = 3.3793,$$

$$\hat{\sigma} = 1.236.$$

With these parameters, the copper endowment of the region can be computed for any specified cut-off

TABLE 9.1. *Copper data, calculations, and endowment estimates.* (*Source:* Agterberg and Divi 1978, p. 237.)

(1) Cut-off grade q' (per cent Cu)	(2) Observed tonnage $R_{q'}$ (metric tons)	(3) Probability $P(Q > q') = R_{q'}/W$	(4) $\hat{\sigma}$	(5) Average grade $\bar{q}_{q'}$ (per cent Cu)	(6) Model estimates $\hat{R}_{q'}$ (metric tons)	(7) Model estimates $\hat{\bar{q}}_{q'}$ (per cent Cu)	(8) Model estimates $\hat{E}_{q'} = \hat{R}_{q'} \cdot \hat{\bar{q}}_{q'}$ (metric tons)	(9) Observed metal (metric tons)
5.0	0.198×10^6	1.013×10^{-9}	1.244	9.22	0.169×10^6	6.25	0.106×10^5	0.183×10^5
3.0	3.015×10^6	1.543×10^{-8}	1.256	3.73	2.003×10^6	3.81	0.763×10^5	0.112×10^6
2.0	13.466×10^6	6.892×10^{-8}	1.239	2.71	12.853×10^6	2.45	0.315×10^6	0.365×10^6
1.0	0.148×10^9	7.574×10^{-7}	1.204	1.53	0.232×10^9	1.25	0.290×10^7	0.226×10^7
0.5	0.197×10^9	1.008×10^{-6}	1.033	1.36	3.140×10^9	0.68	0.214×10^8	0.268×10^7
0.3	0.638×10^9	3.265×10^{-6}	0.770	0.72	17.662×10^9	0.42	0.742×10^8	0.459×10^7
0.2	0.661×10^9	3.383×10^{-6}	0.684	0.70	62.071×10^9	0.29	0.180×10^9	0.463×10^7
0.0	0.690×10^9	3.531×10^{-6}	—	0.68	0.1954×10^{15}	0.0063	0.123×10^{11}	0.469×10^7

$\hat{\sigma} = 1.236$ (bracketing the 1.244, 1.256, 1.239, 1.204 values).

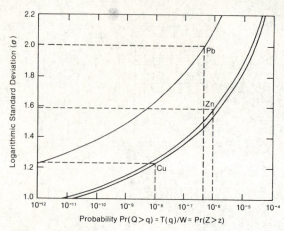

Fig. 9.2. Relationship between logarithmic (base e) standard deviation σ and $Pr\,(Q > q)$ for fixed crustal-abundance values and with minimal copper, lead, and zinc grades equal to 3, 3, and 5 per cent, respectively. (After Agterberg and Divi 1978, p. 241.)

grade. Columns (6), (7), and (8) of Table 9.1 show the estimates of $R_{q'}$, $\bar{q}_{q'}$, and $E_{q'} = \bar{q}_{q'} \cdot R_{q'}$ for each of the seven cut-off grades used to estimate the

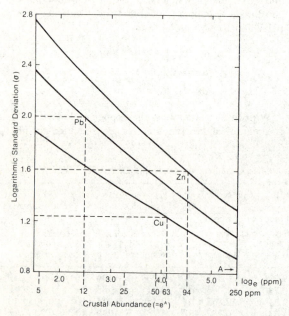

Fig. 9.3. Relationship between logarithmic (base e) standard deviation σ and crustal abundance for fixed values of $T_e(q)$ with copper, lead, and zinc grades equal to 3, 3, and 5 per cent, respectively. (After: Agterberg and Divi 1978, p. 242.)

unknown parameters. Endowment estimates by the crustal-abundance model, column (8), can be compared with observed quantities of copper metal for the various cut-off grades: for cut-off grades of 3.0 and 5.0 per cent Cu, model estimates are less than observed quantities of metal; for cut-off grades of 2.0 and 1.0 per cent Cu, model estimates agree closely with observed quantities; for cut-off grades below 1.0 per cent Cu, model estimates exceed observed quantities by ever-increasing amounts as cut-off grade is decreased. For the cut-off grade of 0.2 per cent Cu, the estimated copper endowment is approximately 40 times observed quantities of copper.

Because of the ways that the parameters of the lognormal model are estimated, both the selected value for crustal abundance and the specified weight of the earth's crust within the region affect parameter estimates. Consequently, questions arise naturally about the sensitivity of estimates of the parameters to these values. Figs. 9.2 and 9.3 were presented by Agterberg and Divi (1978) as a means of exploring this sensitivity. They concluded that estimates of σ are not highly sensitive to values of crustal abundance and the weight of the earth's crust; however, they cautioned that all parameters are interrelated and that small variations in σ may have a large effect on endowment estimates by the model.

9.3. US uranium endowment [3]

9.3.1. *Estimates by the approach of Agterberg and Divi*

The main objective of this section is to estimate the U_3O_8 endowment of the United States using the approach demonstrated by Agterberg and Divi (1978) for base metals of the Canadian Appalachian region. The data required to perform the exercise consist of a cut-off grade, the cumulative tonnage containing grades above the cut-off grade, and the average grade of this tonnage. This information is published by the Department of Energy (US DOE) of the United States under the label of pre-production inventory (i.e. uranium originally present) and can be used for this exercise.

Initially, it is necessary to estimate W, the weight of the segment of the earth's crust represented by the pre-production inventory

$$W = S \cdot h \cdot \lambda,$$

where W is the weight of the segment of the crust being analysed, S is the surface of the region, h the average depth of bedrock in which the majority of deposits have been discovered, and λ is the average rock density. For the conterminous United States, S equals $7.82 \times 10^6 \, \text{km}^2$; the average density ($\lambda$) of uranium-hosting rock was calculated as $2.59 \, \text{g/cm}^3$; and h was initially set to 600 ft. The total weight W of this environment is 4.06×10^{15} tonnes.

The results obtained when eqns (9.7), (9.12), and (9.13) were applied to the uranium data are presented in Table 9.2. Column (4) of this table exhibits the standard deviations calculated for each cut-off grade; for the higher cut-off grades, the estimated values for σ are quite similar, suggesting that all describe the same distribution. However, as grades are lowered, possibly below 0.12 per cent, there is a departure from this consistency. Thus, following Agterberg and Divi (1978), the averages of the standard deviations for the higher grades are considered good approximations to the true value; the average standard deviation for grades in the range 0.12–0.25 per cent U_3O_8 is 1.3561.

Once the parameters of the lognormal distribution have been defined, the calculation of tonnages above a specified cut-off grade is straightforward; Table 9.3 presents these results. For purposes of comparison, this table also provides the quantities reported by US DOE. These data show that the model underestimates the inventory tonnages above the cut-off grade of 0.18 per cent U_3O_8. It is noteworthy that underestimation of metal endowment for high grades also characterized the estimates of copper made by the model of Agterberg and Divi (1978). However, when grade is lowered to 0.12 per cent, the cumulative tonnage estimated by the model is already almost $2\frac{1}{2}$ times more than that reported by US DOE. At the lowest grade considered 0.01 per cent, the model estimates a cumulative tonnage of 2.2×10^{12} tonnes of U_3O_8, or more than 700 times the quantity re-

TABLE 9.2. *Standard deviations of uranium inventory grade categories calculated using Agterberg's endowment model. (Source: Harris et al. 1981.)*

(1) Cut-off grade q' (per cent U_3O_8)	(2) Observed tonnage of material $R_{q'}$ ($\times 10^6$ tons)	(3) Observed average grade $\bar{q}_{q'}$ (per cent U_3O_8)	(4) Estimates of the logarithmic standard deviation $\hat{\sigma}$
0.25	84	0.43	1.4092
0.24	90	0.42	1.4033
0.23	97	0.40	1.3974
0.22	105	0.39	1.3911
0.21	114	0.37	1.3849
0.20	123	0.36	1.3772
0.19	134	0.35	1.3700
0.18	147	0.33	1.3620
0.17	161	0.32	1.3533
0.16	177	0.30	1.3441
0.15	196	0.29	1.3338
0.14	217	0.27	1.3228
0.13	243	0.26	1.3109
0.12	274	0.24	1.2980
0.11	310	0.23	1.2835†
0.10	353	0.21	1.2672
0.09	407	0.20	1.2486
0.08	474	0.18	1.2281
0.07	562	0.16	1.2039
0.06	677	0.15	1.1752
0.05	838	0.13	1.1406
0.04	1069	0.11	1.0968
0.03	1429	0.09	1.0387
0.02	2068	0.07	0.9535
0.01	3128	0.05	0.7980

† Average of 15 values (0.11–0.25 per cent) = 1.3561.

TABLE 9.3. *Calculated tonnages and average grades above specified cut-off grades of US uranium resources, estimated using Agterberg's endowment model.* (*Source: Harris et al. 1981.*)

(1) Cut-off grade q' (per cent U_3O_8)	(2) Observed tonnage of material $R_{q'}$ ($\times 10^6$ tons)	(3) Observed tonnage of U_3O_8 ($\times 10^6$ tons)	(4) Observed average grade $\bar{q}_{q'}$ (per cent U_3O_8)	(5) Model estimates of material $\hat{R}_{q'}$ ($\times 10^6$ tons)	(6) Model average grade $\hat{\bar{q}}_{q'}$ (per cent U_3O_8)	(7) Model endowment $\hat{E}_{q'} = \hat{R}_{q'} \cdot \hat{\bar{q}}_{q'}$ ($\times 10^6$ tons U_3O_8)
0.25>	84	0.361	0.43	35	0.462	0.16
0.24	90	0.378	0.42	42	0.443	0.19
0.23	97	0.388	0.40	50	0.424	0.21
0.22	105	0.410	0.39	60	0.405	0.24
0.21	114	0.422	0.37	73	0.387	0.28
0.20	123	0.433	0.36	90	0.368	0.33
0.19	134	0.469	0.35	111	0.350	0.39
0.18	147	0.485	0.33	138	0.331	0.46
0.17	161	0.515	0.32	175	0.312	0.55
0.16	177	0.531	0.30	224	0.293	0.66
0.15	196	0.568	0.29	294	0.274	0.81
0.14	217	0.586	0.27	383	0.256	0.98
0.13	243	0.632	0.26	515	0.237	1.22
0.12	274	0.656	0.24	704	0.219	1.54
0.11	310	0.713	0.23	985	0.200	1.97
0.10	353	0.741	0.21	1416	0.182	2.58
0.09	407	0.814	0.20	2110	0.163	3.43
0.08	474	0.853	0.18	3253	0.145	4.72
0.07	562	0.899	0.16	5307	0.127	6.74
0.06	677	1.016	0.15	9215	0.108	9.95
0.05	838	1.089	0.13	17000	0.090	15.30
0.04	1069	1.176	0.11	36000	0.070	25.20
0.03	1429	1.286	0.09	93000	0.050	46.50
0.02	2068	1.448	0.07	324000	0.030	97.20
0.01	3128	1.564	0.05	2206000	0.018	397.10

ported by US DOE. The estimated average grades of the calculated tonnages are lower as the amount of material increases; for example, the average grade reported for material having grades above the cut-off grade of 0.05 per cent is 0.13 per cent, whereas the calculated one is only 0.09 per cent.

In this exercise, and the demonstration by Agterberg, the estimate of the standard deviation that was used is the average value of the standard deviations computed for the higher grades. The individual standard deviations for each cut-off grade are calculated from the specific values of the variables Z, x, and A. The choice of values for Z and A cannot be considered as the exact values either. Although no sensitivity analysis was performed in the uranium analysis, Agterberg and Divi (1978) document the fact that the estimate of the standard deviation by their approach is not sensitive to 'rather large changes in the value of depth or A,' at least when these variables are modified individually. Neverthe-

less, the four variables, σ, Z, x, and A, are all interrelated, and it is observed that even a small change in σ results in a large change in $P(Q > q)$ and, therefore, in the endowment estimate.

9.3.2. *Estimation of an asymptotic σ, a modification of the approach of Agterberg and Divi*

Concepts

Agterberg and Divi's basic proposition was that because of less complete exploration for the lower-grade deposits, estimates of σ for these grades will fluctuate. Therefore, Agterberg and Divi examined the estimates of σ for a pattern of stability of estimates for high cut-off grades and a break in this stability as cut-off grade is lowered. This is a reasonable procedure. Let us carry the reasoning one step further. Suppose that exploration is progressively and systematically less thorough for successively lower cut-off grades. Such a pattern would result in recorded measures of $R_{q'}$ that are progressively less than they should be for the lognormal law. Continuing this reasoning suggests that if values of $R_{q'}$ are progressively less than they should be for the lower cut-off grades, the probabilities represented by $R_{q'}/W$ also are less. And, if values of $R_{q'}/W$ are less than they should be, so also are the Z values. For a given and constant value of crustal abundance, the effect of progressive bias to small values of Z as cut-off grade is decreased is that the resulting estimates of σ are progressively negatively biased (tend to progressively smaller values). Given these circumstances, the preferred estimate of σ would be that value to which the estimates tend as cut-off grade *increases*. In the real world, grade is only one of many variables that affects the economics of exploration and mining; consequently, estimates of σ for successively lower cut-off grades may exhibit some random variation. Even so, an overall asymptotic trend may exist; and, given that it does, there seems to be good argument for employing it to estimate σ.

Estimation

Fig. 9.4 shows the estimated standard deviations associated with each cut-off grade. This figure suggests that as the value of the cut-off grade increases, the associated estimate of σ approaches asymptotically the true value of σ. If this is so, then an alternative to averaging the estimates of σ for the higher cut-off grades is to estimate the asymptotic value. A mathematical curve that exhibits a pattern similar to that of the estimates of σ, shown in Fig. 9.4, is the modified exponential: $\sigma = \sigma^* + ab^{q'}$, $a > 0$,

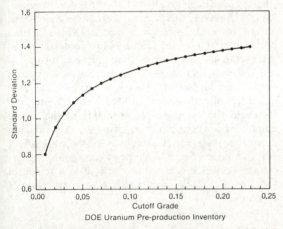

Fig. 9.4. Estimated standard deviations calculated using Agterberg's endowment model—US uranium inventory grade categories. (Source: Harris *et al.* 1981.)

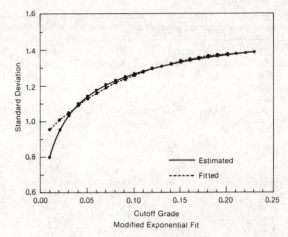

Fig. 9.5. Modified exponential curve fitted to estimated standard deviations of US uranium inventory grade categories. (Source: Harris *et al.* 1981.)

$0 < b < 1$. Thus, as q' approaches infinity, σ approaches σ^*. Fig. 9.5 shows the modified exponential fitted to the standard deviation estimates. The asymptotic value of the equation of this fitted function is 1.437, a value slightly larger than 1.3561, which was obtained by averaging the standard deviations of the high cut-off grades.

Cumulative tonnages and their average grades were calculated using the asymptotic standard deviation; these results are shown in Table 9.4. It is interesting to note that no underestimation is evident: the calculated tonnages are all greater than the observed ones, in amounts that vary from 0.55 times for the 0.25 per cent cut-off grade to 3.1 times for 0.18 per cent, and to 70 times for 0.12 per cent. The calculated average grades for these tonnages are considerably below those reported by DOE. The average grades estimated using the asymptotic variance do not match the DOE grades nearly as well as do those estimated using the averaged variance.

Column (7) of Table 9.4 shows the quantity of U_3O_8 implied by the endowment model estimates of mineralized material $R_{q'}$ and average grade, $\bar{q}_{q'}$: $E_{q'} = R_{q'} \cdot \bar{q}_{q'}$.

9.3.3. A comparison of estimates

Estimates of U_3O_8 endowment using models based upon an averaging of selected estimates of σ and an asymptotic σ are plotted in Fig. 9.6, as also is the DOE inventory of U_3O_8. Fig. 9.6 shows that the endowment model based upon the asymptotic standard deviation has the desirable property that for all

TABLE 9.4. *Calculated tonnages and average grades above specified cut-off grades of US uranium resources, estimated using the asymptotic value of the standard deviation. (Source: Harris et al. 1981.)*

(1) Cut-off grade q' (per cent U_3O_8)	(2) Observed tonnage of material $R_{q'}$ ($\times 10^6$ tons)	(3) Observed tonnage of U_3O_8 ($\times 10^6$ tons)	(4) Observed average grade $\bar{q}_{q'}$ (per cent U_3O_8)	(5) Model estimates of material $\hat{R}_{q'}$ ($\times 10^6$ tons)	(6) Model average grade $\hat{\bar{q}}_{q'}$ (per cent U_3O_8)	(7) Model endowment $\hat{E}_{q'} = \hat{R}_{q'} \cdot \hat{\bar{q}}_{q'}$ ($\times 10^6$ tons U_3O_8)
0.25 >	84	0.361	0.43	136	0.332	0.452
0.24	90	0.378	0.42	159	0.320	0.509
0.23	97	0.388	0.40	187	0.307	0.574
0.22	105	0.410	0.39	223	0.294	0.656
0.21	114	0.422	0.37	265	0.281	0.745
0.20	123	0.433	0.36	319	0.268	0.855
0.19	134	0.469	0.35	385	0.256	0.916
0.18	147	0.485	0.33	473	0.243	1.150
0.17	161	0.515	0.32	585	0.230	1.346
0.16	177	0.531	0.30	731	0.217	1.586
0.15	196	0.568	0.29	925	0.204	1.887
0.14	217	0.586	0.27	1188	0.191	2.269
0.13	243	0.632	0.26	1553	0.178	2.764
0.12	274	0.656	0.24	2068	0.164	3.392
0.11	310	0.713	0.23	2799	0.151	4.226
0.10	353	0.741	0.21	3891	0.138	5.370
0.09	407	0.814	0.20	5600	0.125	7.000
0.08	474	0.853	0.18	8293	0.112	9.288
0.07	562	0.899	0.16	13000	0.098	12.740
0.06	677	1.016	0.15	21000	0.085	17.850
0.05	838	1.089	0.13	38000	0.071	26.980
0.04	1069	1.176	0.11	76000	0.058	40.410
0.03	1429	1.286	0.09	177000	0.044	77.880
0.02	2068	1.448	0.07	551000	0.030	165.300
0.01	3128	1.564	0.05	3180000	0.0161	511.980

cut-off grades, estimated U_3O_8 exceeds the known inventory. Inasmuch as exploration for uranium in the US is far from exhaustive, this is a desirable result. Estimates of U_3O_8 endowment by the model based upon the average of estimates of σ for the high cut-off grades does not possess this property. Endowment estimates for cut-off grades in excess of 0.175 are less than the known inventory, which is a disturbing result [4]. By this criteria of evaluation, the model based upon the asymptotic σ is superior to that based upon the average of selected estimates of σ. While the foregoing seems a reasonable assessment, endowment estimates by the asymptotic model may be more difficult to accept than those by the other model because they are so much greater and exceed the known inventory by rather large quantities for subeconomic grades. Generally, the large estimates of endowment that are produced by CAG models have been a barrier to the acceptance by many geologists of these models. In part, this may result from failure by the geologist to differentiate

endowment (that which exists) from potential supply (that which can be discovered and produced economically). However, there are concerns of a more basic nature to some geologists, one of which is that crustal material having grades below some threshold value consists of common rock silicates, instead of ore minerals, in which the metal can be extracted only at very high costs. Those who attribute the large quantities of endowment to this effect may find little solace in the even greater estimates of the model employing an asymptotic σ. Even so, this model is more appealing, because it allows for the existence of yet undiscovered U_3O_8 at the higher grades, a circumstance which is certain to prevail in a region of the size of the US and which is not exhaustively explored.

9.4. An important qualification

The approach to the estimation of σ employed by Agterberg and Divi (1978)—average of estimates of

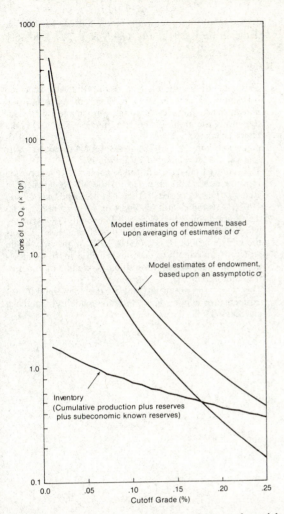

Fig. 9.6. Comparison of estimates by lognormal models of uranium endowment and uranium inventory.

quantities of mineralized material for lower grades reflect the left-hand side of the second mode. If that were so, then the practice of averaging or of seeking the asymptotic σ, as demonstrated in this section, is improper, for both demonstrations employed the lognormal law. So far, no one has demonstrated by data the existence of a bimodal distribution, but, it is likely that no one yet has had sufficient data to perform a credible test of this hypothesis.

9.5. Endowment is not resources or potential supply

It has been stated that the lognormal distribution is a widely accepted model of the distribution of grades within the earth's crust. In this case, this model has been used to represent the endowment of uranium in the US crust, given a cut-off grade of 0.01 per cent U_3O_8. When a crustal-abundance model is employed to make inferences about the amount of the estimated endowment that can actually be found and extracted at a profit for a given set of economic conditions, factors beyond those captured in the crustal-abundance model must be considered. Changing economic conditions do not affect the existing endowment, but they do affect resources and potential supply. In response to changing economics and technology, new modes of occurrence become recognized; greater depths are reached; and previously subeconomic grades of known modes of occurrence become economic. When the objective of the resource analysis is to estimate those resources available for a given set of economic circumstances, the endowment base becomes an exogenous factor to the problem, and a linkage between the physical occurrences (endowment) in the earth's crust and the economics of resources and potential supply must be defined. This task then becomes two separate tasks

1. Estimation of the natural availability (endowment) of uranium in the earth's crust,
2. Describing the economic circumstances required to find and extract concentrations having certain characteristics.

σ for high cut-off grades—and that employed by Harris *et al.* (1981)—an asymptotic σ—rests upon the assumptions that grades are continuous and that they are distributed according to a unimodal (lognormal) distribution. As indicated in § 9.3.2 ('Concepts'), given a measure of crustal abundance, the tendency to smaller estimates of σ as cut-off grade is decreased is equivalent to the tendency to smaller quantities of mineralized material than expected, given the *quantities observed for higher grades and the assumption of the lognormal law.* An obvious competing hypothesis is that the distribution of crustal grades is bimodal and that the less than expected

References

Agterberg, F. P. and Divi, S. R. (1978). A statistical model for the distribution of copper, lead, and zinc in the Canadian Appalachian Region. *Econ. Geol.* **73,** 230–45.

Ahrens, L. H. (1953). A fundamental law of geochemistry. *Nature* **172** (4390), 1148.

Brinck, J. W. (1967). Note on the distribution and predictability of mineral resources. *Euratom 3461*, Brussels.

—— (1972). Prediction of mineral resources and long-term price trends in the nonferrous metal mining industry. In *Section 4-Mineral deposits, twenty-fourth session International Geological Congress, Montreal.*, pp. 3–15. 24th International Geological Congress, Ottawa, Canada.

Drew, M. W. (1977). US uranium deposits—a geostatistical model. *Resources Policy* **3** (1), 60–70.

Harris, D. P., Ortiz-Vértiz, S. R., Chavez, M. L., and Agbolosoo, E. K. (1981). *Systems and economics for the estimation of uranium potential supply.* Report prepared for US Department of Energy, Grand Junction Office, Colorado, Subcontract No. 78-238-E.

Tan, L. and Chi-Lung, Y. (1965). Abundance of chemical elements in the earth's crust and its major tectonic units. *Acta Geol. Sinica*, **45**, 82–91. [English translation, *Int. Geol. Rev.* **12**, 778–86.]

Notes

1. This value differs slightly from 1.244, the value reported by Agterberg and Divi (1978); this difference is insignificant since these calculations were made by the author using the graph of the erfc function (Fig. 9.1) and a hand calculator.

2. Agterberg and Divi (1978) do not report estimates of μ; this value was calculated by the author.

3. The material described in this section was first reported in a research report prepared for the US Department of Energy (Harris, Ortiz-Vértiz, Chavez, and Agbolosoo 1981). This material is also part of a forthcoming Ph.D. dissertation by Luis Chavez, University of Arizona, which explores in depth CAG models and also extends the initial work of Brinck (1967, 1972) to provide 'grade structure' and depth to deposits which comprise endowment, thus facilitating the credible modelling of exploration and mining.

4. This same feature characterizes the lognormal CAG estimates for copper, lead, and zinc made by Agterberg and Divi (1978).

10 THE BIVARIATE LOGNORMAL DEPOSIT MODEL OF PAU—A CRUSTAL-ABUNDANCE GEOSTATISTICAL MODEL

10.1. General perspective

The Programmes Analysis Unit (PAU) of Great Britain has developed a very interesting, comprehensive model (Drew 1977) for the description of mineral resources. This section explores PAU's deposit (endowment) model, which is a submodel of the resource model.

The approach of PAU is based upon the assumption that the entire crust of a region is composed of a collection of deposits of varying sizes and grades. Further, this collection of deposits is described by a bivariate, independent lognormal distribution of size and grade.

Since the crust of the earth to some specified depth in the region of interest is considered to be totally comprised of deposits, the expected quantity of mineralized material R occurring in the region is computed by multiplying a probability ρ by the weight of the crust W

$$R = \rho \cdot W.$$

The probability ρ is the probability for the occurrence of deposits having grades of at least q and tonnage of at least t

$$\rho = P(Q \geq q, T \geq t).$$

The PAU model defines $P(Q \geq q, T \geq t)$ by a bivariate lognormal probability distribution having grade parameters of μ_x and σ_x^2 and tonnage parameters of μ_y and σ_y^2 where $x = \ln q$ and $y = \ln t$. Furthermore, the assumption is made by PAU that a measure of crustal abundance is a reasonable measure of the average concentration γ_q of an element in the crust. This measure is related to the mean and variance of the lognormal grade distribution, μ_x and σ_x^2, respectively, according to the equation

$$\gamma_q = e^{\mu_x + \sigma_x^2/2}$$

or

$$\mu_x = \ln \gamma_q - \sigma_x^2/2.$$

Thus, given crustal abundance γ_q, μ_x is dependent solely upon the variance σ_x^2: Knowledge of σ_x^2 is knowledge of μ_x, given γ_q.

Initially, PAU based its estimate of σ_x^2 upon the coefficient of mineralizability developed by Brinck (1967) in his crustal-abundance geostatistical model. Subsequently, PAU concluded that estimation of the coefficient of mineralizability by the method described by Brinck for large regions for which geochemical data were not available was based upon a questionable assumption: all deposits in the region of interest which have grades and sizes making them economic to produce have been discovered. Consequently, PAU developed an alternative method for estimating σ_x. Conceptually, this alternative method is more appealing than that based upon Brinck's coefficient of mineralizability, because the only assumption required is that the data on economic deposits constitute a representative sample of deposits in the truncated part of the bivariate population. Comments in this section apply only to this modified (alternative) model.

Stated in its most general and elementary form, PAU's approach to estimating the unknown parameters, σ_x, μ_y, and σ_y is to base these estimates upon statistics on the average grade $\bar{q}$, average tonnage $\bar{t}$, and average metal content $\bar{m}$ of known exploitable and exploited deposits. However, PAU recognized that these statistics are biased estimators of the unknown parameters because of the 'filtering' effect of economics: statistics reflect only those deposits which have been economic to explore for and to produce. Using these statistics would tend to overstate the values of the parameters μ_x and μ_y and to understate σ_x and σ_y.

In statistical jargon, the statistics represent a bivariate population which has been truncated by a cost surface. The approach described by PAU requires specification of the cost surface so that its effects can be explicitly accounted for in estimating the desired parameters from the available statistics. Simply stated, the cost surface defines the region of the population of deposits from which the data originated and which gives the statistics, $\bar{q}$, $\bar{t}$, and $\bar{m}$. The parameters of the full (untruncated) population are estimated by determining those values of μ_x, μ_y, σ_x, and σ_y such that the expectations (averages) for Q,

T, and M of the truncated theoretical distribution agree with the statistics for known deposits.

Determining the unknown parameters of the bivariate distribution requires integration of truncated lognormal probability functions, a task that cannot be performed directly because of the functional form of the normal probability density function (p.d.f.). The approach used for solution is to manipulate the expressions under the integrals to as useful a form as possible and then to solve for the parameters by numerical approximation methods.

10.2. Demonstration of concepts

10.2.1. A simpler model

In order to demonstrate the concepts of the PAU model and the approach to estimation, let us depart from the specifics of tonnage and grade and examine an analogous situation in which the mathematics are more manageable. Consider a product called Z which is marketed in units of Z, but which, as it occurs in nature in its raw form, is described in terms of characteristics X_1 and X_2. Let us suppose that the probability for Z in its raw form is described by two statistically independent probability distributions of the simple exponential variety

$$\gamma(x_1) = \alpha e^{-\alpha x_1} \quad 0 \le x_1 \le \infty, \quad (10.1)$$

$$\lambda(x_2) = \beta e^{-\beta x_2} \quad 0 \le x_2 \le \infty. \quad (10.2)$$

It follows from the independence of X_1 and X_2 that their joint occurrence, which is the occurrence of Z in raw form, is the product of γ and λ

$$\phi(x_1, x_2) = \gamma(x_1) \cdot \lambda(x_2),$$

or

$$\phi(x_1, x_2) = \alpha \beta e^{-\alpha x_1 - \beta x_2}. \quad (10.3)$$

Let us suppose that the cost of producing a marketable unit of Z is measured in US dollars per pound of Z and is a function of the characteristics X_1 and X_2

$$C = b_0 - b_1 x_1 - b_2 x_2, \quad (10.4)$$

where C is in dollars/lb of Z, b_0 is a fixed cost component, b_1, b_2 are coefficients which reflect the contribution of x_1 and x_2, respectively, to the cost of a unit of Z, and x_1 and x_2 are characteristics of Z as it occurs in raw form.

Now, let us suppose that, although the forms of the distributions in eqns (10.1)–(10.3), are known, their parameters are not known. But, those occurrences from which Z has been produced provide

statistical data on X_1 and X_2, a fact which suggests the use of these data to estimate the unknown parameters. However, since these data are only for occurrences which have been produced, they represent that part of $\phi(x_1, x_2)$ truncated by the cost surface. Thus, we have average values for X_1 and X_2 from our data which represent estimated expected values from a truncated bivariate distribution. Clearly, these data do not constitute a random sample from the populations of X_1 and X_2. The task is to use these biased data to obtain unbiased estimates of the unknown parameters.

10.2.2. Mathematical expectation

Let us digress a moment to basic concepts of probability theory. Recall that the expected value of a random variable W described by $f(w)$ is $E[W]$

$$E[W] = \int_{-\infty}^{\infty} w \cdot f(w)\, dw, \quad a \le w \le b; \quad (10.5)$$

$$f(w) = 0, \quad \text{otherwise}.$$

Computation of $E[W]$ requires integrating over the entire domain of the p.d.f., $f(w)$. Of course, one requirement of a function as a p.d.f. is that

$$\int_a^b f(w)\, dw = 1.0.$$

The act of truncating a p.d.f. by some value c, $a < c < b$, makes the total probability for $c \le w \le b$ or for $a \le w \le c$ less than one. Therefore, a new function f^* must be defined from f such that the total probability in the region of interest is 1.0. For example, suppose that we wish to compute the expected value for W for all values of $c < w$, $a < c < b$. We must first derive a p.d.f. for W on the region $c \le w \le b$. This p.d.f. is derived from f

$$f^*(w) = \frac{f(w)}{\int_c^b f(w)\, dw}, \quad c \le w \le b; \quad (10.6)$$

$$f^*(w) = 0, \quad \text{otherwise}.$$

The expected value of W for f^* is

$$E[W] = \int_c^b \frac{w \cdot f(w)}{\int_c^b f(w)\, dw}\, dw = \frac{\int_c^b w \cdot f(w)\, dw}{\int_c^b f(w)\, dw},$$
$$c \le w \le b. \quad (10.7)$$

As a simple numeric example, consider the p.d.f.,

$f(x) = x^2/9$, $0 \leq x \leq 3$. Obviously,

$$\int_0^3 \frac{x^2}{9} \, dx = 1.0, \quad \text{and} \quad E[X] = \int_0^3 x \cdot \left(\frac{x^2}{9}\right) dx$$

$$= \frac{x^4}{36}\bigg|_0^3 = \frac{81}{36} = \underline{2.25}. \quad (10.8)$$

Now, suppose we truncate $f(x)$ at $X = 1$. Before the mean of this truncated distribution can be computed, we must form a new p.d.f.

$$f^*(x) = \frac{\dfrac{x^2}{9}}{\displaystyle\int_1^3 \frac{x^2}{9} \, dx}, \quad 1 \leq x \leq 3; \quad (10.9)$$

$$f^*(x) = 0, \quad \text{otherwise.}$$

$$f^*(x) = \frac{\dfrac{x^2}{9}}{\dfrac{x^3}{27}\bigg|_1^3} = \frac{\dfrac{x^2}{9}}{1 - \dfrac{1}{27}} = \left(\frac{x^2}{9}\right)\left(\frac{27}{26}\right) = \frac{3x^2}{26}. \quad (10.10)$$

Then, the expectation for X on f^* is defined as

$$E[X] = \int_1^3 (x)\left(\frac{3x^2}{26}\right) dx = \frac{3x^4}{(4)(26)}\bigg|_1^3$$

$$= \frac{(3)(81)}{(4)(26)} - \frac{3}{(4)(26)},$$

$$E[X] = \frac{243 - 3}{104} = \frac{240}{104} = \underline{2.31}. \quad (10.11)$$

10.2.3. Truncation by a cost surface and expectations

The expectation of a truncated distribution is at the core of the analysis by PAU and is required in the hypothetical example provided here. However, a complication is introduced because of the fact that the truncation surface is jointly determined by X_1 and X_2; therefore, the expectations for X_1 and X_2 for the truncated part of the bivariate distribution must be determined on the joint p.d.f. ϕ using variable lower limits of integration.

In our example and in the PAU model, the truncation point is itself a variable which is determined from the cost function

$$C = b_0 - b_1 x_1 - b_2 x_2 \Rightarrow x_1 = \frac{b_0 - b_2 x_2 - C}{b_1}. \quad (10.12)$$

And, since from our initial condition x_1 cannot be

negative, x_2 must be restricted

$$x_2 \geq \frac{C - b_0}{b_2}. \quad (10.13)$$

Therefore, our new joint p.d.f. ϕ^* is described as

$$\phi^*(x_1, x_2) = \frac{\phi(x_1, x_2)}{\displaystyle\int_{\frac{C-b_0}{b_2}}^{\infty} \int_{\frac{b_0-b_2x_2-C}{b_1}}^{\infty} \phi(x_1, x_2) \, dx_1 \, dx_2},$$

$$b_0 - b_2 x_2 - C \leq x_1 \leq \infty, \quad (10.14)$$

$$\frac{C - b_0}{b_2} \leq x_2 \leq \infty;$$

$\phi^*(x_1, x_2) = 0$, otherwise.

The expectations, $E[X_1]^*$ and $E[X_2]^*$, for X_1 and X_2 from ϕ^* would be computed as

$$E[X_1]^* = \int_{\frac{C-b_0}{b_2}}^{\infty} \int_{\frac{b_0-b_2x_2-C}{b_1}}^{\infty} x_1 \cdot \phi^*(x_1, x_2) \, dx_1 \, dx_2, \quad (10.15)$$

$$E[X_2]^* = \int_{\frac{C-b_0}{b_1}}^{\infty} \int_{\frac{b_0-b_1x_1-C}{b_2}}^{\infty} x_2 \cdot \phi^*(x_1, x_2) \, dx_2 \, dx_1. \quad (10.16)$$

Therefore, we have in terms of ϕ instead of ϕ^*

$$E[X_1]^* = \frac{\displaystyle\int_{\frac{C-b_0}{b_2}}^{\infty} \int_{\frac{b_0-b_2x_2-C}{b_1}}^{\infty} x_1 \cdot \phi(x_1, x_2) \, dx_1 \, dx_2}{\displaystyle\int_{\frac{C-b_0}{b_2}}^{\infty} \int_{\frac{b_0-b_2x_2-C}{b_1}}^{\infty} \phi(x_1, x_2) \, dx_1 \, dx_2}, \quad (10.17)$$

$$E[X_2]^* = \frac{\displaystyle\int_{\frac{C-b_0}{b_1}}^{\infty} \int_{\frac{b_0-b_1x_1-C}{b_2}}^{\infty} x_2 \cdot \phi(x_1, x_2) \, dx_2 \, dx_1}{\displaystyle\int_{\frac{C-b_0}{b_1}}^{\infty} \int_{\frac{b_0-b_1x_1-C}{b_2}}^{\infty} \phi(x_1, x_2) \, dx_2 \, dx_1}. \quad (10.18)$$

Substituting the exponential function of (10.3) for $\phi(x_1, x_2)$, we have

$$E[X_1]^* = \frac{\displaystyle\int_{\frac{C-b_0}{b_2}}^{\infty} \int_{\frac{b_0-b_2x_2-C}{b_1}}^{\infty} (x_1)\alpha\beta e^{-\alpha x_1 - \beta x_2} \, dx_1 \, dx_2}{\displaystyle\int_{\frac{C-b_0}{b_2}}^{\infty} \int_{\frac{b_0-b_2x_2-C}{b_1}}^{\infty} \alpha\beta e^{-\alpha x_1 - \beta x_2} \, dx_1 \, dx_2} \quad (10.19)$$

and

$$E[X_2]^* = \frac{\displaystyle\int_{\frac{C-b_0}{b_1}}^{\infty} \int_{\frac{b_0-b_1x_1-C}{b_2}}^{\infty} (x_2)\alpha\beta e^{-\alpha x_1 - \beta x_2} \, dx_2 \, dx_1}{\displaystyle\int_{\frac{C-b_0}{b_1}}^{\infty} \int_{\frac{b_0-b_1x_1-C}{b_2}}^{\infty} \alpha\beta e^{-\alpha x_1 - \beta x_2} \, dx_2 \, dx_1}. \quad (10.20)$$

Now, although the parameters α and β may not be known, we do have estimates of $E[X_1]^*$ and $E[X_2]^*$ from statistical data on Z; therefore, we have two unknowns and two equations, a condition which indicates a unique solution for α and β.

10.2.4. The solution for α and β

§ 10.2.3 defined $E[X_1]^*$ and $E[X_2]^*$, the means of the bivariate exponential population which was truncated by the cost surface $C = b_0 - b_1 x_1 - b_2 x_2$, as integral functions of the parameters of the cost function (b_0, b_1, and b_2), the maximum cost C, and the parameters of the exponential probability functions α and β. In § 10.5 these integral functions—eqns (10.19) and (10.20)—are evaluated, yielding the two equations

$$E[X_1]^* = \frac{b_0 - C}{b_1} - \frac{(C - b_0)}{b_1} - \frac{b_2}{b_1\beta - \alpha b_2} + \frac{1}{\alpha}$$

$$= \frac{2(b_0 - C)}{b_1} - \frac{b_2}{b_1\beta - \alpha b_2} + \frac{1}{\alpha}, \quad (10.21)$$

$$E[X_2]^* = \frac{b_0 - C}{b_2} - \frac{(C - b_0)}{b_2} - \frac{b_1}{b_2\alpha - \beta b_1} + \frac{1}{\beta}$$

$$= \frac{2(b_0 - C)}{b_2} - \frac{b_1}{b_2\alpha - \beta b_1} + \frac{1}{\beta}. \quad (10.22)$$

Now, the fictitious situation that is analogous to the problem formulation by PAU is that estimates of $E[X_1]^*$ and $E[X_2]^*$ are available from data on the raw material for Z. Similarly, from information on production costs, values can be estimated for b_0, C, b_1, and b_2. The quantities that are unknown are the two parameters, α and β. Thus, we have two unknowns and two equations. The known quantities could be substituted into (10.21) and (10.22) and the equations could be solved simultaneously for α and β. The following section provides a numerical example of such a solution.

10.2.5. A numerical example using the simplified hypothetical model

Suppose that statistical analysis of data on known raw material yielded

$$\bar{x}_1 = 15.83,$$

$$\bar{x}_2 = 11.67. \quad (10.23)$$

Ignoring the fact that these data are from truncated distributions would yield the following maximum likelihood estimates of α and β

$$\hat{\alpha} = 1/90 = 0.0632, \quad (10.24)$$

$$\hat{\beta} = 1/20 = 0.0857. \quad (10.25)$$

Let us hold these estimates in reserve for a moment, to be compared with estimates of α and β which take into account truncation effects.

Let us suppose that we know that the truncation surface is described by $C = 10 - 1.0 x_1 - 2.0 x_2$ and that no raw material (described by characteristics X_1 and X_2) has been utilized which yielded a total cost per unit of good Z above US \$5.00. With this information, we can make the identification

$$C = 5, \quad b_1 = 1, \quad \bar{x}_1 = 15.83;$$

$$b_0 = 10, \quad b_2 = 2, \quad \bar{x}_2 = 11.67. \quad (10.26)$$

Using this information and relationships (10.21) and (10.22), we can write

$$15.83 = 2\left(\frac{10 - 5}{1}\right) - \frac{2}{(1)\beta - 2\alpha} + \frac{1}{\alpha}, \quad (10.27)$$

$$11.67 = 2\left(\frac{10 - 5}{2}\right) - \frac{1}{2\alpha - (1)\beta} + \frac{1}{\beta}. \quad (10.28)$$

We have two unknowns and two equations in these unknowns. Simultaneous solution of (10.27) and (10.28) yields these estimates for α and β,

$$\alpha = 0.4,$$

$$\beta = 0.2. \quad (10.29)$$

Thus, in this case, the effect of ignoring the truncation is negatively-biased estimates of α and β

0.0632 compared to 0.4,

0.0857 compared to 0.2. (10.30)

Moreover, the effect of this bias is to overstate the probabilities for large values of X_1 and X_2. For example, the probability for the joint occurrence of values for X_1 greater than 5 and X_2 greater than 10 is correctly described by the expression

$$P(X_1 \geq 5, X_2 \geq 10) = \int_{10}^{\infty} \int_{5}^{\infty} (0.4)$$

$$(0.2) \exp(-0.4 x_1 - 0.2 x_2) \, dx_1 \, dx_2.$$

Because of statistical independence,

$$P(X_1 \geq 5, X_2 \geq 10) = P(X_1 \geq 5) \cdot P(X_2 \geq 10)$$

$$= \int_{5}^{\infty} 0.4 \exp(-0.4 x_1) \, dx_1 \cdot \int_{10}^{\infty} 0.2 \exp(-0.2 x_2) \, dx_2$$

$$= \left[-\exp(-0.4 x_1)\Big|_{5}^{\infty}\right] \cdot \left[-\exp(-0.2 x_2)\Big|_{10}^{\infty}\right]$$

$$= e^{-0.4(5)} \cdot e^{-0.2(10)} = e^{-2} \cdot e^{-2} = e^{-4} = 0.0183.$$

But, if the estimates of the parameters that were made directly without consideration of the truncation effects were used ($P(X_1 \geq 5, X_2 \geq 10) = 0.309$ instead of 0.0183),

$P(X_1 \geq 5, X_2 \geq 10) =$

$$= \int_5^\infty (0.0632) \exp(-0.0632 x_1)\, dx_1 \times$$

$$\times \int_{10}^\infty (0.0857) \exp(-0.0857 x_2)\, dx_2$$

$$= \exp(-0.0632(5)) \cdot \exp(-0.0857(10))$$

$$= \exp(-0.316) \cdot \exp(-0.857)$$

$$= \exp(-1.173)$$

$$= 0.309.$$

Thus, by not accounting for the truncation effect in estimation of the parameters, we would have computed the probability for the high values of X_1 and X_2 to be 0.309 instead of 0.0183. Obviously, neglecting the truncation would have led to a significant overstatement of this probability.

10.3. The PAU model

10.3.1. *The mathematical form*

Basically, the foregoing case demonstrates the concepts embodied in the PAU deposit model and in the estimation of its parameters. In this case, quantification of the bivariate exponential distribution for X_1 and X_2 required estimates for only two parameters. Consequently, given the cost information and averages for X_1 and X_2 from data, there was a unique solution for α and β. While this example provides the ideas employed by PAU in its deposit model, the task of estimating the parameters of the PAU model is much more complex. This complexity derives from the fact that the distribution employed by PAU is bivariate lognormal, which requires estimates for four parameters. The PAU model in its elementary form is expressed as

$$\phi(x, y) = \frac{\exp\left(-\frac{1}{2}\left(\frac{x-\mu_x}{\sigma_x}\right)^2 - \frac{1}{2}\left(\frac{y-\mu_y}{\sigma_y}\right)^2\right)}{\sigma_x \sigma_y (2\pi)},$$

$$-\infty \leq x \leq \infty$$
$$-\infty \leq y \leq \infty. \quad (10.31)$$

This is simply a bivariate normal p.d.f. where $x = \ln q$ and $y = \ln t$. Quantification of this model requires estimation of the four parameters μ_x, σ_x, μ_y, and σ_y.

Obviously, the statistics for mean tonnage and grade from truncated samples do not yield enough information to estimate four parameters. To get around this, PAU employs the fact that tonnage × grade = metal

$$M = T \cdot Q. \quad (10.32)$$

If the forms of the probability distributions for T and Q are known, the probability distribution for M can be obtained from the joint probability density function (p.d.f.) for T and Q by a transformation of variable. Suppose that $\phi(t, q)$ is the joint p.d.f. for tonnage and grade; then, a p.d.f. for metal M relates to $\phi(t, q)$ according to the expression

$$f(m) = \int_Q \phi\left(\frac{m}{q}, q\right) \frac{1}{q}\, dq, \quad (10.33)$$

where $t = m/q$ and $\phi(t, q)$ is the joint p.d.f. for T and Q; in the PAU model this is a bivariate lognormal. Then, we have a bivariate lognormal distribution and a univariate lognormal distribution. Taken together, these distributions require six parameters, but two of these, μ_m and σ_m, can be described in terms of the other four, the effect being that we must estimate from the three statistics, $\bar{t}$, $\bar{q}$, and $\bar{m}$, four parameters, μ_y, σ_y, μ_x, and σ_x instead of six. Solution is possible only if one of the four unknown (parameters) is known (or can be assumed to be known with reasonable confidence) or if an additional relationship can be introduced. Such is the approach employed by PAU: a crustal-abundance measure was taken to be a reasonably accurate estimate of the arithmetic average grade γ_q of the full population of deposits. With this assumption and the relationship [1] of $\mu_x = \ln \gamma_q - \sigma_x^2/2$, we have four unknown parameters and four relationships involving these unknowns, a situation that should be solvable. Although these conditions make a solution conceptually feasible, a numerical solution is not trivial, for the probability relationships of the unknown parameters are integrals. In our example, integration was performed on the integrals to yield tractable algebraic forms. The PAU model employs the bivariate lognormal p.d.f., a functional form that cannot be integrated directly. For this reason, estimates of the unknown parameters can be made only by numerical approximation methods which involve some sort of search algorithm to converge on the values of σ_x, μ_y, σ_y, and μ_x implied by the statistics $\bar{t}$, $\bar{q}$, and $\bar{m}$ and the measure γ_q.

PAU estimates the unknown parameters using relationships of the truncated bivariate distribution and statistical data on known and exploited deposits. These statistics represent data from the bivariate tonnage and grade population which has been truncated by a cost surface which is assumed by PAU to be of the form of $C = (K-1)y - x$. Thus, the average grade and average tonnage of ore per deposit computed from the data represent estimates of γ_q^* and γ_t^*, the means of deposit grade and tonnage of the *truncated* population [2]. In terms of the basic probability function, these quantities are related as

$$\bar{q} \Rightarrow \gamma_q^* =$$

$$\frac{\displaystyle\int_{-\infty}^{\infty}\int_{(K-1)y-C}^{\infty} e^x \exp\left(-\frac{1}{2}\left(\frac{x-\mu_x}{\sigma_x}\right)^2 - \frac{1}{2}\left(\frac{y-\mu_y}{\sigma_y}\right)^2\right) dx\, dy}{\displaystyle\int_{-\infty}^{\infty}\int_{(K-1)y-C}^{\infty} \exp\left(-\frac{1}{2}\left(\frac{x-\mu_x}{\sigma_x}\right)^2 - \frac{1}{2}\left(\frac{y-\mu_y}{\sigma_y}\right)^2\right) dx\, dy},$$

$$(10.34)$$

$$\bar{t} \Rightarrow \gamma_t^* = \frac{\displaystyle\int_{-\infty}^{\infty}\int_{\frac{C+x}{(K-1)}}^{\infty} e^y \exp\left(-\frac{1}{2}\left(\frac{x-\mu_x}{\sigma_x}\right)^2 - \frac{1}{2}\left(\frac{y-\mu_y}{\sigma_y}\right)^2\right) dy\, dx}{\displaystyle\int_{-\infty}^{\infty}\int_{\frac{C+x}{(K-1)}}^{\infty} \exp\left(-\frac{1}{2}\left(\frac{x-\mu_x}{\sigma_x}\right)^2 - \frac{1}{2}\left(\frac{y-\mu_y}{\sigma_y}\right)^2\right) dy\, dx}.$$

$$(10.35)$$

Through mathematical manipulation, PAU reduced the relationships of (10.34) and (10.35), and a similar one for metal, to

$$\gamma_q^* = \frac{\exp(\mu_x + \sigma_x^2/2)\displaystyle\int_{-\infty}^{C}\exp\left(-\frac{1}{2}\left(\frac{C-\mu_C}{\sigma_C}\right)^2\right)dC}{\displaystyle\int_{-\infty}^{C}\exp\left(-\frac{1}{2}\left(\frac{C-\mu_C'}{\sigma_C}\right)^2\right)dC},$$

$$(10.36)$$

$$\gamma_t^* = \frac{\exp(\mu_y + \sigma_y^2/2)\displaystyle\int_{-\infty}^{C}\exp\left(-\frac{1}{2}\left(\frac{C-\mu_C''}{\sigma_C}\right)^2\right)dC}{\displaystyle\int_{-\infty}^{C}\exp\left(-\frac{1}{2}\left(\frac{C-\mu_C'}{\sigma_C}\right)^2\right)dC},$$

$$(10.37)$$

$$\gamma_m^* = \frac{\exp(\mu_x + \sigma_x^2/2 + \mu_y + \sigma_y^2/2)\times\displaystyle\int_{-\infty}^{C}\exp\left(-\frac{1}{2}\left(\frac{C-\mu_C'''}{\sigma_C}\right)^2\right)dC}{\displaystyle\int_{-\infty}^{C}\exp\left(-\frac{1}{2}\left(\frac{C-\mu_C'}{\sigma_C}\right)^2\right)dC},$$

$$(10.38)$$

where

$$\mu_x = \ln \gamma_q - \sigma_x^2/2;\quad C = (K-1)y - x;$$

$$\mu_C = (K-1)\mu_y - \mu_x - \sigma_x^2;$$

$$\sigma_C^2 = (K-1)^2\sigma_y^2 + \sigma_x^2;\quad \mu_C' = (K-1)\mu_y - \mu_x;$$

$$\mu_C'' = (K-1)(\mu_y + \sigma_y^2) - (\mu_x + \sigma_x^2);$$

$$\mu_C''' = (K-1)(\mu_y + \sigma_y^2) - \mu_x.$$

Since K, C, and γ_q (crustal abundance) are known or assumed so, there are three unknowns, σ_x, μ_y, σ_y. All other quantities are functions of these unknowns and K, C, and γ_q.

Solution of these equations requires a search algorithm, which manipulates μ_x, σ_x, μ_y, and σ_y until a measure of difference of γ_q^*, γ_t^*, and γ_m^* and the statistical estimates from the data $\bar{q}$, $\bar{t}$, and $\bar{m}$ is acceptably close to zero.

A computer program named SEARCH was created by PAU to estimate the unknown parameters μ_x, σ_x, μ_y, and σ_y. This program performs a simple iterative search for those values within specified ranges of the unknown parameters that provide the minimum difference of γ_q^*, γ_t^*, and γ_m^* and $\bar{q}$, $\bar{t}$, and $\bar{m}$. Since the search is executed only within the specified ranges, successful use of the program requires good judgement and successive runs. Otherwise, the solution may reflect a saddle or a local minimum.

The PAU search routine was modified in this study to make the iterative search for the best parameters automatic. This was done by including a search routine called MINSER, which was obtained from the Computer Centre of the University of Arizona. While this search routine appears to work well, it, too, must be cautiously employed. Effectiveness of the automatic search is dependent upon the appropriateness of the initial starting values, the search grid, and the irregularity of the search surface. A listing of this program is provided in § 10.6.

10.3.2. *Demonstration by PAU on US uranium*

From data available from the United States Atomic Energy Commission (1 January 1970), now DOE, PAU computed values for $\bar{q}$, $\bar{t}$, and $\bar{m}$ for all uranium deposits in the United States

$$\bar{q} = 0.002577 \rightarrow 0.2577 \text{ per cent } U_3O_8,$$

$$\bar{t} = 99\,285 \text{ tonnes},$$

$$\bar{m} = 190.28 \text{ tonnes}. \qquad (10.38a)$$

PAU analysed cost data for the United States and

derived the cost equation

$$COST = 0.0657t^{-0.159}q^{-1}. \qquad (10.38b)$$

Taking logarithms of both sides of (10.38b), we have

$$\ln COST = -2.7227 - 0.159 \ln t - \ln q. \qquad (10.38c)$$

If we let $C = \ln COST$, $x = \ln q$, and $y = \ln t$, as was done in the foregoing development of theory and method of analysis, we have the cost expression

$$C = -2.7227 - 0.159y - x \qquad (10.38d)$$

or, alternatively,

$$x = -2.7227 - 0.159y - C$$

and

$$x = (0.841 - 1.0)y - 2.7227 - C, \qquad (10.38e)$$

where $K = 0.841$ and $K - 1 = 0.841 - 1.0 = -0.159$.

Suppose that we set $COST = $ US \$8.00/lb. Then, $C = 2.0794$ and eqn (10.38e) can be further specified

$$x = (0.841 - 1.0)y - 2.7227 - 2.0794,$$
$$x = (0.841 - 1.0)y - 4.8021 \qquad (10.38f)$$

or

$$x = -0.159y - 4.8021. \qquad (10.38g)$$

Eqn (10.38g) can be recognized to be of the algebraic form employed in the development of theory and estimation methods

$$C = (K - 1)y - x$$

or

$$x = (K - 1)y - C.$$

With the above values for $\bar{q}$, $\bar{t}$, and $\bar{m}$ and the cost relationship of (10.38b), PAU estimated the parameters of the bivariate lognormal distribution for deposits of uranium in the United States, given that γ_q (crustal abundance) = 0.000002,

$$\hat{\mu}_x = -15.102$$
$$\hat{\sigma}_x = 1.9897; \hat{\sigma}_x^2 = 3.959$$
$$\hat{\mu}_y = 7.517 \ [3]$$
$$\hat{\sigma}_y = 1.1670; \hat{\sigma}_y^2 = 1.362 \qquad (10.38h)$$

Thus, although γ_q, the arithmetic average of grade (crustal abundance), was given as 0.000002, the geometric mean grade, e^{μ_x}, which should also be the modal value for Q is approximately 0.00000027. As previously indicated, these values are related

$$\ln \gamma_q = \mu_x + \sigma_x^2/2 = -15.102 + 1.9795 = -13.1225,$$
$$\gamma_q = e^{-13.1225} \approx 0.000002.$$

The average grade of all US \$8.00/lb U_3O_8 deposits known at the time of PAU's analysis was greater than this modal grade by a factor of approximately 10^4: 0.0026/0.00000027.

The modal (geometric mean $= e^{\mu_y}$) size of United States uranium deposits was found to be approximately 1840 tonnes of mineralized rock. PAU found that the average size of all known US \$8.00/lb U_3O_8 deposits was 99 285 tonnes, approximately 54 times larger than the modal tonnage. Thus, if we assume that the analysis performed by PAU provides an accurate view of the population of uranium deposits of the United States, we must conclude that the economics of exploration and exploitation has served as a strong filter (truncation device): our statistical data on tonnage and grade reflect strongly man's economic activities.

For further demonstration of the PAU deposit model for uranium deposits of the United States, we will take the estimates made by PAU of the parameters of the independent bivariate population of size and grade and estimate the U_3O_8 resources of the United States in deposits having grades of at least 0.1 per cent U_3O_8 and tonnage of mineralized rock of at least 10 000 tonnes. In the introduction to this section, expected quantity of resources was defined as the product of a probability ρ and a tonnage W

$$\text{Expected quantity of resources} = \rho \cdot W.$$

W represents the weight of the crust of the United States, which is taken to be 2.118×10^{16} tonnes; ρ is the probability for the joint occurrence of $Q \geq 0.001$ and $T \geq 10\ 000$. Since by assumption Q and T are statistically independent,

$$P(Q \geq 0.001, T \geq 10\ 000)$$
$$= P(Q \geq 0.001) \cdot P(T \geq 10\ 000).$$

These probabilities are computed using PAU's deposit model as

$$P(Q \geq 0.001) = \frac{1}{1.9897(2\pi)^{\frac{1}{2}}} \times$$
$$\int_{\ln(0.001)}^{\infty} \exp\left(-\frac{1}{2}\left(\frac{\ln q - (-15.102)}{1.9897}\right)^2\right) d\ln q,$$

$$P(T \geq 10\ 000) = \frac{1}{1.1670(2\pi)^{\frac{1}{2}}} \times$$
$$\int_{\ln(10000)}^{\infty} \exp\left(-\frac{1}{2}\left(\frac{\ln t - 7.517}{1.1670}\right)^2\right) d\ln t.$$

Each of these probabilities is a normal probability which can be determined using tabled values of the standard unit normal probability distribution

$$P(Q \geq 0.001) = 1 - F\left(\frac{\ln (0.001) - (-15.102)}{1.9897}\right)$$

$$= 1 - F\left(\frac{8.194}{1.9897}\right)$$

$$= 1 - F(4.118) = 0.0000191$$

$$P(T \geq 10\,000) = 1 - F\left(\frac{\ln (10\,000) - 7.517}{1.1670}\right)$$

$$= 1 - F\left(\frac{1.693}{1.1670}\right)$$

$$= 1 - F(1.451) = 0.0734.$$

Thus,

$$P = (0.0000191)(0.0734) = 1.4 \times 10^{-6},$$

And

$$\text{Resources} = (1.4 \times 10^{-6})(2.118 \times 10^{16}),$$

$$\text{Resources} = 3.0 \times 10^{10} \text{ tonnes.}$$

Thus, the inference by the PAU model is that we have approximately 30 billion tonnes of rock material in the United States having grades of at least 0.10 per cent U_3O_8.

10.3.3. *PAU's African model*

Perspective. PAU concluded that although there is a large amount of data on United States uranium deposits, these data do not constitute a satisfactory base for the development of its deposit model. Reasons for this include the dominance of sandstone deposits in the limited geological environments represented by United States data. PAU selected the African continent as the region upon which to estimate and apply its model, for it was the judgement of PAU that this continent had received a more uniform, although less intensive, coverage of exploration than the United States, and uranium deposits of Africa represent a wider variety of deposit types and a broader spectrum of geological environments.

Input data and estimated parameters. PAU acknowledges considerable problems in acquiring adequate and reliable data, particularly for production and exploration costs. Special problems are posed by the presence of considerable by-product uranium and by the use of different units and accounting procedures for costs. PAU made the decision to exclude from the data on reserves those properties from which by-product uranium originated if the uranium could not be extracted profitably as the primary product.

Tonnage per deposit ranged from approximately 60 000 to approximately 250 000 000 tonnes. The plot of tonnage and grade shows a reasonably well defined inverse correlation of tonnage and grade.

PAU concluded that cost data on Africa were inadequate to justify the estimation of the cost function representing the truncation surface. The estimated cost function is a blending of United States and African cost data

$$COST = 0.05076t^{-0.15033}q^{-1.1311}. \quad (10.38\text{i})$$

Table 10.1 summarizes the basic information which was input to the computer program SEARCH to estimate the parameters of the bivariate lognormal distribution.

TABLE 10.1. *Input data for the Africa model*

Symbol	Value	Description
$\bar{q}$	0.002716 ⇒ 0.2716 per cent U_3O_8	Average grade of deposits
$\bar{t}$	16 705 928 tonnes	Average size of deposits (ore)
$\bar{m}$	11 907 tonnes	Average metal content of deposits
W	8.075×10^{16}	Weight of African crust
C	US \$15/lb U_3O_8	Base price (maximum cost)
γ_q	2×10^{-6}	Crustal abundance

The best estimates of the parameters of the bivariate lognormal population are

$$\mu_x = -15.03 \quad \mu_y = -3.73$$

$$\sigma_x^2 = 3.82 \quad \sigma_y^2 = 11.399. \quad (10.38\text{j})$$

Table 10.2 compares the values of the averages of the theoretical distribution having the above parameters and truncated by the cost function of (10.38i) with the statistics on the known deposits given in Table 10.1. Thus, Table 10.2 confirms that the bivariate lognormal distribution described by the estimated parameters of (10.38j) when truncated by

TABLE 10.2. *Values of the statistics on known deposits and theoretical averages of the truncated population defined by estimated parameters*

Statistics		Theoretical averages (expectations) of the truncated distribution	
Symbol	Value	Symbol	Value
$\bar{q}$	0.002716	γ_q^*	0.00271
$\bar{t}$	16 705 928	γ_t^*	16 699 000
$\bar{m}$	11 907	γ_m^*	11 899

TABLE 10.3. *Estimated parameters of the lognormal distribution for tonnage for the United States and Africa*

	United States	Africa
$\hat{\mu}_y$	7.517	-3.730
$\hat{\sigma}_y^2$	1.362	11.399

TABLE 10.4. *Variations in estimates of parameters and crustal abundance*

Crustal abundance ($\times 10^{-6}$)	$\hat{\mu}_x$	$\hat{\sigma}_x^2$	$\hat{\mu}_y$	$\hat{\sigma}_y^2$
2	-15.04	3.83	-3.73	11.40
4	-14.15	3.44	-3.95	11.54
6	-13.63	3.22	-4.12	11.64
10	-12.98	2.93	-4.35	11.79
20	-12.08	2.54	-4.79	12.05

the cost surface indicated by equation (10.38i) for a maximum cost of US $15.00/lb U_3O_8 yields averages approximately equal to those computed on known deposits.

Especially noteworthy is the fact that although the average grade of known deposits of Africa is very similar to that for US deposits (0.2716 per cent U_3O_8 compared to 0.2577 per cent U_3O_8), the average size of African deposits in tonnes of ore is much larger than that for United States deposits: 16 705 928 compared to 99 285. Moreover, the tonnage distributions, as described by estimated parameters, of Africa and the United States are very dissimilar (see Table 10.3). Note, however, that the expectations for logarithm of size of deposit on the truncated regions of these two populations are much more similar: 7.669 [4] compared to 8.879.

One is prompted to attribute much of the difference in the parameters of the tonnage distributions for Africa and the United States to the fact that the United States data represent primarily one type of deposit while the data on Africa represent several types of deposits in a variety of geological environments. Conceivably, an aggregate such as that for African deposits could be reflected in a large variance in size, as is indicated by the estimated variance of size of African deposits.

Some sensitivities. As indicated, a measure of crustal abundance γ_q is taken by PAU as a reliable estimate of the average concentration of an element in the crust of a region. The values of all four parameters, μ_x, σ_x, μ_y, and σ_y, are influenced to some degree by the assumed value for γ_q; this is most easily seen by examining the manner in which γ_q, μ_x, and σ_x are related in the deposit model

$$\mu_x = \ln \gamma_q - \sigma_x^2/2.$$

Table 10.4 shows the estimates of the four parameters, given assumed values for γ_q ranging from 2 to 20×10^{-6}. While one would expect $\hat{\mu}_x$ and $\hat{\sigma}_x^2$ to show considerable variation, the variations in $\hat{\mu}_y$ and $\hat{\sigma}_y^2$ may come as a surprise. Of course, if we consider

the fact that both tonnage and grade are combined in the cost function, for a given cost function and statistics on known deposits, a change in any parameter will have some effect on estimates of the other parameters. Thus, it is intuitively acceptable that an increase in crustal abundance results in an increase in $\hat{\mu}_x$, a decrease in $\hat{\sigma}_x^2$, a decrease in $\hat{\mu}_y$, and an increase in $\hat{\sigma}_y^2$.

Fig. 10.1 shows the overall effect on the estimates of ultimate resources of U_3O_8 for Africa of assuming values for γ_q ranging from 2 to 20×10^{-6} and for values for maximum cost ranging from US $6/lb U_3O_8 to US $30/lb U_3O_8. Increasing maximum cost from $6 to $30 increases resources of U_3O_8 by a

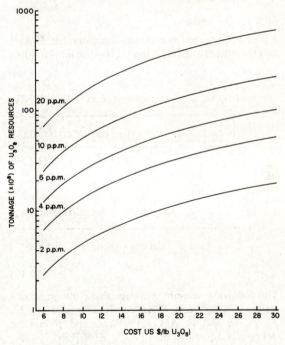

Fig. 10.1. Resources of U_3O_8 for Africa.

factor of approximately 8. Thus, a multiple of 5 applied to costs (price) results in a multiple of approximately 8. A multiple of 5 applied to crustal abundance increases ultimate resources by a factor of approximately 10 for all cost levels, showing the sensitivity of resources to the assumed value of crustal abundance.

10.4. The assumption of independence of grade and tonnage in crustal abundance models

The simplification that independence of grade and tonnage provides to statistical analysis induces receptiveness to the suggestion from empirical data or arguments from geological theory for such a relationship. Caution is in order, for the usefulness of the assumption of independency is seductive, for the concept of deposit is intimately involved in the issue of dependency of grade and tonnage. For samples of rock ranging from, say a few pounds to billions of tons, is the assumption of independence of deposit size and grade reasonable? This question and others are considered in the next section as part of a broader examination of the statistical relationship of deposit size to deposit grade.

10.5. Appendix A: The mathematics of a solution for α and β

10.5.1. The problem

§ 10.2.3 developed two expressions, one for $E[X_1]^*$ and the other for $E[X_2]^*$ (eqns (10.19) and (10.20))

$$E[X_1]^* =$$

$$\frac{\int_{\frac{C-b_0}{b_2}}^{\infty} \int_{\frac{b_0-b_2x_2-C}{b_1}}^{\infty} (x_1)\alpha\beta \exp(-\alpha x_1 - \beta x_2)\, dx_1\, dx_2}{\int_{\frac{C-b_0}{b_2}}^{\infty} \int_{\frac{b_0-b_2x_2-C}{b_1}}^{\infty} \alpha\beta \exp(-\alpha x_1 - \beta x_2)\, dx_1\, dx_2}$$

$$\text{(10.39)}$$

and

$$E[X_2]^* =$$

$$\frac{\int_{\frac{C-b_0}{b_1}}^{\infty} \int_{\frac{b_0-b_1x_1-C}{b_2}}^{\infty} (x_2)\alpha\beta \exp(-\alpha x_1 - \beta x_2)\, dx_1\, dx_2}{\int_{\frac{C-b_0}{b_1}}^{\infty} \int_{\frac{b_0-b_1x_1-C}{b_2}}^{\infty} \alpha\beta \exp(-\alpha x_1 - \beta x_2)\, dx_1\, dx_2}.$$

$$\text{(10.40)}$$

The following sections evaluate these integrals, describing $E[X_1]^*$ and $E[X_2]^*$ as functions of C_1, b_0, b_1, b_2, α, and β. Alternatively, α and β can be defined as functions of $E[X_1]^*$, $E[X_2]^*$, C, b_0, b_1, and b_2.

10.5.2. Evaluating the denominator D_1 of (10.39)

Let

$$\frac{b_0-C}{b_1} = K_1; \quad \frac{C-b_0}{b_2} = K_2; \quad \text{and} \quad Z = \frac{b_2}{b_1}.$$

Then,

$$D_1 = \int_{K_2}^{\infty} \int_{K_1-Zx_2}^{\infty} \alpha\beta \exp(-\alpha x_1 - \beta x_2)\, dx_1\, dx_2$$

$$D_1 = \int_{K_2}^{\infty} -\beta \exp(-\alpha x_1 - \beta x_2)\Big|_{K_1-Zx_2}^{\infty} dx_2 = 0+$$

$$+ \int_{K_2}^{\infty} \beta \exp(-\alpha(K_1 - Zx_2) - \beta x_2)\, dx_2 \quad \text{(10.41)}$$

$$D_1 = \exp(-\alpha K_1)\int_{K_2}^{\infty} \beta \exp(-(\beta - \alpha Z)x_2)\, dx_2$$

$$= \left[\frac{\beta \exp(-\alpha K_1)}{(\beta - \alpha Z)}\right]\left[-\exp(-(\beta - \alpha Z)x_2)\Big|_{K_2}^{\infty}\right]$$

$$D_1 = \left[\frac{\beta \exp(-\alpha K_1)}{(\beta - \alpha Z)}\right][\exp(-(\beta - \alpha Z)K_2)]$$

$$= \frac{\beta \exp(-\alpha K_1 - \beta K_2 + \alpha Z K_2)}{(\beta - \alpha Z)}$$

$$D_1 = \frac{\beta \exp(-\alpha K_1 - \beta K_2 + \alpha Z K_2)}{(\beta - \alpha Z)}. \quad \text{(10.42)}$$

10.5.3. Evaluating the numerator N_1 of (10.39)

$$N_1 = \int_{K_2}^{\infty} \int_{K_1-Zx_2}^{\infty} \alpha\beta x_1 \exp(-\alpha x_1 - \beta x_2)\, dx_1\, dx_2$$

$$\text{(10.43)}$$

$$N_1 = \beta \int_{K_2}^{\infty} \left[-x_1 \exp(-\alpha x_1 - \beta x_2) - \right.$$

$$\left. - \int_{K_1-Zx_2}^{\infty} -\exp(-\alpha x_1 - \beta x_2)\, dx_1\right] dx_2 \quad \text{(10.44)}$$

$$N_1 = \beta \int_{K_2}^{\infty} \left[-x_1 \exp(-\alpha x_1 - \beta x_2) + \right.$$

$$\left. + \int_{K_1-Zx_2}^{\infty} \exp(-\alpha x_1 - \beta x_2)\, dx_1\right] dx_2$$

$$N_1 = \beta \int_{K_2}^{\infty} \left[-x_1 \exp(-\alpha x_1 - \beta x_2) - \right.$$

$$\left. - \frac{\exp(-\alpha x_1 - \beta x_2)}{\alpha}\Big|_{K_1-Zx_2}^{\infty}\right] dx_2$$

$$N_1 = \beta \int_{K_2}^{\infty} (K_1 Z x_2) \exp(-\alpha(K_1 - Zx_2) - \beta x_2) +$$

$$+ \frac{\exp(-\alpha(K_1 - Zx_2) - \beta x_2)}{\alpha}\, dx_2$$

$$N_1 = \int_{K_2}^{\infty} \beta K_1 \exp\left(-\alpha(K_1 - Zx_2) - \beta x_2\right) -$$

$$- \int_{K_2}^{\infty} \beta Z x_2 \exp\left(-\alpha(K_1 - Zx_2) - \beta x_2\right) dx_2 +$$

$$+ \int_{K_2}^{\infty} \frac{\beta}{\alpha} \exp\left(-\alpha(K_1 - Zx_2) - \beta x_2\right) dx_2. \quad (10.45)$$

$$N_1 = I_1 - I_2 + I_3. \quad (10.46)$$

$$I_1 = \int_{K_2}^{\infty} \beta K_1 \exp\left(-\alpha K_1 - (\beta - \alpha Z)x_2\right) dx_2 \quad (10.47)$$

$$I_1 = \beta K_1 \exp\left(-\alpha K_1\right) \int_{K_2}^{\infty} \exp\left(-(\beta - \alpha Z)x_2\right) dx_2$$

$$I_1 = \left[\frac{\beta K_1 \exp\left(-\alpha K_1\right)}{(\beta - \alpha Z)}\right]\left[-\exp\left(-(\beta - \alpha Z)x_2\right)\Big|_{K_2}^{\infty}\right]$$

$$I_1 = \left[\frac{\beta K_1 \exp\left(-\alpha K_1\right)}{(\beta - \alpha Z)}\right]\left[\exp\left(-(\beta - \alpha Z)K_2\right)\right]$$

$$I_1 = \frac{\beta K_1 \exp\left(-\alpha K_1 - \beta K_2 + \alpha Z K_2\right)}{(\beta - \alpha Z)}. \quad (10.48)$$

Similarly,

$$I_3 = \frac{\beta \exp\left(-\alpha K_1 - \beta K_2 + \alpha Z K_2\right)}{\alpha(\beta - \alpha Z)}. \quad (10.49)$$

Now, for I_2

$$I_2 = \int_{K_2}^{\infty} -\beta Z x_2 \exp\left(-\alpha(K_1 - Zx_2) - \beta x_2\right) dx_2 \quad (10.50)$$

$$I_2 = \int_{K_2}^{\infty} -\beta Z x_2 \exp\left(-\alpha K_1 - (\beta - \alpha Z)x_2\right) dx_2$$

$$I_2 = -\beta Z \exp\left(-\alpha K_1\right) \int_{K_2}^{\infty} x_2 \exp\left(-(\beta - \alpha Z)x_2\right) dx_2$$

$$I_2 = -\beta Z \exp\left(-\alpha K_1\right) \left[\frac{-x_2 \exp\left(-(\beta - \alpha Z)x_2\right)}{(\beta - \alpha Z)} - \right.$$

$$\left. - \int_{K_2}^{\infty} \frac{-\exp\left(-(\beta - \alpha Z)x_2\right)}{(\beta - \alpha Z)} dx_2 \right]$$

$$I_2 = \left[\frac{-\beta Z \exp\left(-\alpha K_1\right)}{(\beta - \alpha Z)}\right] \times$$

$$\times \left[-x_2 \exp\left(-(\beta - \alpha Z)x_2\right) \frac{-\exp\left(-(\beta - \alpha Z)x_2\right)}{(\beta - \alpha Z)}\Big|_{K_2}^{\infty}\right]$$

$$I_2 = \left[\frac{-\beta Z \exp\left(-\alpha K_1\right)}{(\beta - \alpha Z)}\right] \times$$

$$\times \left[K_2 \exp\left(-\beta K_2 - \alpha Z K_2\right) + \frac{\exp\left(-\beta K_2 + \alpha Z K_2\right)}{(\beta - \alpha Z)}\right]$$

$$I_2 = \left[\frac{-\beta Z}{(\beta - \alpha Z)}\right] \times$$

$$\times \left[K_2 \exp\left(-\alpha K_1 - \beta K_2 + \alpha Z K_2\right) \right.$$

$$\left. + \frac{\exp\left(-\alpha K_1 - \beta K_2 + \alpha Z K_2\right)}{(\beta - \alpha Z)}\right]$$

$$I_2 = \left[\frac{-\beta Z}{(\beta - \alpha Z)}\right]\left[K_2 + \frac{1}{(\beta - \alpha Z)}\right] \times$$

$$\times \left[\exp\left(-\alpha K_1 - \beta K_2 + \alpha Z K_2\right)\right]. \quad (10.51)$$

10.5.4. Putting the parts together for $E[X_1]^*$

Gathering terms of the numerator and denominator, we have

$$E[X_1]^* = \left[\frac{\beta K_1 \exp\left(-\alpha K_1 - \beta K_2 + \alpha Z K_2\right)}{(\beta - \alpha Z)} \frac{-\beta Z}{(\beta - \alpha Z)} \times \right.$$

$$\times \left[K_2 + \frac{1}{(\beta - \alpha Z)}\right] \exp\left(-\alpha K_1 - \beta K_2\right)$$

$$+ \alpha Z K_2) +$$

$$\left. + \frac{\beta \exp\left(-\alpha K_1 - \beta K_2 + \alpha Z K_2\right)}{\alpha(\beta - \alpha Z)}\right] \Big/$$

$$\Big/ \left[\frac{\beta \exp\left(-\alpha K_1 - \beta K_2 + \alpha K_2\right)}{(\beta - \alpha Z)}\right] \quad (10.52)$$

$$E[X_1]^* = K_1 - ZK_2 - \frac{Z}{(\beta - \alpha Z)} + \frac{1}{\alpha}.$$

Now, resubstituting, we have

$$E[X_1]^* = \frac{b_0 - C}{b_1} - \frac{b_2}{b_1}\left(\frac{C - b_0}{b_2}\right) - \frac{b_2/b_1}{\left\{\beta - \alpha \frac{b_2}{b_1}\right\}} + \frac{1}{\alpha}. \quad (10.53)$$

10.5.5. Evaluating the denominator D_2 of (10.40)

From (10.20), we have

$$E[X_2]^* =$$

$$\frac{\displaystyle\int_{\frac{C-b_0}{b_1}}^{\infty} \int_{\frac{b_0 - b_1 x_1 - C}{b_2}}^{\infty} x_2 \alpha\beta \exp\left(-\alpha x_1 - \beta x_2\right) dx_2\, dx_1}{\displaystyle\int_{\frac{C-b_0}{b_1}}^{\infty} \int_{\frac{b_0 - b_1 x_1 - C}{b_2}}^{\infty} \alpha\beta \exp\left(-\alpha x_1 - \beta x_2\right) dx_2\, dx_1}.$$

$$(10.54)$$

Let us simplify the notation by letting $(b_0 - C)/b_2$ be a constant K_1 and $(C - b_0)/b_1 = -K_1(b_2/b_1) = K_2$

another constant. Further let $b_1/b_2 = Z$. Then,

$$E[X_2]^* = \frac{\int_{K_2}^{\infty} \int_{K_1-Zx_1}^{\infty} x_2 \alpha\beta \exp(-\alpha x_1 - \beta x_2)\, dx_2\, dx_1}{\int_{K_2}^{\infty} \int_{K_1-Zx_1}^{\infty} \alpha\beta \exp(-\alpha x_1 - \beta x_2)\, dx_2\, dx_1}.$$

(10.55)

Let us take the denominator D_2 first,

$$D_2 = \int_{K_2}^{\infty} \int_{K_1-Zx_1}^{\infty} \alpha\beta \exp(-\alpha x_1 - \beta x_2)\, dx_2\, dx_1$$

(10.56)

$$D_2 = \int_{K_2}^{\infty} \left. -\alpha \exp(-\alpha x_1 - \beta x_2) \right|_{K_1-Zx_1}^{\infty} dx_1$$

$$D_2 = \int_{K_2}^{\infty} [0 + \alpha \exp(-\alpha x_1 - \beta(K_1 - Zx_1))]\, dx_1$$

$$D_2 = \int_{K_2}^{\infty} \alpha \exp(-\alpha x_1 - \beta K_1 + \beta Z x_1)\, dx_1$$

$$D_2 = e^{-\beta K_1} \int_{K_2}^{\infty} \alpha \exp(-(\alpha - \beta Z)x_1)\, dx_1$$

$$D_2 = \left[\frac{\alpha \exp(-\beta K_1)}{(\alpha - \beta Z)}\right] \times$$

$$\times \left[\left. \exp(-(\alpha - \beta Z)x_1)\, dx_1) \right|_{K_2}^{\infty} \right]$$

$$D_2 = \left[\frac{\alpha \exp(-\beta K_1)}{(\alpha - \beta Z)}\right][\exp(-(\alpha - \beta Z)K_2)]$$

$$= \left[\frac{\alpha \exp(-\beta K_1)}{(\alpha - \beta Z)}\right][\exp(-\alpha K_2 + \beta Z K_2)]$$

$$D_2 = \frac{\alpha \exp(-\beta K_1 + \beta Z K_2 - \alpha K_2)}{\alpha - \beta Z}.$$

(10.57)

10.5.6. Evaluating the numerator N_2 of (10.40)

Let us represent the numerator by N_2

$$N_2 = \int_{K_2}^{\infty} \int_{K_1-Zx_1}^{\infty} x_2 \alpha\beta \exp(-\alpha x_1 - \beta x_2)\, dx_2\, dx_1.$$

Letting

$$u = x_1 \quad \text{and} \quad dv = \alpha\beta \exp(-\alpha x_1 - \beta x_2),$$

(10.58)

we have

$$N_2 = \int_{K_2}^{\infty} \left[-\alpha X_2 \exp(-\alpha x_1 - \beta x_2) - \right.$$

$$\left. - \int_{K_1-Zx_1}^{\infty} -\alpha \exp(-\alpha x_1 - \beta x_2)\, dx_2 \right] dx_1$$

$$N_2 = \int_{K_2}^{\infty} \left[-\alpha x_2 \exp(-\alpha x_1 - \beta x_2) - \right.$$

$$\left. - \frac{\alpha \exp(\alpha x_1 - \beta x_2)}{\beta} \Big|_{K_1-Zx_1}^{\infty} \right] dx_1$$

$$N_2 = \int_{K_2}^{\infty} \left[\alpha(K_1 - Zx_1)\exp(-\alpha x_1 - \beta(K_1 - Zx_1)) + \right.$$

$$\left. + \frac{\alpha}{\beta}\exp(-\alpha x_1 - \beta(K_1 - Zx_1)) \right] dx_1$$

$$N_2 = \int_{K_2}^{\infty} \alpha K_1 \exp(-\alpha x_1 - \beta(K_1 - Zx_1)) -$$

$$- \alpha Z \int_{K_2}^{\infty} x_1 \exp(-\alpha x_1 - \beta(K_1 - Zx_1))\, dx_1 +$$

$$+ \frac{\alpha}{\beta} \int_{K_2}^{\infty} \exp(-\alpha x_1 - \beta(K_1 - Zx_1))\, dx_1.$$

(10.59)

$$N_2 = I_1 + I_2 + I_3.$$

(10.60)

Let us take I_3 first

$$I_3 = \frac{\alpha}{\beta} \exp(-\beta K_1) \int_{K_2}^{\infty} \exp(-(\alpha - \beta Z)x_1)\, dx_1$$

(10.61)

$$I_3 = \frac{\alpha \exp(-\beta K_1)}{\beta(\alpha - \beta Z)} \left[\left. -\exp(-(\alpha - \beta Z)x_1) \right|_{K_2}^{\infty} \right]$$

$$= 0 + \left[\frac{\alpha \exp(-\beta K_1)}{\beta(\alpha - \beta Z)}\right][\exp(-(\alpha - \beta Z)K_2)]$$

$$I_3 = \frac{\alpha \exp(-\beta K_1 - \alpha K_2 + \beta Z K_2)}{\beta(\alpha - \beta Z)}.$$

(10.62)

Similarly,

$$I_1 = \frac{\alpha K_1 \exp(-\beta K_1 - \alpha K_2 + \beta Z K_2)}{(\alpha - \beta Z)}.$$

(10.63)

Now, we consider I_2

$$I_2 = -\alpha Z \int_{K_2}^{\infty} x_1 \exp(-\alpha x_1 - \beta K_1 + \beta Z x_1)$$

(10.64)

$$I_2 = (-\alpha Z) \exp(-\beta K_1) \int_{K_2}^{\infty} x_1 \exp(-(\alpha - \beta Z)x_1)\, dx_1$$

$$I_2 = (-\alpha Z) \exp(-\beta K_1) \left[\frac{-x_1 \exp(-(\alpha - \beta Z)x_1)}{(\alpha - \beta Z)} - \right.$$

$$\left. - \int_{K_2}^{\infty} \frac{-\exp(-(\alpha - \beta Z)x_1)}{(\alpha - \beta Z)}\, dx_1 \right]$$

$$I_2 = \frac{(-\alpha Z) \exp{(-\beta K_1)}}{(\alpha - \beta Z)} \left[-x_1 \exp{(-(\alpha - \beta Z)x_1)} - \right.$$

$$\left. - \frac{\exp{(-(\alpha - \beta Z)x_1)}}{(\alpha - \beta Z)} \bigg|_{K_2}^{\infty} \right]$$

$$I_2 = \left[\frac{(-\alpha Z) \exp{(-\beta K_1)}}{(\alpha - \beta Z)} \right] \left[K_1 \exp{(-(\alpha - \beta Z)K_2)} + \right.$$

$$\left. + \frac{\exp{(-(\alpha - \beta Z)K_2)}}{(\alpha - \beta Z)} \right]$$

$$I_2 = \left[\frac{(-\alpha Z) \exp{(-\beta K_1)}}{(\alpha - \beta Z)} \right] \left[K_2 + \frac{1}{(\alpha - \beta Z)} \right] \times$$

$$\times [\exp{(-(\alpha - \beta Z)K_2)}]$$

$$I_2 = \left[\frac{(-\alpha Z) \exp{(-\beta K_1 + \beta Z K_2 - \alpha K_2)}}{(\alpha - \beta Z)} \right] \times$$

$$\times \left[K_2 + \frac{1}{(\alpha - \beta Z)} \right]. \quad (10.65)$$

10.5.7. *Putting the parts together for $E[X_2]^*$*

Now, let us put all of these terms together

$$E[X_2]^* = \left[\frac{\alpha K_1 \exp{(-\beta K_1 - \alpha K_2 + \beta Z K_2)}}{(\alpha - \beta Z)} + \right.$$

$$+ \left[\frac{(-\alpha Z) \exp{(-\beta K_1 + \beta Z K_2 - \alpha K_2)}}{(\alpha - \beta Z)} \right] \times$$

$$\times \left[K_2 + \frac{1}{(\alpha - \beta Z)} \right] +$$

$$+ \frac{\alpha \exp{(-\beta K_1 - \alpha K_2 + \beta Z K_2)}}{\beta(\alpha - \beta Z)} \right] \Bigg/$$

$$\Bigg/ \left[\frac{\alpha \exp{(-\beta K_1 - \beta Z K_2 - \alpha K_2)}}{(\alpha - \beta Z)} \right]$$

$$(10.66)$$

$$E[X_2]^* = \left\{ \left[\frac{\alpha \exp{(-\beta K_1 - \alpha K_2 + \beta Z K_2)}}{(\alpha - \beta Z)} \right] \times \right.$$

$$\times \left[K_1 - Z \left[K_2 + \frac{1}{(\alpha - \beta Z)} \right] + \frac{1}{\beta} \right] \right\} \Bigg/$$

$$\Bigg/ \left\{ \left[\frac{\alpha \exp{(-\beta K_1 + \beta Z K_2 - \alpha K_2)}}{(\alpha - \beta Z)} \right] \right\}$$

$$(10.67)$$

$$E[X_2]^* = K_1 - Z K_2 - \frac{Z}{(\alpha - \beta Z)} + \frac{1}{\beta}. \quad (10.68)$$

Now, resubstituting for K_1, K_2, and Z_1,

$$E[X_2]^* = \frac{b_0 - C}{b_2} - \frac{b_1}{b_2} \left(\frac{C - b_0}{b_1} \right) -$$

$$- \frac{b_1/b_2}{\left(\alpha - \beta \frac{b_1}{b_2} \right)} + \frac{1}{\beta} \quad (10.69)$$

or, alternatively,

$$\frac{b_1/b_2}{\left(\alpha - \beta \frac{b_1}{b_2} \right)} - \frac{1}{\beta} = \frac{b_0 - C}{b_2} - \frac{b_1}{b_2} \left(\frac{C - b_0}{b_1} \right) - \mu^*_{x_2}. \quad (10.70)$$

10.6. Appendix B: Computer program

```
C----THIS PROGRAM CALCULATES THE BEST ESTIMATED
C----MEAN AND VARIANCE FOR SIZE AND GRADE FOR THE
C----INPUTTED DEPOSIT DESCRIPTION.
        DIMENSION DUM(5),E(5)
        COMMON ALPH,CA,CB,GR,CONT,SIZE,CLARK,COST,XBAR,XPAVS,
       1XPAVX,XPAVZ,CO
        IOUT = 23
        IPT = 20
        CALL IFILE(20,'RESD')
        READ(IPT,6)ALPH,CA,CB,GR,CONT,SIZE
        READ(IPT,6)CLARK,COST
     WRITE(IOUT,90)GR,CONT,SIZE,CLARK
        WRITE(IOUT,91) COST,ALPH,CA,CB
90      FORMAT(' INPUT DATA',/,' AVERAGE DEPOSIT GRADE',F10.4,
       1/,' AVERAGE DEPOSIT METAL CONTENT',F10.0,/,
       2' AVERAGE DEPOSIT SIZE',F10.0,/,' CLARK',F10.6)
91    . FORMAT('0COST PARAMETERS',/,' BASE PRICE',F5.0,/,
       1' ALPH = ',F10.4,' CA = ',F10.4,' CB = ',F10.4)
        READ(IPT,6)YBAR,YBU,YVAR,YVU,XVAR,XVU,ESCALE
```

```
6          FORMAT(7F)
           CO = ALOG(COST/ALPH)
           DUM(1) = XVAR
           E(1) = XVU
           DUM(2) = YBAR
           E(2) = YBU
           DUM(3) = YVAR
           E(3) = YVU
           F = 10.
           CALL MINSER(DUM,E,3,F,ESCALE,2,1,10)
           WRITE(IOUT,25)
25         FORMAT(1HO,21X,'BEST ESTIMATES')
           WRITE(IOUT,26)
26         FORMAT(1H ,6X,'XPAVX',8X,'XPAVY',8X,'XPAVS',8X,'ERROR')
           WRITE(IOUT,27)XPAVX,XPAVZ,XPAVS,F
27         FORMAT(1H ,4E13.5)
           WRITE(IOUT,28)
28         FORMAT(1HO,6X,' AVX',8X,'SIGSX',8X,' AVY',8X,'SIGSY')
           WRITE(IOUT,27)XBAR,DUM(1),DUM(2),DUM(3)
104        CONTINUE
        STOP
        END
        FUNCTION PNORM(X)
        Z = 0.0
        IF(X.EQ.0.0) GO TO 2
        Z = 1.0
        V = ABS(X)*0.5
        IF(Y.GE.3.0) GO TO 2
        IF(Y.GE.1.0) GO TO 1
        W = Y*Y
        Z = (((((((((0.000124818987*W−0.001075204047)*W+0.005198775019)
       1*W−0.019198292004)*W+0.059054035642)*W−0.151968751364)*W
       2+0.31915293294)*W−0.5319230073)*W+0.797884560593)*Y*2.0
        GO TO 2
1       Y = Y−2.0
        Z = ((((((((((((−0.000045255659*Y+0.00015252929)*Y−
       10.000019538132)*Y−0.000676904986)*Y+0.001390604284)*Y−
       20.00079462082)*Y−0.002034254874)*Y+0.006549791214)*Y−
       30.010557625006)*Y+0.011630447319)*Y−0.009279453341)*Y+
       40.005353579108)*Y−0.002141268741)*Y+0.000535310849)*Y
       5+0.999936657524
2       PNORM = (1.0+SIGN(Z,X))*0.5
        RETURN
        END
        SUBROUTINE CALCFX(NI,DUM,F)
        DIMENSION DUM(1),E(1)
        COMMON ALPH,CA,CB,GR,CONT,SIZE,CLARK,COST,XBAR,XPAVS,
       1XPAVX,XPAVZ,CO
        XVAR = DUM(1)
        YBAR = DUM(2)
        YVAR = DUM(3)
C--- CALCULATE XBAR
        XBAR = ALOG(CLARK)−XVAR/2.0
C--- CALCULATE COST PARAMS
        CVAR2 = CA*CA*YVAR+CB*CB*XVAR
        CVAR = SQRT(CVAR2)
```

```
          CBAR = CA*YBAR+CB*(XBAR+XVAR)
          CBAR1 = CA*YBAR+CB*XBAR
          CBAR2 = CA*(YBAR+YVAR)+CB*(XBAR+XVAR)
          CBAR3 = CA*(YBAR+YVAR)+CB*XBAR
C --- CALCULATE Z VALUES
          Z1 = (CO-CBAR)/CVAR
          Z2 = (CO-CBAR1)/CVAR
          Z3 = (CO-CBAR2)/CVAR
          Z4 = (CO-CBAR3)/CVAR
C --- FIND PROBABILITY VALUES
          P1 = PNORM (Z1)
          P2 = PNORM(Z2)
          P3 = PNORM(Z3)
          P4 = PNORM(Z4)
C --- CALCULATE XPAVX, XPAVZ, AND XPAVS
          XPAVX = EXP(X3AR+XVAR/2.0)*P1/P2
          XPAVZ = EXP(XBAR+XVAR/2.+YBAR+YVAR/2.)*P3/P2
         XPAVS = EXP(YBAR+YVAR/2.0)*P4/P2
C ---- CALCULATE ERROR MEASURE
       F = (ALOG(XPAVX/GR))**2+(ALOG(XPAVS/SIZE))**2+(ALOG(XPAVZ/CONT))**2


          RETURN
          END
          SUBROUTINE MINSER (X,E,N,F,ESCALE,IPRINT,ICON,MAXIT)
          common/min/w(40)
          DIMENSION x(1),e(1)
          IOUT = 23
          DDMAG = 0.1*ESCALE
          SCER = 0.05/ESCALE
          JJ = N*N+N
          JJJ = JJ+N
          K = N+1
          NFCC = 1
          IND = 1
          INN = 1
          DO 1 I = 1,N
          DO 2 J = 1,N
          W(K) = 0.
          IF(I-J)4,3,4
   3      W(K) = ABS(E(I))
          W(I) = ESCALE
   4      K = K+1
   2      CONTINUE
   1      CONTINUE
          ITERC = 1
          ISGRAD = 2
          CALL CALCFX(N,X,F)
          FKEEP = ABS(F)+ABS(F)
   5      ITONE = 1
          FP = F
          SUM = 0.
          IXP = JJ
          DO 6 I = 1,N
          IXP = IXP+1
          W(IXP) = X(I)
   6      CONTINUE
```

```
        IDIRN = N + 1
        ILINE = 1
    7   DMAX = W(ILINE)
        DACC = DMAX * SCER
        DMAG = AMIN1(DDMAG,0.1*DMAX)
        DMAG = AMAX1(DMAG,20.*DACC)
        DDMAX = 10.*DMAG
        GO TO (70,70,71),ITONE
   70   DL = 0.
        D = DMAG
        FPREV = F
        IS = 5
        FA = F
        DA = DL
    8   DD = D - DL
        DL = D
   58   K = IDIRN
        DO 9 I = 1,N
        X(I) = X(I) + DD*W(K)
        K = K + 1
    9   CONTINUE
        CALL CALCFX(N,X,F)
        NFCC = NFCC + 1
        GO TO (10,11,12,13,14,96),IS
   14   IF(F-FA)15,16,24
   16   IF (ABS(D)-DMAX) 17,17,18
   17   D = D + D
        GO TO 8
   18   WRITE(IOUT,19)
   19   FORMAT (5X,45HMINSER MAXIMUM CHANGE DOES NOT ALTER FUNCTION)
        GO TO 20
   15   FB = F
        DB = D
        GO TO 21
   24   FB = FA
        DB = DA
        FA = F
        DA = D
   21   GO TO (83,23),ISGRAD
   23   D = DB + DB - DA
        IS = 1
        GO TO 8
   83   D = 0.5*(DA+DB-(FA-FB)/(DA-DB))
        IS = 4
        IF((DA-D)*(D-DB))25,8,8
   25   IS = 1
        IF (ABS(D-DB)-DDMAX) 8,8,26
   26   D = DB+SIGN(DDMAX,DB-DA)
        IS = 1
        DDMAX = DDMAX + DDMAX
        DDMAG = DDMAG + DDMAG
        IF(DDMAX-DMAX)8,8,27
   27   DDMAX = DMAX
        GO TO 8
   13   IF(F-FA)28,23,23
   28   FC = FB
```

```
      DC = DB
29    FB = F
      DB = D
      GO TO 30
12    IF(F − FB)28,28,31
31    FA = F
      DA = D
      GO TO 30
11    IF(F − FB)32,10,10
32    FA = FB
      DA = DB
      GO TO 29
71    DL = 1.
      DDMAX = 5.
      FA = FP
      DA = −1.
      FB = FHOLD
      DB = 0.
      D = 1.
10    FC = F
      DC = D
30    A = (DB − DC)*(FA − FC)
      B = (DC − DA)*(FB − FC)
      IF((A + B)*(DA − DC))33,33,34
33    FA = FB
      DA = DB
      FB = FC
      DB = DC
      GO TO 26
34    D = 0.5*(A*(DB + DC) + B*(DA + DC))/(A + B)
      DI = DB
      FI = FB
      IF(FB − FC)44,44,43
43    DI = DC
      FI = FC
44    GO TO (86,86,85),ITONE
85    ITONE = 2
      GO TO 45
86    IF (ABS(D − DI) − DACC) 41,41,93
93    IF (ABS(D − DI) − 0.03*ABS(D)) 41,41,45
45    IF ((DA − DC)*(DC − D)) 47,46,46
46    FA = FB
      DA = DB
      FB = FC
      DB = DC
      GO TO 25
47    IS = 2
      IF ((DB − D)*(D − DC)) 48,8,8
48    IS = 3
      GO TO 8
41    F = FI
      D = DI − DL
      DD = SQRT((DC − DB)*(DC − DA)*(DA − DB)/(A + B))
      DO 49 I = 1,N
      X(I) = X(I) + D*W(IDIRN)
      W(IDIRN) = DD*W(IDIRN)
```

```
         IDIRN = IDIRN + 1
   49    CONTINUE
         W(ILINE) = W(ILINE)/DD
         ILINE = ILINE + 1
         IF(IPRINT − 1)51,50,51
   50    WRITE(IOUT,52) ITERC,NFCC,F
   52    FORMAT (/1X,9HITERATION,I5,I15,16H FUNCTION VALUES,
         11OX,3HF = ,E21.9)
         WRITE(IOUT,54) (X(I),I = 1,N)
   54    FORMAT (5E24.9)
         GO TO (51,53),IPRINT
   51    GO TO (55,38),ITONE
   55    IF (FPREV − F − SUM) 94,95,95
   95    SUM = FPREV − F
         JIL = ILINE
   94    IF (IDIRN − JJ) 7,7,84
   84    GO TO (92,72),IND
   92    FHOLD = F
         IS = 6
         IXP = JJ
         DO 59 I = 1,N
         IXP = IXP + 1
         W(IXP) = X(I) − W(IXP)
   59    CONTINUE
         DD = 1.
         GO TO 58
   96    GO TO (112,87),IND
  112    IF (FP − F) 37,91,91
   91    D = 2.*(FP + F − 2.*FHOLD)/(FP − F)**2
         IF   (D*(FP − FHOLD − SUM)**2 − SUM) 87,37,37
   87    J = JIL*N + 1
         IF (J − JJ) 60,60,61
   60    DO 62 I = J,JJ
         K = I − N
         W(K) = W(I)
   62    CONTINUE
         DO 97 I = JIL,N
         W(I − 1) = W(I)
   97    CONTINUE
   61    IDIRN = IDIRN − N
         ITONE = 3
         K = IDIRN
         IXP = JJ
         AAA = 0.
         DO 65 I = 1,N
         IXP = IXP + 1
         W(K) = W(IXP)
         IF (AAA − ABS(W(K)/E(I))) 66,67,67
   66    AAA = ABS(W(K)/E(I))
   67    K = K + 1
   65    CONTINUE
         DDMAG = 1.
         W(N) = ESCALE/AAA
         ILINE = N
         GO TO 7
   37    IXP = JJ
```

```
          AAA = 0.
          F = FHOLD
          DO 99 I = 1,N
          IXP = IXP + 1
          X(I) = X(I) − W(IXP)
          IF (AAA*ABS(E(I)) − ABS(W(IXP))) 98,99,99
   98     AAA = ABS(W(IXP)/E(I))
   99     CONTINUE
          GO TO 72
   38     AAA = AAA*(1.+DI)
          GO TO (72,106),IND
   72     IF (IPRINT−2) 53,50,50
   53     GO TO (109,88),IND
  109     IF (AAA−0.1) 89,89,76
   89     GO TO (20,116),ICON
  116     IND = 2
          GO TO (100,101),INN
  100     INN = 2
          K = JJJ
          DO 102 I = 1,N
          K = K + 1
          W(K) = X(I)
          X(I) = X(I) + 10.*E(I)
  102     CONTINUE
          FKEEP = F
          CALL CALCFX (N,X,F)
          NFCC = NFCC + 1
          DDMAG = 0.
          GO TO 108
   76     IF (F−FP) 35,78,78
   78     WRITE(IOUT,80)
   80     FORMAT (5X,38HMINSER ACCURACY LIMITED BY ERRORS IN F)
          GO TO 20
   88     IND = 1
   35     DDMAG = 0.4*SQRT(FP−F)
          ISGRAD = 1
  108     ITERC = ITERC + 1
          IF (ITERC−MAXIT) 5,5,81
   81     WRITE(IOUT,82) MAXIT
   82     FORMAT (I5,31H ITERATIONS COMPLETED BY MINSER)
          IF (F−FKEEP) 20,20,110
  110     F = FKEEP
          DO 111 I = 1,N
          JJJ = JJJ + 1
          X(I) = W(JJJ)
  111     CONTINUE
          GO TO 20
  101     JIL = 1
          FP = FKEEP
          IF (F−FKEEP) 105,78,104
  104     JIL = 2
          FP = F
          F = FKEEP
  105     IXP = JJ
          DO 113 I = 1,N
          IXP = IXP + 1
```

```
          K = IXP + N
          GO TO (114,115),JIL
    114   W(IXP) = W(K)
          GO TO 113
    115   W(IXP) = X(I)
          X(I) = W(K)
    113   CONTINUE
          JIL = 2
          GO TO 92
    106   IF (AAA − 0.1) 20,20,107
     20   RETURN
    107   INN = 1
          GO TO 35
          END
```

References

Brinck, J. W. (1967). Note on the distribution and predictability of mineral resources. *Euratom 3461*, Brussels.

Drew, M. W. (1977). U.S. uranium deposits: a geostatistical model. *Resources Policy* **3**(1), 60–70.

Notes

1. This relationship is a restatement of a relationship derived for lognormal distributions in general: arithmetic mean $= e^{a + b^2/2}$, where a is the mean of logarithms of the variable and b^2 is the logarithmic variance. Here $x = \ln q$; γ_q is the arithmetic mean of q; $\mu_x = E(\ln q)$; $\sigma_x^2 = E(\ln q - \mu_x)$.

2. $\gamma_q^* = E(Q)^*$, $\gamma_t^* = E(T)^*$, the expectations of grade and tonnage on the truncated population.

3. The PAU report gives the value of 8.879 as $\hat{\mu}_y$, but in PAU notation μ_y is the parameter of the biased (truncated) distribution. The mean of the full population is $7.517 = 8.879 - 1.362$ (biased mean minus variance).

4. Note: $\mu_y' = \mu_y + \sigma_y^2$ where μ_y' is the expectation of the biased (truncated) population. For Africa, $\mu_y' = 7.669 = -3.73 + 11.399$; for the US, $\mu_y' = 8.879 = 7.517 + 1.362$.

11 THE STATISTICAL RELATIONSHIP OF DEPOSIT SIZE TO GRADE—A GRADE–TONNAGE RELATIONSHIP

11.1. Perspective

The topic of this chapter is commonly referred to as a grade–tonnage relation. While this terminology is appropriate, it is important that it be understood that the nature of the relationship explored here is markedly different from the Lasky-type relationship (see 'Quantity–quality relations', Chapter 3), which is that relationship envisioned by many in response to the expression 'grade–tonnage relation'. Precisely stated, this chapter examines the *correlation* between deposit size (tonnage) and deposit grade. Proper perspective is achieved by considering the following question: considering the entire population of deposits of a specific kind, is the expectation for deposit grade the same for a deposit of size X as it is for one of size $10X$? If the answer to this question were to be yes, then deposit tonnage and grade would be statistically independent. On the other hand, if the expectation for grade for the deposit of size $10X$ were to be smaller than for a deposit of size X, deposit tonnage and grade would be said to be dependent and negatively correlated or inversely related. Conversely, if 'on average' grade were to be larger for large deposit tonnages than for small ones, deposit grade and tonnage would be said to be dependent and positively correlated. The correlation coefficient, ρ, describes the strength of correlation: $\rho = -1$ and $+1$ connotes perfect inverse (negative) and perfect direct (positive) relations, respectively; $\rho = 0$ connotes no relation (statistical independence); for $0 < \rho < 1$ and $-1 < \rho < 0$, the relation is less than perfect.

In contrast to the grade–tonnage relation of this chapter, the grade–tonnage relationship of Chapter 3 is non-statistical, being instead a description of a stock of material by quality. While this characterization and contrasting of the two very different relations is an accurate statement of their overall nature and is, therefore, useful in the instruction and discussion of them, it is a somewhat simplistic statement of their use. Specifically, the statistical relationship, either directly or indirectly as a part of a crustal-abundance model, may influence either the perception of or the estimation of the magnitude of mineral resources and endowment. Thus, a statistical grade–tonnage relation also may have quantity implications.

11.2. Why the concern about this issue?

The correlation of deposit tonnage and grade is important in the economics of exploration and in models of this process. Explorationists are concerned with the sizes and grades of the remaining undiscovered deposits. For, having to explore for and develop deposits having lower grades is one thing if, as we turn to the lower-grade deposits, those deposits are, on average, larger; it is quite another thing if deposit tonnage and grade are statistically independent or positively correlated. In the case of statistical independence, deposits with lower grades have proportionately less metal. Therefore, having to turn to lower-grade deposits means that production costs will increase unless technical change results in cost savings sufficient to offset grade depletion.

The correlation of deposit tonnage and grade is a very important issue in resource adequacy and potential supply. Usually, these issues are relevant only in the very long run of time. Of course, in the very long run, technology can change significantly. In the past, this change has resulted in the identification of new modes of occurrence for specific metals and in the ability to produce low-grade, large deposits at ever-decreasing costs. Since the very long run implies large increases in cumulative production for a given metal, the quantities of metal present in low-grade deposits may affect significantly the perception and assessment of resource adequacy. With regards to resource adequacy, the following questions merit consideration: what happens to the amounts of metal and mineralized material when grade of deposits is decreased by an order of magnitude? Are there very low-grade deposits that contain huge quantities of mineralized rock? And, do these deposits permit significant economics in exploration, development, and production?

The PAU crustal-abundance geostatistical model of the previous chapter is one attempt to examine the potential supply of uranium for prices significantly higher than those that prevailed at the time of the analysis. Of course, these prices imply deposit grades considerably below those of known deposits. The grade–tonnage relation, either implied by a CAG model or explicitly expressed in the model, strongly affects estimates of mineral endowment and potential supply. Therefore, the grade–tonnage relation employed in CAG models is deserving of critical examination and thought.

11.3. Perceptions and beliefs

In a survey of the copper resources of Sonora, Mexico, Harris (1973) found that each geologist interviewed believed in an inverse relationship of deposit grade and tonnage separately for each mode of occurrence: vein and porphyry. This belief was strongly expressed in probabilities for tonnage and grade combinations. However, when the probability distribution for *all geologists*, collectively, was determined for a given mode of occurrence, there was so much disagreement among the geologists on the numerical specification of this relationship that for the group as a whole there was no statistically meaningful relationship between deposit size and grade within the porphyry class. However, for the group a strong relationship was found for grade and deposit size across both modes of occurrence.

Generally, it is a fact that geologists have in the past perceived an inverse relationship (correlation) of deposit tonnage to deposit grade. The extent of and strength of this perception are particularly interesting in view of the fact that until 1973, this relation had not been systematically analysed by statistical methods. This prompts one to question the reason for the commonality of this perception: is it because of some 'super sense' of the geologist, a sense born either of field observation or of geoscientific principles? Or, is it a misinterpretation of some other effects, such as economics and technology, as a physical relation?

Man's experience is that he has depleted the high-grade, easily located deposits; therefore, he has been forced to exploit lower-grade deposits (see Fig. 11.1). In the case of copper deposits in this country, history documents the early exploitation of high-grade vein deposits, primary and enriched, and the

Fig. 11.1. Economics of copper mining in the United States 1925–65 (data from US Bureau of Mines). (Source: Lovering 1969, p. 124.) (Reproduced from *Resources and Man* with the permission of the National Academy Press, Washington, D.C., 1969.)

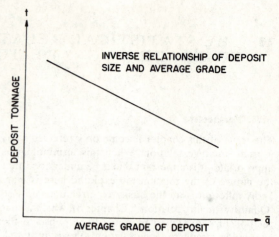

Fig. 11.2. Belief of geologists about the relationship of deposit size and average grade.

later transition to the low-grade porphyries, generally with larger tonnages of ore than were contained in the high-grade veins (see Fig. 11.1). Technological advances made this transition to lower-grade ores possible without increases in copper prices; in fact, real prices continued to decline during and after this transition. In effect, technology created copper resources by allowing the exploitation of a different kind of deposit. An equally striking example of the effect of technology in expanding our resources is the application of concentrating and pelletizing technologies to low-grade taconite material, creating a usable source of iron for the blast furnace. Here, as with copper, technology expanded considerably our resources by allowing the exploitation of lower-grade ore, ore that was relatively abundant in the Great Lakes Region. With experience such as the foregoing, it is hardly surprising that mineral scientists and engineers commonly believe that as cut-off grade decreases, we can expect deposits of larger size (see Fig. 11.2). But, this experience neither proves nor disproves the presence of a dependency (correlation) between deposit size and grade. Rather, it suggests that determining the actual relationship between deposit size and grade from available data is a complex and difficult task.

11.4. Empirical studies

The first comprehensive and statistical investigation of the relationship of deposit size to grade was made by the US Geological Survey (Singer, Cox, and Drew 1975). It is argued in that investigation that geological reasoning dictates that deposit size and deposit

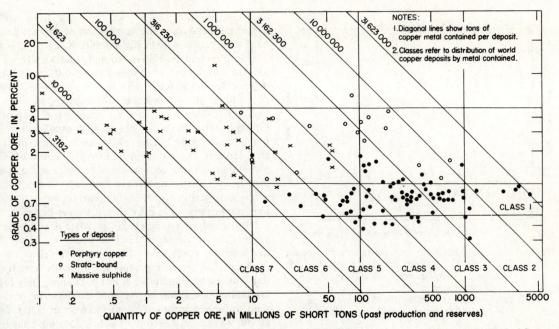

Fig. 11.3. Size and grade characteristics of copper deposits of the three main geological types (After US Geological Survey, presentation at COMRATE Colloquium, 1973, Estes Park, Colorado.)

grade are statistically independent, because they are controlled by different geological processes. This conceptual argument is followed by a statistical analysis of deposit size and deposit grade for the copper deposits of the world. Fig. 11.3 shows the plot of tonnage and grade for these deposits. The results of this investigation are that there is no statistically significant relationship between deposit size and grade for porphyry or stratabound copper deposits. However, there is a significant relationship between deposit size and grade for the mixed class of massive sulphide deposits and for the aggregate of all deposits ($r = -0.42$ and -0.67, respectively, which are significant at the 1 per cent level). The presence of the inverse relationship between deposit tonnage and grade across all deposits is evident in the downward slope of the bivariate plot of Fig. 11.3 as deposit tonnage increases.

Agterberg and Divi (1978) investigated the correlation of deposit size and grade for 180 base metal deposits of the Canadian Appalachian Region. By genetic type, these 180 deposits were classified as follows (Agterberg and Divi 1978, p. 233): 108 volcanogenic massive sulphide type (includes some disseminated sulphide deposits interpreted as alteration pipes); 31 vein and replacement types (exclusive of skarn); 15 skarn, contact-metasomatic, and por-

phyry types; 13 sedimentary type; 7 magmatic type; and 6 unclassified. For 145 of the 180 deposits, data were compiled on ore reserves (measured, indicated, or inferred) and added to cumulative production. Fig. 11.4 is a bivariate scattergram of deposit tonnage and grade for 127 copper deposits; statistical analysis of these data produced a correlation of -0.60, which is significantly different from zero at the 0.01 level of significance. For 66 lead deposits, Agterberg and Divi also found size and grade to be negatively correlated: $\rho = -0.34$, which is significantly different from zero at the 0.01 level of significance. However, they found the correlation (-0.18) of deposit size and grade for 78 zinc deposits to be not significantly different from zero at the 0.01 level of significance.

Harris (1977) examined the correlation of size and grade for uranium deposits of the San Juan Basin of New Mexico. The basic data consisted of cumulative production and estimated ore reserves for mining properties. To the extent possible, which was very limited, mining properties were grouped to conform to recognized deposits. Statistical analysis of all data showed size and grade to be positively correlated. However, this result appeared to be highly influenced by a high density of deposits/properties having very small size, less than 150 s.t. (see Fig.

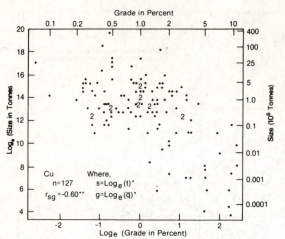

Fig. 11.4. Size (in tonnes of ore) plotted against mean grade for 127 deposits with reported values for copper. [* Explanation added by author. ** Correlation coefficient $r_{sg} = -0.60$ is significantly different from zero at 0.01 level of significance.] (After Agterberg and Divi 1978, p. 235.)

12.3). Harris found that eliminating these deposits/properties and subjecting the remaining 167 deposits/properties to statistical analysis resulted in a weak negative correlation, -0.070. While this correlation is small, it is significantly different from zero at the 0.01 level of significance. Although this result is interesting, the fact that some of the data were not included in the analysis calls for an explanation. The explanation offered is that since the data for sizes greater than 150 s.t. (see Fig. 12.3) exhibit a distinctly different pattern than those having sizes less than 150 s.t., there is either (1) more than one population represented in the data, or (2) some of the data have been 'filtered' by economic criteria, while some (deposits/properties having sizes less than 150 s.t.) have not. Chapter 12 develops a method for the analysis of the correlation of deposit size with grade in which consideration is given to the economic effect; some general comment on this issue is provided in § 11.5.

Singer and DeYoung (1980) applied statistical analysis to differentiated massive sulphide copper deposits (mafic volcanogenic and felsic volcanogenic), nickel deposits (komatiite, laterite, and small intrusive), porphyry molybdenum, and tactite tungsten deposits. Table 11.1 shows the results of their analysis. It is noteworthy that when massive sulphide copper deposits are differentiated into mafic

and felsic volcanogenic types, only for felsic volcanogenic deposits is the correlation of deposit tonnage and grade statistically significant, even at the 0.05 probability level. For copper, statistically significant correlations were found at the 0.01 probability level for skarn, felsic volcanogenic, and mixed (all deposits; in all of these cases correlations are negative. For nickel deposits, the correlation of deposit tonnage with grade is statistically significant for komatiite deposits, but not for laterite or small intrusive deposits. As with copper, for the mixture of all nickel deposits, the correlation of tonnage and grade also is statistically significant, but only at the 0.05 probability level; however, this correlation is positive, not negative as it is for mixed copper deposits.

Singer and DeYoung (1980, p. 94) point out that while deposit tonnages tend to increase, given a decrease in grade, for skarn copper, felsic volcanogenic copper, mixed copper, and tactite tungsten deposits, metal content tends not to change. Only for komatiite nickel deposits does a decrease in grade tend to be accompanied by an increase in metal. In all other cases, metal content either does not change or decreases with a decrease in grade.

11.5. Difficulties in the statistical analysis of ore-deposit data

11.5.1. *Contamination of statistical data by economics*

A critical and definitive examination of the dependency between deposit tonnage and grade is impeded by the fact that statistical data reflect, among other things, a biased sample of the bivariate population. To some degree, a plot of tonnage and grade per deposit is a plot of the economics and technology of exploration, mining, and processing of the metals. This may be particularly significant when tonnages and grades are examined over a wide range of deposit types.

A seemingly reasonable approach to determining the presence of dependency (correlation) between deposit tonnage and grade is to examine their statistical correlation on data of known deposits. Unfortunately, such an approach alone may not prove or disprove dependency, for the tonnage–grade data represent a truncated sample, not a random sample of tonnages and grades. Furthermore, the effect of profit maximization of mining is that data on deposits are translated as well as truncated.

TABLE 11.1. Grade and tonnage correlations and regression coefficients. (Source: Singer and DeYoung 1980, p. 94.)

Deposit type	Commodity	Number of deposits	$\log_{10} G = a + b \cdot \log_{10} T$			$\log_{10} M = a + b \cdot \log_{10} T$			$\log_{10} M = a + b \cdot \log_{10} G$			Estimated grade for crust (10^{-6})
			Correlation coefficient	a (intercept)	b (slope)	Correlation coefficient‡	a (intercept)	b (slope)	Correlation coefficient	a (intercept)	b (slope)	
Komatiite	nickel	52	−0.6156‡	−0.5411	−0.1963	0.9545	−0.5411	0.8037	−0.3524†	3.2706	−0.9309	89
Laterite	nickel	54	−0.1259	−1.7436	−0.0161	0.9918	−1.7436	0.9839	0.0019	5.8163	0.0151	14 000
Small intrusive	nickel	50	−0.0874	−1.9815	−0.0390	0.9075	−1.9815	0.9610	0.3391‡	5.6682	0.8044	6 400
All deposits	nickel	156	0.1690†	−2.3196	0.0473	0.9669	−2.3196	1.0473	0.4145‡	8.1214	1.6020	36 000
Skarn	copper	35	−0.4703‡	−0.9973	−0.1224	0.9674	−0.9973	0.8776	−0.2315	3.0089	−0.8072	660
Mafic volcanogenic	copper	37	−0.1334	−1.4269	−0.0379	0.9598	−1.4269	0.9621	0.1502	5.5792	0.5302	22 000
Felsic volcanogenic	copper	92	−0.4000‡	−0.5027	−0.2000	0.8677	−0.5027	0.8000	0.1085	4.8996	0.2002	92
Porphyry	copper	165	0.1463	−2.6042	0.0420	0.9648	−2.6042	1.0420	0.4011‡	9.3842	1.5098	5700
All deposits§	copper	395	−0.4183‡	−1.0811	−0.1376	0.9449	−1.0811	0.8624	−0.0979	4.4815	−0.2718	320
Porphyry	molybdenum	34	−0.1271	−2.6919	−0.0287	0.9744	−2.6919	0.9713	0.0989	5.8467	0.4369	1300
Tactite	tungsten	32	−0.3948†	−1.7665	−0.0920	0.9733	−1.7665	0.9080	−0.1734	1.9400	−0.6941	400

T = tonnage of mineralized material ('ore') in each deposit; M = contained metal in each deposit; G = average grade of mineralized material in each deposit.
† Significant at 5 per cent level.
‡ Significant at 1 per cent level.
§ Include copper in 46 small intrusive nickel deposits and 20 komatiite nickel deposits.

11.5.2. *Truncation*

Truncation derives from a combination of circumstances

1. Data on known deposits are primarily data on economic sizes and concentrations.
2. Preferential discovery of large deposits.
3. Economies of scale in mining.
4. A dependency of milling cost on grade of ore.

Because of the relationships of cost to both tonnage and grade, it is conceptually possible that a correlation analysis of grade and tonnage data would reflect primarily the cost surface, the truncation effect. The truncation effect of the cost surface can impart an apparent but false dependency of grade and tonnage, as in case A of Fig. 11.5, or it can confuse a real dependency, as in cases B and C of Fig. 11.5.

Where the cost surface is very gently sloping but the dependency relationship is steeply sloping, it is conceivable, conceptually, that statistical data on grade and tonnage may indicate a lack of dependency. Schematically, such a set of circumstances is portrayed in case D of Fig. 11.5. In case B, the strength of the statistically estimated dependency would be understated by correlation analysis, while in case C it would be overstated. Obviously, the relative effects depend upon the relative slopes of the dependency relationship and the truncation surface. Of course, non-linearity of either of these further confounds interpretation of the statistical data. In all cases, the estimated identification and description of dependency is distorted by the cost surface. The real dependency can be estimated only by compensating for the truncating effects of economics.

11.5.3. *Translation*

The foregoing section identified one effect of economics and technology of exploration, mining,

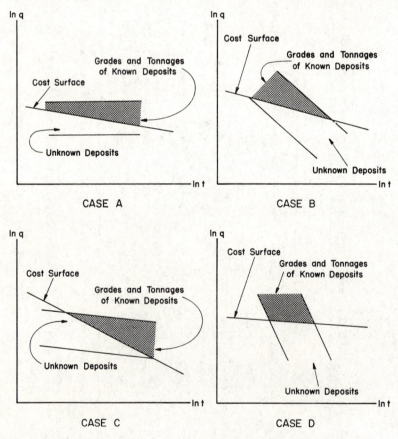

Fig. 11.5. A schematic representation of the effects of the truncation surface on the apparent correlation of grade and tonnage.

and processing to be a nonrandom sample of deposit sizes and grades. This sample is referred to as a truncated sample, or as a sample from a truncated population. If each deposit were homogeneous as to grade and other physical parameters, this truncation would be the only major data anomaly. However, matters are more complex than this: since some deposits have a wide range of grades, the optimization of profits in mining often results in the development and mining of only the high-grade part of the deposit. In other words, tonnage and grade data that are routinely reported are for the ore deposit, not the geologic deposit (total mineralized material). The general result of mine optimization is to represent the deposit by a smaller tonnage and higher grade than apply to the geological deposit. In terms of a map of the deposit tonnage–grade space, the effect of the optimization of mine profits is to translate the deposit to a new position of higher grade but lower tonnage. Fig. 11.6 shows both the translation and truncation effects. The importance of translation as a distortion varies with the mineral commodity and the age or maturity of the exploitation activity. For those mineral commodities or modes of occurrences for which the material within any given deposit typically exhibits small variations in grade, the distortion of data by translation may be minor. Furthermore, the longer the deposit has been mined, the greater the reserve additions and the more representative the revised ore tonnage and grade data are of the geologic deposit.

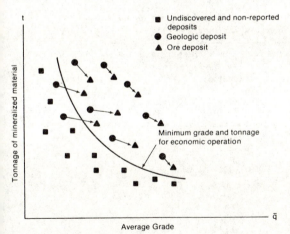

Fig. 11.6. Schematic illustration of truncation and translation resulting from economics of exploration and exploitation. (Source: Harris and Agterberg 1981.)

11.5.4. *Possible remedies*

Conceptually, the simplest of remedies would be that for translation. Replacing tonnages and grades of all ore deposits by tonnages and grades of the geological deposit would be a completely satisfactory solution. While this is conceptually appealing, it may not be achievable, at least not with a high level of accuracy. For one thing, data on geological deposits are seldom reported to the public, and those entities (mining companies) possessing the desired data are reluctant to release them. Second, in the early stages of development and mining of a deposit even the mining company may not have good estimates of the total tonnage and average grade of the deposit.

When data on geological deposits cannot be obtained directly for all deposits, the analyst may have to employ other methods to approximate these data. For example, if tonnages and average grades are known for two cut-off grades, statistical analysis may be employed to estimate the quantity of material for some sufficiently low cut-off grade. The methods of Chapter 3 ('Quantity–quality relations') or a generalized search for the total tonnage and the parameters of the implied grade distribution may be useful approaches (Charles River Associates 1978).

The foregoing comments apply to correcting for the translation effect only. When truncation is also present, an additional remedy must be sought. Generally speaking, treating the truncation effect requires first the identification of the truncation relationship, and second the explicit consideration of this relationship in the estimation of parameters, one of which is the correlation of deposit tonnage with grade. The first attempt at such analysis was made by Harris (1977) and is reported on in Chapter 12. Since the investigation by Harris, a sophisticated mathematical method of analysis has been employed (Kroch [1]).

11.6. Grade–tonnage relations and crustal abundance

11.6.1. *Perspective*

The amount of metal ultimately available, or the average concentration of a metal in crustal material (crustal abundance), has been employed variously as a basis for inference as to the quantities of the metal that are available at higher, but subeconomic grades. For example, Brinck (1967), Agterberg and Divi (1978), and Harris, Ortiz-Vértiz, Chavez, and Agbolosoo (1981) have employed lognormal distributions of element concentration in crustal material as a means to estimating mineral endowment or mineral resources. Use of these relations implies a continuity of grades down to and beyond crustal abundance. Such a continuity has been questioned by Skinner (1976), who proposes that the concentration of an element in the earth's crust is more likely to be bimodal, one mode representing concentrations in ore minerals (sulphides and oxides) and the other the much lower concentrations in common rocks. § 11.6.2 describes the effort by Singer and DeYoung (1980) to test the assumption of grade continuity by grade–tonnage models.

The PAU model described in Chapter 10 employed an independent bivariate lognormal distribution of deposit size and grade as a crustal-abundance model for the estimation of mineral endowment and mineral resources. While the representation of deposit grade and tonnage for familiar modes of occurrence of deposits as being statistically independent often seems to be justified, independence of deposit size and grade in a crustal-abundance model, which by its nature represents all modes of occurrence of that element, may be problematic. This issue is explored in § 11.6.3.

11.6.2. Singer and DeYoung's analysis

Singer and DeYoung (1980, pp. 94–5) test the usefulness of estimated grade–tonnage equations by substituting for deposit tonnage the tonnage of the continental crust of the earth, which was taken to be 10^{18} tonnes (Brinck 1971). Their reasoning was that

a useful relationship (equation) should provide an estimate for grade that is approximately equal to the measured crustal abundance for that element when tonnage of deposit is set equal to total crustal material. Consider, for example, the mixed copper equation (Singer and DeYoung 1980)

$$\log(\bar{q}) = -1.0811 - 0.1376 \log t.$$

Substituting $t = 10^{18}$, we have

$$\log(\bar{q}) = -1.0811 - 0.1376(18) - 3.5579$$
$$\bar{q} = 0.000320 \rightarrow 320 \times 10^{-6}.$$

The crustal abundance of copper reported by Lee and Yao (1970) is 63×10^{-6}; thus, the crustal abundance estimated by the grade–tonnage relation for mixed copper is approximately 5 times that measured. Table 11.2 compares crustal abundance estimated in this fashion (tonnage–grade relation) with the values reported by Lee and Yao (1970). The estimate of crustal abundance for komatiite nickel is identical to that reported by Lee and Yao, and the estimate for felsic volcanogenic is a close estimate. But, in all other cases estimates of crustal abundance by the grade–tonnage relations exceed, often by very large multiples, measured crustal abundances.

In addition to comparing estimated and measured crustal abundance, Singer and DeYoung (1980, p. 95) compare slopes of the grade–tonnage equations with the slopes of that line which passes through the measured crustal abundance and the average grade and total tonnage of known deposits. They found for

TABLE 11.2. Comparison of crustal abundance estimated by grade–tonnage equation with measured values. (After Singer and DeYoung 1980.)

Deposit Type	Commodity	Crustal abundance	
		Estimated by equation ($\times 10^{-6}$)	Measured[†] ($\times 10^{-6}$)
Komatiite	Nickel	89	89
Laterite	Nickel	14 000	89
Small intrusive	Nickel	6 400	89
Mixed (all)	Nickel	36 000	89
Skarn	Copper	660	63
Mafic volcanogenic	Copper	22 000	63
Felsic volcanogenic	Copper	92	63
Porphyry	Copper	5700	63
Mixed (all)	Copper	320	63
Porphyry	Molybdenum	1300	1.3
Tactite	Tungsten	400	1.1

† Lee and Yao (1970).

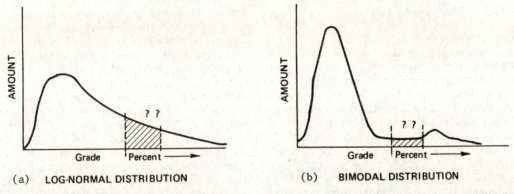

Fig. 11.7. Competing hypotheses for grade distributions: (a) lognormal versus (b) Skinner's (1976) bimodal distribution. (Source: Harris 1978.)

the mixed copper and mixed nickel deposits that the slopes of the crustal abundance lines are significantly lower (at the 0.01 probability level) than those of the estimated grade–tonnage models. They concluded that this raises questions about the validity of assuming continuity of grades to crustal abundance and supports Skinner's (1976) hypothesis of a bimodal grade distribution (see Fig. 11.7).

Singer and DeYoung may be correct with regard to the relevance of a bimodal element distribution. Furthermore, their analysis is a valuable commentary, for it is the most definitive available at this time. Even so, because of the possibility that the deposit data analysed may contain unresolved translation and truncation effects, the grade–tonnage models which they estimated do not make a convincing case for the abandonment of the assumption of the continuity of grades implied by a lognormal crustal abundance model. To the extent that data were available, Singer and DeYoung (1980, p. 92) attempted to remedy the translation effect.

> The grade and tonnage data came from two kinds of sources: those that represent the economic portion of deposits and therefore have relatively high cutoff grades, and those that represent the total endowment of mineralized rock in a deposit and therefore have relatively low cutoff grades. Combining these two kinds of sources means that tonnages and average grades in these analyses are associated with cutoff grades that are typically lower than those now economic to mine but higher than the endowment of deposits.

As indicated in this quote, some data were for geological deposits while other data were for ore deposits; consequently, it is difficult to assess what unresolved translation effects may have contributed to the results of their analysis.

The second statistical problem, that of truncation, was not considered in the estimation of the grade–tonnage models. Essentially, the mixture of geological-deposit and ore-deposit data was considered to be a random sample of deposit sizes and grades. On *a priori* grounds, such a treatment would be less than satisfying if the objective were to estimate all parameters of a dependent bivariate model of deposit grade and tonnage. Even so, it is difficult to say just what the impact of economic truncation is on the estimation of correlation. As indicated in Fig. 11.5, various effects can result from ignoring truncation, depending on the slope of the cost function and nature of and strength of correlation between size and grade in the population of geological deposits. A rather persuasive argument seems to be that because of failure to account for the truncation effect in the analysis of the correlation of deposit tonnages and grades, conclusions about continuity and modality of the distribution of grades within the Earth's crust are severely weakened. When due consideration is given to (1) the very small part—in the high-grade tail—of the distribution of crustal grade that is represented by economic mineral deposits, (2) the magnitude of the extrapolation required of the estimated equation to reach crustal abundance and the weight of the crust, and (3) the large error in such an estimate even under the best of conditions, the almost certainty that the data on deposit tonnages and grades contain systematic biases suggests strongly that grade–tonnage relations based upon such data say very little about the continuity of grades or the modality of the distribution of crustal grades. Unfortunately, a useful test of the Skinner hypothesis will require much more and better data than that available at this time.

11.6.3. *The PAU model*

This section explores the credibility of basing a crustal-abundance geostatistical model on the independence of deposit grade and tonnage. The demonstration in Chapter 10 of the PAU crustal-abundance geostatistical model for Africa is useful for the exploration of this issue, for deposit tonnage was considered to be statistically independent (uncorrelated) of deposit grade. In that demonstration, $\hat{\mu}_y$, given a crustal abundance of 2×10^{-6}, is estimated to be -3.73. Therefore, the geometric mean $(e^{\hat{\mu}_y})$ is 0.024 tonnes; this is the estimated geometric mean tonnage of the full (nontruncated) population and corresponds to the modal (most likely or most typical) tonnage. What kind of a deposit is it for which the most typical size is approximately 50 lb of mineralized material? Is a deposit population of this nature compatible with man's geological understanding? And, what can be said about dependency of grade and tonnage for such a population? For samples of rock ranging from, say a few pounds to billions of tons, is the assumption of independence of grade and tonnage reasonable? Can we really accept the implication of this assumption that the probability for a given grade is the same for 10 lb of rock as it is for 1×10^9 tonnes of rock? These are pertinent questions to be directed to a crustal-abundance-type of model, such as that developed by PAU.

The concept of deposit accommodates various morphologies, reflecting the different geological processes involved in the formation of deposits of the various modes. Although man's experience must allow for considerable variation in morphology, it also recognizes known economic deposits as anomalies in the domain of rock material. Usually the bounds of these anomalies are well defined. What is the deposit morphology when grades are lowered to an order above crustal abundance? Are there distinct morphologies? What about deposits having grades below crustal abundance? We simply do not know the answers to these questions.

If the deposit model is generalized to represent all rock material to some specified depth in a given region, as are the models of Brinck and PAU, the assumption of statistical independence of grade and tonnage for a set of deposits that comprises all of this rock and has a mean grade of crustal abundance may not be appropriate. Unfortunately, there has not been assembled a set of data which could test this hypothesis in a comprehensive way. Available data represent only a small segment of the bivariate grade and tonnage distribution conceptualized by PAU,

one having a mean grade of crustal abundance and all possible sizes from grains to our largest porphyries or stratabound deposits, or larger.

Elsewhere the position often has been taken by the author that models restricted to a given mode are preferred, for a number of reasons. That position is here underscored. However, it must be recognized that taking this position is not without cost for very generalized models of the crustal abundance variety. Once a model is restricted to a given mode, it does not represent the totality of material in a given region; therefore, there is no assurance that the mean of grade for this mode is crustal abundance. The impact of this upon the quantification of a deposit model of the PAU variety is that instead of having to estimate three parameters from three relationships, one must estimate four. Furthermore, if the model does not represent the totality of material in a region, then an additional distribution is required, one which defines number of deposits. The simplicity of modelling of resources afforded by crustal-abundance models is, of course, one of their most appealing features. Another such feature is the ease of inferring resources in deposits having grades well below current economic grades. Consequently, those having strong preference for this simplicity may be reluctant to restrict models to a single mode of occurrence unless very strong arguments can be made to do so.

One approach to modelling, that employed by Brinck, ascribes to the distribution of metal a totally stochastic character and abandons the concept of deposit as a morphological constraint, a constraint which reflects structured geological processes in deposit formation. Instead, deposits are blocks of some specified size, arbitrarily drawn. But, if blocks, hence deposits, can be arbitrarily drawn, what is the basic morphological embodiment of grade which physically relates to the geological process by which grades were created? Is it the crystal size of the major metal-bearing minerals? This unit is as reasonable as any. The fact that in Brinck's model, grades of blocks (deposits) of any size can be computed simply by modifying appropriately the variance volume relationship denies any structure in the formation of deposits. The probability for a large block having a grade of X per cent is really the probability for that block having an *average* grade of X per cent. This conceptualization of deposit occurrence demands that grade and size of block (deposit) are not independent. As shown clearly by DeWijs (1953), for blocks of ore within a deposit, as the block size increases, the probabilities for extreme grades, either high or low, decreases. The limit of this argument in terms of a resource model is one deposit having a probability of 1.0 of having an average grade of crustal abundance.

The only escape from a dependency of grade and tonnage is for deposits to represent structured geological processes which preferentially ascribe different distributions of grade to deposits of various modes. In this kind of a geological world, we could have independency of grade and tonnage at least within a mode of occurrence of a metal. But, are there *a priori* grounds for independency of grade and tonnage for deposits across modes? Let us consider this case by examining an extreme situation. Suppose we define as our unit for observation of grade the average size of the mineral crystals of the most typical ore mineral of a particular element. If in a given region, say the United States, the crust to a depth of one mile were divided into samples of rock of this size and a relative frequency distribution of concentration of the element were constructed, there would be an exceedingly small, but *nonzero*, relative frequency for between 99 and 100 per cent concentration for those elements which can occur in an elemental form. Man's experience includes such an observation. But, if this region were divided into samples of rock of 100 000 000 tonnes, from man's experience we would be forced to conclude that the probability for a grade within the interval (99–100 per cent) is zero; we have no evidence that such an event has ever occurred.

Similarly, for the grain or crystal-sized rock samples, reason suggests that there would be a very small, but *nonzero*, relative frequency for a grade in the interval $(0-10^{-10}$ per cent) if our equipment could measure perfectly. But, if the samples of rock were of the volume which yields 100 000 000 tonnes, the relative frequency for a concentration within this interval would most likely be zero.

Clearly, statistical dependency of grade and tonnage is an enigmatic issue. The presence of a dependency seems to be consciously or subconsciously ingrained in the minds of most practising geologists and explorationists. Only recently have significant efforts been directed to an objective investigation of this issue.

11.7. Final comment

This chapter explored the issue of dependency of deposit size on deposit grade, examined statistical analysis of available data on size and grade, and identified difficulties in the analysis of this dependency by estimation of the statistical correlation of size and grade data that are routinely available because of economic truncation of the population, hence sample, and because of the translation of deposit size and grade (geological deposit to ore deposit) that results from profit maximization. The following chapter explores the dependency of size and grade in the uranium deposits of the San Juan Basin, New Mexico, when explicit consideration is given to compensating for the truncating effect of economic factors on the population (sample).

References

Agterberg, F. P. and Divi, S. R. (1978). A statistical model for the distribution of copper, lead, and zinc in the Canadian Appalachian Region. *Econ. Geol.* **73**, 230–45.

Brinck, J. W. (1967). Note on the distribution and predictability of mineral resources. *Euratom 3461*, Brussels.

—— (1971). MIMIC. *Eurospectra* **X** (2), Brussels.

Charles River Associates, Inc (1978). *The economics and geology of mineral supply: an integrated framework for long run policy analysis*, Report No. 327. Prepared for National Science Foundation, Washington, DC.

DeWijs, H. J. (1953). Statistics of ore distribution, Part II. *J. R. Netherlands Min. Soc.*, January.

Harris, D. P. (1973). A subjective probability appraisal of metal endowment of Northern Sonora, Mexico. *Econ. Geol.* **68**(2), 222–42.

—— (1977). *Mineral endowment, resources, and potential supply: theory, methods for appraisal, and case studies.* MINRESCO, 3330 N. Jackson Ave., Tucson, Arizona.

—— (1978). Undiscovered uranium resources and potential supply. *Concepts of uranium resources and producibility*, pp. 51–81. The National Research Council, National Academy of Sciences, Washington, DC.

—— and Agterberg, F. P. (1981). The appraisal of mineral resources. *75th Anniversary Volume, Econ. Geol.* pp. 897–938.

——, Ortiz-Vértiz, S. R., Chavez, M. L., and Agbolosoo, E. K. (1981). *Systems and economics for the estimation of uranium potential supply.* Report to US Department of Energy, Grand Junction Office, Colorado, Subcontract No. 78-238-E.

Lee, T. and Yao, C. (1970). Abundance of chemical elements in the earth's crust and its major tectonic units. *Int. Geol. Rev.*, **12**(7), 778–86.

Lovering, T. S. (1969). Mineral resources from the land. In *Resources and man* (A study and recommendations by the Committee on Resources and Man., National Academy of Sciences—National Research Council) Chapter 6, pp. 109–34. W. H. Freeman & Company, San Francisco (For National Academy of Sciences.)

Singer, D. A. and DeYoung, J. H., Jr. (1980). What can grade-tonnage relations really tell us? in *Ressources minérales—mineral resources* (ed. Claude Guillemin and Philippe Lagny), pp. 91–101. 26th CGI, Bur. Recherches Géol. et Minières Mém. 106, Orleans, France.

——, Cox, D. P., and Drew, L. J. (1975). *Grade and tonnage relationships among copper deposits, Professional Paper 907-A*, pp. A1–A11. US Geological Survey, Washington, DC.

Skinner, B. J. (1976). A second iron age ahead? *Am. Scientist* **64**(3), 258–69.

Notes

1. Kroch, E. (1980). Estimating long-run marginal cost for mineral deposits (the case of uranium). Presentation at Workshop on Uncertainty in Uranium Resource and Cost Assessments (NUS Corporation), sponsored by EPRI, Denver, Colorado.

12 SIZE AND GRADE DEPENDENCY AND AN EXPLICIT TREATMENT OF ECONOMIC TRUNCATION: THEORY, METHOD OF ANALYSIS, DEMONSTRATION, AND A CASE STUDY (NEW MEXICO URANIUM)

12.1. Overview

Chapter 11 examined the concept of dependency of deposit grade and tonnage and attempts to explore dependency by statistical analysis of deposit data. That examination led to the investigation in this chapter of a more general method of analysis which allows for either dependency or independency of grade and tonnage and is not based upon a measure of crustal abundance. Application of such a general model requires not only identification of the presence or absence of a dependency between grade and tonnage, but the quantitative specification of the dependency relationship, if such is present, and estimation of parameters of the relevant probability distributions. No conditions are specified *a priori*, such as crustal abundance as the mean of the grade distribution.

If the average of the grade distribution is crustal abundance, and grade and tonnage are independent, such results should emerge from the general analysis. Implementing a more general analysis places more burden upon the analyst because estimation of the parameters of such an unconstrained model requires statistical data on grades and tonnages and a general algorithm for analysis of these data.

While a generalized model which allows for dependency is appealing conceptually, it is not without cost in a real application. One cost is the necessity of determining from statistical data the form of the dependency relationship. Identification problems arise in attempting to determine this relationship, because of the influence of economics in the sampling of the deposit population. The form of the dependency between tonnage and grade cannot be determined without removing the effect of economics.

A cost of another kind may arise if the average grade of the bivariate distribution is greater than crustal abundance in the region. Such a result implies that the region contains non-deposit material as well as deposits. Therefore, the bivariate distribution would be incomplete as a resource appraisal model.

To make it complete would require a number-of-deposits distribution (see Chapter 5, 'Geostatistical models of metal endowment—a conceptual framework').

In this chapter a general methodology is described which allows for the removal of the economic effects, the estimation of the dependency relationship, and estimation of the parameters of the grade and tonnage distributions. This methodology first is tested and validated on synthetic data generated from a known model. Then, the methodology is applied to the uranium deposits of New Mexico.

12.2. Two hypotheses

The case study of the uranium deposits of New Mexico tests two hypotheses. One of these is the hypothesis that deposit grade and size (tonnage of ore) are statistically independent. The other hypothesis is that the average grade of the New Mexico population of uranium deposits is crustal abundance.

12.3. Theory and model form

12.3.1. *Theory*

A complete deposit model for metal endowment consists of three separate probability models: one for number of deposits conditional upon geology and grade $h(n \mid q, G_D)$, one for deposit size conditional upon grade and geology $j(t \mid q, G_D)$, and one for deposit grade conditional upon geology, $k(q \mid G_D)$. These three models combine to define metal endowment conditional upon geology $f(m \mid G_D)$

$$f(m \mid G_D) = \int_T \int_Q h\left(\frac{m}{t \cdot q} \,\middle|\, q, G_D\right) \cdot j(t \mid q, G_D) \times$$

$$\times k(q \mid G_D) \cdot \frac{1}{t} \cdot \frac{1}{q} \, dq \, dt.$$

Suppose that the effect of geology on the probability for number of deposits, deposit tonnage, and deposit grade is to be ignored in a deposit model. This is equivalent to forming new probability models by integrating out the effects of geology. Letting $u(G_D)$ be the joint probability density function for the D geological variables, we have

$$\tilde{h}(n \mid q) = \int_{*G_D} h(n \mid q, G_D) \cdot u(G_D)\, dG_D,$$

$$\tilde{j}(t \mid q) = \int_{*G_D} j(t \mid q, G_D) \cdot u(G_D)\, dG_D,$$

$$\bar{k}(q) = \int_{*G_D} k(q \mid G_D) \cdot u(G_D)\, dG_D$$

and

$$\bar{f}(m) = \int_T \int_Q \tilde{h}\left(\frac{m}{t \cdot q} \,\bigg|\, q\right) \cdot \tilde{j}(t \mid q) \cdot \bar{k}(q) \frac{1}{q} \cdot \frac{1}{t}\, dq\, dt,$$

$$(12.1)$$

where $*G_D$ represents the domain of the D geological variables.

The CAG model by Drew (1977) can be viewed generally in terms of $\tilde{j}$ and $\bar{k}$

$$\bar{m}_{q',t'} = w \cdot \bar{q}_{q'} \int_{t'}^{\infty} \int_{q'}^{\infty} \overset{*}{\tilde{j}}(t) \cdot \overset{*}{\bar{k}}(q)\, dq\, dt, \quad (12.2)$$

where $\bar{m}_{q',t'}$ is the expectation for metal occurring in deposits having grades of at least q' and size of at least t' and $\overset{*}{\tilde{j}}(t) = \int_Q \tilde{j}(t \mid q)\bar{k}(q)\, dq$. $\overset{*}{\bar{k}}(q)$ is a special form of $\bar{k}(q)$ which meets the requirement $\gamma = \int_Q q \cdot \bar{k}(q)\, dq$ where γ is crustal abundance. W is the weight of the earth's crust in the region of interest and $\bar{q}_{q'} = \int_{q'}^{\infty} q \cdot \overset{*}{\bar{k}}(q)\, dq / \int_{q'}^{\infty} \overset{*}{\bar{k}}(q)\, dq$. As indicated in (12.2), a number distribution is not included in the PAU model, the reason being that the region is assumed to consist entirely of deposits.

This section is devoted to an examination of the relationship of specific forms of $\tilde{j}(t \mid q)$ and $\bar{k}(q)$ and to the estimation of their parameters. Dependency of deposit grade and tonnage is assumed to be present unless statistical analysis indicates its absence. In the process of quantifying the dependency relationship, the parameters of the specified forms of $\tilde{j}$ and $\bar{k}$ are estimated.

If the case study on New Mexico uranium deposits should show that the deposit size and grade are statistically independent and that the average grade of the grade distribution is crustal abundance, then the PAU model would be appropriate. If analysis should contradict either of these requirements, then a more general model is required.

12.3.2. Specification of the model

For simplicity of notation, let us represent $\ln T$ and $\ln Q$ by

$$Y = \ln T, \quad (12.3)$$
$$X = \ln Q. \quad (12.4)$$

Let us suppose that Y is normally distributed having a mean of μ_y and variance of σ_y^2. Suppose further that the probability for X is dependent upon the value for Y. For a given value of Y, X is normally distributed having a mean of $\mu_x(y)$ and variance of $\sigma_x^2(y)$. Then, the joint probability density function (p.d.f.) for X and Y, $\lambda(x, y)$, is defined as

$$\lambda(x, y) = \frac{\exp\left(-\frac{1}{2}\left(\frac{x - \mu_x(y)}{\sigma_x(y)}\right)^2 - \frac{1}{2}\left(\frac{y - \mu_y}{\sigma_y}\right)^2\right)}{\sigma_y \cdot \sigma_x(y) \cdot (2\pi)},$$

$$(12.5)$$

for $-\infty \le x \le x_{\max}$; $-\infty \le y \le \infty$. Let us suppose further that the form of the functions $\mu_x(y)$ and $\sigma_x(y)$ are known

$$\mu_x(y) = \alpha_0 + \alpha_1 y, \quad (12.6)$$
$$\sigma_x(y) = \beta_0 + \beta_1 y. \quad (12.7)$$

Then, we have

$$\lambda(x, y) = \frac{\exp\left(-\frac{1}{2}\left(\frac{x - \alpha_0 - \alpha_1 y}{\beta_0 + \beta_1 y}\right)^2 - \frac{1}{2}\left(\frac{y - \mu_y}{\sigma_y}\right)^2\right)}{(\sigma_y)(\beta_0 + \beta_1 y)(2\pi)},$$

$$(12.8)$$

for $-\infty \le y \le \infty$; $-\infty \le x \le x_{\max}$. Now, suppose that λ is truncated by a cost surface C

$$C = (K-1)y - x \rightarrow x = (K-1)y - C. \quad (12.9)$$

Then, the mean values for Q and T from the truncated distribution are defined as

$$\gamma_q^* = \frac{\displaystyle\int_{-\infty}^{\infty} \int_{(K-1)y-C}^{x_{\max}} e^x \cdot \exp\left(-\frac{1}{2}\left(\frac{x - \alpha_0 - \alpha_1 y}{\beta_0 + \beta_1 y}\right)^2 - \frac{1}{2}\left(\frac{y - \mu_y}{\sigma_y}\right)^2\right) dx\, dy}{\displaystyle\int_{-\infty}^{\infty} \int_{(K-1)y-C}^{x_{\max}} \exp\left(-\frac{1}{2}\left(\frac{x - \alpha_0 - \alpha_1 y}{\beta_0 + \beta_1 y}\right)^2 - \frac{1}{2}\left(\frac{y - \mu_y}{\sigma_y}\right)^2\right) dx\, dy},$$

$$\gamma_t^* = \frac{\displaystyle\int_{-\infty}^{\infty} \int_{\frac{C+x}{K-1}}^{x_{\max}} e^y \cdot \exp\left(-\frac{1}{2}\left(\frac{x - \alpha_0 - \alpha_1 y}{\beta_0 + \beta_1 y}\right)^2 - \frac{1}{2}\left(\frac{y - \mu_y}{\sigma_y}\right)^2\right) dy\, dx}{\displaystyle\int_{-\infty}^{\infty} \int_{\frac{C+x}{K-1}}^{x_{\max}} \exp\left(-\frac{1}{2}\left(\frac{x - \alpha_0 - \alpha_1 y}{\beta_0 + \beta_1 y}\right)^2 - \frac{1}{2}\left(\frac{y - \mu_y}{\sigma_y}\right)^2\right) dy\, dx}.$$

These expressions parallel those of the PAU model, except that they allow for dependency between tonnage and grade. While expressions such as these were employed in the quantification of the PAU model, quantification of this model is based upon a different approach and does not require arithmetic averages; consequently, these expressions will not be employed in quantifying this generalized model. Relationships to be used are developed in the following section.

12.4. A compromise of theory to facilitate estimation

Generalizing the deposit model of PAU to allow for a dependency between grade and tonnage and to free the estimation of the grade parameters from the crustal-abundance constraint compounds the already difficult task of quantifying the model, for none of the parameters (α_0, α_1, β_0, β_1, μ_y, and σ_y) are known. They must be estimated from data on known deposits; such estimation also requires identification of the appropriate cost surface

$$C = (K-1)y - x. \quad (12.10)$$

Let us adopt some approximations so that estimates of these unknown parameters can be made. Divide the range of sample values of $y = \ln t$ into n equally spaced intervals, $(y_i'' - y_i')$, $i = 1, 2, \ldots, n$. Let us represent the ith interval by its average value y_i^0 and let us approximate the truncation effect of the cost surface on this interval by the value of the cost surface evaluated at y_i^0. Then, given some upper bound for cost C_0 we have the approximate lower truncation value for x, x_{1i}, over the ith interval on y

$$x_{1i} = (K-1)y_i^0 - C_0. \quad (12.11)$$

Let us suppose that from *a priori* considerations, we can identify a maximum upper truncation value for x, x_{2i}, for the ith interval on Y. Then, for the ith interval, we have the expression for the average value

$$\gamma_i = \frac{\dfrac{1}{\sigma_i(2\pi)^{\frac{1}{2}}}\displaystyle\int_{x_{1i}}^{x_{2i}} x \cdot \exp\left(-\frac{1}{2}\left(\frac{x-\mu_i}{\sigma_i}\right)^2\right)dx}{\dfrac{1}{\sigma_i(2\pi)^{\frac{1}{2}}}\displaystyle\int_{x_{1i}}^{x_{2i}} \exp\left(-\frac{1}{2}\left(\frac{x-\mu_i}{\sigma_i}\right)^2\right)dx},$$
$$i = 1, 2, \ldots, n. \quad (12.12)$$

Similarly, for the variance of X on the range $(x_{1i} - x_{2i})$, we have

$$\nabla_i^2 = \frac{\dfrac{1}{\sigma_i(2\pi)^{\frac{1}{2}}}\displaystyle\int_{x_{1i}}^{x_{2i}} x^2 \cdot \exp\left(-\frac{1}{2}\left(\frac{x-\mu_i}{\sigma_i}\right)^2\right)dx}{\dfrac{1}{\sigma_i(2\pi)^{\frac{1}{2}}}\displaystyle\int_{x_{1i}}^{x_{2i}} \exp\left(-\frac{1}{2}\left(\frac{x-\mu_i}{\sigma_i}\right)^2\right)dx} - \gamma_i^2,$$
$$i = 1, 2, \ldots, n. \quad (12.13)$$

Expressions (12.12) and (12.13) define the mean and variance of a doubly-truncated normal probability distribution. Of course, computation of γ_i and ∇_i^2 require that μ_i and σ_i are known, $i = 1, 2, \ldots, n$. Our situation is the inverse of this; we have estimates of γ_i and ∇_i^2, $i = 1, 2, \ldots, n$, but unknown parameters. Basically, quantification of our model requires estimation of μ_i and σ_i, given estimates from data of γ_i and ∇_i^2, $i = 1, 2, \ldots, n$. This estimation could be made by a computer search routine, but a more efficient method is to employ Cohen's solution, an approach that will be explained later. For now, let us suppose that analysis has produced the n pairs of parameters, μ_i and σ_i, $i = 1, 2, \ldots, n$.

Now, define γ_y as the expectation of Y over the truncated part of the joint probability distribution. An approximation of γ_y can be described in terms of our n conditional probability distributions and the unknown marginal p.d.f. for Y

$$\gamma_y = \frac{\displaystyle\sum_{i=1}^{n} y_i^0 \cdot \int_{x_{1i}}^{x_{2i}} \frac{\exp\left(-\frac{1}{2}\left(\frac{x-\mu_i}{\sigma_i}\right)^2\right)}{\sigma_i(2\pi)^{\frac{1}{2}}}dx \times \int_{y_i''}^{y_i'} \frac{\exp\left(-\frac{1}{2}\left(\frac{y-\mu_y}{\sigma_y}\right)^2\right)}{\sigma_y(2\pi)^{\frac{1}{2}}}dy}{\displaystyle\sum_{i=1}^{n} \cdot \int_{x_{1i}}^{x_{2i}} \frac{\exp\left(-\frac{1}{2}\left(\frac{x-\mu_i}{\sigma_i}\right)^2\right)}{\sigma_i(2\pi)^{\frac{1}{2}}}dx \times \int_{y_i''}^{y_i'} \frac{\exp\left(-\frac{1}{2}\left(\frac{y-\mu_y}{\sigma_y}\right)^2\right)}{\sigma_y(2\pi)^{\frac{1}{2}}}dy}.$$
$$(12.14)$$

Similarly, the variance of Y over this truncated area is approximated by

$$V_y^2 = \frac{\displaystyle\sum_{i=1}^{n} (y_i^0)^2 \int_{x_{1i}}^{x_{2i}} \frac{\exp\left(-\frac{1}{2}\left(\frac{x-\mu_i}{\sigma_i}\right)^2\right)}{\sigma_i(2\pi)^{\frac{1}{2}}}dx \times \int_{y_i''}^{y_i'} \frac{\exp\left(-\frac{1}{2}\left(\frac{y-\mu_y}{\sigma_y}\right)^2\right)}{\sigma_y(2\pi)^{\frac{1}{2}}}dy}{\displaystyle\sum_{i=1}^{n} \int_{x_{1i}}^{x_{2i}} \frac{\exp\left(-\frac{1}{2}\left(\frac{x-\mu_i}{\sigma_i}\right)^2\right)}{\sigma_i(2\pi)^{\frac{1}{2}}}dx \times \int_{y_i''}^{y_i'} \frac{\exp\left(-\frac{1}{2}\left(\frac{y-\mu_y}{\sigma_y}\right)^2\right)}{\sigma_y(2\pi)^{\frac{1}{2}}}dy} - (\gamma_y)^2.$$
$$(12.15)$$

Again, let us suppose that we have estimates of γ_y and V_y^2 from data which represent a random sample from the truncated area of the joint p.d.f. Further, let us substitute our estimates of the n pairs of parameters, μ_i and σ_i, $i = 1, 2, \ldots, n$ for the actual parameters of the conditional probability distributions. Then, if we also use estimates of y_i^0 from our data, we have estimates of all quantities and parameters except for μ_y and σ_y. These unknown parameters would be estimated by searching for values of them such that computed values for γ_y and V_y^2 approximate to some specified degree of accuracy the values calculated from data. Define

$$D = \left(1 - \frac{\gamma_y}{\bar{y}}\right)^2 + \left(1 - \frac{V_y^2}{S^2}\right)^2.$$

Then a search would be made for μ_y and σ_y such that D approaches zero.

The development of this approach employed y_i^0, $i = 1, 2, \ldots, n$, in expression (12.11) and again in (12.14) and (12.15). Obviously, exact values for the expectation of Y on each of the n intervals of Y cannot be known, because the parameters of the distribution of Y are not known. y^0 must be approximated for each of the n intervals. Three alternatives are available

1. Use the midpoint of the ith interval, $y_i^0 = (y_i'' + y_i')/2$.
2. Estimate y_i^0 by averaging the values of Y from observed data that fall within the limits of the ith interval.
3. Leave y^0 to be defined by the search algorithm as it varies μ_y and σ_y.

Both alternatives 2 and 3 were used in the New Mexico study: Alternative 2 was used to compute the truncation grade, but alternative 3 was used in the search for the parameters of the distribution for Y. Alternative 1 was used in the demonstration and validation of the procedures on the synthetic data from the known model.

12.5. Estimation methods

12.5.1. Perspective

Given the simplifications described in the foregoing section, quantification of the generalized model consists of four main steps

1. Estimation of the parameters μ_i and σ_i for each of the n conditional probability distributions for $X = \ln Q$;
2. Given the n pairs of estimated parameters (μ_i

and σ_i, $i = 1, 2, \ldots, n$), estimation of the dependency relationships

$$\mu_i = \alpha_0 + \alpha_1 y_i^0,$$
$$\sigma_i = \beta_0 + \beta_1 y_i^0;$$

3. Estimation of μ_y and σ_y, the parameters of the marginal distribution for $Y = \ln T$;
4. Iteration over 1 through 3 for refinement of estimates.

The first step can be achieved by a procedure developed by Cohen (1950) for the estimation of the parameters of a doubly truncated normal probability distribution. Cohen's solution requires identification of the truncation values and the first and second moments about the lower truncation value. Thus, these measures must be computed for X on each of the n intervals on Y.

Application of Cohen's solution is facilitated through employing Newton's algorithm for the numerical evaluation of two nonlinear equations in two unknowns. Both Cohen's solution and Newton's algorithm are explained in detail in subsequent sections.

Step 2 is accomplished simply by plotting the estimates of μ and σ against y^0 for each of the n intervals. Examination of these two bivariate plots should give evidence for the presence or absence of a dependency relationship between X and Y. Any relationship that appears to be present can be estimated by regressing $\hat{\mu}$ against y^0 and $\hat{\sigma}$ against y^0.

Step 3 takes the estimated values for μ_i, σ_i, and y_i^0 as given and estimates by a computer search routine the values for μ_y and σ_y. Basically, this step generates a two-dimensional grid for μ_y and σ_y^2 and associates with each grid location a value for γ_y and V_y^2. These calculated values are compared to those which were computed from data, $\bar{y}$ and S^2, searching for that grid location at which statistical and expected values are in the closest agreement.

Completion of steps 1 through 3 provides a quantification of the model. Step 4 is optional; it allows for further refinement if such is desired. Since quantification began by substituting averages of Y within each interval for actual mean values in at least the cost function and possibly in the equation for γ_y and V_y^2 (depending upon which of the three alternatives were selected), subsequent calculations are predicated upon these averages. Initial quantification of the model would allow for a computation of mathematical expectations. These could be substituted in place of the averages computed on the data, and the whole procedure could be repeated. Iterations could be made in this manner until some convergence criterion were met.

12.5.2. Cohen's solution

Cohen (1950) derived the following set of equations, which when solved simultaneously give estimates of σ and μ, the parameters of a normal probability distribution for the random variable X', which is truncated at x_0' and x_0''

$$\sigma[Z_1 - Z_2 - \varepsilon'] - v_1 = 0 \qquad (12.16)$$

$$\sigma^2[1 - \varepsilon'(Z_1 - Z_2 - \varepsilon') - Z_2 R/\sigma] - v_2 = 0, \quad (12.17)$$

where

$$Z_1 = \frac{\phi'}{I_0' - I_0''}, \quad Z_2 = \frac{\phi''}{I_0' - I_0''}, \qquad (12.18)$$

where ϕ' and ϕ'' are ordinate values of the normal probability function for ε' and ε'';

$$\varepsilon' = \frac{x_0' - \mu}{\sigma}, \quad \text{where } x_0' \text{ is the lower truncation value;}$$

$$(12.19)$$

$$\varepsilon'' = \varepsilon' + \frac{R}{\sigma}, \quad \text{where } R = x_0' - x_0'',$$

(the upper truncation value); $\quad$ (12.20)

$$I_0' = \frac{1}{(2\pi)^{\frac{1}{2}}} \int_{\varepsilon'}^{\infty} \exp(-t^2/2) \, dt;$$

$$I_0'' = \frac{1}{(2\pi)^{\frac{1}{2}}} \int_{\varepsilon''}^{\infty} \exp(-t^2/2) \, dt; \qquad (12.21)$$

$$\phi' = \frac{1}{(2\pi)^{\frac{1}{2}}} \exp\left(-\frac{\varepsilon'^2}{2}\right); \qquad (12.22)$$

$$\phi'' = \frac{1}{(2\pi)^{\frac{1}{2}}} \exp\left(-\frac{(\varepsilon'')^2}{2}\right); \qquad (12.23)$$

$$v_1 = \sum_{i=1}^{n} x_i/n, \qquad (12.24)$$

where $x_i = x_i' - x_0'$; x_i' are the sample values from the truncated distribution;

$$v_2 = \sum_{i=1}^{n} x_i^2/n. \qquad (12.25)$$

We can rewrite (12.16)

$$\sigma = v_1/[Z_1 - Z_2 - \varepsilon'] \qquad (12.26)$$

or

$$\sigma = v_1 \left/ \left[\frac{\phi'}{I_0' - I_0''} - \frac{\phi''}{I_0' - I_0''} - \varepsilon' \right] \right. \qquad (12.27)$$

and

$$\sigma = v_1 \left/ \left[\frac{\phi' - \phi''}{I_0' - I_0''} - \varepsilon' \right] \right. . \qquad (12.28)$$

Similarly, we can rewrite (12.17)

$$\sigma^2[1 - \varepsilon'(Z_1 - Z_2 - \varepsilon')] - Z_2 R\sigma - v_2 = 0. \quad (12.29)$$

In this form, (12.29) can be recognized as a quadratic in σ. Substituting for Z_1 and Z_2 from (12.18), we have

$$\sigma^2 \left[1 - \varepsilon'\left(\frac{\phi' - \phi''}{(I_0' - I_0'')} - \varepsilon' \right) \right] -$$

$$- \left(\frac{\phi''}{I_0' - I_0''} \right) R\sigma - v_2 = 0. \quad (12.30)$$

By making the following identifications, the solution of (12.30) can be made by the quadratic formula for given values for ϕ', ϕ'', ε', R, and v_2

$$A = \left[1 - \left(\frac{\phi' - \phi''}{I_0' - I_0''} - \varepsilon' \right) \right]; \qquad (12.31)$$

$$B = -R \frac{\phi''}{I_0' - I_0''}; \qquad (12.32)$$

$$C = -v_2; \qquad (12.33)$$

and

$$\sigma = \frac{-B \pm (B^2 - 4AC)^{\frac{1}{2}}}{2A}. \qquad (12.34)$$

Of course, this provides a solution for only one of the parameters in one of the equations. A complete solution requires values of σ and ε' which satisfy both (12.16) and (12.17). Cohen's solution is obtained by trying various values of the two parameters in both equations and moving the direction that makes the difference Δ between the values of (12.28) and (12.30) the smallest

$$\Delta = \sigma^2 \left[1 - \varepsilon'\left(\frac{\phi' - \phi''}{I_0' - I_0''} - \varepsilon' \right) \right] -$$

$$- \left(R \frac{\phi''}{I_0' - I_0''} \right) \sigma - v_2 - \left[\sigma\left(\frac{\phi' - \phi''}{I_0' - I_0''} - \varepsilon' \right) - v_1 \right],$$

$$(12.35)$$

where variables are defined in definitions (12.18) through (12.25). Thus, $\hat{\sigma}$ and $\hat{\varepsilon}_1$ are found by converging on $\Delta = 0$ to some accepted degree of error. From $\hat{\sigma}$ and $\hat{\varepsilon}_1$, μ can be calculated

$$\hat{\mu} = x_0' - \hat{\varepsilon}'\hat{\sigma}. \qquad (12.36)$$

Cohen suggests that for a first approximation one

should use

$$\sigma = S_x,$$
$$\varepsilon' = v_1/S_x,$$

(12.37)

where S_x^2 is the sample variance of x (not x') and v_1 is the sample first moment (mean) on x.

While Cohen's solution could be achieved through a computer search algorithm, a more direct solution can be achieved through application of Newton's algorithm for a numerical solution of two equations in two unknowns. This algorithm is described in the following section.

12.5.3. The Newton algorithm applied to Cohen's solution

Newton's algorithm. Whittaker and Robinson (1944) provide a description of methods for the numerical solution of algebraic and transcendental equations. One case of this set of problems is the solution of a pair of equations in two unknowns. For this problem, Whittaker and Robinson describe Newton's numeric solution. The description that follows is reproduced intact from Whittaker and Robinson (1944, p. 90). [Reproduced by kind permission of the Blackie Publishing Group Ltd, Glasgow, Scotland.]

Let two equations be given

$$f(x, y) = 0; \quad g(x, y) = 0;$$

(12.38)

from which the unknowns (x, y) are to be determined.

Let (x_0, y_0) be an approximate solution of the equations. Write

$$x = x_0 + h,$$
$$y = y_0 + k.$$

(12.39)

Then, by Taylor's Theorem, neglecting powers of h and k above the first, we have

$$0 = f(x_0, y_0) + h \frac{\partial f}{\partial x_0} + k \frac{\partial f}{\partial y_0},$$

(12.40)

$$0 = g(x_0, y_0) + h \frac{\partial g}{\partial x_0} + k \frac{\partial g}{\partial y_0},$$

(12.41)

giving

$$h = \frac{g \dfrac{\partial f}{\partial y_0} - f \dfrac{\partial g}{\partial y_0}}{\dfrac{\partial f}{\partial x_0} \dfrac{\partial g}{\partial x_0} - \dfrac{\partial f}{\partial y_0} \dfrac{\partial g}{\partial x_0}},$$

(12.42)

$$k = \frac{f \dfrac{\partial g}{\partial x_0} - g \dfrac{\partial f}{\partial x_0}}{\dfrac{\partial f}{\partial x_0} \dfrac{\partial g}{\partial y_0} - \dfrac{\partial f}{\partial y_0} \dfrac{\partial g}{\partial x_0}}.$$

(12.43)

Therefore an improved pair of values for the roots is

$$x_1 = x_0 + \frac{g \dfrac{\partial f}{\partial y_0} - f \dfrac{\partial g}{\partial y_0}}{\dfrac{\partial f}{\partial x_0} \dfrac{\partial g}{\partial y_0} - \dfrac{\partial f}{\partial y_0} \dfrac{\partial g}{\partial x_0}},$$

(12.44)

$$y_1 = y_0 + \frac{f \dfrac{\partial g}{\partial x_0} - g \dfrac{\partial f}{\partial x_0}}{\dfrac{\partial f}{\partial x_0} \dfrac{\partial g}{\partial y_0} - \dfrac{\partial f}{\partial y_0} \dfrac{\partial g}{\partial x_0}}.$$

(12.45)

A solution for the two unknowns, x and y, is obtained by iterating on the above relationship, converging upon the true solution.

Cohen's solution by Newton's algorithm. From Cohen (1950), we have that the unknown parameters μ and σ of a truncated normal distribution can be determined by the simultaneous solution of two equations in two unknowns (ε' and σ)

$$0 = \sigma^2 - \sigma^2 \varepsilon' \left(\frac{\phi' - \phi''}{I' - I''} \right) +$$
$$+ \sigma^2 \varepsilon'^2 - (\sigma R) \left(\frac{\phi''}{I' - I''} \right) - v_2,$$

$$0 = \sigma \left(\frac{\phi' - \phi''}{I' - I''} \right) - \sigma \varepsilon' - v_1.$$

Besides the obvious presence of σ and ε' in the expression for f and g, these unknowns (parameters) are involved in ϕ', ϕ'', I', and I'', which are symbols for the partial derivatives with respect to the unknowns of the ordinate and interval probability forms of the normal probability density function, as noted in eqns (12.21)–(12.23). Because of these terms, derivation of the partial derivatives of f and g, which are required to cast our problem in a form that is solvable by Newton's algorithm, is somewhat messy and tedious. Derivation of the expressions for the partial derivatives is provided in § 12.9. The results of the mathematical analysis are summarized, as follows.

Let us make the identifications

$$f = \sigma^2 - \sigma^2 \varepsilon' \left(\frac{\phi' - \phi''}{I' - I''} \right) + \sigma^2 \varepsilon'^2 -$$
$$- (\sigma R) \left(\frac{\phi''}{I' - I''} \right) - v_2,$$

(12.46)

$$g = \sigma \left(\frac{\phi' - \phi''}{I' - I''} \right) - \sigma \varepsilon' - v_1.$$

(12.47)

Then

$$\frac{\partial f}{\partial \sigma} = 2\sigma - \left\{ 2\sigma\varepsilon' \left(\frac{\phi' - \phi''}{I' - I''} \right) + \right.$$

$$+ \left[\left(-\frac{1}{(2\pi)^{\frac{1}{2}}} \right) \left(\frac{\varepsilon' R}{\sigma^2} + \frac{R^2}{\sigma^3} \right) \right.$$

$$\times \left(\exp \left(\frac{-\left(\varepsilon' + \frac{R}{\sigma} \right)^2}{2} \right) \right) \times$$

$$\times (I' - I'')^{-1} + \left(\frac{\frac{\partial I''}{\partial \sigma}}{(I' - I'')^2} \right) (\phi' - \phi'') \right] (\sigma^2 \varepsilon') \right\}$$

$$+ 2\sigma\varepsilon'^2 - \left\{ \frac{R\phi''}{(I' - I'')} \right.$$

$$+ \sigma R \left[\left(\frac{1}{(2\pi)^{\frac{1}{2}}} \right) \left(\frac{\varepsilon' R}{\sigma^2} + \frac{R^2}{\sigma^3} \right) \times \right.$$

$$\times \left(\exp \left(\frac{-\left(\varepsilon' + \frac{R}{\sigma} \right)^2}{2} \right) \right) (I' - I'')^{-1} -$$

$$- \left(\frac{\frac{\partial I''}{\partial \sigma}}{(I' - I'')^2} \right) \phi'' \right] \right\}, \qquad (12.48)$$

$$\frac{\partial f}{\partial \varepsilon'} = -\left\{ \sigma^2 \left(\frac{\phi' - \phi''}{I' - I''} \right) + \right.$$

$$+ \left[\left[\left(\frac{1}{(2\pi)^{\frac{1}{2}}} \right) \left(\varepsilon' + \frac{R}{\sigma} \right) \left(\exp \left(\frac{-\left(\varepsilon' + \frac{R}{\sigma} \right)^2}{2} \right) \right) - \right.$$

$$- \left(\frac{\varepsilon'}{(2\pi)^{\frac{1}{2}}} \right) \left(\exp \left(\frac{-\varepsilon'^2}{2} \right) \right) \right] (I' - I'')^{-1} -$$

$$- \left[\frac{\left(\frac{\partial I'}{\partial \varepsilon'} - \frac{\partial I''}{\partial \varepsilon'} \right)}{(I' - I'')^2} \right] (\phi' - \phi'') \right] (\sigma^2 \varepsilon') \right\} +$$

$$+ 2\sigma\varepsilon'^2 - (\sigma R) \left[\left[\left(-\frac{1}{(2\pi)^{\frac{1}{2}}} \right) \left(\varepsilon' + \frac{R}{\sigma} \right) \times \right. \right.$$

$$\times \left(\exp \left(\frac{-\left(\varepsilon' + \frac{R}{\sigma} \right)^2}{2} \right) \right) \right] (I' - I'')^{-1} -$$

$$- \left[\frac{\left(\frac{\partial I'}{\partial \varepsilon'} - \frac{\partial I''}{\partial \varepsilon'} \right)}{(I' - I'')^2} \right] (\phi'') \right], \qquad (12.49)$$

$$\frac{\partial g}{\partial \varepsilon'} = (\sigma) \left\{ \left[\left[\left(\frac{1}{(2\pi)^{\frac{1}{2}}} \right) \left(\varepsilon' + \frac{R}{\sigma} \right) \left(\exp \left(\frac{-\left(\varepsilon' + \frac{R}{\sigma} \right)^2}{2} \right) \right) \right] - \right. \right.$$

$$- \left(\frac{\varepsilon'}{(2\pi)^{\frac{1}{2}}} \right) \left(\exp \left(\frac{-\varepsilon'^2}{2} \right) \right) \right] (I' - I'')^{-1} -$$

$$- \left[\frac{\left(\frac{\partial I'}{\partial \varepsilon'} - \frac{\partial I''}{\partial \varepsilon'} \right)}{(I' - I'')^2} \right] (\phi' - \phi'') \right\} - \sigma, \qquad (12.50)$$

$$\frac{\partial g}{\partial \sigma} = \left(\frac{\phi' - \phi''}{I' - I''} \right) +$$

$$+ (\sigma) \left\{ \left[\left(-\frac{1}{(2\pi)^{\frac{1}{2}}} \right) \left(\frac{\varepsilon' R}{\sigma^3} + \frac{R^2}{\sigma^3} \right) \times \right. \right.$$

$$\times \left(\exp \left(\frac{-\left(\varepsilon' + \frac{R}{\sigma} \right)^2}{2} \right) \right) \right] (I' - I'')^{-1} +$$

$$+ \left[\frac{\frac{\partial I''}{\partial \sigma}}{(I' - I'')^2} \right] (\phi' - \phi'') \right\} - \varepsilon', \qquad (12.51)$$

where

$$\frac{\partial I'}{\partial \varepsilon'} = \left(-\frac{1}{(2\pi)^{\frac{1}{2}}} \right) \left[\exp \left(\frac{-\varepsilon'^2}{2} \right) \right], \quad \frac{\partial I'}{\partial \sigma} = 0, \quad (12.52)$$

$$\frac{\partial I''}{\varepsilon'} = \left(-\frac{1}{(2\pi)^{\frac{1}{2}}} \right) \left[\exp \left(\frac{-\left(\varepsilon' + \frac{R}{\sigma} \right)^2}{2} \right) \right],$$

$$\frac{\partial I''}{\partial \sigma} = \left(\frac{R}{(\sigma^2)(2\pi)^{\frac{1}{2}}} \right) \left[\exp \left(\frac{-\left(\varepsilon' + \frac{R}{\sigma} \right)^2}{2} \right) \right], \qquad (12.53)$$

$$I'_0 = \frac{1}{(2\pi)^{\frac{1}{2}}} \int_{\varepsilon'}^{\infty} \exp \left(-t^2/2 \right) dt, \qquad (12.54)$$

$$I''_0 = \frac{1}{(2\pi)^{\frac{1}{2}}} \int_{\varepsilon''}^{\infty} \exp \left(-t^2/2 \right) dt, \qquad (12.55)$$

$$\phi' = \frac{1}{(2\pi)^{\frac{1}{2}}} \exp \left(-\frac{\varepsilon'^2}{2} \right), \qquad (12.56)$$

$$\phi'' = \frac{1}{(2\pi)^{\frac{1}{2}}} \exp \left(\frac{-\varepsilon''^2}{2} \right). \qquad (12.57)$$

Eqns (12.46)–(12.57) are required for the estimation of ε' and σ. These equations include terms that are derivatives of integrals: $\partial I'/\partial \varepsilon'$, $\partial I''/\partial \varepsilon'$, and $\partial I''/\partial \sigma$. The evaluation of these integrals is provided in § 12.9.2. Given estimates of ε' and σ, an estimate of μ is obtained from the relationship of (12.36) $\hat{\mu} = x_0' - \hat{\varepsilon}' \hat{\sigma}$.

12.5.4. *Estimation of the parameters μ_y and σ_y by computer search*

In this section, we consider the task of estimating the parameters of the marginal distribution, the distribution for Y given that estimates have been made of the parameters of the conditional distributions, a distribution for X for each of the n intervals on Y.

The estimated parameters of the n conditional distributions provide a basis for exploring the dependency between X and Y. Regression analysis of $\hat{\mu}_i$ and $\hat{\sigma}_i$ against y_i^0, the mean tonnage of an interval on Y, would provide estimates of the parameters of the dependency relationship. For example, a linear model of dependency would require estimates of two parameters for each of two equations

$$\hat{\mu}_i = \hat{\alpha}_0 + \hat{\alpha}_1 y_i^0,$$
$$\hat{\sigma}_i = \hat{\beta}_0 + \hat{\beta}_1 y_i^0,$$

where y_i^0 is the arithmetic average of values of Y in the ith interval $[y_i'' - y_i']$, $i = 1, 2, \ldots, n$. If there is no dependency, regression analysis would indicate that the coefficients of y^0 in both equations are statistically not significantly different from zero at some specified significance level. In such a case, we would then adopt a simpler model

$$\mu_i = \alpha \quad \text{and} \quad \sigma_i = \beta.$$

We could use as estimates of α and β the arithmetic mean values of $\hat{\mu}_i$ and $\hat{\sigma}_i$, $i = 1, 2, \ldots, n$

$$\hat{\alpha} = \frac{1}{n} \sum_{i=1}^{n} \hat{\mu}_i, \tag{12.58}$$

$$\hat{\beta} = \frac{1}{n} \sum_{i=1}^{n} \hat{\sigma}_i. \tag{12.59}$$

Regardless of the outcome of the investigation of the dependency relationship, estimation of the parameters of the marginal distribution for Y must consider the fact that the presence of a truncation of grades by a cost function makes a simple straightforward estimation of μ_y and σ_y^2 by $\bar{y}$ and S^2 computed on tonnage data inappropriate. A cost function serving to truncate grade means that our sample of tonnage is weighted by probabilities for grade P_i, $i = 1, 2, \ldots, n$. This is reflected in eqns (12.60) and

(12.61)

$$\gamma_y = \frac{\sum_{i=1}^{n} P_i \dfrac{y_i^0}{\sigma_y (2\pi)^{\frac{1}{2}}} \times \displaystyle\int_{y_i''}^{y_i'} \exp\left(-\frac{1}{2}\left(\frac{y - \mu_y}{\sigma_y}\right)^2\right) dy}{\sum \dfrac{P_i}{\sigma_y (2\pi)^{\frac{1}{2}}} \times \displaystyle\int_{y_i''}^{y_i'} \exp\left(-\frac{1}{2}\left(\frac{y - \mu_y}{\sigma_y}\right)^2\right) dy}, \tag{12.60}$$

$$V_y^2 = \frac{\sum_{i=1}^{n} P_i \dfrac{(y_i^0)^2}{\sigma_y (2\pi)^{\frac{1}{2}}} \times \displaystyle\int_{y_i''}^{y_i} \exp\left(-\frac{1}{2}\left(\frac{y - \mu_y}{\sigma_y}\right)^2\right) dy}{\sum \dfrac{P_i}{\sigma_y (2\pi)^{\frac{1}{2}}} \times \displaystyle\int_{y_i''}^{y_i'} \exp\left(-\frac{1}{2}\left(\frac{y - \mu_y}{\sigma_y}\right)^2\right) dy} - \gamma_y^2, \tag{12.61}$$

where γ_y and V_y^2 are the mean and variance of Y on the truncated population.

Since analysis of the previous section would have provided estimates of the dependency relationship and of the cost function, P_i can be estimated

$$\hat{P}_i = \frac{1}{\hat{\sigma}_i (2\pi)^{\frac{1}{2}}} \int_{x_{1i}}^{x_{2i}} \exp\left(-\frac{1}{2}\left(\frac{x - \hat{\mu}_i}{\hat{\sigma}_i}\right)^2\right) dx \tag{12.62}$$

or, equivalently,

$$\hat{P}_i = \frac{1}{(\hat{\beta}_0 + \hat{\beta}_1 y_i^0)(2\pi)^{\frac{1}{2}}} \times$$
$$\times \int_{\phi(y_i^0)}^{x_{2i}} \exp\left(-\frac{1}{2}\left(\frac{x - \hat{\alpha}_0 - \hat{\alpha}_1 y_i^0}{\hat{\beta}_0 + \hat{\beta}_1 y_i^0}\right)^2\right) dx, \tag{12.63}$$

where $\phi(y_i^0)$ is the cost function which defines values for x as a function of the average y_i^0, $i = 1, 2, \ldots, n$. The arithmetic average values of data on Y on the ith interval would be substituted for the actual value of y_i^0 for determining the cut-off value x_{1i}. Therefore, estimated values for P_i in (12.60) and (12.61) would be specified.

Additionally, $\bar{y}$ and S^2 would be computed from statistical data on Y. These would serve as estimates of γ_y and V^2. Therefore, the only unknowns in (12.60) and (12.61) are y_i^0 and the value of the integral for each interval of Y. As was done in calculating cut-off values x_{1i}, we could use arithmetic averages of Y on each interval as estimates of y_i^0. But this is not necessary. y_i^0 could be defined as a function of the unknown parameters, μ_y and σ_y

$$\gamma_y = \frac{\left\{\sum_{i=1}^{n}\left(\dfrac{P_i}{\sigma_y(2\pi)^{\frac{1}{2}}}\right) \times \left[\dfrac{\sigma_y}{(2\pi)^{\frac{1}{2}}} \times \dfrac{\left(\exp\left(-\frac{1}{2}\left(\frac{y_i'-\mu_y}{\sigma_y}\right)^2\right) - \exp\left(-\frac{1}{2}\left(\frac{y_i''-\mu_y}{\sigma_y}\right)^2\right)\right)}{\dfrac{1}{\sigma_y(2\pi)^{\frac{1}{2}}}\int_{y_i''}^{y_i'}\exp\left(-\frac{1}{2}\left(\frac{y-\mu_y}{\sigma_y}\right)^2\right)dy} + \mu_y \right]\int_{y_i''}^{y_i'}\exp\left(-\frac{1}{2}\left(\frac{y-\mu_y}{\sigma_y}\right)^2\right)dy\right\}}{\left\{\sum_{i=1}^{n}\dfrac{\hat{P}_i}{\sigma_y(2\pi)^{\frac{1}{2}}}\int_{y_i''}^{y_i'}\exp\left(-\frac{1}{2}\left(\frac{y-\mu_y}{\sigma_y}\right)^2\right)dy\right\}},$$

$$(12.64)$$

$$V_y^2 = \frac{\left\{\sum_{i=1}^{n}\left(\dfrac{P_i}{\sigma_y(2\pi)^{\frac{1}{2}}}\right) \times \left[\dfrac{\sigma_y}{(2\pi)^{\frac{1}{2}}} \times \dfrac{\left(\exp\left(-\frac{1}{2}\left(\frac{y_i'-\mu_y}{\sigma_y}\right)^2\right) - \exp\left(-\frac{1}{2}\left(\frac{y_i''-\mu_y}{\sigma_y}\right)^2\right)\right)}{\dfrac{1}{\sigma_y(2\pi)^{\frac{1}{2}}}\int_{y_i''}^{y_i'}\exp\left(-\frac{1}{2}\left(\frac{y-\mu_y}{\sigma_y}\right)^2\right)dy} + \mu_y \right]\int_{y_i''}^{y_i'}\exp\left(-\frac{1}{2}\left(\frac{y-\mu_y}{\sigma_y}\right)^2\right)dy\right\}}{\left\{\sum_{i=1}^{n}\dfrac{P_i}{\sigma_y(2\pi)^{\frac{1}{2}}}\int_{y_i''}^{y_i'}\exp\left(-\frac{1}{2}\left(\frac{y-\mu_y}{\sigma_y}\right)^2\right)dy\right\}} - \gamma^2.$$

$$(12.65)$$

If we have estimates for γ_y, V_y^2, and P_i, $i = 1, 2, \ldots, n$, then the remaining unknowns are the quantities in the brackets and the integral that it multiplies. It follows that if y_i'' and y_i' are specified, then the value of the right-hand side can be varied only by changing the values of μ_y and σ_y. But, there is only one pair of values that will make the right-hand sides of these equations equal to $\bar{y}$ and S^2, estimates of γ_y and V^2 from our data on Y. Thus, estimation of the parameters μ_y and σ_y consists of a search for those values that satisfy (12.64) and (12.65).

In order to aid this search, a single response characteristic of these relations is defined

$$D = \left(1 - \frac{\gamma_y}{\bar{y}}\right)^2 + \left(1 - \frac{V_y^2}{S^2}\right)^2, \qquad (12.66)$$

where γ_y and V_y^2 are values of the right-hand side of (12.64) and (12.65) for values of μ_y and σ_y selected in the search and $\bar{y}$ and S^2 are the statistics computed from our data.

With this response characteristic D an approximation of μ_y and σ_y can be achieved by a two dimensional search, a dimension for μ_y and a dimension for σ_y. Values of D can be associated with each grid intersection (combination of μ_y and σ_y) and a search made for that pair of values that yields the smallest value for D. Obviously, for such a search to be successful requires that either the response pattern of D is smooth and well-behaved, thereby hav-

ing only one minimum, or that the search routine in the μ_y-σ_y space can distinguish between a local extremum and a global extremum. This problem of successful search is not independent of the search scale and initial values.

Rather than design a program for this particular problem, a library subroutine of the Computer Center of the University of Arizona by the name of MINSER was employed. This subroutine is called by the main program, SEARCH. The listings of SEARCH and MINSER are provided in § 12.9.3.

Basically, the program requires a statement of the response function and search parameters, such as scale and initial (starting) values. The use of this generalized search routine on the problem posed in this paper, the estimation of μ_y and σ_y from probability weighted data is validated on synthetic data before it is employed as an estimation tool. This validation is demonstrated in § 12.6. § 12.7 is a case study of the uranium deposits of New Mexico. In this case study, this search routine is employed to estimate the parameters of the marginal distribution, $Y = \ln(\text{tonnage})$.

12.6. Demonstration on a synthetic truncated normal distribution

12.6.1. Overview

§ 12.3 described the conceptual form of the grade-tonnage dependent deposit model, and § 12.4 restated the model in a form that may allow quantification. § 12.5 examined numerical analysis methods which may be helpful in estimating the parameters of the approximate form of the model. This section demonstrates the methods of § 12.5 applied to the model as described in § 12.4. For this demonstration to serve as a form of validation, it must be made on data from a known situation so that the estimated parameters can be compared with the actual parameters. This is achieved by constructing a model and generating from the model data which would be consistent with that available in a real situation. Then, proceeding as if the parameters of the model were unknown, the estimation methods previously described are applied to these data, and the estimates of the parameters are compared with the parameters of the known model. There are two possible ways of generating synthetic test data

1. Generate by Monte Carlo methods data from each of the truncated distributions and compute statistical estimates of γ_i and V_i^2, $i = 1, 2, \ldots, n$, the true means and variances of the truncated conditional distribution;

2. Compute mathematically the exact values for γ_i and V_i^2, $i = 1, 2, \ldots, n$.

Approach 2 is selected here. Computational formulae for these values are derived in the next section. The results of the mathematical development explained in § 12.6.2 are two equations, one for γ and one for V^2

$$\gamma = \frac{\frac{\sigma}{(2\pi)^{\frac{1}{2}}}(\exp(-\frac{1}{2}z_1^2) - \exp(-\frac{1}{2}z_2^2))}{[F(z_2) - F(z_1)]} + \mu, \quad (12.67)$$

$$V^2 = \left\{ \left[\frac{z_1\sigma^2 \exp(-\frac{1}{2}z_1^2)}{(2\pi)^{\frac{1}{2}}} - \frac{z_2\sigma^2 \exp(-\frac{1}{2}z_2^2)}{(2\pi)^{\frac{1}{2}}} \right] + \right.$$

$$\left. + \frac{2\mu\sigma}{(2\pi)^{\frac{1}{2}}} [\exp(-\frac{1}{2}z_1^2) - \exp(-\frac{1}{2}z_2^2)] \right\} \Big/$$

$$\Big/ \{[F(z_2) - F(z_1)]\} + \sigma^2 + \mu^2 - \gamma^2, \quad (12.68)$$

where

$$z_1 = \frac{x_1 - \mu}{\sigma}, \quad z_2 = \frac{x_2 - \mu}{\sigma}, \quad (12.69)$$

and x_1, x_2 are lower and upper truncation values for X.

$$F(z) = \frac{1}{(2\pi)^{\frac{1}{2}}} \int_{-\infty}^{z} \exp(-\frac{1}{2}z^2) \, dz \quad (12.70)$$

is the value from a table or function for the standard unit normal evaluated for the standardized score of $z = (x - \mu)/\sigma$; Z has mean of zero and variance of 1.0.

Thus, substituting appropriately the values for $\mu_i = \mu_x(y_i^0)$, $\sigma_i = \sigma_x(y_i^0)$, and $x_i = \phi(y_i^0)$, $i = 1, 2, \ldots, n$, we can compute γ and V^2 for each of the n truncated grade distributions. This generates a data set from a model with specified parameters. The estimation methodology can be tested by attempting to estimate μ_i and σ_i, given only γ_i, V_i^2, x_{1i}, and x_{2i}, $i = 1, 2, \ldots, n$. Values for $\hat{\mu}$ and $\hat{\sigma}$ can be plotted against y^0 for each of the n intervals on Y and estimates made by regression analysis of the parameters of the dependency relationships α_0, α_1, β_0, and β_1

$$\mu_x(y) = \alpha_0 - \alpha_1 y,$$
$$\sigma_x(y) = \beta_0 - \beta_1 y.$$

Then, using the estimates made for μ_i and σ_i, $i = 1, 2, \ldots, n$, the parameters μ_y and σ_y for the marginal tonnage distribution are estimated by the search algorithm.

12.6.2. *Generating synthetic sample data from a model*

Perspective. In order to test and examine the usefulness and reliability of the approximation procedure outlined for the estimation of the parameters of a grade–tonnage dependent bivariate lognormal distribution, we need data from a known population, a model. Given a model and data generated by the model, the estimates can be compared to the known parameters of the generating process.

The model. Let us adopt as our model the joint normal probability density function λ for X and Y that was defined in § 12.3

$$\lambda(x, y) = \frac{1}{\sigma_x(y) \cdot \sigma_y(2\pi)} \times$$

$$\times \exp\left(-\frac{1}{2}\left(\frac{x - \mu_x(y)}{\sigma_x(y)}\right)^2 - \frac{1}{2}\left(\frac{y - \mu_y}{\sigma_y}\right)^2\right).$$

Let us specify

$$\mu_y = 1000,$$
$$\sigma_y = 200,$$
$$\mu_x(y) = 300 - 0.1y, \quad (12.71)$$
$$\sigma_x(y) = 100 - 0.05y. \quad (12.72)$$

Now, let us adopt as our cost function

$$C = 50 - 0.015y - 0.1x = \phi^{-1}(x). \quad (12.73)$$

And let us suppose that no raw material has been consumed in production for which production costs were in excess of US $10. Thus, from (12.72), we have

$$x = \frac{50 - 10 - 0.015y}{0.1}$$

$$= \frac{40 - 0.015y}{0.1} = 400 - 0.15y, \quad (12.74)$$

$$x = 400 - 0.15y = \phi(x).$$

Now, let us suppose that the largest known quantity of y is of a size of 1400 lb and that the smallest is of a size of 400 lb. Let us divide this interval (1400, 400) into 10 equally-spaced 100-lb intervals and for each interval compute its midpoint y^0 and the implied truncation value for X. For example, the first interval is (400–500), which has a midpoint of 450. The truncation value for X for $y^0 = 450$ is determined by substituting 450 into (12.74)

$$x = 400 - 0.15(450) = 332.5.$$

Similarly, we can compute, using y^0, the parameters $\mu_x(y^0)$ and $\sigma_x(y^0)$: For $y^0 = 450$, we have

$$\mu_x(450) = 300 - 0.1y^0 = 300 - 45 = 255,$$

$$\sigma_x(y) = 100 - 0.05y^0 = 100 - (0.05)(4.50) = 77.5.$$

Thus, for each interval on Y, we have a truncation value for X and the mean and standard deviation for X. Data for the ten intervals on Y over the range 400–1400 are presented in Table 12.1.

In effect, we have the parameters and lower truncation value for X on each of ten intervals on Y. In order to test the estimation procedure, we need to have the mean value and variance for X for each of these truncated distributions. These statistics were generated by evaluating eqns (12.67)–(12.68) at the means, variances, and truncation values for each of the conditional probability distributions. This procedure produced the data of Table 12.1.

Next we present the derivation of eqns (12.67) and (12.68). The reader who is not interested in the mathematical detail should skip this section and proceed to the subsection entitled 'Generating the data'.

Derivation of the generating equations. From probability theory we have that the mean μ of a probability distribution $f(x)$ ($a < x < b$, $f(x) = 0$, otherwise) is the mathematical expectation for X on f

$$\mu = E[X] = \int_{-\infty}^{\infty} x \cdot f(x) \, dx.$$

Furthermore, we have from theory that the variance of X on f is computed as

$$\sigma^2 = E[X^2] - \mu^2 = \int_{-\infty}^{\infty} x^2 \cdot f(x) \, dx - \mu^2.$$

Now, suppose that $f(x)$ is specified as

$$f(x) = \frac{\frac{1}{\sigma(2\pi)^{\frac{1}{2}}} \exp\left(-\frac{1}{2}\left(\frac{x-\mu}{\sigma}\right)^2\right)}{\frac{1}{\sigma(2\pi)^{\frac{1}{2}}} \int_{x_1}^{x_2} \exp\left(-\frac{1}{2}\left(\frac{x-\mu}{\sigma}\right)^2\right) dx}, \quad x_1 \le x \le x_2;$$

$$f(x) = 0, \quad \text{otherwise}.$$

TABLE 12.1. *Synthetic data generated from a model*

Interval on Y	Midpoint of§ tonnage interval $(y^0) = (y'' + y')/2$	The mean of X,‡ conditional upon y^0 (μ)	Variance of X,‡ conditional upon y^0 (σ)	Truncation value,† given y^0 (x_1)
1	450	255	77.5	332.5
2	550	245	72.5	317.5
3	650	235	67.5	302.5
4	750	225	62.5	287.5
5	850	215	57.5	272.5
6	950	205	52.5	257.5
7	1050	195	47.5	242.5
8	1150	185	42.5	227.5
9	1250	175	37.5	212.5
10	1350	165	32.5	197.5

† From cost equation: $C = 50 - 0.015y - 0.1x$ and the fact that an upper cost bound is US $10, which implies $x = 400 - 0.15y$.

‡ The dependency relationships are $\mu_i = 300 - 0.1y_i^0$; $\sigma_i = 100 - 0.05y_i^0$.

§ Y is normally distributed having a mean μ_y of 1000 and a variance σ_y^2 of 1600.

Then, γ, the expectation of this truncated normal distribution, is defined as

$$\gamma = E[X] = \dfrac{\dfrac{1}{\sigma(2\pi)^{\frac{1}{2}}} \displaystyle\int_{x_1}^{x_2} x \cdot \exp\left(-\dfrac{1}{2}\left(\dfrac{x-\mu}{\sigma}\right)^2\right) dx}{\dfrac{1}{\sigma(2\pi)^{\frac{1}{2}}} \displaystyle\int_{x_1}^{x_2} \exp\left(-\dfrac{1}{2}\left(\dfrac{x-\mu}{\sigma}\right)^2\right) dx}$$

and

$$V^2 = E[X^2] - \gamma^2$$

$$= \dfrac{\dfrac{1}{\sigma(2\pi)^{\frac{1}{2}}} \displaystyle\int_{x_1}^{x_2} x^2 \cdot \exp\left(-\dfrac{1}{2}\left(\dfrac{x-\mu}{\sigma}\right)^2\right) dx}{\dfrac{1}{\sigma(2\pi)^{\frac{1}{2}}} \displaystyle\int_{x_1}^{x_2} \exp\left(-\dfrac{1}{2}\left(\dfrac{x-\mu}{\sigma}\right)^2\right) dx} - \gamma^2.$$

Since these relationships involve integrals, they are not easy to employ. Let us make a transformation of integrals and simplify them. Let $z = (x-\mu)/\sigma$. Then $x = z\sigma + \mu$, $dx = dz\sigma$, and

$$\gamma = \dfrac{\dfrac{1}{(2\pi)^{\frac{1}{2}}} \displaystyle\int_{z_1}^{z_2} (z\sigma + \mu) \exp\left(-\tfrac{1}{2}z^2\right) dz}{\dfrac{1}{(2\pi)^{\frac{1}{2}}} \displaystyle\int_{z_1}^{z_2} \exp\left(-\tfrac{1}{2}z^2\right) dz},$$

where $z_1 = (x_1 - \mu)/\sigma$ and $z_2 = (x_2 - \mu)/\sigma$;

$$\gamma = \dfrac{\dfrac{1}{(2\pi)^{\frac{1}{2}}} \displaystyle\int_{z_1}^{z_2} (z\sigma + \mu) \exp\left(-\tfrac{1}{2}z^2\right) dz}{F(z_2) - F(z_1)},$$

where $F(z) = (2\pi)^{-\frac{1}{2}} \int_{-\infty}^{z} \exp\left(-\tfrac{1}{2}z^2\right) dz$, which is the probability for $Z \leq z$, where Z is normally distributed, having a mean of zero and a standard deviation of one. The values for this function are available from tables for the standard unit normal probability distribution.

Let us simplify the numerator N of the expression for γ.

$$N = \dfrac{\sigma}{(2\pi)^{\frac{1}{2}}} \int_{z_1}^{z_2} z \exp\left(-\tfrac{1}{2}z^2\right) dz +$$

$$+ \dfrac{\mu}{(2\pi)^{\frac{1}{2}}} \int_{z_1}^{z_2} \exp\left(-\tfrac{1}{2}z^2\right) dz$$

$$N = \left(\dfrac{\sigma}{(2\pi)^{\frac{1}{2}}}\right)\left(-\exp\left(-\tfrac{1}{2}z^2\right)\big|_{z_1}^{z_2}\right) + \mu[F(z_2) - F(z_1)]$$

$$N = \left(\dfrac{\sigma}{(2\pi)^{\frac{1}{2}}}\right)\left(\exp\left(-\tfrac{1}{2}z_1^2\right) - \exp\left(-\tfrac{1}{2}z_2^2\right)\right) +$$

$$+ \mu[F(z_2) - F(z_1)].$$

Then

$$\gamma = \dfrac{\left(\dfrac{\sigma}{(2\pi)^{\frac{1}{2}}}\right)\left(\exp\left(-\tfrac{1}{2}z_1^2\right) - \exp\left(-\tfrac{1}{2}z_2^2\right)\right) + \mu[F(z_2) - F(z_1)]}{[F(z_2) - F(z_1)]}$$

$$\gamma = \dfrac{\left(\dfrac{\sigma}{(2\pi)^{\frac{1}{2}}}\right)\left(\exp\left(-\tfrac{1}{2}z_1^2\right) - \exp\left(-\tfrac{1}{2}z_2^2\right)\right)}{[F(z_2) - F(z_1)]} + \mu. \qquad (12.75)$$

Now, for the variance V^2,

$$V^2 = \left\{\dfrac{\dfrac{1}{(2\pi)^{\frac{1}{2}}} \displaystyle\int_{z_1}^{z_2} (z\sigma + \mu)^2 \exp\left(-\tfrac{1}{2}z^2\right) dz}{\dfrac{1}{(2\pi)^{\frac{1}{2}}} \displaystyle\int_{z_1}^{z_2} \exp\left(-\tfrac{1}{2}z^2\right) dz}\right\} - \gamma^2.$$

Take the numerator N

$$N = \dfrac{\sigma^2}{(2\pi)^{\frac{1}{2}}} \int_{z_1}^{z_2} z^2 \exp\left(-\tfrac{1}{2}z^2\right) dz + \dfrac{2\sigma\mu}{(2\pi)^{\frac{1}{2}}} \int_{z_1}^{z_2} z \times$$

$$\times \exp\left(-\tfrac{1}{2}z^2\right) dz + \dfrac{\mu^2}{(2\pi)^{\frac{1}{2}}} \int_{z_1}^{z_2} \exp\left(-\tfrac{1}{2}z^2\right) dz$$

$$N = N_1 + N_2 + N_3.$$

Clearly, $N_3 = \mu^2[F(z_2) - F(z_1)]$ and

$$N_2 = \dfrac{2\mu\sigma}{(2\pi)^{\frac{1}{2}}} \int_{z_1}^{z_2} z \cdot \exp\left(-\tfrac{1}{2}z^2\right) dz$$

$$= \dfrac{2\mu\sigma}{(2\pi)^{\frac{1}{2}}} [-\exp\left(-\tfrac{1}{2}z^2\right)|_{z_1}^{z_2}],$$

$$N_2 = \dfrac{2\mu\sigma}{(2\pi)^{\frac{1}{2}}} [\exp\left(-\tfrac{1}{2}z_1^2\right) - \exp\left(-\tfrac{1}{2}z_2^2\right)].$$

Now,

$$N_1 = \dfrac{\sigma^2}{(2\pi)^{\frac{1}{2}}} \int_{z_1}^{z_2} z^2 \cdot \exp\left(-\tfrac{1}{2}z^2\right) dz.$$

Let $u = z$ and $dv = (2\pi)^{-\frac{1}{2}}\sigma^2 z \exp\left(-\tfrac{1}{2}z^2\right)$. Then $du = dz$ and $v = -(2\pi)^{-\frac{1}{2}}\sigma^2 \exp\left(-\tfrac{1}{2}z^2\right)$. Employing the relationship from calculus for integration by parts, $\int u\, dv = uv - \int v\, du$, we have

$$\int u\, dv = -\dfrac{z\sigma^2}{(2\pi)^{\frac{1}{2}}} \exp\left(-\tfrac{1}{2}z^2\right) -$$

$$- \left(\int -\dfrac{\sigma^2}{(2\pi)^{\frac{1}{2}}} \exp\left(-\tfrac{1}{2}z^2\right)\right) dz$$

$$\int u\, dv = -\dfrac{z\sigma^2}{(2\pi)^{\frac{1}{2}}} \exp\left(-\tfrac{1}{2}z^2\right) + \dfrac{\sigma^2}{(2\pi)^{\frac{1}{2}}} \int \exp\left(-\tfrac{1}{2}z^2\right) dz.$$

Then,

$$N_1 = \left[-\frac{z\sigma^2}{(2\pi)^{\frac{1}{2}}} \exp\left(-\tfrac{1}{2}z^2\right)\big|_{z_1}^{z_2} \right] + \sigma^2[F(z_2) - F(z_1)]$$

$$N_1 = \left[\frac{z_1\sigma^2}{(2\pi)^{\frac{1}{2}}} \exp\left(-\tfrac{1}{2}z_1^2\right) - \frac{z_2\sigma^2}{(2\pi)^{\frac{1}{2}}} \exp\left(-\tfrac{1}{2}z_2^2\right) \right] +$$
$$+ \sigma^2[F(z_2) - F(z_1)]$$

and

$$V^2 = -\gamma^2 + \Bigg\{ \left[\frac{z_1\sigma^2}{(2\pi)^{\frac{1}{2}}} \exp\left(-\tfrac{1}{2}z_1^2\right) - \frac{z_2\sigma^2}{(2\pi)^{\frac{1}{2}}} \exp\left(-\tfrac{1}{2}z_2^2\right) \right] +$$

$$+ \sigma^2[F(z_2) - F(z_1)] + \frac{2\mu\sigma}{(2\pi)^{\frac{1}{2}}} \left[\exp\left(-\tfrac{1}{2}z_1^2\right) - \right.$$

$$\left. - \exp\left(-\tfrac{1}{2}z_2^2\right) \right] + \mu^2[F(z_2) - F(z_1)] \Bigg\}\Bigg/$$

$$\Big/ \{F(z_2) - F(z_1)\}$$

Finally,

$$V^2 = \sigma^2 + \mu^2 - \gamma^2$$

$$+ \Bigg\{ \left[\frac{-z_1\sigma^2}{(2\pi)^{\frac{1}{2}}} \exp\left(-\tfrac{1}{2}z_1^2\right) - \frac{z_2\sigma^2}{(2\pi)^{\frac{1}{2}}} \exp\left(-\tfrac{1}{2}z_2^2\right) \right] +$$

$$+ \frac{2\mu\sigma}{(2\pi)^{\frac{1}{2}}} \left[\exp\left(-\tfrac{1}{2}z_1^2\right) - \exp\left(-\tfrac{1}{2}z_2^2\right) \right] \Bigg\}\Bigg/$$

$$\Big/ \{F(z_2) - F(z_1)\} \qquad (12.76)$$

Generating the data. Eqns (12.75) and (12.76) derived in the foregoing subsection [identical to eqns (12.67) and (12.68) of § 12.6.1] were used to generate means and variances for each of the ten intervals identified in Table 12.1. Essentially, μ, σ, x_1 the lower truncation value, and x_2 the upper truncation value of X for each of the ten intervals on Y, were

substituted into these equations, generating the means and standard deviations, γ and V, listed in Table 12.2.

Cohen's solution requires data different from but related to γ and V: v_1, v_2, ε', and R. To clearly indicate what these data requirements are, let x_1 and x_2 be the lower and upper truncation values for the random variable X and let $W = X - x_1$.

The data for Cohen's solution (v_1, v_2, R_1, and ε') can be described as functions of w, x_1, and x_2

$$w_i = x_i - x_1, \quad i = 1, 2, \ldots, n, \qquad (12.77)$$

$$v_1 = \frac{1}{n} \sum w_i, \qquad (12.78)$$

$$v_2 = \frac{1}{n} \sum w_i^2 \Rightarrow E[W], \qquad (12.79)$$

$$R = x_2 - x_1, \qquad (12.80)$$

$$\varepsilon' = -\frac{v_1}{S}, \qquad (12.81)$$

where

$$S = (v_2 - v_1^2)^{\frac{1}{2}} \Rightarrow (E[W^2] - E[W]^2)^{\frac{1}{2}}. \quad (12.82)$$

In a real application v_1 and v_2 could be computed directly from data by simply subtracting x_1 from every observed value of X and performing the indicated operations; however, in this contrived situation, all values are exact, being determined mathematically from a probability distribution with known parameters. A previous section developed the equations to generate the exact values for γ and V^2, the mean and variance from a doubly-truncated normal probability distribution. Similarly, v_1 and v_2 must be derived mathematically from the probability distribution.

TABLE 12.2. *Data and parameters*

Interval (on Y)	Parameters of the complete distribution		Truncation values		Parameters of the truncated distribution	
	μ	σ	x_2	x_1	γ	V
1	255	77.5	500	332.5	372.5	33.0
2	245	72.5	500	317.5	355.3	31.8
3	235	67.5	500	302.5	337.9	29.9
4	225	62.5	500	287.5	320.3	27.8
5	215	57.5	500	272.5	302.7	25.6
6	205	52.5	500	257.5	285.1	23.4
7	195	47.5	500	242.5	267.4	21.1
8	185	42.5	500	227.5	249.8	18.9
9	175	37.5	500	212.5	232.2	16.7
10	165	32.5	500	197.5	214.6	14.5

Theoretical statistics comparable to sample values for v_1 and v_2 can be computed by recognizing that the theoretical equivalent statistical expectation of v_1 is $E[W]$ and that for v_2 is $E[W^2]$. These could be computed directly from the truncated p.d.f.; but by employing properties of expectations, they can be computed using γ and V^2, the exact mean and variance of the truncated part of the normal probability distribution.

From our definition of $X = W + x_1$ and the definition of γ, we can state

$$\gamma = E[X] = E[W + x_1] = E[W] + x_1. \quad (12.83)$$

Therefore,

$$E[W] = \gamma - x_1. \quad (12.84)$$

And, from (12.78) and (12.84), we have

$$v_1 = E[W] = \gamma - x_1 \quad (12.85)$$

or

$$v_1 = \gamma - x_1. \quad (12.86)$$

Similarly, by definition of V^2 and by substituting $X = W + x_1$ we have

$$
\begin{aligned}
V^2 &= E[X^2] - \gamma^2 \\
V^2 &= E[(W + x_1)^2] - \gamma^2 \\
V^2 &= E[W^2 + 2x_1 W + x_1^2] - \gamma^2 \\
V^2 &= E[W^2] + 2x_1 E[W] + x_1^2 - \gamma^2.
\end{aligned}
\quad (12.87)
$$

Substituting $E[W] = \gamma - x_1$ from (12.84), we have

$$V^2 = E[W^2] + 2x_1(\gamma - x_1) + x_1^2 - \gamma^2. \quad (12.88)$$

Then,

$$
\begin{aligned}
E[W^2] &= V^2 - 2x_1(\gamma - x_1) - x_1^2 + \gamma^2 \\
E[W^2] &= V^2 - 2x_1\gamma + 2x_1^2 - x_1^2 + \gamma^2 \\
E[W^2] &= V^2 - 2x_1\gamma + x_1^2 + \gamma^2 \\
E[W^2] &= V^2 + \gamma^2 - 2x_1\gamma + x_1^2.
\end{aligned}
\quad (12.89)
$$

From (12.79) we have $v_2 = E[W^2]$; therefore using (12.89), we have

$$v_2 = V^2 + \gamma^2 - 2x_1\gamma + x_1^2. \quad (12.90)$$

Finally, exact values for v_1 and v_2 can be computed from (12.86) and (12.90)

$$v_1 = \gamma - x_1,$$
$$v_2 = V^2 + \gamma^2 - 2x_1\gamma + x_1^2.$$

These relations and eqn (12.81) were employed to compute v_1 and v_2 for each of the hypothetical truncated distributions of Table 12.2, generating the complete data of Table 12.3.

TABLE 12.3. *Data input to Cohen's solution*

Interval (on Y)	R	ε'	σ	v_1	v_2
1	167.5	−1.21210	33.0	40.0	2689.00
2	182.5	−1.18870	31.8	37.8	2440.08
3	197.5	−1.18395	29.9	35.4	2147.17
4	212.5	−1.17986	27.8	32.8	1848.68
5	227.5	−1.17969	25.6	30.2	1567.40
6	242.5	−1.17949	23.4	27.6	1309.32
7	257.5	−1.18009	21.1	24.9	1065.22
8	272.5	−1.17989	18.9	22.3	854.50
9	287.5	−1.17964	16.7	19.7	666.98
10	302.5	−1.17931	14.5	17.1	502.66

12.6.3. *Estimating the parameters of the conditional distributions for $(X \mid Y_i)$*

The Newton algorithm for Cohen's solution of the parameters of a doubly-truncated normal distribution was programmed on a digital computer. The data of Table 12.4 were input to this program. Estimating the parameters of the 10 truncated conditional distributions required 10 separate solutions. The 10 pairs of estimated parameters $\hat{\mu}_i$ and $\hat{\sigma}_i$, $i = 1, 2, \ldots, 10$, are listed in Table 12.5, along with the actual parameters. Visual inspection reveals close agreement of estimates with actual parameters. Although there is close agreement of estimates with actual parameters, there does seem to be a slight positive bias in the estimates of μ, but a slight negative bias in the estimates of σ. However, since the lower truncation values were well above the means, by at least one standard deviation, the estimation methodology seems to perform quite well.

TABLE 12.4. *Data tableau for computer program of Newton's algorithm for Cohen's solution*

Interval (on Y)	Data input				
	X01	X011	XBAR	SX	V2
1	332.5	500	40.0	33.0	2689.00
2	317.5	500	37.8	31.8	2440.08
3	302.5	500	35.4	29.9	2147.17
4	287.5	500	32.8	27.8	1848.68
5	272.5	500	30.2	25.6	1567.40
6	257.5	500	27.6	23.4	1309.32
7	242.5	500	24.9	21.1	1065.22
8	227.5	500	22.3	18.9	854.50
9	212.5	500	19.7	16.7	666.98
10	197.5	500	17.1	14.5	502.66

TABLE 12.5. *Comparison of actual and estimated parameters of conditional distributions*

Interval (on Y)	Actual parameters		Estimated parameters	
	μ	σ	$\hat{\mu}$	$\hat{\sigma}$
1	255	77.5	257.5	76.8
2	245	72.5	243.3	72.9
3	235	67.5	238.1	66.6
4	225	62.5	227.0	61.9
5	215	57.5	217.1	56.9
6	205	52.5	206.8	52.1
7	195	47.5	197.1	46.9
8	185	42.5	186.7	42.0
9	175	37.5	176.4	37.1
10	165	32.5	166.0	32.3

12.6.4. *Investigating the dependency relationship*

Figs. 12.1 and 12.2 are plots of data in Table 12.6 and demonstrate the relationship of the estimated parameters to y. These plots demonstrate a strong dependency between X and Y, as there should be, since the test data were generated by a model in which this dependency was explicitly expressed by linear relationships

$$\mu_x(y) = 300 - 0.1y,$$
$$\sigma_x(y) = 100 - 0.05y.$$

Least-squares fits of linear relationships to the data

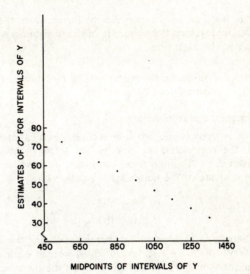

Fig. 12.2. Estimates of σ for conditional distributions for X, given intervals of Y.

of Table 12.6 yield the following estimates of dependency

$$\hat{\mu}_x(y) = 301.550 - 0.0999y,$$
$$\hat{\sigma}_x(y) = 99.543 - 0.0500y.$$

Obviously the constants and slopes of these linear equations compare very favourably with those of the model which was used to generate the data, particularly when consideration is given to the fact that the lower truncation value of X was greater than the mean value of X for each of the conditional distributions. In other words, the parameters of these distributions were estimated from data representing less

TABLE 12.6. *Estimated parameters of the conditional distributions for $(X \mid Y)$ compared with values of Y*

Interval (on Y)	Parameters of conditional distributions		Midpoint of intervals of Y
	$\hat{\mu}$	$\hat{\sigma}$	y
1	257.5	76.8	450
2	243.3	72.9	550
3	238.1	66.6	650
4	227.0	61.9	750
5	217.1	56.9	850
6	206.8	52.1	950
7	197.1	46.9	1050
8	186.7	42.0	1150
9	176.4	37.1	1250
10	166.0	32.3	1350

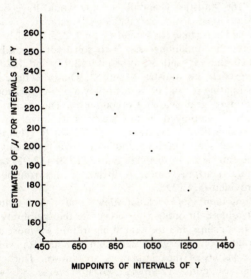

Fig. 12.1. Estimates of μ for conditional distributions for X, given intervals of Y.

than one-half of the population; furthermore these data represented only one side of the distributions of values, the high side.

12.6.5. *Estimating the parameters of the marginal distribution (Y)*

Perspective and procedure

The analysis of the previous section yields estimates of the parameters μ_i and σ_i for each of the n intervals on Y. From these estimates, we have made an estimate of the dependency relationships

$$\mu_i = \alpha_0 + \sigma_1 y_i^0,$$
$$\sigma_i = \beta_0 + \beta_1 y_i^0,$$

where y_i^0 is the arithmetic average of Y for the ith interval of Y, $i = 1, 2, \ldots, n$. Thus, we can estimate the probability P_i for X falling within the interval of $[x_{1i} - x_{2i}]$

$$P_i(x_{1i} \leq X \leq x_{2i} \mid y_i^0)$$
$$= \frac{1}{\sigma_i (2\pi)^{\frac{1}{2}}} \int_{x_{1i}}^{x_{2i}} \exp\left(-\frac{1}{2}\left(\frac{x - \mu_i}{\sigma_i}\right)^2\right) dx \quad (12.91)$$

or

$$P_i(x_{1i} \leq X \leq x_{2i} \mid y_i^0) = \frac{1}{(\beta_0 + \beta_1 y_i^0)(2\pi)^{\frac{1}{2}}} \times$$
$$\times \int_{\phi(y_i^0)}^{x_{2i}} \exp\left(-\frac{1}{2}\left(\frac{x - \alpha_0 - \alpha_1 y_i}{\beta_0 - \beta_1 y_i^0}\right)^2\right) dx, \quad (12.92)$$

where $\phi(y_i^0)$ is the cost function stated in terms of truncation value for x as a function of y; $\phi(y_i^0)$ gives the lower truncation value for x for the ith interval of Y, $i = 1, 2, \ldots, n$. In this example $\phi(y_i^0) = 400 - 0.15 y_i^0$. We do not yet have estimates of the parameters μ_y and σ_y of the marginal distribution for Y from the joint probability space for X and Y

$$f(y) = \frac{1}{\sigma_y (2\pi)^{\frac{1}{2}}} \exp\left(-\frac{1}{2}\left(\frac{y - \mu_y}{\sigma_y}\right)^2\right).$$

But, we do have statistics $\bar{y}$ and S^2 computed from data on Y. These data represent a sample from the cost-truncated population of deposits.

As a simplification, we divided the distribution of values for Y into n class intervals: $[y_i'' - y_i']$, $i = 1, 2, \ldots, n$. y_i^0 is the arithmetic mean of Y for the ith interval, and P_i described in (12.91) and (12.92) is the probability for X being within the interval $(\phi(y_i^0), x_{2i})$ for the ith partition of Y of the joint population of X and Y. With regard to this discretizing, the statistics $\bar{y}$ and S^2 computed on known and economic occurrences can be considered to represent

sample estimates of the relations

$$\bar{y} \Rightarrow \gamma_y = \frac{\sum_{i=1}^{n}\left\{y_i^0 \cdot P_i\left(\frac{1}{\sigma_y(2\pi)^{\frac{1}{2}}}\right) \times \right.}{\left. \times \int_{y_i''}^{y_i'} \exp\left(-\frac{1}{2}\left(\frac{y - \mu_y}{\sigma_y}\right)^2\right) dy\right\}}{\sum_{i=1}^{n}\left\{P_i\left(\frac{1}{\sigma_y(2\pi)^{\frac{1}{2}}}\right) \times \right.}{\left. \times \int_{y_i''}^{y_i'} \exp\left(-\frac{1}{2}\left(\frac{y - \mu_y}{\sigma_y}\right)^2\right) dy\right\}}, \quad (12.93)$$

$$S^2 \Rightarrow V_y^2 = \frac{\sum_{i=1}^{n}\left\{(y_i^0)^2 \cdot P_i\left(\frac{1}{\sigma_y(2\pi)^{\frac{1}{2}}}\right) \times \right.}{\left. \times \int_{y_i''}^{y_i'} \exp\left(-\frac{1}{2}\left(\frac{y - \mu_y}{\sigma_y}\right)^2\right) dy\right\}}{\sum_{i=1}^{n}\left\{P_i\left(\frac{1}{\sigma_y(2\pi)^{\frac{1}{2}}}\right) \times \right.}{\left. \times \int_{y_i''}^{y_i'} \exp\left(-\frac{1}{2}\left(\frac{y - \mu_y}{\sigma_y}\right)^2\right) dy\right\}} - \gamma_y^2, \quad (12.94)$$

where

$$y_i^0 = \frac{\frac{\sigma_y}{(2\pi)^{\frac{1}{2}}}\left[\exp\left(-\frac{1}{2}\left(\frac{y_i'' - \mu_y}{\sigma_y}\right)^2\right) - \right.}{\left. - \exp\left(-\frac{1}{2}\left(\frac{y_i - \mu_y}{\sigma_y}\right)^2\right)\right]}{\left[F\left(\frac{y' - \mu_y}{\sigma_y}\right) - F\left(\frac{y'' - \mu_y}{\sigma_y}\right)\right]} + \mu. \quad (12.95)$$

The statistics $\bar{y}$ and S^2 already would have been determined from our data and, estimates would have been made for y_i^0 and P_i, $i = 1, 2, \ldots, n$. Therefore, the remaining task is to solve for μ_y and σ_y such that γ_y and V_y^2 of eqns (12.93) and (12.94) approach the statistics $\bar{y}$ and S^2. The procedure for estimating μ_y and σ_y is to employ a two-dimensional iterative grid search by computer. The computer routine employed in this study is a University of Arizona library program called MINSER. This is a general search routine and requires a statement of the functions, in this case eqns (12.93)–(12.95), and initial starting values. A listing of this routine is provided in § 12.9.3.

Validation of relationships and the search algorithm. In order to demonstrate the credibility of relationships and the search algorithm, we must operate upon data generated from a model for which the values of the parameters are known. Thus, we will use eqns (12.93)–(12.95) in reverse; we will compute P_i, y_i^0, $\bar{y}$, and S^2 by specifying the parameters. Then, we will take these values as data from a bivariate dependent population for which μ_y and σ_y are unknown and show that the computer search routine can make reasonably accurate estimates of them.

First, let us show that eqns (12.93) and (12.94) provide reasonable estimates of $\bar{y}$ and S^2 when a large number of intervals on Y is selected. To do this in simplest form, let us specify P_i as equal for all i; in other words, there is no dependency and no truncation. And, let us construct 100 intervals over Y and specify $\mu_y = 1000$ and $\sigma_y = 200$. Under these conditions, eqns (12.93) and (12.94) give $\bar{y} = 1000$ and $S = 198.64$. Now, let us treat these as statistics from a population for which μ_y and σ_y are unknown. Let us give the search algorithm initial values of $\mu_y = 900$ and $\sigma_y = 170$, the statistics $\bar{y} = 1000$ and $S^2 = 39457.85$, the test criterion of (12.66), and have it search for the population values. The population values determined by the search routine were $\hat{\mu}_y = 999.999$ and $\hat{\sigma}_y = 200.006$. Obviously, these are very close to the exact values of 1000 and 200.

Now, let us make conditions slightly less favourable by assuming that data on the lower 1/3 of the 100 class intervals are not available; that is, the data are truncated. This means that $\bar{y}$ and S^2 will be computed over only 70 of the 100 intervals, yielding $\bar{y} = 1037.52$ and $S^2 = 28\,412.47$. These statistics and starting values of $\mu_y = 1082.54$ and $\sigma_y = 175.36$ were provided to the search algorithm, which produced the estimates

$$\hat{\mu}_y = 999.999,$$

$$\hat{\sigma}_y = 200.000.$$

Finally, let us give it a difficult test by imposing the truncating effects of the cost function. Stated as a truncation of X, we will impose $x_{1i} = 400 - 0.2y_i^0$, $i = 1, 2, \ldots, 100$. Furthermore, let us build in a dependency of X upon Y

$$\mu_i = 300 - 0.1y_i^0,$$
$$\sigma_i = 100 - 0.05y_i^0, \quad i = 1, 2, \ldots, 100.$$

Finally, we will truncate the observations on Y by ignoring the first 30 intervals, which means computing the statistics over Y from 740 to 1650. The resulting statistics from this doubly truncated, dependent population are $\bar{y} = 1082.54$ and $S^2 = 30751.13$. The search routine was given the statistics and initial values of $\mu_y = 900$ and $\sigma_y = 170$. The resulting estimates of the parameters were $\hat{\mu}_y = 999.960$ and $\hat{\sigma}_y = 200.003$.

The last validation test is similar to that described except that Y is truncated at 1000. In other words,

the lower one-half of the data is discarded. For this doubly-truncated, dependent population, we have $\bar{y} = 1180.92$ and $S^2 = 16090.92$ ($S = 126.95$). These values are quite far removed from the parameter values of 1000 and 200. Initial values given the search routine were $\mu = 900$ and $\sigma = 170$. The estimates of the population parameters are still very close to the actual values: $\hat{\mu}_y = 999.832$ and $\hat{\sigma}_y = 200.067$.

The conclusion of the testing is that the relationships of (12.93) and (12.94) are internally consistent and that the search routine, using the criterion of (12.66), provides reasonably accurate estimates of parameters even when statistics derive from a severely truncated population. The testing results lend encouragement to the use of this search algorithm for estimation from real data on tonnages and grades of known deposits of the parameters of the underlying, full (non-truncated) populations. The next section is a case study of uranium deposits of New Mexico.

12.7. Analysis of uranium deposits of New Mexico

12.7.1. The data

Normally, available data on tonnages and grades are primarily for mining properties. In some cases these properties represent a deposit, but in others, one deposit may comprise two or more mines or one mine may comprise two or more deposits. The former of these two latter possibilities is more often the case than the latter. The data of Fig. 12.3 represent as completely as possible tonnages and grades of all uranium deposits, not mining properties, in New Mexico. While these data represent all deposits, hence all modes of occurrence, the preponderance of the deposits are of the sandstone type. The few that are not of this mode are limestone deposits and vein deposits. Fig. 12.3 exhibits considerable scatter and only a very weak relationship. Just what this relationship is depends upon what is taken to be relevant data. The thesis previously advanced in this book is that a plot of tonnages and grades represents a combination of things: the tonnage–grade relationship and the truncating effects of the cost function.

If we consider all of the data of Fig. 12.3 to represent both of these effects, we at once are faced with a dilemma: We have production from very small deposits, say less than 150 s.t., which also have very low grades, grades lower than deposits having many times greater tonnages. Such a result conceptually

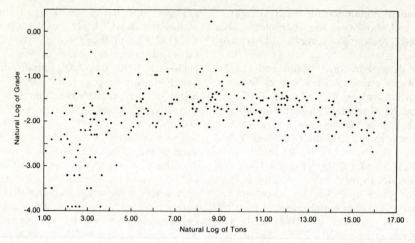

Fig. 12.3. Uranium deposits of New Mexico. (Source: Personal communication, US Energy Research and Developmen
   Administration 1976.)

could arise two ways

  1. These data are not constrained at all by cost, but reflect only the fact that low grades at intermediate tonnages do not occur.

  2. The production of small tonnages, say of the order of 150 or less tons, does not necessarily represent an economic activity. Small quantities of material could be produced while examining the limits of a mineralized area even though that production is not of an economic grade, given the tonnage of the deposit.

Interpretation 2 is adopted. Examination of Fig. 12.3 shows quite a different pattern of the data for tonnages greater than 150 s.t. The decision was made that only deposits having reported tonnages greater than 150 s.t. have passed the test of economics, hence are of a common kind. It was upon this subset of data that the analysis of tonnage–grade relations and parameter estimation was performed.

  The data on tonnages greater than 150 tons were subjected to correlation and regression analysis to estimate the parameters of an equation of the form

$$\ln q = \ln a + b \ln t.$$

Results of the analysis are

$$(0.382)\ (0.00923)$$
$$\ln q = -1.319 - 0.0336 \ln t,$$
$$R^2 = 0.070, \quad n = 167. \qquad (12.96)$$

The coefficient of $\ln t$ is significantly different from zero at the 0.10 per cent level of significance. There-

fore, by a straightforward statistical analysis of the data, tonnage and grade appear to be inversely related. Of course, an inverse relationship between tonnage and grade may be real, or it may be only apparent, reflecting primarily the truncation effects of economics. § 12.7.2 examines cost relationships with the objective of defining the truncation effect of economics on grade so that this effect can be removed. This removal would allow for an uncluttered examination of the real relationship of tonnage to grade.

12.7.2. Costs: components, relations, and estimates

Basis. The cost relationships employed in this model were adopted from the appraisal by Ellis, Harris, and Van Wie (1975) of the uranium resources of New Mexico. In that study, four general cost categories were recognized: mining, milling, transportation, and costs that were constant on a per-lb-U_3O_8 basis. While a host of particulars affect these costs in an actual practice, for that study, costs were defined to reflect only those physical factors that were explicitly considered in the assessment of undiscovered endowment

> Deposit tonnage,
> Deposit grade,
> Depth to deposit,
> Location.

Mining cost was considered to be primarily a function of depth and size of the orebody, decreasing with size and increasing with depth. Fig. 12.4 shows

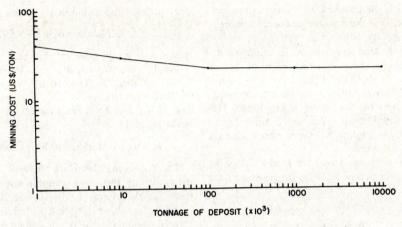

Fig. 12.4. The relationship of mining cost to tonnage of deposit.

graphically the profile of mining costs by tonnage. This figure shows that sizeable reduction in cost per ton occurs with increased tonnages up to about 100 000 s.t., after which scale economies level off.

Engineering cost analysis was performed for typical operations of each of several combinations of tonnages and depth, producing the data in Table 12.7.

Statistical analysis of milling cost data produced two milling cost functions, one for 500 ton/day and another for 1000 ton/day throughput

For the 500 ton/day mill,

$$\text{US \$/ton} = 7.8414 + 6.0214q.$$

For the 1000 ton/day mill,

$$\text{US \$/ton} = 6.2186 + 5.5500q,$$

where q is in per cent. Transportation costs per ton were estimated to vary with haulage distance $T =$

TABLE 12.7. *Estimating mining cost† per ton of ore (as of 1/1/74). (Source: Ellis et al. 1975.)*

Depth (ft)	Estimated mining cost (US $)/ton of ore				
	$0–1 \times 10^3$ tons	10×10^3 tons	100×10^3 tons	1000×10^3 tons	$\geq 10\,000 \times 10^3$ tons
Open pit					
0–100	21.00	19.00	17.00	15.50	12.50
150	21.00	19.00	17.00	16.50	12.50
200	22.50	21.50	19.00	16.50	15.50
300	29.00	27.00	21.50	19.50	19.00
Underground					
300	29.00	27.00	21.50	19.50	19.00
400	260.00	45.00	23.50	21.50	21.50
500	400.00	51.00	23.50	21.50	21.50
1000	1215.00	133.00	26.50	23.50	21.50
1500	1815.00	195.00	31.00	24.50	24.50
2000	2615.00	283.00	38.50	24.50	24.50
3000	4150.00	405.00	55.00	26.50	26.50
4000	5615.00	575.00	70.00	29.00	29.00
≥ 5000	7515.00	780.00	90.00	32.00	32.00

† 1/1/74 estimates include only mine surface plant, equipment, primary development, direct, and indirect mining costs.

$H \cdot D$, where H is the cost in US dollars per ton mile of U_3O_8 ore and D is the haulage distance in miles.

H was estimated by Ellis *et al.* (1975) to be US $0.08/ton-mile. In that same study, locations of deposits were explicitly defined as the centre of the cell (intergrid area). In this model there is no locational information. Consequently, a constant (average) value for D in New Mexico, must be employed. This value was estimated at 10 miles, since much of the ore in the Grants region has very short haulage distances: $D = 10$ mile.

In the New Mexico study by Ellis *et al.* (1975), the following costs were considered to be constant on a per-lb-U_3O_8 basis

Acquisition	US $0.158 = K_1$,
Exploration drilling	US $0.526 = K_2$,
Development drilling	US $0.263 = K_3$.

The unit royalty charge R used in that same study was US $0.368 for an underground mine and US $0.355 for an open-pit mine.

While the tableau of mining costs (Table 12.7) by depth and size (tonnage of ore) was useful in the New Mexico study by Ellis *et al.* it cannot be used in the general model of this study, for it does not include the depth dimension. Consequently, the cost data of Table 12.7 were aggregated across depths by weighting each cost element of the table by that fraction of the total number of mining properties characterized by the depth and tonnage associated with that cost and then summing across depth. This produced a vector of weighted average costs by depth. These costs are listed in Table 12.8.

Similarly, a weighted average milling cost relationship was computed by weighting the coefficients of the two cost equations by the estimated fractions of ore milled in 500- and 1000-s.t./day mills: 0.10 for 500 s.t./day and 0.90 for 1000 s.t./day. This proce-

TABLE 12.8. *Mining costs by tonnage class*

Tonnage (short tons)	Mining cost US $/ton of ore
≤1000	41.72
10 000	29.79
100 000	21.89
1 000 000	21.47[a]
≥10 000 000	21.04

[a] Weighted averaging produced US $23.37/ton for a 1 000 000-ton deposit, but this value was changed to US $21.47 to provide a smooth cost relationship.

dure yielded the milling cost function:

$$US \, \$/ton = 6.381 + 5.597q,$$

where q is grade as a percentage.

Finally, the two royalty rates were combined to a single weighted average royalty by weighting 0.355 by 0.16, the fraction of all mines that are open pit and 0.368 by 0.84, fraction of all mines that are underground

$$R = (0.16)(0.355) + (0.84)(0.368) = 0.366.$$

The foregoing describes the cost framework and estimates of the cost components; however, as a basis for describing a cost surface, the components must be combined so that either one of the pair (grade, tonnage) can be described in terms of the other. The selection was made in this study of defining the cost surface as a grade effect; consequently, these cost components must be combined so that given a cost level C_0 and the tonnage of a deposit, we can solve for the associated grade, which will represent a minimum minable grade, hence a truncation grade. The next subsection derives the equation for this grade.

Derivation of equations for the cost surface and the truncation grade. Let us begin by writing an equation which defines the cost C per pound of U_3O_8. Let

CM = cost of mining per s.t. U_3O_8 ore
CML = cost of milling per s.t. U_3O_8 ore
H = haulage cost per s.t. U_3O_8 ore
K_1 = acquisition costs per lb U_3O_8
K_2 = exploration drilling cost per lb U_3O_8
K_3 = development drilling cost per lb U_3O_8
t = tons of ore
q = grade of ore, as a percentage
C_0 = stated cost level on a per-lb-U_3O_8 basis
D = distance of transport
R = royalty charge per lb U_3O_8
e = recovery expressed as a decimal fraction.

Then,

$$C = \frac{CM}{(2000)(e)(q/100)} + \frac{CML}{(2000)(e)(q/100)} + \frac{H \cdot D}{(2000)(e)(q/100)} + K_1 + K_2 + K_3 + R.$$

But, suppose that $CM = \phi_t(t)$ and $CML = \phi_q(q)$

$$C = \frac{\phi_t(t)}{(200)(e)(q/100)} + \frac{\phi_q(q)}{2000e(q/100)} + \frac{H \cdot D}{2000e(q/100)} + K_1 + K_2 + K_3 + R.$$

For a given cost C_0 we have

$$(C_0)(2000)e(q/100) = \phi_t(t) + \phi_q(q) + H \cdot D +$$
$$+ 2000e(q/100)(K_1 + K_2 + K_3 + R)$$

or

$$2000C_0e(q/100) - \phi_q(q) -$$
$$- 2000e(q/100)(K_1 + K_2 + K_3 + R) = \phi_t(t) + H \cdot D.$$

Suppose that $\phi_q(q)$ is linear

$$\phi_q(q) = \alpha_0 + \alpha_1 q.$$

Then,

$$2000C_0e(q/100) - \alpha_0 - \alpha_1 q -$$
$$- 2000e(q/100)(K_1 + K_2 + K_3 + R) = \phi_t(t) + H \cdot D,$$

$$q\left[\frac{2000C_0e}{100} - \alpha_1 - \frac{2000e}{100}(K_1 + K_2 + K_3 + R)\right]$$
$$= \phi_t(t) + H \cdot D + \alpha_0,$$

$$q = \frac{[\phi_t(t) + H \cdot D + \alpha_0]}{\left[\dfrac{2000C_0e}{100} - \alpha_1 - \dfrac{2000e(K_1 + K_2 + K_3 + R)}{100}\right]},$$

or

$$q = \frac{\phi_t(t) + H \cdot D + \alpha_0}{20C_0e - \alpha_1 - 20e(K_1 + K_2 + K_3 + R)}.$$

Let us substitute known values for all quantities

but $\phi_t(t)$ and C_0

$$q = \frac{(\phi_t(t) + (0.08) \cdot (10) + 6.381)}{(20(C_0)(0.96) - 5.597 -}$$
$$- 20(0.96)(0.158 + 0.526 + 0.263 + 0.366))$$

or, more simply,

$$q = \frac{\phi_t(t) + 7.181}{19.20C_0 - 30.807}. \qquad (12.97)$$

This is our basic relationship, expressed as a grade (percentage). For example, suppose that we have a 10 000-s.t. deposit and that our maximum production cost is US $15.00 = C_0$. Examination of Table 12.8 shows that the mining cost portion $\phi_t(10\,000) =$ US \$29.79. The truncation grade would be

$$q = \frac{29.79 + 7.181}{19.2(15) - 30.807} = \frac{36.971}{257.193} \approx 0.144 \text{ per cent}$$

and $x = \ln q = -1.93794$. Eqn (12.97) has been evaluated at selected tonnages, and the resulting truncation grades are plotted in Fig. 12.5.

12.7.3. *Parameters of the grade distribution*

A first look. The first analysis of the tonnage–grade data on New Mexico uranium was made by dividing the tonnage range of 150 s.t. to 18 million s.t. into 10 intervals of equal lengths in the logarithmic scale (intervals of y). The limits of these intervals are provided in the first column of Table 12.9. The

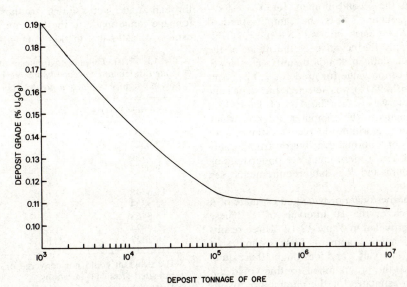

Fig. 12.5. Truncation (lowest minable) grade, given a cost of US \$15/lb U$_3$O$_8$ (US \$ 1975).

TABLE 12.9. *Data for the initial estimation of parameters of conditional grade distributions (10 intervals on Y, depo* tonnage >150 s.t.)

(1) Intervals of Y† $(y''-y')$	(2) Mean Y† (y^0)	(3) Number of deposits	(4) Truncation value for X‡ (x_1)	(5) v_1§	(6) v_2	(7) S	(8) ε'
5.0106– 6.1802	5.6787	9	−1.6636	0.4621	0.3137	0.3165	−1.4599
6.1802– 7.3497	6.9172	6	−1.6648	0.2678	0.1379	0.2571	−1.0415
7.3497– 8.5192	8.1166	12	−1.7281	0.3061	0.1843	0.3010	−1.0168
8.5192– 9.6887	9.0042	19	−1.8770	0.5178	0.4752	0.4551	−1.1376
9.6887–10.8582	10.4291	19	−2.0023	0.3929	0.2121	0.2404	−1.6347
10.8582–12.0277	11.5859	18	−2.1863	0.5557	0.3649	0.2370	−2.3446
12.0277–13.1973	12.5269	14	−2.1890	0.6818	0.5577	0.3047	−2.2377
13.1973–14.3667	13.7888	12	−2.2003	0.5224	0.3075	0.1861	−2.8067
14.3667–15.5363	14.9929	12	−2.2047	0.4537	0.2903	0.2906	−1.5612
15.5363–16.7059	16.1834	9	−2.2160	0.3907	0.2280	0.2745	−1.4233

† $Y = \ln(T)$, where T = tonnage.
‡ $X = \ln(Q)$, where Q = grade.
§ v_1 = mean of truncated data.

second column of this table lists the mean of each interval of Y, y_0, where y is the natural logarithm of tonnage. The truncation grade x_1 as a natural logarithm of grade (percentage), was computed by evaluating eqn (12.97) at the mean of Y for that interval. These values are provided in column 4 of Table 12.9. Column 5 lists the first moment for $X_i - x_{1i}$, where x_{1i} is the truncation value of X for the ith interval on Y, and X_i is a value of X for which the associated Y lies in the ith interval of Y. Column 6 lists the second moment for $X_i - x_{1i}$, $i = 1, 2, \ldots, 10$. Column 7 lists the sample standard deviation of X for each interval: $S = (v_2 - v_1^2)^{\frac{1}{2}}$. Finally, ε' is simply the negative of the mean of the truncated grade data in standard units: $\varepsilon' = -v_1/S$. An upper truncation value for grade of 2.0 per cent $(x_{2i} = \ln(2.0) = 0.69315)$ was selected and kept constant for all intervals of Y. The data of Table 12.9 are required inputs to the computer program which applies Newton's algorithm to Cohen's estimation of the parameters of a normal distribution from doubly truncated data. For a more complete understanding of this procedure and the data requirements, see § 12.6.

Processing of these data provided an estimate of μ and σ for each of the 10 intervals of Y. These estimates are provided in Table 12.10. Three results of this analysis merit comment. First, estimates of parameters for intervals 1 and 5 through 10 are quite similar. Second, the programmed routine could not converge upon estimates for the parameters for intervals 2 and 3. Third, the estimates of the parame-

ters for interval 4 disagree considerably with those o the other intervals. This estimation routine appear to be data-sensitive to some degree. In order t explore the issue, a second run was made using onl six intervals, thereby introducing a different parti tioning of the data and greater frequencies of de posits within the intervals. Data input to this secon analysis are provided in Table 12.11, and the result ing estimates are provided in Table 12.12. Thre results merit comment. First, estimates for intervals through 6 are very similar to those of the sam tonnage range made in the first run, indicating rob ustness of estimates in this tonnage range. Second

TABLE 12.10. *Estimated parameters of 10 conditional grade distributions for deposits having US $15 reserves plus cumulative production greater than 150 s.t.*

Average $\ln(t)$	$\hat{\mu}$	$\hat{\sigma}$
5.7830	−1.4205	0.4487
7.0321	†	†
8.1750	†	†
9.0951	−4.2662‡	1.3214‡
10.4725	−1.6927	0.3009
11.6548	−1.6392	0.2468
12.5854	−1.5223	0.3212
13.8468	−1.6797	0.1884
15.0924	−1.8839	0.3805
16.2227	−2.0484	0.4032

† The program could not converge on estimates and terminated after 500 iterations.
‡ These estimates were provided by the program but appear to be at great variance to the other estimates.

TABLE 12.11. *Data for second estimation of parameters of conditional grade distributions (six intervals on* Y, *deposit tonnage > 150 s.t.*)

Intervals of Y† ($y''-y'$)	Mean Y† (y^0)	Number of deposits	Truncation value for X‡ (x_1)	v_1§	v_2	S	ε'
5.0106– 6.9598	6.0636	13	−1.6636	0.3991	0.2652	0.3254	−1.2264
6.9598– 8.9091	8.2500	22	−1.7436	0.4109	0.3545	0.4309	−0.9536
8.9091–10.8583	10.1329	30	−1.9813	0.4113	0.2411	0.2683	−1.5329
10.8583–12.8075	11.9507	28	−2.1870	0.5969	0.4135	0.2391	−2.4963
12.8075–14.7567	13.8426	19	−2.2008	0.5259	0.3597	0.2882	−1.8250
14.7567–16.7059	15.7217	19	−2.2104	0.4269	0.2769	0.3077	−1.3872

† $Y = \ln(T)$, where T = tonnage.
‡ $X = \ln(Q)$, where Q = grade.
§ v_1 = mean of truncated data.

TABLE 12.12. *Estimated parameters of six conditional grade distributions for deposits having US $15 reserves plus cumulative production greater than 150 s.t.*

Average $\ln(t)$	$\hat{\mu}$	$\hat{\sigma}$
6.1683	−2.0393	0.6445
8.3377	†	†
10.1284	−1.7072	0.3583
11.9040	−1.5955	0.2459
13.8586	−1.7267	0.3321
15.7524	−2.0793	0.4700

† The program could not converge on estimates and terminated after 500 iterations.

the routine again could not converge for data in the interval containing tonnages around 4000 s.t. Finally, merely regrouping of the data for the second run gave estimates for μ and σ for tonnages of the order of 14 000 s.t. which were very different from those

made in the initial run (specifically, those of the fourth interval).

Because of the instability of the estimates for lower tonnages and the inability of the routine to provide estimates for some of the lower tonnage intervals, the decision was made to restrict analysis to tonnages greater than 16 000 s.t. As has already been noted, parameter estimates appear to be robust in this range (16 000–18 000 000).

A second look. Pursuant to the restriction of analysis as described, eight class intervals for Y were constructed for the range 16 000–18 000 000—this was done in the logarithmic scale, as previously noted. Data for this analysis are provided in Table 12.13, and the resulting parameter estimates are provided in Table 12.14. An additional analysis was made using only seven class intervals solely for the purpose of examining sensitivity of the parameter estimates to data regrouping. The data input for this analysis

TABLE 12.13. *Data for estimation of conditional grade distributions using truncated tonnage data (eight intervals on* Y; *deposit tonnage > 16 000 s.t.*)

Intervals of Y† ($y''-y'$)	Mean Y† (y^0)	Number of deposits	Truncation value for X‡ (x_1)	v_1§	v_2	S	ε'
9.6803–10.5585	10.1690	11	−1.9836	0.3873	0.2198	0.2642	−1.4658
10.5585–11.4367	10.8831	13	−2.0534	0.4051	0.2030	0.1972	−2.0545
11.4367–12.3149	11.8655	19	−2.1868	0.6154	0.4500	0.2671	−2.3038
12.3149–13.1931	12.7614	8	−2.1902	0.6670	0.5480	0.3212	−2.0761
13.1931–14.0713	13.6353	10	−2.1981	0.5194	0.3077	0.1947	−2.6672
14.0713–14.9495	14.5649	8	−2.2027	0.4887	0.3167	0.2791	−1.7508
14.9495–15.8277	15.3585	8	−2.2070	0.3709	0.2074	0.2642	−1.4035
15.8277–16.7059	16.2593	7	−2.2160	0.4464	0.2759	0.2769	−1.6123

† $Y = \ln(T)$, where T = tonnage.
‡ $X = \ln(Q)$, where Q = grade.
§ v_1 = mean of truncated data.

TABLE 12.14. *Estimated parameters of eight conditional grade distributions for deposits having US $15 reserves plus cumulative production in excess of 16 000 s.t.*

Average ln (t)	$\hat{\mu}$	$\hat{\sigma}$
10.1605	−1.7743	0.3725
10.8831	−1.6654	0.2141
11.8577	−1.5823	0.2794
12.7582	−1.5494	0.3473
13.7008	−1.6813	0.1983
14.5978	−1.7783	0.3306
15.3280	−2.0713	0.3963
16.3004	−1.8738	0.3510

TABLE 12.16. *Estimated parameters of seven conditional grade distributions for deposits having US $15 reserves plus cumulative production greater than 16 000 s.t.*

Average ln (t)	$\hat{\mu}$	$\hat{\sigma}$
10.3039	−1.6251	0.2871
11.2625	−1.7025	0.2285
12.1109	−1.4966	0.1896
13.2287	−1.6520	0.3706
14.1894	−1.7776	0.1963
15.1797	−1.9210	0.4058
16.3004	−1.8738	0.3510

and the resulting parameters are provided in Tables 12.15 and 12.16. Comparison of the estimates for the seven-group analysis with those of the eight-group confirms the robustness of estimates from the data in the restricted range.

12.7.4. *The dependency relationship*

Estimates for μ made using both the eight and seven intervals on Y are plotted against the average tonnages of the intervals in Fig. 12.6. Two observations can now be made

1. Estimates made by using eight or seven groups are very similar;
2. The plot of μ against y^0 is very flat, suggesting that tonnage and grade may be statistically independent.

This proposition was explored formally. The model selected was $\mu = \alpha_0 + \alpha_1 y^0$. The hypothesis to be tested H_0 is that α_1, the coefficient of y^0, is zero. This hypothesis is tested at the 5 per cent significance

level against the alternative H_1 that $\gamma \neq 0$. Regression analysis of the estimates of μ for the eight intervals yielded estimates of the parameters and their standard errors

$$(0.1478)\ (0.02575)$$
$$\hat{\mu} = -1.1428 - 0.04784y^0,$$
$$R^2 = 0.345.$$

The computed t is 1.858, while $t_{0.025}$ for 6 degrees of freedom is 2.447; consequently, we accept H_0 and conclude that there is no statistically significant relationship between the means of the conditional grade distributions and tonnage.

A similar analysis (see Fig. 12.7 for a plot of $\hat{\sigma}$ for each tonnage interval) was made for $\sigma = \beta_0 + \beta_1 y^0$

$$(0.07521)\ (0.0131)$$
$$\hat{\sigma} = 0.1748 + 0.01033y^0,$$
$$R^2 = 0.094.$$

The hypothesis to be tested H_0 is that $\beta_1 = 0$. This hypothesis is tested against the alternative hypothesis

TABLE 12.15. *Data for estimation of parameters of conditional distributions using truncated tonnage data (seven intervals on Y; deposit tonnage $> 16\,000$ s.t.)*

Intervals of Y† $(y''-y')$	Mean Y† (y^0)	Number of deposits	Truncation value for X‡ (x_1)	v_1§	v_2	S	ε'
9.6803–10.6840	10.3010	15	−1.9927	0.4237	0.2382	0.2422	−1.7492
10.6840–11.6876	11.2904	15	−2.1273	0.4415	0.2397	0.2117	−2.0852
11.6876–12.6913	12.0920	15	−2.1874	0.6909	0.5132	0.1894	−3.6468
12.6913–13.6949	13.2374	11	−2.1936	0.5964	0.4604	0.3236	−1.8431
13.6949–14.6986	14.1878	8	−2.2015	0.4316	0.2215	0.1876	−2.3012
14.6986–15.7022	15.1712	12	−2.2056	0.4516	0.2932	0.2989	−1.5109
15.7022–16.7059	16.2130	7	−2.2160	0.4464	0.2759	0.2769	−1.6123

† $Y = \ln(T)$, where $T =$ tonnage.
‡ $X = \ln(Q)$, where $Q =$ grade.
§ $v_1 =$ mean of truncated data.

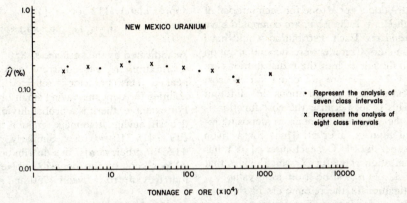

Fig. 12.6. The relationship $\hat{\mu}$ (per cent U_3O_8) to tonnage.

H_1 that $\beta_1 \neq 0$ at the 5 per cent level of significance. The 't' statistic for β_1 is 0.789. This value is less than $t_{0.025}$ for 6 degrees of freedom: $t = 0.789 < t_{0.025}^{(6)} = 2.447$. Therefore, we cannot reject the hypothesis that the coefficient of $\beta_1 = 0$. In effect, we conclude that the standard deviation of grade is not related to tonnage.

Since the statistical analysis indicates no statistically significant relationship between either μ or σ and $\ln t$, we must conclude that grade and tonnage of uranium deposits are statistically independent. Therefore, instead of having a $\hat{\mu}$ and $\hat{\sigma}$ for each tonnage interval, we will have only one $\hat{\mu}$ and one $\hat{\sigma}$. These estimates are the averages of the eight separate estimates

$$\hat{\mu} = -1.7470 = \tfrac{1}{8}\sum_{i=1}^{8}\hat{\mu}_i,$$
$$\hat{\sigma} = 0.3112 = \tfrac{1}{8}\sum_{i=1}^{8}\hat{\sigma}_i. \tag{12.98}$$

This means that the geometrical mean grade of uranium deposits of New Mexico is 0.174 per cent U_3O_8. The arithmetic mean grade is obtained by evaluating $e^{-1.7470+(0.3112)^2/2} = 0.174e^{(0.3112)^2/2} = \underline{0.183}$. Only about 5 per cent of the total uranium resources have grades less than 0.1045 per cent U_3O_8

$$F\left(\frac{\ln(0.1045) - (-1.7470)}{0.3112}\right) = F(-1.644) \approx 0.05.$$

The next section utilizes the results of this analysis, data on deposit tonnages, and the cost function to estimate the parameters of the distribution for $Y = \ln(T)$, where T is deposit tonnage.

12.7.5. *The parameters of the tonnage distribution*

Finding grade and tonnage to be statistically independent does not alter the procedure for analysis described in § 12.5. The parameters for the tonnage distribution still are appropriately estimated by eqns (12.64) and (12.65). Independence merely means

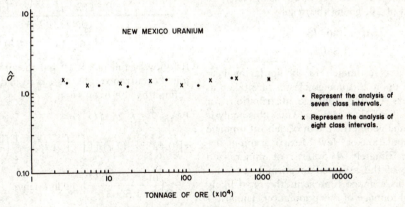

Fig. 12.7. The relationship $\hat{\sigma}$ to tonnage.

that the n distributions for x (one for each interval of Y) from which P_i, $i = 1, 2, \ldots, n$, are computed have the *same parameters*. Each distribution would have different parameters if grade were dependent upon tonnage. Even though each of the n distributions are equal, P_i, $i = 1, 2, \ldots, n$, are not equal, for the cost surface truncates these distributions at different levels of x. This is so, because the cost function is evaluated at the geometrical mean of deposit tonnage for each tonnage interval. Thus, for a given maximum cost per lb of U_3O_8, each interval of Y has a different truncation value for X, which means that each P_i, $i = 1, 2, \ldots, n$, will be a different value.

For the estimation of the parameters of the tonnage distribution, deposits having tonnage greater than 150 s.t. were classified into 20 classes. These classes were determined by dividing the range of 18 000 000 to 150 into 20 intervals of equal size in the logarithmic scale

Size of interval = (ln (18 000 000) − ln (150))/20.

The mean of ln (t) for deposits having a size greater than 150 s.t. was computed to be 10.9852 (58 985 s.t.), and the associated logarithmic variance was computed to be 2.9213. In the computation of these statistics, deposits having grades lower than the lower truncation grade of an interval were excluded, just as they were in the estimation of the grade parameters. The sample mean and variance and the grade probabilities, P_i, $i = 1, 2, \ldots, 20$, constituted input data for the computer search for the tonnage parameters. The result of this search is

$$\hat{\mu}_y = 10.7034,$$
$$\hat{\sigma}_y^2 = 1.8505. \tag{12.99}$$

As a check on the data sensitivity of the search routine, the analysis was repeated using only 10 classes instead of 20, giving the results

$$\hat{\mu}_y = 10.6278,$$
$$\hat{\sigma}_y^2 = 1.8401.$$

The parameters estimated in the initial analysis (12.99), based upon 20 tonnage classes, are taken as the parameters of the tonnage distribution for uranium deposits of New Mexico. Thus, this analysis indicates that the geometric mean of deposit tonnage in the full population of New Mexico uranium deposits is approximately 44 500 s.t. of mineralized rock. Because of the assumed lognormality of this distribution, this tonnage represents the most likely or most typical tonnage of this population. The arithmetic mean of deposit tonnage for this population is

approximately 112 300 s.t. [1]

$$112\ 300 \approx e^{10.7034 + (1.8505/2)}.$$

As indicated by the variance (1.8505), this lognormal distribution is very narrow and rather sharply peaked. This character is reflected in the low probabilities for deposits having small or large tonnages. For example, there is a probability of only 0.05 for a deposit having a tonnage greater than 415 710 s.t. $P(T \geq 415\ 710) \approx 0.05$. Similarly, $P(T \leq 4750) \approx 0.05$. In other words, this distribution indicates that 90 per cent of the deposits in New Mexico have tonnages of ore between 4750 and 415 710.

12.7.6. The model

The analyses in §§ 12.7.3–12.7.5 lead to the conclusion that tonnage and grade of uranium deposits in New Mexico are statistically independent. Thus, the probability density function for the joint occurrence of a deposit tonnage of t and a grade of q is the product of two statistically independent lognormal probability density functions

$$\phi(\ln t, \ln q) = \frac{\exp\left(-\frac{1}{2}\left(\dfrac{\ln q - (-1.7470)}{0.3112}\right)^2\right)}{(0.3112) \cdot (2\pi)^{\frac{1}{2}}} \times$$

$$\times \frac{\exp\left(-\frac{1}{2}\left(\dfrac{\ln t - 10.7034}{1.3603}\right)^2\right)}{(1.3603) \cdot (2\pi)^{\frac{1}{2}}},$$

$$-\infty \leq \ln q \leq \infty$$
$$-\infty \leq \ln t \leq \infty. \tag{12.100}$$

Or, in simpler form

$$\phi(\ln t, \ln q)$$

$$= \frac{\exp\left(-\frac{1}{2}\left(\dfrac{\ln q + 1.7470}{0.3112}\right)^2 - \frac{1}{2}\left(\dfrac{\ln t - 10.7034}{1.3603}\right)^2\right)}{(0.4233)(2\pi)},$$

$$-\infty \leq \ln q \leq \infty; \quad -\infty \leq \ln t \leq \infty. \tag{12.101}$$

It follows from (12.101) that the probability for the joint occurrence of $t_1 \leq T \leq t_2$ and $q_1 \leq Q \leq q_2$ is defined by the expression

$$P(t_1 \leq T \leq t_2, q_1 \leq Q \leq q_2)$$

$$= [(0.4233) \cdot (2\pi)]^{-1} \int_{q_1}^{q_2} \int_{t_1}^{t_2} \exp\left(-\frac{1}{2}\left(\dfrac{\ln q + 1.7470}{0.3112}\right)^2 - \right.$$

$$\left. -\frac{1}{2}\left(\dfrac{\ln t - 10.7034}{1.3603}\right)^2\right) d\ln t\, d\ln q. \tag{12.102}$$

Of course, because of the independency of grade and

tonnage, this probability can be determined by using tabled values or a computer routine for the standard unit normal probability distribution

$$P(t_1 \le T \le t_2, q_1 \le Q \le q_2)$$
$$= \left[F\left(\frac{\ln q_2 + 1.7470}{0.3112}\right) - F\left(\frac{\ln q_1 + 1.7470}{0.3112}\right) \right] \times$$
$$\times \left[F\left(\frac{\ln t_2 - 10.7034}{1.3603}\right) - F\left(\frac{\ln t_1 - 10.7034}{1.3603}\right) \right],$$

where $F(z)$ is the probability that the standardized random variable Z is less than z.

12.8. Conclusions and some criticisms

Subject to the probabilistic qualifications attendant to all conclusions which result from statistical analyses, two major conclusions are indicated

1. Grade and tonnage of uranium deposits of New Mexico are statistically independent.
2. Average grade U_3O_8 of this population of deposits is far greater than crustal abundance:

$$1800 \times 10^{-6} \text{ compared to } 2 \times 10^{-6}.$$

The finding of independency of grade and tonnage is an interesting one in view of the fact that correlation analysis of grades and tonnage of deposits having a size greater than 150 s.t. showed a highly significant negative correlation. The finding of independency implies that the strength of the negative correlation derived primarily from the effects of deposit size and grade on the technologies and economies of mining, milling, and processing. Removal of the economic effects removed the apparent dependency of grade and tonnage. Such a result prompts a general admonition. Straightforward correlation analysis of grade and tonnage of deposits for which grade and size may reflect primarily the economic effects may be deceptive. For such circumstance, neglecting to explicitly account for the economic effects in the analysis may lead to an incorrect assessment of the statistical relationship of grade and tonnage.

The finding that the arithmetic average grade of the New Mexico population of uranium deposits is approximately 900 times that of crustal abundance is equally interesting because of the manner in which the parameters of the lognormal grade distribution were estimated. The procedure for estimation recognized the truncation of grades by economics and in effect compensated for the truncation in the estimation of the parameters of the grade distribution.

Thus, if the average grade over the full population of deposits were crustal abundance, such a fact should emerge from the analysis. But, instead, the parameters of the grade distribution indicate an average grade much greater than crustal abundance. This result has further ramifications. One of these is that the bivariate tonnage and grade distribution does not represent the totality of material in the region; consequently, an appraisal of the endowment of New Mexico in uranium deposits typical of those currently known cannot be made by multiplying a probability for the joint occurrence of tonnage and grade with the weight of the crust, as is done in Brinck's geochemical model or in PAU's deposit model. Such a procedure would overstate endowment in these kinds of deposits. In this case, the correct appraisal of endowment in these deposits requires an additional distribution, one which describes number of deposits.

Care must be exercised to not overinterpret the results of this analysis. The results are not a definitive commentary upon the practice by PAU and Brinck of basing the specification of their models on crustal abundance. A definitive commentary can be made only when data on grade and tonnage for a region represent all, or at least a majority, of the modes of occurrence. The bulk of the deposits in New Mexico are in sandstone; only a few represent other modes of occurrence, and these are restricted to vein deposits and limestone deposits. Deposits of modes of occurrence which are important in other regions are not represented in the New Mexico data on tonnage and grade. Consequently, allowance must be made for the occurrence of deposits of these other modes in New Mexico. Or, stated differently, for the estimating of endowment by the methods of Brinck or PAU to be appropriate requires that at least some of these other modes of occurrence are present in New Mexico and that these modes have very low grades. At this time, our knowledge of the geology of New Mexico is insufficient to rule out completely the possibility for the presence of deposits of other modes. If there is such a thing as a continuous, master grade distribution and it applies to New Mexico, then other modes of occurrence must be present.

About all that can be said with some degree of confidence, as a result of this research, is that the deposits that are currently typical of New Mexico do not constitute a population with an average grade of crustal abundance, and only a small part of the crust of New Mexico constitutes the rock material contained in the deposits of this population.

A number of issues are raised by the procedures described in this section. Few of these received any more than a superficial exploration. In this regard, this study is embryonic, for time did not permit the pursuit of these issues. In a sense, this analysis serves to raise more questions than it answers.

One bothersome issue is the loss of information which results from the removal of the economic effect by procedures described herein. Whereas there may be observations on grade and tonnage for as many as several hundred deposits, the size of the sample used to test for dependency of grade and tonnage is determined by the number of classes of tonnage constructed, one class for each conditional grade distribution. A constraint is imposed on the creation of a large number of classes, for each class must have a number of deposits large enough to make the estimation of the parameters of the grade distribution for that class reliable. For a given total number of deposits, increasing the number of tonnage classes decreases the average number of deposits per class. Furthermore, if the frequency of deposits is uneven across the tonnage scale (in logarithms), the number of deposits in some of these classes may be so small as to preclude reliable estimation of grade parameters when a large number of classes is employed.

In this study, the number of deposits having a size greater than 150 s.t. is 98, but the number of observations used to test the hypothesis of no relationship was 8 (the number of pairs of estimated parameters, $\hat{\mu}$ and $\hat{\sigma}$). As a means of examining the sensitivity of the statistical result to number of classes, the number was increased until the estimates for one of the tonnage classes departed markedly from those of the remaining classes. This occurred at 12 classes. Therefore, the hypothesis of no relationship (H_0: γ (the coefficient of ln t) = 0) was tested for 11 classes. The result was the same as it was for 8 classes: failure to reject the hypothesis at the 5 per cent significant level.

Comment is in order concerning SIGMU, the computer program of Newton's algorithm for Cohen's solution (estimation) for the parameters of a doubly-truncated normal distribution. This computer routine seems to work very well when the truncation value is only 1 or 2 or even 3 standard deviations from the mean. The ability of the routine to perform well when this truncation value is a large number of standard units away is limited by the accuracy of the numerical analysis of the subroutine which computes the normal probability. A systems function called PNORM is used in the routine as programmed for the CDC computer of the University of Arizona. Standard scores of 4 and 5 tax the reliability of this

program, and scores of 6 exceed it. For this reason, when one or both of the truncation values are far out in the tails of the distribution, convergence by SIGMU on the parameters of the full distribution breaks down. Instead of converging on an error of zero, the routine cycles as it moves one way, then the next, seeking a smaller error. Under these conditions, the algorithm is prevented from successful convergence by errors generated in the normal probability subroutine. A truncation value which is very far out in the tail may even cause over- or underflow of computer registers and the termination of computation by system control.

So far as most statistical analysis and inference is concerned, the loss of reliability for truncation values so far out in the tails is of no consequence. However, the performance of an estimation algorithm under such circumstances would be a concern if the mean of the full population were near crustal abundance. In this case, the lower truncation value of the statistical data is far out in the tail of large values. In fact, many of the demonstrations by Brinck of his geochemical element distribution employ standard scores in the 6–8 range. It is apparent that estimation under these circumstances can be questioned not just because of limitations of numerical analysis algorithms but on the proposition that such a small and non-representative sample of a population be used to estimate the parameters of the distribution.

Had time permitted, it would have been both interesting and useful to have explored the relative merits of Newton's algorithm for the estimation of the parameters of a doubly truncated normal distribution with the computer search routine, MINSER, under various conditions of truncation.

Perhaps the most important unanswered question with respect to analysis is, 'Why did Newton's algorithm perform so badly (erratically) on the grade distributions for tonnage classes in the 150–16 000 tons range?' What are the mechanical-type explanations, and are there underlying geological factors? Since completing the analysis, it has been brought to the author's attention that many of the deposits in this tonnage range are the limestone-type of uranium deposit, while the majority of those having sizes greater than 16 000 s.t. are the sandstone-type of deposit. While this is interesting and should be investigated further, it does not provide understanding in terms of the mechanics of statistical analysis.

Obviously, this study is no more than a beginning. Considerable work needs to be done on the analysis of grade–tonnage relations and the estimation of the parameters of the grade and tonnage distributions when the data which supports the analysis have, so to speak, passed through an economic filter.

12.9. Appendices

12.9.1. *Derivation of equations for Newton's algorithm for Cohen's solution*

Given

$$f = \sigma^2 - \sigma^2 \varepsilon'\left(\frac{\phi' - \phi''}{I' - I''}\right) + \sigma^2 \varepsilon'^2 - \sigma R \frac{\phi''}{(I' - I'')} - v_2,$$

$$g = \sigma\left(\frac{\phi' - \phi''}{I' - I''}\right) - \sigma \varepsilon' - v_1,$$

calculate: $\partial f/\partial \varepsilon'$, $\partial f/\partial \sigma$, $\partial g/\partial \varepsilon'$, and $\partial g/\partial \sigma$.

1. *Derivation of $\partial f/\partial \sigma$.*

$$\frac{\partial f}{\partial \sigma} = 2\sigma - \left\{ 2\sigma\varepsilon'\left(\frac{\phi' - \phi''}{I' - I''}\right) + \right.$$

$$\left. + \frac{\partial[(\phi' - \phi'')(I' - I'')^{-1}]}{\partial \sigma}\sigma^2\varepsilon' \right\} + 2\sigma\varepsilon'^2 -$$

$$- \left\{ \frac{R\phi''}{(I' - I'')} + \sigma R \frac{\partial[(\phi'')(I' - I'')^{-1}]}{\partial \sigma} \right\}$$

and

$$\frac{\partial[(\phi' - \phi'')(I' - I'')^{-1}]}{\partial \sigma}$$

$$= \frac{\partial(\phi' - \phi'')}{\partial \sigma}(I' - I'')^{-1} + \frac{\partial[(I' - I'')^{-1}]}{\partial \sigma}(\phi' - \phi'').$$

Thus,

$$\frac{\partial[(\phi' - \phi'')(I' - I'')^{-1}]}{\partial \sigma}$$

$$= \left[\left(-\frac{1}{(2\pi)^{\frac{1}{2}}}\right)\left(\frac{\varepsilon'R}{\sigma^2} + \frac{R^2}{\sigma^3}\right)\exp\left(\frac{-\left(\varepsilon' + \frac{R}{\sigma}\right)^2}{2}\right) \right] \times$$

$$\times (I' - I'')^{-1} + \left[\frac{\frac{\partial I''}{\partial \sigma}}{(I' - I'')^2} \right](\phi' - \phi'').$$

Also,

$$\frac{\partial[\phi''(I' - I'')^{-1}]}{\partial \sigma} = \frac{-\partial[(\phi' - \phi'')(I' - I'')^{-1}]}{\partial \sigma}.$$

Therefore,

$$\frac{\partial f}{\partial \sigma} = 2\sigma - \left\{ 2\sigma\varepsilon'\left(\frac{\phi' - \phi''}{I' - I''}\right) + \right.$$

$$+ \left[-\left(\frac{1}{(2\pi)^{\frac{1}{2}}}\right)\left(\frac{\varepsilon'R}{\sigma^2} + \frac{R^2}{\sigma^3}\right)\exp\left(\frac{-\left(\varepsilon' + \frac{R}{\sigma}\right)^2}{2}\right)(I' - I'')^{-1} + \right.$$

$$+ \left(\frac{\frac{\partial I''}{\partial \sigma}}{(I' - I'')^2}\right)(\phi' - \phi'') \right]\sigma^2\varepsilon' \right\} +$$

$$+ 2\sigma\varepsilon'^2 - \left\{ \frac{R\phi''}{(I' - I'')} + \right.$$

$$+ \sigma R\left[\left(\frac{1}{(2\pi)^{\frac{1}{2}}}\right)\left(\frac{\varepsilon'R}{\sigma^2} + \frac{R^2}{\sigma^3}\right)\exp\left(\frac{-\left(\varepsilon' + \frac{R}{\sigma}\right)^2}{2}\right)(I' - I'')^{-1} - \right.$$

$$\left.\left. - \left(\frac{\frac{\partial I''}{\partial \sigma}}{(I' - I'')^2}\right)(\phi'') \right] \right\}.$$

2. *Derivation of $\partial f/\partial \varepsilon'$.*

$$\frac{\partial f}{\partial \varepsilon'} = -\left\{ \sigma^2\left(\frac{\phi' - \phi''}{I' - I''}\right) + \frac{\partial[(\phi' - \phi'')(I' - I'')^{-1}]}{\partial \varepsilon'}(\sigma^2\varepsilon') \right\} +$$

$$+ 2\sigma^2\varepsilon' - \sigma R\left\{ \frac{\partial[\phi''(I' - I'')^{-1}]}{\partial \varepsilon'} \right\}.$$

But, since

$$\frac{\partial[\phi' - \phi'']}{\partial \varepsilon'} = -\frac{\varepsilon'}{(2\pi)^{\frac{1}{2}}}\exp\left(\frac{-\varepsilon'^2}{2}\right) +$$

$$+ \left(\frac{1}{(2\pi)^{\frac{1}{2}}}\right)\left(\varepsilon' + \frac{R}{\sigma}\right)\exp\left(\frac{-\left(\varepsilon' + \frac{R}{\sigma}\right)^2}{2}\right),$$

$$\frac{\partial f}{\partial \varepsilon'} = -\left\{ \sigma^2\left(\frac{\phi' - \phi''}{I' - I''}\right) + \left[\left[\frac{1}{(2\pi)^{\frac{1}{2}}}\left(\varepsilon' + \frac{R}{\sigma}\right) \times \right.\right.\right.$$

$$\times \exp\left(\frac{-\left(\varepsilon' + \frac{R}{\sigma}\right)^2}{2}\right) - \frac{\varepsilon'}{(2\pi)^{\frac{1}{2}}}\exp\left(\frac{-\varepsilon'^2}{2}\right) \right](I' - I'')^{-1} -$$

$$\left. - \left[\frac{\frac{\partial I'}{\partial \varepsilon'} - \frac{\partial I''}{\partial \varepsilon'}}{(I' - I'')^2} \right](\phi' - \phi'') \right](\sigma^2\varepsilon') \right\} +$$

$$+ 2\sigma^2\varepsilon' - \sigma R\left\{ \left[\left(-\frac{1}{(2\pi)^{\frac{1}{2}}}\right)\left(\varepsilon' + \frac{R}{\sigma}\right) \right.\right.$$

$$\times \exp\left(\frac{-\left(\varepsilon' + \frac{R}{\sigma}\right)^2}{2}\right) \right] \times$$

$$\left.\left. \times (I' - I'')^{-1} - \left[\frac{\frac{\partial I'}{\partial \varepsilon'} - \frac{\partial I''}{\partial \varepsilon'}}{(I' - I'')^2} \right](\phi'') \right\}.$$

3. Derivation of $\partial g/\partial \sigma$.

$$\frac{\partial g}{\partial \sigma} = \left\{ \left(\frac{\phi' - \phi''}{I' - I''} \right) + \sigma \left[\frac{\partial [(\phi' - \phi'')(I' - I'')^{-1}]}{\partial \sigma} \right] \right\} - \varepsilon'$$

$$\frac{\partial g}{\partial \sigma} = \left(\frac{\phi' - \phi''}{I' - I''} \right) +$$

$$+ \sigma \left\{ \left[\left(-\frac{1}{(2\pi)^{\frac{1}{2}}} \right) \left(\frac{\varepsilon' R}{\sigma^2} + \frac{R^2}{\sigma^3} \right) \exp \left(\frac{-\left(\varepsilon' + \frac{R}{\sigma} \right)^2}{2} \right) \right] \times \right.$$

$$\times (I' - I'')^{-1} + \left[\frac{\frac{\partial I''}{\partial \sigma}}{(I' - I'')^2} \right] (\phi' - \phi'') \bigg\} - \varepsilon'.$$

4. Derivation of $\partial g/\partial \varepsilon'$.

$$\frac{\partial g}{\partial \varepsilon'} = \sigma \left\{ \frac{\partial [(\phi' - \phi'')(I' - I'')^{-1}]}{\partial \varepsilon'} \right\} - \sigma$$

$$\frac{\partial g}{\partial \varepsilon'} = \sigma \left\{ \left[\left(\frac{1}{(2\pi)^{\frac{1}{2}}} \right) \left(\varepsilon' + \frac{R}{\sigma} \right) \exp \left(\frac{-\left(\varepsilon' + \frac{R}{\sigma} \right)^2}{2} \right) - \right. \right.$$

$$\left. - \frac{\varepsilon'}{(2\pi)^{\frac{1}{2}}} \exp \left(\frac{-\varepsilon'^2}{2} \right) \right] (I' - I'')^{-1} -$$

$$\left. - \left[\frac{\frac{\partial I'}{\partial \varepsilon'} - \frac{\partial I''}{\partial \varepsilon''}}{(I' - I'')^2} \right] (\phi' - \phi'') \right\} - \sigma$$

where

(a) $\quad \dfrac{\partial (\phi' - \phi'')}{\partial \sigma} = \dfrac{\partial \phi'}{\partial \sigma} - \dfrac{\partial \phi''}{\partial \sigma},$

but, since ϕ' is not a function of σ,

$$\frac{\partial \phi'}{\partial \sigma} = 0,$$

$$\phi'' = \frac{1}{(2\pi)^{\frac{1}{2}}} \exp \left(\frac{-\left(\varepsilon' + \frac{R}{\sigma} \right)^2}{2} \right)$$

$$= \frac{1}{(2\pi)^{\frac{1}{2}}} \exp \left(\frac{-\left(\varepsilon'^2 + \frac{2\varepsilon' R}{\sigma} + \frac{R^2}{\sigma^2} \right)}{2} \right),$$

and

$$\frac{\partial \phi''}{\partial \sigma} = \left(\frac{1}{(2\pi)^{\frac{1}{2}}} \right) (-1) \left(\frac{-\frac{2\varepsilon' R}{\sigma^2} - \frac{2R^2}{\sigma^3}}{2} \right) \times$$

$$\times \exp \left(\frac{-\left(\varepsilon'^2 + \frac{2\varepsilon' R}{\sigma} + \frac{R^2}{\sigma^2} \right)}{2} \right).$$

Thus,

$$\frac{\partial \phi''}{\partial \sigma} = \frac{1}{(2\pi)^{\frac{1}{2}}} \left(\frac{\varepsilon' R}{\sigma^2} + \frac{R^2}{\sigma^3} \right) \exp \left(\frac{-\left(\varepsilon' + \frac{R}{\sigma} \right)^2}{2} \right).$$

Therefore,

$$\frac{\partial (\phi' - \phi'')}{\partial \sigma} = \left(-\frac{1}{(2\pi)^{\frac{1}{2}}} \right) \left(\frac{\varepsilon' R}{\sigma^2} + \frac{R^2}{\sigma^3} \right) \exp \left(\frac{-\left(\varepsilon' + \frac{R}{\sigma} \right)^2}{2} \right).$$

(b) $\quad \dfrac{\partial [(I' - I'')^{-1}]}{\partial \sigma} = [(-1)(I' - I'')^{-2}] \left[\dfrac{\partial I'}{\partial \sigma} - \dfrac{\partial I''}{\partial \sigma} \right],$

but $\partial I'/\partial \sigma = 0$. Thus,

$$\frac{\partial [(I' - I'')^{-1}]}{\partial \sigma} = [(I' - I'')^{-2}] \left[\frac{\partial I''}{\partial \sigma} \right] = \frac{\frac{\partial I''}{\partial \sigma}}{(I' - I'')^2}.$$

(c) $\quad \dfrac{\partial [\phi' - \phi'']}{\partial \varepsilon'} = \dfrac{\partial \phi'}{\partial \varepsilon'} - \dfrac{\partial \phi''}{\partial \varepsilon'}$

and

$$\frac{\partial \phi'}{\partial \varepsilon'} = \frac{\partial \left[\frac{1}{(2\pi)^{\frac{1}{2}}} \exp \left(\frac{-\varepsilon'^2}{2} \right) \right]}{\partial \varepsilon'} = \left(\frac{1}{(2\pi)^{\frac{1}{2}}} \right) \left(\frac{-2\varepsilon'}{2} \right) \times$$

$$\times \exp \left(\frac{-\varepsilon'^2}{2} \right) = \frac{-\varepsilon'}{(2\pi)^{\frac{1}{2}}} \exp \left(\frac{-\varepsilon'^2}{2} \right).$$

Since

$$\phi'' = \frac{1}{(2\pi)^{\frac{1}{2}}} \exp \left(\frac{-\left(\varepsilon' + \frac{R}{\sigma} \right)^2}{2} \right),$$

$$\frac{\partial \phi''}{\partial \varepsilon'} = \frac{\partial \left\{ \frac{1}{(2\pi)^{\frac{1}{2}}} \exp \left[-\left(\varepsilon' + \frac{R}{\sigma} \right)^2 / 2 \right] \right\}}{\partial \varepsilon'}$$

$$\frac{\partial \phi''}{\partial \varepsilon'} = \frac{\partial \left\{ \frac{1}{(2\pi)^{\frac{1}{2}}} \exp \left[-\left(\varepsilon'^2 + \frac{2R\varepsilon'}{\sigma} + \frac{R^2}{\sigma^2} \right) / 2 \right] \right\}}{\partial \varepsilon'}$$

$$\frac{\partial \phi''}{\partial \varepsilon'} = \left(\frac{1}{(2\pi)^{\frac{1}{2}}} \right) (-1) \left(\frac{2\varepsilon' + \frac{2R}{\sigma}}{2} \right) \exp \left(\frac{\left(\varepsilon' + \frac{R}{\sigma} \right)^2}{2} \right)$$

$$\frac{\partial \phi''}{\partial \varepsilon'} = - \left(\frac{1}{(2\pi)^{\frac{1}{2}}} \right) \left(\varepsilon' + \frac{R}{\sigma} \right) \exp \left(\frac{-\left(\varepsilon' + \frac{R}{\sigma} \right)^2}{2} \right).$$

Therefore,

$$\frac{\partial[\phi' - \phi'']}{\partial\varepsilon'} = \left(\frac{1}{(2\pi)^{\frac{1}{2}}}\right)\left(\varepsilon' + \frac{R}{\sigma}\right) \times$$

$$\times \exp\left(\frac{-\left(\varepsilon' + \frac{R}{\sigma}\right)^2}{2}\right) - \frac{\varepsilon'}{(2\pi)^{\frac{1}{2}}}\exp\left(\frac{-\varepsilon'^2}{2}\right).$$

12.9.2. Differentiation of the integrals I', I''

Method: differentiation of integrals

The formula for taking derivatives of integrals is as follows (adapted to the single variable case).

Let $f(x)$ be the function and $F(z)$ be the integral of $f(x)$

$$F(z) = \int_{a(z)}^{b(z)} f(x)\, dx.$$

Then, the derivative of $F(z)$ is determined by the equation

$$\frac{\partial F(z)}{\partial z} = \overbrace{\int_{a(z)}^{b(z)} \frac{\partial f(x)}{\partial(z)}\, dx}^{1} + \overbrace{f(b(z))b'(z)}^{2} - \overbrace{f(a(z))a'(z)}^{3}.$$

Note, the first term is undefined in the single variable case; only the second and third terms are relevant.

Application

1. *Evaluate* $\partial I'/\partial\varepsilon'$. In this case, the function is

$$f(x) = \frac{1}{(2\pi)^{\frac{1}{2}}}\exp\left(\frac{-x^2}{2}\right)dx.$$

The integral function is

$$F(\varepsilon') = I' = \frac{1}{(2\pi)^{\frac{1}{2}}}\int_{\varepsilon'}^{\infty}\exp\left(\frac{-x^2}{2}\right)dx.$$

Make the identifications

$$b(\varepsilon') = \infty, \quad b'(\varepsilon') = 0;$$
$$a(\varepsilon') = \varepsilon', \quad a'(\varepsilon') = 1.$$

Therefore,

$$f(b(\varepsilon')) \cdot b'(\varepsilon') = \left(\frac{1}{(2\pi)^{\frac{1}{2}}}\exp\left(\frac{-\infty^2}{2}\right)\right)(0) = 0,$$

$$f(a(\varepsilon')) \cdot a'(\varepsilon') = \left(\frac{1}{(2\pi)^{\frac{1}{2}}}\exp\left(\frac{-\varepsilon'^2}{2}\right)\right)(1)$$

$$= \frac{1}{(2\pi)^{\frac{1}{2}}}\exp\left(\frac{-\varepsilon'^2}{2}\right).$$

Since $\partial I'/\partial\varepsilon' = f(b(\varepsilon')) \cdot b'(\varepsilon') - f(a(\varepsilon')) \cdot a'(\varepsilon')$,

$$\frac{\partial I'}{\partial\varepsilon'} = -\frac{1}{(2\pi)^{\frac{1}{2}}}\exp\left(\frac{-\varepsilon'^2}{2}\right).$$

2. *Evaluate* $\partial I''/\partial\varepsilon'$.

$$I'' = F(\varepsilon'') = \frac{1}{(2\pi)^{\frac{1}{2}}}\int_{\varepsilon''}^{\infty}\exp\left(\frac{-x^2}{2}\right)dx.$$

Since we desire $\partial I''/\partial\varepsilon'$, the limits of the integral must be based upon ε', not ε''

$$\varepsilon'' = \varepsilon' + \frac{R}{\sigma}.$$

Therefore,

$$I'' = F\left(\varepsilon' + \frac{R}{\sigma}\right) = \frac{1}{(2\pi)^{\frac{1}{2}}}\int_{\varepsilon' + \frac{R}{\sigma}}^{\infty}\exp\left(\frac{-x^2}{2}\right)dx.$$

Here $a(\varepsilon') = \varepsilon' + (R/\sigma)$ and $a'(\varepsilon') = 1$; $b(\varepsilon') = \infty$ and $b'(\varepsilon') = 0$. Thus,

$$\frac{\partial I''}{\partial\varepsilon''} = \frac{\partial F\left(\varepsilon' + \frac{R}{\sigma}\right)}{\partial\varepsilon'}$$

$$= -\left[\frac{1}{(2\pi)^{\frac{1}{2}}}\exp\left(\frac{-\left(\varepsilon' + \frac{R}{\sigma}\right)^2}{2}\right)\right]\quad(1)$$

$$= \frac{-1}{(2\pi)^{\frac{1}{2}}}\exp\left(\frac{-\left(\varepsilon' + \frac{R}{\sigma}\right)^2}{2}\right).$$

3. *Evaluate* $\partial I''/\partial\sigma$.

$$I'' = F(\varepsilon'') = \frac{1}{(2\pi)^{\frac{1}{2}}}\int_{\varepsilon''}^{\infty}\exp\left(\frac{-x^2}{2}\right)dx.$$

Substituting $\varepsilon' + (R/\sigma) = \varepsilon''$

$$I'' = F\left(\varepsilon' + \frac{R}{\sigma}\right) = \frac{1}{(2\pi)^{\frac{1}{2}}}\int_{\varepsilon' + \frac{R}{\sigma}}^{\infty}\exp\left(\frac{-x^2}{2}\right)dx.$$

Thus, we have

$$\frac{\partial I''}{\partial\sigma} = -f(a(\sigma)) \cdot a'(\sigma).$$

Since

$$f(a(\sigma)) = \frac{1}{(2\pi)^{\frac{1}{2}}}\exp\left(-\frac{1}{2}\left(\varepsilon' + \frac{R}{\sigma}\right)^2\right)$$

and $a'(\sigma) = -R/\sigma^2$,

$$\frac{\partial I''}{\partial\sigma} = \frac{R}{\sigma^2(2\pi)^{\frac{1}{2}}}\exp\left(-\frac{1}{2}\left(\varepsilon' + \frac{R}{\sigma}\right)^2\right).$$

12.9.3. *Computer programs* SIGMU *and* SEARCH

```
C      PROGRAM SIGMU
C      **********************************************************************
C      *                                                                  **
C      *    THIS PROGRAM WILL ESTIMATE THE MEAN AND STANDARD DEVIATION    **
C      *    OF A NORMALLY DISTRIBUTED POPULATION FROM A TRUNCATED SAMPLE  **
C      **********************************************************************
       CALL IFILE(21,'SIG')
       IPT = 21
       IOUT = 23
       DIF = 0.000006
       IOUT2 = 24
 51    J = 0
       KOUNTER = 0
C      **********************************************************************
C      *    READ IN SAMPLE PARAMETERS                                     **
C      *    X01 = LOWER TRUNCATION LIMIT                                  **
C      *    X011 = UPPER TRUNCATION LIMIT                                 **
C      *    XBAR = SAMPLE MEAN                                            **
C      *    SX = SAMPLE STANDARD DEVIATION                               **
C      *    V2 = SECOND SAMPLE MOMENT                                    **
C      **********************************************************************
       READ(IPT,10,END = 50)X01,X011,XBAR,SX,V2
 10    FORMAT (5F)
C      **********************************************************************
C      *    INITIALIZE VI (FIRST SAMPLE MOMENT)                          **
C      *             EPS1(INDEPENDENT PARAMETER OF LOCATION)             **
C      *             SIGMA (ESTIMATE FOR POPULATION STANDARD DEVIATION)  **
C      *             (RANGE)                                             **
C      **********************************************************************
       V1 = ABS(XBAR)
       EPS1 = -V1/SX
       SIGMA = SX
       R = X011 - X01
C      **********************************************************************
C      *    PRINT OUT STARTING VALUES                                    **
C      **********************************************************************
       WRITE(IOUT,60)X01,X011,R,XBAR,SX,V2,SIGMA,EPS1
 20    EPS2 = EPS1 + (R/SIGMA)
C      **********************************************************************
C      *    ORDINATE PROBABILITIES FROM STANDARDIZED NORMAL              **
C      **********************************************************************
       PSI1 = (1./SQRT(2.*3.14159))*EXP(-(EPS1**2)/2.)
       PSI2 = (1./SQRT(2.*3.14159))*EXP(-(EPS2**2)/2.)
C      **********************************************************************
C      *    AREA PROBABILITIES FOR NORMAL CURVE                          **
C      **********************************************************************
       SUM1 = PNORM(EPS1)
       SUM2 = PNORM(EPS2)
       P = (PSI1 - PSI2)/(SUM1 - SUM2)
       Q = PSI2/(SUM1 - SUM2)
C      **********************************************************************
C      *    FIND THE DIFFERENCE (DELTA) BETWEEN ESTIMATING EQUATIONS     **
C      *            FOR SIGMA AND EPS1                                   **
C      **********************************************************************
```

```
      DELTA = ((SIGMA**2)*(1.-EPS1*(P-EPS1)))-(R*Q*SIGMA)-V2-(SIGMA*(P-1EPS1)
     -V1)
2       KOUNTER = KOUNTER+1
        IF(KOUNTER.GT.500) GO TO 999
```

```
C     ********************************************************************
C     *     IF WE ARE WITHIN SPECIFIED ERROR LEVEL CALCULATE            *
C     *     POPULATION MEAN (GO TO 52) OTHERWISE ADJUST SIGMA AND        *
C     *     EPS1 BY USE OF A MODIFIED NEWTON RAPHSON NUMERICAL           *
C     *     ANALYSIS TECHNIQUE AND LOOP THROUGH STATEMENT 20 AGAIN       *
C     ********************************************************************
      IF (DELTA.GT.-DIF.AND.DELTA.LT.DIF) GO TO 52
```

```
C     ********************************************************************
C     *     SET UP CONSTANTS FOR NEWTON RAPHSON FORMULAS                *
C     ********************************************************************
      PI2 = 1./(SQRT(2.*3.14159))
      P1 = (EPS1*R/SIGMA**2)+(R**2/SIGMA**3)
      P2 = EXP ((-(EPS1+(R/SIGMA))**2)/2.)
      P3 = 1./(SUM1-SUM2)
      P4 = (SUM1-SUM2)**2
      P5 = PSI1-PSI2
      P6 = SIGMA**2
      P7 = EPS1+(R/SIGMA)
      P8 = EXP((-(EPS1**2))/2.)
      P9 = (-PI2)*P8
      P10 = (-PI2)*P2
      P11 = 0.0
      P12 = ((R/P6)*PI2)*P2
      P13 = EPS1**2
      P14 = 2.*EPS1*P6
```

```
C     ********************************************************************
C     *     ESTIMATING EQUATIONS FOR SIGMA AND EPSILON                  *
C     ********************************************************************
      F = P6-(P6*EPS1*P)+(P6*P13)-(SIGMA*R*Q)-V2
      G = (SIGMA*P)-(SIGMA*EPS1)-V1
```

```
C     ********************************************************************
C     *     PARTIAL DERIVATIVE OF F WITH RESPECT TO SIGMA               *
C     ********************************************************************
      PFS = 2.*SIGMA-((2.*SIGMA*EPS1*P)+(((( -PI2)*
     1P1*P2*P3)+(P12/P4*P5))*(P6*EPS1)))+(2.*
     2 SIGMA*P13 )-(( R*Q)+((SIGMA*R)*((P12*P1*P2*
     3P3)-(P12/P4*PSI2))))
```

```
C     ********************************************************************
C     *     PARTIAL DERIVATIVE OF F WITH RESPECT TO EPSILON             *
C     ********************************************************************
      PFE = -((P6*P)+((((PI2*P7*P2)-(EPS1 *PI2*P8
     1))*P3)-(((P9-P10)/P4)*P5))*(P6*EPS1)))+P14
     2-((SIGMA*R)*(((-PI2)*P7*P2*P3)-((P9-P10)/P4
     3*PSI2)))
```

```
C     ********************************************************************
C     *     PARTIAL DERIVATIVE OF G WITH RESPECT TO SIGMA               *
C     ********************************************************************
      PGS = P+(SIGMA*(((-PI2)*P1*P2*P3)+(P12/P4*25)))-EPS1
```

```
C     ********************************************************************
C     *     PARTIAL DERIVATIVE OF G WITH RESPECT TO EPSILON             *
C     ********************************************************************
```

```
        PGE = SIGMA*((((PI2*P7*P2)-(EPS1*PI2*P8))*P3)-((P9-P10)/P4*P5)
       1)-SIGMA
C       ************************************************************
C       *                                                          *
C       *     RECURSIVE RELATIONSHIPS                              *
C       *                                                          *
C       ************************************************************
        PDEN = (PFS*PGE)-(PFE*PGS)
        S1 = SIGMA+(((G*PFE)-(F*PGE))/PDEN)
        E1 = EPS1+(((F*PGS)-(G*PFS))/PDEN)
        SIGMA = S1
        EPS1 = E1
        GO TO 20
    50  STOP
   999      WRITE(IOUT,80)KOUNTER,SIGMA,EPS1,DELTA
    52  AMU = X01-(SIGMA*EPS1)
        WRITE(IOUT,90)SIGMA,EPS1,AMU
          WRITE(IOUT2,91)AMU,SIGMA
    91      FORMAT(2F12.5)
        GO TO 51
    60      FORMAT(//' LOWER TRUNCATION LIMIT          =',E14.8,/,
       1'UPPER TRUNCATION LIMIT          =',E14.8,/,'RANGE',27X,
       2'=',E14.8,/,'SAMPLE MEAN',21X,'=',E14.8,/,
       3'SAMPLE STANDARD DEVIATION',7X,'=',E14.8,/,'SECOND
       4 SAMPLE MOMENT V2 ',8X,'=',E14.8,//,'INITIAL VALUES ARE',
       5/,5X,'SIGMA',6X,'=',E14.8,/,5X,'EPSILON',4X,'=',E14.8)
    70  FORMAT ('1',21X,'KOUNTER',17X,'SIGMA',10X,'EPSILON', 12X,'DELTA')
    80  FORMAT(21X,I4,15X,3(E14.8, 6X))
    90      FORMAT('OFINAL VALUES ARE',/,'STANDARD DEVIATION',5X,E14.8,/,
       1'EPSILON',16X,E14.8,/,'POPULATION MEAN'8X,E14.8)
        END
        FUNCTION PNORM(X)
        Z = 0.0
        IF(X.EQ.0.0) GO TO 2
        Z = 1.0
        Y = ABS(X)*0.5
        IF(Y.GE.3.0) GO TO 2
        IF(Y.GE.1.0) GO TO 1
        W = Y*Y
        Z = (((((((0.000124818987*W-0.001075204047)*W+0.005198775019)
       1*W-0.019198292004)*W+0.059054035642)*W-0.151968751364)*W
       2+0.31915293294)*W-0.5319230073)*W+0.797884560593)*Y*2.0
        GO TO 2
     1  Y = Y-2.0
        Z = ((((((((((((-0.000045255659*Y+0.00015252929)*Y-
       10.000019538132)*Y-0.000676904986)*Y+0.001390604284)*Y-
       20.00079462082)*Y-0.002034254874)*Y+0.006549791214)*Y-
       30.010557625006)*Y+0.011630447319)*Y-0.009279453341)*Y+
       40.005353579108)*Y-0.002141268741)*Y+0.000535310849)*Y
       5+0.999936657524
     2  PNORM = (1.0+SIGN(Z,X))*0.5
        PNORM = 1.0-PNORM
        RETURN
        END
```

```
C     PROGRAM SEARCH–EMPLOYS SUBROUTINE MINSER
C---PROGRAM TO CALCULATE THE MEAN AND VARIANCE OF A DISTRIBUTION
C---GIVEN CERTAIN INFORMATION ABOUT TRUNCATED INTERVALS OF IT.
      DIMENSION X1(100),X2(100),U1(100),SIG1(100),DUM(5),E(5)
      COMMON Y1(100),Y2(100),P(100),Y(100),YBAR,SIGO,N
      COMMON/MIN/W(40)
      CALL IFILE(21,'HAR2')
      IPT = 21
      IOUT = 23
      READ(IPT,10)N,YBAR,SIGO
10    FORMAT(I,2F)
      DO 35 I = 1,N
      READ(IPT,30)U1(I),SIG1(I),X1(I),X2(I),Y1(I),Y2(I)
30    FORMAT(6F)
      Z1 = (X1(I) – U1(I))/SIG1(I)
      Z2 = (X2(I) – U1(I))/SIG1(I)
      V1 = PNORM(Z1)
      V2 = PNORM(Z2)
C     TYPE 101,Z1,Z2,V1,V2
      P(I) = ABS(V2 – V1)
35    CONTINUE
      TYPE 101,(P(I),I = 1,N)
101   FORMAT(10F10.5)
      READ(IPT,30)U,S,UDIF,SDIF,ESCALE
      DUM(1) = U
      DUM(2) = S
      E(1) = UDIF
      E(2) = SDIF
      F = 10.
      CALL MINSER(DUM,E,2,F,ESCALE,2,1,10)
      WRITE(IOUT,65)DUM(1),DUM(2),F
65    FORMAT(' ESTIMATED MEAN (Y) = ',E14.8,/,' ESTIMATED V
     1ARIANCE = ',E14.8,/,' ERROR = ',E14.8)
      STOP
      END
      SUBROUTINE CALCFX(N1,DUM,F)
      COMMON Y1(100),Y2(100),P(100),Y(100),YBAR,SIGO,N
      DIMENSION DUM(1)
      SQ2P = SQRT (2.0*3.141592654)
      U = DUM(1)
      S = DUM(2)
      SUMYP = 0.0
      SUMP = 0.0
      SUM2Y = 0.0
      DO 60 I = 1,N
      Z1 = (Y1(I) – U)/S
      Z2 = (Y2(I) – U)/S
      VY1 = PNORM(Z1)
      VY2 = PNORM(Z2)
      FDIF = ABS(VY1 – VY2)
      Y(I) = (EXP(–0.5*Z2**2) – EXP(–0.5*Z1**2))*S*SQ2P/FDIF + U
      PF = P(I)*FDIF
C     TYPE 101,Z1,Z2,VY1,VY2,FDIF,PF
101   FORMAT(10F10.5)
```

```
                 SUMP = SUMP + PF
                 SUMYP = SUMYP + PF * Y(I)
                 SUM2Y = SUM2Y + PF * Y(I) * Y(I)
60               CONTINUE
C                TYPE 102,SUM2Y,SUMP,SUMYP
102              FORMAT(5E12.5)
                 YHAT = SUMYP/SUMP
                 SIG = SUM2Y/SUMP − YHAT * YHAT
                 F = (1. − YHAT/YBAR) * *2 + (1. − SIG/SIGO) * *2
                 TYPE 102,U,S,YHAT,SIG,F
                 RETURN
                 END
             SUBROUTINE MINSER (X,E,N,F,ESCALE,IPRINT,ICON,MAXIT)
                 COMMON  /MIN/W(40)
             DIMENSION X(1),E(1)
                 IOUT = 23
             DDMAG = 0.1 * ESCALE
             SCER = 0.05/ESCALE
             JJ = N * N + N
             JJJ = JJ + N
             K = N + 1
             NFCC = 1
             IND = 1
             INN = 1
             DO 1 I = 1,N
             DO  2 J = 1,N
             W(K) = 0.
             IF(I − J)4,3,4
    3        W(K) = ABS(E(I))
             W(I) = ESCALE
    4        K = K + 1
    2        CONTINUE
    1        CONTINUE
             ITERC = 1
             ISGRAD = 2
             CALL CALCFX(N,X,F)
             FKEEP = ABS(F) + ABS(F)
    5        ITONE = 1
             FP = F
             SUM = 0.
             IXP = JJ
             DO 6 I = 1,N
             IXP = IXP + 1
             W(IXP) = X(I)
    6        CONTINUE
             IDIRN = N + 1
             ILINE = 1
    7        DMAX = W(ILINE)
             DACC = DMAX * SCER
             DMAG = AMIN1(DDMAG,0.1 * DMAX)
             DMAG = AMAX1(DMAG,20. * DACC)
             DDMAX = 10. * DMAG
             GO TO (70,70,71),ITONE
   70        DL = 0.
```

```
          D = DMAG
          FPREV = F
          IS = 5
          FA = F
          DA = DL
   8      DD = D − DL
          DL = D
  58      K = IDIRN
          DO 9 I = 1,N
          X(I) = X(I) + DD*W(K)
          K = K + 1
   9      CONTINUE
          CALL CALCFX(N,X,F)
          NFCC = NFCC + 1
          GO TO (10,11,12,13,14,96), IS
  14      IF(F − FA)15,16,24
  16      IF (ABS(D) − DMAX) 17,17,18
  17      D = D + D
          GO TO 8
  18      WRITE(IOUT,19)
  19      FORMAT (5X,45HMINSER MAXIMUM CHANGE DOES NOT ALTER FUNCTION)
          GO TO 20
  15      FB = F
          DB = D
          GO TO 21
  24      FB = FA
          DB = DA
          FA = F
          DA = D
  21      GO TO (83,23),ISGRAD
  23      D = DB + DB − DA
          IS = 1
          GO TO 8
  83      D = 0.5*(DA + DB − (FA − FB)/(DA − DB))
          IS = 4
          IF((DA − D)*(D − DB))25,8,8
  25      IS = 1
          IF (ABS(D − DB) − DDMAX) 8,8,26
  26      D = DB + SIGN(DDMAX,DB − DA)
          IS = 1
          DDMAX = DDMAX + DDMAX
          DDMAG = DDMAG + DDMAG
          IF(DDMAX − DMAX)8,8,27
  27      DDMAX = DMAX
          GO TO 8
  13      IF(F − FA)28,23,23
  28      FC = FB
          DC = DB
  29      FB = F
          DB = D
          GO TO 30
  12      IF(F − FB)28,28,31
  31      FA = F
          DA = D
          GO TO 30
```

```
   11   IF(F−FB)32,10,10
   32   FA = FB
        DA = DB
        GO TO 29
   71   DL = 1.
        DDMAX = 5.
        FA = FP
        DA = −1.
        FB = FHOLD
        DB = 0.
        D = 1.
   10   FC = F
        DC = D
   30   A = (DB−DC)*(FA−FC)
        B = (DC−DA)*(FB−FC)
        IF((A+B)*(DA−DC))33,33,34
   33   FA = FB
        DA = DB
        FB = FC
        DB = DC
        GO TO 26
   34   D = 0.5*(A*(DB+DC)+B*(DA+DC))/(A+B)
        DI = DB
        FI = FB
        IF(FB−FC)44,44,43
   43   DI = DC
        FI = FC
   44   GO TO (86,86,85),ITONE
   85   ITONE = 2
        GO TO 45
   86   IF (ABS(D−DI)−DACC) 41,41,93
   93   IF (ABS(D−DI)−0.03*ABS(D)) 41,41,45
   45   IF ((DA−DC)*(DC−D)) 47,46,46
   46   FA = FB
        DA = DB
        FB = FC
        DB = DC
        GO TO 25
   47   IS = 2
        IF ((DB−D)*(D−DC)) 48,8,8
   48   IS = 3
        GO TO 8
   41   F = FI
        D = DI−DL
        DD = SQRT((DC−DB)*(DC−DA)*(DA−DB)/(A+B))
        DO 49 I = 1,N
        X(I) = X(I)+D*W(IDIRN)
        W(IDIRN) = DD*W(IDIRN)
        IDIRN = IDIRN+1
   49   CONTINUE
        W(ILINE) = W(ILINE)/DD
        ILINE = ILINE+1
        IF(IPRINT−1)51,50,51
   50   WRITE(IOUT,52) ITERC,NFCC,F
   52   FORMAT (/1X,9HITERATION,I5,I15,16H FUNCTION VALUES,
        110X,3HF = ,E21.9)
```

```
      WRITE(IOUT,54) (X(I),I = 1,N)
  54  FORMAT (5E24.9)
      GO TO(51,53),IPRINT
  51  GO TO (55,38),ITONE
  55  IF (FPREV - F - SUM) 94,95,95
  95  SUM = FPREV - F
      JIL = ILINE
  94  IF (IDIRN - JJ) 7,7,84
  84  GO TO (92,72),IND
  92  FHOLD = F
      IS = 6
      IXP = JJ
      DO 59 I = 1,N
      IXP = IXP + 1
      W(IXP) = X(I) - W(IXP)
  59  CONTINUE
      DD = 1.
      GO TO 58
  96  GO TO (112,89),IND
 112  IF (FP - F) 37,91,91
  91  D = 2.*(FP + F - 2.*FHOLD)/(FP - F)**2
      IF (D*(FP - FHOLD - SUM)**2 - SUM) 87,37,37
  87  J = JIL*N + 1
      IF (J - JJ) 60,60,61
  60  DO 62 I = J,JJ
      K = I - N
      W(K) = W(I)
  62  CONTINUE
      DO 97 I = JIL,N
      W(I - 1) = W(I)
  97  CONTINUE
  61  IDIRN = IDIRN - N
      ITONE = 3
      K = IDIRN
      IXP = JJ
      AAA = 0.
      DO 65 I = 1,N
      IXP = IXP + 1
      W(K) = W(IXP)
      IF (AAA - ABS(W(K)/E(I))) 66,67,67
  66  AAA = ABS(W(K)/E(I))
  67  K = K + 1
  65  CONTINUE
      DDMAG = 1.
      W(N) = ESCALE/AAA
      ILINE = N
      GO TO 7
  37  IXP = JJ
      AAA = 0.
      F = FHOLD
      DO 99 I = 1,N
      IXP = IXP + 1
      X(I) = X(I) - W(IXP)
      IF (AAA*ABS(E(I)) - ABS(W(IXP))) 98,99,99
  98  AAA = ABS(W(IXP)/E(I))
  99  CONTINUE
```

```
          GO TO 72
     38   AAA = AAA*(1.+DI)
          GO TO (72,106),IND
     72   IF (IPRINT-2) 53,50,50
     53   GO TO (109,88),IND
    109   IF (AAA-0.1) 89,89,76
     89   GO TO (20,116),ICON
    116   IND = 2
          GO TO (100,101),INN
    100   INN = 2
          K = JJJ
          DO 102 I = 1,N
          K = K+1
          W(K) = X(I)
          X(I) = X(I)+10.*E(I)
    102   CONTINUE
          FKEEP = F
          CALL CALCFX (N,X,F)
          NFCC = NFCC+1
          DDMAG = 0.
          GO TO 108
     76   IF (F-FP) 36,78,78
     78   WRITE(IOUT,80)
     80   FORMAT (5X,38HMINSER ACCURACY LIMITED BY ERRORS IN F)
          GO TO 20
     88   IND = 1
     35   DDMAG = 0.4*SQRT(FP-F)
          ISGRAD = 1
    108   ITERC = ITERC+1
          IF (ITERC-MAXIT) 5,5,81
     81   WRITE(IOUT,82) MAXIT
     82   FORMAT (I5, 31H ITERATIONS COMPLETED BY MINSER)
          IF (F-FKEEP) 20,20,110
    110   F = FKEEP
          DO 111 I = 1,N
          JJJ = JJJ+1
          X(I) = W(JJJ)
    111   CONTINUE
          GO TO 20
    101   JIL = 1
          FP = FKEEP
          IF (F-FKEEP) 105,78,104
    104   JIL = 2
          FP = F
          F = FKEEP
    105   IXP = JJ
          DO 113 I = 1,N
          IXP = IXP+1
          K = IXP+N
          GO TO (114,115),JIL
    114   W(IXP) = W(K)
          GO TO 113
    115   W(IXP) = X(I)
          X(I) = W(K)
    113   CONTINUE
          JIL = 2
```

```
          GO TO 92
  106     IF (AAA−0.1) 20,20,107
   20     RETURN
  107     INN = 1
          GO TO 35
          END
  ·       FUNCTION PNORM(X)
          Z = 0.0
          IF(X.EQ.0.0) GO TO 2
          Z = 1.0
          Y = ABS(X)*0.5
          IF(Y.GE.3.0) GO TO 2
          IF(Y.GE.1.0) GO TO 1
          W = Y*Y
          Z = (((((((((0.000124818987*W−0.001075204047)*W+0.005198775019)
         1*W−0.019198292004)*W+0.059054035642)*W−0.151968751364)*W
         2+0.31915293294)*W−0.5319230073)*W+0.797884560593)*Y*2.0
          GO TO 2
    1     Y = Y−2.0
          Z = ((((((((((((((−0.000045255659*Y+0.00015252929)*Y−
         10.000019538132)*Y−0.000676904986)*Y+0.001390604284)*Y−
         20.00079462082)*Y−0.002034254874)*Y+0.006549791214)*Y−
         30.010557625006)*Y+0.011630447319)*Y−0.009279453341)*Y+
         40.005353579108)*Y−0.002141268741)*Y+0.000535310849)*Y
         5+0.999936657524
    2     PNORM = (1.0+SIGN(Z,X))*0.5
          RETURN
          END
C         PROGRAM ORDER.F4
C−−−−THE MIDPOINT OF THE CLASS INTERVAL IS USED TO DETERMINE THE
C−−−−TRUNCATION POINT OF EACH INTERVAL
          DIMENSION VARX(102),BARX(102),VARZ(102),XTRUN(102)
          DIMENSION V1(102),V2(102),BARV(102),R(300),EPSILN(102)
          DIMENSION SUMX(102),SUMXQ(102),CNT(102),SUMZ(102),SUMW(102)
          DIMENSION CL(102),SUMWQ(102),FIRST(5,102),P(300),GP(300)
          DIMENSION GR(300),SUMZW(102),CNTW(102),BARZW(102)
          DIMENSION BARXW(102),BARZ(102),VARV(102)
          CALL IFILE(21,'AEC')
          IPT = 21
          IOUT = 23
          IOUT2 = 24
          READ(IPT,10) NF,M,XL,XU,IFLG
   10     FORMAT(2I,2F,I)
          I = 0
   15     READ(IPT,25,END = 20)PD,GG,RP,GRR
          I = I+1
          P(I) = ALOG(PD+RP)
          GP(I) = GG*PD+RP*GRR)/(PD+RP)
          GP(I) = ALOG(GP(I))
          R(I) = PD+RP
   25     FORMAT(21X,F9.0,F5.3,F8.0,F5.3)
          GO TO 15
   20     N = I
          XM = M
          M = M+1
          YL = ALOG(XL)
```

```
              YU = ALOG(XU)
              D = (YU − YL)/XM
C***SET UP CLASS INTERVALS
              DO 30 I = 1,N
              CL(I) = YL + (I − 1)*D
30            CONTINUE
C***CALCULATE STATISTICS FOR UNTRUNCATED DATA
              DO 4 I = 1,N
              IF(P(I).GT.YU.OR.P(I).LT.YL) GO TO 4
              DO 5 J = 1,M
              IF(P(I).GT.CL(J)) GO TO 5
              SUMX(J) = SUMX(J) + GP(I)
              SUMXQ(J) = SUMXQ(J) + GP(I)*GP(I)
              SUMZ(J) = SUMZ(J) + R(I)
              SUMY = SUMY + P(I)
              SUMYQ = SUMYQ + P(I)*P(I)
              CNT(J) = CNT(J) + 1.0
              XKNT = XKNT + 1.0
              GO TO 4
5             CONTINUE
4             CONTINUE
              DO 11 J = 2,M
              VARX(J) = SQRT(SUMXQ(J)/CNT(J) − (SUMX(J)/CNT(J))**2)
              BARX(J) = SUMX(J) /CNT(J)
              BARZ(J) = EXP((CL(J) + CL(J − 1))/2.0)
11            CONTINUE
              BARY = SUMY/XKNT
              VARY = SQRT(SUMYQ/XKNT − BARY*BARY)
C***NOW PERFORM THE TRUNCATION
              IF(IFLG.GT.0) GO TO 200
              DO 35 I = 1,N
              IF(P(I).LT.YL.OR.P(I).GT.YU) GO TO 35
              DO 34 J = 2,M
              IF(P(I).GT.CL(J)) GO TO 34
              CALL ARANGE(GP(I),FIRST,NF,M,J)
              GO TO 35
34            CONTINUE
35            CONTINUE
              CALL TRUNK(FIRST,NF,M,XTRUN)
              GO TO 66
200           CALL TRNCT(BARZ,XTRUN,M)
66            DO 40 I = 1,N
              IF(P(I).GT.YU.OR.P(I).LT.YL) GO TO 40
              DO 45 J = 1,M
              IF(P(I).GT.CL(J)) GO TO 45
              IF(GP(I).LE.XTRUN(J)) GO TO 40
              CNTW(J) = CNTW(J) + 1.0
              GX = GP(I) − XTRUN(J)
              SUMW(J) = SUMW(J) + GX
              SUMWQ(J) = SUMWQ(J) + GX*GX
              XKNTW = XKNTW + 1.0
              SUMZW(J) = SUMZW(J) + P(I)
              SUMYW = SUMYW + P(I)
              SUMYWQ = SUMYWQ + P(I)*P(I)
              GO TO 40
45            CONTINUE
```

```
40        CONTINUE
          DO 50 J = 2,M
          V1(J) = SUM(J)/CNTW(J)
          V2(J) = SUMWQ(J)/CNTW(J)
          VARV(J) = SQRT(V2(J) − (V1(J)**2))
          BARV(J) = V1(J)
          EPSILN(J) = − V1(J)/VARV(J)
          BARZW(J) = SUMZW(J)/CNTW(J)
50        CONTINUE
          BARYW = SUMYW/XKNTW
          VARYW = SQRT(SUMYWQ/XKNTW − BARYW*BARYW)
          WRITE(IOUT,60)
60        FORMAT(' ',9X,'INTERVAL',8X,'EPSILON',7X,'R',8X,
          1'SIGMAX',5X,'MEANX',7X,'XO1',8X,'V1',9X,'V2',5X,
          2'FREQ',4X,'MEANY')
          M11 = M − 1
          WRITE(IOUT2,81)M11,BARYW,VARYW
          DO 70 I = 2,M
          WRITE(IOUT,75)CL(I − 1),CL(I),EPSILN(I),D,VARV(I),BARV(I)
          1,XTRUN(I),VI(I),V2(I),CNTW(I),BARZW(I)
          WRITE(IOUT2,77)XTRUN(I),CL(I − 1),CL(I),BARZW(I)
77        FORMAT(' − 1.74703 0.3117 ',F12.5, '.69 ',3F12.4)
75        FORMAT(' ',9E11.5,1X,F4.0,E11.5)
70        CONTINUE
          WRITE(IOUT,80)BARYW,VARYW
81        FORMAT(I10,2F12.4)
80        FORMAT(' MEAN Y = ',E12.5,10X,'VARIANCE Y  = ',E12.5,///)
          WRITE(IOUT,85)
85        FORMAT(7X,' INTERVAL Y', 8X,'SIGMAX',6X,'MEANX', 7X, 'FREQX',
          15X,'MEANY')
          DO 90 I = 2,M
          WRITE(IOUT,76)CL(I − 1),CL(I),VARX(I),BARX(I),CNT(I),BARZ(I)
76        FORMAT(' ',4E11.5,3X,F5.U,3X,E11.5)
90        CONTINUE
          WRITE(IOUT,80)BARY,VARY
          STOP
          END
          SUBROUTINE TRUNK(FIRST,NF,M,XTRUN)
          DIMENSION XTRUN(1),FIRST(5,100)
          XN = NF
          DO 10 J = 2,M
          SUM = 0.0
          DO 20 I = 1,NF
          SUM = SUM + FIRST(I,J)
20        CONTINUE
          XTRUN(J) = SUM/XN
10        CONTINUE
          RETURN
          END
          SUBROUTINE ARANGE(X,FIRST,NF,M,J)
          DIMENSION FIRST(5,100),SECOND(5)
          DO 10 K = 1,NF
10        SECOND(K) = FIRST(K,J)
          DO 20 K = 1,NF
          IF(FIRST(K,J).NE.0.0) GO TO 400
          FIRST(K,J) = X
```

```
              GO TO 30
400           IF(X.GT.FIRST(K,J)) GO TO 20
              FIRST(K,J) = X
              L = K + 1
              GO TO 22
20            CONTINUE
22            KL = L - 1
              IF(KL.EQ.NF) GO TO 30
              DO 25 K = L,NF
25            FIRST(K,J) = SECOND(K - 1)
30            CONTINUE
              RETURN
              END
              SUBROUTINE TRNCT(Z,XTRUN,M)
              DIMENSION XTRUN(100),Z(100),BASE(5),CMINE(5)
C             Z = MATRIX OF TONNAGES
C             H = $/TON/MILE OF HAULAGE
C             K1 = ACQUISITION COST $/LB U308
C             K2 = EXPLORATION DRILLING COST $/LB
C             K3 = DEVELOPMENT DRILL $/LB
C             CO = COST BOUNDARY:(RESERVE CATEGORY)
C             D = AVERAGE HAULAGE DISTANCE
C             FC = FRACTION OF ALL ORE THAT IS MILLED
C                IN 500 TON/DAY MILLS
C             FUND = FRACTION OF ALL MINING THAT IS UNDERGROUND
C             R1 = ROYALTY FOR UNDG OPERATION
C             R2 = ROYALTY FOR OPEN PIT OPERATIONS
C             K = NUMBER OF TONNAGE CLASSES ON COST TABLE
C             M = NUMBER OF TONNAGE CLASSES IN GRADE TON DIST.
              DATA BASE/1000., 10000., 100000., 1000000., 10000000./
              DATA CMINE/41.72,29.79,21.89,21.47,21.04/
              DATA RHO,H,K1,K2,K3/.96,.08,.158,.526,.263/
              DATA CO,D,R1,R2,FC,FUND/15.,10.,.368,.355,.10,.84/
              DATA GAMMA,GAMMA1,BETA,BETA1/7.8414,6.0214,6.2186,5.55/
              REAL K1,K2,K3
              K = 5
              IOUT = 23
C****COMPUTE ALFA AND ALFA1
              ALFA = FC*GAMMA + (1. - FC)*GAMMA1
              ALFA1 = FC*BETA + (1. - FC)*BETA1
C****COMPUTE ROYALTY
              R = FUND*R1 + (1. - FUND)*R2
C****COMPUTE PHIY
              DO 10 I = 2,M
              Y = Z(I)
              IF(Y.GT.BASE(1)) GO TO 6
              PHIY = CMINE(1)
              GO TO 9
6             DO 4 J = 2,K
              L = J
              IF(Y.GT.BASE(J - 1).AND.Y.LE.BASE(J)) GO TO 5
4             CONTINUE
              PHIY = CMINE(K)
              GO TO 9
5             PHIY = CMINE(L - 1) + (Y - BASE(L - 1))/(BASE(L) - BASE(L - 1))*
              1(CMINE(L) - CMINE(L - 1))
```

```
9        XTT = (PHIY + H*D + ALFA)/(20.*RHO*CO − ALFA1 − 20.*RHO*
         1(K1 + K2 + K3 + R))
         XTRUN(I) = ALOG(XTT)
10       CONTINUE
         WRITE(IOUT,25)
25       FORMAT(' MEAN TONNAGES',10X,' TRUNCATION GRADE',//)
         DO 30 I = 2,M
         WRITE(IOUT,26)Z(I),XTRUN(I)
26       FORMAT(' ',E12.5,12X,E12.5)
30       CONTINUE
         RETURN
         END
```

References

Cohen, A. C., Jr. (1950). Estimating parameters of Pearson Type III populations from truncated samples. *Am. statist. Ass. J.*, September, 1950, pp. 411–23.

Drew, M. W. (1977). U.S. uranium deposits—a geostatistical model. *Resources Policy* **3**(1), 60–70.

Ellis, J. R., Harris, D. P., and Van Wie, N. H. (1975). *A subjective probability appraisal of uranium resources in the state of New Mexico.* Open File Report GJO-110(76). US Energy Research and Development Administration, Grand Junction, Colorado.

Whittaker, E. T. and Robinson, G. (1944). *The calculus of observations; a treatise on numerical mathematics* (4th edn). Blackie, London.

Notes

1. This is calculated using a relationship which applies generally to all lognormal distributions: the arithmetic average of X, $\bar{X} = e^{\mu + (\sigma^2/2)}$.

13 RESOURCE ANALYSES WHICH USED GEOLOGICAL ANALYSIS AND CONVENTIONAL ASSESSMENTS OF SUBJECTIVE PROBABILITIES FOR MINERAL OCCURRENCE AND DISCOVERY: CONCEPTS, METHODS, AND CASE STUDIES

13.1. The concept of subjective probability

The use of the opinion or judgement of an informed person or set of informed persons as a statement of nature is as old as is history of modern man and has found application in all avenues of inquiry and action. This chapter examines a small part of the host of applications, those that state judgement about some aspect of mineral resources in terms of probabilities.

Good (1965) describes various kinds of probability, one of which is psychological probability, which is defined as 'a degree of belief or intensity of conviction that is used for betting purposes, for making decisions, or for any other purpose, not necessarily after mature consideration and not necessarily with any consistency with one's opinions'. According to Good's terminology, subjective probability is the special case of psychological probability, the case in which the psychological probabilities are consistent: 'when a person . . . uses a fairly consistent set of probabilities, they are called subjective ("personal") or multisubjective ("multipersonal") probabilities.' Good (1965) states further that . . . 'a consistent set of probabilities obeys the usual axioms of probability except that Kolmogorov's axiom (complete additivity) is inessential' (© MIT).

Other kinds of probability described by Good (1965) include physical probability and mathematical probability. A mathematical probability is tautological, for it exists by reason of definition. Physical probability is considered by some (Poisson 1837; Bartlett 1933; Jeffreys 1961; Ramsey 1931) as an intrinsic character of the physical system. As pointed out by Good (1965) there is disagreement as to the existence of physical probabilities and the distinction between them and the nonphysical varieties.

The perspective advocated here is apparent from the dissertation on geostatistical theory; namely, that so-called 'physical probabilities' reflect the knowledge about a phenomenon for which either our understanding of the underlying physics is incomplete or our ability to measure the phenomenon is limited. So, in a sense, physical probabilities exist because of incomplete knowledge. Even so, the physical probabilities are distinct from what are here considered subjective probabilities. The author's view of subjective probabilities in the context of resource appraisal is that subjective probabilities are the estimates by informed persons of the physical probabilities that are held to exist. In other words, although, for some level of knowledge of earth physics, the occurrence of a deposit having some specified tonnage of ore and grade would be appropriately defined by 'physical' probability laws, the exact form of these laws is unknown. Subjective estimates of probabilities that would be described by these laws for specified conditions are subjective probabilities.

Consistent with this view, a mineral resource appraisal for a region by subjective probability methods is considered to reflect *estimates* of the probabilities that would be described by some form(s) of the basic deposit models: $h(n \mid q, G_D)$, $k(q \mid G_D)$, $j(t \mid q, G_D)$. In essence the mind of the geologist is substituted for a specified mathematical form and the associated statistical inference. By making this substitution some of the sampling and purely statistical problems are avoided, such as multicollinearity and autocorrelation; however, information issues are not avoided, although some of them are ameliorated somewhat.

Obviously, the actual making of an appraisal of mineral resources by subjective probability methods raises issues of psychometrics and communications as well as those of mineral resources and their relationships to geology. Discussion of the psychometric and communications issues are deferred to a later chapter, after we have examined some of the mineral resource appraisals that have been made using conventional subjective probability methods.

13.2. Scope

The content of Chapter 13 is limited first to those methods and case studies that have relied upon expert geologists to employ geoscience to infer from observed geology to the magnitude of mineral endowment or resources. Second, only those geologically-based appraisals which have used conventional methods to elicit the judgements of geologists as subjective probabilities qualify for this chapter. Specifically, methods which formalize geological reasoning, such as Bayesian and decision methods, are excluded from this chapter; these excluded subjective probability methods are examined in Chapter 15. Finally, since assessing subjective probabilities by conventional methods is to some degree an intuitive process, heuristics and hedging are issues that are relevant to all of these appraisals; consequently, in order to avoid repetition, examination of these issues is deferred to Chapter 14.

13.3. Mineral endowment and potential supply of British Columbia and the Yukon Territory

13.3.1. *Overview*

The first published application of subjective probabilities to the analysis of mineral resources and potential mineral supply was made on British Columbia and the Yukon Territory of Canada (Harris, Freyman, and Barry 1971; Barry and Freyman 1970). This study included undiscovered deposits of 11 mineral commodities or commodity groups: copper, lead–zinc, molybdenum, nickel, tungsten, asbestos, coal, iron, uranium, mercury, and silver–gold.

The motivation for this study was the selection of a route for the construction of a railroad from Vancouver, British Columbia, north through the province of British Columbia and across the Yukon Territory. Several different routes appeared feasible. The Canadian government desired to select that route which had the greatest benefit–cost ratio. Since the construction of the railroad would take place over a long period of time and when completed would impact upon economic activities within the two regions through which it traversed, the measurement of benefits had to include the economic activities of the future that would be promoted by the railroad. Benefits were considered to derive from three major sectors: minerals, forestry, and agriculture.

Assessment of future economic benefits from the mineral sector required appraisal of the benefits due to improved infrastructure and the production from not only currently operating mines and known prospects but also deposits that exist and have not yet been discovered but which may be discovered and

exploited in the future. Obviously, an estimate of potential mineral supply and the benefits that may be derived from the generation of such supply was necessary. However, rather than attempt to estimate potential supply directly, the approach taken was to estimate endowment of the regions in each of the mineral commodities and then to assess potential supply by interacting exploration and exploitation with the estimated endowment through computer simulation models.

The decision to employ a subjective probability assessment was predicated upon the simultaneous satisfying of three requirements

(1) the need for tonnage and grade estimates so as to allow for the assessment of the effect of varying production and transportation costs;
(2) the need for locational (geographic) information on the expected endowment;
(3) the short time period allowed for the study— approximately three months.

13.3.2. *The study design for mineral endowment*

The basic scheme employed to assess the undiscovered mineral endowment was to construct a grid network of cells and to ask each of a selected panel of 20 experts to describe the undiscovered endowment of each cell in terms of probabilities for various numbers of deposits and for tonnage and grade combinations for each of the mineral commodities. Fig. 13.1 shows the questionnaire employed to elicit this information. Prior to leaving the expert to struggle with the probability assessment, probability and resource concepts were reviewed for him; he was provided statistical data on currently known mines and prospects and a geological map with an overlay of the cell grid design; and, he was led through the assessment of one or more cells to make sure that he understood the procedure. The first information that the geologist was asked for was that in the last table to the extreme right in the second row of Fig. 13.1. The information (opinion) requested in this table was for the likelihood of occurrence of deposits of all eleven kinds considered in aggregate. The intended use of this information was to compute a probability distribution for number of deposits without regard to the kinds of mineral commodities. Even though the intent of the questionnaire was to elicit from the respondent probabilities for number of aggregate deposits, probabilities were not requested. Instead, the respondent was asked merely to scale the number of deposit events on a rating scale of 10. In other words, he was asked to place 10 in the space

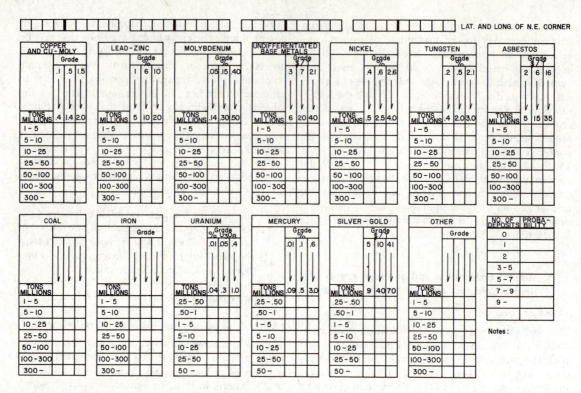

Fig. 13.1. Questionnaire for geological opinion about the occurrence of mineral deposits—Canadian Northwest. (After Harris *et al.* 1971.)

opposite the number of aggregate deposits which in his considered judgement were most likely. He was asked then to scale all other number-of-deposit possibilities provided for in the table in a way which reflected their likelihood in comparison to the most likely event. For example, if in the respondent's opinion the most likely number of aggregate deposits were 2, a 10 would have been placed opposite that number. If the geologist believed that 1 and 3 deposits were equally but just slightly less likely than 2, he might have placed a 9 opposite each of these numbers. Completing the exercise, he might have judged the occurrence of zero deposits to be about half as likely as 2 deposits, the likelihood of (5–7) deposits to be very small, and the likelihood of more than 7 deposits to be 0. Thus, his completed table would display his judgement in the form of the probability index numbers of Table 13.1.

These probability index numbers were converted to probabilities by employing one of the axioms of probability: the sum of the probabilities over the probability space must equal 1.0

$$P_l = PI_l \bigg/ \sum_{l=1}^{7} PI_l, \qquad (13.1)$$

where PI_l, P_l are the probability index number and probability for the lth number of deposit entry (class). In this hypothetical example, the probabilities associated with the probability index numbers would be 5/34, 9/34, 10/34, 9/34, and 1/34, 0, and 0.

TABLE 13.1. *Hypothetical responses for the occurrence of aggregate deposits*

Number of deposits	Probability index
0	5
1	9
2	10
3–5	9
5–7	1
7–9	0
9+	0

Geostatistical theory, as set forth in Chapter 5, described a number-of-deposits distribution for only one metal or mineral commodity. Preferably, as indicated in the theory, the distribution refers to a single mode of occurrence of a metal. Thus, the method of extracting opinion on endowment in this study does not appear to conform well to preferred theory. However, the disparity is not as great as may seem indicated, for in addition to the aggregate number distribution, information was obtained about the composition of these deposits. Specifically, a respondent was asked to take the number of deposits that he believed to be most likely and to break that composite down to numbers of deposits of each of the 11 mineral commodities. For example, the geologist might have placed the highest probability index number opposite the number of deposits interval of 7–9. Taking the midpoint of this interval as representative, the geologist would then have allocated the 8 deposits to the 11 commodities. For example, he might have provided the allocation

Copper	3
Molybdenum	2
Lead–zinc	1
Nickel	1
Silver–gold	1.

The allocation made by the geologist was to be placed in the blank space provided in the upper left-hand corner of the tonnage–grade table of each of the mineral commodities. In this example a 3 would have been placed in the copper table, a 2 in the molybdenum table, and so on. Commodities other than copper, molybdenum, lead–zinc, nickel, and silver–gold would have been allocated zero deposits, meaning that, in the opinion of the geologist, deposits of these commodities simply are not present within the cell.

Although the foregoing represents the intended procedure, in the course of the survey, it was found that some geologists reversed the procedure: in arriving at the most likely number of aggregate deposits, the geologist would estimate first the most likely number of deposits of each kind, placing this number in the open space of the grade–tonnage table of the appropriate commodity and then sum these numbers across the commodities to give the most likely number of aggregate deposits, which would be identified in the number table by a rating of 10.

Probabilities for number of deposits for each mineral commodity. Since the information provided for number of aggregate deposits and the composition of the aggregate was made only after considering a

cell's geology (G_D), probabilities for number of deposits and mineral commodity were computed by the relationship

$$P(R = r, N = n \mid G_D) = P(R = r \mid G_D) \cdot P(N = n \mid G_D),$$

$$n > 0, \quad r = 1, 2, \ldots, 11,$$

$$P(R = r, N = 0 \mid G_D) = 1.0 - \sum_{n=1}^{n_{max}} P(N = n \mid G_D),$$

$$(13.2)$$

where $P(R = r, N = n)$ is the probability that the cell contains n deposits of the rth mineral commodity, $P(R = r)$ is the probability that a deposit which occurs in the cell is of the rth mineral commodity, $P(N = n)$ is the probability that the total number of deposits (all kinds) in the cell is n, and G_D is the observed geology.

Implicit in the relationship of (13.2) is the assumption that $P(R = r \mid G_D)$ does not change with the size of the aggregate of deposits. The presence of this assumption is underscored by the manner in which these probabilities were estimated

$$P(R = r \mid G_D) = \frac{Z(r)}{a}, \quad Z(r) \le a; \quad r = 1, 2, \ldots, 11,$$

$$(13.3)$$

where a is the most likely number of aggregate deposits of the 11 mineral commodities, $Z(r)$ is the number of deposits which were allocated to the rth commodity (Z is a numbering or counting function). Obviously for (13.3) to be appropriate requires that $a = Z(1) + Z(2) + \ldots + Z(11)$ for all a. This may be a strong assumption, for in the geologist's mind the occurrence of a large number of deposits may be associated preferentially with selected mineral commodities, especially when the 11 mineral commodities vary so much in geological habitat as do these eleven. A more general model would allow for the probability for r to be conditional upon number

$$P(R = r, N = n \mid G_D)$$

$$= P(R = r \mid G_D, n) \cdot P(N = n \mid G_D). \quad (13.4)$$

Probabilities for grade and tonnage per deposit. Information about the tonnage and grade properties of the deposits of a given mineral commodity that were envisioned by the geologist as occurring in the cell was obtained in a manner similar to that described for number of deposits. Suppose, for example, that the number of deposits allocated to uranium (U_3O_8) were greater than 0. The geologist was then asked to reflect upon the occurrence of any one of the n deposits of U_3O_8 and to select from the grade–tonnage table for U_3O_8 that combination of grade and tonnage that he believed to be the most likely of the alternatives specified. An entry of 10 was made in the box of the tonnage–grade table associated with the selected combination. The respondent was then asked to move laterally and vertically from this combination and enter numbers from 0 to 10 indicating the likelihood of other grade–tonnage combinations relative to the most likely combination. As was done in the case of the number table, the probability index numbers were converted to probabilities

$$P(K = k, L = l) = PI_{kl} \bigg/ \sum_{k=1}^{7} \sum_{l=1}^{3} PI_{kl}, \quad (13.5)$$

where k, l are indices of the tonnage and grade classes, respectively, PI_{kl} is the probability index number of the kth tonnage and lth grade class, and $P(K = k, L = l)$ is the probability for the joint occurrence of a tonnage of the kth tonnage class and a grade of the lth grade class. Thus, the result of the survey was a set of these probabilities for each of the mineral commodities believed to occur in the cell and given by each of the 20 geologists participating in the study, unless the geologist by virtue of limited knowledge and experience did not feel capable of making useful probability assessments. Each respondent was allowed to indicate his lack of qualifications and to not provide estimates for selected cells or commodities. For a given commodity, up to 20 separate estimates of the matrix of probabilities were provided, one matrix for each qualified geologist. These separate estimates were averaged to yield a representative (average) matrix.

The computation of composite grade–tonnage probabilities by simple averaging of probabilities across geologists is strictly appropriate only if there is no correlation across the geologists of number of deposits with grade or tonnage of ore per deposit. If, on average, the geologists providing higher probabilities for large numbers of deposits also reported higher probabilities for high grades and low tonnages than did the geologists giving high probabilities for small numbers, then simple averaging is not appropriate. The appropriate average in this case would weight each geologist's probabilities for grade and tonnage by his expected number of deposits.

An unweighted average was computed by Harris et al. (1971). Subsequent analysis by Barry and Freyman (1970) showed that weak correlation did in fact exist across the responses of the geologists between number of deposits and grade and tonnage per de-

posit. The presence of this correlation had the effect of introducing a positive bias in average endowment as computed by Harris et al. (1971). Barry and Freyman employed a weighting scheme to avoid such bias. Their maps of expected mineral endowment exhibited a very slight tendency to smaller areas of high potential than those resulting from the simple unweighted averaging.

Of course, one way to avoid the necessity of weighting by number of deposits is to request the geologist to provide probabilities for a two-way table, a table which allows for probability to vary with both number of deposits and grade, much as does tonnage and grade.

Although the primary purpose of the survey was to represent the estimated endowment of the regions in each of the 11 commodities for the purpose of economic analysis, the endowment estimates themselves were of interest to engineers and scientists involved in mineral exploration. Consequently, an endowment map was prepared for each of the 11 commodities (see Barry and Freyman 1970). Figs. 13.2 and 13.3 are the endowment maps for tungsten and copper.

13.3.3. Economic analysis

Perspective and overview

The motivation of the Canadian Northwest (CN) study was to determine which of several routes would be the preferred route for the construction of a railroad through the province of British Columbia and the Yukon Territory. The alternative routes were compared on the basis of net present value of costs and benefits of the construction and use of the railroad. These costs and benefits were determined by simulating the construction of the railway and all consequent economic activity in the regions, with particular attention given to the movement of goods over the railroad. Procedures of accounting and regional economic analysis were employed for the measurement of benefits and costs. No further comment will be given in this section concerning the overall economic model or method of analysis. Comment in this section will be restricted to the costing models for exploration and exploitation and their interaction with the mineral endowment model.

The character of the resource model of the CN study contrasts considerably with the character of the PAU and Brinck resource models, as described in preceding chapters. Whereas those models described endowment by mathematical functions, the CN model describes endowment by relative frequency

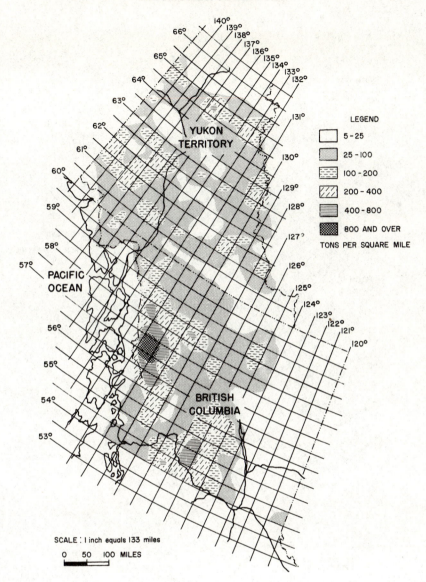

Fig. 13.2. Geographical distribution of the endowment of copper in undiscovered but expected deposits–Canadian Northwest. (After Barry and Freyman 1970.)

histograms of number of deposits, deposit grade, and deposit ore tonnage obtained by the polling of qualified geologists.

Potential mineral supply was determined by interacting an exploration model and an exploitation model with the endowment model by computer simulation, using Monte Carlo methods. Simply stated, the histograms of the endowment model were sampled to give the number of deposits which occur in the cell; then, the tonnage and grade histograms were sampled to ascribe a tonnage and a grade of ore to each deposit (see Fig. 13.4). Exploration for and production of deposits were simulated for specified price and cost conditions to determine those deposits that would be discovered and would be economic to produce. Thus, the quantity of metal that could be produced, given unlimited markets at the price specified, could be determined by simply summing

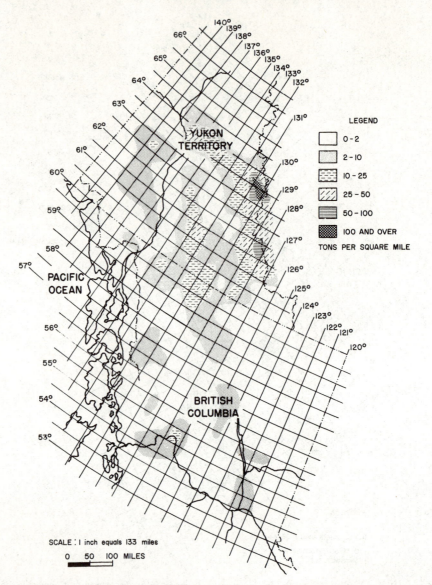

Fig. 13.3. Geographical distribution of the endowment of tungsten in undiscovered but expected deposits–Canadian Northwest. (After Barry and Freyman 1970.)

the producible metal in discovered deposits. In this economic analysis, the economic viability of a deposit was determined by performing a discounted cash flow analysis according to standard procedures.

The discounted cash flow analysis included seven cost components: return on investment, exploration cost, operating cost, capital cost, transportation cost, provincial tax, and federal tax. The computation of taxes considered the conditions which prevailed at

that time with respect to accelerated depreciation of capital, depletion allowance, the expensing of exploration costs, and a tax-free start-up period. Thus, by iterating the sampling of the endowment model and the economic analysis, a probability distribution for the amount of potential supply for the economic conditions specified could be computed. Furthermore, by varying the overall levels of transportation cost, operating and capital cost, and price, the simulation

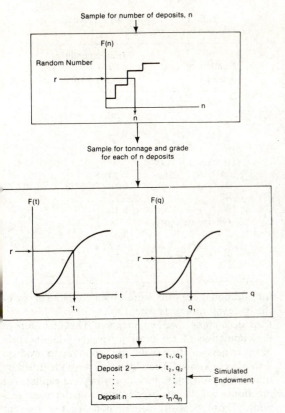

Sample for number of deposits, n

Random Number

F(n)

r

n

n

Sample for tonnage and grade
for each of n deposits

F(t)

F(q)

r

r

t

q

t_1

q_1

Deposit 1 ⟶ t_1, q_1
Deposit 2 ⟶ t_2, q_2
⋮
Deposit n ⟶ t_n, q_n

Simulated
Endowment

Fig. 13.4. Simulating endowment.

model was used to generate data on potential supply for each combination of conditions. Statistical analysis of these data provided a means of describing potential supply as a function of the economic parameters that were manipulated. For example, suppose that the level of capital and operating costs are held constant and only price and the level of transportation costs to and along the prospective railway are varied for the 36 cells that lie adjacent to the Yukon–British Columbia border. The following equations describe the response of potential supply of ore of copper, nickel, and uranium to these two economic variables with costs held at the base level

$$t_{cu} = 10^{7.93+0.83\log(pr)-0.76\log(tr)}, \qquad (13.6)$$

$$t_u = 10^{5.01+1.52\log(pr)-1.69\log(tr)}, \qquad (13.7)$$

$$t_{ni} = 10^{6.92+1.55\log(pr)-0.83\log(tr)}, \qquad (13.8)$$

where *pr* is the price per pound of metal, *tr* is a multiple of basic transportation cost for the cell, and t_{cu}, t_u, t_{ni} are the tonnage of ore of copper, uranium, and nickel, respectively.

A more comprehensive and useful statement of potential supply would describe the quantity of metal as a function of price, level of operating capital cost, and level of transportation cost. Such an equation could be generated from the resource model simply by manipulating the level of operating and capital costs as well as price and transportation cost and by multiplying grade by tonnage of ore. The simulator could be used to generate potential supply of metal for combinations of these economic conditions, and statistical analysis of these generated data would provide a means of quantitatively describing the response of potential supply to variation in price, operating and capital cost, and transportation cost. Of course, resource characteristics other than potential supply of ore or metal could be described in a similar manner. For example, the number of deposits of copper for the 36 cells previously referred to was described as a function of price and level of transportation cost

$$n_{cu} = 10^{0.79+0.61\log(pr)-0.80\log(tr)}.$$

Thus, for a copper price of US $0.65/lb and a transportation cost of one-half the base cost, the expected number of copper deposits is

$$n_{cu} = 10^{0.79+0.61(-0.187)-0.80(-0.301)}$$

$$n_{cu} = 10^{0.917} \approx 8 \text{ deposits.}$$

The following sections describe the exploration, operating, and capital cost relationships. No further description is given of the cash flow relations or the overall system design. (For further description see Harris and Azis 1970.)

The exploration model

Structure. The basic proposition that served to set the structure of the exploration model of the CN study is that the probability for discovery of a deposit in a region, given that a deposit is present, reflects the influence of four factors.

1. Deposit tonnage;
2. Amount of cover (glacial debris, alluvium, or gravel);
3. The type of terrain;
4. The intensity of search.

Rather than attempt to define a single relationship in which each of these four factors is an explanatory variable, the decision was made to identify three tonnage classes, three kinds of terrain, and three conditions of cover, and to define a relationship of intensity of effort to probability for discovery for each of the 27 combinations of the three factors. The basic model form is

$$p = 1 - (\exp(-bE^c))^4,$$

where b and c are unknown parameters. Thus, 27 of these equations were required to define the model. If we let the subscripts i, j, and k represent cover condition, terrain type, and tonnage category, then the exploration model is described by

$$p_{ijk} = 1 - (\exp(-b_{ikj}E^{c_{iki}}))^4, \qquad (13.9)$$
$$i, j, k = 1, 2, 3.$$

Use of this model required the estimation of the 54 unknown parameters (two parameters for each of the 27 combinations of cover, terrain, and tonnage class). In order to estimate these parameters, a survey was made of 18 explorationists of the probability of discovery for three levels of exploration effort in dollars (these levels were selected by the explorationist) for each of the 27 conditions. Statistical analysis of these responses provided estimates of the 27 parameters. For example, the probability for discovery of a deposit in a 1000-square mile cell, given the presence of the deposit, mountainous terrain (2000 to 5000 ft relief), normal (average) amount of cover, and a deposit of over 50×10^6 tons is described by the expression

$$p_{223} = 1 - (\exp(-0.065E^{0.333}))^4,$$

where E is in millions of US dollars. For an expenditure of US \$4 000 000, the conditional probability of discovery is 0.34 (34 per cent)

$$p_{223} = 1 - (\exp(-0.065(4)^{0.333}))^4,$$
$$p_{223} = 1 - (\exp(-0.065(1.587)))^4$$
$$= 1 - (\exp(-0.103))^4 = 1 - 0.66 = 0.34.$$

For *each* deposit generated by the previous sampling of the endowment model, a number on the interval $(0, 1)$ was selected at random in the Monte Carlo simulation of exploration. This number was compared to the probability for discovery resulting from the evaluation of the appropriate probability function, as indicated by the deposit tonnage and the cover and terrain of the cell being evaluated. If the random number was less than or equal to the probability so computed, the deposit was considered to be discovered. Thus, an expenditure on a regional exploration programme of E could have resulted in the discovery of several deposits. In the case of multiple discoveries, additional costs would be incurred in the testing and proving of the deposits. Estimates of costs

TABLE 13.2. *Exploration expenditures for additional deposits*

Number of deposits	Mean expenditure in 1970 US dollars ($\times 10^6$)
Tonnage category 1	
2	3.50
4	5.33
8	8.77
16	13.30
Tonnage category 2	
2	6.15
4	10.58
8	17.65
16	28.10
Tonnage category 3	
2	8.33
4	14.92
8	26.21
16	52.37

for additional deposits were obtained by a survey of the 18 explorationists (see Table 13.2).

Cost accounting and optimization. The first step in the simulation of exploration was the identification of those deposits that would be economic to produce if they were known. These deposits were identified by simulating production with operating and capital cost functions, which will be described in the next sections. Those deposits with a non-negative present value, exclusive of exploration cost, were the targets of exploration. Then, the cell was explored by allocating to exploration 3 per cent of the total present value of all economic deposits: $E = (0.03)$(total present value)$/(1 \times 10^6)$. The total exploration expenditure was apportioned to those deposits discovered on the basis of their contribution to the total present value of all deposits *discovered* at the expenditure E. Then, with the exploration charge calculated in this manner, the present value of each deposit discovered was recomputed. This process was repeated for various levels of E, searching for that level of exploration effort which balanced the contribution to total present value from the additional discoveries due to a greater exploration expenditure against the decrease in present value of a given deposit due to the greater exploration costs. The amount of metal producible from those deposits discovered by the optimum exploration expenditure constituted potential supply for the economic conditions specified.

Capital cost for mining

Structure. The structure of each capital cost model was dictated by two factors

1. The only physical characteristics ascribed to the hypothetical deposit by the simulator were deposit tonnage, deposit type, and deposit grade.
2. The capital cost model had to be quantified from statistical analysis of cost data.

As a consequence of factor 1, capital cost was postulated to be a function of deposit tonnage

$$cap = 10^{\alpha_0 + \alpha_1 t + \alpha_2 z}, \qquad (13.10)$$

where cap is the capital cost of plant, t is the deposit tonnage, z is a standard unit normal variate (mean of zero and a standard deviation of one), α_0, α_1 are unknown parameters to be estimated by regression analysis, and α_2 is the standard error of the estimate of cap by the regression equation with parameters of α_0 and α_1.

The presence of z in eqn (13.10) provides a means for introducing variation in the capital cost for a given tonnage. In other words, it represents the error in the estimate of cap due to those factors that affect capital cost but have been excluded from the model.

The cost model was employed in this manner: In the simulation, a sampling of the endowment model would have provided a deposit tonnage t_0 and grade q_0. Then, a standard unit normal probability distribution was sampled to give z_0. t_0 and z_0 are substituted into (13.10) to provide a capital cost $\widehat{cap}$ ($\widehat{cap}$ is an estimate of cap). The value $\widehat{cap}$ was passed to the routine which performs the discounted cash flow analysis.

Because of very different mining operations for near surface deposits as compared to deeply buried deposits, it was recognized that the parameters α_0, α_1, and α_2 would vary for open pit and underground operations; consequently, a separate model of the form of (13.10) was estimated for each of these kinds of mining operations.

Although eqn (13.10) represents the basic model form for capital cost, the necessity for estimation of the unknown parameters from statistical data on t and cap did not allow the implementation of this model for all commodity groups. For example, statistical analysis of the available data failed to provide a statistically significant value for α_1 for iron mining; consequently, the capital cost model for iron was modified to

$$cap = \overline{cap} + \hat{\sigma} z,$$

where $\overline{cap}$ is the average of available data on capital costs, $\hat{\sigma}$ is the estimated standard error, and z is the standard unit normal variate.

Specific models. Although production costs per pound of refined metal varies for each of the base and precious metals, mining costs reflect only the size and type of deposit, not the kind of metal; consequently, instead of a capital cost model for each of the eleven commodity groups, only four models were constructed: base and precious metals, iron, asbestos, and uranium. The models employed for the base and precious metals group and for uranium are given below (note, log means base ten logarithm).

Base and precious metals

Open pit: $cap = 10^{3.100 + 0.554 \log(t) + 0.307z}$.

Underground: $cap = 10^{2.174 + 0.724 \log(t) + 0.321z}$.

Uranium

$$cap = 288\,000\,000 + 48\,000\,000z$$

or, alternatively,

$$cap/\text{annual tons capacity} = 24.5 + 1.5z$$

Mining life

The execution of a discounted cash flow analysis of a mining operation requires the estimated life of the mine. As with the capital cost relationship, mining life l ultimately in this simulator had to be related to deposit tonnage

$$l = t/300h, \qquad (13.11)$$

where h is annual production. However, rather than estimating l directly from tonnage, the procedure employed in this study was to estimate h as a function of deposit tonnage

$$h = 10^{\beta_0 + \beta_1 t + \beta_2 z} \quad \text{or} \quad h = \exp(\beta_0 + \beta_1 t + \beta_2 z), \qquad (13.12)$$

where β_0, β_1 are unknown parameters to be estimated, β_2 is the standard error of the estimate, and z is a standard unit normal variate.

The models for h employed for capital cost for the base and precious metals group are

Base and precious metals

Open pit: $h = \exp(-2.344 + 0.639 \ln(t) + 0.540z)$

Underground: $h = 10^{0.0444 + 0.475 \log(t) + 0.204z}$.

Operating cost

A scheme similar to that for capital cost was adopted for operating cost: relating, where possible, operating cost per ton of ore to deposit tonnage. The models employed for the base and precious metals group are

Base and precious metals

Open Pit: $op = 3.4 + 1.9z$,

where op are the operating costs per ton of ore and z is the standard unit normal variate.

Underground: $op = 39.084 - 5.129 \log(t) + 2.981z$.

For uranium, operating costs were considered to consist of two components

$op = $ (mining costs/ton of ore +

+ (milling costs/lb U_3O_8) $\cdot$ (2000) $\cdot$ (q),

where $q = $ grade, as a decimal fraction.

Data did not permit the quantification of a relationship of deposit tonnage to mining costs; therefore, the resulting model employed an average cost (US $6.20/ton)

$$op = \frac{\text{uranium}}{6.20/2000q} + F^{-1}(rn) + z, \quad (13.13)$$

where $F^{-1}(rn)$ represents a milling cost per lb U_3O_8 determined by sampling the cumulative probability distribution for milling costs with random number rn.

The values in Table 13.3 represent F, the cumulative probability distribution for milling costs/lb U_3O_8. Thus, in the simulator, an operating cost was ascribed to a uranium deposit by selecting two random numbers rn_1 and rn_2. The first of these numbers was used to sample the unit normal probability distribution for a value for z, and the second was used to sample F for a milling cost. For example, suppose that previous sampling of the endowment model has described a uranium deposit with a tonnage of ore of 6 435 680 tons and a grade of 0.5 per cent uranium (0.59 per cent U_3O_8), and that the two random numbers drawn are 0.603 and 0.775. Operating cost per lb of U_3O_8 would be calculated as

$op = 6.20/((2000)(0.0059)) + 2.23 + 0.26$

$= $ US $3.02/lb U_3O_8,

TABLE 13.3. *Distribution of milling costs*

Cumulative probability (F)	Milling cost/lb U_3O_8 (US $)
0.350	1.38
0.666	2.00
0.775	2.23
1.000	3.23

where 0.26 is the z score from the tables for the standard unit normal distribution for a probability (random number) of 0.603 and 2.23 is the milling cost from Table 13.3 for a probability (random number) of 0.775. The expected value for milling cost is US $2.08/lb U_3O_8. Since the expected value for z is zero, the expected (average) operating cost for uranium for a deposit having a grade of 0.59 per cent U_3O_8 is US $2.61/lb U_3O_8

$op = 6.20/2000(0.0059) + 2.08$

$= $ US $2.61/lb U_3O_8.

13.4. Northern Sonora, Mexico

13.4.1. *Estimation of copper endowment*

Overview and general scheme

Through support by the Ford Foundation, four studies were made upon various aspects of base and precious metals resources development in Mexico, particularly in northern Sonora (Donald [1]; Harris 1973; Harris and Azis 1970; Harris and Euresty 1973). The study by Harris and Azis examined the capability of Mexico to meet its requirements in base and precious metals to 1990. The remaining three studies focused upon northern Sonora as a region, hereafter referred to only as Sonora. Estimation of the copper resources of the region was an essential part of these studies and is detailed by Harris (1973). The study by Donald [1] examines the economics of exploration and resource development in Sonora by interacting exploration and exploitation simulation models with the estimated metal endowment. The study by Harris and Euresty (1973) examines the effect of and adequacy of existing infrastructure for the development of the region's metal resources. This section examines only two of these four studies: (1) the estimation of mineral endowment of northern Sonora, and (2) analysis of the economics of infrastructure and resource development.

While the scope of the study on Sonora included base and precious metals, evidence on known mines and prospects and the characteristics of the more recent discoveries suggested that copper would be the dominant metal in future discoveries and that resources of the region in molybdenum, lead, zinc, gold, and silver derive mainly from the presence of these metals in deposits that are primarily copper. Consequently, the endowment survey was primarily a survey of copper endowment. However, since the economics of exploration and resource development are favourably influenced by associated metals, the

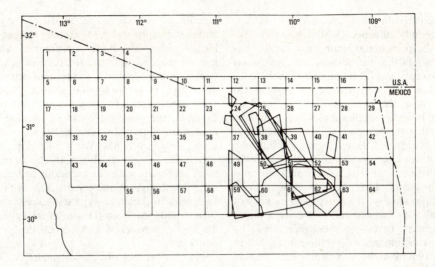

Fig. 13.5. Locations of highest-priority prospecting zones. (Source: Harris 1973, p. 227.)

possible presence of these metals could not be ignored. Therefore, the respondents were asked to provide probabilities for tonnage and grade in terms of copper plus the copper equivalent of associated metals. A set of prices for the metals was provided to facilitate the conversion to copper equivalent.

The survey design differed from that employed in the Canadian study in two important aspects

1. It was not only restricted to one metal, but it recognized two main modes of occurrence of that

metal and solicited judgement on each mode separately;

2. It allowed the geologist to construct prospecting zones and to provide judgement information on number of deposits, grade, and tonnage per deposit for each of his prospecting zones and for the total study area, including the prospecting zones.

Figs. 13.5 and 13.6 show the highest priority prospecting zones and the prospecting zones of all lower priorities, respectively, identified by the nine geolog-

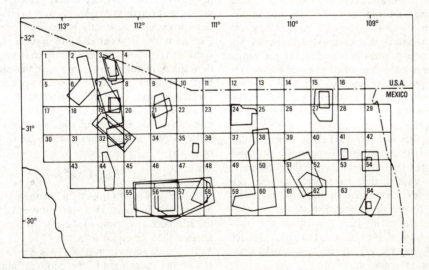

Fig. 13.6. Locations of prospecting zones of priority other than the highest. (Source: Harris 1973, p. 228.)

ists who participated in the estimation of metal endowment. The only influence exerted upon the respondent by the person conducting the survey was
(1) to make certain that the respondent understood
probability concepts and (2) to suggest that the construction of a few very large prospecting zones would
not be as useful in the characterization of endowment as would be many smaller zones. Nevertheless,
it was agreed that the respondent would select that
size of zone that reflected the exploration philosophy
of the firm and was large enough so that the firm did
not fear the divulgence of critical locational information on its prospects. The rationale behind these
flexible guidelines are first, the size of and number of
the prospecting zones should reflect the exploration
practice of the firm, because a subsequent study by
Donald [1] was to simulate exploration of each firm
separately as described by the firm; the size and
number of prospecting zones is just one of many
features that characterize the architecture of regional
exploration. Second, from the consideration of the
endowment estimate alone, it is preferable to have
honest answers on large zones than to risk dishonest
ones on small zones, particularly when dishonesty is
prompted by the fear of divulging proprietary locational information about prospects. Third, it was
recognized that a careful completion of the entire
survey (endowment as well as exploration practice
and economics) would constitute quite an imposition
upon the time and patience of those participating in
the study, particularly since these individuals were
the critical personnel of the major exploration and
mining firms of Sonora. Therefore, steps were taken
to minimize the time required of these individuals.
Asking the participants to respond carefully to several prospecting zones that comprised the chief potential of the region and then to evaluate the entire
area as one large zone instead of responding to each
of many cells seemed to minimize the time required
of them without significantly sacrificing endowment
information. Finally, it may be more compatible with
the way that geologists think to allow them to locate
zones, because they can construct these zones around
geologic features, and it is the complex of these
features that most directly reflects metal endowment.
Furthermore, within the zone defined by this
geologic complex, the geologist may be relatively
indifferent as to the likely location of the inferred
deposit. Therefore, asking him to partition the complex by a grid network into cells and to appraise each
cell separately may merely create 'busy work' without any gain in information.

While the foregoing constitutes arguments for a
flexible cell or zone design, merits of the use of such
a design must be weighed carefully against two possible liabilities. The most important of these is that
leaving the geologist the freedom of selecting zone
size as well as location, shape, and orientation may
encourage the geologist who is predisposed to 'game'
the entire exercise to carry out such disposition. For
example, the geologist could be cavalier and avoid
much mental effort by dividing the study area in half,
giving only two zones. While such a zone selection
was made by one geologist in the Sonora survey,
most geologists were conscientious and devoted considerable thought to the construction of the prospecting zones. In some cases, these zones were smaller
than would have been the size of the cells delineated
by a grid network if a fixed-cell design had been
employed.

Fig. 13.7 shows the questionnaire for number of
deposits of copper. As has already been indicated,
two modes of occurrence of copper deposits were
recognized.

> Vein deposits: usually low tonnage and high grade;
> Porphry deposits: usually high tonnage and low
> grade.

The ore tonnage selected as separating these two
modes was 25×10^6 short tons.

Probabilities: their form and their elicitation

Initially, the plan of the survey was to request probability index numbers for selected numbers or intervals of numbers of deposits; however, early in the
field work it was found that the geologists were well
versed in probability concepts and preferred to provide probabilities directly instead of index numbers.
Furthermore, it seemed more natural for them to
think in terms of the probability that the number of
deposits is greater than some specified number than
that the number is equal to some specified number.
For this reason, the number table used in the elicitation of subjective probability provides for the probability that the number of deposits occurring in the
cell exceeds the quantities at the head of the number
table (n)

$$P_{zjg}(N \geq n \mid G_D^0),$$

where $P_{zjg}(N \geq n \mid G_D^0)$ is the probability estimated
by the gth geologist that the number of deposits of
the jth mode occurring in the zth prospecting zone is
greater than or equal to n.

The table shown in Fig. 13.8 was employed to
record the judgement of the geologist about the tonnage of ore of a deposit, given that one of the

		NUMBER OF DEPOSITS								
		≥1	≥2	≥3	≥4	≥5-8	≥9-16	≥17-32	≥33-64	≥65-128
SELECTED AREA (NO.) — 1	BULK LOW GRADE	0.65	0.50	0.25	0.05	0.003	0.00	–	–	–
	HIGH GRADE	0.80	0.75	0.60	0.50	0.35	0.025	0.00	–	–
2	BULK LOW GRADE	0.65	0.55	0.32	0.12	0.003	0.00	–	–	–
	HIGH GRADE	0.80	0.75	0.60	0.50	0.35	0.025	0.00	–	–
3	BULK LOW GRADE	0.55	0.35	0.20	0.05	0.001	0.00	–	–	–
	HIGH GRADE	0.60	0.50	0.38	0.25	0.015	0.00	–	–	–
ENTIRE AREA	BULK LOW GRADE	1.00	1.00	1.00	1.00	0.90	0.82	0.65	0.50	0.01
	HIGH GRADE	1.00	1.00	1.00	1.00	1.00	1.00	1.00	1.75	0.02

MINIMUM TONNAGE AND MINIMUM GRADE CONSIDERED SIGNIFICANT:
BULK LOW GRADE, 25 MILLION TONS AND 0.45% COPPER EQUIVALENT.
HIGH GRADE, 200,000 TONS AND US $16.00/TON.

Fig. 13.7. Probability for occurrence of deposits. (Source: Harris 1973, p. 224.)

deposits conceptualized in the number distribution does occur. As indicated in this table, judgement was elicited separately for each of the two modes of occurrence. As with the number distribution, judgement was provided directly as probabilities

$$P_{zjg}(t_k'' \leq T \leq t_k' \mid G_D^0),$$

where $P_{zjg}(t_k'' \leq T \leq t_k' \mid G_D^0)$ is the probability provided by the gth geologist that a deposit of the jth mode and occurring in the zth prospecting zone would have an ore tonnage greater than or equal to the lower bound of the kth tonnage class but less than or equal to the upper bound of the kth tonnage class, given observed geology G_D^0.

The judgements provided by the geologists for grade were given as conditional probabilities, the probability for grade being conditional upon tonnage of ore

$$P_{zjg}(q_l'' \leq Q \leq q_l' \mid t_k'' \leq T \leq t_k'; G_D^0),$$

where $P_{zjg}(q_l'' \leq Q \leq q_l' \mid t_k'' \leq T \leq t_k'; G_D^0)$ is the probability provided by the gth geologist that a deposit of the jth mode and occurring in the zth prospecting zone has an average grade greater than or equal to the lower bound of the lth grade class but less than or equal to the upper bound of the lth class, given that deposit tonnage is within the kth tonnage class and given the observed geology G_D^0.

		1	2	3	4	5	6	REMAINING AREA	ENTIRE AREA	
TONS (2000 LBS)	≥ 200,000	1.00	1.00						1.00	HIGH GRADE
	≥1M	0.21	0.21						0.21	
	≥5M	0.04	0.04						0.04	
	≥25M	1.00	1.00						1.00	LOW GRADE
	≥100M	0.35	0.35						0.35	
	≥300M	0.05	0.05						0.05	
	600M	0.00	0.00						0.00	

MINIMUM TONNAGE AND MINIMUM GRADE CONSIDERED SIGNIFICANT:
BULK LOW GRADE, 25 MILLION TONS AND 0.45% COPPER EQUIVALENT.
HIGH GRADE, 200 000 TONS AND US $16.00/TON.

Fig. 13.8. Probability for any occurrence having a tonnage ≥ tonnage class specified. (Source: Harris 1973, p. 225.)

Resolution of multiple opinions (from zone to cell)

Number of deposits. The polling of a geologist provided a set of these distributions of probability for each of his zones and for the entire area. Obviously the polling of nine geologists provides nine complete and separate appraisals; thus we have a multiplicity of opinion. However, since these opinions had not been provided on a cell design common to all geologists, they could not be averaged as they were given. Rather, resolution of the multiple opinions was effected by superimposing a grid network upon the region and relating the prospecting zones to the common unit of reference, a cell defined by the grid network. In this way, a set of average probability distributions was computed for each of the 64 cells of the study area. Projection to the cell and subsequent averaging were effected by Monte Carlo methods, which are described generally by Euresty [2]. Rather than repeating a description of this analysis, a description of how the resolution of opinions should be made by mathematical analysis is here provided. For the mathematical resolution, one more measure D_{zg} and sets of probabilities, each set representing a probability distribution, for the areas excluded from the prospecting zones are required. The additional measure needed D_{zg} is that fraction of the zth prospecting zone of the gth geologist lying within the

cell. Then, if the area excluded by the gth geologist is treated simply as another zone, one of the NZ_g zones, multiple opinions can be resolved by probability analysis. In the notation of the following description, reference to mode of occurrence and cell are suppressed, unless specifically required for explanation. It is to be understood, unless explained otherwise, that probabilities, quantities, and functions represent a single cell and one mode of occurrence.

Consider the cell of the hypothetical study area of Fig. 13.9. This cell lies within three prospecting zones, one of which (zone 2) is the composite zone which consists of the excluded area. The numbers in the boxes are the probabilities for one deposit occurring in each of the three zones. The numbers in parentheses are the fractions of the zones lying within the cell. Then the probability that a deposit lies within each of the parts of the cell, when considered separately, would be calculated as

$$(0.36)(0.15) = 0.054$$
$$(0.5)(0.1) = 0.05$$
$$(0.8)(0.2) = 0.16.$$

But, the probability for exactly one deposit occurring is the probability that the deposit occurs in one part times the probability that it doesn't occur in the

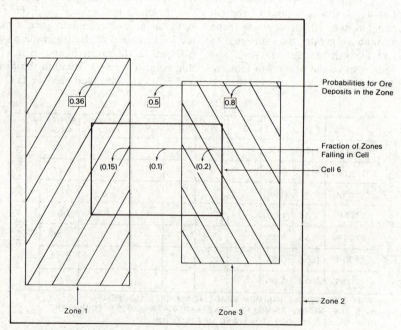

Fig. 13.9. Hypothetical configuration of area, prospecting zone, and cell.

other parts summed over all combinations

$$P(N = 1) = (0.054)(1-0.05)(1-0.16) +$$
$$+ (0.05)(1-0.054)(1-0.16) +$$
$$+ (0.16)(1-0.05)(1-0.054),$$
$$P(N = 1) = 0.04309 + 0.03973 + 0.14379 = 0.22661.$$

Let us represent symbolically the above calculations. Suppose that the prospecting zones are zones 1, 2, and 3, and that we are dealing with information provided by the fourth geologist for a given mode of occurrence. Then the probabilities for each part of the cell considered separately represent

$$0.054 = P_{14}(N = 1 \mid G_D^0)$$
$$0.05 = P_{24}(N = 1 \mid G_D^0)$$
$$0.16 = P_{34}(N = 1 \mid G_D^0).$$

Calculation of the desired probability can be symbolized by the equation

$$P_g(N = 1 \mid G_D^0) = \sum_{z=1}^{NZ_g} \left\{ D_{zg} \cdot P_{zg}(N = 1 \mid G_D^0) \times \right.$$
$$\left. \times \prod_{y \neq z} [1 - D_{yg} \cdot P_{zg}(N = 1 \mid G_D^0)] \right\}, \quad (13.14)$$

where $P_g(N = 1 \mid G_D^0)$ is the probability implied by the gth geologist that one deposit occurs in the cell.

Eqn (13.14) is useful only for the calculation for exactly one deposit in the cell. Calculation of probabilities for N having values other than 1 are more complex. For example, in calculating the probability for $N = 2$, we must consider the fact that 2 deposits can occur as the sum of 1 deposit in each of 2 parts and 0 in the remaining parts or as 2 deposits in 1 part and 0 in all other parts. Greater numbers of combinations must be considered as the number of deposits increases [3].

Once $P_g(N = n \mid G_D^0)$ has been computed for each cell, computation of the average probability distribution for the cell is simply the averaging of $P_g(N = n \mid G_D^0)$ over the geologists

$$\bar{P}(N = n \mid G_D^0) = \frac{1}{NG} \sum_{g=1}^{NG} P_g(N = n \mid G_D^0).$$
$$(13.15)$$

In the foregoing description, it was assumed that a probability distribution existed for the excluded area. The study could easily be designed so that probabilities of this distribution are supplied by the geologists; however in the Sonoran study, this was not the case. Instead, the probabilities were re-

quested for each of the zones and then separately for the *entire* study area, not the excluded area. Since the resolution of multiple opinion and the entire probability analysis of the study was via Monte Carlo analysis and computer simulation, obtaining an approximation of the probabilities for the excluded area from those of the zones and the entire area was achieved through numerical analysis. The procedure is described in some detail by Euresty [2]. Basically, it amounted to random sampling of the distributions of the zones and of the entire area for number of deposits, then summing the numbers for the zones and subtracting this number from the number for the entire area; the difference was the number in the excluded area. If this procedure were iterated a large number of times and the results classified into a histogram, the histogram would constitute an approximation to the number distribution for the excluded area.

Tonnage and grade distributions. The survey yielded probabilities by geologist for tonnage and for grade, conditional upon deposit tonnage, for each of the geologist's zones. These multiple opinions (tonnage–grade distributions by each of the nine geologists) were resolved by projecting them onto a fixed grid network of cells and averaging the projected information across the geologists. However, before this could be done, joint tonnage–grade probabilities were computed for each zone of each geologist by combining the marginal probabilities for tonnage with the conditional probabilities for grade

$$P_{zg}(q_l'' \leq Q \leq q_l', t_k'' \leq T \leq t_k' \mid G_D^0)$$
$$= P_{zg}(q_l'' \leq Q \leq q_l' \mid t_k'' \leq T \leq t_k'; G_D^0) \times \quad (13.16)$$
$$\times P_{zg}(t_k'' \leq T \leq t_k' \mid G_D^0).$$

The average joint probabilities for tonnage and grade for the ith cell could be computed by weighting these probabilities by the expectation for number of deposits and by consideration of the spatial geometry of the cell and zones

$$\bar{P}(q_l'' \leq Q \leq q_l', t_k'' \leq T \leq t_k' \mid G_D^0)$$
$$= \left[\sum_{g=1}^{NG} \sum_{z=1}^{NZ_g} \bar{n}_{zg} \cdot D_{zg} \times \right.$$
$$\left. \times P_{zg}(q_l'' \leq Q \leq q_l', t_k'' \leq T \leq t_k' \mid G_D^0) \right] \Big/ \sum_{g=1}^{NG} \sum_{z=1}^{NZ_g} \cdot \bar{n}_{zg}.$$
$$(13.17)$$

Thus, the operations described provide the average probability distribution of the geologists participating in the survey for grade and tonnage of ore in a copper deposit occurring in a cell, given that cell's geology G_D^0. As indicated previously, this straightforward averaging was not employed in the Sonoran study. Approximations to these averages were obtained by Monte Carlo methods on a digital computer (for a description, see Euresty [2]). In addition to determining the number, tonnage, and grade distributions during the computer analysis, a data file on tonnage and grade was generated for each cell. This data file was subjected to regression analysis to yield a grade–tonnage equation, an equation describing the relationship of grade of the ore of a copper deposit to its tonnage of ore. An equation was computed for each cell. Additionally, during the computer analysis the expected tonnage of ore per deposit and the expected number of deposits across all modes were computed. By substituting the expected tonnage of ore into the grade–tonnage equation, the expected grade given the expected tonnage was computed. Combining of these three quantities yielded the expected copper metal for the cell. Eqn (13.18) describes this relationship.

$$\bar{m} = \bar{n} \cdot \bar{t} \cdot \bar{q}(\bar{t}), \qquad (13.18)$$

where $\bar{q}(\bar{t})$ is the average grade given the average tonnage of $\bar{t}$. Fig. 13.10 shows the distribution of the expectation of copper metal in the cells of northern Sonora. $\bar{m}$ is an approximation to the $\bar{m}$ defined in the section on geostatistical theory

$$\bar{m} = \int_M m \cdot f(m \mid G_D^0)\, dm.$$

13.4.2. *The economic analysis of infrastructure development and potential copper supply*

Perspective

The objectives of this study (SI) were

1. To examine the adequacy of infrastructure in northern Sonora, Mexico;
2. To examine the sensitivity of potential supply to infrastructure;
3. To describe the potential supply of copper or copper equivalent for each of the 64 cells (sub-areas of 400 mi^2).

The overall approach was similar to that described for the Canadian Northwest (CN): Monte Carlo simulation of mineral endowment, exploration, and exploitation combined with a discounted cash flow analysis. As in the CN study, the SI required the construction of the exploration and exploitation models and their integration with an economic framework. However, besides some differences in the design of the endowment model, the SI model differed from the CN model in a very significant way: the SI model contained an algorithm to determine the least cost transportation (capital plus operating costs) path over the terrain of a cell from its center to the nearest existing transportation link. The cost of construction for this link was charged as a capital cost to the economic deposits of the cell, and the carrying charge over the linkage and along the existing infrastructure to Hermosillo, Mexico, was treated as an operating cost. The following sections describe

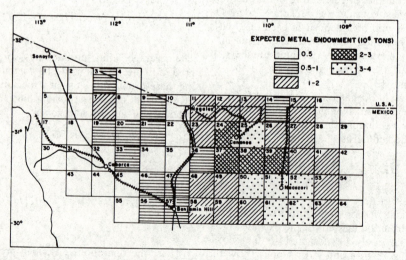

Fig. 13.10. Spatial distribution of expected metal endowment (copper equivalent) of Northern Sonora, Mexico. (Source: Harris 1973, p. 235.)

the way that the computerized model was used to explore the economics of infrastructure and resource development. No details are provided on the exploration and exploitation models or on particulars of the system; for these, see Euresty [2].

The potential supply–infrastructure model

General procedure. Simply stated, the topography of a cell was input to the computer as a matrix of elevations, each elevation on a grid intersection. The optimum transportation route, one having the shortest distance and at the same time meeting gradient constraints, was determined by dynamic programming. Since the primary focus of this study was the effect of infrastructure on potential supply, price, transportation capital costs, and carrying costs were varied and the simulation model was employed to estimate expected potential supply for each combination of circumstances. The data generated by this manipulation served as the data base for the estimation of potential supply functions.

Specific relations. Let us define potential supply of the jth metal as

$$ps_j = K_j T, \qquad (13.19)$$

where T is the ore in tons and K_j is the proportion of ore consisting of the jth metal. Let us further define K_j

$$K_j = Z \cdot (h_j/r_j). \qquad (13.20)$$

Thus,

$$ps_j = (h_j/r_j) \cdot Z \cdot T, \qquad (13.21)$$

where h_j is the proportion of value per ton constituted by the jth metal; r_j is the price of the jth metal (consistent with Z); and Z is the grade in US dollars per ton, based on 1970 prices. If a different set of prices, $\acute{r}_j$, is to be used, h_j must be adjusted

$$\acute{h}_j = h_j \cdot (\acute{r}_j/r_j)$$

and

$$ps_j = (\acute{h}_j/\acute{r}_j) \cdot Z \cdot T, \qquad (13.22)$$

where $\acute{h}_j$ and $\acute{r}_j$ are the new value proportion and price, respectively, of the jth metal.

Define TRC as the multiple of the basic transportation construction schedule, CCC as the fraction of government sharing of construction costs, and CMC as the multiple of construction costs. Then, T and Z are functions, f_1 and f_2, respectively, of TRC, CMC,

and CCC

$$T = f_1(TRC, CMC, CCC) \qquad (13.23)$$
$$Z = f_2(TRC, CMC, CCC). \qquad (13.24)$$

Let us specify further that functions f_1 and f_2 are of the form

$$A_0(TRC)^{A_1} \cdot (CMC)^{A_2} \cdot (CCC)^{A_3}$$
$$= f_2(TRC, CMC, CCC), \qquad (13.25)$$
$$\beta_0(TRC)^{\beta_1} \cdot (CMC)^{\beta_2} \cdot (CCC)^{\beta_3}$$
$$= f_1(TRC, CMC, CCC). \qquad (13.26)$$

Then, using (13.21)–(13.26), potential supply can be written as

$$ps_j = (\acute{h}_j/\acute{r}_j) A_0 \beta_0 (TRC)^{A_1+\beta_1} \times$$
$$\times (CMC)^{A_2+\beta_2} \cdot (CCC)^{A_3+\beta_3}. \qquad (13.27)$$

In this form, $A_1 + \beta_1$ is $ETRC$, the elasticity of potential metal supply relative to carrying rates

$$ETRC = A_1 + \beta_1.$$

Similarly,

$ECMC = A_2 + \beta_2 =$ elasticity of ps_j with respect to transportation construction.

$ECCC = A_3 + \beta_3 =$ elasticity of ps_j with respect to government sharing of construction costs.

Thus, we can write (13.27) as

$$ps_j = (\acute{h}_j/\acute{r}_j) A_0 \beta_0 (TRC)^{ETRC}(CMC)^{ECMC}(CCC)^{ECCC}. \qquad (13.28)$$

However, *a priori* reasoning suggests that these elasticities for any particular cell should vary with the transportation construction distance and the carrying distance (the greater the distance, the larger the elasticities)

$$ETRC = \alpha(CD)^{\alpha_1}(TD)^{\alpha_2}$$
$$ECMC = \omega(CD)^{\omega_1}(TD)^{\omega_2}$$
$$ECCC = \gamma(CD)^{\gamma_1}(TD)^{\gamma_2},$$

where CD is the construction distance and TD is the transportation (carrying) distance; α, ω, and γ are multipliers and α_1, α_2, ω_1, ω_2, γ_1, and γ_2 are exponents that are to be estimated.

Finally, we can write potential supply of the jth metal as a function of $\acute{h}_j$, $\acute{r}_j$, TRC, CMC, CCC, CD, and TD

$$ps_j = (\acute{h}_j/\acute{r}_j) A_0 \beta_0 (TRC)^{\alpha(CD)^{\alpha_1}(TD)^{\alpha_2}} \times$$
$$\times (CMC)^{\omega(CD)^{\omega_1}(TD)^{\omega_2}}(CCC)^{\gamma(CD)^{\gamma_1}(TD)^{\gamma_2}}. \qquad (13.29)$$

The potential metal supply of an area could be computed by (13.21), (13.27), or (13.29). When estimates only of Z and T, for a given (h_i/r_i), are available potential supply could be estimated by eqn (13.21). If the analysis has yielded elasticities as functions of distances, (13.29) is appropriate. If the ultimate objective were the charting of a transportation route, expressions of the type of (13.29) computed for each cell would provide useful auxiliary information for selection of the overall optimum route.

Analysis

Conditions. Occurrence of deposits, exploration for deposits, and exploitation of those deposits discovered were simulated under various levels of the pertinent transportation variables *TRC, CMC,* and *CCC.* All other economic variables, such as exploration expenditures, price level, capital costs, discount rate, and overall level of operating costs were held constant. This does not mean, for example, that operating and capital costs were the same for every deposit, nor does it mean that the stochastic properties of the estimated cost functions were ignored. On the contrary, the operating and capital costs were defined, where applicable, to be functions of the tonnage of the simulated deposits, and a random error term consistent with the standard error of each cost equation was added to the estimated cost. When it is stated that capital costs and operating costs were held constant, this means that the relationships of the basic cost equations were employed, rather than modifying the costs by multiplying the basic relationships by some selected constant. Similarly, an average regional exploration expenditure was employed as typical of a regional exploration programme. However, the results of exploration for a given deposit varied according to its tonnage and the effect of a stochastic error term (see Harris *et al.* 1971; Euresty [2]).

The basic construction cost employed in this study was that of a crushed stone surfaced road in Mexico, about US $26 000 per mile. The basic carrying rate employed was 0.021 US $/ton-mile.

Elasticities. Inasmuch as the effect of transportation upon potential metal supply was the objective of this study, a sensitivity analysis was performed by varying the transportation variables and observing the output of the simulation model. Of course, the effect of transportation on metal supply varies with the cell, depending upon the metal endowment of the cell, terrain, and location. However, a more general analysis of cells was performed by changing arbitrar-

ily the transportation construction distance and the carrying distances. Statistical analysis of the output of the simulator yielded response functions of tonnage and grade of ore as a function of the transportation variables and the construction and carrying distances. The following equation defines the expected metal supply of cell 39, conditional upon the basic relationships of the economic variables

$$p\hat{s}_j = (7 \times 10^8) \cdot [(TRC)^{-(TD^{2.59}/7.12)}] \times$$
$$\times [(CMC)^{-(CD^{0.41}/2.14)}] \cdot (\acute{h}_j/\acute{r}_j), \quad (13.30)$$

where $p\hat{s}_j$ is the estimated potential metal supply in units compatible with $\acute{r}_j$; TD is the transportation distance in units of 100 miles; CD is the construction distance in units of 100 miles; TRC and CMC are the multiple of basic carrying charge and the multiple of basic construction cost, respectively, and $\acute{h}_j$ is the new proportion of value per ton comprised by the jth metal, caused by using specified price $\acute{r}_j$ instead of the base price r_j for the jth metal.

The variable representing government sharing of construction cost does not appear in the equation because in a statistical sense it was not a significant variable (5 per cent level of significance), given the necessary simultaneous estimation of coefficients of TRC and CMC. In order to explore the properties of this equation, let us assume that carrying distance is 400 miles and construction distance is zero. In this case the potential metal supply is a function only of $\acute{h}_j$, $\acute{r}_j$ and TRC

$$p\hat{s}_j = (7 \times 10^8)(TRC)^{-(36.2/7.12)}(\acute{h}_j/\acute{r}_j). \quad (13.31)$$

Now, suppose that the carrying distance is decreased to 200 miles

$$p\hat{s}_j = (6 \times 10^8)(TRC)^{-(6.03)/7.12}(\acute{h}_j/\acute{r}_j).$$
$$(13.32)$$

The elasticity of potential metal supply with respect to TRC decreases correspondingly from about 5.1 to about 0.85. This is equivalent to saying that given a carrying distance of 400 miles, a 100 per cent increase in transportation rates (charge per ton-mile for concentrate) decreases potential metal supply by 510 per cent. For a carrying distance of 200 miles, the 100 per cent increase in transportation rates decreases the potential metal supply by only about 85 per cent.

Because of the small exponent of CD [expression (13.30)], the elasticity of potential metal supply does not increase as rapidly for increased construction distances as does the elasticity with respect to carrying rates. However, because of the small denominator in the exponent of *CMC*, small-to-moderate construction distances are seen to have a greater impact upon supply than do small-to-moderate transportation distances. In the case of $TD = CD = 100$ miles, the elasticity of supply relative to *TRC* is $-1/7.12$, while relative to *CMC* it is $-1/2.14$. Because of the definition of *TRC* and *CMC* as multiples of basic cost schedules, eqn (13.30) is not meaningful (from the point of view of elasticities) for *TRC* or *CMC* = 1.0, for at these levels potential metal supply is invariant to transportation and construction distances.

Potential supply of cell 39—an example. For comparative purposes, let us evaluate the potential supply of cell 39 under the following states of the variables and parameters: $TRC = 1.5$, $CMC = 1.5$, $TD = 2.0$, $CD = 2.0$, $h_1 = 1.0$, $h_2 = h_3 = h_4 = h_5 = 0$, $r_1 = $ US \$0.56/lb.

In the above set of conditions h_1 and r_1 refer to copper. The implication of setting $h_2 = h_3 = h_4 = h_5 = 0$ is that potential metal supply will be in terms of copper equivalent. This will allow the comparison of expected potential metal supply to expected metal endowment.

$$ps_j = \frac{(7 \times 10^8)(1.5)^{-0.85}(1.5)^{-0.62}}{(0.56)}$$

= 344 100 short tons (s.t.) copper equivalent.

Referring to Fig. 13.10, the expected metal endowment for cell 39 in terms of copper equivalent is 2 000 000–3 000 000 s.t. Taking the midpoint of this range, it appears that the potential metal supply of cell 39 for the conditions specified is approximately 14 per cent of that expected to occur in the cell. If construction and transportation distances were near zero, the potential metal supply would approach 600 000 s.t.

Adequacy of existing transportation network. To test the adequacy of the existing transportation network, the potential metal supply of the cells of the study area was evaluated by simulating the supply of metals using the transportation links of each cell to the existing transportation network (see Fig. 13.10). These links are the paths determined by dynamic programming. Concentrates of the simulated deposits were transported south to Hermosillo.

In general, the existing transportation network is fairly well situated, as it passes through the richly endowed areas (see Fig. 13.10). This was verified by the coefficients of the transportation variables in the potential supply functions for the cells. Only minor construction was required to connect the rich cells to the existing network. Consequently, the elasticity of potential supply relative to the multiple of construction costs was small for the well endowed cells. The effect of transportation rates, while greater than construction costs, was also moderate; the elasticity of potential supply relative to *TRC* never exceeded 40 per cent.

Concentrates from deposits in the southeast part of the study area must be transported north across the United States–Mexican border, then west, before they can be transported south to Hermosillo. Naturally, this is a much longer route than would be direct shipping south to Hermosillo, but there is no major transportation link south to Hermosillo, except an old unsurfaced road. In view of this indirect shipping route for some of the cells, it seemed appropriate to use the model of this study to determine if construction of a surfaced road from Nacozari to Hermosillo and construction of the links from the pertinent cells to the road could be justified by the benefits of a shorter carrying route. Only three cells were considered: cells 51, 52, and 53. The discounted benefits of potential metal supply from these three cells outweighed the costs of construction by approximately US \$2 000 000. For details of the analysis, see Euresty [2].

Potential supply of the study area. Simulation of exploration and exploitation, with special provision for including costs for construction of required transportation links and the cost of transporting concentrate to Hermosillo, indicated a potential supply of approximately 15 430 000 tonnes of copper equivalent. Thus, the requirement that only the metal in those deposits that were discovered in the simulation and were economic to develop and produce would contribute to potential supply reduced potential supply of metal to about 26 per cent of the metal endowment. The remaining 74 per cent of metal endowment either was not discovered by the simulated exploration, or it was not economic to develop and produce.

The potential supply of the entire study area was determined for the standard economic conditions and for the basic carrying rate and construction cost, given the existing transportation network and required links. Estimation of the expected quantity of each of the five metals that would be supplied was based upon the assumption that the proportions of value of the metals in ore discovered in the future will be similar, on the average, to the proportion of value of metals in ore produced from Arizona and

New Mexico

Copper	0.26303
Zinc	0.14066
Gold	0.13196
Lead	0.21115
Silver	0.25321.

These value proportions are based upon 1968 prices. $\hat{h}_i$ and $\hat{r}_i$ were based upon 1970 prices since these were the prices used in estimating Z. The results of this analysis of potential supply are as follows:

Copper	7 709 000 tonnes
Lead	10 314 000 tonnes
Zinc	6 951 000 tonnes
Silver	76 498 000 kg
Gold	1 764 000 kg.

13.5. Mineral Endowment of Manitoba, Canada

The undiscovered mineral wealth of Manitoba, Canada, (Azis, Barry, and Haugh 1972) was appraised using the same survey design as was described in the previous section for British Columbia and the Yukon Territory of Canada. The survey employed the same questionnaire design and included the same 11 commodity groups. Since the survey and methods of analysis were described in the previous section, the reader is referred to that section for such description and to the paper by Azis *et al.* (1972) for results of the survey.

13.6. Estimation of uranium resources of New Mexico by Delphi procedures

13.6.1. *Background*

In 1973 a subjective probability appraisal of the uranium resources of New Mexico was initiated by the Grand Junction Office of the Energy Research and Development Administration (ERDA) (Ellis, Harris, and Van Wie 1975). Objectives of this study included the examination of the application of subjective probability methods to the appraisal of uranium resources and comparison of estimates made by subjective probability to those made by ERDA using conventional methods. The study was conducted by the Grand Junction Office of ERDA. Through the efforts of this office, the participation of 36 geologists was obtained. This group of experts consisted of 26 geologists from industry, 7 from government, and 3 from universities.

13.6.2. *Survey design*

Mechanics and probabilities.

The State of New Mexico was subdivided into 62 cells. The dimensions of the cells were approximately $\frac{1}{2}$ degree latitude by 1 degree longitude, imparting an area of approximately 1970 square miles to each cell, except for two fractional cells.

Except for the fact that this study dealt with only one metal, uranium, the format for eliciting the judgements of the 36 experts was much the same as that used in the British Columbia and Yukon Territory survey and the survey on Manitoba, Canada, (see Fig. 13.11). The background information, including statistical data on uranium deposits, and the instructions given to the respondents are described in Ellis *et al.* (1975). Subjective probabilities were provided independently by each of the geologists for number of deposits and for tonnage–grade combinations for each of the 62 cells

$$P_g(N = n \mid G_D^0);\ P_g(q_i'' \leq Q \leq q_i',\ t_k'' \leq T \leq t_k' \mid G_D^0).$$

Initially, there was no differentiation of modes of occurrence.

Although the survey design as described to this point offers nothing new, this study is of particular interest because it extended the methodology in two interesting ways

1. It attempted to take into consideration the variation in knowledge among experts;
2. It provided for a revision (Delphi) of probabilities.

Issues raised in selecting experts

Let us digress from the mechanics of the survey for a moment and consider a proverbial problem in subjective assessment: the quality of judgement of the experts and its variability. Conceptually, a rather strong case can be made that for a limited region, there exists one expert who is the most informed of all possible experts and that if the identity of that individual were known, the best appraisal of the mineral resources of the region should reflect his judgement alone. Including judgements of other individuals merely dilutes the best available information. While the foregoing states what appears to be an intrinsic truth, the utilization of this truth in many applications may be operationally impossible, for it requires identification of this expert by the person or persons conducting the survey. Such identification could be made in only two ways.

SUBJECTIVE PROBABILITY ASSESSMENT
OF URANIUM POTENTIAL
STATE OF NEW MEXICO

Cell No. 14   Respondent's No. 7   Date 1 / 5 / 73

MATRIX NO. II

MATRIX NO. I

NO. OF DEPOSITS	PROBABILITY
0	
1-4	8
5-9	10
10-24	2
25-49	
50-99	
100-	

TONS ORE THOUSANDS	GRADE (% U3O8)			
	.01-.04	.05-.14	.15-.25	.26-1.0
0-1				
1-3				
3-10		3	5	1
10-30		5	7	1
30-100		2	2	1
100-300				
300-1000				
1000-3000				
3000-10 000				
10 000-30 000				

10   Your best estimate on average thickness of deposits in cell (Nearest foot)

150   Your best estimate on average depth of deposits in cell (Nearest 50 feet)

Please check appropriate boxes to indicate your familiarity with the geology and uranium occurrences in this cell.

GEOLOGY
☐ High
☑ Medium
☐ Low

URANIUM OCCURRENCES
☐ High
☐ Medium
☑ Low

Fig. 13.11. Completed questionnaire form. (Source: Ellis *et al.* 1975.)

1. By the judgement of the person or persons conducting the survey as to overall professional expertise;
2. By some performance characteristic.

It takes only a moment's thought to conclude that selection of the most qualified expert by the person conducting the survey requires that person to be the most qualified expert. Thus, he alone should provide the subjective probabilities. When the person con-
ducting the survey does not qualify in this manner, his selection of the most qualified expert at best would be a 'noisy' choice, because the selection would reflect a host of 'shadowy' impressions, such as the affiliation of a geologist with the most active firm in exploration of the region, the reserves hold-ings of the firm, conformity of the geologists' science with the theories of ore genesis that are most current at the moment, the professional competency of the person or persons conducting the survey, and how

well he is acquainted with exploration personnel and geoscientists. While a well-informed individual using such criteria as outlined may identify a subset of experts that contains the most qualified individual, he is limited by his own capabilities in selecting the one best expert. Actually, there is no guarantee that a well-informed individual selecting a set of experts will include in the set the 'super expert', for the 'super expert' may espouse scientific theories that run counter to tradition; it has not been uncommon for a scientific genius to be rejected by his peers because he was considered to espouse what then appeared to be unsupported theories but which later were proven to be correct, to wit, continental drift, which only two decades ago was not a popular theory but which now is considered to be a proven fact.

If a reliable performance characteristic were available, its use has some appeal, for it relieves those conducting the survey from the dilemma of identifying the expert or experts on the basis of their own professional expertise. However, such a measure is not publicly available. Furthermore, it is not clear how this measure would be determined. Typically, exploration conducted by large firms is a team effort of geoscientists of varied specializations. To what single individual is the discovery of a major deposit to be credited? Crediting it to the chief geologist or exploration manager would probably result if such crediting had to be done, and, perhaps, in some cases, such a choice may be appropriate, but in other cases, it may have been the genius of a junior, highly specialized sceintist in the organization who provided the greatest single insight. In most cases, it may be impossible to make such an assignment.

The implication of the foregoing argument is that unless the person conducting the survey is the 'super expert', it is impossible for him to base the survey on the opinion of the singly most capable individual. And, even if he were the most capable of all experts, there is little chance that he would be universally accepted as such. Use of a performance characteristic appears equally fruitless as an approach to identifying the 'super expert'. Therefore, the identification of the 'super expert' is not a realistic goal. A much looser approach must be taken, the selection of a group of experts recognized by their peers merely as well informed in geology and mineral resources of the study area.

Kinds of expertise and self-rating

For the appraisal of mineral endowment, it is useful to recognize two general kinds of expertise, both of which are useful but for different reasons or in different ways

(1) knowledge of the geoscience of the ore-formation process;
(2) knowledge of the physical characteristics of the uranium deposits and associated geology.

These kinds of expertise are referred to by Ellis *et al.* (1975) as expertise in geology and uranium occurrences. Obviously, these two kinds of expertise are not mutually exclusive; even so, such classification is useful because it emphasizes the contributions of the theorists and of those with extensive field experience.

While the expert with the field experience may provide much more specific knowledge on and estimates of deposit occurrence, as deposits are currently defined, he may not (though not necessarily so) be as capable as the more science-trained person of generalizing to resources in deposits having physical characteristics different from those currently sought in traditional regions or to resources in new modes of occurrence in traditional regions, particularly in new regions having environments different from those of the traditional regions.

The survey of uranium resources in New Mexico was designed to allow the geologist to rate himself on each cell as to how well informed he believed himself to be in geology and uranium occurrences. The respondent was given three levels of expertise by which to describe himself: high, medium, and low. In the subsequent combining of the multiple responses (averaging), these levels were assigned numerical values: high = 3, medium = 2, and low = 1. Then, an overall expertise score was computed by summing the two scores and dividing by 6. Thus, a geologist's overall expertise on a cell would be represented by one of the numbers

High–high	= 1.000
High–medium or medium–high	= 0.833
High–low, low–high or medium–medium	= 0.666
Medium–low or low–medium	= 0.500
Low–low	= 0.333

Additional information

In addition to the probabilities (number of deposits, grade, and tonnage of ore per deposit) and a self-rating, the geologist was asked to estimate the representative depth to and thickness of the deposits he envisioned while completing the probability survey. This information was solicited to improve the economic assessment of the physical endowment described by the probabilities.

13.6.3. *Analysis by cell of initial information*

Approach

The initial step in the processing of the survey results was to compute probabilities from the probability index numbers provided by each geologist for each cell. The procedure followed was identical to that employed on the Canadian study, which was described earlier in this chapter; consequently, these relations will not be repeated here.

Subsequent to the transforming of the probability index numbers to probabilities, the probabilistic responses of the 36 geologists were combined to provide a set of average probability distributions, a univariate one for number and a bivariate one for grade and tonnage. However, in the averaging process, the responses of each geologist were weighted by his self-rating of expertise, w_{ig}

$$\bar{P}_i(N=n \mid G_D^0) = \sum_{g=1}^{NG} w_{ig} \cdot P_{ig}(N=n \mid G_D^0) \bigg/ \sum_{g=1}^{NG} w_{ig},$$
$$(13.33)$$

$$\bar{P}_i(q_l'' \le Q \le q_l', t_k'' \le T \le t_k' \mid G_D^0)$$
$$= \sum_{g=1}^{NG} w_{ig} \cdot \bar{n}_{ig} \cdot P_{ig}(q_l'' \le Q \le q_l', t_k'' \le T \le t_k' \mid G_D^0)$$
$$\bigg/ \sum_{g=1}^{NG} \bar{n}_{ig} \cdot w_{ig}, \quad (13.34)$$

where w_{ig} is the self-rating of the gth geologist on the ith cell and $\bar{n}_{ig}$ is the expectation for number of deposits for the ith cell by the gth geologist.

The self-rating information was examined on a cell-to-cell basis to see if such information could be used to provide a more reliable estimate of a cell's endowment. The manner in which this was done was to convert each geologist's estimates to tons of U_3O_8

$$\bar{u}_{ig} = \bar{n}_{ig} \cdot \bar{t}_{ig} \cdot \bar{q}_{ig}, \quad (13.35)$$

where $\bar{u}_{ig}$, $\bar{n}_{ig}$, $\bar{t}_{ig}$, $\bar{q}_{ig}$ are the means of tonnage of U_3O_8, number of deposits, tonnage of ore per deposit, and grade of ore per deposit, respectively, for the ith cell by the gth geologist. Then, the self-ratings of the geologists were examined, starting with the highest possible level, 1.0. Those geologists having a value of 1.0 were identified. If there were at least ten geologists having a self-rating on the cell of 1.0, a high-rating subset of data was formed consisting only of the $\bar{u}_{ig}$ of the geologists in this subset. However, if the number of geologists having a self-rating of 1.0 were less than 10, the next highest possible level of expertise, 0.833, was used to identify a subset of geologists having a self-rating of at

least 0.833. Again, the number of such geologists was determined, and if this number were still less than 10, the procedure was repeated using the next lower level 0.666. The extremes of this process could be a subset consisting of all 36 geologists

(1) if all geologists believed themselves to be well informed on both geology and deposit occurrences;

(2) if more than 26 geologists believed themselves to be poorly informed on geology and deposit occurrence.

If either of the two cases were to eventuate, it was not possible by the scheme adopted in this study to identify two subsets. Otherwise, two subsets were identified and for each subset two statistics were computed

$$\bar{u}_i^{(1)} = \frac{1}{NG^{(1)}} \sum_{g=1}^{NG^{(1)}} u_{ig}^{(1)} \quad (13.36)$$

$$\bar{u}_i^{(2)} = \frac{1}{NG^{(2)}} \sum_{g=1}^{NG^{(2)}} u_{ig}^{(2)}$$

$$S_i^{(1)} = \left\{ \frac{\sum_{g=1}^{NG^{(1)}} (u_{ig}^{(1)} - \bar{u}_i^{(1)})^2}{NG^{(1)} - 1} \right\}^{\frac{1}{2}}$$

$$S_i^{(2)} = \left\{ \frac{\sum_{g=1}^{NG^{(2)}} (u_{ig}^{(2)} - \bar{u}_i^{(2)})^2}{NG^{(2)} - 1} \right\}^{\frac{1}{2}}.$$

The superscript identifies the subset to which the geologist's responses and the statistics are associated. The next step in the analysis was to test $\bar{u}_i^{(1)}$ against $\bar{u}_i^{(2)}$ to see if there was a statistically significant difference between the endowment estimates of the two subsets. The statistic employed for this test was

$$t_i = \frac{|\bar{u}_i^{(1)} - \bar{u}_i^{(2)}|}{\left\{ \frac{(S_i^{(1)})^2 + (S_i^{(2)})^2}{(NG^{(1)} + NG^{(2)} - 2)} \times \left(\frac{1}{NG^{(1)}} + \frac{1}{NG^{(2)}} \right) \right\}^{\frac{1}{2}}}$$
$$(13.37)$$

This statistic was compared to t^*, an effective student-t measure at the 5 per cent significance level

$$t_i^* = \frac{\dfrac{t_1 \cdot (S_i^{(1)})^2}{NG^{(1)} - 1} + \dfrac{t_2 \cdot (S_i^{(2)})^2}{NG^{(2)} - 1}}{\dfrac{(S_i^{(1)})^2}{NG^{(1)} - 1} + \dfrac{(S_i^{(2)})^2}{NG^{(2)} - 1}}, \quad (13.38)$$

where t_1 and t_2 are values for the 't' distribution for

TABLE 13.4. *Estimates of U_3O_8 endowment characteristics averaged over all respondents—cell 20 and the State of New Mexico. (Source: Ellis et al. 1975.)*

	Cell 20		New Mexico	
	Weighted	Unweighted	Weighted	Unweighted
No. of deposits	41.4	40.0	577.8	553.8
Thousand tons ore/deposit	1896.7	1874.4	296	298
Thousand tons ore	70 269	68 082	170 751	165 000
Grade (per cent)	0.276	0.276	0.229	0.224
Depth (ft)	2702	2650	540	544
Thickness (ft)	11.9	11.8	4.7	4.5
Tons U_3O_8/square mile	102.9	96.2	3.3	3.1
Thousand tons U_3O_8	179.1	173.1	382.0	368.8

degrees of freedom $NG^{(1)} - 1$ and $NG^{(2)} - 1$, respectively. If $t_i > t_i^*$ for the 5 per cent level of significance, the difference in the U_3O_8 estimated by the two subsets was considered to be significant, and the endowment of the cell was based upon the responses of the high-confidence subset alone; otherwise, the endowment reflected the responses of all geologists.

Evaluation of usefulness of self-ratings of expertise

The effects of weighting endowment information by a geologist's self-rating were analysed by comparing weighted to unweighted averages, leading to the following observations (Ellis *et al.* 1975).

1. The estimate of U_3O_8 by the high-confidence subset was greater than that for the remaining set in 39 of the 62 cells, but not by a significant amount.

2. A significant difference between the high-confidence subset and the remaining geologists was observed in 6 of the 62 cells: cells 7, 16, 22, 36, 48, and 60. The high-confidence subset estimated greater quantities of U_3O_8 than the remaining geologists.

3. When weighting was utilized in combining the opinions of all respondents, as opposed to no weighting, the estimates of U_3O_8 endowment increased, but not by a statistically significant amount, as indicated in Table 13.4.

From this limited study of the use of self-rating indices as weights in the resolution of multiple opinions, the conclusion seems indicated that self-ratings are of limited usefulness. Subsequent to the completion of this study, the literature on subjective probability assessment was consulted, and it was found that a similar conclusion was reached by Campbell [4] and Dalkey (1969).

There are three possible explanations for the finding of limited usefulness of self-ratings.

1. Careful selection of a panel of experts could create a subpopulation that is relatively homogeneous in capability.
2. Since self-rating involves the individual's ego, it is bound to be a somewhat noisy measure of actual capability.
3. Professional expertise has little to do with estimation of unknown endowment.

The argument for 1 would hold that, perhaps, across the *entire population* of *geologists* who work in New Mexico, a self-rating on knowledge about the geology and occurrence of U_3O_8 may be more closely associated with actual differences than for a relatively homogeneous subset. If such were the case, then the fact that self-rating must by its involvement of the ego be somewhat noisy may make actual differences non-discernible in the subset of experts on U_3O_8.

Although the last possible explanation is not one which we would like to accept, it must be given consideration for there is no guarantee that high expertise in the profession of geology leads to definitive estimates of such a complex and unknown quantity, mineral endowment. Estimation of unknown endowment involves mental processes other than understanding of geoscience. Some of these processes are discussed later in the section on psychometrics.

3.6.4. *Modified Delphi reassessment*

Justification

Analysis of the initial survey data revealed an unexpected result: of the expected U_3O_8 endowment remaining in New Mexico, the relative frequencies of low grades were *lower* than the relative frequencies of the same grades in past production and known ore reserves. It had been anticipated that the remaining endowment would consist of lower-grade material. While the remaining endowment may consist of a smaller proportion of low grades, there was some concern that it reflected either the preoccupation of the geologists with characteristics of exploitable deposits, hence a truncation or censorship induced by economics, or a bias induced by the survey design. The potential for bias due to the survey design was considered to have been created by asking the geologist to provide an estimated depth to the deposits envisioned while completing the probability tables. It was reasoned that requesting one depth may have preempted the including of endowment at greater depth than deposits currently being mined and may have preempted the including of endowment of deposits of different environments. These possibilities led to the consideration of a second-round assessment with the specific intent to encourage the geologists to consider additional modes of occurrence. Additional argument for a second round was found in the benefits that are customarily ascribed to Delphi procedures for the assessment in general of judgement, one of which is the narrowing of variation in responses to a consensus of the group. While a consensus was never an objective in this study, a decrease in the variation seemed at the time to be a worthwhile goal. As pointed out in a subsequent section, these benefits are not without a price and may not warrant the sacrifice required to achieve them. The decision was made to conduct a modified Delphi by providing feedback information from the initial survey to the respondents and encouraging a reassessment of their initial responses. Only one iteration of feedback-reassessment was made. The information obtained from the second-round survey (reassessment) constituted the data from which was described the endowment of New Mexico in U_3O_8.

Each respondent was asked to do two things on each cell.

1. Re-examine his original responses and the cell's geology while considering whether or not additional deposits could be present at greater depths or in a geological setting somewhat different from the conventional modes. If additional deposits could exist in this fashion, then the respondent was asked to complete additional survey sheets, one for each mode of occurrence, where mode of occurrence was taken to be different depth or geologic environment.

2. Re-examine his original responses and the 'feedback' information from the analysis of the initial survey data from all geologists to see if any changes in his responses were appropriate.

Kinds of and use of 'feedback' information

Fig. 13.12 and Tables 13.5 and 13.6 show actual first-round information for cell 20 that was returned to each geologist to be used in his reassessment of the endowment of the cell. Information in this form for each cell was returned to each of the participating geologists. In addition, each geologist received Fig. 13.13 which shows the geographic distribution of the average endowment across all geologists for all 62 cells.

Table 13.7 shows for cell 20 the expectations for the various features and characteristics of endowment by each of the 36 geologists and the average across all geologists. In addition the numerical code of each geologist and his self-rating of expertise is provided. This table allows each geologist to compare the statistics of his responses and his self-rating to those of the other geologists while preserving anonymity of the respondents.

Fig. 13.12 (before Delphi) provides histograms for number of deposits, tonnage of ore per deposit, and grade of ore within the modal tonnage class. These histograms show the frequency of geologists who provided responses within the intervals indicated on the abscissa of the graphs. The intent of the histograms was to provide the geologist with a quick view of the variation in the responses across the geologists for a given feature.

The purpose for Fig. 13.13 was to assist the geologist in the evaluation of cells which are barren or relatively poor in known deposits by providing him with a view of the geography of the first-round assessment of endowment. The idea behind providing this figure was that it would assist in the extrapolation or integration of geology and endowment relationships.

Tables 13.5 and 13.6 are perhaps the most useful in actual reassessment, for they provide for a cell, in this case cell 20, an average of the judgements of the 36 geologists in the same format as the information provided by the geologists, namely, probability index numbers for number of deposits and grade–tonnage

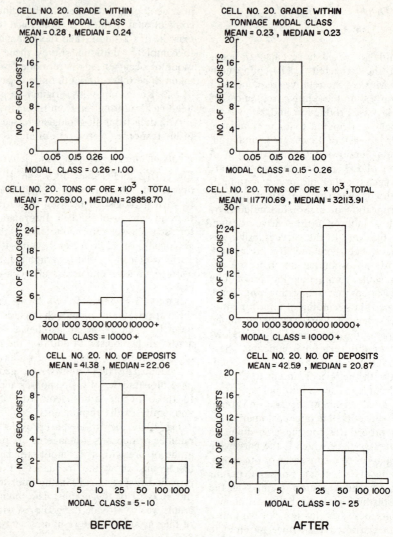

Fig. 13.12. Cell 20 histograms, before and after Delphi reassessment. (Source: Ellis *et al.* 1975.)

combinations. A geologist could make a direct comparison of his original responses to the average of all geologists. Such a direct comparison should facilitate the making of the decision as to whether or not he deserves to modify his initial responses, and if so, just what modification is appropriate. As indicated in these tables, average probability index distributions were provided for the high self-rated subset and for all geologists, with a statement as to whether there exists a statistically significant difference between the responses of the two subsets comprised by the high-confidence geologists and all remaining geologists. In

this way, the decision was left to the geologist as to which of the tables he employed in his reassessment.

Analysis of second-round survey (reassessment) by cell

Upon receipt of the data from the second-round survey, the endowment of each cell was computed by the relationships employed in the first round except allowance was made for multiple modes. Each mode was analysed separately. The effect of the second round was an increase in overall U_3O_8 for the State of New Mexico, but not by much. Cell 20 contains

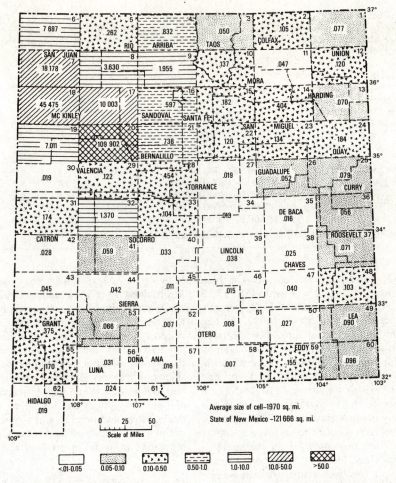

Fig. 13.13. Spatial distribution of U_3O_8 (tons/mi^2) prior to the Delphi reassessment. (Source: Ellis *et al.* 1975.)

TABLE 13.5. *Probability index numbers for all geologists* (*pre-Delphi*). (*Source: Ellis* et al. *1975.*)

Number of deposits	Probability index	Tons (×10³)	Grade (per cent U_3O_8)			
			0.01–0.04	0.05–0.14	0.15–0.25	0.26–1.00
0.– 0.	0.3	0.0– 1.0	0.0	0.0	0.0	0.0
1.– 4.	4.0	1.0– 3.0	0.0	0.0	0.0	0.0
5.– 9.	7.6	3.0– 10.0	0.0	0.2	0.5	0.5
10.– 24.	10.0	10.0– 30.0	0.0	0.4	0.8	0.8
25.– 49.	7.1	30.0– 100.0	0.0	3.8	4.0	3.5
50.– 99.	5.3	100.0– 300.0	0.0	4.3	6.4	4.2
GE 100.	2.4	300.0– 1000.0	0.1	7.0	10.0	5.7
		1000.0– 3000.0	0.1	4.6	8.8	5.5
		3000.0–10 000.0	0.2	1.4	6.3	2.6
		10 000.0–30 000.0	0.0	0.0	0.0	0.0

TABLE 13.6. *Probability index numbers for high-confidence subset.* (*Source: Ellis* et al. *1975.*)

High-confidence subset of 24 geologists (minimum of 10 specified). Minimum expertise level = 1.000

Number of deposits	Probability index	Tons (×10³)	Grade (per cent U_3O_8) 0.01–0.04	0.05–0.14	0.15–0.25	0.26–1.00
0.- 0.	0.0	0.0– 1.0	0.0	0.0	0.0	0.0
1.- 4.	2.9	1.0– 3.0	0.0	0.0	0.0	0.0
5.- 9.	6.2	3.0– 10.0	0.0	0.0	0.0	0.0
10.- 24.	10.0	10.0– 30.0	0.0	0.1	0.1	0.1
25.- 49.	7.3	30.0– 100.0	0.0	4.0	4.1	3.7
50.- 99.	5.3	100.0– 300.0	0.0	4.8	6.8	4.2
GE 100.	2.3	300.0– 1000.0	0.1	7.4	10.0	5.7
		1000.0– 3000.0	0.1	4.6	8.8	6.1
		3000.0–10 000.0	0.1	1.1	6.9	3.0
		10 000.0–30 000.0	0.0	0.0	0.0	0.0

Non-significant difference in estimates between high-confidence subset and remaining geologists

the major U_3O_8 mining districts of the San Juan Basin. Comparison of Fig. 13.14 with Fig. 13.13 shows that the expectation for tons of U_3O_8 per mile for this cell increased from 109.9 to 137.9. Fig. 13.12 reveals how this change came about through changed responses of the geologists. For example, the histogram for number of deposits shows a shift in the geologists' opinions from both the high- and low-number intervals to the interval (10–25). There was little change in the histogram for tonnage per deposit, probably because class intervals for tonnage did not extend to large enough tonnages, and in this cell most geologists' responses fell in the greater-than-10 000 tons class. Since this is an open-ended class, the effect of feedback information and reassessment would not be discernible unless changes were made in the low tonnage classes. On the other hand, feedback and reassessment of the grade for deposits in the greater-than-10 000 tons of ore class did decrease the variation in grade, showing an increase in number of geologists whose expectation for grade was in the grade interval (0.15–0.26 per cent).

While for the entire state the expectation for U_3O_8 increased with reassessment, the expectation by cell increased for some but decreased for others. For example, the expectation for U_3O_8 for cell 18 increased considerably, from 45.475 to 63.583 s.t., but that for cell 28 decreased from 0.454 to 0.032 s.t. (compare Figs. 13.13 and 13.14).

Although some decrease in variation among the geologists resulted from the feedback and reassessment, considerable variation still remained after the second round. Fig. 13.15 shows the considerable variation among the geologists in total U_3O_8 for the

State of New Mexico, where this total for a geologist is obtained simply by adding his expectations for U_3O_8 across the 62 cells. It should be carefully noted that no judgement on the usefulness of Delphi procedures in decreasing the variation in opinions can be drawn from this study, because instructions for the second round encouraged the respondent to consider multiple modes (depth as well as environment) and low grades. While such instructions may be well motivated by policy considerations, it violates statistical control and precludes any conclusion about the usefulness of feedback and reassessment in decreasing variation in the opinions of the geologists.

13.6.5. *Probability distributions for the State of New Mexico*

Analysis of the second-round survey provided average subjective probability distributions for deposits of each mode and for each cell. No information was requested of the respondents concerning these probability distributions for the entire state. Rather, probability distributions for total tonnage of ore, tonnage of U_3O_8, and grade of ore for the entire State of New Mexico were derived from cell distributions by Monte Carlo methods and computer processing. The procedure employed was to sample the distribution of a geologist for a cell for number of deposits n and then to sample the bivariate distribution for grade and tonnage for each of the n deposits, giving n triplets of data, each triplet consisting of a measure of grade of ore, tonnage of ore, and tonnage of U_3O_8; performing this sampling on all cells made it possible to compute the total ore and

ABLE 13.7. *Averages endowment characteristics for cell number 20 by geologists, New Mexico (pre-Delphi). (Source: Ellis : al. 1975.)*

| | Geologist Index | | | | Summary of geologist estimates for this cell | | | | | |
ode	GE	OC	RTG.	Number of deposits	Tons of ore per deposit (×10³)	Total	Grade (percent)	Ore depth	Average thickness	U₃O₈ content tons/mi²
2	H	H	1.000	37.78	2435.48	92 015.6	0.233	2800.0	10.0	109.562
3	H	H	1.000	24.22	753.85	18 259.8	0.227	4000.0	10.0	21.268
4	H	H	1.000	90.38	1043.75	94 328.9	0.229	850.0	34.0	110.848
5	H	H	1.000	22.56	2266.67	51 125.9	0.248	2500.0	10.0	64.880
6	H	H	1.000	6.20	89.37	554.1	0.294	2800.0	20.0	0.835
7	H	H	1.000	9.82	246.02	2415.5	0.235	2500.0	18.0	2.903
8	H	H	1.000	102.81	2441.18	250 983.3	0.280	2000.0	10.0	359.369
9	H	H	1.000	77.87	4375.00	340 678.9	0.403	4000.0	10.0	703.789
2	H	H	1.000	35.63	950.00	33 843.7	0.207	1000.0	10.0	35.800
3	H	H	1.000	74.50	4250.00	316 625.0	0.301	3000.0	10.0	488.349
4	M	M	0.667	15.42	84.09	1296.8	0.219	3000.0	25.0	1.452
5	M	M	0.667	9.10	314.43	2861.3	0.293	2500.0	5.0	4.291
6	H	M	0.833	22.45	1000.00	22 454.5	0.200	2000.0	8.0	22.998
7	M	L	0.500	49.61	5326.09	264 246.4	0.114	600.0	20.0	154.462
8	H	H	1.000	356.17	268.02	95 460.9	0.286	1000.0	5.0	140.027
9	H	H	1.000	29.65	2820.59	83 622.1	0.401	2000.0	10.0	171.862
0	M	M	0.667	4.97	623.95	3098.9	0.104	2500.0	15.0	1.653
1	H	H	1.000	39.16	2450.00	95 939.7	0.436	5000.0	16.0	214.284
2	H	M	0.833	7.47	944.83	7056.7	0.283	3000.0	10.0	10.231
3	M	M	0.667	2.73	2368.18	6458.7	0.215	1200.0	8.0	7.100
4	H	H	1.000	8.38	2387.00	19 991.1	0.240	3500.0	12.0	24.591
5	H	H	1.000	6.83	4000.00	27 333.3	0.461	3750.0	15.0	64.500
6	H	H	1.000	6.71	907.14	6090.8	0.198	4000.0	10.0	6.181
7	H	H	1.000	38.20	301.47	11 514.8	0.186	2000.0	15.0	10.973
8	H	H	1.000	9.21	1351.47	12 447.7	0.242	3500.0	10.0	15.417
9	M	M	0.667	18.00	2414.47	43 460.5	0.225	3000.0	7.0	50.101
0	H	H	1.000	19.22	1100.00	21 144.4	0.311	3000.0	9.0	33.691
3	H	H	1.000	10.48	2900.00	30 384.1	0.122	1500.0	6.0	18.954
5	H	M	0.667	6.39	2739.83	17 520.5	0.263	3900.0	6.0	23.618
6	H	H	1.000	34.74	3894.74	135 295.6	0.237	2500.0	6.0	164.227
7	H	H	1.000	44.25	3775.00	167 043.7	0.194	4000.0	20.0	165.802
8	M	M	0.667	82.95	922.73	76 537.7	0.277	2500.0	10.0	108.542
9	H	H	1.000	21.67	2013.23	43 620.0	0.263	3000.0	8.0	58.855
0	M	M	0.667	90.00	25.35	2281.6	0.346	1000.0	4.0	4.040
1	M	M	0.667	7.68	946.05	7269.7	0.289	2500.0	12.0	10.763
2	H	H	1.000	16.64	2746.59	45 703.3	0.329	3500.0	12.0	77.080
Average†				41.38	1896.68	70 269.0	0.281	2702.0	11.9	102.902
Standard deviation				61.56		89 126.9		1308.0	6.9	

† Weighted averages, using geologists' self-ratings (RTG) as weights.

U_3O_8 for the State of New Mexico for a particular geologist. The distributions of each of the 36 geologists were sampled in this fashion and the total ore, total U_3O_8 tonnages, and total number of deposits were averaged across the geologists, first for each cell and then for all cells, giving t'_s, u'_s, and n_s, the average of total tonnage of ore, tonnage of U_3O_8, and number of deposits for the State of New Mexico on the sth iteration

$$t'_s = \sum_{i=1}^{62} t'_{is}; \quad u'_s = \sum_{i=1}^{62} u'_{is}; \quad n_s = \sum_{i=1}^{62} n_{is},$$

where t'_{is}, u'_{is}, and n_{is} are the average (across geologists) tonnage of ore, average tonnage of U_3O_8, and average number of deposits for the ith cell on the sth iteration of sampling.

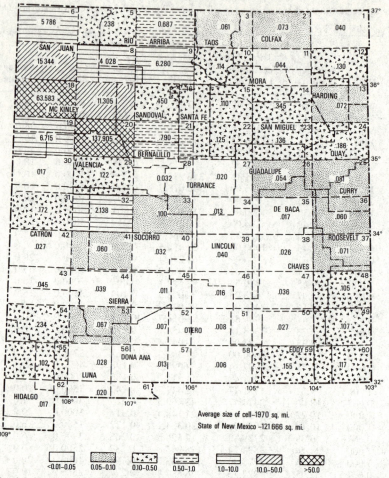

Fig. 13.14. Spatial distribution of U_3O_8 (tons/mi^2) after the Delphi reassessment. (Source: Ellis *et al.* 1975.)

Completion of the process just described constituted one iteration of sampling, creating one value each for t', u', and n for the state. By performing 1000 iterations, a data file for each of these quantities was generated. These data files were analysed statistically to yield histograms of n, t', and u'. The histogram of t' was used to decompose the histogram of u' to yield a histogram of grade q. These histograms for t', u', and q are exhibited in Fig. 13.16. The probabilities in Table 13.8 were obtained from the histogram for u'.

The numerical analysis performed using Monte Carlo methods approximates the true distributions only if there is no correlation between grade and number of deposits. The reasoning here is that the survey of opinion on number of deposits for a cell

provided probabilities that represent the conceptuali zation of $\bar{h}(n \mid G_D^0)$ instead of $h(n \mid q, G_D^0)$ where

$$\bar{h}(n \mid G_D) = \int_Q h(n \mid q, G_D) \cdot k(q \mid G_D)\, dQ.$$

Only if no correlation exists between grade and number of deposits is this consistent with regard t the geostatistical theory.

13.7. The oil resource appraisal by the US Geological Survey (circular 725): description critique, and comparison with Hubbert

13.7.1. *The nature of the appraisal*

The resource assessment reported in Circular 725 i basically a probabilistic appraisal of the potentia

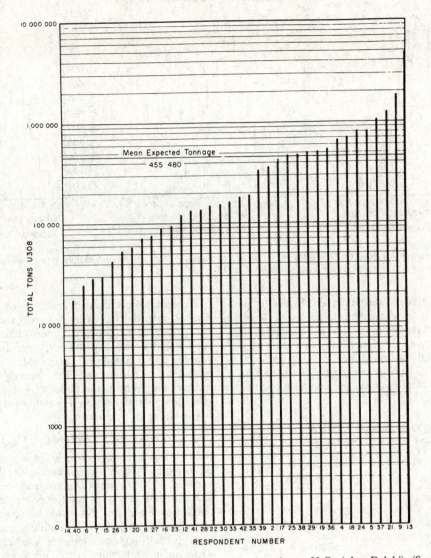

Fig. 13.15. Respondents' range of estimates in increasing order of total tons U_3O_8 (after Delphi). (Source: Ellis *et al.* 1975.)

supply of oil and gas from undiscovered deposits (Miller, Thomsen, Dolton, Coury, Hendricks, Lennartz, Powers, Sable, and Varnes 1975, p. 1).

> The estimates of undiscovered recoverable resources take into account relevant past history and experience and are based on assumptions that undiscovered recoverable resources will be found in the future under conditions represented by a continuation of price–cost relationships and technological trends generally prevailing in the recent years prior to 1974.

As thus described, Circular 725 reports on what

has been defined in this book as potential supply, not endowment or resources. Thus, it reflects not only the undiscovered endowment indicated by the geology of an oil province, but also the impact of economics and technology in transforming this endowment to potential supply. While the foregoing quote from Circular 725 makes it clear that an implicit economic assessment was made using pre-1974 prices and costs, it leaves some doubt as to the technologic conditions considered in the appraisal. What does the 'continuation of ... technologic

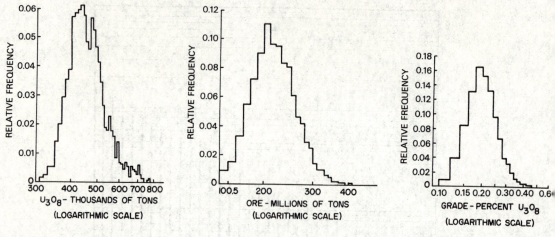

Fig. 13.16. Resources derived by New Mexico subjective probability study. Based on Delphi phase and aggregation b
Monte Carlo methods. (Source: Ellis *et al.* 1975.)

trends' imply? While this statement leaves technology undefined by suggesting some future level of technologic efficiency, the author has concluded from other accounts of the procedures that estimates of potential supply assumed pre-1974 technology as well as pre-1974 prices and costs. The use of a 32 per cent rate of recovery in the appraisal testifies to this fact.

TABLE 13.8. *Probability for U_3O_8 exceeding stated amount. (Source: Ellis et al. 1975.)*

Tons U_3O_8	Probability
740 000	0.025
675 500	0.05
598 800	0.10
566 300	0.15
540 000	0.20
509 200	0.30
490 500	0.40
471 100	0.50
451 900	0.60
435 300	0.70
418 300	0.80
396 000	0.90
380 300	0.95
367 100	0.975
320 000	1.000
Arithmetic mean U_3O_8	480 793
Modal U_3O_8	435 000
Median	471 100

95 per cent confidence interval:

$$367\,100 \leq M_{U_3O_8} \leq 740\,000$$

A geostatistical character was given to the ap
praised potential supply by requiring the participat
ing geologists to provide a most likely potentia
supply and a 5th and a 95th percentile potentia
supply. These quantities were used to construct a
probability distribution. The Survey's appraisa
methodology reflects the philosophy that the proba
bility for potential supply is conditional upon geol
ogy, economics, and technology

$$P(PS \geq ps \mid G_D, E) = \phi(ps \mid G_D, E), \quad (13.39)$$

where PS is a random variable, ps is a specific leve
of potential supply, a realization of the random
variable, G_D is the set of D geological conditions, and
E is the set of economic and technologic conditions.

For a given region, G_D would be observed and E
was specified as pre-1974 conditions and was con
stant for all regions. Since E was constant, the
variation in probability distributions across oil pro
vinces reflects variation in geology and deposit
parameters only, such as depth and reservoir charac
teristics. Nevertheless, eqn (13.39) which includes E,
is useful in establishing the perspective that the
probabilistic appraisal of potential supply reflects
both geological assessment and the implicit assess
ment of the impact of an assumed state of E in
transforming geologically-based endowment poten
tial to potential supply. Conceptually, the effect of
geological assessment by the geologist and the consid
eration of the specified economic and technologic
conditions was to define a probability distribution in
the mind of the geologist for potential supply. The
three quantities (most likely and the 5th and 95th

percentiles) provided by the geologist reflect the probability distribution indicated by the geological and economic assessment.

On the basis of empirical evidence and *a priori* reasoning, the Survey specified the form of ϕ

$$\phi(ps \mid G_D, E) = 1 - F\left[\frac{\ln ps - \mu}{\sigma}\right],$$

where F is the probability distribution function of a normal population having a mean of μ and a variance of σ^2

$$F\left[\frac{\ln ps - \mu}{\sigma}\right] = \frac{1}{\sigma(2\pi)^{\frac{1}{2}}}\int_{-\infty}^{ps} \times$$

$$\times \exp\left(-\frac{1}{2}\left(\frac{\ln(x) - \mu}{\sigma}\right)^2\right) d\ln(x).$$

The three quantities of potential supply that were provided in the subjective assessment were used to estimate the parameters μ and σ^2 of the lognormal distribution of potential supply for the area being evaluated.

13.7.2. *Methodology*

The appraisal can be viewed as consisting of seven phases

1. Gathering of primary data:
   a. basic geoscience data;
   b. previously made resource estimates.
2. Estimation of resources by geological analysis and assorted methods for inference or extrapolation:
   a. volumetric techniques using geological analogues for estimating yield factors;
   b. volumetric techniques employing arbitrarily selected yield factors when direct analogues were not available, such as in frontier regions;
   c. extrapolation of known producibility into untested regions of a province;
   d. using Hendricks (1965) potential-area categories.
3. Initial assessment of the subjective probability distribution by a representative of the Resource Appraisal Group, based upon consideration of data of 1 and 2.
4. Comprehensive review by the Resource Appraisal Committee and assessment by each member of the committee of his subjective probability distribution.
5. Review of estimates made by committee members and achievement of a consensus of the

committee about the subjective probability distribution.
6. Fitting of a lognormal probability distribution to the consensus subjective probabilities.
7. Monte Carlo analyses of the lognormal distributions of selected provinces to give a lognormal probability distribution for the aggregate of provinces, such as a probability distribution representing the lower 48 states, or one representing the entire US.

Approximately 70 geologists participated in the gathering of the primary data. For a mature, producing province, approximately 85 basic categories of information were reported on the data form. For frontier and offshore areas, approximately 60 categories of geological data were examined. These data were analysed and a one-page summary was passed on to the Resource Appraisal Committee. Among the data included in this summary were reserves, cumulative production, resource estimates previously made by 'outside' sources, the single-point estimate made by the geologist of the Survey who was responsible for the province, and the areas used for the geological analogies by which the estimate was made (see Fig. 13.17).

The summary information on geology, reserves, and production for a province was assigned to a member of the Resource Appraisal Group who completed stage two of the appraisal: the estimation of in-place resources, total recoverable resources, and remaining undiscovered recoverable resources. The estimates made by the member of the Resource Appraisal Group and all published and documented estimates were compiled on a summary form (Fig. 13.18). This completed phase two of the appraisal.

The representative of the Resource Appraisal Group who had been assigned to the province made a comprehensive review of the information and appraisals made in phase two and, on the basis of this review and on the assumption of the 'occurrence of oil and gas in commerical quantities', identified the most likely quantity of his subjective probability distribution and the 5th and 95th percentile values (see Fig. 13.19). In addition, these three quantities were summed and divided by three to give a 'statistical mean'. This completed phase three of the appraisal.

The representative of the Resource Appraisal Group responsible for a province presented a comprehensive summary of the geology and all pertinent information to the Resource Appraisal Group Committee. This committee reviewed summary sheets,

FORM #3

Region #8
RAC No. _____

PROVINCE SUMMARY SHEET

PROVINCE ___MICHIGAN BASIN___

*Stage of Exploration: Early SIL & ORD Intermediate DEV & U SIL Late PENN, MISS, U DEV
*Area (Mi²)-----Total Sed. Province: __122,000__ % Productive ≅ 25-35%
   Areas by Depth Units: 5000' ≅ 73,200   5000-10,000' ≅ 36,600
          10,000'-15,000' ≅ 12,200   15,000-20,000' _____
          20,000'-30,000' _____   30,000' _____

*Thickness of sediments (Ft.): Avg. __4,674__   Max. __14,000 - 15,000__

*Volume of sediments (Mi.³) __108,000__
   Total Province: _____
   % Drilled ≅ 60 %
   % Explored > 75 %

Stratigraphic Age Range: From __CAMBRIAN__   Through __JURASSIC & PLEISTOCENE__

*Producing and/or Prospective Horizons _____
   Age: a. SILURIAN b. DEVONIAN c. ORD, ORD-CAM d. MISS
   Gross Thickness: ≅4,130   3,655   3,660   760   Total: 12,205

*Dominant Lithology (Total Province)
   Type __CARBONATE, SANDSTONE, SHALE, EVAPORITES__
   % of Volume 47%   23%   18%   12%
   Ratio, Marine/non-marine ≅ 10:1

Types of Traps
   Stratigraphic __DOLOMITIZED CARBONATES, SAND PINCHOUTS, REEFS__
   Structural __ANTICLINAL, GRABEN FAULTING AND ALTERED CARBONATES__

*Structural Aspects
   Type Basin __INTERIOR BASIN, CRATON CENTER__
   Geometry __SYMMETRICAL -- GENTLE SLOPES (NEARLY SO)__

Indications of Hydrocarbons
   Producing Trends MISS & PENN - GAS, DEV TO ORD - COMBINED OIL & GAS, TAR GROSS AREA ≅ 38,455 M²
   Seeps, Tar Sands, etc. __OIL & GAS SEEPS - MINOR EXTENT__

Probable Source Beds (Age and Lithology) DEV MAJOR-CARB MINOR-SHALES, SIL CARB-50 SHALE-50, ORD SHALE-60 CARB-40

Major Seals (Age and Lithology) DEV THROUGH ORD, CARBONATE, EVAPORITES, & SHALE

Field Size Distribution: Avg.   R.Min.   R.Max.
   Oil (mill.bbls):   ≅ 5   < 1   > 150
   Gas (bcf):   ≅ 30   < 6   > 200

Nature of Hydrocarbons: Avg.   R.Min.   R. Max.
   API Gravity
   Sulfur Content
   *Recovery Factor   31.8   ≅ 10   ≅ 45

*Production, Reserves, & Resources: Crude Oil   NGL   Nat. Gas
   Cum. Production (bill.bbls.;tcf) 624,136,000 MILL   434,476 MILL CU FT.
   Measured Reserves   "   81,028,000 MILL   1,296,815 MILL CU FT.
   Indicated Reserves   "
   Inferred Reserves   "

*Wells Drilled to Date: __27,149__   Date: 1 / 1 / 73
   Exploratory Wells __13,800 (1/1/73)__
   Development Wells __13,349 (1/1/73)__

*Resource Estimates (Undiscovered--In Billion BBLS or Trillion Cu.Ft.)
                        Recoverable   In Place
   Outside Sources (MEM 15) .673-1.223 BILL BBLS , RECOVERABLE UNDISCOVERED RES.
   U.S.G.S. Evaluator ≅ 1 BILL BBLS , RECOVERABLE UNDISCOVERED RES.
   Analogs W ALBERTA, HUDSON BAY BASIN, ILLINOIS BASIN (PORTIONS OF THIS BASIN)
   RAG Estimate _____

*Province Qualitative Rating: Oil __GOOD__   Gas __FAIR__

Posted by: __KURT CARLSON__   Date __2-13-75__   Approved __S. Miller__ Date __2-17-75__

* Data most pertinent to resource appraisals.   2/4/75

Fig. 13.17. Province summary sheet (phase I). (Source: Miller *et al.* 1975.)

FORM # 4-A   REGION 8

Region # 8 MICHIGAN BASIN AREA   RAG No. _____
Province   MICHIGAN BASIN AREA
Province Area ____122,000____ (mi²) Province Volume: __108,000__ (mi³)

RESOURCE APPRAISAL --PROVINCE ESTIMATE

PRODUCTION AND RESERVES	OIL (Bill. BBLS)	NGL (Bill. BBLS)	GAS (TCF)
Cumulative Production: 12/73 API →	.627	.011 ← API 12/72 →	.135 12/72
Identified Reserves:			
Measured Reserves	.072	.025	1.549
Indicated Reserves			
Inferred Reserves (³/p = 3.19)	≅ .229	≅ .009	≅ .802 (³/p = .518)
Total (Cumulative & Identified):	.928	.045	2.786

UNDISCOVERED RESOURCES Resource Appraisal Methods	OIL (Billion Barrels) In-Place	Total Rec. Resource	Undiscovered Rec. Resource	NGL EST (Billion Barrels) In-Place	Total Rec. Resource	Undiscovered Rec. Resource	GAS (Trillion Cubic Feet) In-Place	Total Rec. Resource	Undiscovered Rec. Resource
METHOD I--VOLUMETRIC-ANALOG Yield Factors: Analog 1: MICHIGAN BASIN Analog 2: ILLINOIS BASIN									
Oil: 16,000 34,000	1. 5,400	1.728	.800	.108	.086 **	.0414	4.155	3.564	.778
Gas: 25 MM 20 MM									
Rec. Factors: 32/80/80	2. 11.475	3.672	2.744	.086	.069 **	.0241	2.70	2.16 TOO LOW	LOW —
METHOD IV: HENDRICKS' CATEGORIES Dis.-Rec. Factors: Category #: 4 (25/50/50)	12.200	3.05	2.122	1.220	.610	.565	30.5	15.25	12.464
Category #: 3	30.500	7.625	6.697	2.440	1.220	1.175	61.0	30.50	27.714
							ALL GAS FIGURES TOO HIGH		CAT 5 TOO LOW
METHOD: (III PRODUCTIVE - RECOVERY) PROCEDURE Yield Factors: Oil: 23 MM/M.² Gas: 4 MM/M.²	4.294	1.379	.451	.109	.087	.042	3.413	2.730	TOO LOW
Prod. Area/Unexpl. Area: 229 M.² / 7,527 M.²	5.694	1.914	.986	.151	.121	.076	4.733	3.786	1.000
DOCUMENTED RESOURCE APPRAISAL ESTIMATES: (UNDIS.)									
AAPG, Memoir 15, 1971 POSSIBLE	650	.293	1.179						
ALL HYDROCARBONS PROBABLE SPECULATIVE	680 7.343	.306 .886							
National Petroleum Council Estimates, 1973	1290 UNDIS - IN PLACE —		.413						4.8 (6.00 IN-PLACE)
ANOGRE Estimates									
OTHER METHOD II	2) 5,003 —	1601 —	673 —						
	6.722	2.151	1.223 1)						

Posted by DI   Date 2-20-75 Approved B. Miller Date 12/21/74

1) RANGE IS DEPENDENT UPON ASSUMPTION OF EXCLUDING OR INCLUDING ANOTHER ALBION - SCIPIO TREND.

** CONVERSION FACTOR : 32 BBLS NGL / 1 MM CUFT GAS (HENDRICKS, 1965)

DOCUMENTATION FOR RESOURCE APPRAISAL METHODS USED ON FORM 4-A

METHOD I Volumetric - Analog	METHOD II Explored Area - Recovery Procedures	METHOD III Productive Area - Recovery Procedure	METHOD IV Hendricks' Categories
Analog I Basin or Province Name: MICHIGAN BASIN (PRODUCTIVE AREAS) Yield factors used: /M.³ OIL 16,000 GAS 33 MM NGL PROPORTION Recovery factors used: 32/80/80	Areas Explored: 1. 6,943 M.² PENN-DEV 2. 1,232 M.² SIL 3. 5,608 M.² TRENTON & BLACK RIVER Areas Unexplored: 1. 6,857 M.² PENN-DEV 2. 18,840 M.² SIL 3. 35,622 M.² TRENTON-BLACK RIVER Yield per mi² of explored areas: 1. 397,315,157 BBLS/M.² PENN-DEV 2. 373,333,440 BBLS/M.² SIL 3. 38,863,602 BBLS/M.² T-BR (A-S EXCLUDED) 588,796,038 BBLS/M.³ (A-S INCLUDED)	Areas Productive (proved areas): 1. 172 M.² PENN-DEV 2. 34 M.² SIL 3. 23 M.² TRENTON - BLACK RIVER Areas Unexplored: 1. 6,857 M.² PENN-DEV 2. 528 M.² SIL 3. 36-142 M.² T-BR Yield per mi² of productive areas: 1. 2,338,963 BBLS/M.² P-D 2. 718,038 BBLS/M.² SIL 3. 1,019,908 - 4030,194 BBLS/M.² T-BR 1) SEE FOOTNOTE - P 4-A REC 32/80/80	Category # ___4___ Discovery-Recovery Factors: 25/50/50 Modifications: NONE Category # ___3___ Discovery-Recovery Factors: 25/50/50 Modifications: NONE
Analog II Basin or Province Name: ILLINOIS BASIN Yield factors used: OIL 34,000 GAS 20 MM NGL PROPORTION Recovery factors used: 32/80/80			

AAPG, Memoir 15, 1971: Tables: 10	Pages: 1160
NPC Estimates, 1973: Tables: 99, 292	Pages: 171, 367
ANOGRE Estimates:	
Other Published Sources: Date:	Pages:
Other Procedures:	

DEFINITIONS FOR RESOURCE APPRAISAL METHODS USED ON FORM 4-B

REASONABLE MINIMUM -- That quantity which the estimator associates with a 95% probability that there is at least this amount.

MOST LIKELY -- That quantity which the estimator associates with the highest probability (of occurrence) that there will be this amount.

REASONABLE MAXIMUM -- That quantity which the estimator associates with a 5% probability that there is at least this amount.

EXPECTATION --Also called "EXPECTED VALUE" or "BEST ESTIMATE" -- A mathematical term. It is the only value we are entitled to add if we combine estimates of similar quantities in other provinces.

$$E = \frac{R.\ Min. + M.\ L. + R.\ Max.}{3} = \frac{50 + 300 + 850}{3} = 400$$

MARGINAL PROBABILITY -- That probability which the estimator would assign to his basic assumptions that oil and gas accumulations are actually present in the province to be evaluated.

/27/75

Fig. 13.18. Initial appraisals of potential supply (phase 2). (Source: Miller et al. 1975.)

FORM # 4-B

Region #8 MICHIGAN BASIN   RAG No. _____
Province
RESOURCE APPRAISAL --PROVINCE ESTIMATE
Province Area   122,000   (mi²)
Province Volume: 108,000   (mi³)

PRODUCTION AND RESERVES	OIL (Bill. BBLS)	NGL (Bill. BBLS)	GAS (TCF)
Total (Cumulative & Identified)	.928	.045	2.786

REGIONAL REPRESENTATIVE Resource Appraisal	OIL (Billion Barrels) In-Place	Total Rec. Resource	Undiscovered Rec. Resource	NGL (Billion Barrels) In-Place	Total Rec. Resource	Undiscovered Rec. Resource	GAS (Trillion Cubic Feet) In-Place	Total Rec. Resource	Undiscovered Rec. Resource
a. Reasonable Min. (95% "at least")	3.681	1.178	.250 Anal	.113	.090	.045	4.1825	3.586	.800
b. Reasonable Max. (5% "at least")	9.15	2.928	2.000 *1	.681	.545	.500	5.983	4.786	2.000
c. Most Likely	5.40	1.728	.800 Anal	.181	.145	.100	4.858	3.886	1.100
d. Expectation: $\frac{a+b+c}{3}$	6.075	1.944	1.016	.325	.260	.215	5.108	4.086	1.300
Method:									
Rec.--Yield Factors:									
Classify: Hypothetical ___ Speculative ___									

Posted by B. Miller   Date 2-28-75

RESOURCE APPRAISAL GROUP Recommended Appraisal:									
a. Reasonable Min. (95% "at least")	3.85	1.23	0.300				4.482	3.586	0.800
b. Reasonable Max. (5% "at least")	9.16	2.928	2.000				5.982	4.786	2.000
c. Most Likely	5.10	1.630	0.700				4.807	3.886	1.100
d. Expectation: $\frac{a+b+c}{3}$	6.03	1.928	1.000				5.107	4.086	1.300
Method:									
Rec.--Yield Factors:									
Marginal Probability:									

Posted by B. Miller for RAG committee   Date March 7/75   Approved _____   Date _____

Fig. 13.19. Subjective estimates (phases 3, 4, and 5). (Source: Miller *et al.* 1975.)

data, all resource estimates, and the procedures of the representative. After completion of this review, each member of the committee identified the most likely and the 5th and 95th percentile quantities of his subjective probability distribution for resources. This completed phase four of the appraisal.

The estimates made by each member of the Resource Appraisal Group Committee were posted for review. Differences in estimates were discussed and resolved, and a consensus of the group was determined for the most likely and the 5th and 95th percentile potential supply quantities (see lower part of Fig. 13.19). The last step in phase five was a review of the consensus estimates by the representative and the geologist of the US Geological Survey who made the geological investigation and the initial single-point estimate for the region. If there were major disagreements, the entire evaluation was reconsidered.

Given the assumption that 'undiscovered recoverable resources' are distributed lognormally, and given the three consensus quantities (most likely and the 5th and 95th percentiles), estimation of the parameters of the lognormal is straightforward, provided that the consensus quantities describe a positively skewed distribution (the most likely value is closer to the small value than to the large value).

The analysis described through step 6 provided a probability distribution for 'undiscovered, recoverable resources' for each province. Given the identity of a probability distribution for each of n provinces, the probability distribution for the aggregate of the n regions requires the convolution of the n distributions. For example, let $f_1(x_1), \ldots, f_n(x_n)$ be the probability density functions for the n regions. Then, on the assumption that $X_1, \ldots, X_n$ are statistically independent, the probability density function for the joint occurrence of $X_1, \ldots, X_n$ is $\phi(x_1, \ldots, x_n)$, the product of the n densities

$$\phi(x_1, \ldots, x_n) = f_1(x_1) \cdot f_2(x_2) \cdot \ldots \cdot f_n(x_n). \quad (13.40)$$

Then, if the random variable Z is defined as the sum of the n random variables, $Z = X_1 + X_2 + \ldots + X_n$ the probability distribution for Z, $f(z)$, is computed from the joint density for the n Xs

$$f(z) = \int_{X_n} \ldots \int_{X_2} \phi(z - x_2 - x_3 \ldots - x_n; $$
$$x_2, \ldots, x_n) \, dx_2 \ldots dx_n \quad (13.41)$$

or, alternatively,

$$f(z) = \int_{X_n} \ldots \int_{X_2} f_1(z - x_2 - x_3 \ldots - x_n) \cdot f_2(x_2) \cdot \ldots$$
$$\ldots f_n(x_n) \, dx_2 \ldots dx_n. \quad (13.42)$$

The Monte Carlo analysis referred to in step 7 provides an approximation to $f(z)$ defined in (13.41). This is effected by a stimulated sampling of the populations represented by n distributions for $x_1, \ldots, x_n$ and the summing of these values to give a value for z. This is repeated many times to create a synthetic population of z values. This population is analysed statistically to give an approximation of $f(z)$. The approximation can be made as close as desired by increasing the number of iterations.

13.7.3. *Comments on methodology*

General

The effort made by the Survey to assemble relevant geological and resource data and to base its appraisal of undiscovered, recoverable resources on a systematic analysis of these data is commendable. Commendable also is the break with traditional practice indicated by the description of undiscovered, recoverable resources by a probability distribution. In this regard, Circular 725, overall, was well received by resource analysts. However, the appraisal has been criticized on a number of other grounds. Of course, this fact does not make the appraisal unique, for such is the fate of all appraisals.

It is well understood by most individuals engaged in oil or mineral resource appraisal that since estimation of the unknown involves models, the person or persons responsible for the model identification and for the probabilities are in a sense, 'damned if they do and damned if they don't!' No matter the model form that is selected, criticism will be forthcoming from some 'quarter'; so to speak, 'this goes with the territory'.

Hubbert's scholarly analysis is depreciated by some as nothing but 'curve fitting.' But, to others, it is a professional, courageous (since its result was not popular), and forthright analysis, because it was based upon rigorous analysis of 'hard' data, and these data were provided, along with equations and results, for anyone and everyone to scrutinize.

Similarly, the Survey is to be commended for its recent study because it incorporates comprehensive geological–resource analysis within a probabilistic structure; nevertheless, its methods will be criticized, perhaps just as strongly as were Hubbert's, but for different reasons. While some of those who depreciated the curve fitting of Hubbert are pleased with the basing of the resource estimates upon geology, others criticize this study because it constitutes 'guesstimates' which cannot be rigorously documented by an equation, hard data, or a fixed logic sequence.

Others, who fancy themselves to be the greatest of experts, will never accept a subjective probability study performed by anyone else but themselves. Surprising as it may seem, geologists commonly place little credibility in their fellow geologists when it comes to resource estimation or exploration decisions. This tendency seems to follow from the exploration failures experienced by the exploration geologist. Because an exploration geologist must live with these failures on a day-to-day basis, he is strongly aware of the inadequacies of his understanding of the geology–resource relationships. What the geologist would like to see is something new, something that significantly improves his decision-making by giving him additional data or new knowledge of relationships. Unfortunately, a resource appraisal generally must be made at the current level of information, which for the public may be less than it is for industry. Furthermore, a probability survey methodology does not add new geological theory. The best it can do is to encourage a critical use of theory and to provide data enhancement, data review, and consistent analysis. Some geologists prefer the multivariate geostatistical models to the subjective probability models. While these models are appealing for conceptual reasons, practical application on a large region is often hampered by the nonuniformity of data, a problem not easily treated in standard multivariate procedures. In addition building multivariate models takes considerable time, time that may not be available. Consequently, subjective probability assessment is an attractive and useful procedure, but it also has its pitfalls and problems. Comment on these will be made in Chapter 14, but first let us consider the issue of usefulness.

Usefulness

The appraisal reported in Circular 725, although much improved from the traditional single-point estimates, was found inadequate in one respect, the usefulness of the appraisal in addressing the economic issues raised by OPEC's oil embargo. As indicated in § 13.7.1, Circular 725 reports on potential supply from undiscovered deposits. This simultaneous appraisal of endowment potential and economics makes it difficult for resource economists to evaluate the impact of economic conditions different from those prior to 1974, such as the dramatic increase in oil prices caused by the embargo, on potential supply. The implicit economic analysis employed in Circular 725 reflects a synthesis of exploration cost and effectiveness, production technology, production costs, endowment, and probability. For the analysis of economic and technologic impact on potential supply, a probabilistic description of oil and gas endowment in terms of physical parameters of the deposits expected to occur would have been considerably preferred. In addition, such a decomposition may promote a more definitive geological assessment of resource potential.

A reasonable case can be made for restricting the purview of the geologist to the potential endowment indicated by geology. Even so, for the geologist to provide estimates, endowment must be defined as some bounded set of occurrences of oil and gas, as was indicated in the introduction to this book. This bounding should be based upon physical parameters, not economic ones. For example, oil endowment could be defined as all oil to a depth of 30 000 ft which occurs in anticlinal traps [5] having at least 500 000 barrels (bbl) of oil. Then, given a population bounded in this manner, endowment could be represented by a probability distribution for number of occurrences and a set of probability distributions for the physical characteristics of the occurrences. The complexity of the endowment model could be considerable, depending on the specification of the many physical characteristics, e.g. permeability and porosity of reservoir rock, oil–gas ratio, reservoir drive, sand thickness, etc.

The maximum value of decomposition would be achieved by relating size, concentration, permeability, and depth to economics and technology. This could be achieved through computer simulation of exploration and production, employing Monte Carlo analysis. Basically, such an analysis would require the definition of the probability of discovery as a function of amount of effort and the physical characteristics of the occurrences. Similarly, production costs (operating and capital) would be expressed probabilistically, given the physical characteristics of the deposits and the overall cost level. Sampling on the population of occurrences would yield a set of occurrences, each with its size, concentration, permeability, and depth. Simulation of exploration on this simulated population would yield a set of occurrences discovered, and simulation of production, given economic and technologic conditions (cost level, prices, exploration effectiveness, and per cent recovery), would yield the quantity of oil that could be produced, given unconstrained markets. The quantity produced, given an optimum allocation of exploration, would constitute potential supply. Iteration of this procedure and variation of the economic and technologic conditions would provide a set of data on potential supply for various conditions.

Statistical analysis of these data would allow the probabilistic description of potential supply conditional upon economics and technology.

An appraisal methodology similar in form to this stylized one but carefully constructed to represent best relationships would achieve two goals: the decomposition of the subjective probability assessment to the components of endowment and the description of potential supply in a manner such that the effects of economics and technology upon potential supply could be assessed and described probabilistically. Both goals are very worthwhile: the first one because it promotes critical analysis and introspection and thereby diminishes the potential for biases that can result from the heuristics (see Chapter 14) which usually are employed in subjective assessment and the second one because it yields an appraisal that is useful in answering the economic questions that face policy-makers in establishing a sound mineral policy.

The foregoing conceptualization is useful, because when potential oil supply is viewed as a system of components and interrelationships, the weight of the burden placed upon the geologist to appraise the resultant of this system (potential supply) becomes abundantly clear. The benefits of restructuring of the appraisal methodology to a systematic specification of the components of the system also are evident.

Comparison of the appraisal methodology of Circular 725 to this disaggregated system indicates the *possibility* for distortion or bias resulting from the use of heuristics to simplify the mental burden of assessing potential supply of oil and gas directly. That such bias is present or absent can not be proven; all that can be said is that the possibility for such is greater than it would have been had the appraisal been made using a system in which endowment and economics are separated and endowment is decomposed to its components.

Psychometric issues

A discussion of psychometric issues in the assessment of subjective probabilities is appropriate here, as it is for other appraisals reviewed in Chapter 13. Such a discussion is especially relevant as a commentary on this appraisal of potential oil supply

1. Because of the high level of aggregation—the estimation by a geologist of percentiles for the quantity of oil that exists in all traps within the region;
2. Because of the use of a group in assessing these percentiles.

Both of these practices carry the potential for introducing biases in estimates, the first because of heuristics that appraisers use, and the second because of interpersonal relations and psychological reactions. Since some psychometric issues are present in every appraisal that employs subjective probabilities, a description of these issues is made once, in Chapter 14, rather than repeating it in the discussion of each appraisal.

Setting aside heuristic bias and group dynamics, the Resource Appraisal Group Committee adopted some commendable procedures. One of these was the estimation privately, prior to group assessment, of the most likely and the 5th and 95th percentile quantities and then the posting of these estimates for review. A second one, and perhaps the most important one, was the discussion of the *geological reasons* for differences in opinions prior to the seeking of a consensus of the group.

13.7.4. *The supposed unanimity of recent oil resources estimates (Hubbert versus the Survey)*

The setting

If any one phrase could describe the various estimates of potential petroleum resources of the US in the last 10–15 years, it must be marked disagreement. In the case of oil and natural gas liquids, estimates made as recently as 1972 ranged from 53×10^9 bbl (Unidentified oil company 1973) to 458×10^9 bbl (Theobald *et al.* 1972). Other more recently made estimates fall within this range but still display great variation: 72×10^9 bbl (Hubbert 1974), 89×10^9 bbl (Unidentified company 1974), and 200–400×10^9 bbl (US Geological Survey—Gillette 1974). Notably, the high estimates were by scientists of the US Geological Survey using various forms of geologic analogy.

For many years, M. King Hubbert has staunchly defended lower estimates, challenging those made by the US Geological Survey. The battle between Hubbert and the Survey has not been restricted to numbers but also to methods.

The extrapolation by Hubbert of a time series of production and of discovery rates stands in marked contrast to the geology-based approach used by the Survey. The fact that the estimates made by these two very different methods also differed so greatly brought what were at times sharp criticisms of methods.

The publication of Circular 725, *Geological estimates of undiscovered oil and gas resources in the United States* brought a peace of sorts, for the esti-

mates of Circular 725 *appeared* to be not far from those of Hubbert, in a *strictly numerical sense.*

In the spring of 1975, shortly after release of Circular 725, Resources for the Future, under sponsorship of NSF, held a workshop on oil and gas resources. The fact that the study by the US Geological Survey had just been released gave this workshop a different character than it would have had otherwise. Although there was still interest in critiquing and comparing various methods, some of the urgency for critical examination had been dampened by a '*perceived unanimity*' of opinion about the size of the undiscovered oil and gas resources of the United States. Such perceived unanimity arose from a simplistic and improper comparison of the lower estimate made by the US Geological Survey of 50×10^9 bbl (using geological and probability methods) of undiscovered, recoverable resources to the 55×10^9 bbl estimated by Hubbert. Although the numbers are nearly equal, the conclusion that the two estimates are in general agreement is incorrect, as will be demonstrated in this section.

Prerequisite to a comparison of estimates is an understanding of what Hubbert attempts to estimate by his Q_∞. Examination of his methods makes it clear that Q_∞ is an estimate of the total quantity of oil that will ever be produced by a region. To arrive at undiscovered, recoverable resources, Hubbert subtracts from Q_∞ the sum of cumulative production plus reserves and that quantity which in the future will be added to reserves of producing reservoirs as 'extensions and revisions'

$$URS = Q_\infty - CP - RS - A, \qquad (13.43)$$

where CP is cumulative production, RS is reserves, URS is undiscovered, recoverable resources, and A is additions through extensions and revisions.

Just how reliably Hubbert's methods estimate Q_∞ is a relevant question, a question that was addressed in Chapter 2. That chapter demonstrated that Hubbert's approach leads to a conservatively biased estimate of Q_∞. While such a finding is an overriding consideration in evaluating Hubbert's estimates, the perspective in this chapter is to set this issue aside and focus on the 'kind of thing' that Hubbert estimates: just what is a proper comparison of his estimate with that of the US Geological Survey, and how much agreement is there between these two estimates?

The estimates [6]

Hubbert's 1969 estimate of Q_∞ for the conterminous US was about 165×10^9 bbl (Hubbert 1969). On the basis of later data revisions, Hubbert recalculated Q_∞ to be 172×10^9 bbl (Hubbert 1974). Just what this quantity means in terms of undiscovered, recoverable resources depends upon what is taken as reserves. Based upon 1972 data, Hubbert estimated the sum of all past, present, and future reserve additions to be approximately 143×10^9 bbl, implying 29×10^9 bbl as the estimate of undiscovered, recoverable resources for the conterminous United States.

Still employing Hubbert's estimate of Q_∞ but subtracting from it reserves of all categories for the conterminous US (45.7×10^9 bbl) as estimated by the US Geological Survey (Miller *et al* 1975) and the cumulative production through 1974 (105.5×10^9 bbl) we would arrive at a somewhat lower figure for the size of undiscovered resources in the conterminous United States

$$172 \times 10^9 - 105.5 \times 10^9 - 45.7 \times 10^9 \approx 21 \times 10^9 \text{ bbl.}$$

Based upon Hubbert's $\hat{Q}_\infty$ (172×10^9 bbl), the total quantity of oil to be forthcoming from the conterminous US, as of the end of 1974, is $172 \times 10^9 - 105.5 \times 10^9 = 66.5 \times 10^9$ bbl. Let's round this to 67×10^9 bbl as the estimate of potential supply from the conterminous US, based upon Hubbert's analysis. This quantity represents reserves plus undiscovered resources for the conterminous United States.

For Alaska, reserves have been estimated (Miller *et al.* 1975) at 16.3×10^9 bbl. Cumulative production has amounted to only 0.61×10^9 bbl. Thus, cumulative production plus reserves amounts to approximately 17×10^9 barrels. Hubbert is quoted (Miller *et al.* 1975) as estimating the degree of advancement of the petroleum and natural gas discovery in Alaska to be approximately 40 per cent, implying ultimate recoverable reserves of approximately 43×10^9 bbl, of which approximately 26×10^9 bbl consists of undiscovered resources.

To be consistent in the use of Hubbert's numbers, let us take 29×10^9 bbl as his estimate of the undiscovered resources of the conterminous US and add to it the 26×10^9 bbl of Alaska, giving 55×10^9 bbl as his estimate of the undiscovered resources for the total United States. Similarly, adding potential supply for the conterminous US (67×10^9 bbl) to 43×10^9 bbl of Alaska, gives 110×10^9 bbl as the estimate of the quantity of oil to be forthcoming from the total United States, based upon Hubbert's analysis and US Geological Survey reserves data. These estimates are summarized in Table 13.9.

The previous sections described the recently completed study of recoverable oil and gas resources in

TABLE 13.9. *Estimates based upon Hubbert's work*† *(as of the close of 1974. (Source: Harris 1977)*

	Conterminous US ($\times 10^9$ bbl)	Alaska ($\times 10^9$ bbl)	Total US ($\times 10^9$ bbl)
Undiscovered resources	29	26	55
Total future supply	67	43	110

† Figures are rounded.

the United States by the US Geological Survey (Miller *et al.* 1975). (From here on, the estimates described by Miller *et al.* (1975) will be referred to as the Survey's estimates.) The Survey's appraisal procedure yielded a lognormal probability distribution for undiscovered, recoverable resources.

Fig. 13.20 is the probability distribution representing undiscovered, recoverable oil resources of the total United States. It was from this probability distribution that the Survey determined the 90 per cent confidence interval for undiscovered, recoverable resources (*URS*) of the total US

$$50 \times 10^9 \text{ bbl} \le URS \le 127 \times 10^9 \text{ bbl.}$$

This interval should be interpreted in this way. On the basis of the probability analysis, Survey found that the probability for *URS* being greater than 50×10^9 but less than 127×10^9 is 0.90, or 90 per cent. It follows that there is a probability of 10 per cent that *URS* lies outside of these limits, i.e. it is not within this interval.

Besides the 90 per cent confidence interval, the Survey computed the expectation for the undiscovered, recoverable resources for the total United

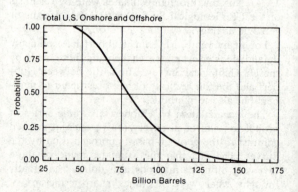

Fig. 13.20. Lognormal probability distributions for the undiscovered recoverable oil resources for total United States, onshore and offshore (0–200 m). (Source: Miller *et al.* 1975, p. 44.)

tates to be 82×10^9 bbl. This is the arithmetic mean (average) of the probability distribution. Similarly, expectations for the undiscovered, recoverable oil resources of Alaska and the conterminous US were computed to be 27×10^9 bbl and 55×10^9 bbl, respectively.

Misinterpretation of the Survey's estimates.

An effective means of introducing the erroneous interpretation of the Survey's analysis is through this following quotation from the *New York Times* (8 July 1975).

On June 20, the Interior Department, releasing results of a special two-year review, revised the estimate [of undiscovered recoverable oil resources] to 50 billion to 127 billion barrels. The review described as the 'most rigorous' ever, was under the direction of Harry Thomsen of the Survey's Denver office.

The Department explained that the lower figure represented a 95 per cent probability of accuracy and the higher figure a 5 per cent probability. Dr. Hubbert said that the lower figure roughly coincided with his own calculations.

The lower figure has been accepted by policymakers, who have renewed emphasis on coal, shale and uranium, a theme the Nixon–Ford Administration has sounded for at least four years.

The note within the brackets was inserted by the author.)

Let's examine paragraph 2. The first sentence of this paragraph represents a complete violation of probability laws. In truth, the probability for 50×10^9 is the *same* as the probability for 127×10^9, *exactly zero*

$$P(URS = 50 \times 10^9) = P(URS = 127 \times 10^9) = 0!$$

This result follows from the fact that *URS*, undiscovered resources, is a continuous random variable; therefore, the probability for it having any single value is zero.

The *correct* interpretation of the Survey's results is the probability that the undiscovered resources, *URS*, are *greater than* 127×10^9 is *exactly equal* to the probability that they are *less than* 50×10^9, 5.0 per cent.

$$P(URS < 50 \times 10^9) = P(URS > 127 \times 10^9)$$
$$= 0.05 \quad \text{or} \quad 5.0 \text{ per cent}$$

Or, alternatively, the probability that *URS* is *greater* than 50×10^9 is exactly equal to the probability that *URS* is *less* than 127×10^9.

If a single value is to be selected to represent this distribution of values, why should it be the 5th percentile value, 50×10^9 bbl? The 95th percentile,

127×10^9 bbl is just as reliable an estimate! In keeping with most statistical practice, if a distribution is to be represented by one number, it generally is one of the standard measures of central tendency

> Arithmetic mean (expectation)
> Median value
> Modal value
> Geometric mean.

The Survey computed the arithmetic mean to represent the entire distribution: $\overline{URS} = 82 \times 10^9$ bbl. The misinterpretation of the 90 per cent confidence statement provided by the Survey is common, even among persons engaged in the making of or the use of oil and gas resources appraisals. The same interpretation indicated in the above quotation was witnessed at the RFF conference on oil and gas resources, June 1975, a conference attended by resource specialists.

Consider the last paragraph of the news article. Why should policy-makers select the lower figure of 50×10^9? Possible reasons include

1. They have misinterpreted the probabilistic significance of the number, as demonstrated above;

2. They believe it is corroborated by Hubbert's analysis;

3. They understand correctly its meaning in a probability sense and purposefully adopt it because of their preference to be safe, meaning adopting policies that will assure at least adequate supplies of oil.

A word is in order concerning reason 3. The practice of being safe in making estimates of uncertain events has received much approval in the past on the premise that it is better to be pleasantly surprised than to find that you have overestimated. Such approval seems to stem from ascribing to underestimation virtues akin to those of modesty and ignores the interdependency of the economic system. When energy policy impacts upon programmes for the development of all energy sources, to predicate such policy upon a highly conservative estimate of the contribution of one energy source may result in just as large an economic cost as one based upon an overestimation. The impact of non-optimal energy policy can be likened to a sword that cuts on both edges. We should predicate policy on our best estimates, giving consideration to the spectrum of possibilities; we cannot afford to preferentially select a highly conservative estimate as the basis for policy.

As indicated in the second paragraph, Hubbert contributes to the adoption of the lower figure by drawing attention to its supposed similarity to his own. Such a comparison commits two errors:

1. Comparing the Survey's estimate of undiscovered resources to Hubbert's indirect estimate (an estimate made using $\hat{Q}_\infty$) is like comparing apples to oranges—they do not represent the same thing.

2. Even if both estimates represented the same thing, it is inconsistent on statistical grounds to compare a 5th percentile figure with Hubbert's estimate.

Let us examine the second error first. Consistency would require the comparison of 5th percentile values from each approach. But, what is Hubbert's 5th percentile estimate? No one knows, for it cannot be deduced from his nonstatistical approach.

Even so, a moment's thought leads to the conclusion that conceptually Hubbert's estimate is one value of a probability distribution of values. This implied probability distribution would reflect the joint probabilities for the continuation of past trends of the economy into the future.

A reasonable approach is to treat Hubbert's estimate as a central tendency, an average value, and to compare it to a measure of central tendency of the Survey's probability distribution; let us adopt the one computed by the Survey, the arithmetic mean: $\underline{URS} = 82 \times 10^9$ bbl. Note: this assumes that the two estimates represent the same things. If they did, we could compare 82×10^9 bbl with 55×10^9 bbl. The fact of the matter is that these estimates *differ far more* than is indicated by the numerical difference of 27×10^9 bbl.

The reasoning behind this statement is that Hubbert determines undiscovered recoverable reserves by subtracting what amounts to the sum of cumulative production, remaining proved reserves, and future reserve additions to known deposits from $\hat{Q}_\infty$, the ultimate recoverable reserves. By Hubbert's own admission and implicit to the models he employs, $\hat{Q}_\infty$ embodies all future extensions and revisions in reserves, future economic incentives, and future improved efficiencies of exploration, recovery, and exploration (Hubbert 1962).

> Thus, we do not have to worry about how much oil may be contained in known oil fields over and above the API estimates of proved reserves, or how much improvement may be effected in the future in both exploration and production techniques, for these will all be added in the future, as they have been in the past, by revisions and extensions to new discoveries. [Reproduced with permission from *Energy resources: A report to the Committee on National Resources*, Pub. 1000-D, National Academy Press, Washington, D.C., 1962.]

$\hat{Q}_\infty$ *is not* an estimate of the oil that ultimately will be produced under *static* conditions. Quite the contrary, it embodies changes in structure of the economy and in technology. In short, it represents the fulfilment of dynamics that have been present in the economy. Unfortunately, these dynamics are implicit and not explicitly noted or stated. Therefore, the degree of attainment of technology in the future must be inferred from supplementary analysis. One very important issue is the per cent of oil recovery that is implied by $\hat{Q}_\infty$. Is it the current average of 32 per cent? If, as has been suggested, $\hat{Q}_\infty$ embodies past trends in technologies and economic factors, then the answer must be that it is 32 per cent if, and only if, recovery efficiency has been constant over the years. What has been the improvement in recovery? A study on recovery efficiency by the National Petroleum Council concluded that recovery efficiency has improved by approximately 0.5 per cent per year over two decades (1945–65) (Elkins [7], personal communication). Since oil prices during this period remained relatively constant, such an increase in recovery efficiency has been attributed to improved technology.

Comparison

For comparative purposes, let us suppose that the Arab oil embargo had not occurred. Then, a reasonable assumption, one based upon the NPC study, seems to be that recovery efficiencies will continue to improve by 0.5 per cent per year to year 2000 [8]. Given these conditions, we would expect recovery to reach 42 per cent. What additional impact would the high prices, say US $13.00 per bbl for old oil as well as new oil, have on future recovery? Is it unreasonable to expect that if recovery could have reached 42 per cent by an extension of pre-embargo trends that it could reach 50 per cent by year 2000, given the high prices that are likely to prevail?

Now, Hubbert's full analysis was applied only to the conterminous US so, for comparative purposes, let us restrict our attention to this region. For the conterminous US, $\hat{Q}_\infty$ was estimated at 172×10^9 bbl. If we subtract cumulative production from $\hat{Q}_\infty$, we have 67×10^9 bbl as the sum of *new discoveries and the contribution from all improved technologies*, including *recovery* of *known deposits* as well as those to be discovered in the future.

In order to obtain a figure of like kind from the Survey's work, we need to do a little arithmetic; namely, we need to compute the oil in place in the conterminous US implied by production, reserves, and undiscovered recoverable resources

$$\text{Oil in place} = \frac{\begin{array}{c}\text{Cumulative prod.} + \text{reserves} \\ + \text{undiscovered recoverable} \\ \text{reserves}\end{array}}{\text{Recovery percentage}/100}$$

$$= \frac{(105.53 + 45.78 + 55) \times 10^9}{0.32}$$

$$= \frac{206.31 \times 10^9}{0.32} = 644.72 \times 10^9 \text{ bbl}$$

$$\approx 645 \times 10^9 \text{ bbl}.$$

Taking this figure as our estimate of oil in place within the conterminous US, the quantities of recoverable oil for selected recovery rates up to 60 per cent were computed; for example, given a recovery rate of 42 per cent, that which might have been expected if pre-Arab embargo trends were continued into the future, the quantity of recoverable oil that originally was available in known plus unknown deposits is estimated at 270.90×10^9 bbl. But, 105.53×10^9 bbl of this have been produced. Subtracting this quantity from 270.90×10^9 bbl suggests that the future supply of oil from the conterminous US under pre-Arab embargo conditions would have been 2.5 times that estimated by Hubbert (67×10^9 compared to 165.37×10^9 bbl). Should higher recoveries be reached, the estimates would be even more divergent. At 50 per cent recovery, the estimate increases to approximately 217×10^9 bbl, approximately 3.2 times Hubbert's estimate. Fig. 13.21 shows the estimated contributions of oil in known and unknown deposits (separately and combined) for recoveries ranging from 32 to 60 per cent.

Similar calculations were made for total US (conterminous US plus Alaska)

$$\text{Oil in place} = \frac{(106.136 + 61.99 + 82) \times 10^9 \text{ bbl}}{0.32}$$

$$= \frac{250.12 \times 10^9 \text{ bbl}}{0.32}$$

$$= 781.63 \times 10^9 \text{ bbl}.$$

Multiplying various recovery rates by this oil in place and subtracting cumulative total US production yielded estimates of remaining resources in known and unknown oil deposits. The results of these calculations are graphed in Fig. 13.22. For example, for a recovery rate of 50 per cent, remaining recoverable resources are estimated to be approximately 285×10^9 bbl. This estimate is approximately 2.6

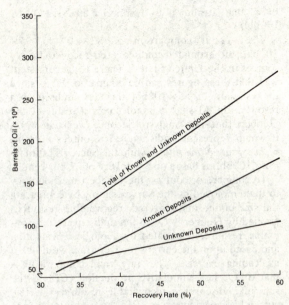

Fig. 13.21. Oil resource of conterminous US in known plus unknown deposits at specified recoveries. (Based upon 1975 US Geological Survey reserve and resource estimates.) (Source: Harris 1977.)

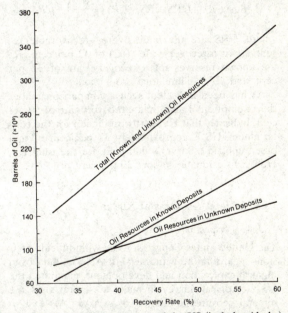

Fig. 13.22. Total oil resources of the US (includes Alaska) in known and unknown deposits at specified recoveries. (Based upon 1975 US Geological Survey resource and reserves estimates.) (Source: Harris 1977.)

times that attributed to Hubbert's analysis (110×10^9 bbl).

What about comparison of 82×10^9 to 55×10^9 bbl, the estimated undiscovered recoverable resources in the United States? There is no consistent way that these figures can be compared. First, since the estimate of 55×10^9 bbl includes undiscovered resources in Alaska, it is not solely a result of the Hubbert time-rate analysis. Second, even if it were, it would represent undiscovered resources at *some recovery rate of the future*, while the Survey's estimate (82×10^9 bbl) is based on a recovery of 32 per cent.

To compare or contrast the Hubbert methodology to that employed by the Survey simply by comparing the size of the undiscovered, recoverable resources implied by Hubbert's $\hat{Q}_\infty$ to the undiscovered, recoverable resources estimated by geological evaluation and based upon the current recovery rate would be a misleading exercise. The only valid comparison is that of $\hat{Q}_\infty$ less cumulative production (CP) to the sum of undiscovered recoverable resources (URS), currently known reserves (RS), and additional production from old fields at some improved recovery rate of the future (RC)

$$\text{Hubbert: } \hat{Q}_\infty - CP$$

$$\text{Survey: } \left((URS + RS + CP) \cdot \frac{(RC)}{(32)} \right) - CP$$

where URS are the undiscovered recoverable resources for a recovery rate (RC) of 32 per cent, RS are known reserves for a recovery rate of 32 per cent, and CP is cumulative production.

As has been indicated, such a comparison, under the assumption of an ultimate recovery rate of 50 per cent, indicates that Hubbert's prediction for the conterminous US is approximately 31 per cent of that based upon the Survey's data and, for the total US, Hubbert's estimate is about 39 per cent.

13.8. Mineral resources of Alaska

13.8.1. *Perspective*

The United States Congress, faced with difficult decisions regarding the withdrawal of Alaskan land from mineral exploration and development, mandated the US Geological Survey to make an appraisal of the mineral resources potential of Alaska. At least in concept, land withdrawals should reflect a rational evaluation of alternative and competing uses of the lands. Of course, Alaska's being rather unexplored required that this appraisal be of potential as well as

known mineral occurrences. Because of the urgency of the politics involved, the time allowed for the appraisal permitted only the use of existing geological and resource data and expert geologists as a means to responding to the mandate. Consequently, this appraisal employed the judgements of expert geologists, stated as subjective probabilities. The results of this appraisal can be found in the maps and tables of US Geological Survey Open File Reports 78-1-B through F (see Grybeck and DeYoung, Jr. [9]; Hudson and DeYoung, Jr. [10]; Eberlein and Menzie [11]; MacKevett, Jr., Singer, and Holloway [12]; and Patton, Jr. [13]; see also Singer and Ovenshine 1979).

13.8.2. *Methodology*

The methodology employed is similar in one respect to that employed by Harris (1973) in the appraisal of base metal resources of northern Sonora: namely, the geologist delineated on a map what were referred to as favourable areas—these were called prospecting zones in the Sonoran study. An area was delineated as favourable if it contained known mineral occurrences or if it exhibited geological conditions favourable for their occurrences. Some areas thought to have potential were not appraised because information was not sufficient to make estimates of number of deposits or grade and tonnage (personal communication, D. Singer 1978 [14]).

The procedure for estimating the endowment of a favourable region differed in a very important respect from previous subjective appraisals: the geologists did not estimate probabilistically the sizes and grades of the postulated undiscovered deposits. Quite the contrary, the availability of tonnage–grade models or data for a particular kind of deposit was viewed as a prerequisite condition for appraisal. In the author's mind, there are two possible rationalizations of this procedure.

1. Probability statements by the geologist about number of deposits are more credible if he has a good perception of the distributions of size and grade of known deposits and of their tonnage–grade relations (correlation).

2. The ability of the typical geologist to credibly describe distributions of sizes and average grades is somewhat suspect. Even more suspect is knowledge of the nature of the correlation between deposit size and grade.

There can be little argument that providing the geologist who is performing the appraisal with tonnage and grade models in advance of the appraisal is

TABLE 13.10. *Grade and tonnage models. (Source: Hudson and De Young, Jr. [10].)*

Deposit type	Tonnage and grade variables (units in parenthesis)	Number of deposits used in developing model	Correlation coefficient of listed variable with variable on line with it in column 2	90 per cent of deposits have at least	50 per cent of deposits have at least	10 per cent of deposits have at least
porphyry copper	Tonnage of ore (millions of tons)	41		20	100	430
	Average copper grade (per cent)	41	with tonnage of ore = −0.07 NS	0.1	0.3	0.55
	Average molybdenum grade (per cent Mo)	41		0.0	0.008	0.031
land porphyry copper	Tonnage of ore (millions of tons)	41		20	100	430
	Average copper grade (per cent)	41	with tonnage of ore = −0.07 NS	0.1	0.3	0.55
	Average molybdenum grade (percent Mo)	41		0.0	0.008	0.031
	Average gold grade- locally significant but not determined					
porphyry molybdenum	Tonnage of ore (millions of tons)	31		1.6	24	340
	Average molybdenum grade (per cent Mo)	31	with tonnage of ore = −0.05 NS	0.065	0.13	0.26
podiform chromite	Tonnage of Cr_2O_3 (tons)	268		15	200	2700
copper skarn	Tonnage of ore (millions of tons)	38		0.08	1.4	24
	Average copper grade (per cent)	38	with tonnage of ore = −0.44‡	0.86	1.7	3.5
	Average gold grade— locally significant but not determined					
mafic volcanogenic	Tonnage of ore (millions of tons)	37		0.24	2.3	22.0
	Average copper grade (percent)	37	with tonnage of ore = −0.13 NS	1.1	2.2	4.1
	Average zinc grade excluding deposits without reported grades (per cent)	19	with tonnage of ore = 0.03 NS	0.3	1.3	5.5
	Average gold grade— locally significant but not determined					
felsic and intermediate volcanogenic massive sulphide	Tonnage of ore (millions of tons)	89		0.19	1.9	18.0
	Average copper grade (per cent)	89	with tonnage of ore = −0.41‡	0.54	1.70	5.40
	Average zinc grade excluding deposits without reported grades (per cent)	41	with tonnage of ore = 0.25 NS	1.40	3.80	10.00
	Average lead grade excluding deposits without reported grades (per cent)	14	with tonnage of ore = −0.02 NS	0.20	0.95	4.80
	Tonnage contained gold	38	with tonnage of ore =	0.27	2.90	32.00

TABLE 13.10. *Continued*

Deposit type	Tonnage and grade variables (units in parenthesis)	Number of deposits used in developing model	Correlation coefficient of listed variable with variable on line with it in column 2	90 per cent of deposits have at least	50 per cent of deposits have at least	10 per cent of deposits have at least
	excluding deposits without reported gold (tons)		0.78‡			
	Tonnage contained silver excluding deposits without reported silver (tons)	46	with tonnage of ore = 0.82‡	5.00	80.00	1300.00
	Tonnage of ore (millions of tons)	48		0.23	1.20	5.90
Nickel sulphide	Average nickel grade (per cent)	48	with tonnage of ore = −0.03 NS	0.32	0.61	1.20
	Average copper grade (per cent)	48	with tonnage of ore = 0.03 NS with nickel grade = 0.04 NS	0.18	0.47	1.20
Mercury	Tonnage of contained mercury (tons)	165		0.09	3.10	120.00
Vein gold	Tonnage of contained gold (tons)	43		0.29	3.30	38.00
Skarn/tactite tungsten	Tonnage of ore (millions of tons)	31		0.024	0.63	17
	Average tungsten grade (per cent W)	31	with tonnage of ore = −0.34 NS	0.24	0.51	1.10

Related data occur on line from column to column; all data in metric units. NS, not significant;
† significant at 5-per cent level;
‡ significant at 1-per cent level.

preferred practice. For, even if the geologist does not believe, for geological reasons, that these models apply to his region, these models provide him with the only data that are available and a basis for exploring and describing the effects of the special geological circumstances on size and grade. More usually, the geological information for endowment appraisal—and sometimes the science—does not provide for discriminating differences in grades and tonnages of postulated deposits from known deposits of a like kind (mode of occurrence). When that is the case, the statistical models, which are based upon data of deposit size and grade, are far superior to distributions based upon subjective probabilities. Table 13.10 shows the deposit tonnage and grade models developed and employed in the appraisal of the mineral resources of Alaska.

Having delineated the favourable areas and having the tonnage and grade models for reference, the task of appraisal consisted of providing subjective esti-

mates of the 10th, 50th, and 90th percentile values for number of deposits for each mode of occurrence in each of the favourable areas. MacKevett *et al.* ([12], pp. 9–10) describe this estimation.

The general procedure followed in deriving the resource estimates consisted of: (1) using geology to delineate areas that either have known deposits of a particular type or areas that are favorable for containing them, (2) where possible, providing information on grades and tonnages of similar deposits based upon careful study of geology and grades and tonnages of well explored deposits, and (3) where possible, subjectively estimating the number of deposits of each type in each delineated area using the number of known deposits, the amount of favorable geology, the extent of exploration, and in some cases supplementary geochemical and geophysical data.

It should be noted that the 10th, 50th, and 90th percentile values are for a cumulative distribution in which probability is cumulated from the right to the left; in other words, the 90th percentile value is that number for which there is a probability of 0.90 that

TABLE 13.11. *Subjective probabilities and number distributions.* (*Source: Charles River Associates 1978.*)

Region in aska	(2) Percentiles 90	(3) 50	(4) 10	(5) Distribution	(6) Parameters k or λ	(7) p	(8) Error	(9) Expectation	(10) Mode of occurrence
astern Southern 8	1	2	4	Poisson	1.742		0.85×10^{-2}	1.74	Mafic vol. m.s.
astern Southern 10	2	4	8	Neg. binomial	5.793	0.692	0.57×10^{-2}	4.01	Mafic vol. m.s.
astern Southern 21	1	2	5	Neg. binomial	3.073	0.661	0.19×10^{-1}	2.03	Mafic vol. m.s.
astern Southern 22	2	3	4	Poisson	1.873		0.37	1.87	Porphyry
astern Southern 23	2	3	5	Poisson	2.488		0.59×10^{-1}	2.49	Porphyry
astern Southern 24	0	1	2	Poisson	0.550		0.27×10^{-1}	0.55	Porphyry
astern Southern 25	0	1	2	Poisson	0.550		0.27×10^{-1}	0.55	Porphyry
astern Southern 26	0	1	3	Neg. binomial	1.371	0.658	0.14×10^{-9}	0.90	Porphyry
astern Southern 28	0	1	3	Neg. binomial	1.371	0.658	0.14×10^{-9}	0.90	Porphyry
astern Southern 30	1	2	5	Neg. binomial	3.073	0.661	0.19×10^{-1}	2.03	Porphyry
astern Southern 31	6	8	11	Poisson	7.151		0.73×10^{-1}	7.15	Porphyry
astern Southern 32	4	6	9	Poisson	5.484		0.19×10^{-1}	5.48	Porphyry
astern Southern 32	8	10	14	Poisson	9.544		0.36×10^{-1}	9.54	Skarn
astern Southern 33	3	5	9	Neg. binomial	9.622	0.509	0.19×10^{-1}	4.90	Contact metamorphic
astern Southern 33	0	1	3	Neg. binomial	1.371	0.658	0.14×10^{-9}	0.90	Porphyry
astern Southern 34	4	6	10	Neg. binomial	20.880	0.281	0.13×10^{-1}	5.87	Porphyry
astern Southern 34	2	4	9	Neg. binomial	3.300	1.297	0.11×10^{-1}	4.28	Felsic & inter. vol. m.s.
astern Southern 35	1	3	9	Neg. binomial	1.381	2.646	0.72×10^{-2}	3.65	Felsic & inter. vol. m.s.
astern Southern 35	1	2	5	Neg. binomial	3.073	0.661	0.19×10^{-1}	2.03	Porphyry
astern Southern 36	0	1	4	Neg. binomial	0.676	1.786	0.31×10^{-8}	1.21	Porphyry
astern Southern 38	1	2	4	Poisson	1.742		0.85×10^{-2}	1.74	Porphyry
astern Southern 41	4	9	20	Neg. binomial	2.682	3.780	0.42×10^{-2}	10.14	Felsic & inter. vol. m.s.
astern Southern 41	1	2	4	Poisson	1.74		0.85×10^{-2}	1.74	Porphyry
astern Southern 42	5	7	12	Neg. binomial	14.374	0.497	0.23×10^{-1}	7.14	Felsic & inter. vol. m.s.
Vestern Southern 2	0	1	3	Neg. binomial	1.371	0.658	0.14×10^{-9}	0.90	Mafic vol. m.s.
Vestern Southern 3	0	1	3	Neg. binomial	1.371	0.658	0.14×10^{-9}	0.90	Mafic vol. m.s.
Vestern Southern 3	0	1	2	Poisson	0.550		0.27×10^{-1}	0.55	Porphyry
Vestern Southern 5	5	9	15	Neg. binomial	10.329	0.873	0.84×10^{-3}	9.02	Porphyry
Vestern Southern 6	1	3	8	Neg. binomial	1.8072	1.856	0.38×10^{-2}	3.36	Porphyry
Vestern Southern 13	10	20	35	Neg. binomial	5.422	3.869	0.41×10^{-4}	20.97	Island arc porphyry
Vestern Southern 7	5	7	10	Poisson	6.313		0.44×10^{-1}	6.31	Skarn
Vestern Southern 7	1	2	6	Neg. binomial	1.657	1.408	0.29×10^{-1}	2.33	Porphyry
Vestern Southern 9	30	50	75	Neg. binomial	10.250	4.996	0.15×10^{-3}	51.21	Island arc porphyry
Central 28	5	9	13	Poisson	8.646		0.13×10^{-2}	8.65	Porphyry
Central 29	0	2	4	Poisson	1.736		0.15×10^{-2}	1.74	Felsic & inter. vol. m.s.
Brooks Range 12a	15	20	30	Neg. binomial	16.927	1.213	0.13×10^{-1}	20.54	Felsic & inter. vol. m.s.
Brooks Range 12b	3	8	30	Neg. binomial	0.985	12.624	0.20×10^{-1}	12.43	Felsic & inter. vol. m.s.
Brooks Range 12c	1	5	20	Neg. binomial	0.805	9.671	0.37×10^{-2}	7.78	Felsic & inter. vol. m.s.
Brooks Range 17	1	3	5	Poisson	2.464		0.39×10^{-1}	2.46	Porphyry

the actual number equals or exceeds it. Table 13.11 shows the three percentiles for number of copper deposits for those favourable areas thought to have copper potential. Note also, that the last column of this table identifies the mode of copper occurrence. Furthermore, Table 13.10 provides the tonnage and grade models for each of these modes. For example, Eastern Southern Region 32 is estimated to have potential for two modes of copper deposits: porphyry and skarn. For porphyry deposits we have the following description of copper endowment.

Number of porphyry deposits n:
$$P(N \geq 4) = 0.90,$$
$$P(N \geq 6) = 0.50,$$
$$P(N \geq 9) = 0.10.$$
Deposit size (tonnage of material), t (tonnes) (Table 13.10):
$$P(T \geq 20 \times 10^6) = 0.90,$$
$$P(T \geq 100 \times 10^6) = 0.50,$$
$$P(T \geq 430 \times 10^6) = 0.10.$$

Deposit average grade q (per cent):

$$P(Q \geq 0.1) = 0.90,$$

$$P(Q \geq 0.3) = 0.50,$$

$$P(Q \geq 0.55) = 0.10.$$

Note that for this same region, but for skarn copper deposits, the percentile values for number of deposits are somewhat larger, deposit tonnages are much smaller, and deposit grades are much higher.

13.8.3. *An estimate of expected copper in porphyry deposits*

Suppose that we wished to have an estimate of the expected number of porphyry deposits for the collection of all favourable areas. Provided that we had an expected number for each favourable area, this expectation could be obtained simply by summing the expectations of the favourable areas. However, the appraisal of endowment did not provide expected values for number of deposits for each favourable area. Instead, we have for each area the three percentile values, shown in Table 13.11, and expectations cannot be computed directly from these values. But, one way that the expectations can be computed is to fit a probability distribution to the percentile values and then determine the expectation of the fitted model.

Two common discrete probability models are the Poisson and the negative binomial (see Table 13.12).

Usually, these distributions are fitted from moment computed on statistical data. In this case, such data are not available; instead we have three percentile and associated values. Each of the two distribution was fitted to the percentile data by computer search (see Charles River Associates 1978). This procedure requires computing for the given value of the parameter(s) a theoretical probability, by the equations of Table 13.12, for each percentile value and comparing the theoretical probability (percentile) with that specified in the subjective survey. The parameters were varied until values were found for which the theoretical percentiles matched closely those that were specified in the appraisal.

Table 13.11 provides the identity of the best fitting distribution (column 5), the parameter(s) of that distribution, an error measurement (see Table 13.12 for a definition), and an expected value for number of deposits (column 9). For each mode of occurrence, these expectations were summed across all favourable areas; these are reported in Table 13.13. Thus, analysis of the appraisal by the US Geological Survey shows that 136 porphyry deposits are expected to occur in Alaska, and lesser numbers of the four other modes of occurrence.

So far, we have expected numbers of copper deposits of various kinds. In order to compute the expected endowment of Alaska in copper metal, we must first compute the expected quantity of metal per deposit. Since for porphyry deposits the correlation between deposit tonnage and grade is not statis-

---

TABLE 13.12. *Mathematical relations for fitting probability models to subjective probability statements on Alaska. (Source: Charles River Associates 1978.)*

1. Poisson: $p(N = n) = \dfrac{\lambda^n e^{\lambda}}{n!} = f(n)$.

2. Negative binomial: $p(N = n) = (q^{-k}) \dfrac{(k + n - 1)!}{n!\,(k-1)!} \left(\dfrac{p}{q}\right)^n = f(n)$,

where $p = \dfrac{S_n^2 - \bar{n}}{\bar{n}}$, $k = \dfrac{\bar{n}^2}{S^2 - \bar{n}}$, $q = 1 + p$,

S_n^2 = variance of n; $\bar{n}$ = mean of n.

3. Let $p'(N \geq n) = f(n) + f(n+1) + \ldots + f(n+m)$,

where $f(n + m + 1) < 0.0001$.

4. DIF† $= \left(1 - \dfrac{p'(N \geq n_1)}{p(N \geq n_1)}\right)^2 + \left(1 - \dfrac{p'(N \geq n_2)}{p(N \geq n_2)}\right)^2 + \left(1 - \dfrac{p'(N \geq n_3)}{p(N \geq n_3)}\right)^2$,

where $p(N \geq n_i)$, $i = 1, 2, 3$ are the subjective probabilities
$p'(N \geq n_i)$, $i = 1, 2, 3$ are the theoretical probabilities.

---

† DIF is an error measure.

TABLE 13.13. *Expected number of copper deposits in Alaska. (Source: Charles River Associates 1978.)*

Mode of occurrence	Expected number of deposits
Porphyry	136
Mafic volcanogenic massive sulphide	8
Felsic and intermediate volcanogenic massive sulphide	68
Skarn	16
Contact metamorphic	5

tically significant (see Table 13.10), parameters of the lognormal distributions for tonnage and for grade can be estimated separately. The parameters of these independent lognormal distributions have been estimated (D. Singer, personal communication, 1978 [14]):

Deposit tonnage $\mu_t = 7.9764$, $\sigma_t = 0.5161$

Deposit grade $\mu_q = -2.590$, $\sigma_q = 0.268$.

The expectations for tonnage and grade computed from these parameters are approximately: 192 000 000 tonnes and 0.31 per cent Cu, respectively, giving an expectation of 595 200 tonnes of copper per porphyry deposit. Thus, given an expectation of 136 deposits, the copper expected to occur in porphyry deposits is approximately 81 000 000 tonnes. At a price of US \$1.00 per pound, this amounts to a gross value of approximately 160×10^9 US dollars.

Of course, the Alaskan appraisal is of endowment only, not potential supply. Estimation of potential copper supply for specified prices would require the subjecting of this endowment to analysis of the economics of exploration and production in the physical and economic environments of that region.

13.9. Uranium endowment estimates by NURE

13.9.1. *General commentary on the NURE appraisal*

In October 1980, a report entitled 'An assessment report on uranium in the United States' was issued by the US Department of Energy. This report is the culmination (1974–80) of the largest and most intensive single effort ever undertaken anywhere in the world for the evaluation of the endowment and resources of a nation in a mineral or in an energy source.

The assessment described in the aforementioned report was part of the United States NURE (National Uranium Resource Evaluation) programme. This programme consisted of many elements, including aerial radiometric and magnetic reconnaissance, hydrogeochemical and stream sediment reconnaissance, drilling and logging, geological mapping, and resource appraisal. The report is comprehensive, covering uranium supply, reserves, potential resources, and undiscovered endowment. Only one of these topics, the estimation of undiscovered endowment, is considered in this section.

The contribution made by NURE to promoting and supporting 'resource' appraisal as a geological activity has been very great. This judgement does not require that the methodology developed in the NURE programme is of the best or ultimate form—in fact, later in this section, this methodology is criticized for the way that it was applied—or that the estimates are highly credible. What this judgement *does* recognize is the fact that apart from meeting a national need for uranium resource and potential supply numbers, the NURE programme can be seen as a valuable experiment in the large-scale, real-time, implementation of geoscience and a probabilistic appraisal methodology in a consistent manner. The magnitude of this task needs proper appreciation, for besides the usual problems attendant to managing large, mandated national programmes, this programme had to pioneer both the *cause* of and *method* for using geology to estimate unknown uranium endowment. Not the least of the problems encountered was the resistance of some geologists to the appraisal task because of an imagined corruption of pure geoscience by having to use it to estimate potential uranium endowment. It must be true that among the services of NURE are (1) the involvement of a large number of geologists in generating basic geoscience (geology, geophysics, and geochemistry) information on many quadrangles for which such information had been meagre and (2) the exposure of some of these geologists to the concepts, challenges, and difficulties of translating geoscience to uranium endowment. For most this was at least enlightening, and for some disturbing, because it exposed otherwise unrecognized deficiencies in methodology and in geoscience–resource theory. A most important result of this effort is the educational impact of this involvement. Future appraisals will benefit considerably from this contribution.

Because of the importance of uranium resources to

national energy policy at the time that NURE was initiated, NURE had to contend with greatly increased standards of credibility for estimates. One result of this was the abandonment of point (single number) estimates made by geological analogy (see Chapter 4) for a probabilistic description. Since such methodology was, and still is, in an emerging state, the NURE programme had to pioneer the identification of a probabilistic methodology that could be applied on grand scale and could be used consistently by many geologists, some of whom were not experienced in resource assessment. In retrospect, which is a privileged perspective, one of the important lessons taught by the NURE appraisal is how too little effort can be devoted to the resource and probability estimation, particularly in view of the years devoted to geoscience. Because of the importance of this lesson to future appraisals, an in-depth critique will be provided later in this chapter on the elicitation of estimates.

In view of the criticisms that will be made of part of the NURE methodology, it is essential that it be recognized that any real appraisal effort always requires a compromise of methodology because of time, availability of geoscience data, expertise, cost, and intended use of the estimates. In some cases, best practice must be severely compromised. To some extent the NURE appraisal was compromised by attempting to do too much in too short of a time. Probably, this compromise is, to a great degree, responsible for some of the shortcomings that are identified later in this chapter. Finally, at the same time that this national appraisal was being made, DOE was actively exploring other methods of appraisal and ways of improving upon the NURE methodology. One result of research supported by NURE is the substance of Chapter 15.

13.9.2. *Scope of this section*

Some comment on the scope of this section has already been offered; namely, that it examines only the appraisal methodology of potential (unknown) uranium endowment. Thus, no description is provided of the economic analysis of the endowment for the description of resources or potential supply that this endowment may provide for specified economic conditions. Furthermore, this section will not examine or describe, except very superficially, the statistical processing of subjective estimates and the geological analysis that preceded the endowment estimation stage. The emphasis of this section is mainly upon the overall appraisal design and upon

the elicitation of the geologists' judgements (percentile values and probabilities). This emphasis is purposeful, because these are critical, but often slighted, steps in the use of geological experts in making appraisals of uranium endowment, and, the NURE appraisal affords a useful and effective means for commentary.

13.9.3. *Logistics and approach in general*

The NURE appraisal methodology can be summarized as combining methods of geological analogy and subjective probability elicitation for the probabilistic description of undiscovered uranium endowment. Consequently, the logistics and approach of the appraisal, if well conducted, should be expected to support sound geological analysis and the elicitation of judgement in quantitative terms. The NURE appraisal programme for undiscovered endowment can be viewed as consisting of five major activities.

1. Geological investigation of evaluation (NURE) regions and preparation of a multi-map folio for each 2-degree quadrangle.

2. Support analysis—the organization of geological and resource information to be used for the selection of favourable areas and in estimation of undiscovered endowment.

(a) Selection of the control areas, the areas to be used for analogy, i.e. for the identification of favourable areas and in the estimation of their endowment;

(b) Identification of recognition criteria for each geological environment (represented by one or more control areas);

(c) Construction of quantitative estimates of appraisal factors (components of endowment) on each control area.

3. Selection of favourable areas, areas which were subsequently submitted to resource evaluation.

4. Elicitation of appraiser's subjective probabilities for the components of endowment and of P^0, the probability for at least one deposit of at least 10 tons of U_3O_8 (given the 0.01 per cent U_3O_8 cut-off grade).

5. Statistical analysis of subjective estimates; this required the fitting of probability distributions and their mathematical manipulation.

Activity 1 was performed by a PI (principal investigator), a geologist or team of geologists who contracted to perform the geological evaluation, select the favourable areas, and provide the subjective estimates (or percentile values). Being that Activity 1 equired basic geological investigation and that there were over 600 quadrangles—only 135 were completed—this was on-going throughout the NURE programme. The 2-degree quadrangles were used to coordinate the various kinds of geoscience information—geology, geochemistry, geophysics, mineral occurrence, drilling, and logging—generated by NURE. Geologists spent an average of 4 man-years in field examination and the preparation of the multi-map folio for each of the 135 completed quadrangles (US Department of Energy 1980, p. 4). Concurrent with the basic geological investigations of Activity 1, US DOE and Bendix personnel performed Activity 2, the support analysis. This consisted of compiling in useful form the geological and resource information for the known resource regions which served as control areas for geologic analogy.

On the basis of (1) geological investigation of the evaluation region and (2) recognition criteria developed from control areas, the PI identified favourable areas. The geological bases for these delineations by the PI subsequently were reviewed by a team consisting of DOE, Bendix, and in some cases USGS geologists. This review and subsequent modifications completed Activity 3. Generally, activities 1 through 3, although great in magnitude, were very well done. In fact, the level of data developed and geoscience employed in the identification of the favourable areas is an impressive feature of the NURE appraisal programme.

As originally conceived, once the geologist (PI) had completed Activity 3, he was to prepare himself for Activity 4, which essentially requires the geologist to bridge from geology to uranium endowment. The PI presented himself before a team of geologists who elicited from him probability statements about the states of the components of endowment. These statements were intended to reflect both geological variability—the influence of the geology of that area being appraised upon the levels of the components—and uncertainty in the mind of the PI about the actual states of the components. There is no doubt that Activity 4 was the least satisfying and most poorly executed of the activities. More will be said about this in a later section.

Subsequent to the completion of the elicitation of subjective estimates for the endowment components, these estimates were subjected to mathematical analysis designed to produce for each favourable area a formal probability distribution for the quantity of U_3O_8 in that region. In addition, this activity was designed to compute mathematically distributions for various aggregates of areas and stratigraphical units.

13.9.4. *The methodology in perspective and in comparison with other subjective probability appraisal methodologies*

Some features of other, previous appraisals described in Chapter 13 are present in this methodology. Favourable areas, first used by Harris (1973) and Donald [1] in the Sonoran appraisal and later by the US Geological Survey's appraisal of Alaska (Grybeck and DeYoung, Jr. [9]; Hudson and DeYoung, Jr. [10]; Eberlein and Menzie [11]; Mac-Kevett, Jr. *et al.* [12], are at the very foundation of the NURE methodology. Similarly, the use of control areas and formal geological analogy is a carry-over of earlier practice, initiated by forerunners of DOE (ERDA, AEC), as demonstrated by Hetland (1979)—see Chapter 4. Decomposition of uranium endowment to components is similar in concept to decompositions of previous appraisals, e.g. number of deposits and deposit tonnage and grade, but different in identity of components. Finally, the elicitation of expert opinion about these components is similar in concept to other, earlier appraisals, particularly that by the US Geological Survey for oil resources (Miller *et al.* 1975) in which the geologist was asked for a modal value and two percentile values.

One major innovation of the NURE programme over previous appraisals is the definition of the objective of the appraisal as endowment, not resources, and the support of this estimation by a formal description of an endowment cut-off size and grade that were below those of economic interest at that time

$$\text{Minimum size} = 10 \text{ tons of } U_3O_8,$$

$$\text{Minimum grade} = 0.01 \text{ per cent } U_3O_8.$$

In addition, the appraisal of endowment for these unfamiliar conditions was supported by appropriate tonnage and grade relations developed on each of the control areas. These models were employed by the geologist in inferring from magnitude and quality of endowment for familiar grades and sizes to endowment for the cut-off conditions.

While the concept of decomposing endowments to components was not new, the identities of the components used in NURE are different from those of other appraisals. U_c, the magnitude of endowment conditional upon the presence of at least one deposit of at least 10 tons of U_3O_8 and having a grade of at least 0.01 per cent U_3O_8, was decomposed to four components A, F, T, G

$$U_c = A \cdot F \cdot T \cdot G, \tag{13.44}$$

where A is the projected surface area of favourable area in square miles [15], F is the fraction of A that is underlain by endowment, T are tons of endowed rock per square mile within $A \cdot F$ [15], and G is the average grade of endowment, in decimal fraction form.

The decomposition appears to be in part a carry-over from the format of previous appraisals designed to produce point estimates by geological analogy (see Chapter 4). If this were the only explanation for the decomposition, it would be inadequate, for decomposition is itself a very important part of an appraisal methodology which requires a geologist to infer from geological relations to the magnitude of endowment. Conceptually, decomposed endowment should consist of components that can be related by the geologist to the geological evidence available to him and to concepts of his geoscience. Of course, this is a very big order, one which cannot be met fully because of limited geoscience and limited geological and deposit data. Even so, any decomposition should be the best possible, given all other considerations, in terms of facilitating this inference and at the same time producing a description of endowment that satisfies the intended use of the estimate.

The decomposition decision has consequences that extend beyond the geoscience issue. Specifically, support of the geologist's estimation requires that data on the components in control areas be made available to him. Thus, the decomposition also must be compatible with available data on mineral, in this case uranium, occurrence. It is noteworthy in this regard, for example, that research initiated by the US Geological Survey on deposit tonnage and grade models was compatible with the decomposition of endowment made by the Survey in the appraisal of Alaska, namely number of deposits, deposit tonnage, and deposit grade. Herein lies one explanation of the A, F, T, G components: years of previous appraisal activities under ERDA and AEC had yielded data bases on these components.

Another important consideration in decomposition of endowment to components is that the components are compatible with the experience of the geologists performing the evaluation. When a large number of geologists from various kinds of professional experience are involved in an appraisal that employs a standard format, this requirement may not be fully met, for the nature of mineral occurrence may be perceived differently by geologists having different training and professional experience. In part, this must reflect the type of professional experience, but in part it must also reflect the nature of the modes of

occurrences of that element. For example, while a perception of uranium occurrences as discrete occurrences may satisfy the geologist appraising uranium endowment in a vein-type of environment, the geologist appraising endowment of geologic environments of the roll-type of sandstone deposit may have difficulty in thinking of number of deposits because of the continuity and sinuosity of these deposits and the effect of cut-off grade on number of reported occurrences. For this type of environment, the decomposition adopted by the NURE programme may be more compatible with geological experience and evidence than one based upon number of deposits.

As indicated earlier in this discussion, the geologists were asked for a modal value and two percentile values for each of the components of endowment that were considered to be stochastic: F, T, G. Subsequent to the elicitation of probabilities, a three-parameter lognormal probability distribution was fitted to these three values (modal and percentile values) for each component. This is a departure from practice in other appraisals. For example, while the appraisal of oil resources by the US Geological Survey requested the same three values (modal and percentile values), these were for *undecomposed* oil endowment. In the Alaskan appraisal, the three values were all percentile values—the mode was not requested. Other appraisals, such as those of Harris (1973) and Ellis *et al.* (1975), requested probability (or probability index numbers) estimates for tabled values of the variable; these tables were converted to relative frequency distributions; and, an endowment distribution and selected statistics were computed directly from the relative frequency distributions instead of from fitted functions. Of course, when the geologist is required to provide only two percentile values and a modal value, statistics can be computed only from a probability distribution which has been fitted to these estimates; similarly, a probability distribution for endowment cannot be determined from the components unless the estimates (modal and percentiles) for each component have been fitted by probability distributions.

The magnitude of data-processing and computation in the NURE appraisal was considerable. For, not only were there many evaluation regions (135 completed quadrangles plus parts of 45 quadrangles), but high-potential regions could have several different stratigraphic units, and for any such unit, there could be more than one favourable area. The statistical analysis that followed the elicitation of subjective estimates required for each elicitation the fitting of probability distributions to the three components of endowment and the subsequent mathematical combining of them to produce a probability distribution of U_3O_8 endowment. Furthermore, probability distributions for various aggregates, such as regions, mode of occurrence, and for the nation, were computed. Considerable and careful research by Ford and McLaren (1980) was devoted to the mathematics of combining random variables in various ways, aggregation of regions, and parameter estimation for a number of relevant circumstances, e.g. accounting for P^0, the marginal probability for at least one deposit, and for correlations among areas. These issues and their mathematics are not covered in this chapter; for them, the reader is referred to Ford and McLaren (1980) and to the US Department of Energy (1980) report on uranium assessment.

13.9.5. *Some details on design of elicitation*

The description provided here of the methodology for the elicitation of subjective probability estimates is taken directly from the US Department of Energy (1980, pp. 25–6) report. That report uses the term 'factor' to refer to what the author has called components of endowment

Factor estimation: Estimates of A, F, T, and G are elicited from the PI by the geologic team. The elicitation

process consists of a structured procedure, using standard questions and a consistent approach, for arriving at the values of each factor in the equation. Factors F, T, and G are random variables which are assumed to be mutually independent; factor A is treated as a single-value constant. The three random variables are elicited by the following subjective probability technique: (a) A most likely, or modal, estimate of the variable is prepared, which is the value believed to have a higher probability of being correct than all other values. (b) A low estimate is prepared, corresponding to a 95-percent probability that the factor is at least that large, or a 5-percent probability that the factor is less. (c) A high estimate is prepared, with a 5-percent probability that the factor is at least that large, or a 95-percent probability that the factor is less.

The factors F, T, and G are generated by comparing characteristics in the favourable area with a control area. One or more possible control areas are selected on the basis of the class of deposits expected in the favorable area. The favorability criteria of both the favorable area and the control area(s) are tabulated on the Control Area Selection sheet (Fig. 18) [Fig. 13.23]. The PI uses the form to document the criteria that are considered vital to the existence of uranium in the favorable area. Key criteria for each control area are checked. The degree of similarity between the control areas and the favorable area is observed by noting the number of criteria in common, and a control area is selected. The four factors are generated as follows:

● Factor A: The PI sketches a boundary line, on a

Criteria Classification	F. A. Criterion	Control Area	Control Area	Control Area	Control Area	Control Area
1. Tectonic setting						
2. Regional geology						
3. Regional structure						
4. Local structure						
5. Age of host						
6. Host lithology						
7. Host mineralogy						
8. Host texture						
9. Host geometry						
10. Chemistry						
11. Alteration						
12. Uranium minerals						
13. Nature of mineralization						
14. Geometry of orebodies						
15. Source of U						
16. Reductants/adsorbants						
17. HSSR/ARRS						
18. Other						

What important characteristics from the control area(s) are missing in your area?

Quadrangle _____ Area _____ Date/init _____

Fig. 13.23. Control area selection sheet. (Source: US Department of Energy 1980, Fig. 18, p. 26.)

suitably scaled base map, to represent the most likely extent of the favorable area, based on geologic data, and to define the areas within it where reserves have been delineated. The area, measured in square miles, excluding the area of reserves, is recorded. Although it may seem reasonable to treat factor A as a variable, it is the product of A times F that is important, and variability is introduced through the application of factor F, as described below.

- Factor F: The fraction of the favorable area, A, underlain by endowment may be estimated in several ways. First, following a careful comparison with the selected control area, the endowed area can be estimated in square miles; this value, divided by the total area, gives F. A second method, a variation of the first, is to estimate the number of uranium deposits of a particular size that are likely to exist within the favorable area compared with the known frequency of deposits in various appropriate control areas and to arrive at F by dividing A into the product of the number of deposits and the average area of the deposits. Finally, if insufficient geologic information is available to estimate F by one of the described procedures, F may be taken directly from the selected control area if the size and geologic characteristics of the favorable area and the control area are reasonably comparable. Estimates of modal, upper, and lower values of F are recorded. Regardless of the method used, care is taken to record the geologic reasoning in support of both the method and the estimates.
- Factor T: By comparing the geologic environments of the favorable area with the known geology of similar uraniferous areas including the control area, the average thickness of the endowed portion of the favorable host rock is estimated; multiplying the thickness by the most likely rock density, expressed as tons of rock per square mile per foot of thickness, gives the estimate of T in tons of endowed rock per square mile. If thickness estimates cannot be made from information on the favorable area, T values may be taken directly from the control area if the thicknesses are believed to be comparable. Modal, upper, and lower values of T are estimated, and the geologic reasoning for each estimate is recorded.
- Factor G: The PI also estimates three average grades of endowment: a high value, a modal value, and a low value. Information from known uranium deposits in the favorable area is used whenever available. Alternately, the PI may also use the control area grade directly or adjust it to better represent the impact of geologic conditions in the favorable area. The geologic reasoning for each estimate is recorded. The grade in percent U_3O_8 is converted to a decimal fraction by dividing by 100 so that units are consistent in the equation.

The estimates obtained from the PI were recorded by the elicitation team on the form shown in Fig. 13.24. These are the data that were subjected to statistical analyses, i.e. fitting of three-parameter lognormal distributions, combining of variables, computing of moments, aggregation across regions, etc. Fig. 13.25 presents the probability distributions for endowment and for various categories of resources for the aggregate of all areas, the continental United States.

Quadrangle ____________ PI ____________

Area ____________ Affiliation ____________

Data	Est Min	Est Mode	Est Max	Calc Mean
A				
F				
T				
G				
Total Ue				
Adjust Ue				

We agree that these estimates are acceptable

____
Quadrangle Principal Investigator

____
DOE Regional Geologist

Control Area ____________

Depth: Mode ________ Range ________

Assessment Summary Elicitor(s) ____________ Date ________

Fig. 13.24. Assessment summary form. (Source: US Department of Energy 1980, Fig. 19, p. 27.)

13.9.6. *Critique of endowment estimation, particularly execution of the elicitation*

Qualifying remarks

This section provides a criticism of the execution by the NURE programme of the elicitation of subjective estimates from the geologist (PI). This part of the NURE appraisal programme purposefully is singled out for special emphasis. The reason for this is that the most critical stage of the NURE appraisal programme is the inference from geology to the states of the components of uranium endowment (A, F, T, and G). Part of the challenge of this task is the facilitating of the very difficult bridging by the geologist from observed geology to potential endowment; another part is the promoting of an elicitation that assists the geologist in converting feelings of uncertainty to probabilities, or equivalently percentile quantities.

Some of the comments made in this section are highly critical of the elicitations that were examined. Before stating these criticisms, it is important that

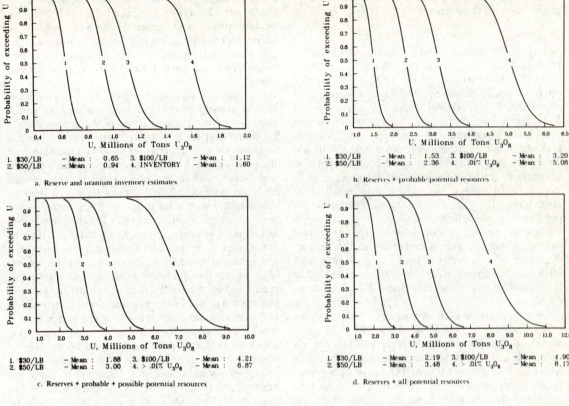

1. $30/LB — Mean : 0.65   3. $100/LB — Mean : 1.12
2. $50/LB — Mean : 0.94   4. INVENTORY — Mean : 1.60

a. Reserve and uranium inventory estimates

1. $30/LB — Mean : 1.53   3. $100/LB — Mean : 3.20
2. $50/LB — Mean : 2.36   4. .01% U_3O_8 — Mean : 5.08

b. Reserves + probable potential resources

1. $30/LB — Mean : 1.88   3. $100/LB — Mean : 4.21
2. $50/LB — Mean : 3.00   4. > .01% U_3O_8 — Mean : 6.87

c. Reserves + probable + possible potential resources

1. $30/LB — Mean : 2.19   3. $100/LB — Mean : 4.90
2. $50/LB — Mean : 3.48   4. > .01% U_3O_8 — Mean : 8.17

d. Reserves + all potential resources

Fig. 13.25. Cumulative probability distributions of reserves plus incremental potential resources of the United States. (Source: US Department of Energy 1980, Fig. 6, p. 6.)

acknowledgement be made of the fact that some of the practices which are criticized came about because of *circumstances attending the application* of the appraisal methodology. Given different circumstances of application, these practices may have been replaced by more appropriate ones. One circumstance which undoubtedly affected the execution of the elicitation was limited time. Another circumstance is the lack of interest by some geologists in learning about and participating in the appraisal task. Many geologists wished to perform the geological investigations only, being more than content to let someone else estimate the endowment. Still another important, if not critical, circumstance was one of poor choice. In order to prevent gaming by the geologist, the decision was made to not provide him with data on the components of endowment on the control areas prior to the elicitation. While this choice was well motivated, it was an unfortunate one, for the cost paid for preventing gaming was high, that of not

supporting and facilitating evaluation by the geologist of how these components vary with geology. It must be remembered that this appraisal was the first of its kind, when allowance is given to its magnitude and the involvement of different groups and institutions and many geologists. Some of these circumstances required special logistics and choices, some of which in retrospect could have been improved upon.

Finally, while these qualifications must be made, it is equally important that we learn what we can from the experience of the NURE programme. To this end, the elicitation stage must be examined critically, for there still exists a 'back-of-the-envelope' mentality among some geologists about the appraisal task, meaning that it is not seen as inconsistent by some geologists to spend years on geological investigations but to spend at most only a few hours in estimating the potential for undiscovered endowment that this geology provides. The NURE elicitation provides an excellent commentary on the problems that can arise in this stage of the evaluation.

Criticisms

Setting. The comments and criticisms which follow were made by the author at the request of US DOE; parts of this report [16] to US DOE (3 July 1980, pp. 6–17, pp. 22–5, and pp. 27–9) are presented here in essentially their original form.

Variation among elicitations. All comments in this section are based upon an admittedly small sample: four elicitations. Furthermore, the comments should be interpreted with respect to the objectives and assumptions noted in the previous sections.

First, even though the sample was small (four elicitations), I found extremes in the elicitation experience. In one elicitation which involved a US Geological Survey geologist, the experience was somewhat unfavourable. Contrasting to this was an elicitation of a contractor team of geologists; this elicitation was made rather smoothly, even though it took considerably more time than the other three elicitations.

Lack of preparation—faulty design. With perhaps minor exceptions, geologists of the US Geological Survey and contract groups received little or no preparation for the elicitation experience. Those with whom I talked knew of the *AFTG* equation but were totally unprepared for the philosophy or procedure by which they were to make the estimates of the variables of the equation. At least for some, and from what I could infer from what was told me, for most, there had been no educational sessions on the philosophy or procedure; furthermore, it appears that the geologists had been provided *no data* on the level of these variables on the control areas.

At this point, I ask you to recall the objectives identified earlier, one of which was to have the geologists participate not only in the geological studies but in the endowment estimation. With that objective in mind, the lack of preparation of the geologist for the elicitation procedure is at best anomalous and reflective of poor design.

The elicitation of F. Consider yourself to be the geologist about to begin the elicitation phase. You have completed a careful, traditional, and professional geological study, but you have not received any preparation for the elicitation. Typically, you have not examined or studied the values of *AFTG* on the control areas.

The elicitation commences with a brief review on the *AFTG* equation, the concepts of modal and extreme estimates, and the overall procedure. Then, a useful discussion on the criteria for the definition of the favourable areas is initiated by the elicitors. This is appropriate and generally is well done. The elicitors press the geologist for his reasons for his selections and explore relevant geological and data issues. This can take from 30 minutes to several hours.

Ultimately, after what has been basically a discussion of geology of the traditional variety, the geologist is asked for F, the fraction of the area underlain by mineralization. It is desired and intended that this estimate be a product of geological reasoning, but the geologist has had no preparation for such reasoning. Since neither the philosophical nor scientific basis has been established to consider F as a geological variable, how is he to provide this estimate? At best, whatever estimate he gives has little credibility as reflective of geological premises, data, and reasoning. Under even the most favourable circumstances, the geologist typically may not feel capable of responding to this question. A typical initial response seems to be, 'I have no idea'. Considering that the geologist has not been prepared for this estimation and that in some cases the geologist has not been a student of uranium deposits, as are economic geologists and explorationists, why should he be able to respond to this question? What has prepared him to introspect about how the amount of uranium mineralization varies with the geology that he has described? Very little, in many cases. It may be argued that when the geologist is of the economic geology-type, he may have a familiarity about the sizes of deposits, at least for economic grades. Even so, he is not prepared to relate the density of deposits and their size at the cut-off grade of 0.01 per cent U_3O_8 to the different geological conditions that he has observed. This would require unhurried, in-depth, and comprehensive examination of the geology of his areas and of the geology and mineral data on all relevant control areas.

So, what happens? The most well prepared and co-operative geologists may look to the elicitor for guidance, which he attempts to provide by reading him the magnitudes of F on one or more control areas. A co-operative geologist may attempt to base an estimate of F upon one or more of these control areas. Or, he will back into F by thinking of the size of the resources defined on the most similar control area. For example, he may reason that the geology is sufficiently similar and the region large enough that it could contain another XY district like that in control area Z. The elicitor assists him by providing from his control area data an estimate of the amount of U_3O_8

in the XY district, given a cut-off of 0.01 per cent U_3O_8. Bear in mind that all of this a 'real time' experience, meaning the geologist does his reasoning and estimation while in the elicitation session, as the elicitors await his response. Seldom does he examine in depth his maps or the basis for the favourable areas of the control areas. Since F is not independent of the size of the area A, a carefully made geological-based estimate of F would require an examination of the geoscience behind the delimiting of the control areas before using F's from those areas to arrive at an estimate of F for the region being evaluated. Furthermore, to the extent that the region differs from the control areas, a science-based F would reflect the geologist's assessment of how these differences affect F. *Even under the best of circumstances, the survey design clearly does not promote the geological and data analysis necessary for a geologically credible estimate of* F.

The elicitation experience can be considerably less favourable than has been alluded to thus far. Consider an elicitation of a geologist who is a fine scientist but has not been a student of uranium deposits nor has he had experience in uranium exploration. Typically, he has not been prepared for the elicitation. Compounding these circumstances considerably may be a preelicitation judgement that uranium endowment cannot be appraised in this fashion or that it cannot be estimated credibly at all. At any rate, for whatever the reasons may be, some geologists enter the elicitation in a contrary frame of mind [17]. When this is the case and the elicitor gets to that place in the elicitation where he seeks an estimate of F, there are many different combinations of psychological responses that are possible. Certainly one of them must be an initial feeling of intimidation, because the geologist feels he simply is incapable of providing what is asked for. This feeling may give way to anger at being compromised as a scientist. After all, he may have reason to feel secure in his skills as a geoscientist but is suddenly presented with a task for which he cannot employ his professional skills. Consequently, he may either provide a negative pronouncement on the entire procedure or become indifferent and attempt to extract himself from the situation as quickly as possible. This is done by accepting quite uncritically control area values or whatever other suggestions the elicitors may provide. Similarly, once he has, so to speak, obtained an F or values for the other variables, he may be quite uncritical about applying them with few variations to all areas. Essentially, under these unfavourable circumstances, the elicitation is some-

thing of a farce with respect to the product of the elicitation representing estimates made by the geologist being elicited. Given the size of the favourable area, which was drawn by the geologist at an earlier time, the sum effect of the elicitation under these unfavourable circumstances is to ascribe in an uncritical, basically mechanical fashion the uranium endowments of a control area or of a composite of areas to the favourable area. Essentially, the only contribution by the geologist has been the delineation of the favourable areas. Otherwise, his function has been to make it possible for the elicitor to complete the mechanics of the appraisal procedure. Unfortunately, the endowment densities produced in such circumstances are essentially those suggested by the elicitor or provided by the control area. A similar result could be produced without the geologist.

The elicitation of T *and* G. Many of the issues commented upon in the previous section on the elicitation of estimates of F apply in concept to the elicitation of estimates for T and G for, like F, these variables reflect the geology of the uranium mineralization. Those comments will not be repeated here; the following statement summarizes their implication: *Given the objectives and assumptions set forth at the beginning of this major section, the elicitation procedure can be faulted with regard to* T *and* G *on the same bases as it was for* F; *namely, the lack of preparation and the lack of geological analyses of these variables prior to the elicitation simply do not support the objective of obtaining independent geological estimates.*

In practice, the geologist does seem to be better disposed to provide an estimate of T than he was for F within the present format of the elicitation. This is especially so when the geologist has examined many deposits. However, there still remains concern about the degree to which this estimate reflects comprehensive geological analysis.

Estimation of average grade of the endowment is especially problematic. The elicitations which I observed reinforced an opinion which I have held for several years: *Most geologists are not able to credibly estimate average grade for a specified cut-off grade.* Consider the following exchange which I noted in one of the elicitations (brackets mine).

Elicitors: We need an estimate of average grade.
Geologist: 0.03 per cent,
Elicitors: We need limits. Now if you wish to skew it [the distribution], it is the time to do so.
[Note leading by elicitors.]
Geologist: Upper value is 1.0 per cent.
[Elicitors reminded the geologist of the cut-off grade of 0.01 per cent.]

Geologist: But, it is easy to collect a 1.0 per cent sample. [Elicitors quoted average grades from a number of control areas. After considering these average grades, the geologist backed off from his estimates of 1.0 per cent.]
Geologist: I'm guessing now; how about 0.07 per cent?
Elicitor: Now we need a minimum average grade.
Geologist: 0.03 per cent.
[Elicitors pointed out to the geologist that 0.03 per cent is his modal (most likely) average grade; therefore, the minimum average must be less than 0.03 per cent.]
Geologist: 0.015 per cent.

The elicitation did produce three average grades (minimum = 0.015, most likely = 0.03, and maximum = 0.07 per cent), and these might be useful estimates for the subsequent probability analysis. However, it is abundantly clear in this case that in no way can these estimates be considered the result of geological investigation. In that regard, this elicitation is a failure. The geologist's only function with regard to the average grade estimates was to serve as a conduit for control area data and to lend his name as the geologist who is accountable for the endowment appraisal, including of course the estimates for average grade. An experience like that just related frustrates the geologist by exposing his ignorance and breeds a certain amount of contempt for the whole appraisal procedure. Furthermore, I cannot believe that the elicitor is unaffected. The pride that comes from contributing to a good product or good cause must suffer to some degree from observing erratic, if not wild, estimates made by the geologist and the uncritical acceptance of values suggested by the elicitor, values which come from one or more control areas. Given the possibilities for these negative experiences and the fact that at least in some instances the geologist contributes no insight to average grades, confusing sample grades with average grades, the current elicitation for average grade constitutes highly questionable procedure. Surely, it is appropriate to ask, 'Why bother?' Why not bypass this procedure and use a histogram of average grades from all relevant control areas? These probably would be as good as the estimates which have been obtained under the current procedure.

If the use of the geologist to estimate average grade is to be justified by his performance, it will be only when the geologist has been prepared with an understanding of cut-off–average grade relations and with cut-off–average grade data from similar regions, and when he has considered grade with respect to those geological factors that affect it. Even within the present format, a better procedure would have been to not ask the geologist about average grade until after reviewing average grades of appropriately selected control areas, where such areas exist. In other words, feed his mental processes information which is relevant to the thing being estimated, average grade for the selected cut-off grade. Of course better procedure would provide him relevant data and information well in advance of the elicitation allowing him time to get a feel for the average grade variable and time to explore geological relations. As far as I could observe, none of these conditions prevailed.

Some of the criticisms made of the elicitation of average grade also apply to the elicitation of estimates of T, the mineralization factor. Within the elicitation procedure, estimating T was reduced to estimating thickness Th for a constant tonnage factor was assumed and Th estimates were elicited after the estimates for F and G. Therefore, both the area and average grade of the postulated mineralization have been described. The only variable left is Th. Geologists did not struggle as much with this as they did with F and G. Even so, as with F, I am not assured that estimates reflected proper geological evaluation. Furthermore, even in those instances that the geologist appeared prepared and conversant, his perception of thickness was relevant primarily to economic cut-off grades and producing deposits.

The geologists used various mental exercises to explore the thickness variable. Some of these were appropriate, for they involved the stratigraphy, outcrop mineralization, and logs. Even so, as with F, the geologist should have been prepared prior to the elicitation to estimate thickness. Some mental exercises were suspect. For example, in one instance, the estimate of the minimum and maximum values for average thickness were obtained by mentally exploring Th when the sands are thin and when they are thick. The danger here is that (1) these may not represent averages, and (2) the relative frequency of these circumstances may not be included in estimating minimum and maximum average thickness. Additional comments about the estimation of T are provided in the following subsections.

Communication and probability perspective in general. Let us for the moment set aside the larger issues of geoscience and its use in appraising endowment and examine the probability elicitation per se. When judged simply as a subjective probability survey, the elicitation has some glaring weaknesses. For example, in the four elicitations which I observed, the efforts to instill a probability perspective were minimal. The geologist was simply and matter-of-factly informed that the elicitors would be seeking minimum and maximum values in addition to the modal value for each of the variables. This was embellished somewhat by the drawing of a curve which included these estimates as a means of placing them in perspective. This cursory explanation was provided at the beginning of the elicitation. No further education or guidance on probability was provided.

A person who is reasonably well informed about probability would have asked what was meant by a minimum or maximum value of a continuous variable, like thickness. Is this to be an absolute minimum and maximum, or is it to be some less extreme value? This hypothetical person also would have wanted to know what percentiles these quantities are supposed to be. But, even well informed persons tend to underestimate the spread between the 5th and 95th percentile. Under the best of circumstances, the extreme values are not unbiased estimates. Is it likely that a person receiving little instruction would provide better estimates? Just what do these so-called minimum and maximum values represent in a probability sense? It is difficult to say.

The estimation of the extreme values usually was so quickly done that it appeared somewhat cavalier. In part, this reflected the geologist making the estimate. For example, one geologist's response for extreme values of Th and for A was simply a ± 25 per cent. However, the format of the elicitation itself is in part responsible for hasty and superficial estimation, for the geologist had not been prepared prior to the elicitation to consider the complex of geology, endowment, and probability. As one geologist put it, 'This is too quick, too much off the cuff.'

Estimation of P^0. A vivid example of a breakdown in communication was the attempt by the elicitor to obtain P^0_{10}. P^0_{10} is intended to be the probability for at least one deposit of at least 10 tons of U_3O_8. Clearly, there are two dimensions to this probability: number of deposits and size of deposit. In my notes of the four elicitations I observed that P^0_{10} was *never* described correctly. Instead, the elicitor asked for 'the probability for one 10-ton deposit', or 'the probability for a ten-ton deposit'.

A strict interpretation of the question as it was asked would require that P^0_{10} be zero. This is because the question seems to be seeking the probability for exactly one deposit of exactly 10 tons U_3O_8. The probability that a continuous variable, like quantity of U_3O_8, has any single value, no matter what it is, is zero by definition. Suppose the interpretation is less strict, allowing that 10 tons means an interval from 9.5 to 10.5 tons. This interpretation allows a nonzero probability, but the magnitude of that probability varies in ways not intended by the elicitor. For example, the probability for exactly one deposit of a size from 9.5 to 10.5 tons of U_3O_8 could be less for a

large and rich region than a smaller poorer one, everything else being equal. This is because in the large rich region the events having the largest probabilities are those of a greater number of deposits and those of larger size deposits.

Clearly, the proper formulation of the question asks for cumulative probability over the number dimension from 1 to ∞ and over the size dimension from 10 tons to ∞:

What is the probability for *at least one* deposit of *at least 10* tons of U_3O_8?

There can be no question that the elicitors in the four elicitations which I observed communicated the concept poorly. However, examination of the responses of the geologists suggests that in most cases the elicitor received estimates not for what he asked for but for what he *should have asked for*. For example, larger rich areas were given P^0_{10} of 1.0, while smaller or poorer ones were given $P^0_{10} < 1.0$. Furthermore, for a given region $P^0_{1000} < P^0_{100} < P^0_{10}$. These relations suggest that the geologist was thinking of cumulative probability. So, the elicitation may have produced 'right' answers in spite of poor communication.

13.9.7. *Some possible modifications*

The strongest recommendation indicated by the observations and analysis of this brief study is that the format of the elicitation and the appraisal should be modified. As it is now, the role of the geologist in the endowment estimation is quite unsatisfactory. Arguments to support this judgement were presented in previous sections. The following sections consider possible changes in structure.

Possible changes and criteria for choice

There are two possible changes

(1) limit the role of the geologist to geological study and mapping, resulting in the delimiting of favourable areas;

(2) involve the geologist totally in the appraisal process, providing him with necessary preparation and all relevant information early in the appraisal process, preferably as he begins his geological studies.

Which of these modifications should be selected depends upon a number of factors, among which are

(1) the assessment of the capability of a geologist to estimate the variables of the endowment

equation by the application of his science;

(2) the availability of geologists who are interested in the endowment appraisal task and committed to its completion;

(3) the time and human resources available to support the appraisal task.

A limited role for the geologist

A negative circumstance for one or more of these factors may be sufficient to justify the decision to limit the role of the geologist to the delimiting of favourable areas. If negative circumstances prevail for all three factors, such a modification is strongly indicated. Of course making such a modification would place the responsibility for ascribing an endowment to the favourable areas on DOE personnel. While such a proposition may be less than satisfying to those who desire to have endowment estimates represent many geologists, it would be appropriate procedure. Furthermore, it would formalize and portray honestly the current contribution of the geologist and the current 'sub rosa' contribution of the elicitors to the endowment estimates. Such a design would undoubtedly lead to a more mechanical use of control areas for appraisal; hence it would place an even greater stress on assembling data on a greater number and diversity of control areas.

A slight variant on the limited role would be to require the geologist to study in depth the geology of all control areas so that he could describe probabilities for each of them being the appropriate control area for the area being evaluated. These probabilities could be used to weight the control area factors of all relevant areas to produce an estimate of endowment for the region being appraised.

An expanded role for the geologist

Structure. The alternative to limiting the role of the geologist is to greatly expand his role and to place upon him much greater responsibilities. Clearly, this can be done only if the geologist is willing to accept this expanded participation and if he is provided both extensive educational and data support. Given that both of these conditions are met, then a possible scenario of the appraisal process may be

An educational session is presented prior to the initiation of geological studies and field work. This session would require several days, for it would develop a resource perspective, grade relations, probability concepts, subjective processes, and the endowment equation.

An important part of the educational session would be examining some actual appraisals and working through a mock appraisal.

The geologist would be provided with all available data on control areas and their factors and asked to make an in-depth study and analysis of them.

Upon completion of the geological investigation of the region to be evaluated, the geologist presents his maps, describes the geology of the region, and identifies areas favourable for uranium endowment.

Subsequent to this geological presentation, a review session on the endowment equation and the topics covered in the initial educational session is presented to the geologist.

Following the review session, on an individual basis, a trial run is made on one of the favourable areas. The purpose of this session is to highlight controversial and vague issues in appraisal and items of greatest uncertainty.

The geologist is required to participate in a probability calibration exercise. This exercise will tell him whether he tends to underestimate or overestimate probabilities for things he feels fairly certain about and for things about which he feels quite uncertain. Hopefully, he will factor this into his probability assessment.

The geologist is given the task of reviewing his geological studies and relevant data as necessary to make estimates for the variables of the endowment equation.

Upon the completion of his appraisals, the geologist presents each evaluation to a review board. The geologist would provide the geological and data bases for his estimates. The responsibility of the board would be to probe the geological, judgemental, and probability issues relevant to the appraisal. To the extent that the geologist could defend his work, it would not be modified. Otherwise, the board and the geologist would jointly arrive at a modification.

Gaming. The appraisal procedure just outlined raises the issue of gaming of estimates or of purposefully biasing them to meet some other goal, e.g. to be 'safe'. Clearly, this appraisal procedure allows for this to take place, for the geologist is provided all relevant information and asked to make his estimates prior to presenting and defending them before the review board. He could certainly 'back into' values of the variables which result in any number he desires. It is likely that some manipulation of this kind would take place, for it already does under the current format. An evaluation of the seriousness of this issue cannot be made without considering the objectives and priorities. If the objective is to promote geological analyses in the estimation of endowment and to have many geologists participate in this task, then it may be that this design is the appropriate one in spite of the opportunity which it provides for gaming. Besides, there is the opportunity for an in-depth examination by the review board. Anticipating that he must face such examination may serve to deter an inclination to purposefully bias or game the estimates.

13.9.8. *Final comments*

At times, we have difficulty in 'seeing the forest because of the trees'. If we are to improve methodology we must always be critical of current methods. Even so, one should not lose sight of what has been accomplished in the NURE programme. Even under the most critical of evaluations, it must be true that the NURE appraisal programme has improved greatly the geological input to the appraisal process. If this greatly improved level of geological analysis influenced nothing more than the identification and delimiting of the control areas, it made a great contribution. I am confident that at the very least, this contribution has been successfully made. The contribution may have been greater than this.

Many of the criticisms of the elicitation process made in this report presuppose that a geologist could credibly estimate the variables of the endowment equation by the exercise of his science if he were properly prepared, sufficiently motivated, supported by relevant data, and given sufficient time for study and research. *It must be clearly understood that this presupposition is at present more an 'article of faith' than a demonstrated fact.* I and others have based research on methodology for endowment appraisal upon this article of faith.

We must admit to the possibility that, with the present level of science and data, the capability of the typical geologist involved in the NURE endowment appraisal programme to estimate geologically the variables of the endowment equation may be very limited. The more limited this capability, the less critical we can be of the current appraisal design. In the limit, the lack of capability would force appraisers to rely completely upon control area factors, which is similar to what in fact took place in the current appraisal programme. The current performance of some geologists does not build faith in the current capability of the geologist. Even so, judgement is not clearly made. Geologists have only very recently been drawn into the appraisal of mineral endowment as a geological activity. At present, we

are struggling to evaluate not just current performance but what the geologist could do under favourable circumstances and just what these circumstances are. This has led to redesigning of appraisal methodologies. The current NURE methodology is one stage of this evolutionary process. The point to be made here is that apart from meeting its primary goal of providing an estimate of the national uranium endowment, the NURE programme has been an experiment in the large-scale application of methodology in a difficult and emerging field of endeavour. Our appraisal designs of the future will unquestionably benefit from what has been learned in the implementation of this programme.

One benefit from the current appraisal effort may be a greater appreciation of the need for geological input to the appraisal task. Another may be an increased willingness of geologists to become involved in the appraisal process. Some of these geologists may still be resistive to the NURE procedure as it has been applied. Nevertheless, they may be willing to participate in an appraisal in which they are more fully involved. Let me elaborate on these points. In view of the telescoping of time and the limitations on science and resources that have attended the NURE endowment appraisal, an attempt by US DOE at the beginning of this programme to prepare and support the geologist in his task as an appraiser may not have met with much success. Factors in the judgement that this effort may have achieved only limited success are (1) insufficient time for some geologists to build expertise and experience for endowment appraisal and (2) a lack of desire and interest on the part of many geologists in being involved in the appraisal phase. It is my perception that even the very limited attempts by US DOE personnel to familiarize geologists with the AFTG equation and its use were not very well received by some geologists. While many geologists welcomed the opportunity for geological study, mapping, and analysis, some of them seemed to be resistant from the very beginning to being involved in the appraisal phase. I think that it would be fair to say that when the programme started, the geologist's perception was that the appraisal phase was so far in the future and, for some, interest in the appraisal phase was so limited, that it would have been difficult to prepare the geologist early in the programme.

I suggested to one geologist that while the elicitation was a 'rough experience' because of lack of preparation, the alternative of being prepared brought responsibility to the geologist for the appraisal effort and that it seemed to me that he, as well as others, had enjoyed not being responsible for the appraisal phase. He acknowledged that this was true. I asked him how he felt about the luxury of non-involvement and the current elicitation experience as compared to a full involvement and the responsibility that this implies. He commented that initially he had resisted involvement, but after going through an elicitation, he definitely feels now that he would much prefer being involved early in the appraisal process. In other words, it may now be possible to do an endowment appraisal with the geologists taking greater responsibility for preparedness and estimation. I wonder if such a change in perception could have taken place without experiencing the appraisal process.

References

Azis, A., Barry, G. S. and Haugh, I. (1972). The undiscovered mineral endowment of the Canadian Shield in Manitoba. *Mineral inform. Bull.* MR 124, Mineral Resources Branch, Department of Energy, Mines, and Resources, Ottawa, Canada.

Barry, G. S. and Freyman, A. J. (1970). Mineral endowment of the Canadian Northwest. *Mineral inform. bull.* MR 105, pp. 57–95. Mineral Resources Branch, Department of Energy, Mines, and Resources, Ottawa, Canada.

Bartlett, M. S. (1933). Probability and chance in the theory of statistics. *Proc. R. Soc. (Lond.)*, **A 141**, 518–34.

Charles River Associates (1978). *The economics and geology of mineral supply: an integrated framework for long run policy analysis.* Report No. 327, Prepared for National Science Foundation, Washington, DC.

Dalkey, N. C. (1969). *The Delphi method: an experimental study of group opinion.* RM-5888-PR, The Rand Corporation.

Ellis, J. R., Harris, D. P., and Van Wie, N. H. (1975). *A subjective probability appraisal of uranium resources in the State of New Mexico.* Open File Report GJO-110(76), US Energy Research and Development Administration, Grand Junction, Colorado.

Ford, C. E. and McLaren, R. A. (1980). *Methods for obtaining distributions of uranium occurrence from estimates of geologic features.* Report no. K/CSD-13, Union Carbide Corporation, Nuclear Division, under Contract No. W-7405-eng-26 for the US Department of Energy, NTIS, Springfield, Virginia.

Gillette, R. (1974). Oil and gas resources: did USGS gush too high? *Science*, **185**, 127–30.

Good, I. J. (1965). *The estimation of probabilities: an essay on modern Bayesian methods.* Research Monogram No. 30, The MIT Press, Cambridge, Massachusetts.

Harris, D. P. (1973). A subjective probability appraisal of metal endowment of Northern Sonora, Mexico. *Econ. Geol.* **68**(2), 222–42.

—— (1977). Conventional crude oil resources of the United States: recent estimates, methods for estimation and policy considerations. *Materials Society* **1**, 263–86.

—— and Azis, A. (1970). Future metal requirements for Mexico to 1990 and potential domestic supply. *Proc. Council Econ.* pp. 245–302. AIME, New York.

—— and Euresty, D. E. (1973). The impact of transportation network upon the potential supply of base and precious metals from Sonora, Mexico. *Proc. 10th Int. Symp. Application of Computer Methods in the Mineral Industry*, pp. 99–108. The South African Institute of Mining and Metallurgy, Johannesburg.

——, Freyman, A. J., and Barry, G. S. (1971). A mineral resource appraisal of the Canadian Northwest using subjective probabilities and geological opinion. *Proc. 9th Int. Symp. Techniques for Decision-Making in the Mineral Industry*, Special Volume 12, pp. 100–16. Canadian Institute of Mining and Metallurgy, Montreal, Canada.

Hendricks, T. A. (1965). *Resources of oil, gas, and natural gas liquids in the U.S. and the world.* Circular 522, US Geological Survey, Washington, DC.

Hetland, D. L. (1979). Estimation of undiscovered uranium resources by US ERDA. In *Evaluation of uranium resources*, pp. 231–50. Proceedings of an Advisory Group Meeting, International Atomic Energy Agency, Vienna.

Hubbert, M. K. (1962). *Energy resources: a report to the Committee on Natural Resources.* Publ. 1000-D, National Research Council, National Academy of Sciences, Washington, DC.

—— (1969). Energy resources. In *Resources and man*, (A study and recommendations by the Committee on Resources and Man, National Academy of Sciences—National Research Council), Chapter 8, pp. 157–242. W. H. Freeman & Company, San Francisco (for National Academy of Sciences).

—— (1974). *U. S. energy resources, a review as of 1972.* Background paper prepared at the request of Henry A. Jackson, Chairman, Committee on Interior and Insular Affairs, US Senate, 93rd Congress, 2nd Session, Committee Print Serial No. 93–40 (92–75). US Government Printing Office, Washington, DC.

effreys, H. (1961). *Theory of probability* (3rd edn). Clarendon Press, Oxford.

Miller, B. M., Thomsen, H. L., Dolton, G. L., Coury, A. B., Hendricks, T. A., Lennartz, F. E., Powers, R. B., Sable, E. G., and Varnes, K. L. (1975). *Geological estimates of undiscovered recoverable oil and gas resources in the United States.* Circular 725, US Geological Survey, Washington, DC 78 p.

Poisson, S. D. (1837). *Calcul des jugements*, Paris.

Ramsey, F. P. (1931). *Foundations of mathematics*, Chapters 7 and 8. Harcourt, New York and Kegan Paul, London.

Singer, D. A. and Ovenshine, A. T. (1979). Assessing metallic resources in Alaska. *Am. Scientist* **67** (5), 582–9.

Theobald, P. K., Schweinfurth, S. P., and Duncan, D. C. (1972). *Energy resources of the United States.* Circular 650 US Geological Survey, Washington, DC.

US Department of Energy (1980). *An assessment report on uranium in the United States of America*, GJO-111(80). US Department of Energy, Grand Junction Office, Colorado.

Notes

1. Donald, P. (1974). Investment decisions in nonferrous metals exploration in Mexico; an economic analysis of discovery probabilities, expected financial returns and tax policy. Unpublished Ph.D. dissertation. Department of Mineral Economics, The Pennsylvania State University.

2. Euresty, D. (1971). A systems approach to the regional evaluation of potential mineral resources using computer simulation, with a case study of the impact of infrastructure on potential supply of base and precious metals of Sonora, Mexico. Ph.D. dissertation. The Pennsylvania State University.

3. This computation requires the convolution of the m probability distributions; for example, let a function $\phi_g(x_1, x_2, \ldots, x_m \mid G_D^0)$ be a continuous approximation of the subjective probability for the joint occurrence of $x_1, x_2, \ldots, x_m$, the number of deposits in each of the m parts of the cell that lie in m zones, and let a random variable N be the sum of these independent events (numbers of deposits): $N = X_1 + X_2 + \cdots + X_m$. Then the probability for $N = n$, which is a sum, would be computed as

$$P_g(N = n \mid G_D^0) = \int_{n-0.5}^{n+0.5} \int_{X_m} \cdots$$

$$\int_{X_2} \phi_g(n - x_2 - x_3 - \ldots - x_m;$$

$$x_2, \ldots, x_m \mid G_D^0) \, dx_2 \ldots dx_m \, dn.$$

4. Campbell, R. M. (1966). A methodological study of the utilization of experts in business forecasting. Unpublished Ph.D. dissertation. University of California, Los Angeles.

5. Such a procedure would be repeated for other modes of occurrence such as oil in stratigraphic traps.

6. The rest of § 13.7.4 is reproduced from Harris (1977, pp. 277–81).

7. National Petroleum Council, Oil subcommittee of the National Petroleum Council's Committee on US Energy Outlook, Lloyd D. Elkins, chairman (1972).

8. This report (p. 11) states, 'If cumulative recovery efficiency continues to advance at the indicated past rate in the range of one-half percent per year, it will be necessary to develop new technology as well as fully apply present technology. Nevertheless, past accomplishments and present research provide reason to believe that technology will be developed which will ultimately enable recovery of at least 50 to 60 percent of the total oil in place discovered.'

9. Grybeck, D. and De Young, J. H., Jr. (1978). Map and tables describing mineral resource potential of the Brooks Range, Alaska. USGS Open File Report 78-1-B, Menlo Park, California.

10. Hudson, T. and De Young, J. H., Jr. (1978). Map and tables describing areas of mineral resource potential, Seward Peninsula, Alaska. USGS Open File Report 78-1-C, Menlo Park, California.

11. Eberlein, G. D. and Menzie, W. D. (1978). Maps and tables describing areas of metalliferous mineral resource potential of central Alaska. USGS Open File Report 78-1-D, Menlo Park, California.

12. MacKevett, E. M., Jr., Singer, D. A., and Holloway, C. D. (1978). Map and tables describing metalliferous mineral resource potential of southern Alaska. USGS Open File Report 78-1-E, Menlo Park, California.

13. Patton, W. W., Jr. (1978). Maps and table describing areas of interest for oil and gas in central Alaska. USGS Open File Report 78-1-F, Menlo Park, California.

14. Dr Donald A. Singer, Office of Resource Analysis, US Geological Survey, Menlo Park, California.

15. If the estimator elects to view the favourable area as a volume or as a length, then A is expressed in cubic or linear miles and T in tons of uranium-bearing rock per cubic or linear mile.

16. Harris, D. P. (1980). Critique of resource estimation methodology. Report prepared for US Department of Energy under Subcontract No. 80-469-S, Grand Junction Office, Colorado, 3 July 1980.

17. I have been informed by Bendix personnel that only about 10 per cent of the geologists were basically of a contrary frame of mind.

14 PSYCHOLOGICAL, PSYCHOMETRIC, AND OTHER ISSUES AND MOTIVATIONS IN THE PERCEPTION OF AND THE ASSESSMENT OF SUBJECTIVE PROBABILITY

14.1. Perspective

The inclination to base an appraisal of metal endowment upon the opinions of experts seems to result naturally from the consideration of three central issues.

1. Limitations on time: a survey of expert opinion can be performed quickly as compared to basing the appraisal on multivariate statistical analysis of 'hard' quantitative geological and mineral resource data.

2. A suitable control area for a multivariate model may not exist or cannot be identified except for very low level, general geological variables.

3. Usually, the level of information possessed by geologists who are experienced in exploration in the region of interest far exceeds that present in data that are available to the public, both with respect to basic geoscience data and deposit characteristics, but particularly concerning geoscience data.

While these considerations lead naturally to the use of the opinions of experts, there are some basic questions that arise concerning the use of opinion.

1. How effectively can the mind, even of the expert, integrate and resolve complex uncertain issues?
2. How does the mind process information to yield a judgement about an uncertain event?
3. Given the manner in which the mind processes information and makes decisions about uncertain events, what is the preferred method of eliciting opinion?
4. What is the best way to resolve differences in opinion?

These questions are not unique to the use of expert opinion for the appraisal of mineral endowment; they are relevant to the use of expert opinion in general. Recognition of this fact leads one into the literature of psychometrics and decision-analysis, most of which relates to business and social science, where the reliance on quantified expert opinion for quantitative analysis has a greater and longer tradi-

tion than it does in the appraisal of mineral endowment. While the particulars of application in other fields may differ considerably from those of mineral endowment appraisal, all applications have one thing in common, the estimation of an uncertain event and the need for the expert to rely upon some sort of a model to make such an estimation. The following sections examine issues raised by recent inquiry in psychometrics.

14.2. The concept of bounded intelligence

The history of the social, economic, and intellectual progress of man testifies of a certain intelligence, imagination, and the capability to solve difficult problems. However, the written record also testifies of serious miscalculations, errors in judgement and estimation. On a smaller scale, each of us encounters daily our considerable limitations in dealing with complex issues, particularly when information is incomplete and knowledge of relationships involved is less than perfect. We can err badly. In short, man appears at the same time to be a marvellous creature and yet to be subject to various imperfections in judgement.

The issue here is not whether man overall is rational or not, but under what conditions does he make rational or irrational decisions. More specifically, what are the mental processes employed to make decisions about an uncertain event?

A normative model of rational behaviour by man regarding an uncertain event could include at least two submodels. The first of these would describe the uncertain event by a probability model; that is, the uncertain event would be viewed as a random variable, the values of which are described by a probability function. The second model would describe man's choice of action regarding an activity which is influenced by the state of the random variable by a decision model; that is, man's course of action is dictated by that decision which in a broad and general sense maximizes his expected utility. This decision model expresses the expected utility of various decisions for given states of nature. The first model, the probability model, as a normative model of uncertainty, is of primary interest here. Basically the proposition is that, if man is rational, his perception of the possible states of nature should correspond to the probability distribution of the event whose state is being contemplated.

Slovic (1972) points out that in most of man's decisions, he bypasses formal statistical or probabilistic reasoning and acts instead as an intuitive statistician. A number of investigations have been made of the performance of man as an intuitive statistician; these investigations disclose some deficiencies in man's ability to assess uncertain events. Overall, these studies (Tversky and Kahneman 1972, 1974; Alpert and Raiffa [1]; Pickhardt and Wallace 1974) suggest that man believes he has more knowledge about the event than he actually possesses. Generally, his subjective probability distribution is much narrower than it should be. Man tends to underestimate the probability for extreme events in both tails of the distribution. For example, Alpert and Raiffa [1] asked 800 Harvard MBA students to provide the 0.01, 0.25, 0.50, 0.75, and 0.99 fractile estimates for each of 20 items, such as the number of automobiles imported into the US in 1967. They found that 41 per cent of the actual values fell outside of the 0.01–0.99 range determined from the responses of 800 students. The ideal result would have been for 2 per cent of the actual values falling outside of this range. Tentative conclusions drawn by Pickhardt and Wallace (1974) from various laboratory studies on man's decision-making are

1. When compared to Bayes' rule, man is a conservative and inefficient information processor.
2. Man is poor at gauging the value of information.
3. Man is reluctant to make probability estimates that are close to 0 or 1.

14.3. Heuristics and biases

Reasons for man's overconfidence in the assessment of probabilities of events were investigated by Tversky and Kahneman (1974). They found that man reduces the complexity and difficulty of assessment by employing a few heuristics.

1. Representativeness;
2. Availability;
3. Adjustment and anchoring.

They concluded that while these heuristics are quite useful, they lead to sizeable and systematic errors.

The heuristic of representativeness is employed in answering questions of the following kinds (Tversky and Kahneman 1974).

1. What is the probability that object A belongs to class B?
2. What is the probability that process B will generate event A?

This heuristic defines probabilities by the degree by which A resembles B. Tversky and Kahneman point out that the heuristic can lead to serious errors because similarity or representativeness is not affected by some of the factors which should affect judgements of probability. One of these factors is prior probabilities, unconditional (marginal) probabilities for group membership. The hypothesis that the representativeness heuristic neglects prior probabilities was tested by Tversky and Kahneman (1974). Subjects were told that the population consisted of two types of individuals, engineers and lawyers: 70 per cent engineers and 30 per cent lawyers. Thus the prior probability that an individual drawn at random from the mixed population would be an engineer was 0.7, a lawyer, 0.3. The subjects were provided descriptions (personality profiles) of individuals alleged to have been drawn at random from the mixed population and were asked to provide probabilities that the individual belonged to the group of engineers or lawyers. It was found that the probabilities provided were essentially the same as they were when the subjects were told that the percentages were 30 per cent for engineers and 70 per cent for lawyers. In other words, the probability that an unknown with a given personality profile belonged to the group of engineers was insensitive to how frequently engineers occur in the mixed population. Judgements on probability reflected similarity only; this is a sharp violation of Bayes' rule, which serves as a normative model. By this standard, the probability for membership in the group of lawyers, given a personality profile, should have reflected both similarity and the prior probabilities

$$P(E \mid C) = \frac{P(C \mid E) \cdot P(E)}{P(C \mid E) \cdot P(E) + P(C \mid L) \cdot P(L)},$$

where C is the set of personality characteristics, E is engineer, and L is lawyer. This experiment indicated that both $P(E)$ and $P(L)$ were ignored in the subjective estimation of $P(E \mid C)$.

Tversky and Kahneman (1974) found that when no personality sketch was given, the probabilities for group membership provided by the subjects reflected, as they should, the prior probabilities; but when a totally uninformative personality sketch was given, the prior probabilities were ignored by the subjects in estimating group membership. The subjects responded differently when given no information than they did when given totally worthless information. Of course, in both of these cases, the probabilities for group membership should have been the prior probabilities.

The manner in which individuals respond to usefulness of information was examined in another experiment in which it was found that prediction of profits for firms varied with the descriptions of the firms even though the descriptions contained no information about factors that affect profitability. For firms described in a favourable setting, high profits were predicted. Thus, subjects were insensitive to predictability and attempted to use meaningless information.

Tversky and Kahneman (1974) also found that there are misconceptions about chance: 'people expect that the essential characteristics of the process will be represented, not only globally in the entire sequence, but also locally in its parts.' [Copyright 1974 by The American Association for the Advancement of Science.]

Another important heuristic in subjective probability is that of availability. Simply stated, the use of this heuristic relates the probability of an event to the ease by which it is mentally envisioned. Such a heuristic is not without some basis, for the relative frequency character of probability suggests, when other things are equal, that events that are highly probable should be more frequently encountered in the experience of an individual. Tversky and Kahneman (1974) point out, however, that mental availability is affected by factors other than relative frequency and that these factors impart bias to the estimated probability. One of these factors is the retrievability of instances. The basis for this factor is that events that come to mind are those that are easily retrievable and that easily retrievable events may not be those whose frequency of occurrence is the greatest. Retrievability may reflect the emotional content of experience in addition to the frequency of occurrence of that experience. To demonstrate this, subjects were presented with names of individuals of both sexes, individuals whose fame varied. In some of the lists, the men were more numerous than were the women. The subjects hearing the lists were asked to estimate the frequency of men and women in the list. These frequencies were judged erroneously, because they reflected the frequencies of the *well*

known men and women, not the proportions of each sex in the entire list.

Enjoyable events, events that favour some aspect of the individuals' life-style, including his professional life, may be recalled more easily than events that are unfavourable or unenjoyable.

Tversky and Kahneman (1974) also pointed out that effectiveness of a search set can provide a bias in availability, hence subjective probability. Their example of this factor was the estimation of the frequency of words beginning with the letter k. It has been shown that the frequency of occurrence of letter k in the third position of a word is three times the frequency of occurrence in the first position. Nevertheless, most persons judge the frequency of occurrence of the letter in the first position as the highest simply because it is easier to search for words beginning with k than for words in which k occurs in subsequent positions.

The third heuristic described by Tversky and Kahneman (1974) is called anchoring and adjustment. In order to ease the strain on the memory and reason, an individual may arrive at his estimate by beginning with a value which represents some familiar feature of the event or is provided as part of the circumstances associated with the event and adjust this value to give the final estimate. As an example of the anchoring and adjustment heuristic, Slovic (1972) discusses an experiment in which subjects were asked to attach monetary values to gambles described by prizes and probabilities for winning. Slovic (1972) observed that the subjects determined the monetary value of the gamble by the size of the prize and then adjusted this value to compensate for the less-than-perfect chance of winning. In essence, the subjects anchored on the prize and then adjusted for risk. Slovic (1972) found that this adjustment is insufficient, explaining why people are led to setting prices that are inconsistent with their preferences.

Anchoring and insufficient adjustment are cited by Slovic (1972) and Tversky and Kahneman (1974) as the reason why probability distributions estimated subjectively are invariably too narrow; this result has been observed for sophisticated as well as naïve subjects.

An experiment by Tversky and Kahneman (1974) demonstrates well the biases due to anchoring and adjustment. Three types of events were described

(1) simple events, such as drawing a red marble from a bag containing 50 per cent red marbles and 50 per cent white;

(2) conjunctional events, such as drawing a red

marble seven times in succession, with replacement, from a population having 90 per cent red marbles and 10 per cent white marbles;

(3) disjunctive events, such as drawing a red marble at least once in seven successive trials, with replacement from a population having 10 per cent red and 90 per cent white marbles.

The probabilities for the simple, conjunctive, and disjunctive events, respectively, were 0.50, 0.48, and 0.52. In spite of the fact that the probability for the simple event is greater than that of the conjunctive event, subjects chose the conjunctive event when presented with these two alternatives. Here it is suggested that the subjects anchored on the proportion of red marbles, which for the conjunctive event was greater than that for red marbles: 0.9 compared to 0.5. Subsequent adjustment for the compound conjunctive event was insufficient. Similarly, subjects chose the conjunctive event in preference to the disjunctive, even though the probability for the conjunctive event was lower than that for the disjunctive event. The proportion of red for conjunctive was 0.9 while that for the disjunctive was 0.10; subsequent adjustment was insufficient to reflect the different combinations implied by these two compound events. Tversky and Kahneman (1974) propose that the direction of bias can sometimes be inferred by examining the structure of the event: 'The chain-like structure of conjunction leads to overestimation, the funnel-like structure of disjunction leads to underestimation.' [Copyright 1974 by The American Association for the Advancement of Science.]

Tversky and Kahneman hypothesize that in estimating probabilities, people search for some calculational algorithm and that their estimates are as valid as is the algorithm. Anchoring and adjustment represents a calculational scheme or algorithm. Slovic (1972) points out that there are two sources of uncertainty in this process: uncertainty of each step in the algorithm and uncertainty of the algorithm itself. Adjustment fails to compensate for the multiplicity of errors.

Slovic (1972) documents how judgements of correlation and causation in experimental circumstances are not compatible with probability theory. To demonstrate departure from theory, he considers a matrix containing the frequency of occurrence of two conditions of A and two of B (see Table 14.1). In the body of the table are frequencies of occurrences of the four possible combinations: A_1B_1, A_1B_2, A_2B_1, and A_2B_2. Probability theory indicates that, given that event A_1 is known to occur, the

TABLE 14.1. *A joint frequency matrix*

Events	B_1	B_2
A_1	$f(A_1, B_1)$	$f(A_1, B_2)$
A_2	$f(A_2, B_1)$	$f(A_2, B_2)$

probability for B_1 would be determined as

$$P(B_1 \mid A_1) = \frac{f(A_1, B_1)}{f(A_1, B_1) + f(A_1, B_2)}.$$

Similarly,

$$P(B_1 \mid A_2) = \frac{f(A_2, B_1)}{f(A_2, B_1) + f(A_2, B_2)}.$$

If a correlation between A and B_1 is present, $P(B_1 \mid A_1)$ will differ from $P(B_1 \mid A_2)$. According to Slovic (1972), research indicates that the presence of correlation is not assessed by comparing these two probabilities. Instead, the strength of a relationship between B_1 and A_1 would be based solely upon the relative size of $f(A_1, B_1)$. The other information was ignored.

The principle of concreteness is suggested by Slovic (1972) as important in understanding the description of information-processing strategies of the mind. This principle explains the tendency of a decision-maker or judge to use only information that is explicitly displayed in the stimulus object and to use it only in the form in which it is presented. Information that has been stored in memory or must be inferred or transformed tends to be discounted or ignored. This principle has been demonstrated by betting situations (Slovic and Lichtenstein 1968; Payne and Braunstein 1971).

Slovic (1972) documents a number of studies that explore the way that man makes decisions (Kates 1962; Burton and Kates 1964; Woods 1966; Cyert and March 1963; and Lindblom 1964) in varied situations (policy, business, and environment). He makes this comment regarding these studies (Slovic 1972, p. 22).

The avoidance of uncertainty, the avoidance of 'weighing relative merits and drawbacks', crisis orientation, and the avoidance of long-range forecasting are just what one would expect, given what the laboratory studies indicate about our cognitive limitations.

Man's considerable accomplishments stand in contrast to the limitations of intellect that have been here described and are described in greater detail in the literature of psychometrics and decision-making. As an explanation of this apparently schizoid being, man, consider the lengthy, but valuable, quote from Slovic (1972, pp. 24–5).

> It is interesting to speculate about why we have such great confidence in our intuitive judgments, in the light of the deficiencies that emerge when they are exposed to scientific scrutiny. For one thing, our basic perceptual motor skills are remarkably good, the product of a long period of evolution, and thus we can process *sensory* information with remarkable ease. This may fool us into thinking that we can process conceptual information with similar facility. Anyone who tries to predict where a baseball will land by calculating its impact against the bat, trajectory of flight, etc., will quickly realize that his analytic skills are inferior to his perceptual–motor abilities. Another reason for our confidence is that the world is structured in such a complex, multiply-determined way that we can usually find some reason for our failures, other than our inherent inadequacies—bad luck is a particularly good excuse in a probabilistic world. . . . He (man) is essentially a trial-and-error learner and there is little evidence that he can change his ways even when errors will be quite costly (see for example, Schrader, 1971).

14.4. Doubts about self-ratings of expertise and about Delphi

14.4.1. *Expertise and self-ratings in other studies*

Subsequent to the completion of the New Mexico uranium survey (Ellis *et al.* 1975; see Chapter 13), inquiry was made of the literature on the use of Delphi methods and applications. Most of this literature concerns the use of Delphi in assessment of values, issues, or future states of society, the economy, or technologic innovation. Not all of the findings presented in these studies apply to the use of opinion survey in the appraisal of mineral resources for, in the case of social issues, individual value structures may dominate judgement of events or of issues. Nevertheless, one problem seems common to all applications, that is the identification of and use of experts. Since problems and issues in the identification of experts for mineral resource appraisal were discussed in the New Mexico study, no additional comment will be made here on identification; however the performance of experts and the manner in which multiple opinion is resolved are considered in this section.

Some non-mineral studies that are reported in literature have examined self-rating (self-confidence) as an index to expertise; two such studies are those of Dalkey (1969) and Campbell [2]. Sackman (1974, pp. 38, 39) summarizes the findings of Campbell and Dalkey.

In Campbell's doctoral dissertation on forecasting short-term economic indicators (1966), level of expertise was tested in terms of self-confidence ratings. He correlated these ratings for each item against forecasting accuracy and found the results did not differ significantly from a median correlation of zero. Campbell concluded that "Selecting the most self-confident members of a group based on the five-point or group self-confidence scales, was not an effective means of identifying the most accurate forecasters" (p. 112).

Dalkey (1969), also using self-confidence ratings of expertness for each item, was able to compare those "more expert" against those "less expert" for almanac-types questions. "The basic hypothesis being tested was that a subgroup of more knowledgeable individuals could be selected in terms of their self-rating, and that this group in general would be more accurate than the total group. In every case this hypothesis was not confirmed" (p. 68).

Similar results were reported by Bedford (1972) with respect to differences between housewives and experts for technological developments and by Reisman, Mantel, Dean, and Eisenberg (1969, p. 40) with respect to responses from laymen and experts in evaluations of social service. Sackman (1974) concludes that 'These studies collectively indicate that it doesn't make any difference how expert the respondent is, or how confident he feels about his opinion, when forecasting or estimating a wide variety of social, economic, and technological phenomena.' Sackman acknowledges, however, that some studies have shown differences in the expected direction (higher self-rated being more accurate) of responses for different levels of expertise, but points out that with exception of a study by Dalkey, Brown, and Cochran (1969), these differences were not statistically significant (Kaplan, Skogstad, and Girshick 1950; Campbell [2]) for an experienced subset.

As indicated in the foregoing quotations, Sackman interprets these studies as a verdict not only against the usefulness of self-ratings but also against the usefulness of experts in a variety of social, economic, and technological assessments. The finding in the New Mexico uranium appraisal seems to support the verdict on self-ratings. Because of the involvement of the ego, self-rating at best would be a very noisy index of accuracy. While self-rating seems highly suspect as a useful measure of degree of expertise and reliability on both *a priori* considerations and empirical studies, Sackman's conclusion that experts provide no better estimates than lay persons should not be universally accepted without further investigation. Such a conclusion may be correct for opinion surveys of social issues in which personal values affect judgement and response or in almanac-type questions, but it would be premature and perhaps incorrect to accept this as a proven fact for the physical sciences in which personal values are not involved and in which lay persons may be relatively naïve of even the *identity* of the elements of the subject matter, let alone its state under specified or hypothesized conditions.

14.4.2. *A critique of Delphi methods*

The conventional Delphi method is characterized by the use of a panel of experts, assured anonymity of experts, simple and direct polling of each expert individually, analysis of the results of the first-round survey, feedback of some statistical summary of the first-round survey such as the average, and successive polling and feedback for as many iterations as required for either a consensus of the panel or some desired degree of convergence.

Conventional Delphi and modified versions have been applied over a wide variety of fields. While adoption as a valid survey tool has been widespread, it has not been without its critics. The most comprehensive analysis and critique of conventional Delphi methods was made by Sackman (1974). Besides surveying the entire field of applied and experimental work involving Delphi methods, Sackman evaluates the method by professional standards that have been promulgated for statistical surveys of opinion by social scientists. Sackman's (1974, p. 70) evaluative recommendations are

Two alternative final recommendations were considered as conclusions of this evaluation. One was to seek to upgrade Delphi by recommending higher standards, more consistent with scientific method in the collection, analysis, and use of questionnaire data. The other was to conclude that the assumptions and principles on which conventional Delphi is based are so unscientific and inherently misleading that they preclude any attempts to improve the technique. This second alternative was tantamount to a recommendation to drop Delphi completely. The evidence adduced in this study clearly indicates that the massive liabilities of Delphi, in principle and in practice, outweigh its highly doubtful assets.

As a preferred alternative to conventional Delphi, professionals, funding agencies, and users are urged to work with psychometrically-trained social scientists who can apply rigorous questionnaire techniques and scientific human experimentation procedures tailored to their particular needs.

Whether or not Sackman's general verdict on Delphi is accurate or appropriate, some of the evidence and reasoning by which he reached this conclusion merits careful consideration. No attempt is made here to represent this thorough and comprehensive critique: only a few of the findings that led to his general conclusion are described. The reader is encouraged to consult the published material for a complete treatment.

One issue criticized by Sackman is the stress in Delphi methods on anonymity, feedback, and consensus, or at least some degree of convergence. To begin with, Sackman draws attention to the fact that professional standards established for statistical analysis of surveys require independent responses. Obviously, only the first-round responses are independent, making analysis of Delphi results meaningless in terms of their reliability in a probabilistic or statistical sense. Furthermore, Sackman questions the desirability for statistical feedback and consensus on the grounds that seeking consensus or convergence may be counter to scientific inquiry, which would seek differing opinions and would examine the assumptions and logic supporting them.

Instead of testing a great variety of flexible alternatives, the method zeroed in on iterative statistical group response. The alternatives could have branched out into structured adversary procedures including dialectical planning (e.g. Mason, 1969), adversary polling between groups with vested interests as in SPRITE (e.g. Bedford, 1972), iterative online teleconferences (e.g., Sackman and Citrenbaum, 1972), and eclectic mixtures of confrontation and isolated responses (e.g., Heller, 1969, Weaver, 1972). All of these areas need vigorous experimental work.

Sackman recognizes the well-documented tendency of individuals to conformity to group norm for purely psychological or social reasons. Such tendency could lead to some convergence even when the facts before the individual have not been modified and logic has not been persuaded.

Experimental results do not lead to clear-cut conclusion as to form of feedback information nor to its processing by the respondents. Chesley (1974) states that experiments have shown that greater accuracy was achieved when estimation was first done individually but was followed by group discussion, which in turn was followed by individual reestimation than by statistical feedback alone (Delphi) or by direct group interaction and estimation. This estimate–discuss–reestimate approach is known as a nominal group approach (Gustafson, Shukla, Delbecq, and Walster 1973). On the other hand, Dalkey (1969) compared face-to-face with anonymous Delphi interaction on almanac-type questions and found a tendency towards greater accuracy in the anonymous setting, but a statistically non-significant tendency (Sackman 1974), and Campbell [2] found that estimates of 16 short-term economic indicators by Delphi groups were significantly more accurate in a statistical sense

than those provided by face-to-face groups—
Sackman (1974) questions the validity of the statistical tests. But, Farquhar (1970) compared group versus anonymous Delphi interaction for a complex
software estimation task and consistently obtained
substantially better results in the face-to-face group
(Sackman 1974). Perhaps, Maier's (1967) conclusion
as summarized by Sackman (1974) sums up the
problem of attempting to resolve the methodological
problem of form of feedback and interaction.

> ...the comparative effectiveness of individuals versus
> groups varies widely and depends upon the tradeoff of
> the assets and liabilities of both approaches in the unique
> applied setting. He emphasizes the crucial role played by
> experienced group leaders acting as neutral facilitators in
> achieving successful group outcomes.

With regard to groups and group leaders, the word
'*neutral*' in the foregoing quotation should be emphasized strongly. An 'in-house' (firm, agency, or
organization) group having a vice-president or high
official with some other label serving as group leader,
hardly meets the intent of this requirement. For even
if he strives earnestly to be impartial, previously held
views, either stated or interpreted by his underlings
within the organization, may affect the opinions of
members of the group. Furthermore, attempts at
impartiality in leading the group to explore the issue
may be less than perfect, and in some cases, the
attempt may be token only. The poor performance
of group estimation as compared to nominal group, as
previously described, is attributed to difficulties with
interacting groups (Chesley 1974; Goodman 1972).

In addition to the nonneutrality of an in-house
leader on group performance, there is the effect of
interpersonal judgements of panel members *vis-à-
vis* other panel members, such as professional pecking order, real or imagined, and the effect of personality clash, which could lead to polarized estimates
for other than scientific, objective reasons. Finally,
there is the irrepressible fact that dominant personalities may have a greater influence than justified
by knowledge or insight.

The potential for personal influence to directly or
indirectly mold group opinion must be recognized as
a liability for groups, particularly 'in-house' varieties.
Perhaps the benefits that derive from the arguing of
assumptions and relevant facts could be better handled through other techniques, such as computer–
man–group interfacing, or teleconferencing, as
suggested by Sackman (1974).

Let us bypass the question of the best means of
feedback and resolution of multiple opinion and
examine the more fundamental question of why

employ feedback or group interaction at all? Knowing that man is psychologically inclined to group
conformity suggests that feedback under controlled
conditions will lead to some kind of convergence.
Convergence that reflects only this tendency is at
best of dubious value, especially when other experiments on psychometrics previously described indicate
that individuals underestimate the true variation due
to the heuristics they employ to estimate uncertain
events. In view of this fact, convergence induced by
statistical feedback of estimates only may have a
negative value to a study. The primary justification
for feedback of any kind must be that of exploration
of assumptions and logic. In this regard, statistical
feedback of estimates only appears to fail totally.
Feedback should consist of information in addition
to the estimate.

Consideration of the criticisms of Delphi suggests
that unless circumstances accommodate the imper-
sonal exchange of information on assumptions and
physical relations, there should be no feedback. Estimates should reflect first-round responses only.

Finally, given the evidence of bounded intelligence
that was examined in the previous section, a reasonable conclusion seems to be that the human resources
available for a subjective opinion survey should be
devoted to obtaining the *best possible* first-round
result, not to modifying hastily made initial estimates
as is done in conventional Delphi, particularly if
these methods rely upon man's emotional or social
tendencies.

The comments of Chesley (1974) provide what
seems to be an appropriate emphasis.

> The three factors which are apparent from literature and
> which can affect how consistent a subject's performance
> will be are the technique for elicitation and the possible
> use of a sequence of techniques, the subject's back-
> ground, and the type of data process used. . . . The major
> factor, however, would seem to be the elicitation techni-
> que because without it the feelings of the subject
> cannot be converted into the usable format of subjective
> probabilities.

14.5. Purposeful hedging

Purposeful hedging of estimates is an important dimension of influence upon estimates provided by a
geologist. In that this influence results at least in part
from a conscious motivation, which overrules the
exercise of best practice of geoscience, it is of a
different dimension than biases due to the use of
heuristics and psychological needs. Furthermore, this
influence is difficult to document by all of its motivations, for some of them carry an aura of non-

professional performance. Others, while equally undesirable and nonprofessional, are motivated by seemingly nonselfish considerations. Even so, any purposeful hedging is undesirable to the resource analyst, for he desires to have an estimate of endowment, or resources, which reflects strictly geological data and the current state of geoscience, in other words, a purely geological estimate. If for policy decisions other issues, such as risk of error of a specific kind, require the use of a conservative estimate, such should be selected in full knowledge of the price of such a choice.

An example of a seemingly unselfish motivation to hedge is the belief by a geologist that conservatism is a virtue. Akin to this motivation is the belief that he is providing society a service by making conservative estimates, because it is *better to always be pleasantly surprised than to be occasionally disappointed.* Some geologists feel strongly justified in providing conservative estimates because of a strongly held conviction that geological estimates usually are misused by the politicians or governmental bodies that set policy.

Selfish motivations to hedge estimates include the desire to protect vested interests. These vested interests are various. One of them is a previously made estimate. Another might be the economic interests of the firm, or other body. A vivid example of this was encountered in the research described in Chapter 15, which deals with formalizing geological decisions. One of the geologists who participated in that study and who was affiliated with a firm engaged in uranium exploration had a concern which persisted throughout the study that the system which formalizes decisions would result in estimates which would be too high. He never once registered concern that the estimates would not be 'good' estimates from a geological point of view, or that they would be too low. Yet, in casual conversation, he gave a clear impression that the region (San Juan Basin of New Mexico) is an area rich in uranium.

Selfish motivations may be political, economic, or professional. A form of the latter is the desire that his estimates—the geologist making the appraisal—be similar to those previously made by other geologists, particularly those who are highly reputable. Given that this motivation exists, it is very difficult to avoid the influence of these previously made estimates. Granted, the geologist can be asked to forget them and base his estimates strictly upon the exercise of geoscience, but because of the poorly understood linkages of geoscience, geodata, and mineral occurrence, this task is very difficult. If purposeful hedging is to be countered, or at least reduced to levels which

are not deemed serious, it will be only through appropriate appraisal design and implementation (see Chapter 15 for such a design and implementation).

14.6. Implications of psychometric issues to the appraisal of mineral resources

The results of the experimental studies cited raise serious doubts about the mental capabilities of man to make decisions about an uncertain event consistent with probability models and consistent with his own stated preferences. Having arrived at such a conclusion, what judgement follows with regard to the use of subjective appraisals of mineral resources? Should we abandon this approach entirely? According to Slovic (1972, p. 5), as a result of their experimental work, Tversky and Kahneman concluded that intuitive reason should be abandoned and replaced by formal statistical analysis. Of course, such an alternative is available to appraisers of mineral resources, as described in the section on multivariate statistical modes of mineral wealth and mineral occurrence. However, such a decision does not necessarily follow for all applied studies. Each case must be considered separately, for the important issues are not restricted just to the ability of man to imitate probability models. Three other issues must be considered

(1) the time available for the study;
(2) the alternative approaches;
(3) the information level of the experts as compared to that available to the public.

The first issue recognizes a fact of life; namely, that mineral resource appraisals are generally initiated by a political body at some level of government and that the time allowed for the appraisal often is too short to construct and validate a multivariate geostatistical model. This issue can only be fully appreciated by imagining the extreme but possible case in which there is no geological map available on the study area. Before a multivariate analysis could be performed, a map would have to be prepared. Preparation of a suitable map could take years. Emphasis should be given to the qualifier 'suitable'. For the common multivariate models which have been applied (regression and discriminant analysis), the level of geological information in the model can be no greater than the level of the least known cell. Furthermore, the level of information usable from a control area cannot exceed the level of information on the study area. Consequently, much of the geological information available on a thoroughly explored control area may not be usable if the study area has been mapped at the reconnaissance level (at a very small scale). Bias can be introduced by the less thorough geological mapping of one area than another. This places an extra premium on uniformity of mapping of the control and study areas and of all sub-areas comprising them.

The appraisal of mineral resources of large regions generally confronts the uniformity of information problem at the very initiation of the effort, either on the control area or study area or both. It is common to find that no single mapping effort covers the entire area of interest, even for well-explored regions. Generally, several maps must be consulted, and it is not unusual to find that as many as 30 years separate the preparation of these maps. Mapping procedures have not been constant over time. It can be an enlightening experience to compare maps made prior to the use of aerial photography to those for which extensive use was made of aerial photography as well as the customary detailed field work. Perhaps, the geological feature that differs most is the intensity of fault occurrences. Maps prepared post-World War II may have a density of faults several times that for maps prepared in the early-1900s.

The second issue warrants careful attention, for other than the multivariate models, the available methods fall into two categories: (1) the traditional nonprobabilistic approach and (2) the univariate spatial models. Given the desire by users of resource numbers for a description of the uncertainty about a subjective estimate, resorting to non-probabilistic methods is not likely to be a viable solution to psychometric issues. With regard to spatial models, if geological information is available, such models have little appeal, for they ignore geological data, which is tantamount to ascribing to all cells within the region a constant endowment.

The second issue is one which often arises when considering the appraisal of the resources of a large undeveloped region, such as part of a developing country. For some of these regions, some very excellent maps recently have been prepared, but there has been little resource development. Consequently, there is insufficient data on mineral occurrences in the region or nearby regions to constitute a control area for the quantification of the relationship of geological conditions to mineral occurrence. The only way a multivariate analysis can be performed, given these conditions, is to select an area for which both occurrence and geological data are available. This may require the use of a control area which is geographically far removed from the study area. While geographical separation is not important of itself, the fact that geological environments and mineral occurrences have a geography causes considerable concern, particularly if the information available from the study area indicates that its geologic environment is different in some respects from any well explored area which might serve as a control area. Various compromises may ease the severity of these differences somewhat, but not without costs. For example, the specificity of the geological variables may be reduced to give variables with a broader geological meaning, or a composite control area may be constructed which consists of several areas each from different geological environments, or the study area may be evaluated separately by several models, each one representing a specific environment. In all cases, the level of information usable in the control area or areas and the study area must be compromised to apply a multivariate analysis. While application of subjective probability analysis does not totally avoid these same problems, compromise of information may be considerably less.

The last issue, that of information, is important to the appraisal of mineral resources, for, as was previously indicated, the information on basic geoscience to which the field geologist has been exposed may exceed by a large margin the information available to the public for the construction of a multivariate model. So, while subjective assessment may provide biased answers because of the heuristics employed by the appraiser, a multivariate model built and validated upon a low level of geological information and then used for inference by evaluating the model upon equally low-level information on the unknowns (cells to be evaluated) may yield estimates that are less desirable than those of the experts, but for different reasons. It should be noted that this information issue was not examined in the experimental studies cited. In fact, some of the experiments employed situations in which the information level was restricted to that of probability for a univariate random variable; information about a causation structure was not an issue. Such limitation was purposeful so that the ability of man to imitate probability models could be examined.

The last issue takes on considerable weight when geologic environments are highly varied within the study area and when this study area is of considerable size. This follows from the possibility of including in the set of experts individuals who are not only generally well informed, but highly informed on different subregions of the study area. The collective information level of a set of experts composed of practicing explorationists could far exceed that available to an analyst from public data sources.

An alternative to abandonment of subjective assessment because of limitations of subjective processes is to use the knowledge of the ways that biases are introduced and the nature of the limitations of the intellect to design and employ subjective appraisal methods that diminish these biases and deficiencies and enhance the intellectual powers that man does possess. To this end, the experimental findings here considered raise some possibilities. These are described in the next section. As an ending to this section and a preface to the following section, consider a quotation from Slovic (1972, p. 25).

How does such a creature learn by experience, yet avoid catastrophe? A pessimist might advise him to take very small steps—small enough so that he can recover from the inevitable miscalculations. An optimist would reply that the technology of decision making will undoubtedly advance rapidly within the next decade. Perhaps an awareness of our limitations, coupled with sophisticated methods for decision analysis, will enable us to minimize many of the judgmental biases discussed in this paper. I'm an optimist.

14.7. Preferred procedures

The previous sections identified some limitations of subjective processes for the estimation of an uncertain event. While these limitations undeniably take some of the gloss off of subjective surveys, rejection of subjective appraisal may not be warranted. For one thing, as previously noted, there are significant advantages of a well-designed subjective survey. In view of these advantages, a good case can be made for examining ways of reducing the limitations through the use of especially designed survey procedures.

Furthermore, it does not follow that all of the limitations of man's subjective processes in imitating probability models of unstructured, random processes apply fully to the appraisal of mineral endowment, which is an exercise in estimating probability by assessing geological–resource information. The presence of structure in the decision process makes possible the design of a survey to enhance the contribution of this structure to definitive and consistent estimation.

The two most important features of a preferred subjective probability survey of mineral resources are

1. The survey should be based upon as

thorough and critical evaluation of geology as data and geology–resource theory permit.

2. The method of eliciting opinion as either single-point estimates or as probabilities should reduce, if possible, or at least not contribute to, the biases that arise from the heuristics that man employs to deal with uncertainty.

These two issues are not unrelated.

Recognition of the fact that man uses various heuristics to ease the strain of contemplating complex and uncertain events and that these heuristics can result in severe biases places considerable responsibility upon those conducting the mineral resources appraisal to take measures to reduce these biases. Such measures include providing education on probability concepts, providing analysis and review of reserves, production, and resources, decomposing the estimation of endowment to the estimation of simpler events, and employing a model for the reconstitution of these quantities to endowment. Companion to this decomposition and reconstitution is the stressing of the use by the geologist of geoscience in making his estimates of endowment. Where the event being estimated can be decomposed to components that interrelate according to known relationships, the persuasion is strong to require the appraiser to estimate the simpler events. Estimates of the simpler events subsequently would be combined through the appropriate relationships to provide the estimate of the compound event.

A simple example of the differences between a decomposed procedure and one that is not decomposed is the asking of a geologist to estimate tonnage of ore and grade of ore separately for each of many subdivisions of the region as contrasted to estimating the quantity of U_3O_8 directly for the entire region. Given the estimate of ore tonnage and grade, the tonnage of U_3O_8 for each subdivision would be determined by the relationship of U_3O_8 = tonnage of ore X grade. Then, the quantity of U_3O_8 for the entire region would be described by aggregating appropriately the U_3O_8 for the subdivisions. While this simple example demonstrates the idea, it understates the differences that could arise by decomposition when potential resources are to be estimated. For another comparison consider the following procedures.

1. The geologist examines the geology and provides an estimate of expected U_3O_8 for the entire region.

2. The geologist examines the geologic environment in general and for the subdivision being

evaluated and follows this by critical introspection of the observed geology and the geology–resource relationship. Subsequent to this critical introspection, the geologist provides estimates of the following for each mode of occurrence anticipated in the subdivision:

(a) probability for adequate sources for U_3O_8.
(b) most likely, high, and low estimates of
    (i) number of traps (collapse structures, stream channels, rollfronts, etc.),
    (ii) size of trap (volume).
(c) probability for favourable timing of trap formation and mobility of uranium.
(d) most likely, high, and low estimates of each of the following:
    (i) per cent of trap that is mineralized (concentration above a specified cut-off grade);
    (ii) average grade of mineralized material for a specified cut-off grade of mineralization;
    (iii) depth to trap.

Suppose also that supportive efforts have provided a probability distribution for tonnage–volume factors and a computer program which converts the above estimates to a probability distribution for U_3O_8 and then combines the distributions for the subdivisions to one distribution for the entire region. In addition, the program interacts exploration and exploitation simulators with endowment to yield probability distributions for quantity of U_3O_8 for cost category.

The point to be made here is *not* that alternative 2 as described is *the* methodology for appraisal of U_3O_8 resources, for the degree of disaggregation was selected arbitrarily and may be too much or too little; furthermore the structure of the decomposition is general and stylized and is solely for the demonstration of ideas. In practice decomposition would be done separately for each mode of occurrence so that the components could reflect the peculiarities of the geological processes involved, and at the same time be consistent with an appropriate model. By the appropriate model, components could then be recombined and integrated through subsequent data analysis. The point is that some degree of disaggregation of the geological phenomena involved is both appropriate and desirable for several reasons

1. It reduces the likelihood of severe bias due to heuristics.
2. It encourages a more critical analysis of the geology.

3. It promotes greater introspection as to caus and effect or association.
4. It allows the geologist to work more close with geoscience relationships and avoids th introduction of economics.
5. It results in a description of endowment in form that subsequently can be interacted wit economics for any economic conditions o interest.

Disaggregation in the spirit of alternative 2 to unit of estimation reflecting physical aspects of th geological setting in which deposits occur creates greater awareness and description of the range o possibilities for potential resources. This is due t greater specification of combinations by disaggrega tion of the factors involved and to the more critica examination of and greater weight given to the geol ogy of the study area by focusing attention o geological features or processes involved in or as sociated with the formation of deposits. At som level, analogies to known deposit occurrences an environments must be made; this is inescapable, bu if this is done at a greater level of decomposition, th greater should be the awareness of possible states o nature. The degree of decomposition and th geologic variables involved should be determine separately for each mode of occurrence; in practic this degree of decomposition is eventually bounde by our understanding of the geology–resource rela tionship and the need to reconstitute the informatio by a reasonable relationship (model), if not soone by limitations on data, time, or resources of expertise

Preferred survey procedures must include educa tion on concepts and principles of probability, th perspective of subjective probability, the objective of the survey, the need for critical and consisten introspection, the mechanics of the survey forms, an the role of the impartial and critical observer. Th need for this education cannot be overemphasized. A common, but not universal practice by geologist when providing a single-point estimate is to purpose fully discount their best estimate. The reasons fo this practice are various. One reason which has bee given is that the geologist realizes only too clearl the limitations on his ability and information and the resulting uncertainty about his estimate, and he fear that too great a confidence will be ascribed to hi estimate by those who use it. Therefore, he adjust his best estimate downward as a compensation fo uncertainty. Related to this motivation is the concep of 'professional modesty.' This motivation is expres sed by a geologist when he defends his estimate by stating that it represents a lower bound, or that 'we have at least that much.'

The tendency to understate single-point estimates of undiscovered resources, for whatever the motivation may be, can impart very undesirable effects to a subjective survey. Consider a geologist who has practised purposeful understating of single-point estimates and who now is asked to participate in a subjective probability survey by first selecting his most likely estimate. The possibility is considerable that in spite of the fact that this single value is described as a most likely estimate, the geologist will purposefully understate it for one of the reasons (motivations) described above. The impact of this purposeful understating can be especially serious, given the biases inherent in the heuristics employed for subjective assessment of an uncertain event. The combined effects of these biases and purposeful discounting could be a distribution having too low of a central tendency and much too narrow of a range.

The author has found that unless a special effort is given to explain to the geologist that he does not need to discount and, indeed, best serves the purpose of the appraisal by not discounting, the chances are considerable that he will do so. A useful perspective to give the geologist is that the providing of a probability distribution is in his best professional interest, for it allows him to express the uncertainty in his appraisal by providing a range of possible states of nature, and it allows him to ascribe relative weights (probabilities) to these states. Thus, the chances for his being proved wrong in an absolute sense are considerably decreased. Such a perspective should be useful in persuading the geologist to refrain from discounting.

A more difficult task is the persuading of the geologist who feels he should serve as a social conscience that purposeful discounting to assure that his estimate will not be 'misused' is not appropriate and that he best serves society and himself by providing honest, best estimates. Useful in this regard is the perspective that purposefully understating the resources of a given mineral may lead to the establishing of mineral policies that are not optimum for the welfare of society.

Preferred procedures will avoid traditional Delphi methods. Where the survey employs several or many participants, communication among participants should be restricted to discussing premises for estimation and basic geological information, not the estimates. Procedures that strive for a consensus by playing upon psychological tendencies to conformity serve no good purpose. Similarly, group assessment

should be avoided because of effects on estimation of dominant personalities, job security, peer acceptance, professional pecking order, etc.

Just what constitutes *the* preferred design should reflect the *best* compromise of probability theory and geology–resources theory in view of time, data, and manpower constraints. This decision should be one that is carefully and thoughtfully made, reflecting the input from (a) one or more geologists well informed in the geology–endowment relationships; (b) someone well informed in probability, geostatistics, and resource-modelling; (c) field personnel who are knowledgeable of data availability; (d) someone knowledgeable on data-processing and computer capabilities; and (e) administrative personnel who can advise as to objectives, time limitations, and budget matters.

The foregoing discussions on preferred procedures and of limitations of the mind lead naturally to the next chapter, which is the estimation of mineral endowment by disaggregating and formalizing the subjective analysis of geology and providing the geologist with the use of an interactive computer program to perform probability computations. Furthermore, this methodology provides a means for an anonymous exchange of geoscience by participating geologists as a prelude to formal analysis, thereby capturing some of the benefits of Delphi without incurring its liabilities.

References

Bedford, M. T. (1972). The value of "Comments" analysis of SPRITE as a planning tool, Delphi. *The Bell Canada experience.* Bell Canada.

Burton, I. and Kates, R. W. (1964). The perception of natural hazards in resource management. *Natural Resources J.* **3**, 412–41.

Chesley, G. R. (1974). Elicitation of subjective probabilities: a review. *ORSA/TIMS* [Operations Research Society of America/The Institute of Management Science] Bulletin, Fall 1974 ORSA/TIMS meeting held in San Juan, Puerto Rico, October 16–17–18, 1974. ORSA/TIMS, Baltimore, Maryland.

Cyert, R. M. and March, J. G. (1963). *A behavioral theory of the firm.* Prentice-Hall, Englewood Cliffs, New Jersey.

Dalkey, N. C. (1969). *The Delphi method: an experimental study of group opinion.* RM-5888-PR, The Rand Corporation.

——, Brown, B., and Cochran, S. W. (1969). *The Delphi method III: use of self-ratings to improve group estimates.* RM-6115-PR, The Rand Corporation.

Ellis, J. R., Harris, D. P., and Van Wie, N. H. (1975). *A subjective probability appraisal of uranium resources in the State of New Mexico.* Open File Report GJO-110(76). US Energy Research and Development Administration, Grand Junction, Colorado.

Farquhar, J. A. (1970). *A preliminary inquiry into the software estimation process.* RM-6271-PR, The Rand Corporation.

Goodman, B. C. (1972). Action selection and likelihood ratio estimation by individuals and groups. *Organizational behavior and human performance,* 7(1), 121–41.

Gustafson, D. H., Shukla, R. K., Delbecq, A., and Walster, G. W. (1973). A comparative study of differences in subjective likelihood estimates made by individuals, interacting groups, Delphi groups, and nominal groups. *Organizational behavior and human performance* 9(2), 280–91.

Heller, F. A. (1969). Group feedback analysis. *Psychol. Bull.* 72(2), 108–17.

Kaplan, A., Skogstad, A. L., and Girshick, M. A. (1950). The prediction of social and technological events. *Public Opinion Quart.* 14(1), 93–110.

Kates, R. W. (1962). *Hazard and choice perception in flood plain management.* Dept. of Geography Research Paper No. 8, University of Chicago.

Lindblom, C. E. (1964). The science of muddling through. In *The making of decisions* (ed. W. J. Gore and J. W. Dyson), pp. 155–69. Free Press, New York.

Maier, N. R. F. (1967). Assets and liabilities in group problem solving: the need for an integrative function. *Psychol. Rev.* 74(4), 239–49.

Mason, R. O. (1969). A dialectical approach to strategic planning, *Management Sci,* 15(8), B403–16.

Payne, J. W. and Braunstein, M. L. (1971). Preferences among gambles with equal underlying distributions. *J. exp. Psychol.* 87, 13–18.

Pickhardt, R. C. and Wallace, J. B. (1974). Applica-

tions and implementation: a study of the performance of subjective probability assessors. *Decision Sci.* 5(3) 347–63.

Reisman, A., Mantel, S. J., Dean, B. V., and Eisenberg, N. (1969). *Evaluation and budgeting model for a system of social agencies.* Technical Memorandum No. 167, Dept. of Operations Research, Case Western Reserve University, Cleveland, Ohio.

Sackman, H. (1974). *Delphi assessment: expert opinion, forecasting, and group process.* R-1283-PR, The Rand Corporation.

—— and Citrenbaum, R. (1972). *Online planning.* Prentice-Hall, Englewood Cliffs, New Jersey.

Schrader, G. (1971). Atomic doubletalk. *The Center Mag.* 4, 29–51.

Slovic, P. (1972). From Shakespeare to Simon: speculations—and some evidence—about man's ability to process information. *Oregon Res. Inst. Monograph* 12(12).

—— and Lichtenstein, S. (1968). Importance of variance preferences in gambling decisions. *J. exp. Psychol.* 78, 546–54.

Tversky, A. and Kahneman, D. (1972). Anchoring and calibration in the assessment of uncertain quantities. *Oregon Res. Inst. Res. Bull.* 12(5).

——, —— (1974). Judgment under uncertainty: heuristics and biases. *Science* 185 (4157), 1124–31.

Weaver, W. T. (1972). *Delphi, a critical review.* RR-7, Syracuse University Research Corporation, Syracuse, New York.

Woods, D. H. (1966). Improving estimates that involve uncertainty. *Harvard Bus. Rev.* 44, 91–8.

Notes

1. Alpert, M. and Raiffa, H. (1969). A progress report on the training of probability assessors. Unpublished draft, Harvard Business School.
2. Campbell, R. M. (1966). A methodological study of the utilization of experts in business forecasting. Unpublished Ph.D. dissertation, University of California, Los Angeles.

15.1. Perspective and scope

The appraisals and methods presented in Chapter 13 relied upon the geologist's qualitative geological analysis to infer from geological evidence to potential mineral occurrence. Uncertainties about the evidence and about inference were the bases for subjective probabilities about mineral endowment, or about its components. This is a highly intuitive and judgemental process. The geoscience relations employed by the geologist and the relative weights given by him to various kinds of geological evidence by this procedure are not identified or documented. Similarly, the roles played by geoscience–endowment relations and geodata in the perceived uncertainties which are reflected in the subjective probabilities are vague. Both the geological and probability analyses can be described as implicitly made. For this reason, such appraisals have been referred to as implicit subjective (Harris and Carrigan 1981) probability appraisals; given that the appraisal is understood to be one of subjective probability, only the term implicit may be employed.

Chapter 14 identified some significant deficiencies in the implicit approach. Everything else being equal, these deficiencies may prompt the turning away from the use of experts to the use of strictly quantitative geostatistical methods as a means of bringing together geology, endowment, and probability. Even if these alternative methods were relatively devoid of special problems, the mere fact that some regions are only superficially explored may make their use problematic; even when the geological environment appears favourable, there often is insufficient data on known mineral deposits to support the development and estimation of a multivariate geostatistical model. The appeal is strong in such circumstances to translate the favourability of the geological environment into potential endowment through the use of the geoscience of the expert geologist, that science which is responsible for identifying the geological environment as favourable. But, because of the difficulties of mentally performing simultaneous geological and probability analysis, there also is the need for (1) capturing and using this geoscience in a way that diminishes the biases due to heuristics of subjective assessment, (2) preventing purposeful hedging, (3) documentation of estimation procedure, and (4) the promotion of thorough data integration.

There are two recently developed approaches which strive to implement geoscience by first identifying the relevant relations of processes and geological conditions and then formally stating these relations as a decision structure. For the moment, these two approaches are referred to simply as A and B (see Fig. 15.1). While A and B are similar in that they employ geoscience and a decision structure, they differ greatly in many other respects. Only one of these is identified here, mode of data use and integration. Fig. 15.1 is a schematic representation of these two approaches, highlighting differences in data use and integration. The schematic diagrams are overly simplified in that they do not show the differences that exist in the design, structure, and function of decision analysis. This is purposefully done so as to expose a basic difference, which is both philosophical and methodological, between approaches A and B.

While both approaches formalize geoscience, the philosophy of approach B is that analyses of geodata should be quantitative, i.e. subjective geological analysis of data is purposefully avoided. In this approach the various forms of geodata are each quantified to binary or ternary form, and these data are submitted directly to decision analysis. Approach B requires that these various kinds of quantified geodata be integrated through quantitative relations (equations) involving the binary or ternary variables and that this be done within the decision module. Once the decision module has been constructed and is ready for use, the geologist who uses it to make estimates functions passively in that he does not perform geological analyses or integrate geodata.

The philosophy represented by approach A runs counter to that of B; namely, the quantifying to a binary or ternary scheme of geodata fails to capture much of the information present in the geodata, and the subsequent integration of such quantified geodata by strictly quantitative relations falls far short of the information captured, integrated, and employed by the mental processes of the geologist. This approach requires the geologist to play an active role in analysing and integrating—through the practice of conventional geoscience—the information present in

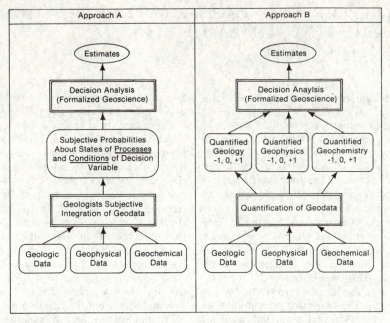

Fig. 15.1. Schematic representation of two approaches to the formal use of geoscience.

the various kinds of geodata when considered collectively. Only after analysis and integration of these data does the geologist use the decision module. He does this by answering questions about the states of processes or geological conditions of his decision module; all answers, which are subjective probabilities, are made only after he has completed his analysis and integration of the basic geodata.

Those who favour approach B would defend their choice by the fact that it is an objective—avoids subjective—geological analysis. They may argue further that only by excluding the subjective analysis of geologists can one avoid the variations in estimates among geologists and the biases due to the psychometric issues discussed in Chapter 14. Those favouring approach A would argue that simplistic coding (binary or ternary) of geodata and simplistic integration of data by quantitative relations may combine data but cannot, at least at present, achieve the same levels of information relevant to geoscience as is achieved by the integration which takes place in the mind of an expert and experienced geologist.

In a broad sense, then, approach B formalizes geoscience and strives for a strictly quantitative use of geodata by this formalized geoscience, while approach A formalizes geoscience as part of a system in which the geologist plays an active role in the

analysis and integration of geodata as a prerequisite to the use of decision analysis. As implied in earlier comments, differences in these two approaches are far greater than this basic difference in the use and integration may suggest. While Fig. 15.1 shows A and B to be similar in that each has a decision module, these modules differ greatly in design and function. These differences have been ignored in this discussion on perspective so as to examine the 'big picture' of the use in a system of the geologist, geoscience, and geodata.

15.2. Formalized geoscience which supports active analysis of data by the geologist (approach A)—the uranium endowment appraisal system of Harris and Carrigan

15.2.1. *Overview of appraisal system* [1]

The endowment appraisal system developed in this study is complex. Consequently, it is useful at the beginning of this report to establish a strong impression of the overall features of the system before taking up the procedures for the design and use of the system.

Fig. 15.2 provides a schematic overview of the components of the appraisal system. The items in the

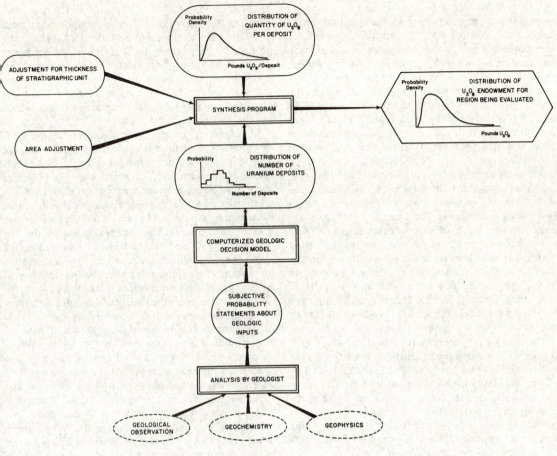

Fig. 15.2. Schematic representation of the endowment appraisal system.

heavily outlined boxes are the active components of the system. The items in the circles are either outputs or inputs. The active components perform computations, decisions, or analyses; these include

- the geologist involved in the appraisal of the mineral endowment of a region;
- a computerized geological decision model (this component consists of the formalized geoscience of uranium cast in an interactive computer program);
- a synthesis computer program (this combines output from the decision model with other information and computes the probability distribution for U_3O_8).

Imagine that you are the geologist who has the responsibility for estimating the uranium endowment of a region in the San Juan Basin and that you are going to make that estimation by using this system. In other words, all other active components have been described and are ready to use. You could be using a geological decision model which you had constructed at an earlier date, or you could be using one previously constructed by someone else. At any rate, consider that such a system is ready to be used to estimate uranium endowment. Your experience in using the system might be, in its simplest form, as follows. A programmer activates the interactive system. This system questions you about the states of some of the earth processes which comprise the decision model. For example, you might be asked if the rate of erosion of the source rock was rapid, intermediate, or slow. You would respond by entering through the interactive computer console your subjective probabilities for each of these states of weathering. You feel a bit uncertain about responding, so you ask for a review of various geological maps. These maps appear on the plasma screen before you. You consider this information plus any supplementary information on geology, geophysics, and geochemistry which you might have in estimating these probabilities. When the geological information available to you makes you feel certain that the rate of erosion was rapid, you provide a probability of 1.0 for this state of the process and 0 for the other two states [2]. Or if, after examination and consideration of all the evidence, you feel that you have no knowledge about the rate of erosion, you give all three states equal probability, entering a probability 0.333 for each of the three states. Usually, examination of the evidence will leave you feeling uncertain but having preferences; for example, you may feel quite strongly, but by no means certain, that the rate of erosion was rapid, and you may feel nearly certain that it was not slow. In this case, depending on the strength of the evidence, you may give a probability of 0.75 for rapid, 0.24 for moderate, and 0.01 for slow. You proceed in this fashion until you have responded to all questions asked by the system about the states of the processes.

The use by a geologist of a system which had previously been designed consists only of the geologist providing these probabilities. Once he has completed this task, his work is completed. The computerized decision model then combines these probabilities with probabilities that exist in the decision model to produce a probability distribution for number of deposits. This is an output of the interactive system, as indicated in Fig. 15.2.

Uranium endowment is only partially described by this probability distribution for number of deposits. First, this probability distribution is for a *reference area*, an area of standard size and a standard thickness of formation (not the area and thickness of the region being appraised), but having the same geology as the region being evaluated, as described by the geologist. Second, our objective is a probability distribution for the magnitude of uranium endowment (not just number of deposits) for the region being evaluated. The endowment probability distribution can only be determined by considering both the probability distribution for number of deposits, which has been computed by the interactive system (geological decision model), and the probability distribution for quantity of uranium per deposit.

The component in Fig. 15.2, referred to as the synthesis program, takes as inputs the thickness of the stratigraphic unit being evaluated, the area underlain by the stratigraphic unit, the probability distribution for number of deposits (which was computed by the geological decision model) for an area of standardized dimensions (reference area), the probability distribution for tonnage of uranium per deposit, and adjustment relations for thickness and area. Given these inputs, the synthesis program computes a probability distribution for the quantity of uranium contained by that stratigraphic unit within the region under evaluation.

In summary, the geologist appraises uranium endowment by using a previously designed system. He does this by functioning as a geoscientist: he considers all of the geoscience information available to him and then subjectively estimates probabilities for the earth processes of the geological decision model (formalized geoscience) having or having had various states. These probabilities are processed by the appraisal system, and a probability distribution for quantities of uranium occurring in the stratigraphic unit within the region being appraised is determined by the system; this distribution is the objective of the analysis and is the principal output of the system.

The foregoing description conveys an overall view of this methodology for the appraisal of mineral endowment. Furthermore, when the geologist is a user of an already constructed system, this portrays simply his function in appraisal. However, when an appraisal system has not been prepared for use, the experience of making an appraisal by this methodology is much different than that just described.

Simply stated, implementation of the system in the latter case requires the construction of the geological model, the definition of the inputs to the synthesis program, and the estimation of the subjective probabilities for the process states for that region being evaluated. This simple statement of work is rather deceptive, for these major tasks involve many smaller but difficult tasks. A more accurate perception of what is involved in implementation of the system is obtained by considering the following activities

- assembling of relevant geological literature and maps;
- assembling of production data and reserves;
- making of 16-mm slides of relevant maps, data, and instructions. (These are placed in a carousel which is mounted on the rear of the PLATO terminal, and upon command projects the slide onto the plasma screen of the terminal.);
- eliciting of the inference net—processes involved in the formation of uranium deposits;
- computerizing of the inference net;
- exchange of geoscience among participants and

finalizing of inference net;

- specifying of a ranking scheme—ranking of process combinations and classifying their favourability;
- calibration of ranking scheme—adjusting favourability groupings of subprocesses so that stratigraphic units are properly described by major process combinations;
- linking of geological decision model to endowment-measure probability distributions;
- specifying of probability distributions for quantity of U_3O_8 per deposit or per mineralized cell;
- specifying of area and thickness adjustment relations;
- calibration of appraisal system—modifying probability distribution for endowment measure (number or fraction);
- estimating for each partition of each stratigraphic unit the probabilities for the states of the end processes of the inference net.

The last activity constitutes use of the system. All other activities are those required for design of the system for a new region, e.g. Wyoming.

15.2.2. *The geological decision model—formalized geoscience*

This section examines (1) the concepts involved in linking probability to geoscience, uranium endowment, and evidence (geological, geophysical, and geochemical information) and (2) procedures employed in the actual formalizing process and in calibration of formalized science (geological decision model).

Probability, geoscience, and endowment—concepts and approach

Consider the following proposition (Harris and Carrigan 1981, p. 1034).

> Given observations of geological features and geoscience measurements for a region, the uncertainty in the mind of a geologist about the number of deposits present in that region consists of incomplete knowledge of the geoscience of that kind of mineral occurrence and uncertainty about the geological history that is suggested by these geological features and geoscience measurements.

'Let us represent the incomplete knowledge about geoscience of mineral endowment simplistically by a conditional probability for number of deposits, $P(N = n \mid X = x)$; that is, given that the state of the earth process, X, within the region is x, the number of deposits present is a random variable, denoted by N' [Harris and Carrigan 1981, p. 1034]. For each

TABLE 15.1. *Probability distribution for number of deposits conditional on earth process having state of x_1*

n	$P(N = n \mid X = x_1)$
0	0.1
1	0.2
2	0.3
3	0.4

value of X, there exists a distribution of probabilities for the random variable N. Suppose for example that X can take on three values (x_1, x_2, and x_3) and that N can take on four values (0, 1, 2, and 3). Suppose that when $X = x_1$ the probabilities for each of the four possible values of N are given in Table 15.1. When X takes on the values of x_2 and x_3, we have different probabilities for the four levels of N, as indicated in Table 15.2. Each of these columns of probabilities is referred to as a conditional probability distribution $h_1(n \mid x_1)$, $h_2(n \mid x_2)$, and $h_3(n \mid x_3)$.

So far, we have dealt only with geoscience. Let us now consider the use of geoscience for *estimation*. More specifically, suppose that our objective is to describe the probability distribution for the number of deposits in a specific region, given the *geological data* available for that region. If the geologist were omniscient with regard to the geological history of the region, he would know which state of nature correctly depicts that region; hence he would select that one of the probability distributions which is conditional upon that state of nature. For example, if he knew that the state of nature in the region were x_1, then he could state that the expected number of deposits is 2.0, but that other events could occur, as indicated by the events noted in Table 15.1 and their probabilities. He could show, for example, by means of the conditional probability distribution, that although the expected value for number of deposits is 2.0, the most likely number is 3 deposits, for which the probability of occurrence is 0.4.

TABLE 15.2. *Probability distributions for number of deposits conditional on earth process having states of x_2 and x_3*

n	$P(N = n \mid X = x_2)$	$P(N = n \mid X = x_3)$
0	0.2	0.3
1	0.3	0.3
2	0.3	0.2
3	0.2	0.2

Typically, a geologist does not know for certain the state of the earth processes in the region being evaluated. However, he does have some ideas about the possible states because of his ability to observe geological features and to make measurements on the chemistry and physics of the earth. Even so, there often is uncertainty in his mind about which state caused these features. Let us capture this uncertainty by describing another probability concept, the probability for the state of process X, conditional upon the geological observations $(g_1, \ldots, g_m)$ made by the geologist

$$P(X = x_1 \mid g_1, g_2, \ldots, g_m).$$

That is, given the m geological observations made by the geologist, there exists uncertainty in his mind as to which state prevails in the region, and this uncertainty is expressed by subjective probabilities for the states. For example, for a given set of observations of the geological features, a geologist may have the subjective probabilities indicated in Table 15.3, reflecting the uncertainty in his mind of the inference from geological features to process states x_1, x_2, and x_3. These probabilities are represented by the probability function ϕ

$$P(X = x \mid g_1, \ldots, g_m) = \phi(x \mid g_1, \ldots, g_m).$$

Recall that it is our objective to make a statement about the probabilities for number of deposits, given that the geologist has made geological observations $(g_1, \ldots, g_m)$. Thus far, we have defined the probability for N conditional on X and the probability for X conditional upon $g_1, \ldots, g_m$. Our objective is the probability for N conditional on $g_1, \ldots, g_m$. Using some basic probability laws, we can compute the desired probabilities from the relations considered thus far. The first thing that we must compute is the probability for the *joint occurrence* of N and X, conditional upon $g_1, \ldots, g_m$ having occurred. For this we rely upon the multiplication law of probability

$$P(A, B) = P(A \mid B) \cdot P(B).$$

This defines the probability for the joint (together) occurrence of events A and B as the product of the probability for A given that B has occurred and the probability for B occurring. In probability jargon, the joint probability is the product of conditional and marginal probabilities. In our case, we can use this law to compute the probability for the joint occurrence of N and X, given $g_1, \ldots, g_m$

$$P(N = n_1, X = x_1 \mid g_1, \ldots, g_m)$$
$$= P(N = n_1 \mid X = x_1) \cdot P(X = x_1 \mid g_1, \ldots, g_m).$$

For example, employing information from Tables 15.1 and 15.3, we can compute the probability for the joint occurrence of $N = 1$ and $X = x_1$

$$P(N = 1, X = x_1 \mid g_1, \ldots, g_m)$$
$$= \underbrace{P(N = 1 \mid X = x_1)}_{(0.2)} \cdot \underbrace{P(X = x_1 \mid g_1, \ldots, g_m)}_{(0.2)} = 0.04.$$

We are only part way to our objective, for we wish to compute the probability for only $N = 1$, conditional upon $g_1, \ldots, g_m$, not the probability for the joint occurrence of $N = 1$ and $X = x_1$. To do this, we must add the probabilities for $N = 1$ when $X = x_1$, $X = x_2$, and $X = x_3$, conditional upon $g_1, \ldots, g_m$. For example, using the multiplicative law, as just demonstrated, we can form the joint probabilities of Table 15.4 (the computation just made is in the first row and third column of this table). As another example, the entry in the uppermost left-hand box of Table 15.4 is computed as

$$P(N = 0, X = x_1 \mid g_1, \ldots, g_m)$$
$$= P(N = 0 \mid X = x_1) \cdot P(X = x_1 \mid g_1, \ldots, g_m)$$
$$= \underbrace{(0.1)}_{\text{(See Table 15.1)}} \cdot \underbrace{(0.2)}_{\text{(See Table 15.3)}} = 0.02$$

The probabilities for $N = 0$, $N = 1$, $N = 2$, and $N = 3$,

TABLE 15.3. *Probability distribution for earth process states given geologic observations*

X	$P(X = x \mid g_1, g_2, \ldots, g_m)$
x_1	0.2
x_2	0.5
x_3	0.3

TABLE 15.4. *Probability distribution for the joint occurrence of number of deposits and earth process states*

X	N 0	1	2	3
x_1	0.02	0.04	0.06	0.08
x_2	0.10	0.15	0.15	0.10
x_3	0.09	0.09	0.06	0.06
	0.21	0.28	0.27	0.24

TABLE 15.5. *Probability distribution for number of deposits conditional upon geologic observations*

n	$P(N = n \mid g_1, \ldots, g_m)$
0	0.21
1	0.28
2	0.27
3	0.24

conditional only on the geological observations $(g_1, \ldots, g_m)$, are obtained by summing the probabilities in each column of Table 15.4, giving the totals at the bottom of the table. These are summarized in Table 15.5 and represent the probability distribution for N, conditional upon $g_1, \ldots, g_m$. These probabilities represent α, the probability distribution conditional only upon the geological observations $\alpha(n \mid g_1, \ldots, g_m)$.

The appraisal system is no more complex in overall concept than the operations demonstrated in Table 15.4, except that instead of one process variable with three states (x_1, x_2, x_3), there are three process variables (X_1, X_2, X_3), each having three states, and the range of N, the number of deposits, is larger.

X_1 = Source and transportation
    x_{11} = excellent
    x_{12} = intermediate
    x_{13} = poor
X_2 = Deposition and mineralization
    x_{21} = excellent
    x_{22} = intermediate
    x_{23} = poor
X_3 = Preservation
    x_{31} = excellent
    x_{32} = intermediate
    x_{33} = poor.

Therefore, there are 27 possible combinations of major process states

$$x_{11} \quad x_{21} \quad x_{31}$$
$$\vdots$$
$$x_{13} \quad x_{23} \quad x_{33}.$$

But, all this means is that the table of joint probabilities, like Table 15.4, would have 27 rows, instead of 3, and more columns [3].

There are two points to be made here. One is that the *major* concepts involved in the integration of

geoscience, endowment, and probability are simple and straightforward, even when geoscience is expanded to greater numbers of processes/geological conditions. The second one is that the complexities of this appraisal system arise mainly in the approach taken to estimating the probabilities for the 27 combinations of the three major earth processes. The simplest approach in terms of the design of a system to support analysis would be to ask the geologist outright for probabilities for these 27 combinations of process states on each region being evaluated. The probabilities given for a region could then be combined with previously specified geoscience relations, the 27 probability distributions for number of deposits, one distribution for each of the 27 combinations of process states, to produce an extended table, like Table 15.4, and the desired probabilities for number of deposits conditional no longer on combinations of process states, but only on geological observations, could be computed by summing the probabilities in each column, as demonstrated in Table 15.4. This approach would rely upon the intuitive processes of the geologist to convert geological evidence to inference about process/condition states. The need for computational support of such an approach would be minor, and meeting this need would be trivial in terms of design and implementation of computer software.

A second approach, and the one adopted by Harris and Carrigan, is to require the geologist to express formally for each of the three major processes the geological relations and the evidence that are used to determine the states of each process. The basic vehicle for description of this formalized geological reasoning is referred to as an inference net. Fig. 15.3 shows the inference net designed by an expert geologist for each of these three major processes. As such, the inference net shows only the identity of processes and conditions that comprise geoscience as it is used in inferring mineral endowment. While defining the inference net is an important achievement, it is not sufficient for the estimation of the states of a process. More information is required; namely, there must be a specification of the relevant states of each subprocess and which combinations of these subprocesses indicate a particular state of the major process. The geological decision model is not complete without these relations, which are referred to by Harris and Carrigan as numerical scalings (groupings) or as a ranking scheme.

A simplified example is here provided to demonstrate how an inference net and its numerical scalings are used in computing probabilities for the states of a

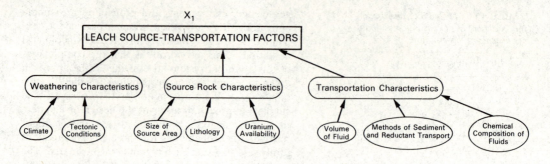

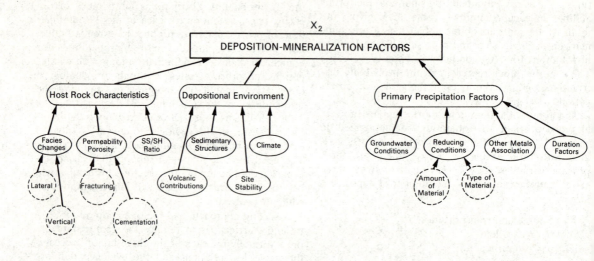

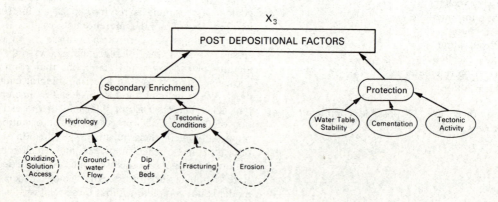

Fig. 15.3. Inference nets for each major variable (process or condition) constructed by Geologist Shiva (code name) for San Juan Basin uranium.

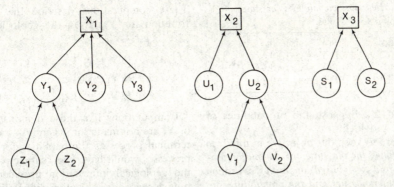

Fig. 15.4. Schematic representations of inference nets for the three major processes.

process. Suppose for each of the three major processes X_1, X_2, and X_3, the expert geologist involved in designing the system has identified inference nets for each of the major processes (see Fig. 15.4). These nets represent the causation structure indicated by the geoscience of uranium. For example, each of the symbols (Y_1, Y_2, Y_3) that feed into X_1 are subprocesses of X_1, and Z_1 and Z_2 are subprocesses of Y_1. Similarly, U_1 and U_2 are subprocesses of X_2, and V_1 and V_2 are subprocesses of U_2. Subprocesses of X_3 are S_1 and S_2. Suppose now for simplicity that subprocesses Y_2 and Y_3 have only two states: $Y_2 = \{y_{21}, y_{22}\}$ and $Y_3 = \{y_{31}, y_{32}\}$. Suppose, however, that Y_1 has three states: $Y_1 = \{y_{11}, y_{12}, y_{13}\}$. Thus, if we look at X_1, there are 12 combinations of subprocesses of the first order $(Y_1, Y_2,$ and $Y_3)$ that determine the state of X_1.

In the construction of the geological decision model, the expert geologist ranks these 12 combinations in terms of favourability for uranium formation on a scale of 0 to 100, as demonstrated in Table 15.6. He then relates the numerical rankings to the three states of X_1. For example, he might state that 90 to 100 is an excellent condition for process X_1, 40 to 90 intermediate, and 0 to 40 poor. In this way, these numerical scalings are related to the states of X_1

$$x_{11} \to (90\text{--}100)$$
$$x_{12} \to (40\text{--}90)$$
$$x_{13} \to (0\text{--}40).$$

Suppose now that an identical analysis is made of *subprocess* Y_1, which in turn consists of subprocesses Z_1 and Z_2 as noted in Table 15.7. Suppose the geologist states that 90 to 100 is excellent, 45 to 90 intermediate, and 0 to 45 poor. It follows that

TABLE 15.6. *Combinations and rankings of Y_1, Y_2, and Y_3*

Combination	Rank
$y_{11}\ y_{21}\ y_{31}$	100
$y_{11}\ y_{21}\ y_{32}$	90
$y_{11}\ y_{22}\ y_{31}$	50
$y_{11}\ y_{22}\ y_{32}$	40
$y_{12}\ y_{21}\ y_{31}$	60
$y_{12}\ y_{21}\ y_{32}$	55
$y_{12}\ y_{22}\ y_{31}$	10
$y_{12}\ y_{22}\ y_{32}$	5
$y_{13}\ y_{21}\ y_{31}$	95
$y_{13}\ y_{21}\ y_{32}$	90
$y_{13}\ y_{22}\ y_{31}$	85
$y_{13}\ y_{22}\ y_{32}$	30

$y_{11} \to (90\text{--}100)$, $y_{12} \to (45\text{--}90)$, and $y_{13} \to (0\text{--}45)$. X_2 and X_3 would be analysed and described similarly.

Let us now examine how this net would be used to determine the probability distribution for a combination of major earth process states. First, a geologist examines all geoscience data; then after evaluating these data, he provides the following subjective probabilities for the subprocess of X_1. Note that subjective probabilities are provided only for the last subprocesses of a net. For X_1, these subprocesses are

TABLE 15.7. *Combinations and rankings of Z_1 and Z_2*

Combination	Rank
$z_{11}\ z_{21}$	50
$z_{11}\ z_{22}$	100
$z_{12}\ z_{21}$	10
$z_{12}\ z_{22}$	30

TABLE 15.8. *Subjective probabilities for states of end processes* (Z_1, Z_2, Y_2, and Y_3)

$P(Z_1 = z_{11}) = 0.8$	$P(Y_2 = y_{21}) = 0.4$
$P(Z_1 = z_{12}) = 0.2$	$P(Y_2 = y_{22}) = 0.6$
$P(Z_2 = z_{21}) = 0.3$	$P(Y_3 = y_{31}) = 0.9$
$P(Z_2 = z_{22}) = 0.7$	$P(Y_3 = y_{32}) = 0.1$

Z_1, Z_2, Y_2, and Y_3. Suppose the probabilities of Table 15.8 were provided.

It is helpful here to keep our objective in mind: *to compute probabilities for the states of the major processes X_1, X_2, and X_3, based upon the causation structure of the inference net and the probabilities for the states of the terminal processes given in Table 15.8.* The first step in computing the probabilities for the states of X_1 is to compute the probability that $Y_1 = y_{11}$ and $Y_1 = y_{12}$. Since the geologist had stated in his inference net that Y_1 is composed of subprocesses Z_1 and Z_2, probabilities for states of Y_1 are computed from probabilities for the states of Z_1 and Z_2. Examination of the geologist's ranking scheme shows that y_{11}, the excellent state of the process, requires a numerical ranking of 90 to 100 for the combinations of states of Z_1 and Z_2. Furthermore, only one combination has a ranking of this magnitude, that is, $z_{11}z_{22}$. Therefore, the probability that $Y_1 = y_{11}$ is the probability for combination $z_{11}z_{22}$. This probability is computed from the geologist's subjective probabilities (Table 15.8), assuming statistical independence of Z_1 and Z_2

$$P(Y_1 = y_{11}) = P(Z_1 = z_{11}, Z_2 = z_{22})$$
$$= P(Z_1 = z_{11}) \cdot P(Z_2 = z_{22})$$
$$= (0.8) \cdot (0.7) = 0.56.$$

Similarly, we can compute $P(Y_1 = y_{12})$. From the geologist's scaling, we see that the state of y_{12} consists of rankings from 50 to 90 and that this includes only one event, $Z_1 = z_{11}$ and $Z_2 = z_{21}$. Thus,

$$P(Y_1 = y_{12}) = P(Z_1 = z_{11}) \cdot P(Z_2 = z_{21})$$
$$= (0.8) \cdot (0.3) = 0.24.$$

The probability for the remaining state of Y_1, y_{13} is computed by observing that the state y_{13} consists of a numerical ranking from 0 to 50 and that two combinations of the states of Z_1 and Z_2 fall within this interval, $z_{12}z_{21}$ and $z_{12}z_{22}$. Therefore, we have

$$P(Y_1 = y_{13}) = P(Z_1 = z_{12}) \cdot P(Z_2 = z_{21}) +$$
$$+ P(Z_1 = z_{12}) \cdot P(Z_2 = z_{22})$$
$$= (0.2) \cdot (0.3) + (0.2) \cdot (0.7)$$
$$= 0.06 + 0.14 = 0.20.$$

These computations describe the probability distribution for Y_1, given the geological observations $g_1, \ldots, g_m$

$$P(Y_1 = y_{11} \mid g_1, \ldots, g_m) = 0.56$$
$$P(Y_1 = y_{12} \mid g_1, \ldots, g_m) = 0.24$$
$$P(Y_1 = y_{13} \mid g_1, \ldots, g_m) = 0.20.$$

Computations like those demonstrated for states of Y_1 are not made for Y_2 and Y_3, because these are terminal processes. Probabilities for states of these processes would have been subjectively made, given the geological information provided, at the same time as were the subjective probabilities for states of Z_1 and Z_2 (see Table 15.8).

Let us summarize where we are. Our objective is to compute the probabilities for states of X_1, given the geologist's observation and evaluation of geological conditions and geoscience measurements. The geologist's science stated that X_1 is made up of subprocesses Y_1, Y_2, and Y_3 and that Y_1 in turn is composed of subprocesses Z_1 and Z_2. He also provided a numerical ranking scheme which equates the subprocesses of Y_1, Y_2, and Y_3 to the three states of X_1 and a ranking scheme which equates the combinations of subprocess states of Z_1 and Z_2 to states of Y_1. These relations are shown in Fig. 15.5. Table 15.9 summarizes our probability information for the states of the subprocesses Y_1, Y_2, and Y_3. As already stated, the probabilities for states of Y_2 and Y_3 are subjectively made and are simply reproduced in this table from Table 15.8. The probabilities for states of Y_1, however, are those that we have just computed.

Employing the probabilities of Table 15.9, we can compute the probabilities for all combinations of the states of Y_1, Y_2, and Y_3. These are provided in column two of Fig. 15.6. In addition, this figure shows how the probabilities for the combinations of earth processes Y_1, Y_2, and Y_3, conditional upon observations $g_1, \ldots, g_m$, are combined, using the ranking scheme for the inference net, to compute probability for the states of X_1, conditional upon the geological observations $g_1, \ldots, g_m$

$$P(X_1 = x_{11} \mid g_1, \ldots, g_n) = 0.2736$$
$$P(X_1 = x_{12} \mid g_1, \ldots, g_m) = 0.5368 \Big\} \rightarrow \phi_1(x_1 \mid g_1, \ldots, g_m).$$
$$P(X_1 = X_{13} \mid g_1, \ldots, g_m) = 0.1896$$

Computations similar to those demonstrated would yield values for $\phi_2(x_2 \mid g_1, \ldots, g_m)$ and $\phi_3(x_3 \mid g_1, \ldots, g_m)$. Thus, these could be combined with the probability distributions for number of deposits, conditional upon the states of the processes,

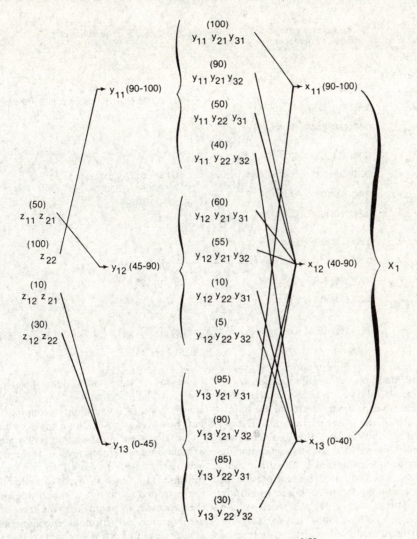

Fig. 15.5. Relations of subprocesses of X_1.

to give a probability distribution for number of deposits n, given the geological observations $g_1, \ldots, g_m$.

Construction of geological decision model

Exchange of geoscience. As described in the foregoing section, relevant geoscience was identified and coordinated as an inference net, a net which consists of three subnets, one for each of the major processes. In the study described by Harris and Carrigan [1, 4] after each of the five participating geologists

TABLE 15.9. *Probabilites for states of* Y_1, Y_2, *and* Y_3

Process	State	Probability
Y_1	y_{11}	0.56
	y_{12}	0.24
	y_{13}	0.20
Y_2	y_{21}	0.4
	y_{22}	0.6
Y_3	y_{31}	0.9
	y_{32}	0.1

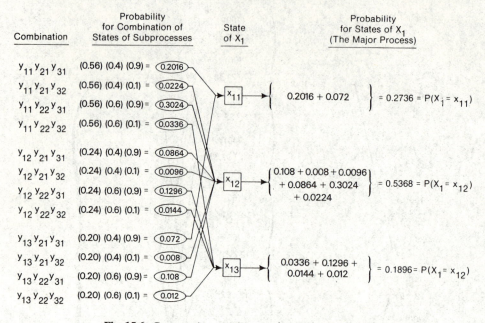

Fig. 15.6. Computation of $P(X_1 = x_{1j} \mid g_1, \ldots, g_m), j = 1, 2, 3.$

individually had made an initial identification of his inference net, he was allowed to access anonymously through an interactive computer terminal the inference nets of each of the other participants. During and subsequent to this review, the geologist was allowed to modify his inference net to accommodate some of the geoscience expressed in the other nets. This modification was facilitated by a provision of the interactive computer terminal to accept certain commands by sensing the geologist's touch of the plasma screen. Upon completion of this exchange of geoscience and final modifications, the structure of his inference net was fixed; subsequently the geologist was asked to rank the various combinations that occur throughout the net and to provide the favourability groupings. As demonstrated in the foregoing section, these rankings and favourability groupings control the relation of the intensities of subprocesses to the states of the major processes. Consequently, they can be seen as the 'control panel' of geoscience. *Calibration of formalized geoscience.* Formalization of geoscience can be viewed as consisting of (1) identifying the elements of geoscience and their interrelations—the inference net—and (2) ranking combinations of subprocesses and specifying the numerical ranges (favourability groupings) that associate the numerically ranked combinations of sub-

processes to states of a higher-level process. Once the geologist has completed his original rankings and specification of favourability groupings for his entire net, he is ready to calibrate his geoscience.

The first step in calibration is the identification of at least one, preferably several, regions for which the geologist considers himself to be geologically well informed. For each of these test regions, the geologist provided subjective probabilities for the states of the processes or geological conditions that comprise his inference net (formalized geoscience). Additionally, for each of a few selected stratigraphic units of the region—in this case the San Juan Basin—the geologist also provided these probabilities for reference circumstances, i.e. poor, intermediate, or excellent Westwater—see Table 15.10 for estimates by Hadrian (code name) for worst Salt Wash Member.

The computerized geological model—the complex of inference net, rankings, favourability groupings, and computational algorithm—accepted the subjective probabilities and printed out computed probabilities for the states of the processes involved at various levels of the inference net. For example, Table 15.11 shows the probabilities for the three states of the major processes—the highest level of geoscience. The expert was asked to review these results for all units to see if the decision model was

TABLE   15.10. *Subjective   probability   index   numbers.* (*Source: Harris and Carrigan* [1].)

Geologist: Hadrian Horizon: Salt Wash Member, worst circumstances Processes and states	Probability index numbers	Geologist: Hadrian Horizon: Salt Wash Member, worst circumstances Processes and states	Probability index numbers
Leach source–transportation factors		Colour	
Leaching agent		light-coloured	1
Inorganic compounds		drab	19
dominant	900	red	980
subordinate	100	Type	
Humic acids		sandstone	49
Climate		limestone	1
favourable	800	shale/mudstone	950
unfavourable	200	Abundant uranium anomalies	
Plant life		abundant	1
abundant	10	moderate	99
moderate	140	sparse	900
sparse	850	Depositional environment factors	
Proper environment		Type	
pervasive	1	fluvial	149
localized	19	marine	1
unfavourable	980	lacustrine	850
Intra-basinal source rock characteristics		Carbonized plant fragments	
Volume of source rock		abundant	1
large	50	moderate	149
moderate	200	sparse	850
small	750	Pyrite	
Available soluble uranium		abundant (1 per cent)	10
abundant	1	moderate ($\frac{1}{2}$ per cent)	90
moderate	9	sparse	900
sparse	140	Mudstone interbeds	
very sparse	850	favourable	200
Volcanic ash contributions		unfavourable	800
abundant	10	Mineralization factors	
moderate	140	Intensity	
sparse	850	high-grade	10
Transport mode		medium-grade	90
Volume of transporting fluid		low-grade	900
large	10	Environment of precipitation	
moderate	140	local acid, swampy	300
small	850	local brackish waters	400
Organo-metal compounds		local abundant clays	300
likely	150	Uranium concentrating agent	
unlikely	850	Humic acid	
Chemical environment		abundant	10
favourable	100	moderate	40
unfavourable	900	absent	950
Deposition–mineralization factors		Inorganic components	
Host rock factors		dominant	900
Geometry		subordinate	100
Thickness		Alteration	
<40	600	Bleaching	
40–300	10	strong, pervasive	1
very thick, massive	390	moderate	49
Lateral continuity		absent	950
excellent	1	Redistributed iron	
moderate	9	locally abundant	10
narrow channels	90	moderate	140
poor	900	sparse	850

TABLE 15.10 (*contd*)

| Geologist: Hadrian | |
| Horizon: Salt Wash Member, worst circumstances | |
Processes and states	Probability index numbers
Post-depositional factors	
Uranium redistribution	
Proximity to primary ore	
near (0–12 miles)	50
moderate	150
distant (>20 miles)	800
Reprecipitation conditions	
adequate	100
inadequate	900
Dispersal	
large	850
moderate	140
small	10
Burial and preservation	
complete	100
incomplete	900

performing in a way that conformed to his geoscience. If he found that the decision model consistently gave high probabilities for moderately favourable major process states to those stratigraphical units which he considered to have poor conditions, he might wish to re-examine his rankings and favourability groupings.

The geologist [5] may find, under the best of circumstances, that he can calibrate his decision model satisfactorily by these high-level adjustments. If not, then he must consider the ranking scheme for lower-level process combinations. Usually, by examining the input geological probabilities of the units under question, it is possible to identify the major process and the subprocess of the major process that

TABLE 15.11. *Probabilities for states of the major processes.* (*Source: Harris and Carrigan* [1].)

| State of process | Process identification | | |
	ST†	DM†	PD†
Excellent	0.66969375	0.12200188	0.10215000
Intermediate	0.27123292	0.00187717	0.00248500
Poor	0.05907332	0.87612096	0.89536500

Geologist: Hadrian	
Horizon: # 12/3 Salt Wash Member	
Worst reference circumstances	

† ST is the source–transportation major process; DM is the depositional–mineralization major process; PD is the post-deposition major process.

contribute to the anomalous responses, thereby guiding the participant to the appropriate modifications in favourability groupings or rankings.

By iteratively modifying selected favourability groupings and examining computed probabilities at all relevant levels, simultaneously for all test areas and reference conditions, the geologist converges on those groupings which cause his formalized geoscience to associate evidence to major process states probabilistically in a manner that pleases him. In this way, the geologist calibrates his geological model (formalized geoscience). Note, that thus far, calibration is of the formalized geoscience only, not of endowment.

It is important [5] to note here that even after identifying the reasons for some unexpected results, the geologist may not choose to change the rankings or favourability groupings, because those changes will affect all units to a greater or lesser degree, depending upon their geology. For many of these units, the process combinations which are associated with them by the original ranking scheme may meet with approval. If modifying the response of the model for one unit would also modify already acceptable responses on other units, the geologist may not make further modifications. Also, as a result of introspection and critical examination required to construct and calibrate the model, the geologist may decide that his preconceived judgement of resource favourability of a particular unit was incorrect and that the unexpected response of the model is acceptable. In fact, such a reaction was observed by Harris and Carrigan [1, 4].

15.2.3. *Preparation and calibration of the appraisal system*

Perspective

The preceding section commented upon the calibration of formalized geoscience. That calibration did not examine the number of deposits implied by the formalized geoscience, even though the geologist had provided initial estimates of the probability distribution for each of the 27 combinations of major process states. This procedure is purposeful, for it allows the geologist to concentrate first solely upon the formalization of his geoscience into a geological decision model that performs to his satisfaction, without complicating the calibration exercise by the endowment which the geological model produces. This procedure is desirable not only because it is piecemeal, therefore simpler, but because the geologist feels more knowledgeable about his geoscience *per se* than about the linkage of geoscience to endowment; furthermore, since the geologist may have perceptions of the magnitude of endowment which reflect either vague geological reasoning or non-geological motivations, it seems a preferred procedure to calibrate the formalized geoscience without considering endowment. Once this has been accomplished, the geologist is not allowed further modification of that formalized geoscience. He then proceeds to the preparation and calibration of the appraisal system.

This calibration [5] could be made by examining only the output of the decision model, e.g. the probability distribution for number of deposits or for fraction of the area that is mineralized; however, there are some arguments for calibrating on the output of the synthesis program, which is a probability distribution for quantity of uranium contained in the evaluation region. There is some appeal to the proposition that the expert's most vivid perception of uranium endowment is in terms of total quantity for a region, like the test region, or for quantity of uranium per unit area of the evaluation region. If there is truth in this proposition, then [calibration] should be made on the output or performance of the entire system. This is the procedure that was followed in this study. The implication here is that before [calibration] can be made, the inputs for the synthesis program must be defined. One of these is a probability distribution for each stratigraphical unit of quantity of uranium per deposit or per unit of mineralized area. There are other inputs besides the distributions for quantity of uranium per deposit or per unit of mineralized area. These include the adjustment relations for thickness of the unit and for size of the area. These adjustments are necessary because in the linkage of endowment to decision model the geologist was asked to predicate all quantity estimates, e.g. number of deposits, on a reference area—a hypothetical area having a reference size and a reference thickness of the stratigraphical unit. Naturally, the test area may have a size and thickness different from these reference conditions. Therefore, [calibration] can only be effected after these adjustments are made.

Additional comment upon the system and its major components

In addition to formalized geoscience, the appraisal system requires the linkage of that geoscience to number of deposits—this is done through the 27 probability distributions for number of deposits, one distribution for each combination of major process states—and the integration of number of deposits

with distributions for quantity of U_3O_8 per deposit and with area and thickness adjustment factors (see Fig. 15.2). This integration is performed by a Monte Carlo simulation program, referred to in Fig. 15.2 as synthesis program. Simply stated, the subjective statements of the geologist about the geology of a region are input to the geological decision model, which produces a probability distribution for number of deposits. This probability distribution is sampled in the synthesis program for a number of deposits; then for each of these deposits, the distribution for quantity of U_3O_8 per deposit is sampled for a quantity; these quantities are summed to give one measure of U_3O_8 endowment for the region. By repeating this sampling procedure many times, a synthetic sample of endowment (histogram) can be produced. This histogram, or a lognormal distribution which has been fitted to it, is adjusted for the departure of the stratigraphical unit from a reference thickness and for the departure of the area of the region from a reference size. Before the appraisal system is prepared for calibration or for actual use, the adjustment relations and the quantity of U_3O_8 per deposit must be specified for each stratigraphical unit. Then during calibration or use, the thickness of the unit within the region and the size of the region are input to the synthesis program, which employs the specified relations in conjunction with appropriate statistical computations to compute the histogram or to fit the lognormal probability distribution.

A word [6] of explanation about the need for the adjustment factors may be helpful. The earth process–endowment relations which comprise the decision model are conceptual and must apply to all areas, irrespective of their size and formation thickness. Yet, the appraisal of endowment by the complete system must take into consideration the size of the region being evaluated for, everything else being equal, the larger the area, the larger the endowment. The relationship of endowment to formation thickness also must be accounted for in computing the endowment of a region. This relationship may be complex. Exploration of this relationship with the participants revealed the concept of a minimum thickness; that is, there is a thickness below which endowment cannot form because of limitations imposed on the physical activities and chemical reactions. Conversely, there is the perception voiced by some that a sandstone can be too thick in that the uranium is too dispersed to be considered endowment.

In order to employ geological concepts which are independent of size of area and formation thickness

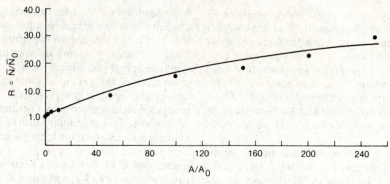

Fig. 15.7. Area adjustment relationship. (Source: Harris and Carrigan [1].)

to appraise endowment and yet have the appraisal reflect the size of the area and formation thickness, the concept of a reference area is employed in the design of the geological decision model. For example, a reference area may be a stratigraphical unit having an areal extent of 100 square miles and a thickness of 100 feet. Those relations which comprise the decision model describe endowment, probabilistically, for the reference area. Adjustment relations in conjunction with statistical relations are used in the synthesis program to compute the endowment and its probability distribution for the actual area appraised.

Figs. 15.7 and 15.8 show the area and thickness adjustment relations specified by one of the participants. Fig. 15.7 shows a curve freely drawn through

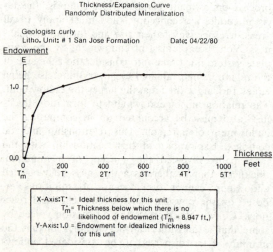

Fig. 15.8. Thickness/expansion curve randomly distributed mineralization. (Source: Harris and Carrigan [1].)

the responses of one of the participants about the effect of size of area on number of deposits. On the ordinate of this figure is the ratio R of the expected number of deposits for a region of size A to the expected number of deposits of the reference area of size A_0. The abscissa shows the ratio of the size of the area of interest A to the size of the reference area A_0. Thus, if the size of the region being evaluated were 60 times that of the reference area, the multiplier (ratio) of approximately 11 would be employed in modifying the probability distribution for endowment for the reference area to an endowment probability distribution for the region of size A. Fig. 15.8 is a PLATO plot of the responses of one of the participants as to the effect of thickness on endowment. On the ordinate of this figure is the ratio of the endowment of a reference area having some specified thickness to the endowment E of the reference area given the ideal thickness of the San Jose formation. Note that the ideal thickness for this unit is specified as 200 feet and that value of the ratio for this thickness is 1.0. Thus, if the thickness of this unit within an evaluation region were 400 feet, the endowment of the region should be increased by approximately 13 per cent over that endowment of the reference case.

The calibration exercise

Calibration of formalized geoscience was achieved by having the geologist select test regions and reference conditions (poor, excellent, and intermediate Westwater, etc.) and to describe each of these by subjective probabilities about the processes and geological conditions that comprise the formalized geoscience (geological decision model). Thus, when this calibration was completed, not only was it fixed—made inaccessible to the geologist—but records were preserved of the geoscience—subjective probabilities—

of each region and reference conditions used in calibration.

Calibration of the appraisal system was based upon records (subjective probabilities) of the same regions and reference conditions used in calibration of geoscience. In this way, the only components of the appraisal system at issue and subject to modification are the conditional distributions for number of deposits, the distribution for U_3O_8 per deposit, and the adjustment relations for thickness and area size. Ideally, statistical data on amount of the mineral (compound or element) per deposit are available for the familiar stratigraphical units of the region. When this is so, calibration of the appraisal system primarily is modification of the conditional number distributions. Such ideal circumstances did not prevail in the study by Harris and Carrigan [1, 4], but, even so, calibration of the appraisal system consisted primarily of modification of the conditional number distributions. Occasionally modifications were made by a geologist of the distributions for quantity of U_3O_8 per deposit for one or more of the stratigraphical units.

Calibration was approached by providing the geologist with expected and modal values of U_3O_8, and probability information if he desired it, computed by the appraisal system for each of the test regions and reference sections. Additional information provided included the expected number of deposits, the pounds of U_3O_8 per square mile, and the marginal probabilities, i.e. the probabilities for each of the 27 major process combinations. These can be viewed by the geologist as relative weights for each of the number of deposit distributions in the computation of the distribution for number that entered the synthesis program. The geologist examined the outputs of the system for all test regions and reference circumstances for patterns that might suggest a modification that would bring the overall response of the system more in line with his experience. Once one or more of these were identified, the procedure was repeated, iterating in this manner until the geologist was satisfied with the output of the system. Once this was achieved, his appraisal system was considered to be calibrated and ready for use in the appraisal of endowment. In the study by Harris and Carrigan, the system was 'locked in' (fixed) and the geologist then became a user of the system, meaning that he appraised the endowment of regions solely by responding to input needs of the system, i.e. the subjective probabilities for the states of the processes and geological conditions of his formalized geoscience. All other inputs and computations leading to the

computation of the probability distribution of U_3O_8 endowment were automatic and beyond his influence.

15.2.4. *Selected comments on features of the appraisal system*

The study by Harris and Carrigan [1, 4; 1981] developed a methodology and software for the appraisal of uranium endowment by the formalization of geoscience. In addition, a demonstration was made of the methodology using five expert geologists. For a detailed description of the many features of this software, the reader is referred to reports submitted to the US Department of Energy (Grand Junction Office). Only a very general description of some of these features is here provided, accompanied by some comment upon the implementation of such a system.

Endowment scheme options [7]

By endowment scheme we are referring to (1) that component of endowment that is to be related (linked) to the processes of the decision model and (2) the way that this component is ultimately combined with the other component of endowment to yield a probability distribution for quantity of uranium.

There are three major endowment scheme options (these have suboptions).

* Earth processes are related directly to quantity of uranium.
* Earth processes are related only to fraction of the stratigraphical unit that is mineralized above a specified cut-off grade and minimum quantity.
* Earth processes are related only to number of deposit, given a cut-off grade and minimum quantity per deposit.

The availability of these three options is an important feature of this appraisal system, for it is *extremely important* that the geologist be able to employ an endowment scheme that is compatible with his resource experience. Formalizing geoscience and describing the linkage to endowment is difficult under the best of circumstances. To compound the difficulty by forcing the expert to link geoscience to an unfamiliar component of endowment is very poor practice for it may obviate his experience. Of the five geologists who participated in the demonstration, three of them—two from industry and one from a governmental agency—selected the number-of-deposit option; the remaining two geologists, both from governmental agencies, selected the 'fraction-of-area-mineralized' option.

Calibration of probability assessment [7]

Since much of the participation of the expert geologist requires him to think in terms of probability and to describe his subjective probabilities for events, he was provided an exercise in the estimation of subjective probabilities. The intent of this exercise was to encourage the geologist to be critical and introspective about probability estimation and to compensate for whatever tendencies to over- or under-estimation that were revealed by the exercise. This exercise consisted of his being asked 240 questions regarding his certainty about the meaning of words. A computer program analysed the expert's responses and provided a graphic display of his performance. Fig. 15.9 is the graph of the performance of one of the participants. The horizontal axis indicates probability responses—the values that an individual may assign to given events, assertions, or situations (in this case, his estimate of the probability that he has correctly defined the word). The vertical axis indicates the actual probabilities that these events, assertions, or situations are true or that they will occur (in this case, the actual percentage of words correctly defined). The straight line on the graph would represent a person with 'perfect calibration'; that is, his probability responses would have the same values as the actual probabilities. Thus, any portion of a curve below the perfect calibration line represents the tendency to overestimate probabilities, and any portion above the perfect calibration line represents the tendency to underestimate probabilities. In Fig. 15.9, the curve for 'easy' words (analogous to geological conditions the participant is fairly certain of) indicates that this user is almost perfectly calibrated. The curve for 'hard' words (analogous to geologic conditions that the participant is less certain of) indicates that when this individual assigns probabilities in the range of 0.1–0.7 as well as around 1.0 he is over confident and should be making a lower estimate. When he is making estimates of around 0.8 (i.e. 0.75–0.95) he knows more than he feels he does; consequently, his estimates should be higher.

Ready review of information

Studies of the subjective estimation of a complex and uncertain event have shown that an appraiser bases his judgements primarily upon the information which is before him. Other relevant information is seldom retrieved and integrated in his judgements. Harris and Carrigan [1, 4] sought to improve the perfor-

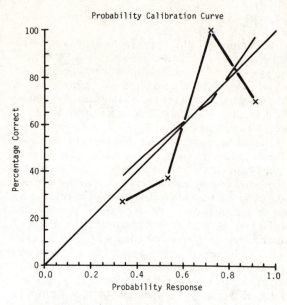

Fig. 15.9. Example probability calibration curve.

mance of the geologist by providing him with ready access to large amounts of information. This was achieved by preparing coloured slides (30 mm) of relevant geological maps (isopachus, outcrop, structural, tectonic, etc.) that were publicly available. In addition, slides were prepared of relevant and available resource data for the region. These slides were projected on the back of the plasma screen of the computer terminal by a projector that had been mounted at the rear of the terminal so as to project forward. This allowed the geologist to review geological and resource data quickly by simply conveying his request to the computer program. This program also would provide appropriate textual descriptions, which had been taken from relevant publications, and instructions for the performance of the various tasks of constructing and using the appraisal system. For the geologist who preferred working with conventional information sources, e.g. geological maps, instead of viewing them through the computer terminal, the original data from which the slides were made were made available to him.

Kinds of expertise [8]

The experience gained in this study about designing five separate uranium endowment appraisal systems, one for each of the five participants, has reaffirmed and emphasized the need for three kinds of expertise in the *design and use* of the appraisal system

* Geoscience;
* Resource and endowment;
* Specific geological knowledge of the region.

The first kind of expertise, geoscience, is called upon in the design of the inference net, the structure of the geological decision model. The second kind of expertise, resource and endowment, is called upon when the decision model is linked to endowment and when the system is validated. And, the third kind of expertise, specific geological knowledge of the region, is called upon when the geologist calibrates the decision model, validates the total system, and uses the system for appraisal. Each of the five experts involved in this study is a different mix of these three kinds of expertise. It is a rare individual who is highly qualified in all three. As would be expected, the degree of difficulty for the five individuals on any part of the design and use of the system varied with this mix of the three kinds of expertise. For example, an excellent geoscientist who has had little resource appraisal experience will 'breeze through' the design of the decision model but agonize over the linkage of this model to endowment. Conversely, an explorationist or resource appraiser may have difficulty with the geological decision model simply because he has become accustomed to using simplistic decision criteria or analogies upon which to base his decisions rather than employing a broad base of geoscience. As the saying goes, 'when you are in elephant country, you simply look for tusks.' Unfortunately, the appraisal of undiscovered endowment requires the identification of the 'kind of country'; therefore, a broader base of geoscience may be required than has been routinely used in exploration, particularly since one must estimate the total endowment, a task quite different from finding the next deposit.

Modelling difficulties and the need for basic data [9]

Universally, the participants in this study who elected the number-of-deposits option struggled with defining a distribution for the quantity of uranium in a deposit and the conditional distributions for number of deposits. On the one hand, they were asked to define a model of the interaction of earth processes, a strictly geological perspective and exercise. But, ultimately, they had to relate the geological decision model to number of deposits and then to describe the magnitude of the uranium deposits. At this point, they found their experience and statistical data were not compatible with the required task. Experience and available data primarily reflected ore

deposits or mining properties, not *geological deposits.* How big are these geological deposits? We cannot at present give an answer to this question in a rigorous way. The need for a formal description of uranium occurrences as geological phenomena cannot be overstated.

This non-conformity of data and experience with the modelling task was most vividly felt when the geologist attempted to provide a probability distribution for number of deposits, given specified states of the earth processes and given the proposed U_3O_8 endowment definition (0.01 per cent U_3O_8 and 500 pounds U_3O_8). The geologist found it impossible to think of number of deposits when a deposit was defined to include discrete accumulations so small as 500 pounds U_3O_8. All three of the geologists using the number-of-deposits option had to redefine the minimum accumulation (500 000 lb, 500 000 lb, and 1 000 000 lb) so that they could provide initial estimates of the number of deposit distributions. Furthermore, two of the geologists also had to raise the minimum grade (endowment cut-off grade) from 0.01 per cent U_3O_8 to 0.10 per cent U_3O_8. Later, during the calibration exercise, the geologist could modify these distributions until the estimates of U_3O_8 endowment for his 'test cases' met with his approval.

Even though the geologist was presented with the opportunity to calibrate his appraisal system on test cases until the system estimates met with his approval, the fact that three of the geologists used endowment definitions quite different from that specified undoubtedly introduces noise in the resulting estimates. As indicated previously in the description of the estimates by geologists, the simplest, most direct way of handling a different endowment definition is to have the geologist calibrate his system conditional upon his endowment definition and then later, during the execution of his system, expand the system estimates by a factor obtained from the US DOE tonnage–grade relation. Only one of the three geologists who used the number-of-deposits option followed this design. The other two used their own endowment definition as a reference for providing initial estimates of the conditional probability distributions for number of deposits, but during calibration, they modified these distributions so that the estimates of U_3O_8 endowment were satisfactory for the originally specified endowment definition (0.01 per cent U_3O_8 and 500 pounds U_3O_8). While estimates produced by systems that were constructed in this fashion may be good estimates, such a non-systematic approach to original specification and calibration is not satisfying, for there is always the question of, did he adequately compensate for the different endowment definitions by this somewhat mixed approach?

Needless to say, construction and validation of an appraisal system would be much simplified and improved if geologists had access to data on the size, average grade, and grade distribution of geological deposits of U_3O_8, given the endowment definition that was originally specified.

The exposure of the difficulties experienced by the geologists in describing the number of deposits and quantity per deposit distributions seems to be a basis for a negative judgement on the feasibility of endowment estimation by an appraisal system. Perhaps, but before making such a judgement, consideration should be given to the following.

 * A geologist could use another option: fraction of the area underlain by mineralization. While this option also has problems, the definition of a deposit and the probability distributions for number of deposits and for quantity of U_3O_8 per deposit can be avoided.

 * In this demonstration, a shortage of time was an ever present problem with the participating geologists, particularly, for the calibration exercise. Had more time been available, design and calibration could have been redone, eliminating some inconsistencies.

 * It is possible to avoid the problem by linking the geological decision model to fraction of area underlain by mineralization by quantitative analysis. This is explained in a later section.

 * While these problems are well exposed by the appraisal system, it is incorrect to suppose that they do not exist in some form in the estimation of endowment by the implicit and other methodologies. True, none of the geologists protested the specified endowment definition when they were asked to provide implicit estimates. But, one must wonder about this, for if the geologist's experience did not allow him to describe number and size of deposits for the system, how adequate can this same experience be in estimating directly the magnitude of U_3O_8 endowment when that endowment includes quantities as small as 500 pounds U_3O_8 and all material having grades above 0.01 per cent U_3O_8? Admittedly, he does not need to know as much about the particulars of uranium occurrences for implicit estimation as for system estimation; even so, to some degree the issue of relevant experience still remains. Similarly, while the NURE methodology employs the fraction of the

area underlain by mineralization and hence avoids the problems attendant to number of deposits, it calls for an estimate of the fraction, given the specified endowment definition (0.01 per cent U_3O_8 and 500 pounds U_3O_8), and of the average grade of that mineralized material. How good are the geologist's estimates of these components of endowment when his experience is with higher-grade material and larger accumulations and when he has little basic data from which to reason and infer? Clearly, estimates by all methodologies suffer from the lack of basic data on uranium deposits as geological phenomena.

 * Even without basic data, a subsequent application of the appraisal system could be improved over this demonstration because of having had this experience. For, at the least, greater stress could be given to preparing the geologist to anticipate and to deal with the problem in a more orderly and structured manner.

 * Finally, selection of a methodology also requires consideration of the use by the geologist(s) of heuristics and hedging.

Construction and use by a group

The need for three kinds of expertise immediately suggests the design and use of the system by a group, such as a subdivision of the US Department of Energy. Everything else being equal, a group could better provide the varied package of talents required in the design and use of the system. In addition and just as important, the system allows for the differentiation of expertise. In other words, a particular geologist does only those things for which he is well qualified.

This last point, the differentiation of expertise, is particularly important when endowment estimation of a large region has been mandated by government and can be achieved only by employing many geologists, like the NURE programme described in Chapter 13, for geologists of various kinds of expertise and degrees of experience may be involved. Some of these are fine geologists but have no resource experience. A properly designed and executed appraisal system could benefit from their talents as field geologists without suffering the penalty of their inexperience in resources and endowment.

To see how this could happen, consider the following scenario. All persons to be involved in the estimation of endowment for a region, say the Wyoming Basins, are brought together to review the tasks of design, validation, and use of the system. Those individuals with high expertise in geoscience assume the dominant role in designing the inference net; however, the geologists (field geologists) who will be using the system also participate so that they are aware of the structure of the system. The field geologists actively participate in the calibration of the decision model. Those individuals with resource experience actively participate in the linkage of the decision model to endowment. In the validation phase, those who have access to statistical data on the size distribution of deposits for each unit could assemble these data and prepare them for input to the synthesis program. Also during this phase, those with high familiarity with the geology and resources of a test area and with the stratigraphical units in general would participate with the resource specialists in the validation of the system. Once the system is validated, it is ready to be used by the *field geologists* who have firsthand experience with the geology of the regions; it matters not that they have little or no resource experience, because all they must do to use the system is function as a geologist and to provide probabilities for the states of processes. The system transforms these probabilities to probabilities for uranium endowment.

A more complex approach, one with more safeguards, would require the field geologist using the system to present his subjective probabilities for process states to a review board. Only after successful defence of these probabilities, or appropriate modification, would they be submitted to the appraisal system. The review board would have on record, as a result of the calibration exercises, the best, poorest, and intermediate geology for each unit. These reference circumstances could be used as a kind of quality control. For example, if a field geologist showed circumstances more favourable than the best reference circumstances for a particular unit, his judgements would be accepted only if he could successfully defend them.

An important point to be made with regard to the design and use of the system by a governmental agency is that the system is a vehicle for integrating various kinds of expertise for the accomplishment of a specific task—the appraisal of uranium endowment. The design and use of a system in this manner could improve the credibility and at the same time facilitate achievement of the objective—the estimate of mineral endowment.

15.2.5. *An improved method for linking formalized geoscience to mineral endowment*

Discussion in previous sections identified the three kinds of expertise required to construct and use the endowment appraisal model. Because of the need for these three kinds of expertise, a good case can be made for the construction and use of such a model by a team of qualified individuals, a team in which the three types of expertise are well represented. The previous section described how such an implementation could take place.

Even with a team effort, there remains a difficult problem in the construction and use of the system: the linkage of earth processes or geological conditions to mineral endowment. This is undoubtedly the most difficult task in the construction of the appraisal system. This difficulty is due in part to two uncertainties

(1) great uncertainty about what constitutes a 'geological' deposit of uranium, as contrasted with a property or ore deposit of uranium;

(2) great uncertainty about how the number of deposits that could occur in a region of a given size varies with the states of the major processes.

Of course, uncertainties about number and size are somewhat related when viewed as integral parts of a process model of uranium deposition, enrichment, and preservation. Even though the geologist's perception of size of geological deposits of uranium is faulty (his experience is with ore deposit size), his knowledge of the total amount of uranium or of the number of deposits that are formed when the major processes have various states is probably even less complete. Linking states of the major processes to probability distributions for number of deposits was, for most of the participants, clearly the most difficult single task, the one for which they felt the least qualified to complete. Because of this difficulty, reference conditions for each stratigraphical unit and one or more test areas were used to help the geologist adjust this linkage so that at least for these circumstances the system performed to his satisfaction. While this may be a reasonable procedure, a procedure which utilizes quantitative rather than subjective means to establish this linkage would be preferred. For one thing, it would remove some of the subjectivity present in construction of the system. This is especially desirable when that component of the system is so vital as is the linkage of process states to endowment.

However, while linking the decision model to endowment by the quantitative analysis of data is immediately appealing in concept, implementation of such a linkage would require data, such as either the number of deposits or the fraction of the partition that is mineralized and data on the states of the earth processes. We have neither of these kinds of data. For one thing, resource data reflect only what has been discovered, not what is there. Even so, we may be able to use such data to achieve our objective. Consider this proposition

> The fraction of an area that is *presently known* to be mineralized is a function of geological favourability of the area and the intensity to which this area has been explored.

Let us formalize this by representing the fraction by f, geological favourability by the 27 probabilities, $P_1, \ldots, P_{27}$, one for each combination of major process states, and exploration by v

$$f = (\alpha_1 P_1 + \alpha_2 P_2 + \ldots + \alpha_{27} P_{27})(1 - e^{-\alpha_0 v})$$

(15.1)

Thus, if the coefficients, $\alpha_0, \alpha_1, \ldots, \alpha_{27}$, were known, given the 27 probabilities and the amount of exploration, the equation would yield an estimate of the fraction of the area known to be mineralized. Of course, our objective is not the fraction known at present but the actual fraction. Even so, if the coefficients were known, by setting v to infinity we could obtain an *estimate* of the *actual fraction*. The advantage of this approach is that it does not require data on the actual f, only on the presently measurable fraction. Of course, to estimate this equation, we must also have data on the 27 probabilities and on the amount of exploration v. The remainder of this section 'walks through' how this approach might be implemented.

Suppose that the geological decision model is complete, meaning that it has been calibrated satisfactorily: the probabilities computed by the system for states of the three major processes, given the probabilities for the states of the minor processes, for each reference condition are satisfactory to the team designing the system. However, the states of the major processes are not yet linked to endowment.

Suppose also that other, independent efforts have recorded for each partition v the amount of exploration per square mile conducted in that partition, or some other description of exploredness, such as drilling density or conditional probability for having missed a target. Suppose also that for every partition which has been explored to any significant degree, the presently known fraction f has been recorded. Finally, suppose that the geologists have described the geology of each partition probabilistically, just as was done in the study by Harris and Carrigan [1, 4]. The input data to the geological decision model—

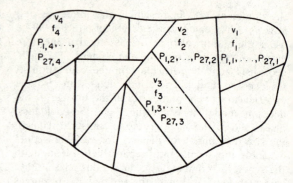

Fig. 15.10. Schematic drawing of data compilation.

probabilities for the states of the minor processes or geological conditions—have been processed by the geological decision model. The output of the decision model for each partition is probabilities for each of the three states of each of the three major processes. Accounting for all combinations of major process states there are 27 probabilities for each partition, one probability for each combination.

Let us summarize what has been postulated. Consider Fig. 15.10, which is a hypothetical map of partitions of some stratigraphical unit. Only those partitions which have received significant exploration are of interest at the moment. For each of these partitions, there are three kinds of information

v_i the exploration effort in the ith partition;
f_i the fraction of the ith partition known at this time to be underlain by uranium mineralization;
$P_{1i}, \ldots, P_{27i}$ the probabilities for each of the 27 combinations of processes states for the ith partition.

v_i and f_i are measured data, but $P_{1i}, \ldots, P_{27i}$ are computed by the decision model. Suppose that this procedure were repeated for each of the geologist's stratigraphical units and that a table of these data over all units were prepared, such as Table 15.12.

TABLE 15.12. *Data tableau*

Case	Exploration (v)	Fraction (f)	Process probabilities $(P_1 P_2, \ldots, P_{27})$
1	v_1	f_1	$P_{1,1} P_{2,1}, \ldots, P_{27,1}$
2	v_2	f_2	$P_{1,2} P_{2,2}, \ldots, P_{27,2}$
.	.	.	.
.	.	.	.
n	v_n	f_n	$P_{1,n} P_{2,n}, \ldots, P_{27,n}$

The data of Table 15.12 could be analysed by statistical and computer methods, e.g. iterative or non-linear regression analysis, to give estimates of $\alpha_0, \alpha_1, \ldots, \alpha_m$, where $m < 27$ [10]

$$\hat{f} = (\hat{\alpha}_1 P_1 + \ldots + \hat{\alpha}_m P_m)(1 - e^{-\hat{\alpha}_0 v}). \quad (15.2)$$

This equation provides an estimate of the fraction of the area that is presently known to be mineralized (contains endowment).

To see how this equation would be used, imagine that by implementing the decision model we have a set of 27 probabilities for each of the partitions. those explored and unexplored. Suppose that for each partition, the intensity of exploration is specified to be infinity. Since $1 - e^{-\alpha_0 \infty}$ evaluates to 1.0, when $v = \infty$, the above relationship is reduced to $\hat{f} = \hat{\alpha}_1 P_1 + \ldots + \hat{\alpha}_m \sum_{j=m}^{26} P_j$. Thus, evaluation of this equation at $v = \infty$ and with the probabilities computed by the decision model for a partition would provide an estimate of the expected actual fraction of the partition that contains endowment.

Regression analysis also provides S, the standard error of the estimate $\hat{f}$. Thus, by employing the assumptions of the regression model and the statistics $\hat{f}$ and S, we would be able to describe a probability distribution for f for each partition, given $P_1, \ldots, P_m$ and $v = \infty$. In this way, it may be possible to avoid the subjective linkage of the decision model to endowment. Of course, implementation requires the measurements of currently known f and of v for each partition that has received any significant amount of exploration. Furthermore, implementation of this approach for appraisal would require the description of a histogram or a probability density for the amount of U_3O_8 in a mineralized cell [11] (subdivision of a partition). This would be an input to the synthesis program. While such data have not routinely been gathered, they could be, given a concerted effort by knowledgeable persons to measure or estimate them.

In summary, by using only the geological decision model component of the appraisal system, data on the states of the major earth processes in each partition can be generated. If for each explored partition, these data were augmented with measurements on exploration and the fraction of the partition currently known to be mineralized, the earth process of the geological decision model could be linked to endowment by a statistical relationship determined by the quantitative analysis of these data. This relationship would replace the subjective conditional probability

distributions for f or number that the system currently employs.

There is another benefit of this linkage approach when the objective is to average the system estimates made by two or more geologists: it would provide a means for weighting the estimates by the geologists. In the demonstration here reported, a simple (unweighted) average was computed because there was no objective way of weighting the responses of the geologists. But, if the statistical analysis described in this section were made separately for each geologist, using the probabilities computed by his system but using the same data on exploration and f, a measure of the fraction of variance in the known fraction that is explained by decision model probabilities and exploration effort could be computed for each geologist. This fraction of explained variance could be employed as a weight for the computation of a weighted average endowment distribution. Simply stated, such a weighting scheme would weight preferentially the estimates of those geologists whose model's estimates were most compatible with known endowment.

15.2.6. *An experiment on the effect of subjective probability methodology on estimates of uranium endowment of San Juan Basin, New Mexico*

Perspective

The five geologists who participated in the demonstration of the appraisal of uranium endowment by the formalization of geoscience were used as the basis for an experiment. Simply stated, each of these geologists estimated uranium endowment for each evaluation region (partition) two ways: one way was through the use of his appraisal system, the other was by conventional assessment of subjective probabilities, referred to as the implicit methodology.

As a means of crystallizing the overall perspective, let mineral endowment be represented only by number of deposits n and consider the eqn (15.3)

$$\begin{aligned} P(N = n \mid g_1, \ldots, g_m) \\ = \sum_i \sum_j \sum_k P(N = n \mid x_{1i}, x_{2j}, x_{3k}) \times \\ \times P(X_1 = x_{1i} \mid g_1, \ldots, g_m) \times \\ \times P(X_2 = x_{2j} \mid g_1, \ldots, g_m) \times \\ \times P(X_3 = x_{3k} \mid g_1, \ldots, g_m), \quad (15.3) \end{aligned}$$

where X_1 is major process 1, and x_{1i} is its ith state; X_2 is major process 2, and x_{2j} is its jth state; X_3 is major process 3, and x_{3k} is its kth state; and

$g_1, \ldots, g_m$ are the m geological observations. The implicit methodology requires the geologist to estimate $P(N = n \mid g_1, \ldots, g_m)$ directly, subsequent to his examination of geodata.

Contrast this implicit approach to one which requires the geologist to express explicitly the linkage of geoscience to endowment, represented by $P(N = n \mid x_{1i}, x_{2j}, x_{3k})$, and to use this geoscience by combining these probabilities with subjective probabilities, determined by the geologist after review and integration of all available geodata, for the states of the geoscience variables X_1, X_2, and X_3. While eqn (15.3) is overly simplistic, it is useful as a broad generalization of the primary issue investigated by Harris and Carrigan [1, 4]: how do estimates made by unconstrained intuitive processes compare with those which require the geologist to formalize his geoscience and employ it as formalized in the estimation of mineral endowment?

The right-hand side of eqn (15.3) is a highly simplified representation of the appraisal system which, as has been shown in foregoing presentations in this section, is quite complex and consists of inference nets of interrelated subprocesses and geological conditions. Consequently, this experiment is an investigation of the use of the appraisal system to estimate uranium endowment and a comparison of these estimates with those made by the implicit methodology. On the basis of considerations in Chapter 14, implicit estimates should reflect biases that arise from the use of heuristics and purposeful hedging. In order to assure the value of the experiment in identifying such effects, two implicit estimates were identified: the first one is a result of the statistical analysis of the initial implicit estimates of the geologist and is referred to as Implicit 1; the second, referred to as Implicit 2, allows the geologist subsequent review of the results of the statistical processing of the initial estimates and modification of initial estimates so that the results of statistical processing more closely satisfy his feelings about uranium endowment. Thus, Implicit 2 estimates purposefully provided opportunity for the full exercise of heuristics and hedging.

Since all participating geologists estimated endowment by Implicit 1, Implicit 2, and Appraisal System methodologies, this experiment provided an opportunity to investigate the effect of methodology on bias and hedging. Estimates made by the NURE methodology (Chapter 13) are also provided for comparison, but since NURE estimates were not made by the same five geologists making the implicit and system estimates, no sharp conclusions can be drawn regarding the NURE estimates and methodology.

Finally, all estimates were initially made on a disaggregated basis, i.e. for each partition of each stratigraphical unit. Only estimates aggregated to Basin totals, employing appropriate statistical methods, are presented here; disaggregated estimates by geologist and by stratigraphical unit are provided by Harris and Carrigan [4].

Logistics [12]

Early in the demonstration, the geologist was asked to examine the stratigraphical column for the San Juan Basin and to identify those lithological or formational units that he would group together for the purpose of uranium endowment appraisal. For example, Table 15.13 shows the groupings, referred to as stratigraphical units, made by one of the geologists who participated in the demonstration.

Subsequent to identifying his stratigraphical units, the geologist was asked to partition the geographical distribution of each stratigraphical unit into geographical subdivisions (partitions) which are homogeneous with respect to the earth processes and geological conditions that comprise his geological decision model. The second column of Table 15.13 shows the number of partitions delineated by one of the geologists for each of his stratigraphical units. Thus, this geologist made 50 (total number of partitions) appraisals of U_3O_8 endowment. Fig. 15.11 shows the geographical locations of partitions for the

TABLE 15.13. *Stratigraphical units selected for endowment appraisal*

Unit	Number of partitions
San Jose formation	3
Nacimiento/Animas formation	2
Ojo Alamo formation	2
Fruitland formation	2
Menefee formation	2
Dakota sandstone	6
Burro Canyon formation	3
Jackpile bed	3
Westwater Canyon/Brushy Basin	8
Recapture member	4
Saltwash member	3
Todilto limestone	5
Chinle formation	2
Cutler/Abo formation	3
Madera limestone	2

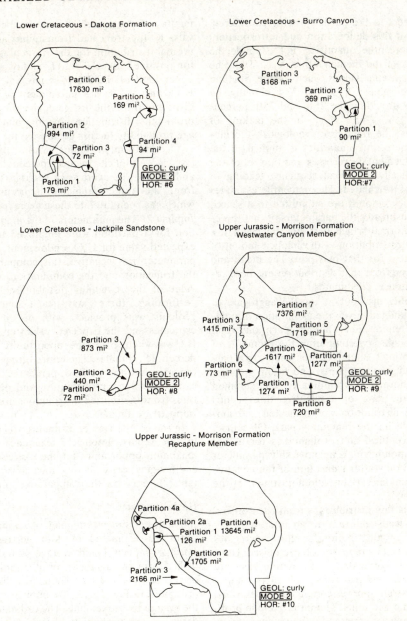

Fig. 15.11. Partitions made by Curly of the Dakota, Burro Canyon, Jackpile, Westwater Canyon, and Recapture units.

Dakota, Burro Canyon, Jackpile, Westwater Canyon, and Recapture units.

All estimates of endowment for aggregated units were derived from estimates made of the endowment of partitions: it is for the partition that a geologist applied his science and inference to make an estimate of the magnitude of U_3O_8 endowment.

Implicit estimation

Implicit 1. The first step by a geologist, after partitioning, in making an implicit estimate is to prepare himself by considering all relevant evidence such as paleogeological maps, outcrop maps, mine locations, reserves, geophysics, geochemistry, and his experience with respect to the partition being considered. On the basis of this deliberation and introspection, he provides percentile quantities. For example, he may first estimate the median value $X_{0.50}$. Then, he may identify extreme values, such as the 5th and 95th percentile values: $X_{0.05}$ and $X_{0.95}$. Finally, he may 'fill in' by providing the 25th and 75th percentile quantities: $X_{0.25}$ and $X_{0.75}$. In the making of these estimates, the relating of geological information to these percentile quantities is implicit to the subjective, judgemental processes and powers of the geologist. Typically, a logical sequence leading to estimates is not articulated. The percentile estimates provided by the geologist are submitted to a search routine which estimates the parameters of that three-parameter lognormal which best fits the estimates. This lognormal distribution is the implicit model of U_3O_8 endowment for that partition. The mean and percentile values from that distribution are here referred to as Implicit 1 estimates.

The probability distribution for the aggregate of partitions is estimated, given the assumption of independency of endowment across partitions and stratigraphical units, by computing the moments of the fitted lognormals, summing moments across partitions and stratigraphical units, and fitting a three-parameter lognormal distribution to the summed moments. In the case of a negative third (shift) parameter, the distribution was truncated and moments computed on the remaining part. Of course, the mean, percentiles, and probabilities for a lognormal distribution having a negative shift parameter were computed only after truncation of the negative range of the random variable and adjustment of the density function.

Having probability distributions from each of several geologists leads naturally to an interest in the average probability distribution for those aggregates of units that are common to all geologists. Units which have been aggregated to a common basis are here referred to as 'merged units'. For each geologist a probability distribution was computed, as described above, for the merged units. Then, the average probability distribution for a merged unit was obtained by fitting a three-parameter lognormal to the probabilities

$$P_i = \frac{1}{NG} \sum_{j=1}^{NG} \left\{ \left[F\left(\frac{\ln(x_i - \alpha_j) - \mu_j}{\sigma_j}\right) - F\left(\frac{\ln(x_{i-1} - \alpha_j) - \mu_j}{\sigma_j}\right) \right] \bigg/ K_j \right\}, \quad (15.4)$$

where $j = 1, 2, \ldots, NG$; $i = 1, 2, \ldots, NC$; NG is the

number of geologists; NC the number of class intervals; K_j the truncated (remaining) area of the lognormal distribution for the jth geologist (probability for positive values of U_3O_8 endowment X); x_i the upper limit of the ith class interval for quantity of U_3O_8; α_j, μ_j, σ_j are parameters of the lognormal distribution for the jth geologist; $F(\ )$ is the normal probability distribution function; and P_i is the average probability (across geologists) for the quantity of U_3O_8 endowment falling within the ith interval $[x_{i-1}, x_i]$. Implicit means, percentiles, and probabilities for the average of geologists are computed from the three-parameter lognormal distribution which has been fitted to these averaged probabilities. *Implicit 2.* The parameters of the lognormal distribution for a partition were employed to compute the expected value for U_3O_8 endowment. When the shift parameter was negative, this computation required the truncation and the computation of the expected value of the remaining distribution. Subsequent to performing these statistical computations, the geologist was provided with his initial percentile estimates and the expected value for each partition. He was then given the opportunity to modify all percentile estimates. The entire fitting procedure was repeated on the revised percentile estimates. All expected values, probabilities, and percentile quantities from the refitted distributions are referred to as Implicit 2 estimates.

In the comparison of estimates which will be made in this report, Implicit 2 estimates represent the maximum opportunity for the exercise of heuristics and hedging; consequently, they constitute an important reference for the comparative analysis.

Basin estimates

Implicit and system estimates. Averaging of the distributions estimated by four geologists produced average Implicit 1 and average system distributions of U_3O_8 for the aggregate of all stratigraphical units of the San Juan Basin. These two distributions are presented in Fig. 15.12, the implicit by asterisk and the system by broken line. The ordinate of this graph describes the probability that U_3O_8 endowment is greater than or equal to the tonnages measured on the abscissa. This figure shows clearly that for a given probability the system-generated distribution describes quantities approximately twice as large as does the Implicit 1 distribution. Table 15.14 is a summary of relevant statistics for the Implicit 1 and system distributions of Fig. 15.12. Table 15.15 shows three of these statistics, the mean and the 5th and 95th percentile quantities, for the Implicit 1, Implicit

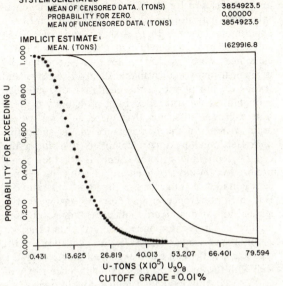

GEOLOGIST: THE AVG. DISTRIBUTION ACROSS ALL GEOLOGISTS

STRATIGRAPHIC HORIZON: THE SUM OF ALL URANIUM BEARING UNITS

SYSTEM GENERATED:
MEAN OF CENSORED DATA. (TONS)   3854923.5
PROBABILITY FOR ZERO.   0.00000
MEAN OF UNCENSORED DATA. (TONS)   3854923.5

IMPLICIT ESTIMATE:
MEAN. (TONS)   1629916.8

Fig. 15.12. System and Implicit 1 (*) probability distributions for initial U_3O_8 endowment for the aggregate of all stratigraphic units. [initial U_3O_8 endowment = cumulative production + reserves + potential]

2, System, and NURE distributions. The statistics for the NURE distribution were determined by adding cumulative production data to the statistics reported by US DOE for the sum of endowment plus mineral inventory. The mineral inventory data represent the Colorado Plateau Resource Region, of which the San Juan Basin is only a part, albeit a major part.

Fig. 15.13 is a graphic display of the data of Table 15.15. The ordinate is an ordinal ranking of opportunity for hedging and of the degree of aggregation (opposite of decomposition). Both of these were described earlier in this report (see the subsection 'Perspective' of this section). Decomposition is a strategy in the subjective estimation of an uncertain complex event and is adopted to mitigate the biases due to the excessive use of heuristics. This figure suggests that the greater the opportunity for hedging and the use of heuristics, the smaller is the estimate of expected (mean or average) U_3O_8 endowment and the narrower is the 90 per cent confidence range.

The general observation of psychometricians is that the use of heuristics results in biases and a

TABLE 15.14. *Selected statistics from the system and implicit distributions of initial U_3O_8 endowment for the aggregate of all stratigraphical units*

Geologist: the avg. distribution across all geologists
Stratigraphic horizon: the sum of all uranium bearing units
System generated.

Censored data:		
	mean. (tons)	3.85492E+6
	mode. (tons)	3.37554E+6
	variance. (tons)	4.10762E+15
	95th percentile. (tons)	6.54097E+6
	5th percentile. (tons)	2.03910E+6
Probability for zero:		0.000000
Uncensored data:		
	mean. (tons)	3.85492E+6
	mode. (tons)	3.37554E+6
	variance. (tons)	4.10762E+15
	95th percentile. (tons)	6.54097E+6
	5th percentile. (tons)	2.03910E+6
First implicit estimate:		
	mean. (tons)	1.62992E+6
	mode. (tons)	1.12699E+6
	variance. (tons)	1.69243E+15
	95th percentile. (tons)	3.36618E+6
	5th percentile. (tons)	5.17704E+5
Second implicit estimate:		
	mean. (tons)	1.53822E+6
	mode. (tons)	1.19495E+6
	variance. (tons)	1.20244E+15
	95th percentile. (tons)	2.97792E+6
	5th percentile. (tons)	5.11458E+5

TABLE 15.15. *Estimates of initial U_3O_8 endowment† for San Juan Basin by four methods—system and implicit estimates represent averaging across four geologists*

Estimation method	Estimates (short tons × 10³)			Spread ($E_{0.95} - E_{0.05}$)
	$E_{0.05}$	$\bar{E}$	$E_{0.95}$	
Implicit 2	511.4	1538	2977	2465.6
Implicit 1	517.7	1629	3366	2848.3
NURE‡	1428	2380	3334	1906
System	2040	3855	6542	4502

† Includes cumulative production, mineral inventory, and potential.
‡ Cumulative production: All units = 138 000 s.t.; Morrison members plus Jackpile Sandstone = 134 750 s.t.; Dakota = 250 s.t.; and Todilto = 3000 s.t. These data were provided by US Department of Energy Oct. 3, 1980.

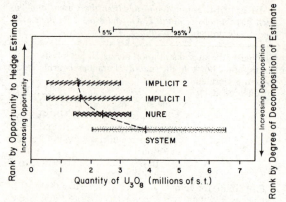

Fig. 15.13. Graphic comparison of estimates of initial U₃O₈ endowment [13] of the San Juan Basin—expected values and 90 per cent confidence ranges.

considerable understatement of the variance of the event—subjective distributions have been observed to exclude 40 to 50 per cent of the states described by the true distribution. In this study, we do not have a statement of 'ground truth', i.e. the true distribution of U_3O_8 endowment for the San Juan Basin; therefore, we cannot make unequivocal judgements as to which methodology produces the most accurate probability distribution. The strongest judgement that can be made is that the 90 per cent confidence ranges for Implicit 1, Implicit 2, and System estimates compare to each other as experimental results and theory of subjective assessment suggest they should. That is, estimation of the compound event by estimating the states of its components and subsequently recomposing the components produces a much broader distribution than the one obtained by unconstrained subjective processes.

Let us for the moment assume that the decomposition and constraints by science and probability relations that constitute the appraisal system are sufficient to capture the true variance in the state of nature. If this were so, the experimental results of research by psychometricians, such as Alpert and Raiffa [14] and Slovic (1972), suggest that if we were to expand the 90 per cent confidence range of the implicit distribution, by dividing it by 0.55 (the average of the 50 per cent and 60 per cent), we should approximate the 90 per cent confidence range of the true distribution, which by assumption is here taken to be the system distribution. But, which of the implicit estimates should be used in this calculation?

Conceptually, the answer is clear: It is the one that most closely represents the circumstances of the experiments by the psychometricians. But, making such an identification for the methodologies employed in this study may not be possible. For, in much of the experimental work, there was no support of the subjective processes, while in this study Implicit 1 estimates were made by experts supported by geological maps and available data on reserves and resources. Furthermore, the elicitation of subjective probabilities was preceded by a probability calibration exercise. It seems that these supports would tend to improve the performance of the subjective appraiser, meaning a more complete capturing of the range of possible events. If this is so, then some preference should be given to selecting the 90 per cent confidence range of the Implicit 2 distribution. But, such preference at best must be very weak. So, let us look at expanded confidence ranges for both implicit estimates. Expanded Implicit 1 and Implicit 2 confidence ranges are 5179×10^3 and 4483×10^3, respectively. Both of these expanded ranges compare well with the system 90 per cent confidence range of 4502×10^3; the expanded range for Implicit 2 is nearly identical. This exercise does not prove that the system distribution is correct. It only suggests that the 90 per cent confidence ranges for the implicit and system distributions are in relationship one to the other as suggested by experimental results on subjective probability assessment. This suggestion is strengthened by the very close comparison of the magnitude of the 90 per cent confidence range of the system distribution and the expanded implicit ranges.

Let us examine further the implication of expanding the 90 per cent confidence range for the implicit estimates. For this exercise let us use Implicit 2 estimates. Expansion of the Implicit 2 90 per cent confidence range was shown to give a range of 4483×10^3. Suppose that we wished to adjust the Implicit 2 estimate to accommodate this information. How would we do it? A simple and intuitive adjustment is a proportional shifting outward of the 5th and 95th percentile values. Accordingly, let us place 41.6 per cent of this range to the left of the mean and 58.4 per cent to the right of the mean. These percentages are derived from the relation of the 5th and 95th percentile quantities to the mean of the Implicit 2 distribution. Performing these calculations gives an expanded 5th and 95th percentile value of -327×10^3 to 4156×10^3. Of course, since negative U_3O_8 endowment has no meaning, this range is not a credible statement about U_3O_8 endowment.

One way of viewing the creation by simple expansion of a noncredible 5th percentile estimate—negative endowment—is that there is more at issue than just the heuristics. To the extent that subjective probability statements reflect an inclination to hedge, the implicit distributions reflect more than the excessive narrowness resulting from the use of heuristics. It is recognized that hedging and heuristic bias may interact in complex ways and that it is overly simplistic to attribute either shape or position to just one or the other of these effects. Nevertheless, it may be useful as a mental exercise to consider the *primary* effect of heuristic bias to be an excessive narrowness of the distribution and the *primary* effect of hedging to be the shifting of the distribution to the left (to smaller values) on the endowment axis. If this were so, then it would come as no surprise to find that adjusting Implicit 2 estimates only for the heuristics effect by shifting outward the 5th and 95th percentile values produces a modified 5th percentile value that is not credible.

What value for the 5th percentile is acceptable? Even the unexpanded 5th percentile may not be a credible estimate. There must be some doubt about 511 400 short tons (s.t.) as a possible state of nature when cumulative production for the greater San Juan Basin is approximately 138 000 s.t. of U_3O_8 and the mineral inventory for the Colorado Plateau Region is estimated at 731 400 s.t. of U_3O_8. Considering that a large part of this inventory derives from the Basin and that to that part must be added cumulative production of approximately 138 000 s.t., the 5th percentile estimate of initial U_3O_8 endowment may be lower than this sum, which is not credible as a 5th percentile estimate of initial endowment. In other words, the motivation to hedge may have overridden the narrowness effect of heuristic biases and produced a 5th percentile value that is not credible. Unfortunately, we have no way of identifying what the 5th percentile value should be, except that it probably is somewhat larger than 511 400 s.t. of U_3O_8.

Since the sum of production for the greater San Juan Basin and the mineral inventory for the Colorado Plateau Region is approximately 870 000 s.t. U_3O_8, let us assume for the purpose of expediting a mental exercise that a credible 5th percentile value for initial U_3O_8 endowment is at least 1 000 000 s.t. U_3O_8. Let us take a simplistic view that correcting for the hedging effect requires no more than a shifting of the Implicit 2 distribution to the right, i.e. adding 488 600 s.t. to all quantities. Then, after making this shift, let us make the adjustment for heuristic biases simply by adding the expanded range

$(\bar{R}_{0.95-0.05})$ to the shifted 5th percentile $(\tilde{U}_{0.05})$

$$\tilde{U}_{0.95} = \tilde{U}_{0.05} + \bar{R}_{0.95-0.05}$$
$$\tilde{U}_{0.95} = 1\,000\,000 + 4\,483\,000 = 5\,483\,000.$$

Given these adjusted percentile estimates, we can estimate the parameters of the implied lognormal by the relations

$$-1.645 = \frac{\ln(1\,000\,000) - \mu}{\sigma}$$

$$+1.645 = \frac{\ln(5\,483\,000) - \mu}{\sigma}.$$

Solving these equations for the two unknowns gives the estimates of parameters

$$\mu = 14.6663,$$
$$\sigma = 0.5172.$$

These computations produce a mean U_3O_8 endowment (2 677 000 s.t.) and a 95th percentile value (5 483 000 s.t.) that are between the NURE and system estimates, the mean being closer to the NURE mean but the 95th percentile value being closer to the system 95th percentile value. Of course, this demonstration is based upon an assumed 5th percentile value and separate adjustments for hedging and heuristic bias, which may not be appropriate. Even so, it demonstrates possible effects of hedging and heuristic bias and that if it were possible to adjust the implicit estimates for these effects, differences between estimates by the two methodologies may be significantly reduced.

NURE estimates. So far, little mention has been made of how the NURE estimates compare to the implicit and system estimates. This has been intentional and reflects the desire to examine not only numerical values but what these values have to say about hedging and heuristic biases in subjective estimation of U_3O_8 endowment by the different methods. In this regard, the NURE estimates cannot be compared with the other estimates, because the four geologists who made the implicit and system estimates of this study were not responsible as a group for the NURE estimates. In other words, the NURE estimates possibly reflect influences other than methodology, e.g. variation among geologists.

Some aspects of the NURE methodology (see Chapter 13) are of particular relevance to this study. One of these is the fact that U_3O_8 endowment is not estimated directly by the geologist. Instead, magnitude of endowment E is decomposed to A area of the region, F fraction of A underlain by U_3O_8

endowment, T tonnage of uranium bearing rock per unit of area, and G the average grade of the mineralized rock. The decomposition of the estimation process imposed by the NURE methodology should, *ceteris paribus*, result in capturing more of the possible variation in E than if E were estimated directly, as is done in the implicit method. Consequently, if the same geologists had been involved in all appraisals (NURE, Implicit 1, Implicit 2, and System) we would expect the 90 per cent confidence range of the NURE estimates to be broader than that of the Implicit 1, but narrower than that of the System. This expectation is noted in Fig. 15.13 by the ranking of NURE between Implicit 1 and System. This expectation is not realized by the estimates made by the NURE methodology; Fig. 15.13 shows a narrower, not a broader, range for NURE than for Implicit 1. Of course, this may be due to the estimation by different geologists instead of methodology.

Which estimate

Endowment appraisal programmes sometimes must meet severe time, data, and personnel constraints; consequently, selection of methodology must reflect these constraints. While this is a fact of life, the selection of methodology, given such constraints is not the issue here. The perspective here is the identification of that method which produces the best estimates irregardless of those considerations which affect the choice of a methodology in a real-time situation.

This question of best methodology cannot be answered unequivocally, because we do not have a 'ground truth' by which to judge the estimates. There are only two possibilities of even remotely approaching such a judgement, given the lack of ground truth. One of these is to ask each of the geologists who participated in this study which estimates he prefers. Of course, the outcome of this approach is pretty certain: They would select Implicit 2 estimates. This probably is so, because the trademark of this methodology is the allowing of the geologist to modify the percentile estimates for each partition so that its expected value is to his liking. If this postulation is correct, it raises a question that merits careful thought: To what degree should methodology selection be based upon preference by the geologist for its estimates? Conceptually, the answer to this question is clear: It is reasonable for a geologist to expect a methodology to produce estimates which *reflect variations* in *geological environment* and *degree of certainty* of *geoscience data*. If the methodology does not produce estimates with these properties, then the

geologist may have grounds for disapproving the methodology. But, it is probably true that all of the estimates examined here meet these loose qualifications. Given such a circumstance, it is natural for the geologist to emphasize the degree by which a methodology produces estimates that most satisfy or please him. As previously stated, the Implicit 2 estimates have this property. Such a basis for selection is a statement of ultimate faith in intuitive processes of judgement. Of course, selecting a methodology on these grounds ignores the deficiencies, observed by psychometricians, of the mind in estimating compound uncertain events.

The second method for judging the merits of the methods is to examine them with respect to the magnitude of heuristic bias and of hedging. This approach, which is the one followed in this study, indicates preference for the appraisal system. The comparative analysis of the previous section suggests the conclusion that when processing and integration of geological information are left to the exercise of mental (subjective) processes, the resulting subjective probability distributions of initial U_3O_8 endowment tend to exhibit narrowness and a conservative bias that decrease with the degree to which the mental processes receive support and aid in the estimation task.

An *a priori* ranking of methods by the degree to which they decompose the estimation process and hence mitigate narrowness of distribution and discourage hedging is also the correct ranking by size of expected endowment produced by these methods. With exception to the NURE estimates, this *a priori* ranking is also the correct one for breadth of the 90 per cent confidence range. The system estimated distributions generally have both the largest expected value and the largest 90 per cent confidence range. Since this methodology employs great decomposition and many decision aids, these results agree well with *a priori* expectations based upon findings and theories of psychometricians regarding the subjective assessment of an uncertain event; furthermore, such agreement indicates preference for the estimation of U_3O_8 endowment by an appraisal system.

Some qualifications

Interpretation of the relationship of methodology to the nature of its estimates has been made given the assumption that the decomposition process and the recomposition were accomplished with no major extraneous effect on the estimates. In other words, it is assumed that the only effect has been the decrease in biases due to the use of heuristics and the preventing of hedging. To the extent that this assumption is violated, the ability to draw sharp conclusions as to preferred methodology and the effect of decomposition and formalization of geological decisions on endowment estimates is weakened. This assumption undoubtedly is violated to some degree; consequently, it is appropriate to consider alternative explanations of the patterns in the estimates. Possible explanations include

1. Formalizing and decomposition are carried to such an extreme that the resulting estimates suffer from the confusion of the mind resulting from having to deal with the frontiers of understanding.

2. Reconstitution is improperly done, because it ignores certain correlations among the processes and conditions.

3. The geological model constitutes simplified geoscience; consequently, it does not capture some relevant information.

Let us examine the last of these possible explanations first. Most certainly, the geological model is, as are all models, a simplification of the real world; consequently, some geological information indeed is excluded. To the extent that the excluded information is relevant to the explanation of uranium endowment, it appeals to reason that this exclusion affects the estimates. Furthermore, one possible result of exclusion of relevant information is that the associated probability distributions exhibit variances that are larger than they would have been if this information had not been excluded. One can argue little with this proposition. Surely, if a geologist were to construct an inference net having all of the processes and geological conditions indicated by theory, it would be much more intricate and complex than those designed in this study. But, this is not the relevant issue. Rather, given that the objective is a model that includes those factors that are employed in the geological estimation of uranium endowment, the relevant question becomes, are there important geological factors used in implicit estimation that were excluded from the geological model? While such exclusion is possible, it is not clearly indicated. In fact, the converse may be a more accurate statement: The simplified geological models represented by the inference nets designed in this study require the explicit consideration by the geologists of more decision factors than usually are considered by the intuitive processes in making explicit estimates. One of the participants commented to this effect, namely that he had never before employed such in-depth geological analysis in estimating uranium endowment

as he did in making the system estimates. Another participant noted that constructing and using his system gave him a greater awareness than he had previously had of limitations of his basic geological data and information. In summary, when a distinction is made between theory and decision factors vis-à-vis the estimation of uranium endowment, the proposition that it is the use of simplified geological models that results in a divergence of the variances of the implicit and system estimates is considerably weakened.

Let us examine the second possible explanation: Reconstitution is improperly done because it ignores certain correlations. The idea here is that the larger variances in the system estimated distributions result from unresolved correlations. Simply stated, the possibility of unresolved correlations among the processes and conditions prompts the speculation that the system distribution may be broader than it should be because of unresolved correlations. Or, both effects, heuristic bias in implicit estimates and unresolved correlations within the inference net of the system may work in tandem to magnify differences in the distributions produced by these methods; this must be considered a possibility. This section explores in some detail the possibility that unresolved dependencies (correlations) challenge some of the findings of this study.

It is the dependency issue that is responsible for the purposeful structuring of the inference net into the three compound major processes: source–transportation; deposition–mineralization; and post-depositional preservation. Specifically, source and transportation were grouped together because of the commonality or intermixing of some processes, agents, or conditions. Deposition and mineralization were treated as a compound process for the same reason. Those geologists who were consulted regarding dependencies of the major processes expressed the opinion that this structuring was acceptable and that they were not concerned geologically about remaining correlations. To the extent that this judgement is accurate, dependencies among the major processes are adequately accommodated by the structure of the decision model; therefore, it is unlikely that unresolved dependencies at this level challenge the findings of this study.

Dependency may still be an issue at a different level. Suppose that the structuring of the major processes does take care of dependencies among the major processes. The dependency issue re-emerges within each major process combination, for within each of these combinations, e.g. the source–transportation process, the geologist identifies minor processes and/or geological conditions which describe the states of source and transportation. Dependencies may exist laterally among these minor processes or conditions. It should be noted carefully here that the dependencies at issue are those between horizontally adjacent processes on a particular level, i.e. processes on parallel branches. Dependencies between a major process and the minor processes that describe it are accounted for in the geological model.

In general, the presence of correlations (dependencies) is not sufficient of itself to make the case for an exaggerated variance of the function of several variables. The variance of the function of the variables will reflect both the ways that the variables are combined by the function and the kind as well as magnitude of the correlations. For example, consider two random variables X and Y that are to be added to produce a new random variable Z: $Z = X + Y$. The variance of Z can be described in terms of the variances of X and Y and the correlation between them

$$V(z) = V(x) + V(y) + 2\rho_{xy} \cdot \{V(x)\}^{\frac{1}{2}} \cdot \{V(y)\}^{\frac{1}{2}},$$

where $V()$ is variance, and ρ_{xy} is the correlation between X and Y. Inspection of this equation shows that if ρ_{xy} is large and positive, the variance of Z is greater than the variance of Z when X and Y are statistically independent ($\rho_{xy} = 0.0$) or when they are negatively correlated. Thus, in this example, if the distribution for Z were obtained by convolving the separate distributions for X and Y, hence ignoring the correlation between them, the resulting distribution could have a *larger or smaller* variance than it should have, depending upon the degree and kind of correlation that actually exists between X and Y. This example is not a close analogue of the operations performed on variables (processes and conditions) of the inference net, but it is useful in making the point that the effect of unresolved correlations is complex. In the appraisal system, unlike the example, one process is not created by adding the numerical values of two or more other processes. More relevant is the perception that the probability for a state of a higher-order process is determined by the probabilities for combinations of states of lower-order processes. Of course, the probability for a specific combination of states of lower-order processes is a joint probability, which is correctly computed as the product of marginal and conditional probabilities. As the system was used in this demonstration, the geologists provided separate estimates of the probabilities for the states of the terminal

(end) minor processes. They were not forced to provide probabilities for a state of one terminal minor process conditional upon the states of another terminal process. Consequently, the computed probabilities for combinations of processes are accurate only if these processes are independent. To the degree that correlations exist between the terminal minor processes, these computed probabilities are not accurate. Even so, this inaccuracy is not necessarily equatable to an exaggerated variance of U_3O_8 endowment. This will be demonstrated by an example.

Complexities in the impact of the kind and magnitude of dependency among the processes and conditions on the variance of endowment can be demonstrated by a simple, contrived example involving two processes X and Y and endowment V. Variables X and Y are considered to be correlated. Therefore, a strictly proper treatment of these variables by an appraisal system would require the geologist to provide probabilities for Y separately for each possible state of X and then to provide probabilities for the states of X. In statistical jargon, the geologist must provide conditional probability distributions for Y and a marginal probability distribution for X. Table 15.16 shows conditional and marginal distributions

TABLE 15.16. *Fictitious marginal and conditional distributions for two processes* X *and* Y

Case I

Distribution for X

X	1	2	3
$P(X)$	0.10	0.30	0.60

Conditional distributions for Y

Y	$P(Y\|X=1)$	$P(Y\|X=2)$	$P(Y\|X=3)$
4	0.1	0.2	0.6
5	0.3	0.5	0.3
6	0.6	0.3	0.1

Case II

Distribution for X

X	1	2	3
$P(X)$	0.20	0.50	0.30

Conditional distributions for Y

Y	$P(Y\|X=1)$	$P(Y\|X=2)$	$P(Y\|X=3)$
4	0.5	0.3	0.2
5	0.3	0.6	0.3
6	0.2	0.1	0.5

Case III

Distribution for X

X	1	2	3
$P(X)$	0.23	0.32	0.45

Conditional distributions for Y

Y	$P(Y\|X=1)$	$P(Y\|X=2)$	$P(Y\|X=3)$
4	0.2174	0.2500	0.2222
5	0.3478	0.3125	0.3333
6	0.4348	0.4375	0.4445

TABLE 15.17. *Joint distributions for* X *and* Y

		Case I		Case II		Case III	
X	Y	$P(Y\|X) \cdot P(X)$	$P(Y) \cdot P(X)$	$P(Y\|X) \cdot P(X)$	$P(Y) \cdot P(X)$	$P(Y\|X) \cdot P(X)$	$P(Y) \cdot P(X)$
1	4	0.0100	0.0430†	0.1000	0.0620	0.0500	0.0529†
1	5	0.0300	0.0360†	0.0600	0.0900†	0.0800	0.0759
1	6	0.0600	0.0210	0.0400	0.0480†	0.1000	0.1012†
2	4	0.0600	0.1290†	0.1500	0.1550†	0.0800	0.0736
2	5	0.1500	0.1080	0.3000	0.2250	0.1000	0.1056†
2	6	0.0900	0.0630	0.0500	0.1200†	0.1400	0.1408†
3	4	0.3600	0.2580	0.0600	0.0930†	0.1000	0.1035†
3	5	0.1800	0.2160†	0.0900	0.1350†	0.1500	0.1485
3	6	0.0600	0.1260†	0.1500	0.0720	0.2000	0.1980

† Combinations of X and Y for which ignoring dependencies produces a higher probability.

for three separate cases. In Cases I and II, X and Y have strong, but different kinds of dependencies (correlations). In Case I, X and Y are inversely correlated, while in Case II, they are positively correlated. In Case III, X and Y are weakly correlated.

Let us compute probabilities for the joint occurrence of X and Y two different ways. The first way is correct, given that X and Y are statistically dependent

$$P(X, Y) = P(Y|X) \cdot P(X).$$

The second way is correct only if X and Y are statistically independent

$$P(X, Y) = P(Y) \cdot P(X).$$

In this second, method, $P(Y)$ and $P(X)$ are correct marginals, having been calculated from the probabilities for the joint occurrence of X and Y

$$P(X = x) = \sum_{y=4}^{6} P(X = x, Y = y)$$

$$P(Y = y) = \sum_{x=1}^{3} P(X = x, Y = y).$$

Table 15.17 shows the joint probabilities calculated by these two ways for each of the three cases. The probabilities $P(Y|X) \cdot P(X)$ represent the probabilities computed by the system if the geologist and the system were to consider all dependencies and if dependencies are present. The probabilities $P(Y) \cdot P(X)$ represent probabilities computed by the system when the geologist and the system treat the processes as though they are statistically independent when in fact they are dependent. In other words, the dependency (correlation) that exists between the processes is ignored by the system and the geologist. This table shows simply that when the dependencies are strong, Cases I and II, probabilities for some of the process combinations are changed considerably, but the pattern of changes varies depending upon the kind of dependency (correlation) among the processes.

Now, suppose that for each of these nine process combinations we have conditional probabilities for magnitude of endowment V: $P(V|X, Y)$. These conditional probabilities for V are shown in Table

TABLE 15.18. *Conditional distributions† for* V, *given combinations of processes* X *and* Y

		V									
X	Y	1	2	3	4	5	6	7	8	9	10
1	4	0.9000	0.0800	0.0200	0.0000	0.0000	0.0000	0.0000	0.0000	0.0000	0.0000
1	5	0.7000	0.1500	0.1000	0.0500	0.0000	0.0000	0.0000	0.0000	0.0000	0.0000
1	6	0.5000	0.3000	0.1000	0.0800	0.0200	0.0000	0.0000	0.0000	0.0000	0.0000
2	4	0.2000	0.4000	0.2000	0.1000	0.0800	0.0200	0.0000	0.0000	0.0000	0.0000
2	5	0.1000	0.4000	0.3000	0.0800	0.0700	0.0500	0.0000	0.0000	0.0000	0.0000
2	6	0.0500	0.2000	0.3000	0.2000	0.1500	0.0800	0.0200	0.0000	0.0000	0.0000
3	4	0.0100	0.1000	0.3500	0.2000	0.1500	0.1000	0.0800	0.0100	0.0000	0.0000
3	5	0.0000	0.0200	0.2000	0.3500	0.2000	0.1000	0.0800	0.0300	0.0200	0.0000
3	6	0.0000	0.0100	0.0900	0.1500	0.3000	0.2000	0.1500	0.0500	0.0300	0.0200

† Numbers in body of table are probabilities for V, given values for X and Y.

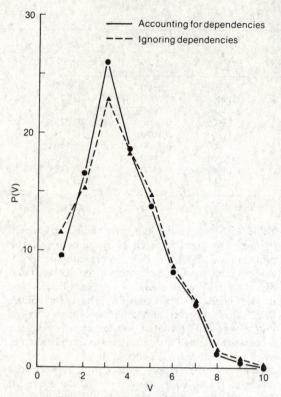

Fig. 15.14. Probability distribution for Case I.

The purpose of this exercise is solely to demonstrate that it cannot be concluded that the simplification of ignoring lateral dependencies between terminal minor processes and conditions imparts an exaggerated variance to the distribution of U_3O_8 endowment. When consideration is given to the fact that different kinds of correlation may be present among different sets of variables, that for each combination of states of the variables there is a different conditional distribution for number of deposits, and that these conditional distributions are combined by weighting them by the probabilities for their associated combination of process states, the presence of unresolved dependencies (correlations) can result in a distribution that is *narrower or broader* than it would be if dependencies had been explicitly accounted for.

The impact of dependencies that are present but unresolved within an inference net is softened somewhat by the manner in which the probabilities for the states of the terminal (furthest out from the apex of the net) processes are related to the higher level

15.18. An unconditional probability that $V = v$ can be computed as

$$P(V = v) = \sum_{x=1}^{3} \sum_{y=4}^{6} P(V = v, X = x, Y = y),$$

where

$$P(V = v, X = x, Y = y)$$
$$= P(V = v \mid X = x, Y = y) \cdot P(X = x, Y = y).$$

These probabilities for Cases I and II are shown in Figs 15.14 and 15.15. Note how the distribution for V is changed differently in these two cases as a result of the different kind of dependency between X and Y. For Case I (inverse correlation) ignoring the dependency between X and Y imparts a larger variance to the distribution of V than should be present: Variance when dependency is considered $= 2.97$; when it is ignored, 3.37. Conversely, for Case II (positive correlation) ignoring the dependency imparts a smaller variance to the distribution of V than actually exists: Variance when dependency is considered $= 3.46$; when it is ignored, 3.11.

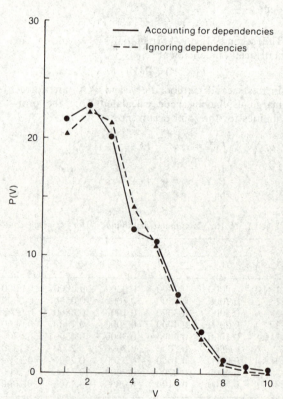

Fig. 15.15. Probability distribution for Case II.

processes. Details of these computations are provided in Harris and Carrigan [1, 4]. Suffice it here to note that in the appraisal of a region the geologist provides probabilities for the states of terminal processes or conditions only. All higher-level processes have only three states: excellent, intermediate, and poor. All combinations of the states of the terminal processes, no matter how numerous they may be, are ascribed to one of the three states (excellent, intermediate, or poor) of the next-higher-level process. This 'telescoping' is perpetuated throughout the net for a major process combination, e.g. source–transportation (ST), having each of the three states (excellent, intermediate, and poor). Such a procedure would tend to soften (diminish) the impact of unresolved correlations. For example, suppose that two of the nine combinations of the states of two terminal processes were linked to an excellent state of a higher-level process. The probability for the excellent state of the higher process would be determined by adding the probabilities for these two states of the terminal process. Suppose that this summing is performed on two different cases, one in which the probabilities for the combinations of the states of the two terminal processes correctly reflect dependencies and the other in which dependencies have been ignored. These two sums would, on average, tend to show less departure, due to unresolved dependencies, than do the unsummed probabilities for the two cases.

There may be dependencies of a different order that affect estimates of merged and aggregated units, for estimates for these units were obtained by treating distributions for the partitions as though they were statistically independent when they were combined. The fact that geologists delineated a partition because of its geological homogeneity seems to support this procedure. However, it can be argued that some processes operate over large regions and some geological conditions have considerable lateral extent. Consequently, by some geological criteria, adjacent partitions may resemble each other, suggesting some dependency in associated U_3O_8 endowment. The fact that partitions and stratigraphical units were assumed to be statistically independent may exaggerate somewhat the variance of U_3O_8 endowment for aggregated units. Even so, such exaggeration probably would affect the implicit and system estimates nearly equally; consequently, the presence of these unresolved dependencies would not prevent the comparative analysis of system and implicit estimates. But, these dependencies may disturb the comparative analysis of NURE with the implicit and

system estimates, for in the NURE analysis some clustering was performed of partitions which were judged to be similar geologically. These were aggregated under the assumption of perfect dependency. Clusters then were aggregated assuming independency. In this way, some correlation was implicitly built into the aggregation.

Let us consider the remaining possible explanation: Formalization and decomposition have been carried to such an extreme that the resulting estimates suffer from the confusion of the mind resulting from having to deal with the frontiers of understanding. The concept here has been eluded to and dramatized by the adage that one need not understand the workings of an internal combustion engine to drive a car. The implication of this adage with respect to mineral exploration is that a geologist need not understand the genesis of uranium deposits in order to discover them (Ridge 1982). Of course, even with regard to mineral exploration not everyone agrees with Ridge, a notable example being Bailly [15], who states that geological modelling is emerging as the most productive exploration tool. The analogy with respect to the appraisal of uranium endowment is that a geologist can estimate uranium endowment without (1) understanding and employing the interrelations of earth processes and geological conditions, (2) understanding how these processes and conditions relate to the density of mineralization (number of deposits or fraction of area underlain by mineralization), and (3) employing information on the quantity of U_3O_8 per deposit or per mineralized cell. An even stronger position can be taken: Requiring a geologist to define, construct, and use such a system creates distortions in estimates because it reveals and plays upon relations about which his understanding is at best vague. In other words, such a method may produce distributions having a greater variance than actually exists simply because it forces the geologist to use poorly understood relations.

In view of the difficulty that the geologists encountered in linking the decision model to endowment— this was commented upon in a previous section—this proposition is appealing. Clearly, linkage of the geological decision model to endowment was the most difficult of all tasks undertaken by the geologists: They struggled with both the conditional distributions for density of mineralization (number of deposits or fraction underlain by uranium endowment) and the distributions of the quantity of U_3O_8 per mineralized unit (deposit or cell). At the heart of this difficulty is the lack of basic data on uranium deposits and occurrences. Had such data been available, the linkage task would have been greatly simplified; it is possible also that a system that would have been constructed and calibrated using such data may have produced distributions of U_3O_8 endowment which would have exhibited smaller variances than those produced in this study. But, this is not the issue. The issue is whether, *given available information*, the true variance is most accurately captured by a system which requires the geologist to deal with his uncertainties about relations or by the implicit methodology, which allows him to suppress or bypass these uncertainties. The fact that the implicit methodology does not expose these uncertainties does not mean that they are not present. On the contrary, *they still exist*. True, the geologist can employ an algorithm for inference that bypasses them. Even so, if the phenomenon of uranium endowment is comprised by deposits which physically exist and if these phenomena are resultants of earth processes—this is the basic tenet of geology—the suggestion is strong that employing an algorithm for inference that bypasses the use of this logic sequence results in distortion of estimates, for the geologist is deceived as to the actual uncertainty which is present. If the basic tenet of geology is taken as given, then one must consider very carefully the proposition that estimation of uranium endowment can be made accurately without dealing with these difficult and vague relations, for they are an integral part of the geology–endowment theory. True, estimates can be generated, as in the case of the implicit methodology, without dealing explicitly with these relations, but is it not possible that this estimation at times is based upon only casual geological analyses? For example, using the implicit methodology it is possible for a geologist to bypass geological reasoning and to predicate an endowment estimate almost exclusively upon geographical proximity of the region to a well known region or upon the locality of the region with respect to a spatial pattern in known producing regions. While this procedure may produce a reasonable estimate, it is not based upon geological analysis. Our interest in Chapter 15 is restricted to subjective geological estimates. Whether or not the endowment of uranium, or any mineral, is best estimated by geological or non-geological methods is a question of a higher order. It must be admitted, however, that the difficulties encountered by the geologist with the linkage of his geological decision model to endowment undermines to some extent confidence in the ability of geologists at this time and with the current level of information and training to estimate endowment, whether it be by implicit or

system methodologies. This does not mean necessarily that we should turn to other non-geological methods, for all methods seem to have their particular problems. It does mean that we need much better data on the nature of uranium deposits and upon the state of exploration to support the building of geology–endowment models. Furthermore, to the degree that data allow, linking the geological decision model to endowment by quantitative statistical analysis should be investigated—this was described in a previous section. In summary, while there is ample reason for concern about difficulties in geological modelling, this concern is not necessarily a justification for the preference of the implicit methodology, for all subjective estimates suffer from insufficient data and knowledge.

A final argument that must be considered when judging the effect of formalization and decomposition on the variance of estimates is that during the calibration exercise the geologist was encouraged to modify the conditional distributions on density and the distributions for quantity per mineralized unit so that the output of the appraisal system on the test areas and reference sections met with his approval. If we assume that this calibration was conscientiously performed, the argument that formalization and decomposition created an exaggeration of variance is further weakened, for one must explain why estimates by the system are suspect when the performance of this same system previously was acceptable to the geologist who designed it and calibrated it on test regions and reference conditions. The system was 'locked in' at the completion of calibration, and system estimates are a result of the use by the geologist of his calibrated system.

15.3. A comment on PROSPECTOR—a second example of approach A

15.3.1. *Perspective and scope*

PROSPECTOR is the name given by Stanford Research Institute International to impressive computer software that initially was employed to capture and imitate the decision process of an expert geologist in determining the favourability of a mineral prospect.

PROSPECTOR is an outgrowth of efforts to employ techniques of artificial intelligence to represent empirical judgement knowledge in a formal way and to use that knowledge to perform plausible reasoning—reasoning which is based upon Bayesian decision theory. While much of the early research and applications were in medical diagnosis (Pople *et al.* 1975; Shortliffe 1976; Weiss, Kulikowski, and Safir 1977), the problems of using observations of various kinds and judgements to make a medical diagnosis have parallels in other disciplines, one of which is mineral exploration. Generically speaking, the techniques of artificial intelligence that constitute PROSPECTOR apply to those situations in which the level of science or data available to support making decisions often does not permit precise scientific formulation. Rather, judgements or decisions are based upon evidences which collectively are suggestive of one or more states. Typically, decisions made in such circumstances are informed, but uncertain, hence probabilistic in nature. The fact that mineral exploration is sometimes referred to as an art–science indicates that exploration decisions are made without unequivocal data and without a complete understanding of the relationship between geological evidence and mineral occurrence.

An important property of PROSPECTOR is that it requires a formal statement of assertions, which can be evidences or hypotheses, and of the strength of the relationship between evidence and hypotheses. The complex of interrelated assertions produces an inference net, much like that described by Harris and Carrigan [1, 4]. The relation between evidence and hypotheses is referred to as a logical relationship, and the statement of strength of relationship is referred to as a plausible (probabilistic) relationship. Thus, PROSPECTOR integrates data, science, and probability. Another important point to be made is that the software and approach of PROSPECTOR are both designed to facilitate the formalization of decision-making. For example, the burden of encoding an inference net is eased by the PROSPECTOR system, which allows the geologist to state the inference rule in terms of evidence, hypotheses, and strength. A computer program accepts these statements and automatically interrelates this rule to other rules that comprise the inference net and to algorithms for the computation of probabilities.

Finally, the PROSPECTOR system represents inference nets and computes probabilities in ways that permit the building and use of large and intricate inference nets. Instead of requiring the geologist, as does the software developed by Harris and Carrigan [1, 4], to identify all combinations at each level and to rank them—as a means of interrelating processes states (see § 15.2.)—the PROSPECTOR methodology requires the geologist to provide odds and likelihood ratios for each rule; all other interrelating and computations are automatically made by the PROS-

PECTOR system. The support by the PROSPECTOR system of formalizing the decision process is a very important feature of that system.

At the time of this writing PROSPECTOR had not been employed to estimate mineral endowment or any of its components. However, impressive deposit models had been developed for the appraisal of the favourability of a prospect, for example a Kuroko-type massive sulphide model (designed by Charles F. Park, Jr.), a Mississippi-Valley-type carbonate lead/zinc model (designed by Neil Campbell), a near-continental-margin porphyry copper model (designed by Marco T. Einaudi), a Komatiitic nickel sulphide model (designed by Anthony J. Naldrett), and a Western-states sandstone uranium model (designed by Ruffin I. Rackley) (Duda, Gaschnig, and Hart 1979). It is noteworthy that at the time of this writing the US Geological Survey is supporting additional development work on PROSPECTOR as a methodology for the appraisal of mineral endowment.

As suggested by the foregoing comments, PROSPECTOR is a complex methodology. General comment on only a few features of the system are provided here. The reader is referred to publications of Stanford Research Institute for in-depth descriptions of the PROSPECTOR system and of applications (Duda, Hart, Barrett, Gaschnig, Konolige, Reboh, and Slocum 1978; Duda, Hart, Nilsson Reboh, Slocum, and Sutherland 1977; and Gaschnig 1980).

15.3.2. *Some specific features*

Capturing and representing geological knowledge

In the foregoing comments, the inference net was cited as an essential feature of PROSPECTOR. This net is essential not only for the functioning of the PROSPECTOR system, but as a means of assisting the geological expert in exploring his decision processes. Simply identifying the evidences and hypotheses and their interrelations is a major task in the construction of a PROSPECTOR model. Even so, demands on the geologist extend far beyond this task. Eventually, the knowledge of the expert must be formally stated in a format that is acceptable to the PROSPECTOR system; that format is termed by the designers of the PROSPECTOR methodology as an inference rule, an example of which is the following (Duda *et al.* 1977, p. 21)

IF   E1 AND E2 AND E3
THEN   H (to degree LS, LN).

This rule states that the presence of all three pieces of evidence suggests hypothesis H to degree LS, LN (these will be explained shortly). Fig. 15.16, shows (under network links) a schematic illustration of this rule. The conjunction AND serves as a logic operator and conveys the idea that it is the joint occurrence of these three evidences that is important to hypothesis H. The logic operator OR represents the disjunctive events, i.e., the presence of any one of the evidences is all that is required for H, and that H is known to degree of certainty LS, LN. An example of evidence and hypothesis for a simple rule is the following (Duda *et al.* 1977], p. 21)

   IF   Abundant quartz sulphide veinlets with no apparent alteration halos

   THEN   Alteration favourable for the potassic stage (to degree LS, LN).

Since the hypothesis of one rule can be the evidence for one or more other rules, a network of interrelated geologic evidences and conditions is produced. The casting of the geological expert's knowledge into these formal statements provides the PROSPECTOR system with an expression of this knowledge in a form that supports computer processing. The principal form of reasoning by PROSPECTOR is by what the designers of the system refer to as propagation of probabilities through the inference net. Some insight to this is obtained by examining the ways that probability is represented in the system; this examination also explains the measures of certainty, LS and LN.

ASSERTION SPACES:

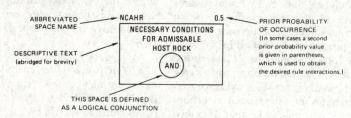

NOTE: If box is dashed rather than solid, then its complete definition (including subnetwork, if any) appears on another page.

NETWORK LINKS:

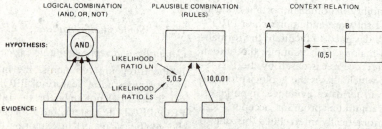

INTERPRETATION:
In the case of an "AND" connection, all pieces of evidence must be present to establish the hypothesis. In the case of an "OR" connection, the hypothesis is established by any piece of evidence.

INTERPRETATION:
LS measures the degree of sufficiency or suggestiveness of the evidence for establishing the hypothesis. (A larger value of LS means greater sufficiency.) LN measures the degree of necessity of the evidence for establishing the hypothesis. (A smaller value of LN means greater necessity.) The value LS = 1 (LN = 1) indicates that the presence (absence) of the evidence is irrelevant to the hypothesis. For example, if LS > 1 and LN = 1, then the presence of the evidence is suggestive of the hypothesis, but its absence does not lower the probability of the hypothesis.

INTERPRETATION:
Do not attempt to establish space B unless and until space A has been established with certainty greater than zero and less than or equal to 5. Context interval [-5,0] indicates A must have negative certainty before attempting to establish B. Context interval [-5,5] indicates simply that one should ask about A (regardless of the answer) before asking about B. Omitted context interval indicates (0,5].

Fig. 15.16. Schematic key to PROSPECTOR model diagrams. (Source: Gaschnig 1980.)

Probability

The previous section identified the use of evidence E and hypothesis H in the representation of the expert's knowledge. The foundation for the measures of degree of certainty, LS and LN, and for some of the probability analysis within PROSPECTOR rests on Bayes rule

$$P(H \mid E) = \frac{P(E \mid H) \cdot P(H)}{P(E)} \qquad (15.5)$$

$$= \frac{P(E \mid H) \cdot P(H)}{P(E \mid H) \cdot P(H) + P(E \mid \bar{H}) \cdot P(\bar{H})} \qquad (15.6)$$

where $\bar{H}$ means not H and $P(\bar{H}) = 1 - P(H)$. Suppose that we define two measures, odds (O) and likelihood ratio (LS) as

$$O(H) = \frac{P(H)}{1 - P(H)}, \qquad (15.7)$$

$$LS = \frac{P(E \mid H)}{P(E \mid \bar{H})}. \qquad (15.8)$$

Then, it can be shown that Bayes rule can be written in terms of odds and likelihood ratios

$$O(H \mid E) = LS \cdot O(H). \qquad (15.9)$$

Suppose that (15.5) is multiplied by $P(\bar{H} \mid E)/P(\bar{H} \mid E)$. Then, we have

$$P(H \mid E) = \frac{P(E \mid H) \cdot P(H) \cdot P(\bar{H} \mid E)}{P(\bar{H} \mid E) \cdot P(E)}$$

$$= \frac{P(E \mid H) \cdot P(H) \cdot P(\bar{H} \mid E)}{P(\bar{H}, E)}$$

and

$$P(H \mid E) = \frac{P(E \mid H) \cdot P(H) \cdot P(\bar{H} \mid E)}{P(E \mid \bar{H}) \cdot P(\bar{H})}. \qquad (15.10)$$

But, eqn (15.10) can be written as the product of three terms

$$P(H \mid E) = \left[\frac{P(E \mid H)}{P(E \mid \bar{H})} \right] \cdot \left[\frac{P(H)}{P(\bar{H})} \right] \cdot P(\bar{H} \mid E). \qquad (15.11)$$

Dividing (15.11) by $P(\bar{H} \mid E)$ and rewriting $P(\bar{H})$ as $1 - P(H)$, we have

$$\frac{P(H \mid E)}{P(\bar{H} \mid E)} = \left[\frac{P(E \mid H)}{P(E \mid \bar{H})} \right] \cdot \left[\frac{P(H)}{1 - P(H)} \right]. \qquad (15.12)$$

Finally, recognizing $P(\bar{H} \mid E)$ as $1 - P(H \mid E)$ and using definitions (15.7) and (15.8), we have Bayes rule in terms of odds and a likelihood ratio

$$O(H \mid E) = LS \cdot O(H).$$

The Bayesian definition of $P(H \mid \bar{E})$ can be described similarly

$$\theta(H \mid \bar{E}) = LN \cdot O(H), \qquad (15.13)$$

where

$$LN = \frac{P(\bar{E} \mid H)}{P(\bar{E} \mid \bar{H})}. \qquad (15.14)$$

The construction of a PROSPECTOR model, as contrasted to the use of an existing model, requires the specification of all quantities on the right-hand side of (15.6). Prior to any information, the probability for H is the prior probability $P(H)$. But, given the observation of evidence E, the appropriate probability is $P(H \mid E)$ and, for the very simple situation of one evidence and one hypothesis, this is computed by eqn (15.6). Thus, in this simple situation, the experience and expertise of the geologist is captured by this Bayesian relationship. Even so, as indicated in the foregoing section and in Fig. 15.16, the geologist is not asked to provide these probabilities. Instead, he provides LS and LN (see 'Plausible combinations' of Fig. 15.16) and odds, $O(H)$ (see 'Prior probability' under 'Assertion spaces' of Fig. 15.16). From these quantities, PROSPECTOR computes the required probabilities.

The straightforward application of Bayes rule requires that the states of the evidences—in the simplest case E or $\bar{E}$—be known with certainty. Often, one or more evidences are not known with certainty. This is represented by $P(E \mid E')$ where E' represents the observations relevant to E. PROSPECTOR uses a linear relationship, shown in Fig. 15.17 to compute $P(H \mid E)$ when E is suspected but not known (Duda et al. 1977).

A more complex situation arises when there are several evidences E_1, E_2, E_3 for a hypothesis and each is known to be true only with some probability. If all E_i were statistically independent, for the conjunctive case, the appropriate probability is $\prod_{i=1}^{N} P(E_i \mid E')$. When E_i are not statistically independent, estimation of the joint probability is much more complex

$$P(E_1, E_2, \ldots, E_n \mid E') = P(E_1 \mid E_2, \ldots, E_n, E') \times$$
$$\times P(E_2 \mid E_3, \ldots, E_n, E') \cdot \ldots \cdot P(E_n \mid E'). \qquad (15.15)$$

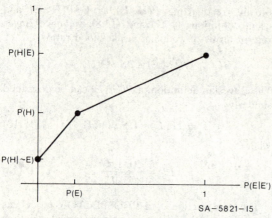

Fig. 15.17. The consequent probability as a function of the antecedent probability. (Source: Duda *et al.* 1977, p. 37, Fig. 5.)

As indicated by relationship (15.15), a theoretically accurate treatment of dependencies would greatly increase the burden on the user of PROSPECTOR by requiring him to specify conditional probabilities. Furthermore, accommodation of such a treatment by PROSPECTOR would create additional complexities. But, ignoring dependencies and treating all probabilities for evidence as statistically independent, when they are not, creates very small probabilities for the joint occurrence, conjunction, of evidences, particularly if the evidences for a hypothesis are numerous. PROSPECTOR does not compute the joint probability; instead, a relationship from the theory of fuzzy sets (Zadeh 1965) is used:

$$P(E_1 \cap E_2 \cap \ldots \cap E_n \mid E') = \min_i \{P(E_i \mid E')\}.$$
$$(15.16)$$

Thus, the smallest marginal probability of the set of N probabilities is taken as the probability for the joint occurrence of all N evidences.

Analogously, for disjunctive events, the probability for the union of the n evidences is not computed. Instead, a relationship proposed by Zadeh (1965) is used

$$P(E_1 \cup E_2 \cup \ldots \cup E_n \mid E') = \max_i \{P(E_i \mid E')\}$$
$$(15.17)$$

Thus, the largest marginal probability is taken as the probability for the union of the n events.

Sometimes a rule is a logical combination of evidences, e.g. E1 OR (E2 AND $\bar{E}$3). The probability for such a combination can be computed by applying

eqns (15.16) and (15.17)

$$\max \{P(E1 \mid E'), \min [P(E2 \mid E'), 1 - P(E3 \mid E')]\}.$$
$$(15.18)$$

When each of several E_i, $i = 1, \ldots, n$, affect H and all E_i are known and are statistically independent, the posterior odds, $O(H \mid E)$ are computed in PROSPECTOR by using the relationship (Duda, Hart, and Nilsson 1976)

$$O(H \mid E) = O(H) \cdot \prod_{i=1}^{n} LS_i.$$
$$(15.19)$$

When the E_i are known only probabilistically, $P(E_i \mid E')$, a heuristic solution is employed (Duda *et al.* 1977)

$$O(H \mid E) = O(H) \cdot \prod_{i=1}^{n} L'_i,$$
$$(15.20)$$

where

$$L'_i = \frac{O(H \mid E'_i)}{O(H)}$$
$$(15.21)$$

and $O(H \mid E'_i)$ are determined using quantities from the linear relationship of Fig. 15.17.

The discussion thus far has commented only on the treatment of one inference rule. A PROSPECTOR model is an interrelated complex of rules, and the desired probability is the Bayesian probability for the highest-level hypothesis. When the probability for the evidence for a hypothesis changes, the probability of H must be updated. Consequently, computation of the desired probability (for highest-level hypotheses) requires the propagation of probabilities throughout the inference net. There are many complexities that arise with regard to this computation; the reader is referred to publications by Stanford Research Institute for commentary on them and on computation procedures.

A summary description of PROSPECTOR *as a computerized system*

One of the most impressive features of PROSPECTOR is the support that it provides both for the construction of a model and for its use. The following overview of the workings of the PROSPECTOR system is reproduced from Duda *et al.* (1978, pp. 7, 9, and 10) (see Fig. 15.18).

A user of Prospector communicates with the system through a simple subsystem called the *Executive*. The Executive accepts commands from the user, interprets them, passes control to other subsystems, and returns responses to the user.

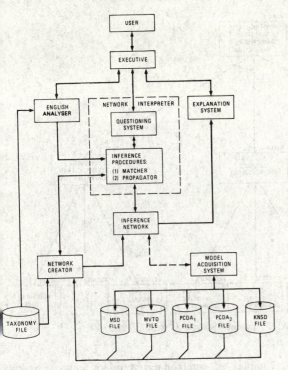

Fig. 15.18. System diagram for PROSPECTOR. (Source: Duda *et al.* 1978, p. 8, Fig. 1.)

In a typical session, the user begins by volunteering relevant facts about the significant rocks, minerals, and alteration products present at the prospect. This is done through a series of simple English sentences, such as "There is a quartz monzonite intrusive," "The host rock is Tertiary granite," "Chalcopyrite is present," and "There is probably some biotite."

The Executive routes this information to the *English Analyzer*, which makes use of an SRI-developed system called LIFER to analyze each sentence (Hendrix, 1977). Those sentences that are successfully analyzed are represented in a network form and a subsystem called the *Matcher* performs the function of matching the observations against the assertions in the Inference Network.

Associated with each assertion in the Inference Network is a probability that the assertion is true. When a match is made between an analyzed observation and an assertion, the probability is changed and the consequences of that change are propagated throughout the network according to the procedures in the *Propagator*.

When the user has finished volunteering observations, the Executive passes control to the *Questioning System*. This subsystem examines the state of the Inference Network and selects the "best-matching" model. Since the user typically has limited observational data and has mentioned only a portion of that, the degree of match with even the best-matching model is usually rather low.

Thus, the Questioning System tries to select the particular piece of unmentioned observational evidence that will be most effective in confirming or refuting a match. [16]

What typically follows is a cycle of questions and answers in which the Questioning System selects a piece of relevant evidence, the Executive asks the user about it, the user provides an answer (which may indicate uncertainty, including a total lack of information), the Propagator assesses the consequences of the answer, and the Questioning System then selects another piece of relevant evidence to inquire about.

Instead of answering a question, the user can take the initiative at any time to do such things as, for example, changing the answer to an earlier question, volunteering additional evidence, asking for a clarification of the question, or requesting an explanation. This latter request is handled by the *Explanation System* and takes one of two forms—an explanation of the reason for that particular question or a summary of the principal conclusions of the system at this point in the consultation. This ability of the system to examine the Inference Network and to produce explanations for its conclusions is quite important, and constitutes a major justification for calling Prospector a consultation program.

To provide its consultation services Prospector draws upon two kinds of geological knowledge—knowledge about specific ore-deposit models that is represented in the Inference Network, and general geological knowledge (such as the classifications of rocks, minerals, ages, and forms) that is represented in the Taxonomy. Both the coded models and the Taxonomy are separated from the Prospector program per se and reside on external disk files. The *Network Creator* reads these files to build the Inference Network. Thus, the geological knowledge in the system can be updated by editing these files and reexecuting the Network Creator.

15.3.3. *A brief comment on the use of PROSPECTOR for regional analysis of uranium favourability* [17]

Figures 15.19, 15.20, and 15.21 display some of the features of an inference net developed in the construction of a PROSPECTOR model for a 'regional scale Western States Sandstone Uranium model (RWSSU)' (Gaschnig 1980). This model was developed by Stanford Research Institute International using Ruffin Rackley's perception of the geoscience of this type of uranium deposit. Fig. 15.19 shows the overall structure of the RWSSU model. Fig. 15.20 shows a bit more detail of the factors that influence one of the nodes, Favourable tectonic and regional conditions. Each factor contained in a box that is delineated by dashed lines is described separately by its own inference net. For example, the factor referred to as Admissible host rock in Fig. 15.20 is described by the inference net in Fig. 15.21. Thus, behind the overall structure in Fig. 15.19 is a

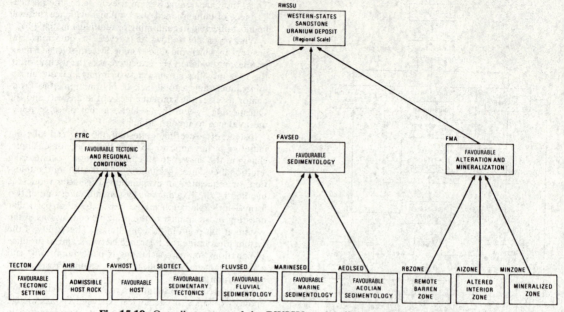

Fig. 15.19. Overall structure of the RWSSU model. (Source: Gaschnig 1980.)

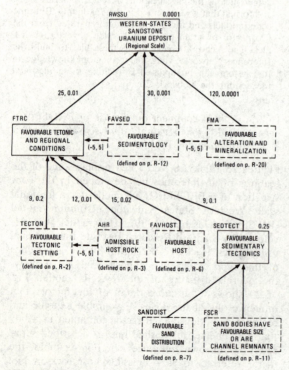

Fig. 15.20. Inference network for the RWSSU model. (Source: Gaschnig 1980.)

complex of interconnected minor nets. It is this entire complex that represents the geoscience of the geologist, in this case, Ruffin Rackley. As described by Gaschnig (1980, p. 18), the PROSPECTOR model consists of assertions, some of which correspond to field observations that PROSPECTOR asks the user about, whereas others correspond to geological conclusions or hypotheses that may be inferred from field observations. An especially impressive feature of PROSPECTOR is the computer software that facilitates the design and implementation of a net-type of decision model. This system is designed to automate net construction through the use of assertion statements and network links, such as logical combination (and, or, not), plausible combination (rules), and context relation. Fig. 15.16 depicts schematically the types of network links.

Gaschnig (1980) describes a test of the RWSSU model in estimating the favourability of a region for the occurrence of at least one uranium deposit. Five regions were selected as the basis for the test: Pumpkin Buttes (Gillette quadrangle), Northwest corner of Gillette quadrangle, Moorcroft (Newcastle quadrangle), Monument Hill (Newcastle quadrangle), and White River (mainly in Casper and Lander quadrangles). The test consisted of two parts. In the first part, the designer of the RWSSU model, Ruffin Rackley, rated each area on a scale of −5 to 5 as to

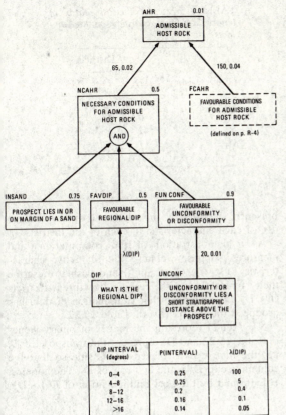

Fig. 15.21. Subnetwork for the RWSSU model. (Source: Gaschnig 1980.)

its favourability for the occurrence of at least one uranium deposit. Then, these same areas were rated by the PROSPECTOR model by the processing of descriptions made by Rackley of the states of the

TABLE 15.19. *Comparison of RWSSU model with Rackley for five test regions.* (*Source: Gaschnig 1980, p. 197.*)

Region	Target value†	PROSPECTOR Score	Difference
Monument Hill	4.40	4.40	0.0
Pumpkin Buttes	4.75	4.40	0.35
Moorcroft	4.20	4.00	0.20
Northwest Gillette	1.00	3.42	2.42
White River	0.80	0.01	0.79
Average			0.75

† These are favourability estimates made directly by Rackley, on a scale of −5 to 5.

geological variables of his inference net. Table 15.19 compares the direct evaluations by Rackley with those of PROSPECTOR, given the input statements about the geology of each region. This table shows overall that the model simulates rather well the intuitive judgements of Rackley. There is very close agreement of favourability estimates for Monument Hill, Pumpkin Buttes, and Moorcroft regions, but considerable departure of estimates for Northwest Gillette.

In the second part of the test, several geologists were asked to use the PROSPECTOR model to estimate the favourability of these same five regions. These geologists provided judgements about the geologic factors in each of the regions and these responses were processed by PROSPECTOR, using the RWSSU model developed by Rackley. Table 15.20 shows the favourability estimates computed by PROSPECTOR, given the responses of four geologists, Rackley, and a team of geologists from the United States Geological Survey.

TABLE 15.20. *Overall conclusions about five test regions.* (*Source: Gaschnig 1980.*)

Region	Geologist				USGS team	Rackley data	Avg.	Range
	A	B	C	D				
Monument Hill	4.17	3.32	3.97			4.40	3.97	1.08
Pumpkin Buttes	4.20	3.30	4.19			4.40	4.02	1.10
Moorcroft			3.92	3.88, 4.00		4.00	3.95	0.12
Northwest Gillette			3.64	0.10		3.42	2.39	3.54
White River					0.13	0.01	0.07	0.12

15.4. Genetic modelling, characteristic analysis, and decision analysis (approach B)—a methodology developed by the US Geological Survey

15.4.1. Perspective

This methodology brings together three separate efforts, some of which have been in development for several years: characteristic analysis (Botbol 1971; Botbol, Sinding-Larsen, McCammon, and Gott 1978), genetic modelling of uranium environments (Finch et al. [18]) and decision analysis (McCammon [19]). This section examines characteristic analysis first; this is followed by a brief review of genetic modelling and the relationship between genetic concepts and geodata. Then, a description is provided of the role of decision analysis in facilitating (1) the use of geodata and genetic concepts and (2) the integration of data by characteristic analysis for the quantitative description of degree of association of a cell of unknown potential with control cells. Finally, comment is provided on the translating of degree of association to probability and the integration of this measure in the appraisal of uranium endowment.

15.4.2. Characteristic analysis

Characteristic analysis was demonstrated (Botbol 1971) as a means for quantitatively describing how typical each of a number of characteristics (stratigraphical, mineralogical, geochemical, structural, etc.) is of a set of mining districts. Table 15.21 identifies the mining districts initially analysed by Botbol. As initially demonstrated, a tableau (matrix) was constructed which showed for each district the

TABLE 15.21. Model base metal mining districts. (Source: Botbol 1971, p. 92.)

Copper districts	Lead districts	Zinc districts
Butte	Park City	Balmat
Ely (Robinson)	Flat River–	Franklin
Elizabeth	Bonne Terre	Joplin
White Pine	Leadville	West Shasta
Santa Rita	Wood River	Upper Mississippi
Ducktown	Rico	Valley
Bingham	East Tintic	Austinville
Antler Peak	Coeur d'Alene	Metaline
Globe–Miami	Darwin	Pioche
Ajo	Shafter	
Banner	Corbin–Wickes	
†Gossan Lead		

† As the production characteristics of the Gossan Lead district were not explicitly defined, it was not considered as a member of any of the three major partitions.

TABLE 15.22. Hypothetical matrix of binary data (characteristics) on three districts

Characteristics	Districts		
	D_1	D_2	D_3
C_1	1	0	1
C_2	0	1	1
C_3	1	1	0
C_4	1	1	1
C_5	0	0	1

presence, denoted by the integer 1 or the absence (0), of each characteristic in each of the districts.

As a demonstration of the computations and measures, suppose we have identified five characteristics (C_1, C_2, C_3, C_4, C_5) and wish to describe their typicalities with respect to three districts (D_1, D_2, D_3). Suppose that examination of data has produced the matrix (D) of Table 15.22.

Now, let D represent the matrix of binary values of Table 15.22 and D' represent the transpose of D, i.e. the matrix D is placed on its side so that the column vector D_1 is the first row of D'. Then, matrix P is formed by the post-multiplication of D by D':

$$P = D \cdot D' = \begin{bmatrix} 2 & 1 & 1 & 2 & 1 \\ 1 & 2 & 1 & 2 & 1 \\ 1 & 1 & 2 & 2 & 0 \\ 2 & 2 & 2 & 3 & 1 \\ 1 & 1 & 0 & 1 & 1 \end{bmatrix}. \quad (15.22)$$

Each of the rows of D shows the frequency of common (joint) occurrence of one variable and all others. If each element $[p_{ij}]$ of matrix P is squared, and all squared elements of each row are summed across the columns, the following column vector is obtained

$$V = \begin{bmatrix} 11 \\ 11 \\ 10 \\ 22 \\ 4 \end{bmatrix}. \quad (15.23)$$

Suppose that the square root of each $[v_i]$ of V is taken; these values are what Botbol (1971) refers to as typicalities of the characteristics (see Table 15.23).

TABLE 15.23. *Computed typicalities of the hypothetical characteristics* ($C_1, \ldots, C_5$)

Characteristics	$\sum_{j=1}^{5} p_{ij}^2$	Typicality $\left(\sum_{j=1}^{5} p_{ij}^2\right)^{\frac{1}{2}}$
C_1	11	3.32
C_2	11	3.32
C_3	10	3.16
C_4	22	4.69
C_5	4	2.00

Thus, this demonstration shows characteristic C_4 to be the most typical of the three districts.

While in this demonstration, the calculations and results are trivial, in the original demonstration, characteristics included 76 rock types, 256 minerals, and structural measurements. Characteristic analysis was performed on all 30 districts and then separately for copper, lead, and zinc districts. Finally, as a test of the approach, Park City district, which has been considered to be a lead–silver district, was deleted and treated as an unknown district. The characteristics of this district were then compared to copper, lead, and zinc districts (see Table 15.24). On the basis of its structure and primary mineralogy, the Park City district does indeed look like a lead district, but by rock and secondary mineralization, it resembles the copper districts.

Through subsequent research and development, the use of characteristic analysis for the evaluation of an unknown—district, regional cell, etc.—was extended in two ways. First, the binary scheme initially employed was replaced by a ternary one: +1 for presence, −1 for absence, and 0 for lack of knowledge. Second, coefficients were estimated for an equation which describes the degree of association of the unknown with the model. Define c_i as the ith characteristic of the model. Then, degree of associa-

tion y is a linear function of the p characteristics

$$y = a_1 c_1 + \ldots + a_i c_i + \ldots + a_p c_p. \quad (15.24)$$

The coefficients (a's) of eqn (15.24) are estimated from the data matrix of characteristics on the control area. McCammon [19, p. 19] describes them as weights which 'characterize the model best in a statistical sense' [20]. Suppose that the characteristic matrix of Table 15.22 is rearranged so that the characteristics are columns in the matrix. Let us refer to the ith column as vector C_i and the collection of vectors as matrix C. If we represent the desired weights (a's) as an n-valued vector A, then the weights are estimated by solving the matrix equation (see § 15.6)

$$C'CA = \lambda A, \quad (15.25)$$

where A is the eigenvector associated with the largest eigenvalue of $C'C$ and C is the data matrix of characteristics and C' its transpose. McCammon [19] describes these weights as reflecting the relative importance of each characteristic with respect to the interactions among the characteristics: the larger the a_i, the more important is the ith characteristic. Table 15.25 shows weights reported by Botbol *et al.* (1978) for 11 characteristics (elements) for Sunshine and Hecla models. These weights show that both areas are characterized strongly by the presence of arsenic, but they differ in that Hecla also is characterized by mercury, sodium, silver, and lead, while Sunshine is characterized strongly by antimony, zinc, and copper. Hecla also differs considerably from Sunshine by the zero weights given to Te and Cu.

Since characteristic analysis requires either binary

TABLE 15.24. *Degrees of association of the Park City District with model copper, lead, and zinc districts.* (*Source: Botbol 1971, p. 98.*)

Vector magnitudes of the degree of association of Park City with

Copper districts	Lead districts	Zinc districts	Variable
33.94	38.68	9.95	Dips of faults
36.99	36.33	28.14	Rock name
243.87	246.77	193.45	Primary mineralogy
271.53	193.16	135.70	Secondary mineralogy

TABLE 15.25. *Characteristic weights for Hecla and Sunshine models.* (*Source: Botbol et al. 1978, p. 542.*)

Characteristic	Weights Hecla	Sunshine
Hg	0.48	0.24
Te	0.00	0.15
Cu	0.00	0.37
Pb	0.38	0.22
Zn	0.10	0.37
Ag	0.38	0.15
Cd	0.01	0.22
Na	0.46	0.26
K	0.14	0.24
As	0.49	0.44
Sb	0.04	0.44

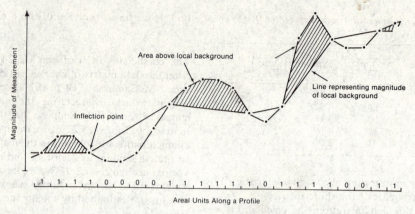

Fig. 15.22. Hypothetical geochemical profile showing areas above local inflection points (second derivative negative) labelled 1 and other locations labelled 0. (Source: Botbol *et al.* [21], p. 33.)

or ternary measurements, geodata which vary continuously in space must be preprocessed to appropriate form before they can be integrated into the analysis. Ideally, such preprocessing should be designed not only to yield the desired form, e.g. binary or ternary, but also to code the responses in a way which conveys the greatest amount of geologic information with respect to the model. In their investigation of the application of characteristic analysis to geochemical exploration data, Botbol *et al.* [21] describe the use of a second-derivative map for data transformation: map locations in which the second derivative is negative were represented by a +1; other locations were given a value of zero. Botbol *et al.* [21] argue that such a procedure is preferable to attempting to separate background (trend) from anomaly; instead, areas are identified which have high values in a relative sense, relative to the surrounding values. Fig. 15.22 shows schematically the kinds of anomalies a second derivative would produce on a profile possessing fluctuations superimposed on a strong trend.

Application of characteristic analysis on a large scale can require great effort in the acquisition of the raw geodata and in the preprocessing of the geodata to binary or ternary form. In assessing magnitude of effort, allowance should be made for the exploration of the data for variable combinations and for different compositions of the control area, i.e. deleting some control cells and/or adding other cells to the control (training) set. These tasks are facilitated by a computer program referred to by Botbol *et al.* (1978) as CHARAN—CHARacteristic ANalysis. This interactive program is designed to guide the user through the steps of characteristic analysis and to

make it easy for him to explore the data and alternative model formulations. Fig. 15.23 provides a flow

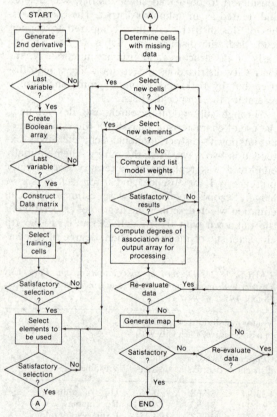

Fig. 15.23. Flowchart of interactive characteristic analytic technique. (Source: Botbol *et al.* [21], p. 37.)

diagram of interactive characteristic analysis. This program also provides the option, using a method derived by Dr Richard McCammon, for the use of probability analysis for the selection of variables [22], i.e. determining which variables (characteristics) should be included and excluded from the model.

Now that the basic ideas of characteristic analysis have been established, let us turn to a brief examination of genetic modelling and its role in the methodology.

15.4.3. *Genetic modelling for decision analysis*

As a result of basic geologic investigations and research, Finch *et al.* [18] identify a sequential scheme of eight general process stages

Precursor processes;
Host-rock formation;
Host-rock preparation;
Uranium-source development;
Transport of uranium;
Primary uranium deposition;
Post-deposition modification;
Preservation.

Each of these process stages is elaborated by Finch *et al.* [18] in terms of the genetic concepts—processes—involved and the geological base (condition or circumstance) which provides some evidence about the state of each process. Table 15.26 shows the processes and geological bases for precursor conditions for a tabular humate-related uranium deposit. Table 15.27 shows the application questions that are prompted by the concepts identified in Table 15.26; furthermore, the second column of Table 15.27 identifies the geodata necessary to answer the application

TABLE 15.26. *The precursor process stage of the tabular humate-related uranium deposit model, San Juan Basin, New Mexico (modified from Granger and others [23]). (Source: Finch* et al. *[18, p. 36].)*

Genetic concept	Geological base
A. Precursor processes 1. A uranium-rich province developed in and south of the San Juan Basin prior to host-rock deposition.	1a. Precambrian crystalline basement rocks contain anomalously uraniferous zircon. 1b. Regional basement rocks are abnormally uraniferous. 1c. Uranium deposits occur in older (Paleozoic, Triassic, earlier Jurassic) and younger (Cretaceous and Tertiary) rocks in the region. 1d. Lead-isotope studies show that regional basement rocks have lost in U in the past.
2. An extended period of marine and later dominantly continental deposition of red beds took place on a broad stable platform.	2a. The underlying strata constitute a sequence of dominantly marine Paleozoic rocks overlain by dominantly continental lower Mesozoic rocks. 2b. The host rock is part of a thick, dominantly red-bed sequence of sedimentary rocks. 2c. The regional dip of the underlying rocks as well as of the host rock is generally low, less than 5°.
3. Host rock deposition was preceded by uplift along the margins of the platform, perhaps coinciding with shallow downwarp of the depositional basin.	3a. Distribution and thickness of the Jurassic Westwater Canyon Member of the Morrison Formation roughly coincides with the present form of the southern San Juan Basin, indicating downwarp prior to and during sedimentation. 3b. Sediment-transport directions indicate a positive area to the south of the Cordilleran foreland margin.

TABLE 15.27. *Application questions and required data for the precursor stage of the tabular humate-related uranium deposit model (after Granger and others [23]) described in Table 15.26. (Source: Finch et al. [18, p. 40].)*

1a. Do regional basement rocks contain abnormally uraniferous zircon?	1a. Uranium analyses of zircons from basement rocks.
1b. Are crystalline basement rocks abnormally uraniferous?	1b. Uranium analyses of basement rocks.
1c. Do associated strata contain uranium deposits?	1c. Knowledge or location of uranium deposits in associated strata.
1d. Do lead-isotope analyses of the nearby basement rocks show loss of U?	1d. Lead-isotope analyses of nearby basement rocks.
2a. Are both marine and continental strata represented in the sequence beneath the host rock?	2a. Presence or absence of marine and continental sequence below host.
2b1. Is the host rock part of a red-bed sequence of rocks?	2b1. Presence/absence of red-bed sequence in host unit.
2b2. Is there evidence of a primary (early-diagenetic) red bed facies of the host unit?	2b2. Knowledge of primary red-bed facies in host unit.
2c1. Is the regional dip of the host rock <5°?	2c1. Regional dip of host rock.
2c2. Is the regional dip of the underlying rocks <5°?	2c2. Regional dip of underlying rocks.
3a1. Is there evidence of basin subsidence during Morrison sedimentation?	3a1. Evidence for subsidence during host-rock sedimentation.
3a2. Is the host rock within X kilometers of the southwestern erosional edge of the basin? (What is the shortest distance in kilometers of this deposit from the Dakota truncation of the Morrison?)	3a2. Distance from eroded edge of host rock.
3b1. Is there evidence of uplift of areas marginal to the Morrison depositional basin?	3b1. Evidence of uplift of nearest margin of basin.
3b2. Are average current directions in the host sandstone as shown by cross-beds, channel trends, lineations, or other features toward the north or east?	3b2. Direction of resultant current directions of host unit (cross-beds, lineation trends, channel trends, etc.).

questions. Thus, for each mode of occurrence of uranium deposits, Finch *et al.* [18] proceeded in an orderly and logical fashion to identify (1) the processes indicated by geoscience and field observation, (2) questions which, when responded to, would comment upon the processes, and (3) the geodata necessary to respond to the questions.

The foregoing steps can be viewed as a partial formalization only of geoscience, for while the concepts, questions, and supportive geodata have been identified, nothing has been said thus far about how these geodata are to be combined to comment upon the processes, which in this case are the precursor processes. To complete the formalization, Finch *et al.* [18] employed what they refer to as logic circuits to combine the geodata so as to reflect genetic concepts. Fig. 15.24 is the logic circuit for the precursor-process questions of Table 15.27. A logic symbol for

logic operators AND, OR, or NOT appears at the node of each branch in this logic circuit. The circuit shows that the joint occurrence, indicated by the symbol for AND, of uranium province and sedimentation framework leads to a favourable state of precursor processes. Tracing the upper branch (uranium province) backwards, we see the symbol for the logic operator OR at the node of the next branch, meaning that if any one of the four conditions— uraniferous zircon, uraniferous basement rocks, associated uranium deposits, or basement lost uranium—is present, a uranium province is present.

15.4.4. *Decision analysis—the integration of characteristic analysis and genetic modelling*

Suppose that logic circuits, like that shown in Fig. 15.24 for the precursor stage, were constructed for all stages and that all conditions at the ends of the

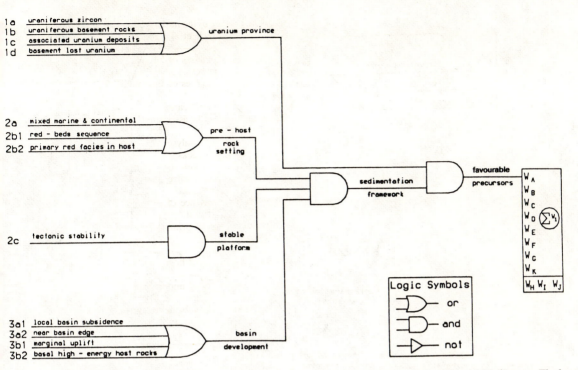

Fig. 15.24. An example of a provisional logic circuit for precursor-process questions given in Table 15.27. (Source: Finch et al. [18], p. 42.)

branches of each circuit—in this example there are twelve end branches—were coordinated into a composite list of attributes. Suppose also that a data matrix were constructed in which a column of the matrix represents one of these attributes and a row represents a cell. Finally, suppose that a ternary coding system were adopted. Then, a given cell could be represented by coding presence (+1), absence (−1), or indeterminacy (0) for each of the characteristics. This is basically the approach employed by the US Geological Survey, as indicated in Fig. 15.25. The steps just described result in the data matrix represented at C in this figure.

Characteristic analysis, as originally demonstrated, could be applied to the matrix at C by selecting a subset of the cells to serve as control cells. However, such analysis would not profit from the combining of measurements in ways that reflect more directly genetic concepts for that type of a deposit (geological environment). It is here that genetic modelling and decision analysis provide an important extension to characteristic analysis. The logic circuits for each stage of the genetic model are used to generate new ternary variables f_i by performing the logic opera-

tions of the circuit on relevant data on the attributes matrix (C of Fig. 15.25). The logic operations of each circuit when applied to the relevant ternary data produce measures which also are ternary—see Table 15.28 for a simplistic example. Thus, the new matrix also contains ternary data.

Subsequent to computation of the fs for each cell, a subset of cells is identified as control cells. In the methodology of the US Geological Survey, it is the matrix of data on fs for these cells that is submitted to characteristic analysis. This analysis, as previously described, yields weights a_i for the genetic variables f_i, $i = 1, 2, \ldots, p$

$$f = a_1 f_1 + \ldots + a_p f_p. \qquad (15.26)$$

By adjusting the coefficients of eqn (15.26) so that the sum of their absolute values is one, the linear equation can be bounded by the limits of −1 and +1

$$f = a_1' f_1 + \ldots + a_n' f_n, \quad -1 \le f \le +1, \quad (15.27)$$

where $a_i' = a_i \Big/ \sum_{j=1}^{n} |a_j|$. Thus, values of +1 and −1 for f would indicate perfect association and no association, respectively, of the unknown with the model.

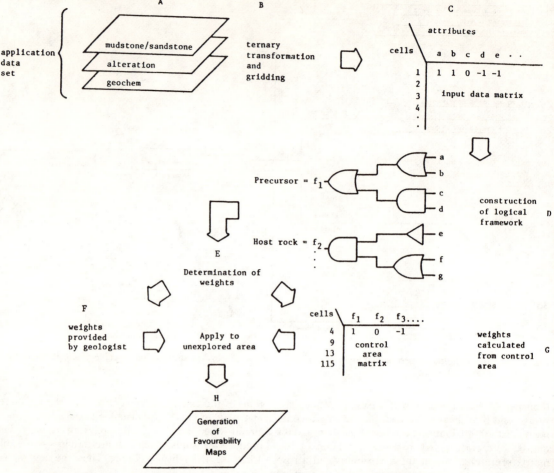

Fig. 15.25. Flow chart showing steps for generating favourability maps. (Source: McCammon [19], p. 22.)

This equation for degree of association is to this methodology what the regression and discriminant equations are to regression and discriminant analyses, respectively. In other words, the equation is a quantitative representation of that information in the large data matrices which is useful in describing degree of association (similarity) of a cell with con-

trol cells by virtue of its values for process variables (fs). Once the equation has been determined, the computation of degree of association is trivial, being simply the evaluation of the equation on the values of the process variables computed for the unknown, f_i, $i = 1, \ldots, p$. For example, suppose that we have only five process variables and that analysis of control cells has provided the equation

$$f = 0.1f_1 + 0.4f_2 - 0.2f_3 + 0.12f_4 + 0.18f_5.$$
$$(15.28)$$

Further, suppose that the attributes of a prospective region have been coded and that these ternary data have been processed through logic circuits to give the measurements

$$f_1 = 1; \quad f_2 = 0; \quad f_3 = 1; \quad f_4 = -1; \quad f_5 = 1.$$

TABLE 15.28. *Example of logic computations on a ternary scheme.* (*Source: Harris and Agterberg 1981.*)

Cell identification	A	B	C	A OR B	$f_i = $ (A OR B) AND C
X	+1	0	+1	+1	+1
Y	−1	+1	0	+1	0

Substituting these values into the eqn (15.28) yields a value of -0.04 for f

$$f = 0.1(1) + 0.4(0) - 0.2(1) + 0.12(-1) + 0.18(1)$$
$$= -0.04.$$

15.4.5. Some comments about this methodology and appraisal of endowment and resources

Description thus far is of a methodology that formalizes geoscience and employs quantified geodata in a novel way to produce a quantitative measure of the similarity of an unknown cell to control cells when unknown and control cells are characterized by ternary scores on attributes. At the time of this writing, the methodology is incomplete for the appraisal of mineral endowment or mineral resources in two basic ways

There is no linkage of geoscience to mineral endowment;

There is no probability dimension.

Because the methodology is novel and does offer *potential* as an appraisal methodology, it is deserving of careful study, for in a complete methodology, it is the formalizing of geoscience *and* the use of quantified geodata that present the greatest modelling problems, and in this regard, the methodology has much to offer the resource geologist. Furthermore, as indicated by McCammon [19], extension of the methodology to include a linkage to endowment and the probability dimension currently is being investigated.

For example, McCammon [19] discusses two ways of transforming the similarity measure (f), which he refers to as favourability, to probability. One way, which he describes as ideal, is to use the model to compute favourability measures for each cell known to have or not to have mineral (in this case uranium) occurrences. Then for each non-overlapping discretized range of favourability, a proportion of number of cells having mineral occurrences to total number of cells could be computed. Each of these proportions can be considered to be an approximation to conditional probability for mineral occurrence. Let $X = 1$ denote occurrence and $X = 0$ denote nonoccurrence. Then,

$$\frac{N(X = 1 \mid f_j'' \leq f \leq f_j')}{N(X = 1 \cup X = 0 \mid f_j'' \leq f \leq f_j')} \rightarrow P(X = 1 \mid f_j'' \leq f \leq f_j')$$
(15.29)

where $N(\ \ )$ is a counting operator, f_j'', f_j' are the lower and upper bounds of the jth nonoverlapping

interval (range) of favourability (association) f, and $\cup$ denotes union, i.e. either $X = 1$ or $X = 0$. While this is a straightforward and logical approach, such detailed data on mineral occurrence are not always available, particularly when consideration is given to the need to *know* whether a cell has or does not have mineral occurrence. Consequently, McCammon [19, pp. 25–6] proposes an alternative approach.

The geologists' best estimates for the probabilities of occurrence of one or more deposits, given that a region cell possesses all the attributes of a particular model or none of the attributes, can be compared with a subjective estimate of the probability of occurrence of one or more uranium deposits.

The relationship between favorability and the probability of occurrence of a particular type of deposit can be expressed as

$$F = \begin{cases} \dfrac{P - P_0}{P_1 - P_0} & P_0 \leq P < P_1 \\ \dfrac{P - P_0}{P_0 - P_T} & P_T < P < P_0 \end{cases}$$

where F is the favorability and P_T, P_0, and P_1 are probabilities. P_1 is the probability of occurrence when $F = 1$ and all the attributes of a model are present. P_T is the probability of occurrence when $F = -1$, and none of the attributes of a model are present. P_0 represents the probability of occurrence when $F = 0$, and information about the attributes of a model is missing or else the combined presence–absence of the attributes yields ambivalent results; if the combined presence–absence of attributes yields ambivalent results, the probability is based on nonmodel evidence for the presence of uranium.

The relationship between favorability and probability is shown in figure 8 [Fig. 15.26]. Even if all the attributes of a model are observed, the probability of occurrence is estimated at being less than one. Similarly, even if none of the attributes are observed, the probability of occurrence can be estimated as being greater than zero. Should information on the attributes of a model be either lacking or contradictory, that is, $F = 0$, the probability of occurrence could be non-zero and would be estimated from the available evidence for the presence of uranium.

Given estimates for P_1, P_T, and P_0 and given that the favorability, F, has been determined within a region cell, the probability of occurrence of one or more deposits within the cell is given by

$$P = \begin{cases} P_0 + F(P_1 - P_0) & F \geq 0 \\ P_0 + F(P_0 - P_T) & F < 0 \end{cases}$$

As more geological information becomes available, the estimates for P_1, P_T, and P_0 will change, and therefore the probability of occurrence within any given region cell should not be regarded as some fixed value.

Whatever the form of the probability relation employed, it must be compatible with other elements of the appraisal methodology. For example, suppose

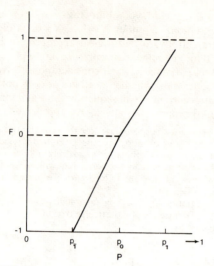

Fig. 15.26. Graph which shows relationship between favourability F and probability of occurrence P. (Source: McCammon [19].)

size and grade distributions could be combined with the probability distribution for number of deposits to compute the probability distribution for quantity of uranium for each large cell. Thus, by adding deposit tonnage and grade models and at the same time keeping cells small, this methodology could be extended to include the probabilistic description of uranium endowment. The ease by which this extension could be made argues for its adoption. Other factors, however, may be important in making this decision; for example, keeping cell size small implies, *ceteris paribus*, that the geodata for a large number of cells must be examined and coded. If there are many kinds of geodata, their acquisition and maintenance can require a great deal of effort. Data availability, acquisition, processing, and management are practical considerations that will vary with the user and with the area and the mode of mineral occurrence. These factors must be considered in determining the extension of the geological decision methodology to the appraisal of mineral endowment.

15.5. Selected comments

The foregoing discussion of the extension of the US Geological Survey's methodology to the appraisal of mineral endowment affords a natural lead into some general comments about methodology for formalizing geoscience.

It is useful here to recall the perspective established in § 15.1 of two general approaches to the formalizing of geoscience and its use in the appraisal of mineral endowment. The methodology developed by Harris and Carrigan (§ 15.2) is representative of one of these: the geologist performs analysis and integration of various kinds of geodata on relatively large areas and then makes probability statements about the states of the processes of his inference net (formalized geoscience); these probabilities are processed to yield a probability distribution for number of deposits for each area. This approach relies heavily upon geological expertise in two ways, other than identifying the genetic concepts: (1) the linkage of geoscience to endowment and (2) integration of geodata and the assessment of subjective probabilities about the geological conditions and processes of the decision model. Given the availability of exploration data, it may be possible to replace the subjective linkage of the decision model by an objective statistical linkage. Even under these ideal circumstances, the geologist still plays an active part in evaluation by performing the data analysis and integration. In other words, that methodology must rely

that the cells being appraised are quite large, say at least 1000 square miles, then the probability, as described, leaves much unsaid about the density of mineral occurrence: in this case, it resembles what the NURE methodology referred to as P^0, the probability for the presence of at least one deposit. But, the NURE methodology supplemented this with other subjectively (geologically) estimated probabilities: conditional on the presence of at least one deposit, probabilities for fraction of area mineralized, tonnage of ore per mineralized square mile, and grade of mineralized material. The point to be made here is that at least two of these measures require geological analysis: P^0 and density of occurrence, i.e. fraction of area mineralized, conditional upon the presence of at least one deposit. Therefore, for large cells, the probability computed by the decision analysis does not provide all that is required of geological analysis, for it provides only P^0. One remedy to this problem is to keep cells small enough that the probability for a second deposit is very small. For such a circumstance, P^0 is also the probability for one deposit. Probability models of deposit size and grade could then be combined with this probability to produce a probability distribution for uranium. Or, many of the small cells could be grouped into large areas and probability relations and computational algorithms could be used to compute probabilities for various numbers of deposits occurring in the large cells. Subsequently, the deposit heavily upon subjective judgements of geologists even apart from the formalizing of geoscience. To some this is seen as a liability, while to others it is seen as an asset.

One appealing feature of the methodology developed by the US Geological Survey—Approach B—is that, apart from identifying the genetic concepts (geoscience) and the data to support its use, the methodology is basically one of quantitative procedures and quantified geodata. Use of an existing model does not require subjective analysis of the geodata. Application of the model to evaluate the degree of association of an unknown region to the control cells is objective and produces a quantitative measure of this association. Everything else being equal, objectivity is preferred to subjectivity. To some degree, everything else may not be equal, even for use, as distinct from construction, of a model. This statement has particular relevance if the geologist's judgement is used to convert degree of association to probability. Introducing a probability dimension to the decision model in this fashion must raise the question of, why? If probability ultimately is to be a judgement call, then asking the geologist to make that judgement about a synthetic measure, like f, the measure of degree of association with control cells, seems like questionable procedure. Why not allow the geologist to estimate probability of occurrence as a result of reviewing the familiar (real) geodata? Furthermore, even if the geologist can provide these probabilities, considerations of Chapter 14 may cast some doubt upon the credibility of his estimates, particularly if the probabilities were to be for number of deposits instead of presence of at least one deposit. For, number of deposits is a complex event in terms of the geological factors which influence it and which would be considered by the geologist in providing estimates of it. Therefore, asking the geologist to provide estimates of this quantity, given only f, provides little support to his reasoning processes. Given such a circumstance, he may be forced to rely heavily upon the heuristics identified in Chapter 14.

Some factors that influence the level of endowment of a region can best be perceived and described for large regions. Furthermore, for some data, e.g., geophysics, pattern of anomaly and its location vis-à-vis other factors may be far more important than a simple description of presence or absence. Recall that §15.4.5 established that for the methodology developed by the US Geological Survey to be extended so that it estimates endowment—instead of describing only degree of association—it should be applied to small cells; otherwise, geology is not effectively used to determine mineral density. The point to be made here is that the use of small cells may carry two costs, one being simply the increased time required to assess a large number of cells; the other one is the cost of information lost by using cell sizes so small that the unit of observation is not easily associated with the geological factors that have affected endowment. Additionally, one must wonder about the cost of information lost due to use of a binary or ternary data scheme. This should be weighed against the benefits of simultaneous consideration of great amounts of data permitted by this approach. Finally, what about the state of indeterminacy that is represented by zero in the ternary scheme? Is it not common for a geologist to *not* know from direct observation but to be *not indifferent* to presence or absence because of the indirect evidence offered from other observations and his geoscience? What is lost when indeterminacy is declared for this circumstance?

A question to be pondered by those studying methodology is how do the gains of objectivity promoted by the US Geological Survey methodology balance against these informational issues? In a larger sense, we need to investigate the benefits of objective data analysis and integration as compared to employing the geologist to analyse and integrate basic geodata. To the extent that the various kinds of geodata provide information which is scale dependent or which interrelates in complex fashions, and to the extent that an experienced geologist understands these complexities, the use of the geologist as an active component of an appraisal system seems desirable. However, if the ability of the geologist in these regards is quite limited, the undesirable features of subjectivity may outweigh the small benefits that derive from his analysis and integration of geodata. At present, we are just recognizing relevant questions. Improved appraisals and appraisal methodologies will require many iterations on theory, methodology, and data.

15.6. Appendix A—mathematical basis for characteristic weights

Consider the equation

$$y = a_1 c_1 + \ldots + a_p c_p, \qquad (15.30)$$

where y is a measure of association of the cell with the control cells of the model. Then, Y is an $n \times 1$ vector of association scores for each control cell with the model

$$Y = C \cdot A, \qquad (15.31)$$

where C is an $n \times p$ matrix of characteristics, one row for each of the n control cells and A is the $p \times 1$ vector of coefficients of eqn (15.30), an element of which is a_i. Then,

$$Y'Y = A'C'CA. \qquad (15.32)$$

Suppose that the elements of A be selected to maximize $Y'Y$. Taking the derivative of $Y'Y$ with respect to A, we have

$$\frac{d[Y'Y]}{dA} = C'CA.$$

Setting $C'CA$ equal to the $p \times 1$ null vector, we have

$$0 = C'CA. \qquad (15.33)$$

Let $[x_{ij}]$ be an element of $C'C$. Then,

$$0 = a_1 x_{11} + a_2 x_{12} + \ldots + a_p x_{1p}$$
$$0 = a_1 x_{21} + a_2 x_{22} + \ldots + a_p x_{2p}$$
$$\vdots$$
$$0 = a_1 x_{p1} + a_2 x_{p2} + \ldots + a_p x_{pp}.$$

This is a linear homogeneous set of equations; nontrivial solutions of this set of equations are given by the determinantal equation

$$|C'C - \lambda I| = 0. \qquad (15.34)$$

The eigenvector associated with the largest value of λ that also is a solution to (15.34) is the desired vector of characteristic weights

$$y = a_1 c_1 + a_2 c_2 + \ldots + a_p c_p.$$

References

Botbol, J. M. (1971). An application of characteristic analysis to mineral exploration. *Proc. 9th Int. Sym. on Techniques for Decision-Making in the Mineral Industry*. Special Volume 12, pp. 92–9. Canadian Institute of Mining and Metallurgy, Montreal, Canada.

——, Sinding-Larsen, R., McCammon, R. B., and Gott, G. B. (1978). A regionalized multivariate approach to target selection in geochemical exploration. *Econ. Geol.* **73**, 534–46.

Duda, R. O., Hart, P. E., and Nilsson, N. J. (1976). Subjective Bayesian methods for rule-based infer-

ence systems. *American Federation of Information Processing Societies (AFIPS) Conference Proceedings*, Vol. 45, pp. 1075–82. AFIPS Press, Montvale, New Jersey.

——, ——, ——, Reboh, R., Slocum, J., and Sutherland, G. L. (1977). *Development of a computer-based consultant for mineral exploration*. Annual Report, SRI Projects 5821 and 6415, Stanford Research Institute International, Menlo Park, California.

——, ——, Barrett, P., Gaschnig, J. G., Konolige, K., Reboh, R., and Slocum, J. (1978). *Development of the Prospector consultation system for mineral exploration*. Final Report, SRI Projects 5821 and 6415, Stanford Research Institute International, Menlo Park, California.

——, Gaschnig, J. G., and Hart, P. E. (1979). Model design in the Prospector consultant system for mineral exploration. In *Expert systems in the microelectronic age* (ed. D. Michie), pp. 153–67. University of Edinburgh Press.

Gaschnig, J. (1980). *Development of uranium exploration models for the Prospector consultant system*. Final Report, SRI Project 7856, Stanford Research Institute International, Menlo Park, California.

Harris, D. P. and Agterberg, F. P. (1981). The appraisal of mineral resources. *Econ. Geol.*, 75th Anniversary Volume, pp. 897–938.

——, and Carrigan, F. J. (1981). Estimation of uranium endowment by subjective geological analysis—a comparison of methods and estimates for the San Juan Basin, New Mexico. *Econ. Geol.* **76**, 1032–55.

Hendrix, G. G. (1977). Human engineering for applied natural language processing. In *Proc. 5th Int. Joint Conf. Artificial Intelligence*, pp. 183–91, Massachusetts Institute of Technology, Cambridge, Massachusetts.

Pople, H. E., Jr., Myers, J. D., and Miller, R. A. (1975). DIALOG: a model of diagnostic logic for internal medicine. *Proc. 4th International Joint Conference on Artificial Intelligence*, pp. 848–55, Tbilisi, Georgia, USSR.

Ridge, J. D. (1982). The economic geologist and exploration for, and exploitation of, non-fuel mineral deposits. In *Future resources: Their geostatistical appraisal* (ed. R. T. Newcomb), pp. 13–27 West Virginia University Press, Morgantown, West Virginia.

Shortliffe, E. H. (1976). *Computer-based medical consultations: MYCIN*. American Elsevier Publishing Co., New York.

Slovic, P. (1972). From Shakespeare to Simon: speculations—and some evidence—about man's ability to process information. *Oregon Res. Inst. Monograph* **12**(12).

Weiss, S. M., Kulikowski, C. A., and Safir, A. (1977). A model-based consultation system for the long-term management of glaucoma. In *Proc. 5th Int. Joint Conf. Artificial Intelligence*, pp. 826–33, Massachusetts Institute of Technology, Cambridge, Massachusetts.

Zadeh, L. A. (1965). Fuzzy sets. *Information and Control* **8**, 338–53.

Notes

1. The material of § 15.2.1 and the subsection 'Probability, geoscience, and endowment—concepts and approach' of § 15.2.2 is reproduced from a research report by D. P. Harris and F. J. Carrigan with some deletions and minor modifications: Harris, D. P. and Carrigan, F. J. (1980). A probabilistic endowment appraisal system based upon the formalization of geological decisions—a general description. US Department of Energy, Grand Junction Office, Colorado, pp. 15–19 and 24–40.

2. In practice, the geologist was discouraged from using zero. Unless some physical circumstances made zero the only answer, he was asked to use small numbers instead of zero. It was hoped that this would encourage greater introspection and avoid simplistic responses.

3. Technically, let $h_{ijk}(n \mid x_{1i}, x_{2j}, x_{3k})$, $i, j, k = 1, 2, 3$, represent the 27 conditional probability distributions, one for each combination of the three states (i, j, k) of the three major processes (X_1, X_2, X_3), for number of deposits. Then, α, the probability distribution for number of deposits, conditional upon the geological observations only (no longer conditional on process states) is written, assuming statistical independence of processes, as

$$\alpha(n \mid g_1, \ldots, g_m) = \sum_{i=1}^{3} \sum_{j=1}^{3} \sum_{k=1}^{3} h_{ijk}(n \mid x_{1i}, x_{2j}, x_{3k}) \times$$
$$\times \phi_1(x_{1i} \mid g_1, \ldots, g_m) \cdot \phi_2(x_{2j} \mid g_1, \ldots, g_m) \times$$
$$\times \phi_3(x_{3k} \mid g_1, \ldots, g_m),$$

where

$$\phi_1(x_{1i} \mid g_1, \ldots, g_m), \quad \phi_2(x_{2j} \mid g_1, \ldots, g_m),$$
$$\phi_3(x_{3k} \mid g_1, \ldots, g_m)$$

are the probability distributions for processes X_1, X_2, and X_3.

4. Harris, D. P. and Carrigan, F. J. (1980). A probabilistic endowment appraisal system based upon the formalization of geological decisions—Final report: demonstration and comparative analysis of estimates and methods. Open File Report No. GJBX-383(81) prepared for US Department of Energy, Grand Junction Office, Grand Junction, Colorado.

5. This paragraph is reproduced from Harris and Carrigan [1].

6. The remainder of this subsection is reproduced from Harris and Carrigan [1].

7. The material of this subsection is reproduced with some deletions and minor modifications from Harris and Carrigan [1].

8. The material in this subsection is reproduced from Harris and Carrigan [4, pp. 126–7].

9. The material in the remainder of § 15.2.4 and in § 15.2.5 is reproduced from Harris and Carrigan [4, pp. 124–34].

10. Since the sum of the 27 probabilities is 1.0, only 26 probabilities are needed to convey the probability information. Furthermore, while conceptually only 26 probabilities are required to convey full information, an analysis may find that with respect to the data analysed on endowment and exploration, less than 26 probabilities convey statistically meaningful information. This is a likely result, since very little, if any, endowment may be present when the states of all major processes are poor. Consequently, P_m the last probability in eqn (15.2) may be the sum of several of the probabilities for the least favourable combinations of process states

$$P_m = \sum_{j=m}^{26} P_j.$$

Thus, the equation which results from the analysis of data may require fewer coefficients than indicated conceptually

$$\hat{f} = \left(\hat{\alpha}_1 P_1 + \ldots + \hat{\alpha}_{m-1} P_{m-1} + \hat{\alpha}_m \sum_{j=m}^{26} P_j \right)(1 - e^{-\hat{\alpha}_0 v}).$$

For example, it is conceivable that statistical analysis could indicate that as few as 10 probabilities are required $(m = 10)$, meaning that probabilities P_{10} through P_{26} are summed and treated as one probability.

11. This replaces the distribution of quantity of U_3O_8 per deposit.

12. The material in the remainder of this section is reproduced from Harris and Carrigan [4, pp. 16–7, 23–5, 84–92, and 111–24].

13. Initial endowment = mineral inventory + cumulative production + potential. The 'System' estimate is an average of estimates by four geologists, each using his own appraisal system. For the calculation of initial endowment in the NURE estimate the assumption was made that the mineral inventory of the Colorado Plateau region is the mineral inventory of the San Juan Basin.

14. Alpert, M. and Raiffa, H. (1969). A progress report on the training of probability assessors. Unpublished draft, Harvard Business School.

15. Bailly, P. A. (1978). Today's resource status—tomorrow's resource problems—the need for research on mineral deposits. Paper presented at the GSA-GAS-MAC Joint Annual Meeting, Toronto, Canada.

16. The exact procedure used by the Questioning System is described in Duda *et al.* (1977).

17. This description is reproduced from Harris and Agterberg (1981).

18. Finch, W. I., Granger, H. C., Lupe, R., and McCammon, R. B. (1980). Genetic–geologic models—a systematic approach to evaluate geologic favorability for undiscovered uranium resources, Part I, Research on uranium resource models, a progress report. US Geological Survey Open-File Report 80–2018A.

19. McCammon, R. B. (1980). Geologic decision analysis and its application to genetic–geological models. Part II, Research on uranium resource models, a progress report. US Geological Survey Open-File Report 80–2018B.

20. These ideas were first set forth by Richard McCammon, Office of Resource Analysis, US Geological Survey, Reston, Virginia in 1976 (personal communication, January 13, 1981).

21. Botbol, J. M., Sinding-Larsen, R., McCammon, R. B., and Gott, G. B. (1977). Characteristic analysis of geochemical exploration data. US Geological Survey Open File Report 77–349.

22. Written correspondence from Dr R. B. McCammon, Office of Resource Analysis, US Geological Survey, Reston, Virginia, 13 January 1981.

23. Granger, H. C., Finch, W. I., Kirk, A. R., and Thaden, R. E. (1980). Genetic-geologic model for tabular humate uranium deposits, Grants Mineral Belt, San Juan Basin, New Mexico-Part III, Research on uranium resource models, a progress report. US Geological Survey Open File Report 80–2018C.

INDEX